THE PRENTICE HALL GUIDE FOR
College Writers

THE PRENTICE HALL GUIDE FOR

College Writers

BRIEF SEVENTH EDITION

STEPHEN REID

Colorado State University

PEARSON

Prentice
Hall

Upper Saddle River, New Jersey 07458

Library of Congress Cataloging-in-Publication Data

Reid, Stephen, (date)
　　The Prentice Hall guide for college writers / Stephen Reid.—7th ed.
　　　　p.　cm.
　　Includes bibliographical references and index.
　　ISBN 0-13-193135-0
　　1.　English language—Rhetoric—Handbooks, manuals, etc.　2.　Report
writing—Handbooks, manuals, etc.　3.　College readers.　I.　Title.
　　PE1408.R424　2005
　　　808′.042—dc22

2004028339

VP, Editorial Director: Leah Jewell
Senior Acquisitions Editor: Brad Potthoff
Assistant Editor: Jennifer Conklin
Director of Marketing: Brandy Dawson
Marketing Manager: Emily Cleary
Marketing Assistant: Kara Pottle
VP, Director of Production and Manufacturing: Barbara Kittle
Production Editor: John Shannon
Prepress and Manufacturing Manager: Nick Sklitsis
Assistant Manufacturing Manager: Mary Ann Gloriande
Director of Marketing: Brandy Dawson
Creative Design Director: Leslie Osher

Interior and Cover Design: Laura Gardner
Cover Illustration/Photo: Thomas McKnight, "Madison Square,"
　16″ × 18″ casein on paper. © 2004 Thomas McKnight
Director, Image Resource Center: Melinda Reo
Manager, Cover Visual Research and Permissions: Karen Sanatar
Manager, Rights and Permissions: Zina Arabia
Manager, Visual Research: Beth Brenzel
Image Permissions Coordinator: Robert Farrell
Photo Researcher: Diana Gongora
Media Editor: Christy Schaack
Media Project Manager: Lynn Pearlman
Full-Service Project Management: Pine Tree Composition

This book was set in 10/12.5 Adobe Caslon by Pine Tree Composition and was printed by Quebecor World Book Services. The cover was printed by Coral Graphics.

Credits and acknowledgments borrowed from other sources and reproduced, with permission, in this textbook appear on appropriate page within text (or on pages 701–702).

Pearson Education LTD.
Pearson Education Singapore, Pte. Ltd
Pearson Education Canada, Ltd
Pearson Education—Japan
Pearson Education Australia PTY, Limited

Pearson Education North Asia Ltd
Pearson Educación de Mexico, S.A. de C.V.
Pearson Education Malaysia, Pte. Ltd
Pearson Education, Upper Saddle River, New Jersey

10 9 8 7 6 5

0-13-193135-0

Brief Contents

Contents

4 Remembering   105

5 Reading   157

6 Investigating   **225**

INVESTIGATING: THE WRITING PROCESS **272**

7 Explaining **303**

TECHNIQUES FOR EXPLAINING **305**

9 Problem Solving   421

TECHNIQUES FOR PROBLEM SOLVING   423

PROBLEM SOLVING: THE WRITING PROCESS   443

10 Arguing   471

TECHNIQUES FOR WRITING: ARGUMENT   472

11 Responding to Literature **553**

Thematic Contents

The Prentice Hall Guide for College Writers, Seventh Edition, contains selections from over 80 writers, artists, poets, and photographers. Thematic clusters of essays, articles, poems, short fiction, and images are indicated below. An asterisk (*) indicates a complete essay.

TECHNOLOGY AND THE INTERNET

ENVIRONMENTAL ISSUES

EDUCATION

Preface

*It seems clear that rhetoric is situational. . . .
[Rhetoric] functions ultimately to
produce action or change in the world.*
—LLOYD F. BITZER, "THE RHETORICAL SITUATION"

At the beginning of each semester, writing teachers usually reexamine their objectives and goals for their course. The Council of Writing Program Administrators has written several position statements (available at http://www.wpacouncil.org) to help writing teachers set their course and program objectives. The WPA Outcomes Statement for First-Year Composition outlines four key goals: building students' *rhetorical knowledge* of purpose, audience, genre, cultural context, voice, and tone; improving students' *critical thinking, reading,* and *writing* skills; developing students' strategies for *writing processes;* and helping students develop their *knowledge of conventions.* In addition to these WPA outcomes, individual states, universities, and departments often have goals for developing critical reading and thinking, improving computer literacy, introducing community-service learning, helping ESL or basic writers, teaching visual literacy skills, and integrating writing across the disciplines.

Although teachers should always set their sights on these goals and objectives, we know that effective teaching begins with the individual students who bring an astonishing variety of language backgrounds, cultural differences, individual learning styles, and academic goals to our classes. The teaching we love begins with meeting these students, dealing with their problems, helping them learn to work individually and together, acknowledging their failures, and celebrating their successes. Every class, every teacher, and every student takes a different path toward these goals of critical thinking and reading, knowledge of rhetoric and its conventions, and flexible writing processes. So each semester, as we think about the goals we hope to accomplish with a course or a writing program, we need to remember that there is not one single way to meet these goals. Just as writing always takes into account the rhetorical situation and the social and cultural context, so teaching is always a unique and situated endeavor. In its seventh edition, *The Prentice Hall Guide for College Writers* has many new and revised features, but it still maintains sufficient flexibility so that, come Monday morning, teachers may select what they need to help the individual students sitting in their classes.

New Features

Revised extensively for the seventh edition, *The Prentice Hall Guide for College Writers* focuses on helping teachers and students meet course and program goals. First, every chapter has been revised to emphasize the *rhetorical situation* in which writers work. Writers' purposes still figure prominently, as they should, but additional coverage of audience, genre, occasion, and cultural contexts for writing builds students' rhetorical knowledge and helps improve their writing. In particular, coverage of a variety of genres—from academic essays and letters to editorials and short articles—has been expanded.

Second, *critical thinking* and *critical reading* are given even more emphasis in the seventh edition. Most teachers recognize the crucial role of teaching critical reading of essays, images, advertisements, and other cultural documents. To prepare students to become citizens in a democracy, we must show them how arguments are constructed, how images and advertisements make their appeals, and how to critically read and respond to a variety of documents in a variety of contexts and genres.

Third, guidelines for *analyzing images and visuals,* from works of art to cartoons to advertisements, have been added throughout the seventh edition. Images have always had a powerful rhetorical effect, and the impact of increased use of images in newspapers and on the Internet has effectively thrust writers—some more willingly than others—into a culture that relies on visuals as a key part of illustrating, explaining, and persuading. The seventh edition includes over forty new works of art, images, cartoons, and graphs for illustration and analysis.

Fourth, guidelines for integrating *community-service-learning* projects into first-year writing courses have been added. Students may wish to keep a journal about their service learning, write assessments of community program needs, produce brochures for a particular agency, and evaluate and reflect on their own learning. For additional treatment of community-service learning, see Cheryl Duffy's excellent reference, *A Student Guide to Service-Learning* (Prentice Hall, 2005).

Fifth, Chapter 11, "Writing about Literature," has been expanded to include guidelines for *reading and responding to poetry* as well as to short fiction. Poems by W. H. Auden, Yusef Komunyakka, Joy Harjo, and Gary Soto illustrate a range of modern and contemporary styles and subject matters.

Sixth, a *Writer's Toolbox* has been added to the inside front cover pages of the seventh edition. Collected on one page are references to passages on reading strategies, invention, strategies for organization, argumentation, research strategies, language of rhetoric, and common fallacies in logic.

Finally, the seventh edition features over *twenty-five new selections*, including poems, student writing, and essays by professional writers such as Margaret Atwood, Ellen Goodman, Richard Alleva, Christopher Caldwell, Cheryl Dellasega, David Sedaris, and James Twitchell.

Continuing Key Features

Annotated Instructor's Edition

The Annotated Instructor's Edition contains additional guidelines for teaching each chapter, including teaching tips on critical reading, critical thinking, responding to assignments, peer group activities, and ESL teaching tips designed to alert teachers to possible problems and solutions for ESL writers.

Emphasis on Writing and Researching with a Computer

In addition to essays focused on current Internet topics such as identity and pornography issues, the seventh edition expands its coverage of new search strategies and search engines as well as strategies for assessing, evaluating, and documenting Internet sources.

Alternate Thematic Table of Contents

The essays, stories, poems, and images in the seventh edition combine to create thematic clusters of topics that reappear throughout the text: Race and Cultural Diversity, Gender Roles, Technology and the Internet, Environmental Issues, Education, Literacy and Language, Advertising and the Media, Social Issues, and Cultural Explorations.

Emphasis on Student Writing

The seventh edition continues to showcase student writing, featuring the work of more than forty student writers from several colleges and universities. The seventh edition contains twenty-five full-length student essays and ten essays with sample prewriting materials, rough drafts, peer-response sheets, and postscripts.

Logical Sequence of Purpose-Based Chapters

Within the rhetorical situation, aims and purposes help guide the reader to select appropriate genres, organizational strategies, appeals to audience, and appropriate styles. Early chapters in *The Prentice Hall Guide for College Writers* focus on observing, remembering, critical reading, and investigating; later chapters emphasize exposition and argumentation (explaining, evaluating, problem solving, and arguing).

Focus on Writing Processes

Every major chapter contains guidelines for writing, journal exercises, reading and writing activities, collaborative activities, peer-response guidelines, revision suggestions, and professional and student samples to assist students with their work-in-progress within their rhetorical situation.

Journal Writing

Throughout the text, write-to-learn activities help writers improve their critical-reading skills, warm up for each assignment, and practice a variety of invention and shaping strategies appropriate for understanding their purpose, audience, genre, and social context.

Marginal Quotations

Nearly a hundred short quotations by composition teachers, researchers, essayists, novelists, and poets personalize for the inexperienced writer a larger community of writers still struggling with the same problems that each student faces.

An Introduction to Myths and Rituals for Writing

Chapter 1, "Writing Myths and Rituals," discounts some common myths about college writing courses, introduces the notion of writing rituals, and outlines the variety of journal writing used throughout the text. Writing-process rituals are crucial for all writers but especially so for novice writers. Illustrating a variety of possible writing rituals are testimonies from a dozen professional writers on the nature of writing. These quotations continue throughout the book, reminding students that writing is not some magical process, but rather a madness that has a method to it, a process born of reading, thinking, observing, remembering, discussing, and writing.

An Orientation to Rhetorical Situation and to Writing Processes

Chapter 2, "Situations, Purposes, and Processes for Writing," bases the writing process in the rhetorical situation. It shows how audience, genre, subject, and context work together with the writer's purpose to achieve a rhetorical end. It demonstrates how meaning evolves from a variety of recursive, multidimensional, and hierarchical activities that we call the writing process. Finally, it reassures students that, because individual writing and learning styles differ, they will be encouraged to discover and articulate their own processes from a range of appropriate possibilities.

Aims and Purposes for Writing

The text then turns to specific purposes and assignments for writing. Chapters 3 through 6 ("Observing," "Remembering," "Reading," and "Investigating") focus on invention and critical-reading strategies. These chapters introduce genres and situations for writing that build students' rhetorical repertoires: observing people, places, objects, and images; remembering people, places and events; developing critical-reading and responding strategies; and investigating and reporting through genres such as interviews, profiles, and multiple source articles.

Chapters 7 through 10 ("Explaining," "Evaluating," "Problem Solving," and "Arguing") emphasize subject-and audience-based purposes and occasions for writing. The sequence in these chapters moves the student smoothly from exposition to argumentation (acknowledging the obvious overlapping), building on the strategies and repertoires of the previous chapters. The teacher may, in fact, use chapters 7 through 10 as a minicourse in argument, teaching students how to develop and argue claims of fact and definition, claims of cause and effect, claims about values, and claims about solutions or policies.

Responding to Literature

Chapter 11 guides students through the process of reading and responding to poetry and short fiction, using many of the critical-reading strategies, invention techniques, and shaping strategies practiced in the earlier chapters.

Writing from Sources

Chapter 12, "Writing a Research Paper," draws on all the reading, writing, and researching strategies presented in the first eleven chapters. Research papers are written for specific purposes, audiences, and contexts, but the invention, drafting, and revising processes are more extended. This chapter helps students select and plan their projects, find and critically evaluate library and Internet sources, record their progress in a research log, and document their sources using MLA or APA styles.

Handbook

A brief handbook includes a review of basic sentence elements, sentence structure and grammar, diction and style, and punctuation and mechanics.

Supplementary Material for Instructors and Students

Supplements

An extensive package of supplements accompanies *The Prentice Hall Guide for College Writers* for both instructors and students.

ONEKEY   OneKey is our new comprehensive Website at www.prenhall.com/reid providing quizzes and exercises to help students better understand the readings in the main text, as well as to reinforce knowledge of the writing process, grammar, and punctuation. Also included and new to this edition are access to personal tutoring, a paper review and exchange tool, visual exercises, additional assignments, exercises and readings, model student essays, an online version of the Critical Skills Thinking Journal, a research tool (Research Navigator™) complete with the *New York Times* archive, bibliography generator and plagiarism tutorial, a mini-handbook and more. An access code to this valuable resource is included automatically with every new copy of this text for no additional fee. Also at www.prenhall.com/reid is an unrestricted access site that contains select quizzes and exercises from OneKey.

CRITICAL SKILLS THINKING JOURNAL (ISBN 0-13-194111-9)   This printed supplement, available for a nominal fee, provides students with additional exercises and freewriting activities, as well as opportunities to consider and respond to opposing viewpoints.

MODEL STUDENT ESSAYS (ISBN 0-13-645516-6)   Compiled by Mark Gallaher, this anthology of twenty-five student essays from around the nation is organized into three broad categories: personal experience, explain and inform, and argue a position.

PRENTICE HALL POCKET READERS   Each reading in our pocket readers has withstood the test of time and teaching, making each the perfect companion for any writing course (limit one free reader per package).

To order the hardback student edition packaged with

ARGUMENT: A Prentice Hall Pocket Reader, by Christy Desmet, Deborah Miller and Kathy Houff, specify package ISBN 0-13-155677-0

LITERATURE: A Prentice Hall Pocket Reader, by Mary Balkun, specify package ISBN 0-13-155678-9

PATTERNS: A Prentice Hall Pocket Reader, by Dorothy Minor, specify package ISBN 0-13-155679-7

THEMES: A Prentice Hall Pocket Reader, by Clyde Moneyhun, specify package ISBN 0-13-155680-0

WRITING ACROSS THE CURRICULUM: A Prentice Hall Pocket Reader, by Stephen Brown, specify package ISBN 0-13-168967-3.

To order the brief paperback student edition (without handbook) with

ARGUMENT: A Prentice Hall Pocket Reader, by Christy Desmet, Deborah Miller and Kathy Houff, specify package ISBN 0-13-155670-3

LITERATURE: A Prentice Hall Pocket Reader, by Mary Balkun, specify package ISBN 0-13-155671-1

PATTERNS: A Prentice Hall Pocket Reader, by Dorothy Minor, specify package ISBN 0-13-155673-8

THEMES: A Prentice Hall Pocket Reader, by Clyde Moneyhun, specify package ISBN 0-13-155674-6

WRITING ACROSS THE CURRICULUM: A Prentice Hall Pocket Reader, by Stephen Brown, specify package ISBN 0-13-168968-1.

THE NEW AMERICAN WEBSTER HANDY COLLEGE DICTIONARY To order the hardback student edition with a free dictionary, specify package ISBN 0-13-155676-2.

To order the brief paperback student edition (without handbook) with a free dictionary, specify package ISBN 0-13-155669-X.

THE NEW AMERICAN ROGET S COLLEGE THESAURUS To order the hardback student edition with a free thesaurus, specify package ISBN 0-13-155682-7.

To order the brief paperback student edition (without handbook) with a free thesaurus, specify package ISBN 0-13-155675-4.

For Instructors

ANNOTATED INSTRUCTOR'S EDITION The Annotated Instructors Edition contains additional guidelines written by Stephen Reid for teaching each chapter, including teaching tips on critical reading, critical thinking, responding to assignments, peer group activities, and ESL teaching tips designed to alert teachers to possible problems and solutions for ESL writers.

ONEKEY OneKey is our new comprehensive Website at www.prenhall.com/reid providing quizzes and exercises to help students better understand the readings in the main text, as well as to reinforce knowledge of the writing process, grammar, and punctuation. Also included and new to this edition are access to personal tutoring, a paper review and exchange tool, visual exercises, additional assignments, exercises and readings, model student essays, an online version of the Critical Skills Thinking Journal, a research tool (Research Navigator™) complete with the *New York Times* archive, bibliography generator and plagiarism tutorial, a mini-handbook and more. The instructor manual for this text is posted on a protected instructor-only version of this site. An access code to this valuable resource automatically accompanies every new copy of this text for no additional fee. Also at www.prenhall.com/reid is an unrestricted access site that contains select quizzes and exercises from the more comprehensive site.

For those instructors who require comprehensive course management, OneKey is also available with preloaded content in WebCT™, Blackboard™, and Course-Compass™. Contact your Prentice Hall representative for more details and a demonstration, or visit www.prenhall.com/onekey.

TEACHING COMPOSITION WITH THE PRENTICE HALL GUIDE (ISBN 0-13-194113-5)   This instructor's manual, prepared by Stephen Reid, is designed to complement the AIE with more activities and more detailed discussions of how to teach composition most effectively. Included are chapter commentaries and answers to discussion questions, as well as sections on composition theory, policy statements, lesson plans, collaborative writing, writing in a computer classroom, teaching ESL writers, small-group learning, write-to-learn exercises, reading/writing exercises, prereading journal assignments, writing assignments, suggestions for student conferences, and ideas for responding to and evaluating writing.

Acknowledgments

Because teaching writing is always a situated enterprise, I would like to thank the members of the composition faculty and staff at Colorado State University whose teaching expertise and enthusiasm have improved every page of the text: Kate Kiefer, Mike Palmquist, Sarah Sloane, Lisa Langstraat, Tobi Jacobi, Kerri Mitchell, Sue Doe, Liz Jackson, Anne Gogela, Laura Thomas, and Bob White. Many of the innovative teaching strategies, resources, and syllabi developed by Colorado State University composition faculty members are available at http://writing.colostate.edu.

In addition, the following teachers offered excellent advice about changes and additions for the seventh edition: M.J. Braun, University of West Florida; Darin Cozzens, Surry Community College; Joan Gilson, Johnson County Community College; Temple West, Old Dominion University; Stephen D. Gibson, Utah Valley State College; Anneliese Homan, State Fair Community College; Susan Sens-Conant, Johnson County Community College; Jon Inglett, Oklahoma City Community College; Robin Bryant, Phillips Community College of the University of Arkanssa; Maurice Hunt, Baylor University; and David Charlson, Oklahoma City

Community College. I wish to thank them for their thorough, honest, constructive, and professional advice.

For the expert crew at Prentice Hall, I am especially grateful. Phil Miller, a fine editor and friend, has enthusiastically supported this text from the first edition. Leah Jewell, Corey Good, and Brad Potthoff provided ongoing revision and editorial advice, while John Sisson and John Shannon gave invaluable developmental and editorial support. Thanks always to Brandy Dawson and Gina Sluss for energy, inspiration, and friendship.

Finally, I wish to thank my family for their continued personal and professional support.

—STEPHEN REID
Colorado State University

THE PRENTICE HALL GUIDE FOR

College Writers

This painting by Edouard Manet shows Monet's love of painting in the outdoors where he could capture the natural outdoor light. In this chapter, the journal exercise on page 12 invites you to consider on what occasions you enjoy reading, writing, or painting outdoors.

Edouard Manet
Monet Painting in His Floating Studio (1874)
Bayerische Staatsgemaldesammlungen, Munich

chapter 1

Writing Myths and Rituals

For me, the most effective writing ritual is to gather up all of my stuff—legal pad and pencil, notes, dictionary, and thesaurus—and get on my bike, ride to campus, and set myself up in the art lounge in the student center. During the week, I'll do this in the evening after dinner. On a weekend, I go any time from 10 A.M. to midnight. I don't write effectively at home because there are always distractions. Some people will be moving around and I'll go see who they are and what they're doing, or I'll go get a cup of coffee or a piece of toast, or I'll snap on the TV, ignoring that tiny voice inside saying, "Get busy—you have to get this done!" So what makes the art lounge better? Simple—no distractions. I can lay out all of my stuff, get a cup of coffee, and go to work. All around me people are doing the same thing, and somehow all of those hardworking people are an encouragement. The art lounge is always quiet, too—quieter than the library—and it doesn't smell like the library.

One myth about writing I have believed my whole life is that "good writers are born, not made." My attitude when beginning this writing course was one of apprehension and dread. I wondered if I *could* improve my writing, or if I was destined to receive B's and C's on every essay for the rest of my life. This writing class has given me concrete examples and suggestions for improvement—not just grammar or essay maps. The freewriting is such a great help that whenever I'm stuck, I immediately turn to my ten-minute freewriting to open up blocked passages. Once I get past my writer's block, I see that I can be a good writer.

> *"A writer is someone who writes, that's all."*
> —GORE VIDAL, NOVELIST AND SOCIAL COMMENTATOR

> *"I've always disliked words like inspiration. Writing is probably like a scientist thinking about some scientific problem or an engineer about an engineering problem."*
> —DORIS LESSING, AUTHOR OF ESSAYS AND FICTION, INCLUDING THE GOLDEN NOTEBOOK

> *"I always worked until I had something done and I always stopped when I knew what was going to happen next. That way I could be sure of going on the next day."*
> —ERNEST HEMINGWAY, JOURNALIST AND NOVELIST, AUTHOR OF THE OLD MAN AND THE SEA

3

AS YOU BEGIN A COLLEGE WRITING COURSE, YOU NEED TO GET RID OF SOME MYTHS ABOUT WRITING THAT YOU MAY HAVE BEEN PACKING AROUND FOR SOME TIME. DON'T ALLOW MISCONCEPTIONS TO RUIN A GOOD EXPERIENCE. Here are a few common myths about writing, followed by some facts compiled from the experiences of working writers.

> *I work at my writing as an athlete does at. . . training, taking it very seriously. What is important is the truth in it and the way that truth is expressed.*
>
> —EDNA O'BRIEN, NOVELIST AND PLAYWRIGHT

MYTH: "Good writers are born, not made. A writing course really won't help my writing."

FACT: *Writers acquire their skills the same way athletes do—through practice and hard work.* There are very few "born" writers. Most writers—even professional writers and journalists—are not continually inspired to write. In fact, they often experience "writer's block," the stressful experience of staring helplessly at a piece of paper, unable to think or to put words down on paper. A writing course will teach you how to cope with your procrastination, anxiety, lack of "inspiration," and false starts by focusing directly on solving the problems that occur during the writing process.

MYTH: "Writing courses are just a review of boring grammar and punctuation. When teachers read your writing, the only thing they mark is that stuff, anyway."

FACT: *Learning and communicating—not grammar and punctuation—come first in college writing courses.* Knowledge of grammar, spelling, punctuation, and usage is essential to editing, but it is secondary to discovering ideas, thinking, learning, and communicating. In a writing course, students learn to revise and improve the content and organization of each other's writing. *Then* they help each other edit for grammar, punctuation, or spelling errors.

MYTH: "College writing courses are really 'creative writing,' which is not what my major requires. If I wanted to be another Shakespeare and write poetry, I'd change my major."

FACT: *Writing courses emphasize rhetoric, not poetry.* Rhetoric involves practicing the most effective means or strategies for informing or persuading an audience. All writing—even technical or business writing—is "creative." Deciding what to write, how to write it, how best to get your reader's attention, and how to inform or persuade your reader requires creativity and imagination. Every major requires the skills that writing courses teach: exploring new ideas, learning concepts and processes, communicating with others, and finding fresh or creative solutions to problems.

MYTH: "Writing courses are not important in college or the real world. I'll never have to write, anyway."

FACT: *Writing courses do have a significant effect on your success in college, on the job, and in life.* Even if you don't have frequent, formal writing assignments in other courses, writing improves your note-taking, reading comprehension, and thinking skills. When you do have other written tasks or assignments, a writing course teaches you to adapt your writing to a variety of different purposes and audiences—whether you are writing a lab report in biology, a letter to an editor, a complaint to the Better Business Bureau, or a memorandum to your boss. Taking a writing course helps you express yourself more clearly, confidently, and persuasively—a skill that comes in handy whether you're writing a philosophy essay, a job application, or a love letter.

The most important fact about writing is that you are already a writer. You have been writing for years. A writer is someone who writes, not someone who writes a nationally syndicated newspaper column, publishes a bestseller, or wins a Pulitzer Prize. To be an effective writer, you don't have to earn a million dollars; you just have to practice writing often enough to get acquainted with its personal benefits for you and its value for others.

WARMING UP: FREEWRITING

Put this book aside—right now—and take out pencil or pen and a piece of paper. Use this free exercise (private, unjudged, ungraded) to remind yourself that you are already a writer. Time yourself for five minutes. Write on the first thing that comes to mind—*anything whatsoever*. Write nonstop. Keep writing even if you have to write, "I can't think of anything to say. This feels stupid!" When you get an idea, pursue it.

When five minutes are up, stop writing and reread what you have written. Whether you write about a genuinely interesting topic or about the weather, freewriting is an excellent way to warm up, to get into the habit of writing, and to establish a writing ritual.

> *My idea of a prewriting ritual is getting the kids on the bus and sitting down.*
>
> —BARBARA KINGSOLVER
> AUTHOR OF PRODIGAL SUMMER

Writing Fitness: Rituals and Practice

Writing is no more magic or inspiration than any other human activity that you admire: figure skating at the Olympics, rebuilding a car engine, cooking a gourmet meal, or acting in a play. Behind every human achievement are many unglamorous hours of practice—working and sweating, falling flat on your face, and picking yourself up again. You can't learn to write just by reading some chapters in a textbook or by memorizing other people's advice. You need help and advice, but you also need practice. Consider the following parable about a Chinese painter:

> A rich patron once gave money to the painter Chu Ta, asking him to paint a picture of a fish. Three years later, when he still had not received the painting, the patron went to Chu Ta's house to ask why the picture was not done. Chu Ta did not answer but dipped a brush in ink and with a few strokes drew a splendid fish. "If it is so easy," asked the patron, "why didn't you give me the picture three years ago?" Again, Chu Ta did not answer. Instead, he opened the door of a large cabinet. Thousands of pictures of fish tumbled out.

Most writers develop little rituals that help them practice their writing. A ritual is a *repeated pattern of behavior* that provides structure, security, and a sense of progress to the one who practices it. Creating your own writing rituals and making them part of your regular routine will help reduce that dreaded initial panic and enable you to call upon your writing process with confidence when you need it.

PLACE, TIME, AND TOOLS

Some writers work best in pen and ink, sprawled on their beds in the afternoon while pets snooze on nearby blankets. Others start at 8 A.M. and rely on hard chairs, clean tables, and a handful of number 2 pencils sharpened to needle points. Still others are most comfortable with their keyboards and word processors at their desks or in the computer lab. Legal-sized pads help some writers produce, while others feel motivated by spiral notebooks with pictures of mountain streams on the covers. Only you can determine which place, time, and tools give you the best support as a writer.

The place where you write is also extremely important. If you are writing in a computer lab, you have to adapt to that place, but if you write a draft in long-hand or on your own word processor, you can choose the place yourself. In selecting a place, keep the following tips in mind:

- **Keep distractions minimal.** Some people simply can't write in the kitchen, where the refrigerator is distractingly close, or in a room that has a TV in it. On the other hand, a public place—a library, an empty classroom, a cafeteria—can be fine as long as the surrounding activity does not disturb you.
- **Control interruptions.** If you can close the door to your room and work without interruptions, fine. But even then, other people often assume that

you want to take a break when they do. Choose a place where you can decide when it's time to take a break.

- **Have access to notes, journal, textbooks, sources, and other materials.** If the place is totally quiet but you don't have room to work or access to important notes or sources, you still may not make much progress. Whatever you need—a desk to spread your work out on, access to notes and sources, extra pens, or computer disks—make sure your place has it.

The time of day you write and the tools you write with can also affect your attitude and efficiency. Some people like to write early in the morning, before their busy days start; others like to write in the evening, after classes or work. Whatever time you choose, try to write regularly—at least three days a week—at about the same time. If you're trying to get in shape by jogging, swimming, or doing aerobics, you wouldn't exercise for five straight hours on Monday and then take four days off. Like exercise, writing requires regular practice and conditioning.

Your writing tools—pen, pencil, paper, legal pads, four-by-six-inch notecards, notebooks, computer—should also be comfortable for you. Some writers like to make notes with pencil and paper and write drafts on computers; some like to do all composing on computers. As you try different combinations of tools, be aware of how you feel and whether your tools make you more effective. If you feel comfortable, it will be easier to establish rituals that lead to regular practice.

Rituals are important because they help you with the most difficult part of writing—getting started. So use your familiar place, time, and tools to trick yourself into getting some words down on paper. Your mind will devise clever schemes to avoid writing those first ten words—watching TV, balancing your checkbook, drinking some more coffee, or calling a friend and whining together about all the writing you have to do. But if your body has been through the ritual before, it will walk calmly to your favorite place, where all your tools are ready (perhaps bringing the mind kicking and screaming all the way). Then, after you get the first ten words down, the

> *"Writers are notorious for using any reason to keep from working: overresearching, retyping, going to meetings, waxing the floors—anything."*
> —GLORIA STEINEM,
> FORMER EDITOR OF
> MS. MAGAZINE

FRANK AND ERNEST ©by Bob Thaves

Frank & Ernst reprinted by permission of Newspaper Enterprise Association, Inc.

mind will say, "Hey, this isn't so bad— I've got something to say about that!" And off you'll go.

Each time you perform your writing ritual, the *next* time you write will be that much easier. Soon, your ritual will let you know: *"This is where you write. This is when you write. This is what you write with."* No fooling around. Just writing.

ENERGY AND ATTITUDE

Once you've tricked yourself into the first ten words, you need to keep your attitude positive and your energy high. When you see an intimidating wall starting to form in front of you, don't ram your head into it; figure out a way to sneak around it. Try these few tricks and techniques:

- **Start anywhere, quickly.** No law says that when you sit down to write a draft, you have to "begin at the beginning." If the first sentence is hard to write, begin with the first thoughts that come to mind. Or begin with a good example from your experience. Use that to get you going; then come back and rewrite your beginning after you've figured out what you want to say.
- **Write the easiest parts first.** Forcing yourself to start a piece of writing by working on the hardest part first is a sure way to make yourself hate writing. Take the path of least resistance. If you can't get your thesis to come out right, jot down more examples. If you can't think of examples, go back to brainstorming.
- **Keep moving.** Once you've plunged in, write as fast as you can—whether you are scribbling ideas out with a pencil or hitting the keys of a typewriter or a computer. Maintain your momentum. Reread if you need to, but then plunge ahead.
- **Quit when you know what comes next.** When you do have to quit for the day, stop at a place where you know what comes next. Don't drain the well dry; stop in the middle of something you know how to finish. Make a few notes about what you need to do next and circle them. Leave yourself an easy place to get started next time.

One of the most important strategies for every writer is to *give yourself a break from the past and begin with a fresh image.* In many fields—mathematics, athletics, art, engineering—some people are late bloomers. Don't let that C or D you got in English back in tenth grade hold you back now like a ball and chain. Imagine yourself cutting the chain and watching the ball roll away for good. Now you are free to start fresh with a clean slate. Your writing rituals should include only positive images about the writer you are right now and realistic expectations about what you can accomplish.

- **Visualize yourself writing.** Successful athletes know how to visualize a successful tennis swing, a basketball free throw, or a baseball swing. When you are planning your activities for the day, visualize yourself writing at your favorite place. Seeing yourself doing your writing will enable you to start writing more quickly and maintain a positive attitude.
- **Discover and emphasize the aspects of writing that are fun for you.** Emphasize whatever is enjoyable for you—discovering an idea, getting the organization of a paragraph to come out right, clearing the unnecessary words and junk out of your writing. Concentrating on the parts you enjoy will help you make it through the tougher parts.
- **Set modest goals for yourself.** Don't aim for the stars; just work on a sentence. Don't measure yourself against some great writer; be your own yardstick. Compare what you write to what *you* have written before.
- **Congratulate yourself for the writing you do.** Writing is hard work; you're using words to create ideas and meanings literally out of nothing. So pat yourself on the back occasionally. Keep in mind the immortal words of comedian and playwright Steve Martin: "I think I did pretty well, considering I started out with nothing but a bunch of blank paper."

KEEPING A JOURNAL

Many writers keep some kind of notebook in which they write down their thoughts, ideas, plans, and important events. Some writers use a journal, a private place for their day-to-day thoughts. Other writers create weblogs, or "blogs," a more public place for their ideas. Both journals and blogs can be a "place for daily writing." If you choose a private, written journal, you can later select what you want others to read; if you use your blog, your thoughts and ideas are there for others to read and respond to. Whatever medium you choose, use it as part of your daily writing ritual. In it can go notes and ideas, bits and pieces of experience, or responses to essays or

> *"I carry a journal with me almost all the time . . ."*
> —NTOZAKE SHANGE, AUTHOR OF THE PLAY FOR COLORED GIRLS WHO HAVE CONSIDERED SUICIDE WHEN THE RAINBOW IS ENUF

> *"The most valuable writing tool I have is my daybook. . . . I write in my lap, in the living room or on the porch, in the car or an airplane, in meetings at the university, in bed, or sitting down on a rock wall during a walk. . . . It is always a form of talking to myself, a way of thinking on paper."*
> —DONALD MURRAY, JOURNALIST, AUTHOR OF BOOKS AND ESSAYS ABOUT WRITING

books you're reading. Sometimes journals or blogs are assigned as part of your class work. In that case, you may do in-class, write-to-learn entries, plans for your essays, postscripts for an essay, or reflections on a portfolio. Your journal or blog can be a place for formal assignments or just a place to practice, a room where all your "fish paintings" go.

As the following list indicates, there are many kinds of journal entries. They fall into three categories: *reading entries, write-to-learn entries,* and *writing entries.* Reading entries help you understand and actively respond to student or professional writing. Write-to-learn entries help you summarize, react to, or question ideas or essays discussed in class. Writing entries help you warm up, test ideas, make writing plans, practice rhetorical strategies, or solve specific writing problems. All three kinds of journal writing, however, take advantage of the unique relationship between thinking, writing, and learning. Simply put, writing helps you learn what you know (and don't know) by shaping your thoughts into language.

Reading Entries

- **Prereading journal entries.** Before you read an essay, read the headnote and write for five minutes on the topic of the essay—what you know about the subject, what related experiences you have had, and what opinions you hold. After you write your entry, the class can discuss the topic before you read the essay. The result? Your reading will be more active, engaged, and responsive.
- **Double-entry logs.** Draw a line vertically down a sheet of paper. On the left-hand side, summarize key ideas as you reread an essay. On the right-hand side, write down your reactions, responses, and questions. Writing while you read helps you understand and respond more thoroughly.
- **Essay annotations.** Writing your comments in the margin as you read is sometimes more efficient than writing separate journal entries. Also, in a small group in class, you can share your annotations and collaboratively annotate a copy of the essay.
- **Vocabulary entries.** Looking up unfamiliar words in a dictionary and writing out definitions in your journal will make you a much more accurate reader. Often an essay's thesis, meaning, or tone hinges on the meanings of a few key words.
- **Summary/response entries.** Double-entry logs help you understand while you reread, but a short one-paragraph summary and one-paragraph response after you finish your rereading helps you focus on both the main ideas of a passage and your own key responses.

Write-to-Learn Entries

- **Lecture/discussion entries.** At key points in a class lecture or discussion, your teacher may ask you to write for five minutes by responding to a few questions: What is the main idea of the discussion? What one question would you like to ask? How does the topic of discussion relate to the essay that you are currently writing?

- **Responses to essays.** Before discussing an essay, write for a few minutes to respond to the following questions: What is the main idea of this essay? What do you like best about the essay? What is confusing, misleading, or wrong in this essay? What strategies illustrated in this essay will help you with your own writing?

- **Time-out responses.** During a controversial discussion or argument about an essay, your teacher may stop the class, take time out, and ask you to write for five minutes to respond to several questions: What key issue is the class debating? What are the main points of disagreement? What is your opinion? What evidence, either in the essay or in your experience, supports your opinion?

Writing Entries

- **Warming up.** Writing, like any other kind of activity, improves when you loosen up, stretch, get the kinks out, practice a few lines. Any daybook or journal entry gives you a chance to warm up.

- **Collecting and shaping exercises.** Some journal entries will help you collect information by observing, remembering, or investigating people, places, events, or objects. You can also record quotations or startling statistics for future writing topics. Other journal entries suggested in each chapter of this book will help you practice organizing your information. Strategies of development, such as comparison/contrast, definition, classification, or process analysis will help you discover and shape ideas.

- **Writing for a specific audience.** In some journal entries, you need to play a role. Imagine that you are in a specific situation, writing for a defined audience. For example, you might write a letter of application for a job or letter to a friend explaining why you've chosen a certain major.

- **Revision plans and postscripts.** Your journal is also the place to keep a log—a running account of your writing plans, revision plans, problems, and solutions. Include your research notes, peer responses, and postscripts on your writing process in this log.

- **Imitating styles of writers.** Use your journal to copy passages from writers you like. Practice imitating their styles on different topics. Also, try simply transcribing a few paragraphs. Even copying effective writers' words will reveal some of their secrets for successful writing.
- **Writing free journal entries.** Use your journal to record ideas, reactions to people on campus, events in the news, reactions to controversial articles in the campus newspaper, conversations after class or work, or just your private thoughts.

WARMING UP: JOURNAL EXERCISES

Choose three of the exercises below and write for ten minutes on each. Date and number each entry.

1. Make an "authority" list of activities, subjects, ideas, places, people, or events that you already know something about. List as many topics as you can. If your reaction is "I'm not really an *authority* on anything," then imagine you've met someone from another school, state, country, or historical period. With that person as your audience, what are you an "authority" on?

2. Choose one activity, sport, or hobby that you do well and that others might admire you for. In the form of a letter to a friend, describe the steps or stages of the process through which you acquired that skill or ability.

3. In two or three sentences, complete the following thought: "I have trouble writing because . . ."

4. In a few sentences, complete the following thought: "In my previous classes and from my own writing experience, I've learned that the three most important rules about writing are . . ."

5. Describe your own writing rituals. *When, where,* and *how* do you write best?

6. Write an open journal entry. Describe events from your day, images, impressions, bits of conversation—anything that catches your interest. For possible ideas for open journal entries, read the following essay by Roy Hoffman.

7. Look again at the chapter opening work of art by Edouard Manet, *Monet Painting in His Floating Studio.* If you have taken an art class, have you drawn or painted outdoors, as Monet is depicted? What are the advantages

or disadvantages of painting outside versus in a studio? Similarly, as a writer or student, can you read or write effectively while sitting outside, or do you need to be inside, in a work environment? Does it depend on what you are reading or writing? Explain.

PROFESSIONAL WRITING

ON KEEPING A JOURNAL

Roy Hoffman

In a Newsweek On Campus *essay, Roy Hoffman describes his own experience, recording events and trying out ideas just as an artist doodles on a sketch pad. Your own journal entries about events, images, descriptions of people, and bits of conversation will not only improve your writing but also become your own personal time capsule, to dig up and reread in the year 2020.*

Wherever I go I carry a small notebook in my coat or back pocket for thoughts, observations and impressions. As a writer I use this notebook as an artist would a sketch pad, for stories and essays, and as a sporadic journal of my comings and goings. When I first started keeping notebooks, though, I was not yet a professional writer. I was still in college.   1

I made my first notebook entries . . . just after my freshman year, in what was actually a travel log. A buddy and I were setting out to trek from our Alabama hometown to the distant tundra of Alaska. With unbounded enthusiasm I began: "Wild, crazy ecstasy wants to wrench my head from my body." The log, written in a university composition book, goes on to chronicle our adventures in the land where the sun never sets, the bars never close and the prepipeline employment prospects were so bleak we ended up taking jobs as night janitors.   2

When I returned to college that fall I had a small revelation: the world around me of libraries, quadrangles, Frisbees and professors was as rich with material for my journals and notebooks as galumphing moose and garrulous fishermen.   3

These college notebooks, which built to a pitch my senior year, are gold mines to me now. Classrooms, girlfriends, cups of coffee and lines of   4 poetry—from mine to John Keats's—float by like clouds. As I lie beneath these clouds again, they take on familiar and distinctive shapes.

Though I can remember the campus's main quadrangle, I see it more 5 vividly when I read my description of school on a visit during summer break: "the muggy, lassitudinal air . . . the bird noises that cannot be pointed to, the summer emptiness that grows emptier with a few students squeaking by the library on poorly oiled bicycles." An economics professor I fondly remember returns with less fondness in my notebooks, "staring down at the class with his equine face." And a girl I had a crush on senior year, whom I now recall mistily, reappears with far more vitality as "the ample, slightly-gawky, whole-wheat, fractured object of my want gangling down the hall in spring heat today."

When, in reading over my notebooks, I am not peering out at quad- 6 rangles, midterm exams, professors or girlfriends, I see a portrait of my parents and hometown during holidays and occasional weekend breaks. Like a wheel, home revolves, each turn regarded differently depending on the novel or political essay I'd been most influenced by the previous semester.

Mostly, though, in wandering back through my notebooks, I meet 7 someone who could be my younger brother: the younger version of myself. The younger me seems moodier, more inquisitive, more fun-loving and surprisingly eager to stay up all night partying or figuring out electron orbitals for a 9 A.M. exam. The younger me wanders through a hall of mirrors of the self, writes of "seeing two or three of myself on every corner," and pens long meditations on God and society before scribbling in the margin, "what a child I am." The younger me also finds humor in trying to keep track of this hall of mirrors, commenting in ragged verse.

> *I hope that one day*
> *Some grandson or cousin*
> *Will read these books,*
> *And know that I was*
> *Once a youth*
> *Sitting in drugstores with*
> *Anguished looks.*
> *And poring over coffee,*
> *And should have poured*
> *The coffee*
> *Over these lines.*

I believe that every college student should attempt to keep some form *8* of notebook, journal or diary. A notebook is a secret garden in which to dance, sing, muse, wander, perform handstands, even cry. In the privacy of this little book, you can make faces, curse, turn somersaults and ask yourself if you're really in love. A notebook or journal is one of the few places you can call just your own.

. . . Journal writing suffers when you let someone, in your mind, look *9* over your shoulder. Honesty wilts when a parent, teacher or friend looms up in your imagination to discourage you from putting your true thoughts on the page. Journal writing also runs a related hazard: the dizzying suspicion that one day your private thoughts, like those of Samuel Pepys or Virginia Woolf, will be published in several volumes and land up required reading for English 401. How can you write comfortably when the eyes of all future readers are upon you? Keep your notebooks with the abandon of one who knows his words will go up in smoke. Then you might really strike fire a hundred years or so from now if anyone cares to pry.

By keeping notebooks, you improve your writing ability, increasing *10* your capacity to communicate both with yourself and others. By keeping notebooks, you discover patterns in yourself, whether lazy ones that need to be broken or healthy ones that can use some nurturing. By keeping notebooks, you heighten some moments and give substance to others: even a journey to the washateria offers potential for some off-beat journal observations. And by keeping notebooks while still in college, you chart a terrain that, for many, is more dynamically charged with ideas and discussions than the practical, workaday world just beyond. Notebooks, I believe, not only help us remember this dynamic charge, but also help us sustain it.

Not long ago, while traveling with a friend in Yorktown, Va., I passed *11* by a time capsule buried in the ground in 1976, intended to be dug up in 2076. Keeping notebooks and journals is rather like burying time capsules into one's own life. There's no telling what old rock song, love note, philosophical complaint or rosy Saturday morning you'll unearth when you dig up these personal time capsules. You'll be able to piece together a remarkable picture of where you've come from, and may well get some important glimmers about where you're going.

Robert Rauschenberg's collage invites the viewer to reconsider images from the mid-twentieth century that are juxtaposed against each other. A journal assignment on page 28 asks you to analyze and evaluate the rhetorical elements in this work of art: the artist's purpose, his genre, the intended audience, and the historical and cultural context.

Robert Rauschenberg
Retroactive I (1964)
Courtesy Wadsworth Athenaeum, Hartford, Connecticut
Art © Robert Rauschenberg/Licensed by VAGA, NY, NY

chapter

2 Situations, Purposes, and Processes for Writing

A veteran smoker, you have become increasingly irritated at the non-smoking regulations that have appeared in restaurants, businesses, and other public places. And it's not just the laws that are irritating, but the holier-than-thou attitude of people who presume that what's good for them should be good for you. Non-smoking laws seem to give people license to censure your behavior while totally ignoring their own offensive behavior: polluting the atmosphere with hydrocarbons, fouling the aquifers with fertilizers, and generally corrupting the social air with odors of false superiority. So after one particularly memorable experience, you write a letter to the editor of the local paper, intending not only to express your own frustration but also to satirize all those smug do-gooders.

A s a Chinese-American woman growing up in America, you decide to write about the difficulty of living in two cultures. You recall how, during your childhood, you rebelled against your mother when she insisted that you learn about your Chinese heritage. You remember how much you hated your Chinese school and how embarrassed you were that your mother could not speak English properly. As you grew older, however, you realized the price you paid for your assimilation into American culture. After discussing this conflict with your friends, you decide to describe your experiences to others who share them or who may want to know what you learned. At that point, you write an autobiographical account of your experiences and send it to a metropolitan newspaper.

> *First and foremost I write for myself. Writing has been for a long time my major tool for self-instruction and self-development.*
> TONI CADE BAMBARA,
> AUTHOR OF
> THE SALT EATERS

> *How do I know what I think until I see what I say?*
> E. M. FORSTER,
> AUTHOR OF
> A PASSAGE TO INDIA

THE WRITING FOR THIS COURSE (AND THE STRUCTURE OF THIS TEXTBOOK) ASSUMES THAT WRITING IS VALUABLE FOR TWO RELATED REASONS. FIRST, WRITING ENABLES YOU TO LEARN ABOUT SOMETHING, TO HELP YOU OBSERVE your surroundings, to remember important ideas and events, and to record what you see and read. Second, writing is an important means to communicate an idea to your readers, to explain or evaluate an idea, to offer a solution, or to argue for your point of view. These two reasons for writing are usually related. If you want to persuade others to agree with your point of view, you'll be more effective if you reflect on how your personal observations, memories, experiences, and things you've read and heard might help you convince your readers. Whatever you write, however, you are always writing in a particular situation or context Understanding how your goals as a writer relate to the writing situation and to your own processes for writing is the focus of this chapter.

Rhetorical Situations

As you begin this writing course, you need to consider how you and your writing fit into a larger context. Anytime you write an e-mail response, a letter to your friends, an essay for your English or history class, an application for a job, a letter to the editor, or an entry in your journal, you are in the middle of a rhetorical situation. If rhetoric is the "art of using language effectively or persuasively," then the rhetorical situation is the overall context in which your writing occurs. The key parts of the rhetorical situation are you, the writer; the immediate occasion that prompts you to write; your intended purpose and audience; your genre or type of writing; and the larger social context in which you are writing. Since these key terms are used repeatedly in this course, you need to know exactly what each term means and how it will help guide your writing.

THE WRITER   You are the writer. Sometimes you write in response to an assignment, but at other times, you choose to write because of something that happened or something that made you think or react. In college or on the job, you often have writing assignments, but in your life, you are often the one who decides to write when you need to remember something, plan, remind others, express your feelings, or solve a problem.

THE OCCASION   The occasion is whatever motivates you to write. Often you are motivated by an assignment that a teacher or a boss gives you. Sometimes, however, a particular event or incident makes you want to write. The cause may be a conversation you had with a friend, an article you read, or something that happened to you recently. The occasion is simply the immediate cause or the pressing need to write, whether assigned to you by someone else or just determined by you to be the reason for your desire to write.

PURPOSE   Your purpose in writing is the effect you wish to have on your intended audience. Major purposes for writing include **expressing** your feelings; investigating a subject and **reporting** your findings; **explaining** an idea or concept; **evaluating** some object, performance, or image; **proposing a solution** to a problem; and **arguing** for your position and responding to alternative or opposing positions.

AUDIENCE   Your knowledge about your intended audience should always guide and shape your writing. If you are writing for yourself, you can just list ideas, express your thoughts, or make informal notes. If you are writing to explain an idea or concept, you should think about who needs or wants to know about your idea. To whom do you want to explain this idea? Are they likely to be novices or experts on the topic? Similarly, if you are arguing for your position, you need to consider the thoughts and feelings of readers who may have several different points of view. What do they believe about your topic? Do they agree or disagree with your position, or are they undecided?

GENRE   The genre you choose is simply the kind, type, or form of writing you select. Everyone is familiar with genres in literature, such as poems, novels, and plays. In nonfiction, typical genres are essays, memoirs, magazine articles, and editorials. In college, you may write in a variety of genres, including e-mail, personal essays, lab reports, summaries, reviews of research, analytical essays, argumentative essays, and even scientific or business reports. Sometimes, you may need to write multigenre or multimedia reports with graphic images or pictures. For community service learning or on the job, you may write reports, analyses, brochures, or flyers. As a citizen of the community, you may write letters to the editor, responses to an online discussion forum, or letters to your representative.

66 Every genre positions those who participate in a text of that kind: as interviewer or interviewee, as listener or storyteller, as a reader or a writer, as a person interested in political matters, as someone to be instructed or as someone who instructs; each of these positionings implies different possibilities for response and for action. 99

—GUNTHER KRESS, AUTHOR OF <u>LITERACY IN THE NEW MEDIA AGE</u>

> *A rhetorically sound definition of genre must be centered not on the substance or form of discourse but on the action it is used to accomplish.*
>
> —CAROLYN MILLER, TEACHER AND AUTHOR OF GENRE AS SOCIAL ACTION

The genre you choose helps create the intellectual, social, or cultural relationship between you and your reader. It helps you communicate your purpose to your reader or makes possible the social action you wish to achieve. If your purpose is to analyze or critique material you are reading in a class, an essay is a genre suitable to your purpose and your intended audience (your teacher and your peers in class). A lab report is a different genre, requiring your notes, observations, and hypothesis about your experiment, presented for members of a scientific community. Finally, the purpose of a one-page brochure for your community crisis center, for example, may be to advertise its services to a wide audience that includes college students and members of the community. The point is to learn what readers expect of each genre and then choose—or modify—a genre that is appropriate for your purpose and audience. Learning which genres are appropriate for each writing situation and learning about the formal features of each genre (such as introduction, presentation of information, paragraphing, and vocabulary) is a key part of each writing task. Remember, however, that genres have rules but are not rule bound. Every text should have recognizable features of a genre but also individual variation appropriate for that particular occasion.

CONTEXT As both a reader and a writer, you must consider the rhetorical and social context. When you read an essay or other text, think about the **author,** the **place of publication,** the **ongoing conversation** about this topic, and the larger **social or cultural context.** First, consider who wrote an essay and where it appeared. Was the essay a citizen's editorial in the *New York Times,* a journalist's feature article in *Vogue,* a scientist's research report in the *New England Journal of Medicine,* or a personal essay on an individual's Web site? Often, who wrote the article, what his or her potential bias or point of view was, and the place of publication can be just as important as what the article says. Next, consider the ongoing conversation to which this essay contributes. What different viewpoints exist on this topic? Which perspectives does this essay address? Finally, the larger sense of culture, politics, and history in which the article appears may be crucial to your understanding.

Similarly, when you write an essay, think about where it might be read or published and what conversation already exists on the topic. What cultural or political points of view are represented in the conversation? How does that ongoing conversation affect what you think? How does your own cultural, political, ethnic, or personal background affect what you believe? Understanding and analyzing the larger rhetorical and social context helps you become a better reader and writer.

REVIEW OF THE RHETORICAL SITUATION

Now that you've finished reading about these terms, notice how they overlap. They are separate, yet they all function together. Go back and reread each of the definitions for occasion, purpose, audience, genre, context, but this time pay attention to how they are interconnected. It's silly, for example, to talk about purpose or about audience without talking about everything else in the writing situation: the writer, the occasion for writing, the purpose, audience, genre, and overall context.

WHY THE RHETORICAL SITUATION IS IMPORTANT

So, you understand each of the elements of the rhetorical situation, and you see how they are interconnected. But how does that knowledge help you as a writer? The answer is both easy and difficult. The easy part is that every decision you make as a writer—how to begin, how much evidence you include, how you organize, whether you can use "I" in your writing, what style or tone you should use—depends on the rhetorical situation. The style and organization of a lab report is different from an essay, which is different from a brochure. If you've ever asked your teacher, "Won't you just tell me what you want?" the answer to that question always is, "Well, it depends." It depends on what is appropriate for the purpose, audience, genre, and context. And that is where the difficult part of writing begins: learning which genres, styles, appeals to your readers, and methods of organization are appropriate for each writing situation. To learn the various approaches to writing and how they are most effectively used is the reason that you continually read and practice writing the major genres taught in your composition class.

FREEWRITING: INVENTORY OF YOUR WRITING

Before you read further in this chapter, take out a pen or open a computer file and make a list of what you have written in the last year or two. Brainstorm a list of all the genres you can think of: shopping lists for a trip, letters to family or friends, applications for jobs, school essays, personal or professional Web sites, science projects, or memos for your boss. Then, for one of your longer writing projects, jot down several sentences describing the situation that called for that piece of writing—what was the occasion, purpose, and audience? What form or genre did your writing take? How did that genre help define a relationship between you and your reader? Where did you write it, and what was your writing process?

Purposes for Writing

Getting a good grade, sharing experiences with a friend, or contributing to society may be among your motives for writing. However, as a writer, you also have more specific rhetorical purposes for writing. These purposes help you make key decisions related to your audience and genre. When your main purpose is to express your feelings, you may write a private entry in your journal. When your main purpose is to explain how your sales promotion increased the number of your company's customers, you may write a formal sales report to your boss. When your main purpose is to persuade others to see a movie that you like, you may write a review for the local newspaper. In each case, the intended rhetorical purpose—your desire to create a certain effect on your audience—helps determine what you write and how you say it.

> *The writer may write to inform, to explain, to entertain, to persuade, but whatever the purpose there should be first of all, the satisfaction of the writer's own learning.*
>
> DONALD MURRAY,
> TEACHER AND
> PULITZER PRIZE-
> WINNING JOURNALIST

WRITER-BASED PURPOSES

Because writing is, or should be, for yourself first of all, everything you write involves at least some purpose that benefits you. Of course, expressing yourself is a fundamental purpose of all writing. Without the satisfaction of expressing your thoughts, feelings, reactions, knowledge, or questions, you might not make the effort to write in the first place.

A closely related purpose is learning: Writing helps you discover what you think or feel, simply by using language to identify and compose your thoughts. Writing not only helps you form ideas but actually promotes observing and remembering. If you write down what you observe about people, places, or things, you can actually "see" them more clearly. Similarly, if you write down facts, ideas, experiences, or reactions to your readings, you will remember them longer. Writing and rewriting facts, dates, definitions, impressions, or personal experiences will improve your powers of recall on such important occasions as examinations and job interviews.

SUBJECT- AND AUDIENCE-BASED PURPOSES

Although some writing is intended only for yourself—such as entries in a diary, lists, class notes, reminders—much of your writing will be read by others, by those readers who constitute your "audience."

- You may write to *inform* others about a particular subject—to tell them about the key facts, data, feelings, people, places, or events.
- You may write to *explain* to your readers what something means, how it works, or why it happens.
- You may write to *persuade* others to believe or do something—to convince others to agree with your judgment about a book, record, or restaurant, or to persuade them to take a certain class, vote for a certain candidate, or buy some product you are advertising.
- You may write to *explore* ideas and "truths," to examine how your ideas have changed, to ask questions that have no easy answers, and then to share your thoughts and reflections with others.
- You may write to *entertain*—as a primary purpose in itself or as a purpose combined with informing, explaining, persuading, or exploring. Whatever your purposes may be, good writing both teaches and pleases. Remember, too, that your readers will learn more, remember more, or be more convinced when your writing contains humor, wit, or imaginative language.

" I think writing is really a process of communication. . . . It's the sense of being in contact with people who are part of a particular audience that really makes a difference to me in writing."

—SHERLEY ANN WILLIAMS,
POET, CRITIC, AND NOVELIST

COMBINATIONS OF PURPOSES

In many cases, you write with more than one purpose in mind. Purposes may appear in combinations, connected in a sequence, or actually overlapping. Initially, you may take notes about a subject to learn and remember, but later you may want to inform others about what you have discovered. Similarly, you may begin by writing to express your feelings about a movie that you loved or that upset you; later, you may wish to persuade others to see it—or not to see it.

Purposes can also contain each other, like Chinese boxes, or overlap, blurring the distinctions. An explanation of how an automobile works will contain information about that vehicle. An attempt to persuade someone to buy an automobile may contain an explanation of how it handles and information about its body style or engine. Usually, writing to persuade others will contain explanations and basic information,

" Writing, as a rhetorical act, is carried out within a web of purpose."

—LINDA FLOWER,
TEACHER AND RESEARCHER IN COMPOSITION

but the reverse is not necessarily true; you can write simply to give information, without trying to persuade anyone to do anything.

SUBJECT, PURPOSE, AND THESIS

The *thesis, claim,* or *main idea* in a piece of writing is related to your purpose. As a writer, you usually have a purpose in mind that serves as a guide while you gather information about your subject and think about your audience. However, as you collect and record information, impressions, and ideas you gradually narrow your subject to a specific topic and thus clarify your purpose. You bring your purpose into sharper and sharper focus—as if progressing on a target from the outer circles to the bull's-eye—until you have narrowed your purpose down to a central thesis. The thesis is the dominant idea, explanation, evaluation, or recommendation that you want to impress upon your readers.

The following examples illustrate how a writer moves from a general subject, guided by purpose, to a specific thesis or claim.

SUBJECT	PURPOSE	THESIS, CLAIM, OR MAIN IDEA
Childhood experiences	To express your feelings and explain how one childhood experience was important.	The relentless competition between my sisters and me distorted my easygoing personality.
Heart disease	To inform readers about relationships between Type A personalities and heart attacks.	Type A personalities do not necessarily have an abnormally high risk of suffering heart attacks.
The death penalty	To persuade readers that the death penalty should be used.	Despite our belief that killing is wrong, a state-administered death penalty is fair, just, and humane.

Purpose and Audience

Writing for yourself is relatively easy; after all, you already know your audience and can make spontaneous judgments about what is essential and what is not. However, when your purpose is to communicate to other readers, you need to analyze your audience. Your writing will be more effective if you can anticipate what your readers know and need to know, what they are interested in, and what their beliefs or attitudes are. As you write for different readers, you will select different kinds of information, organize it in different ways, or write in a more formal or less formal style.

FREEWRITING: WRITING FOR DIFFERENT AUDIENCES

Before you read further, get a pen or pencil and several sheets of paper and do the following exercise:

1. For your eyes only, write about what you did at a recent party. Write for four minutes.

2. On a second sheet of paper, describe for the members of your writing class what you did at this party; you will read it aloud to the class. Stop after four minutes.

3. On a third sheet of paper, write a letter to one of your parents describing what you did at the party. Stop after four minutes.

AUDIENCE ANALYSIS

If you are writing to communicate to other readers, analyzing your probable audience will help you answer some basic questions:

- What genre should I choose? What genre—or combination of genres— would best enable me to communicate with my audience?
- How much information or evidence is enough? What should I assume my audience already knows? What should I not tell them? What do they believe? Will they readily agree with me, or will they be antagonistic?
- How should I organize my writing? How can I get my readers' attention? Can I just describe my subject and tell a story, or should I analyze everything in a logical order? Should I put my best examples or arguments first or last?
- Should I write informally, with simple sentences and easy vocabulary, or should I write in a more elaborate or specialized style, with technical vocabulary?

Analyze your audience by considering the following questions. As you learn more about your audience, the possibilities for your own role as a writer will become clearer.

1. **Audience profile.** How narrow or broad is your audience? Is it a narrow and defined audience—a single person, such as your Aunt Mary, or a group with clear common interests, such as the zoning board in your city or the readers of *Organic Gardening?* Is it a broad and diverse audience: educated readers who wish to be informed on current events, American voters as a whole, or residents of your state? Do your readers have identifiable roles? Can you determine their age, sex, economic status, ethnic background, or occupational category?

2. **Audience–subject relationship.** Consider what your readers know about your subject. If they know very little about it, you'll need to explain the basics; if they already know quite a bit, you can go straight to more difficult or complex issues. Also estimate their probable attitude toward this subject. Are they likely to be sympathetic or hostile?

3. **Audience–writer relationship.** What is your relationship with your readers? Do you know each other personally? Do you have anything in common? Will your audience be likely to trust what you say, or will they be skeptical about your judgments? Are you the expert on this particular subject and the readers the novices? Or are you the novice and your readers the experts?

4. **Writer's role.** To communicate effectively with your audience, you should also consider your own role or perspective. Of the many roles that you could play (friend, big sister or brother, student of psychology, music fan, employee of a fast-food restaurant, and so on), choose one that will be effective for your purpose and audience. If, for example, you are writing to sixth-graders about nutrition, you could choose the perspective of a concerned older brother or sister. Your writing might be more effective, however, if you assume the role of a person who has worked in fast-food restaurants for three years and knows what goes into hamburgers, french fries, and milkshakes.

Writers may write to real audiences, or they may create audiences. Sometimes the relationship between writer and reader is real (sister writing to brother), so the writer starts with a known audience and writes accordingly. Sometimes, however, writers begin and gradually discover or create an audience in the process of writing. Knowing the audience guides the writing, but the writing may construct an audience as well.

Purpose, Audience, and Genre

In addition to considering your purpose and audience, think also about the possible forms or genres your writing might take. If you are writing to observe or remember something, you may want to write an informal essay, a letter, a memoir, or even an e-mail to reach your audience. If you are writing to inform your readers or explain some idea, you may write an article, essay, letter, report, or pamphlet to best achieve your purpose and address your audience. Argumentative writing—writing to evaluate, persuade, or recommend some position or course of action—takes place in many different genres, from e-mails and letters, to reviews and editorials, to proposals and researched documents. As you select a topic, consider which genre would most effectively accomplish your purpose for your intended audience.

Below are some of the common genres that you will read or write while in college, on the job, or as a member of your community. Each genre has certain organization and style features that readers of this genre expect. Knowing the genre that you are writing or reading helps answer questions about how to write or how to respond to a piece of writing.

GENRE	CONVENTIONS OF ORGANIZATION AND STYLE
Personal essay	Some narrative and descriptive passages Informal, uses first person "I" Applies personal experience to larger social question
Research review	Uses concise, accurate summary May be an annotated bibliography or part of a larger thesis Adheres to MLA, APA, Chicago styles
Argumentative essay	Makes a claim about a controversial topic Responds to alternative or opposing positions Carefully considers audience Supports claims with evidence and examples Uses reasonable tone Has formal paragraphing
Laboratory report	May be informal description of materials, procedures, and results May be formal organization with title, abstract, introduction, method, results, and discussion

Brochure	Mixes graphics, text, visuals Visually arresting and appealing layout Concise information and language
Letter to the editor	Refers to issue or topic States opinion, point of view, or recommendation Usually concise to fit into editorial page
Posting to an electronic forum	Connects to specific thread in discussion May be informal style Flaming and trolling occur, but are often censured
E-mail and text messaging	Usually short Informal and personal style Often without salutation, caps, or punctuation May use emoticons such as :-), :-(, :-.) (Cindy Crawford), or 8(:-) (Mickey Mouse), or acronyms such as BTW, LOL, FYI, or THX

FREEWRITING: PURPOSE, AUDIENCE, GENRE, AND CONTEXT IN AN IMAGE

Before you read further in this chapter, analyze the rhetorical elements in the work of art by Robert Rauschenberg that appears at the beginning of this chapter. Who is the artist? What is the purpose of this painting? Who was the intended audience? How would you describe this genre of art? What was the social and cultural context in which this painting appeared? (Use Yahoo!, Google, or your favorite search engine to discover background information.) Overall, how effective is this painting at achieving its rhetorical purpose for its audience and context? Explain.

The Rhetorical Situation

To review, the rhetorical situation consists of the writer, the occasion, the purpose and audience, the genre and the context. Sometimes several of these are assigned to the writer, but at other times, the writer chooses a purpose, audience, and genre. The key point to remember is that these terms are all interrelated and interconnected. Your overall purpose often depends on your selected audience. Deciding on a particular audience may mean choosing a particular genre. Thinking about the context and conversation surrounding a particular topic may help you be more persuasive for your selected audience. Writing and revising require reconsidering and revising each of these elements to make them work harmoniously to achieve your rhetorical goal.

The following scenarios illustrate how the writer's purpose, the occasion, the audience, genre, and context work together to define the rhetorical situation. In the following descriptions, identify each of the key parts of the rhetorical situation.

A student majoring in journalism reads accounts by reporters embedded in military units in the Iraq war. After reading several accounts, the student decides that this war was a good test case in the battle between the public's right to receive accurate information and the military's need for security. The advantages of embedded journalists were their on-the-spot reports and film footage; the disadvantages included the journalists' natural bias toward their military unit, their potential violations of privacy and tactical security, and their inability to present a larger picture of the progress of the war. The student decides to write an essay for a conservative online news magazine in which she recommends policy changes for embedded reporters for any future military engagement.

In response to a request by an editor of a college recruiting pamphlet, a student decides to write an essay explaining the advantages of the social and academic life at his university. According to the editor, the account needs to be realistic but should also promote the university. It shouldn't be too academic and stuffy—the college catalog itself contains all the basic information—but it should give high school seniors a flavor of college life. The student decides to write a narrative account of his most interesting experiences during his first week at college.

PURPOSE, AUDIENCE, AND CONTEXT IN TWO ESSAYS

The two short essays that follow appeared as columns in newspapers. Both relate the writers' own experiences. They are similar in genre but have different purposes, they appeal to different readers, and they have different social and cultural contexts. First, read each essay just to understand each writer's point of view. Then reread each essay, thinking particularly about each writer's main purpose, his or her intended audience, and the social and cultural context surrounding each topic.

PROFESSIONAL WRITING

The Struggle to Be an All-American Girl

Elizabeth Wong

It's still there, the Chinese school on Yale Street where my brother and 1
I used to go. Despite the new coat of paint and the high wire fence, the
school I knew 10 years ago remains remarkably, stoically the same.

Every day at 5 P.M., instead of playing with our fourth- and fifth-grade 2
friends or sneaking out to the empty lot to hunt ghosts and animal bones,
my brother and I had to go to Chinese school. No amount of kicking,
screaming, or pleading could dissuade my mother, who was solidly determined to have us learn the language of our heritage.

Forcibly, she walked us the seven long, hilly blocks from our home to 3
school, depositing our defiant tearful faces before the stern principal. My
only memory of him is that he swayed on his heels like a palm tree, and he
always clasped his impatient twitching hands behind his back. I recognized
him as a repressed maniacal child killer, and knew that if we ever saw his
hands we'd be in big trouble.

We all sat in little chairs in an empty auditorium. The room smelled 4
like Chinese medicine, and imported faraway mustiness. Like ancient moth-
balls or dirty closets. I hated that smell. I favored crisp new scents. Like
the soft French perfume that my American teacher wore in public school.

Although the emphasis at the school was mainly language—speaking, 5
reading, writing—the lessons always began with an exercise in politeness.
With the entrance of the teacher, the best student would tap a bell and
everyone would get up, kowtow, and chant, "sing san ho," the phonetic for
"How are you, teacher?"

Being ten years old, I had better things to learn than ideographs copied 6
painstakingly in lines that ran right to left from the tip of a *moc but,* a real
ink pen that had to be held in an awkward way if blotches were to be
avoided. After all, I could do the multiplication tables, name the satellites
of Mars, and write reports on "Little Women" and "Black Beauty." Nancy
Drew, my favorite book heroine, never spoke Chinese.

The language was a source of embarrassment. More times than not, I had 7
tried to disassociate myself from the nagging loud voice that followed me

wherever I wandered in the nearby American supermarket outside China-town. The voice belonged to my grandmother, a fragile woman in her sev-enties who could outshout the best of the street vendors. Her humor was raunchy, her Chinese rhythmless, patternless. It was quick, it was loud, it was unbeautiful. It was not like the quiet, lilting romance of French or the gen-tle refinement of the American South. Chinese sounded pedestrian. Public.

In Chinatown, the comings and goings of hundreds of Chinese on their 8 daily tasks sounded chaotic and frenzied. I did not want to be thought of as mad, as talking gibberish. When I spoke English, people nodded at me, smiled sweetly, said encouraging words. Even the people in my culture would cluck and say that I'd do well in life. "My, doesn't she move her lips fast," they would say, meaning that I'd be able to keep up with the world outside Chinatown.

My brother was even more fanatical than I about speaking English. He 9 was especially hard on my mother, criticizing her, often cruelly, for her pid-gin speech—smatterings of Chinese scattered like chop suey in her con-versation. "It's not 'What it is,' Mom," he'd say in exasperation. "It's 'What is it, what is it, what is it!' " Sometimes Mom might leave out an occasional "the" or "a," or perhaps a verb of being. He would stop her in mid-sentence: "Say it again, Mom. Say it right." When he tripped over his own tongue, he'd blame it on her: "See, Mom, it's all your fault. You set a bad example."

After two years of writing with a *moc but* and reciting words with mul- 10 tiples of meanings, I finally was granted a cultural divorce. I was permitted to stop Chinese school.

I thought of myself as multicultural. I preferred tacos to egg rolls; I 11 enjoyed Cinco de Mayo more than Chinese New Year.

At last, I was one of you; I wasn't one of them. 12

Sadly, I still am. 13

PROFESSIONAL WRITING

I'M O.K., BUT YOU'RE NOT

Robert Zoellner

The American novelist John Barth, in his early novel, *The Floating* 1 *Opera,* remarks that ordinary, day-to-day life often presents us with embarrassingly obvious, totally unsubtle patterns of symbolism and meaning—life in the midst of death, innocence vindicated, youth versus age, etc.

The truth of Barth's insight was brought home to me recently while having breakfast in a lawn-bordered restaurant on College Avenue near the Colorado State University campus. I had asked to be seated in the smoking section of the restaurant—I have happily gone through three or four packs a day for the past 40 years.

As it happened, the hostess seated me—I was by myself—at a little two-person table on the dividing line between the smoking and non-smoking sections. Presently, a well-dressed couple of advanced years, his hair a magisterial white and hers an electric blue, were seated in the non-smoking section five feet away from me.

It was apparent within a minute that my cigarette smoke was bugging them badly, and soon the husband leaned over and asked me if I would please stop smoking. As a chronic smokestack, I normally comply, out of simple courtesy, with such requests. Even an addict such as myself can quit for as long as 20 minutes.

But his manner was so self-righteous and peremptory—he reminded me of Lee Iacocca boasting about Chrysler—that the promptings of original sin, always a problem with me, took over. I quietly pointed out that I was in the smoking section—if only by five feet—and that that fact meant that I had met my social obligation to non-smokers. Besides, the idea of morning coffee without a cigarette was simply inconceivable to me—might as well ask me to vote Republican.

The two of them ate their eggs-over-easy in hurried and sullen silence, while I chain-smoked over my coffee. As well as be hung for a sheep as a lamb, I reasoned. Presently they got up, paid their bill, and stalked out in an ambiance of affronted righteousness and affluent propriety.

And this is where John Barth comes in. They had parked their car—a diesel Mercedes—where it could be seen from my table. And in the car, waiting impatiently, was a splendidly matched pair of pedigreed poodles, male and female.

Both dogs were clearly in extremis, and when the back door of the car was opened, they made for the restaurant lawn in considerable haste. Without ado (no pun intended), the male did a doo-doo that would have done credit to an animal twice his size, and finished off with a leisurely, ruminative wee-wee. The bitch of the pair, as might be expected of any well-brought-up female of Republican proclivities, confined herself to a modest wee-wee, fastidious, diffident, and quickly executed.

Having thus polluted the restaurant lawn, the four of them marshalled   9
their collective dignity and drove off in a dense cloud of blue smoke—that
lovely white Mercedes was urgently in need of a valve-and-ring job, its
emission sticker an obvious exercise in creative writing.

As I regretfully watched them go—after all, the four of them had made   10
my day—it seemed to me that they were in something of a hurry, and I
uncharitably wondered if the husband was not anxious to get home in order
to light the first Fall fire in his moss-rock fireplace, or apply the Fall ration
of chemical fertilizer to his doubtlessly impeccable lawn, thus adding another half-pound of particulates to the local atmosphere and another 10
pounds of nitrates and other poisons to the regional aquifers. But that, of
course, is pure and unkindly speculation.

In any case, the point of this real-life vignette, as John Barth would   11
insist, is obvious. The current controversy over public smoking in Fort
Collins is a clear instance of selective virtue at work, coming under the
rubric of, what I do is perfectly OK, but what you do is perfectly awful.

QUESTIONS FOR WRITING AND DISCUSSION

1. Choosing only one adjective to describe your main reaction to each
    essay, answer the following question: "When I finished the _____ [Wong,
    Zoellner] essay, I was _____ [intrigued, bored, amused, irritated, curious, con-
    fused, or _____] because _____. Explain your choice of adjectives in one or
    two sentences.

2. Referring to specific passages, explain the purpose and state the thesis or
    main point of each essay.

3. What personality or role does each writer project? Drawing from evidence in
    the essay, describe what you think both writers would be like if you met them.

4. Both of these essays appeared in newspapers. What kind of reader would find
    each essay interesting? What kind of reader would not enjoy each essay? For
    each essay, find examples of specific sentences, word choices, vocabulary, ex-
    periences, or references to culture or politics that would appeal to one reader
    but perhaps irritate another.

5.   These two essays are similar in genre—they are both informal essays narrating personal experiences and explaining what each writer discovered or learned. There are differences, however, in structure and style. What differences do you notice in the way each essay begins and concludes, in the order of the paragraphs, and in vocabulary or style of the sentences?

6.   Each essay has a particular social, cultural, and political context. Describe this context for both essays. Then identify at least three other viewpoints that exist in the cultural, social, or political conversations that surround each of these topics. (For example, what are different points of view about multicultural or bilingual education? What arguments exist both for and against smoking in privately owned business establishments?) How effective is each writer in responding to the ongoing cultural, social, or political context or conversation?

"I don't see writing as communication of something already discovered, as "truths" already known. Rather, I see writing as a job of experiment. It's like any discovery job; you don't know what's going to happen until you try it."

—WILLIAM STAFFORD, TEACHER, POET, AND ESSAYIST

Dimensions of the Writing Process

Processes for writing vary from one writer to the next and from one writing situation to the next. Most writers, however, can identify four basic stages, or dimensions, of their writing process: collecting, shaping, drafting, and revising. The writing situation may precede these stages—particularly if you are assigned a subject, purpose, audience, and form. Usually, however, you continue to narrow your subject, clarify your purpose, meet the needs of your audience, and modify your form as you work through the dimensions of your writing process.

COLLECTING

Mark Twain, author of *Huckleberry Finn,* once observed that if you attempt to carry a cat around the block by its tail, you'll gain a whole lot of information about cats that you'll never forget. You may collect such firsthand information, or you may rely on the data, experience, or expertise of others. In any case, writers constantly collect facts, impressions, opinions, and ideas that are relevant to their subjects, purposes, and audiences. Collecting involves observing, remembering, imagining, thinking, reading, listening, writing, investigating, talking, taking notes, and experimenting. Collecting also involves thinking about the relationships among the bits of information that you have collected.

SHAPING

Writers focus and organize the facts, examples, and ideas that they have collected into the recorded, linear form that is written language. When a hurricane hits the Gulf Coast, for example, residents of Texas, Louisiana, Mississippi, Alabama, and Florida are likely to collect an enormous amount of data in just a few hours. Rain, floods, tree limbs snapping in the wind, unboarded windows shattering, sirens blaring—all of these events occur nearly simultaneously. If you try to write about such devastation, you need to narrow your focus (you can't describe everything that happened) and organize your information (you can't describe all of your experiences at the same time).

The genre of the personal essay, weaving description in a chronological order, is just one of the shapes that a writer may choose to develop and organize experience. Such shaping strategies also help writers collect additional information and ideas. Reconstructing a chronological order, for example, may suggest some additional details—perhaps a wet, miserable-looking dog running through the heavy downpour—that you might not otherwise have remembered.

> *The writing process is not linear, moving smoothly in one direction from start to finish. It is messy, recursive, convoluted, and uneven. Writers write, plan, revise, anticipate, and review throughout the writing process.*
>
> —MAXINE HAIRSTON,
> TEACHER AND AUTHOR OF ARTICLES AND TEXTBOOKS ON WRITING

DRAFTING

At some point, writers actually write down a rough version of what will evolve into the finished piece of writing. Drafting processes vary widely from one writer to the next. Some writers prefer to reread their collecting and shaping notes, find a starting point, and launch themselves—figuring out what they want to say as they write it. Other writers start with a plan—a mental strategy, a short list, or an outline—of how they wish to proceed. Whatever approach you use in your draft, write down as much as possible: You want to see whether the information is clear, whether your overall shape expresses and clarifies your purpose, and whether your content and organization meet the needs and expectations of your audience.

> *We must and do write each our own way.*
>
> EUDORA WELTY,
> NOVELIST AND ESSAYIST

REVISING

When writers revise rough drafts, they literally "resee" their subjects—and then modify drafts to fit new visions. Revision is more than just tinkering with a word here and there; revision leads to larger changes—new examples or details, a different organization, or a new perspective. You accomplish these changes by adding, deleting, substituting, or reordering words, sentences, and paragraphs. Although revision begins the moment you get your first idea, most revisions are based on the reactions—or anticipated reactions—of the audience to your draft. You often play the role of audience yourself by putting the draft aside and rereading it later when you have some distance from your writing. Wherever you feel readers might not get your point, you revise to make it clearer. You may also get feedback from readers in a class workshop, suggesting that you collect more or different information, alter the shape of your draft to improve the flow of ideas, or clarify your terminology. As a result of your rereading and your readers' suggestions, you may change your thesis or write for an entirely different audience.

Editing—in contrast to revising—focuses on the minor changes that you make to improve the accuracy and readability of your language. You usually edit your essay to improve word choice, grammar, usage, or punctuation. You also use a computer spell-check program and proofread to catch typos and other surface errors.

THE WHOLE PROCESS

In practice, a writer's process rarely follows the simple, consecutive order that these four stages or dimensions suggest. The writing process is actually recursive: It begins at one point, goes on to another, comes back to the first, jumps to the third, and so forth. A stage may last hours or only a second or two. While writing a letter to a friend, you may collect, shape, revise, and edit in one quick draft; a research paper may require repeated shaping over a two-week period. As writers draft, they may correct a few mistakes or typos, but they may not proofread until many days later. In the middle of reorganizing an essay, writers often reread drafts, go back and ask more questions, and collect more data. Even while editing, writers may throw out several paragraphs, collect some additional information, and draft new sections.

In addition to the recursive nature of the writing process, keep in mind that writing often occurs during every stage, not just during drafting and revising. During collecting, you will be recording information and jotting down ideas. During shaping, you will be writing out trial versions that you may use later when you draft or revise. Throughout the writing process, you use your writing to modify your subject, purpose, audience, and form.

The most important point to keep in mind is that the writing process is unique to each writer and to each writing situation. What works for one writer may be absolutely wrong for you. Some writers compose nearly everything in their heads. Others write only after discussing the subject with friends or drawing diagrams and pictures.

During the writing process, you need to experiment with several collecting, shaping, and drafting strategies to see what works best for you and for a particular piece of writing. As long as your process works, however, it's legitimate—no matter how many times you backtrack and repeat stages. When you are struggling with a piece of writing, remember that numerous revisions are a normal part of the writing process—even for most professionals.

Circling back over what you have already written—to sharpen your thesis, improve the organization, tighten up a paragraph, or add specific details to your examples—is likely to be the most time-consuming, yet worthwhile, part of your writing process. Most professional writers testify to the necessity and value of writing numerous drafts. When you are reworking a piece of writing, scrawling revisions over what you had hoped would be your finished product, remember what Nobel laureate Isaac Bashevis Singer once pointed out: "The wastepaper basket is the writer's best friend."

Writing with a Computer

Even though you have probably used a computer to help write your essays, you may not have worked in a writing classroom or lab where you have the advantages of a network. Most college writing classes today use many of the advantages of a networked environment, including e-mail, access to a class Web page and class discussion forums, and access to the Internet. In a networked environment, teachers and students can send each other e-mail and can e-mail drafts of their work-in-progress. Students no longer need to be in the same room, building, or city in order to be part of their writing community. They can respond electronically to each other's writing in a discussion forum, chat room, blog, or bulletin board. They can collaboratively conduct research, post results using file sharing, and edit each other's drafts online. In the middle of drafting or revising an essay, they can quickly check the Internet or their library's database for other articles or information that they need. Finally, students often publish their essays online or even create their own Web pages using materials they have written for their writing course. In short, networked computers have totally revolutionized the teaching of writing by allowing discussion and revision to continue even after the class meeting time has finished. Writing in a networked computer environment reinforces the idea that a writing class is a continually supportive, interactive learning community.

WRITING WITH COMPUTERS

The computer can assist you both as a writing tool and as a networking tool. Listed in the left-hand column are writing activities that a standalone computer provides. Listed in the right-hand column are the additional capabilities of computers tied into a network.

The Computer as a Writing Tool
- Freewriting
- Brainstorming
- Double-entry reading log
- Answers to "Wh" questions
- Insert/delete sentences
- Move paragraphs
- Style/usage checkers
- Thesaurus
- Spelling checker
- Print preview

The Computer as a Networking Tool
- Access to bulletin boards
- E-mail messages
- E-mail essays or files
- "Chat" dialogues
- Postings to class forum
- Access to online library catalogs
- Access to the Internet and the World Wide Web

WARMING UP: JOURNAL EXERCISES

The following exercises will help you review and practice the topics covered in this chapter. In addition, you may discover a subject for your own writing. Choose three of the following entries, and write for ten minutes on each.

1. Reread your "authority" list from Chapter 1. Choose one of those topics and then explain your purpose, identify a possible audience, and select a genre you would use.

2. From the resources available to you at home or on your computer, find examples of four different genres, such as advertisements, pamphlets, letters, articles, letters to the editor, and so forth. For each sample genre, identify the purpose, audience, and context. Bring these samples to class and be prepared to explain the rhetorical situation for each genre and why each sample is or is not effective.

3. If you have already been given a writing assignment in another course, explain the purpose, the intended audience, and the genre for that assignment. Be prepared to explain in class (or in a discussion forum) how you plan to complete that assignment.

4. During the first week of the term, one of your friends, Mark Lindstrom, is in an accident and is hospitalized. While still under the effects of anesthesia, he scribbles the following note for you to mail to his parents.

> Dear Mom and Dad,
>
> I arrived here last week. The trip was terrible. Dr. Stevens says that my leg will be better soon. My roommate is very strange. The police say my money is gone forever.
>
> Please send $1,500 to my new address right away.
>
> Thanks!
>
> Your loving son
>
> Mark

Because you were at the accident and can fill in the details, Mark asks you to explain everything to his parents. Write a short letter to them. Next, write a paragraph to your best friend that describes what happened to Mark.

5. Explore the availability of computers on your campus. Where is the English department computer lab? What services does it offer? What other computer facilities are available? Write up your report and post it on your class bulletin board or forum.

6. Read Neil Petrie's essay and postscript at the end of this chapter. Then find the best paper you've written during the past year or two and write a "post-script" for it. Describe (a) the rhetorical situation, (b) your purpose, and (c) the process you used to write it.

A Writing Process at Work: Collecting and Shaping

PROFESSIONAL WRITING

ATHLETES AND EDUCATION

Neil H. Petrie

In the following essay, which appeared in The Chronicle of Higher Education, *Neil H. Petrie argues that colleges have a hypocritical attitude toward student athletes. Although most universities claim that their athletes—both male and female—are in college to get a good education, in reality the pressures on athletes compromise their academic careers. The problem, Petrie argues, is not the old cliché that jocks are dumb, but the endless hours devoted to practice or spent on road trips, which drain even the good student-athlete's physical and mental energies. Colleges point with pride to a tiny number of athletes who become professionals, but much more frequently the collegiate system encourages athletes to settle for lower grades and incomplete programs. In far too many cases, athletes never graduate. These are the students whom, as Petrie says, "the system uses and then discards after the final buzzer."*

I have spent all my adult life in academe, first as a student and then as a professor. During that time I have seen many variations in the role of intercollegiate athletics in the university, and I've developed sharply split opinions on the subject. On one hand, I despise the system, clinging as it does to the academic body like a parasite. On the other hand, I feel sympathy and admiration for most of the young athletes struggling to balance the task of getting an education with the need to devote most of their energies to the excessive demands of the gym and the field.

My earliest experiences with the intrusion of athletics into the classroom came while I was still a freshman at the University of Colorado. While

I was in my English professor's office one day, a colleague of hers came by for a chat. Their talk turned to the football coach's efforts to court the favor of the teachers responsible for his gladiators by treating them to dinner and a solicitous discussion of the academic progress of the players. I vividly recall my professor saying, "He can take me out to dinner if he wants, but if he thinks I'll pass his knuckleheads just because of that, he'd better think again."

Later, as a graduate teaching fellow, a lecturer, and then an assistant professor of English, I had ample opportunity to observe a Division I university's athletics program. I soon discovered that the prevailing stereotypes did not always apply. Athletes turned out to be as diverse as any other group of students in their habits, tastes, and abilities, and they showed a wide range of strategies for coping with the stress of their dual roles.

Some of them were poor students. An extreme example was the All-American football player (later a successful pro) who saw college only as a step to a six-figure contract and openly showed his disdain for the educational process. Others did such marginal work in my courses that I got the feeling they were daring me to give them D's or F's. One woman cross-country star, who almost never attended my composition class, used to push nearly illiterate essays under my office door at odd hours.

Yet many athletes were among the brightest students I had. Not so surprising, when you consider that, in addition to physical prowess, success in athletics requires intelligence, competitive drive, and dedication—all qualities that can translate into success in the classroom as well as on the field. The trouble is that the grinding hours of practice and road trips rob student athletes of precious study time and deplete their reserves of mental and physical energy. A few top athletes have earned A's; most are content to settle for B's or C's, even if they are capable of better.

The athletes' educational experience can't help being marred by their numerous absences and divided loyalties. In this respect, they are little different from the students who attempt to go to college while caring for a family or working long hours at an outside job. The athletes, however, get extra help in juggling their responsibilities. Although I have never been bribed or threatened and have never received a dinner invitation from a coach, I am expected to provide extra time and consideration for athletes, far beyond what I give other students.

Take the midterm grade reports, for example. At my university, the athletic department's academic counselor sends progress questionnaires to every teacher of varsity athletes. While the procedure shows admirable concern for the academic performance of athletes, it also amounts to preferential treatment. It requires teachers to take time from other teaching duties to fill out and return the forms for the athletes. (No other students get such progress reports.) If I were a cynic it would occur to me that the athletic department might actually be more concerned with athletes' eligibility than with their academic work.

Special attendance policies for athletes are another example of preferential treatment. Athletes miss a lot of classes. In fact, I think the road trip is one of the main reasons that athletes receive a deficient education. You simply can't learn as much away from the classroom and the library as on the campus. Nevertheless, professors continue to provide make-up tests, alternative assignments, and special tutoring sessions to accommodate athletes. Any other student would have to have been very sick or the victim of a serious accident to get such dispensations.

It is sad to see bright young athletes knowingly compromise their potential and settle for much less education than they deserve. It is infuriating, though, to see the ones less gifted academically exploited by a system that they do not comprehend and robbed of any possible chance to grow intellectually and to explore other opportunities.

One specific incident illustrates for me the worst aspects of college athletics. It wasn't unusual or extraordinary—just the all-too-ordinary case of an athlete not quite good enough to make a living from athletics and blind to the opportunity afforded by the classroom.

I was sitting in my office near the beginning of a term, talking to a parade of new advisees. I glanced up to see my entire doorway filled with the bulk of a large young man, whom I recognized as one of our basketball stars from several seasons ago who had left for the pros and now apparently come back.

Over the next hour I got an intensive course on what it's like to be a college athlete. In high school, John had never been interested in much outside of basketball, and, like many other indifferent students, he went on to junior college on an athletic scholarship. After graduating, he came to the university, where he played for two more years, finishing out his eligibility. He was picked in a late round of the N.B.A. draft and left college, but in the end he turned out to be a step too slow for the pros. By that time he had a family to support, and when he realized he could never make a career of basketball, he decided to return to college.

We both knew that his previous academic career hadn't been particularly focused, and that because of transferring and taking minimum course loads during the basketball season, he wouldn't be close to a degree. But I don't think either one of us was prepared for what actually emerged from our examination of his transcripts. It was almost as if he had never gone beyond high school. His junior-college transcript was filled with remedial and nonacademic courses.

Credit for those had not transferred to the university. Over the next two 14 years he had taken a hodgepodge of courses, mostly in physical education. He had never received any advice about putting together a coherent program leading to a degree. In short, the academic side of his college experience had been completely neglected by coaches, advisers, and, of course, John himself.

By the time we had evaluated his transcripts and worked out a tenta- 15 tive course of study, John was in shock and I was angry. It was going to take him at least three years of full-time study to complete a degree. He thanked me politely for my time, picked up the planning sheets, and left. I was ashamed to be a part of the university that day. Why hadn't anyone in the athletic department ever told him what it would take to earn a degree? Or at least been honest enough to say, "Listen, we can keep you eligible and give you a chance to play ball, but don't kid yourself into thinking you'll be getting an education, too."

I saw John several more times during the year. He tried for a while. He 16 took classes, worked, supported his family, and then he left again. I lost track of him after that. I can only hope that he found a satisfying job or completed his education at some other institution. I know people say the situation has improved in the last few years, but when I read about the shockingly low percentages of athletes who graduate, I think of John.

Colleges give student athletes preferential treatment. We let them cut 17 classes. We let them slide through. We protect them from harsh realities. We applaud them for entertaining us and wink when they compromise themselves intellectually. We give them special dorms, special meals, special tutors, and a specially reprehensible form of hypocrisy.

I can live with the thought of the athletes who knowingly use the 18 college-athletics system to get their pro contracts or their devalued degrees. But I have trouble living with the thought of the ones whom the system uses and then discards after the final buzzer.

PROFESSIONAL WRITING

ON WRITING "ATHLETES AND EDUCATION"

Neil Petrie

In the following postscript on his writing process, Neil Petrie describes why he wanted to write the paper, how he collected material to support his argument, and how he shaped and focused his ideas as he wrote. His comments illustrate how his purpose—to expose the hypocrisies of collegiate athletics—guided his writing of the essay. In addition, Petrie explains that other key questions affected the shape of his essay: how he should begin, where he should use his best example, and what words he should choose.

This essay has its origin, as all persuasive writing should, in a strongly held opinion. I'm always more comfortable if I care deeply about my subject matter. As a teacher, I hold some powerful convictions about the uneasy marriage of big-time athletics and higher education, and so I wanted to write an essay that would expose what I think are the dangers and hypocrisies of that system. 1

At the beginning of my essay, I wanted to establish some authority to lend credibility to my argument. Rather than gather statistics on drop-out rates of student athletes or collect the opinions of experts, I planned to rely on my own experiences as both a student and teacher. I hoped to convince my readers that my opinions were based on the authority of firsthand knowledge. In this introduction I was also aware of the need to avoid turning off readers who might dismiss me as a "jock hater." I had to project my negative feelings about the athletic system while maintaining my sympathy with the individual student athletes involved in that system. The thesis, then, would emerge gradually as I accumulated the evidence; it would be more implied than explicitly stated. 2

Gathering the material was easy. I selected a series of examples from my personal experiences as a college student and instructor, as well as anecdotes I'd heard from other instructors. Most of these stories were ones that I had shared before, either in private discussions with friends or in classrooms with students. 3

Shaping the material was a little tougher. As I began thinking about   *4*
my examples and how to order them, I saw that I really wanted to make two
main points. The first was that most colleges give preferential treatment to
athletes. The second point was that, despite the extra attention, the success
of the athlete's academic career is often ignored by all parties involved.
Many of my examples, I realized, illustrated the varieties of pressures put
upon both athletes and instructors to make sure that the students at least
get by in class and remain eligible. These examples seemed to cluster together because they showed the frustrations of teachers and the reactions
of athletes trying to juggle sports and academics. This group would make
a good introduction to my general exposé of the system. But I had one
more example I wanted to use that seemed to go beyond the cynicism of
some athletes or the hypocrisy of the educators. This was the case of John,
an athlete who illustrated what I thought were the most exploitative aspects of varsity athletics. I originally planned on devoting the bulk of my
essay to this story and decided to place it near the end where it would make
my second point with maximum emotional effect.

A two-part structure for the essay now emerged. In the first segment   *5*
following my introductory paragraph, I gave a series of shorter examples,
choosing to order them in roughly chronological order (paragraphs 2–4). I
then moved from these specific details to a more general discussion of the
demands placed upon both students and teachers, such as lengthy practice
time, grade reports, road trips, and special attendance policies. This concluded my description of the way the system operates (paragraphs 5–8).

Then it was time to shift gears, to provide a transition to the next part   *6*
of my essay, to what I thought was my strongest example. I wanted the
story of John to show how the system destroyed human potential. To do this,
I needed to increase the seriousness of the tone in order to persuade the
reader that I was dealing in more than a little bureaucratic boondoggling.
I tried to set the tone by my word choice: I moved from words such as
"sad," "compromise," and "settle" to words with much stronger emotional
connotations such as "infuriating," "exploited," and "robbed," all in a single
short transitional paragraph (paragraph 9).

I then introduced my final extended example in equally strong lan-   *7*
guage, identifying it as a worst-case illustration (paragraph 10). I elabo-
rated on John's story, letting the details and my reactions to his situation
carry the more intense outrage that I was trying to convey in this second
part of the essay (paragraphs 10–16). The first version that I tried was a

rambling narrative that had an overly long recounting of John's high school and college careers. So I tightened this section by eliminating such items as his progress through the ranks of professional basketball and his dreams of million-dollar contracts. I also cut down on a discussion of the various courses of study he was considering as options. The result was a sharper focus on the central issue of John's dilemma: the lack of adequate degree counseling for athletes.

After my extended example, all that was left was the conclusion. As I 8 wrote, I was very conscious of using certain devices, such as the repetition of key words and sentence patterns in paragraph seventeen ("We let them . . . We let them . . . We protect them . . . We applaud them . . . We give them . . .") to maintain the heightened emotional tone. I was also conscious of repeating the two-part structure of the essay in the last two paragraphs. I moved from general preferential treatment (paragraph 17) to the concluding and more disturbing idea of devastating exploitation (paragraph 18).

On the whole, I believe that this essay effectively conveys its point 9 through the force of accumulated detail. My personal experience was the primary source of evidence, and that experience led naturally to the order of the paragraphs and to the argument I wished to make: that while some athletes knowingly use the system, others are used and exploited by it.

QUESTIONS FOR WRITING AND DISCUSSION

1. In your journal, describe how your extracurricular activities (athletics, jobs, clubs, or family obligations) have or have not interfered with your education. Recall one specific incident that illustrates how these activities affected your classwork—either positively or negatively.

2. Describe Petrie's audience and purpose for this essay. What sentences reveal his intended audience? What sentences reveal his purpose? What sentences contain his thesis, claim, or main idea? Do you agree with that thesis? Why or why not?

3. Reread Petrie's postscript. Based on his comments and on your reading of the essay, how does Petrie describe or label each of the following sections of his essay:

    paragraphs 1–4

    paragraphs 5–8

    paragraph 9

    paragraphs 10–16

    paragraphs 17–18.

4. Who do you think is most to blame for the situation that Petrie describes: The athletes themselves? The colleges for paying their scholarships and then ignoring them when they drop out? The students and alumni who pay to see their teams win?

5. Petrie does not explicitly suggest a solution to the problem that he describes. Assume, however, that he has been asked by the president of his university to propose a solution. Write the letter that you think Petrie would send to the president.

A Writing Process at Work: Drafting and Revising

While drafting and revising, writers frequently make crucial changes in their ideas and language. The first scribbled sentences, written primarily for ourselves, are often totally different from what we later present to other people in final, polished versions. Take, for example, the final version of Abraham Lincoln's Gettysburg Address. It begins with the famous lines "Four score and seven years ago our fathers brought forth on this continent a new nation. . . ." But his first draft might well have begun, "Eighty-seven years ago, several politicians and other powerful men in the American Colonies got together and decided to start a new country. . . ." It is difficult to imagine that language ingrained in our consciousness was once drafted, revised, drafted again, and edited, as the author or authors added, deleted, reordered, and otherwise altered words, sentences, and ideas. In fact, it usually was.

Carl Becker's study of the American Declaration of Independence assembles the early drafts of that famous document and compares them with the final version. Shown below is Thomas Jefferson's first draft, with revisions made by Benjamin Franklin, John Adams, and other members of the Committee of Five that was charged with developing the new document.

Thomas Jefferson's Rough Draft of the Opening Sentences of the Declaration of Independence

When in the course of human events it becomes necessary for ~~a~~ ^{one} people to

dissolve the political bands which have connected them with another, and to

~~advance from that subordination in which they have hitherto remained, & to~~

assume among the powers of the earth the ~~equal & independent~~ ^{separate and equal} station to which

the laws of nature & of nature's god entitle them, a decent respect to the opinions

of mankind requires that they should declare the causes which impel them to

the separation.
~~the change.~~

We hold these truths ^{self-evident} ~~to be sacred & undeniable~~; that all men are created equal

& ~~independent~~; that ~~from that equal creation they derive in rights~~ ^{they are endowed by their creator with} inherent

& inalienable ^{rights; that} among ~~which~~ ^{these} are ~~the preservation of~~ life, & liberty, & the

pursuit of happiness. . . .

The Final Draft of the Opening Sentences of the Declaration of Independence, as Approved on July 4, 1776.

When in the Course of human events, it becomes necessary for one people to

dissolve the political bands which have connected them with another, and to

assume among the powers of the earth, the separate and equal station to which

the Laws of Nature and of Nature's God entitle them, a decent respect to the

opinions of mankind requires that they should declare the causes which impel

them to the separation.

We hold these truths to be self-evident, that all men are created equal, that they

are endowed by their Creator with certain inalienable Rights, that among these

are Life, Liberty and the pursuit of Happiness.

QUESTIONS FOR WRITING AND DISCUSSION

1. Describe your reaction to the "rough draft" of the Declaration of Independence. Where did it seem strange or make you feel uncomfortable?

2. Select one change in a sentence that most improved the final version. Explain how the revised wording is more effective.

3. Find one change in a word or phrase that constitutes an alteration in meaning rather than just a choice of "smoother" or more appropriate language. How does this change affect the meaning?

4. Upon rereading this passage from the Declaration of Independence, one reader wrote, "I was really irritated by that 'all men are created equal' remark. The writers were white, free, well-to-do, Anglo-Saxon, mostly Protestant males discussing their own 'inalienable rights.' They sure weren't discussing the 'inalienable rights' of female Americans or of a million slaves or of non-white free Americans!" Revise the passage from the Declaration of Independence using this person as your audience.

5. On the Internet, visit the National Archives at *http://www.nara.gov* to see a photograph of the original Declaration of Independence and learn how the Dunlap Broadside of the Declaration was read aloud to troops. What does this historical context add to what you know about the Declaration of Independence? Do the revisions help make the document more revolutionary or propagandistic? In addition, this site has other treasures from the National Archives including the police blotter listing Abraham Lincoln's assassination, the first report of the *Titanic's* collision with an iceberg, and Rosa Parks's arrest records. Do you think these documents are as important to our history and culture as the Declaration itself? Explain.

Norman Rockwell's painting is about the act of observing and recording images and is also a statement about the art of the self-portrait. Take notes describing the details that you observe in this painting, then read the commentary by Charles Rosen and Henri Zerner, reprinted on p. 59 of this chapter.

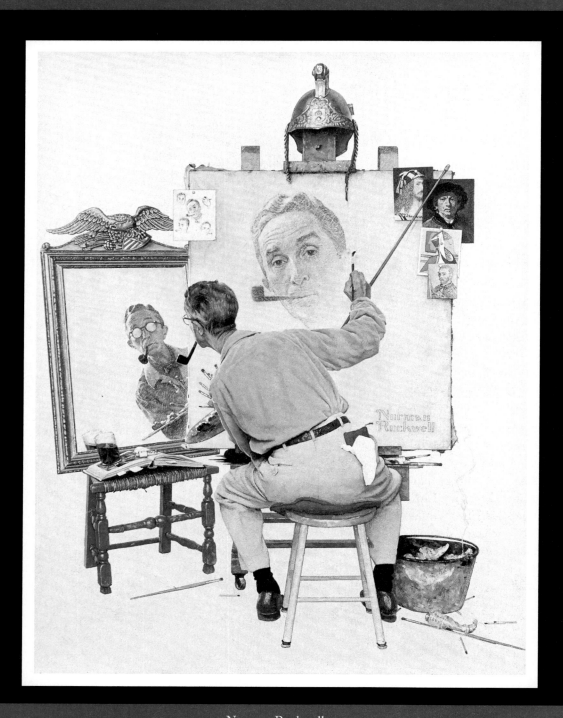

Norman Rockwell
Triple Self-Portrait (1960)
The Norman Rockwell Family Agency
Printed by permission. © 1960 the Norman Rockwell Family Entities.

chapter 3 Observing

In the far corner of a friend's living room is a lighted aquarium. Instead of water, the aquarium has a few inches of white sand, a dish of water, and a small piece of pottery. When you ask about the aquarium, your friend excitedly says, "You mean you haven't met Nino?" In a matter of seconds, you have a small, tannish-brown snake practically in your lap, and your friend is saying, "This is Nino. She—or he—is an African sand boa." You imagined that all boa constrictors were those huge snakes that suffocated and then swallowed babies. "Actually," replies your friend, "Nino is very shy. She prefers to burrow in the sand." The snake is fascinating. It is only fifteen inches long, with a strong, compact body and a stub tail. Before it burrows into your coat pocket, you observe it closely so you can describe it to your younger brother, who loves all kinds of snakes.

In the physics laboratory, you're doing an experiment on light refraction. You need to observe how light rays bend as they go through water, so you take notes describing the procedure and the results. During each phase of the experiment, you observe and record the angles of refraction. The data and your notes will help you write up the lab report that is due next Monday.

> *My task . . . is, by the power of the written word, to make you hear, to make you feel—it is, before all, to make you see.*
>
> —JOSEPH CONRAD, AUTHOR OF <u>HEART OF DARKNESS</u> AND OTHER NOVELS

> *Seeing is of course very much a matter of verbalization. Unless I call my attention to what passes before my eyes, I simply won't see it.*
>
> —ANNIE DILLARD, NATURALIST AND AUTHOR OF <u>PILGRIM AT TINKER CREEK</u>

OBSERVING IS ESSENTIAL TO GOOD WRITING. WHETHER YOU ARE WRITING IN A JOURNAL, DOING A LABORATORY REPORT FOR A SCIENCE CLASS, OR WRITING A LETTER TO THE EDITOR OF A NEWSPAPER, KEEN OBSERVATION is essential. Writing or verbalizing what you see helps you discover and learn more about your environment. Sometimes your purpose is limited to yourself: you observe and record to help you understand your world or yourself better. At other times, your purpose extends to a wider audience: you want to share what you have learned with others to help them learn as well. No matter who your audience is or what your subject may be, however, your task is to see and to help your readers see.

Of course, observing involves more than just "seeing." Good writers draw on all their senses: sight, smell, touch, taste, hearing. In addition, however, experienced writers also notice what is *not* there. The smell of food that should be coming from the kitchen but isn't. A friend who usually is present but now is absent. The absolute quiet in the air that precedes an impending storm. Writers should also look for *changes* in their subjects—from light to dark, from rough to smooth, from bitter to sweet, from noise to sudden silence. Good writers learn to use their previous *experiences* and their *imaginations* to draw comparisons and create images. Does a sea urchin look and feel like a pincushion with the pins stuck in the wrong way? Does the room feel as cramped and airless as the inside of a microwave oven? Finally, good writers write from a specific point of view or role: a student describing basic laws of physics or an experienced worker in a mental health clinic describing the clientele.

The key to effective observing is to *show* your reader the person, place, object, or image through *specific detail*. Good description follows the advice of experienced writers: *Show, don't tell*. Showing through vivid detail allows the reader to reach the conclusions that you may be tempted to just tell them. If your reader is going to learn from your observations, you must give the *exact details that you learned from*, not just your conclusions or generalizations. Even in writing, experience is the best teacher, so use specific details to communicate the look, the feel, the weight, the sights and sounds and smells.

Although effective description depends on detailed observation, what we already know about the subject—and what we can learn during our observations—can be crucial. The people, places, objects, or images that we observe are often *difficult*, *complex*, or *contested*. They do not give up their meaning in our first glance. When we look at Stonehenge, what exactly are we seeing? What does the stone circle really mean? If we look at an Impressionist painting, are we seeing pretty colors in

Photograph of Stonehenge.

Claude Monet, *Impression: Sunrise,* 1872. This painting gave the Impressionists their name.

Ansel Adams, Farm, farm workers, Mount Williamson in background, 1943. Photographs of Japanese-American Internment, Manzanar Relocation Center, California.

shimmering light or just careless, undisciplined brushwork? If we see workers in a field planting or harvesting crops, is it a natural agricultural scene or the exploitation of migrant workers? A key part, then, of effective observation is learning and reading about what we see. An observant eye requires a critical, inquiring mind.

Whether you are a tourist describing the cliff dwellings at Mesa Verde, a student in a chemistry class writing up your laboratory experiment, a social worker observing working and housing conditions of agricultural workers, or a volunteer observing at a community crisis center, your task is to critically observe and then describe your subject—to show your readers, to make them *see*.

Techniques for Writing About Observations

The short passages on the following pages use specific techniques for observing people, places, objects, or images that are described below. In all of the passages the writer *narrows* or *limits* the scope of the observation and selects those specific details which support the *dominant idea* of the passage. The dominant idea reflects the writer's purpose for that particular audience. As you read each passage, notice how the authors use the techniques listed below for making their writing more vivid and effective.

- **Giving sensory details (sight, sound, smell, touch, taste).** Also include *actual dialogue* and *names of things* where appropriate. Good writers often "zoom in" on crucial details. Use *comparisons* and *images* when appropriate.
- **Describing what is *not* there.** Sometimes keen observation requires stepping back and noticing what is absent, what is not happening, or who is not present.
- **Noting changes in the subject's form or condition.** Even when the subject appears static—a landscape, a flower, a building—good writers look for evidence of changes, past or future: a tree being enveloped by tent worms, a six-inch purple-and-white iris that eight hours earlier was just a green bud, a sandstone exterior of a church being eroded by acid rain.
- **Learning about your subject.** An observant eye requires a critical, inquiring mind. Read about your subject. Ask other people or experts on the subject. Probe to find what is *unusual*, *surprising*, or *contested* about your subject.

- **Writing from a distinct point of view.** Good writers assume distinct roles; in turn, perspective helps clarify what they observe. A lover and a botanist, for example, see entirely different things in the same red rose. *What* is seen depends on *who* is doing the seeing.
- **Focusing on a dominant idea.** Good writers focus on those details and images that clarify the main ideas or discoveries. Discovery often depends on the *contrast* between the reality and the writer's expectations.

These techniques for observing are illustrated in the following two paragraphs by Karen Blixen, who wrote *Out of Africa* under the pen name Isak Dinesen. A Danish woman who moved to Kenya to start a coffee plantation, Blixen knew little about the animals in Kenya Reserve. In this excerpt from her journals, she describes a startling change that occurred when she shot a large iguana. (The annotations in the margin identify all six observing techniques.)

In the Reserve I have sometimes come upon the Iguana, the big lizards, as they were sunning themselves upon a flat stone in a riverbed. They are not pretty in shape, but nothing can be imagined more beautiful than their coloring. They shine like a heap of precious stones or like a pane cut out of an old church window. When, as you approach, they swish away, there is a flash of azure, green and purple over the stones, the color seems to be standing behind them in the air, like a comet's luminous tail.

Once I shot an Iguana. I thought that I should be able to make some pretty things from his skin. A strange thing happened then, that I have never afterwards forgotten. As I went up to him, where he was lying dead upon his stone, and actually while I was walking the few steps, he faded and grew pale, all color died out of him as in one long sigh, and by the time that I touched him he was grey and dull like a lump of concrete. It was the live impetuous blood pulsating within the animal, which had radiated out all that glow and splendor. Now that the flame was put out, and the soul had flown, the Iguana was as dead as a sandbag.

Role: a newcomer to the Reserve

Comparisons and images

Sensory details

Comparisons and images

Changes in condition

Sensory detail

Learning about the subject

What is not there

Dominant idea: now colorless and dead

OBSERVING PEOPLE

Observing people—their dress, facial features, body language, attitudes, behavior, skills, quirks, habits, and conversation—is a pastime that we all share. When writers describe people, however, they zero in on specific details that fit overall patterns or impressions. In an *Esquire* magazine article, for example, Joseph Nocera profiles

Steven Jobs, the cocreator of the Apple and Macintosh computers and the ex-chairman of the board of Apple Computer. All of Nocera's details reinforce his dominant idea that Steven Jobs is a temperamental boy genius.

Role: writer as an outsider looks objectively at Jobs, is probably older

Dominant idea: youth

Sensory detail: visual description

Comparison and image

What is not there: facial hair

What is not there: tact

Comparison

With personal computers so ubiquitous today, you tend to forget that . . . the Apple II, the machine that began it all, was unleashed upon an unsuspecting world in 1977. You forget, that is, until you sit in a room full of people who have built them and realize how young they are. Jobs himself is only thirty-one. If anything, he looks younger. He is lithe and wiry. He is wearing faded jeans (no belt), a white cotton shirt (perfectly pressed), and a pair of brown suede wing-tipped shoes. There is a bounce to his step that betrays a certain youthful cockiness; the quarterback of your high school football team used to walk that way. His thin, handsome face does not even appear to need a daily shave. And that impression of eternal youth is reinforced by some guileless, almost childlike traits: by the way, for instance, he can't resist showing off his brutal, withering intelligence whenever he's around someone he doesn't think measures up. Or by his almost willful lack of tact. Or by his inability to hide his boredom when he is forced to endure something that doesn't interest him, like a sixth grader who can't wait for class to end.

OBSERVING PLACES

In the following passage, John Muir describes California and the Yosemite Valley as it looked over 130 years ago. John Muir, of course, was the founder of the Sierra Club, whose first mission was to preserve the vision of Yosemite that Muir paints in the following paragraphs. Notice how Muir uses all of the key techniques for observing as he vividly describes the California Sierra.

Arriving by the Panama steamer, I stopped one day in San Francisco and then inquired for the nearest way out of town. "But where do you want to go?" asked the man to whom I had applied for this important information. "To any place that is wild," I said. This reply startled him. He seemed to fear I might be crazy and therefore the sooner I was out of town the better, so he directed me to the Oakland ferry.

So on the first of April, 1868, I set out afoot for Yosemite. It was the bloom-time of the year over the lowlands and coast ranges; the landscapes of the Santa Clara Valley were fairly drenched with sunshine, all the air was quivering with the songs of the meadow-larks, and the hills were so covered with flowers that they seemed to be painted. Slow indeed was my progress through these glorious gardens, the first of the California flora I had seen. Cattle and cultivation were making few scars as yet, and I wandered enchanted in long wavering curves, knowing by my pocket map that Yosemite Valley lay to the east and that I should surely find it.

Looking eastward from the summit of the Pacheco Pass one shining morning, a landscape was displayed that after all my wanderings still appears as the most beautiful I have ever beheld. At my feet lay the Great Central Valley of California, level and flowery, like a lake of pure sunshine, forty or fifty miles wide, five hundred miles long, one rich furred garden of yellow *Compositae*. And from the eastern boundary of this vast golden flower-bed rose the mighty Sierra, miles in height, and so gloriously colored and so radiant, it seemed not clothed with light, but wholly composed of it, like the wall of some celestial city. Along the top and extending a good way down, was a rich pearl-gray belt of snow; below it a belt of blue and dark purple, marking the extension of the forests; and stretching along the base of the range a broad belt of rose-purple; all these colors, from the blue sky to the yellow valley smoothly blending as they do in a rainbow, making a wall of light ineffably fine. Then it seemed to me that the Sierra should be called, not the Nevada or Snowy Range, but the Range of Light.

In general views no mark of man is visible upon it, nor anything to suggest the wonderful depth and grandeur of its sculpture. None of its magnificent forest-crowned ridges seems to rise much above the general level to publish its wealth. No great valley or river is seen, or group of well-marked features of any kind standing out as distinct pictures. Even the summit peaks, marshaled in glorious array so high in the sky, seem comparatively regular in form. Nevertheless the whole range five hundred miles long is furrowed with canyons 2,000 to 5,000 feet deep, in which once flowed majestic glaciers, and in which now flow and sing the bright rejoicing rivers.

OBSERVING OBJECTS

In observing an inanimate object such as a cookie, Paul Goldberger—architecture critic for *The New York Times*—brings his special point of view to his description. He totally ignores the cookie's taste, ingredients, and calories, focusing instead on the architectural relationships of function and form. Goldberger's architectural perspective helps focus his observations, creating a dominant idea for each passage.

SUGAR WAFER (NABISCO) There is no attempt to imitate the ancient forms of traditional, individually baked cookies here—this is a modern cookie through and through. Its simple rectangular form, clean and pure, just reeks of mass production and modern technological methods. The two wafers, held together by the sugar-cream filling, appear to float . . . this is a machine-age object.

FIG NEWTON (NABISCO) This, too, is a sandwich but different in every way from the Sugar Wafer. Here the imagery is more traditional, more sensual even; a rounded form of cookie dough arcs over the fig concoction inside, and the whole is soft and pliable. Like all good pieces of design, it has an appropriate form for its use, since the insides of Fig Newtons can ooze and would not be held in place by a more rigid form. The thing could have had a somewhat different shape, but the rounded tip is a comfortable, familiar image, and it's easy to hold. Not a revolutionary object but an intelligent one.

OBSERVING IMAGES

Images, works of art, and advertisements require careful observation to bring out their meaning. First, remember that these images have already been constructed by someone else in order to have a particular rhetorical effect, so begin by thinking critically about these images in a rhetorical context.

- Who created this image?
- What was the occasion?
- What was the purpose, and who was the intended audience?
- What is the genre of this image (historical or modern art advertisement, journalistic photograph, or graphic image)?
- What was the cultural, social, or political context in which this image appeared?

As you repeatedly observe the image, pay special attention to how the *composition of the image* (arrangement of figures or objects, balance, color, movement, lines, and contrasts) helps create the overall effect. (For additional ideas for analyzing images, see page 187.)

The following passage, by Charles Rosen and Henri Zerner, appeared originally in the *New York Review of Books*. It describes in detail the *Saturday Evening Post* cover painting by Norman Rockwell, *Triple Self-Portrait, 1960*, which appears at the opening of this chapter. Before you read this passage, study that painting carefully by yourself. What are the important details in the picture? What is the dominant impression of the painting? If necessary, do a background search on Norman Rockwell in your library database or on your favorite search engine. Write out your description and decide what *you* think before you let the following passage influence your reaction to Rockwell's painting.

Triple Self-Portrait of 1960 is clever and witty. It is not simply a portrait of the artist by himself but represents the process of painting a self-portrait, and in the bargain Rockwell takes the opportunity to comment on his brand of "realism" and his relation to the history of art. A sheet of preparatory drawings in different poses is tacked onto the left of the canvas. The artist represents himself from the back; the canvas he works on already has a fully worked-out black-and-white drawing of his face with the pipe in his mouth, based on the central drawing of the sketch sheet. The artist gazes at his own reflection in a mirror propped up on a chair. The reflection we see in the mirror is similar to, but not identical with, the portrait sketched on the canvas. The artist wears glasses, and the glare of the lenses completely obliterates his gaze, while the portrait he works on is without glasses and a little younger-looking, certainly less tense than the reflection. Rockwell seems to confess that the reality of his depicted world, compelling as it may be, is in fact a make-believe.

Tacked on the upper right corner of the canvas is a series of reproductions of historical self-portraits: Durer, Rembrandt, Van Gogh, and Picasso—grand company to measure oneself against, although the humorous tone of the image preserves it from megalomania. But there is a problem: "If Rockwell nodded humbly in Picasso's direction," as Robert Rosenblum suggests, how humbly was it? It is "most surprising," Rosenblum observes, that Rockwell chose "a particularly difficult Picasso that mixes in idealized self-portrait in profile with an id-like female monster attacking from within" rather than something easily recognizable. This was a cover for *The Saturday Evening Post*. The strength of Rockwell is that he knew his public, and knew that such subtleties would be entirely lost on its readers, that most of them would not recognize the Picasso as a self-portrait at all but would consider it as pretentious humbug compared to Rockwell's honest picture and those of the illustrious predecessors he claims. Nor does he seem to have been particularly anxious to change their minds, whatever he himself may have thought.

WARMING UP: JOURNAL EXERCISES

The following topics will help you practice close, detailed observation and may possibly suggest a subject for your assignment on observing. Read the exercises and then write on the two or three that interest you the most.

> *For Godsake, keep your eyes open. Notice what's going on around you.*
>
> —WILLIAM BURROUGHS, NOVELIST

1. Go to a public place (library, bar, restaurant, hospital emergency room, gas station, laundromat, park, shopping mall, hotel lobby, police station, beach, skating rink, beauty salon, city dump, tennis court, church, etc.). Sit and observe everything around you. Use your pencil to help you see, both by drawing sketches and by recording sensory details in words. What do you see that you haven't noticed before? Then *narrow* your attention to a single person, *focus* on a restricted place, or *zoom* in on a single object. What do you see that you haven't noticed before?

2. In one of your classes, use your repeated observations of the total learning environment (the room, the seating arrangements, the blackboards, the audiovisual or computer equipment, the teacher, the daily teaching or learning rituals, and the students) to speculate on who has authority, how knowledge is created or communicated, and what the learning goals are for this course.

3. If you are working on a community-service learning project, for your first assignment, go and observe the place, people, and setting for the agency. Start by taking double-entry notes in your journal. On the left-hand side, record visual and sensory details; on the right-hand side, record your reactions and impressions. Use these notes for a description of your agency that will go in your final portfolio for your learning project.

4. Go to a gallery, studio, or museum where you can observe sculpture, paintings, or other works of art. Choose one work of art and draw it. Then describe it as fully as possible. Return to the gallery the next day, reread your first description, observe the work again, and add details that you didn't notice the first time.

5. Visit a local park. Pretend that you are a landscape architect, a photographer, a bird-watcher, an entomologist, an engineer building a road, a jogger, or a mother with two small children. Describe what you see. Now choose another role—you're a social worker, a woman alone in a park at night, a person

without a home, a Secret Service agent assigned to protect the President of the United States, a Saint Bernard, or a sixth-grader just out of school for the day. Describe what you see. Then reread both descriptions. Compare them. Briefly, explain how and why they are similar or dissimilar.

6. Reprinted below is a painting by Umberto Boccioni entitled *Dynamism of a Cylist*. Write a paragraph describing in detail what you see in this painting. After you finish your description, you may wish to learn more about this painting by researching it in your library database or on Yahoo!, Google, or other search engine. After you finish your research, go back and revise your descriptive paragraph.

7. After the September 11, 2001, attack on the World Trade Center, Robin Morgan wrote the following description of ground zero. The author of *Saturday's Child: A Memoir* (2001), Robin Morgan is a prolific writer of poetry, essays, and feminist tracts. Read the following excerpt from her posting to the Internet on September 18, 2001. What sensory details, statistics, and images help make her description so vivid and memorable? What memories of your own about September 11 does her description bring back?

I'll focus on New York—my firsthand experience—but this doesn't mean any less anguish for the victims of the Washington or Pennsylvania calamities. Today was Day 8. Incredibly, a week has passed. Abnormal normalcy has settled in. Our usually contentious mayor (previously bad news for New Yorkers of color and for artists) has risen to this moment with efficiency, compassion, real leadership. The city is alive and dynamic. Below 14th Street, traffic is flowing again, mail is being delivered, newspapers are back. But very early this morning I walked east, then south almost to the tip of Manhattan Island. The 16-acre site itself is closed off, of course, as is a perimeter surrounding it controlled by the National Guard, used as a command post and staging area for rescue workers. Still, one is able to approach nearer to the area than was possible last weekend, since the law-court district and parts of the financial district are now open and (shakily) working. The closer one gets the more one sees—and smells—what no TV report, and very few print reports, have communicated. I find myself giving way to tears again and again, even as I write this. . . .

From a distance, you can see the lattices of one of the Towers, its skeletal bones the sole remains, eerily beautiful in asymmetry, as if a new work of abstract art had been erected in a public space. Elsewhere, you see the transformation of institutions: The New School and New York University are missing persons' centers. A movie house is now a rest shelter, a Burger King a first-aid center, a Brooks Brother's clothing store a body parts morgue, a record shop a haven for lost animals. Libraries are counseling centers. Ice rinks are morgues. A bank is now a supply depot: in the first four days, it distributed 11,000 respirators and 25,000 pairs of protective gloves and suits. Nearby, a mobile medical unit housed in a McDonald's has administered 70,000 tetanus shots. The brain tries to process the numbers: "only" 50,000 tons of debris had been cleared by yesterday, out of 1.2 million tons. The medical examiner's office has readied up to 20,000 DNA tests for unidentifiable cadaver parts. At all times, night and day, a minimum of 1000 people live and work on the site.

Such numbers daze the mind. It's the details—fragile, individual—that melt numbness into grief. An anklet with "Joyleen" engraved on it—found on an ankle. Just that: an ankle. A pair of hands—one brown, one white—clasped together. Just that. No wrists. A burly welder who drove from Ohio to help, saying softly, "We're working in a cemetery. I'm standing in—not on, in—a graveyard." Each lamp-post, storefront, scaffolding, mailbox, is plastered with homemade photocopied posters, a racial/ethnic rainbow of faces and names: death the great leveler, not only of the financial CEOs—their images usually formal, white, male, older, with suit-and-tie—but the mailroom workers, receptionists, waiters. You pass enough of the MISSING posters and the faces, names, descriptions become familiar. The Albanian window-cleaner guy with the bushy eyebrows. The teenage Mexican dishwasher who had an American flag tattoo. The janitor's assistant who'd emigrated from Ethiopia. The Italian-American grandfather who was a doughnut-cart tender. The 23-year-old Chinese American junior pastry chef at the Windows on the World restaurant who'd gone in early that day so she could prep a business breakfast for 500. The firefighter who'd posed jauntily wearing his green shamrock necktie. The dapper African-American midlevel manager with a small gold ring in his ear who handled "minority affairs" for one of the companies. The middle-aged secretary laughing up at the camera from her wheelchair. The maintenance worker with a Polish name, holding his newborn baby. Most of the faces are smiling; most of the shots are family photos; many are recent wedding pictures. . . .

I have little national patriotism, but I do have a passion for New York, partly for our gritty, secular energy of endurance, and because the world does come here: 80 countries had offices in the Twin Towers; 62 countries lost citizens in the catastrophe; an estimated 300 of our British cousins died, either in the planes or the buildings. My personal comfort is found not in ceremonies or prayer services but in watching the plain, truly heroic (a word usually misused) work of ordinary New Yorkers we take for granted every day, who have risen to this moment unpretentiously, too busy to even notice they're expressing the splendor of the human spirit: fire fighters, medical aides, nurses, ER doctors, police officers, sanitation workers, construction-workers, ambulance drivers, structural engineers, crane operators, rescue worker "tunnel rats." . . .

PROFESSIONAL WRITING

TAKE THIS FISH AND LOOK AT IT

Samuel H. Scudder

In this essay, Samuel H. Scudder (1837–1911), an American entomologist, narrates his early attempts at scientific observation. Scudder recalls how a famous Swiss naturalist, Louis Agassiz, taught him the skills of observation by having him examine a fish—a haemulon or snapper—closely, carefully, and repeatedly. Agassiz, a professor of natural history at Harvard, taught his students that both factual details and general laws are important. "Facts are stupid things," he said, "until brought into connection with some general law." Scudder, writing about his studies under Agassiz, suggests that repeated observation can help us connect facts or specific details with general laws. The essay shows us an important lesson that Scudder learned: To help us see, describe, and connect, "A pencil is one of the best of eyes."

It was more than fifteen years ago that I entered the laboratory of Professor Agassiz, and told him I had enrolled my name in the Scientific School as a student of natural history. He asked me a few questions about my object in coming, my antecedents generally, the mode in which I afterwards proposed to use the knowledge I might acquire, and, finally, whether I wished to study any special branch. To the latter I replied that, while I wished to be well grounded in all departments of zoology, I purposed to devote myself specially to insects.   1

"When do you wish to begin?" he asked.   2

"Now," I replied.   3

This seemed to please him, and with an energetic "Very well!" he reached from a shelf a huge jar of specimens in yellow alcohol. "Take this fish," he said, "and look at it; we call it a haemulon; by and by I will ask what you have seen."   4

With that he left me, but in a moment returned with explicit instructions as to the care of the object entrusted to me.   5

"No man is fit to be a naturalist," said he, "who does not know how to take care of specimens."   6

I was to keep the fish before me in a tin tray, and occasionally moisten the surface with alcohol from the jar, always taking care to replace the stop-   7 per tightly. Those were not the days of ground-glass stoppers and elegantly shaped exhibition jars; all the old students will recall the huge neckless glass bottles with their leaky, wax-besmeared corks, half eaten by insects, and begrimed with cellar dust. Entomology was a cleaner science than ichthyology, but the example of the Professor, who had unhesitatingly plunged to the bottom of the jar to produce the fish, was infectious; and though this alcohol had a "very ancient and fishlike smell," I really dared not show any aversion within these sacred precincts, and treated the alcohol as though it were pure water. Still I was conscious of a passing feeling of disappointment, for gazing at a fish did not commend itself to an ardent entomologist. My friends at home, too, were annoyed when they discovered that no amount of eau-de-Cologne would drown the perfume which haunted me like a shadow.

In ten minutes I had seen all that could be seen in that fish, and started 8 in search of the Professor—who had, however, left the Museum; and when I returned, after lingering over some of the odd animals stored in the upper apartment, my specimen was dry all over. I dashed the fluid over the fish as if to resuscitate the beast from a fainting fit, and looked with anxiety for a return of the normal sloppy appearance. This little excitement over, nothing was to be done but to return to a steadfast gaze at my mute companion. Half an hour passed—an hour—another hour; the fish began to look loathsome. I turned it over and around; looked it in the face—ghastly; from behind, beneath, above, sideways, at three-quarter's view—just as ghastly, I was in despair; at an early hour I concluded that lunch was necessary; so, with infinite relief, the fish was carefully replaced in the jar, and for an hour I was free.

On my return, I learned that Professor Agassiz had been at the Mu- 9 seum, but had gone, and would not return for several hours. My fellow-students were too busy to be disturbed by continued conversation. Slowly I drew forth that hideous fish, and with a feeling of desperation again looked at it. I might not use a magnifying-glass; instruments of all kinds were interdicted. My two hands, my two eyes, and the fish: it seemed a most limited field. I pushed my finger down its throat to feel how sharp the teeth were. I began to count the scales in the different rows, until I was convinced that was nonsense. At last a happy thought struck me—I would draw the fish; and now with surprise I began to discover new features in the creature. Just then the Professor returned.

"That is right," said he; "a pencil is one of the best of eyes. I am glad 10 to notice, too, that you keep your specimen wet, and your bottle corked."

With these encouraging words, he added: "Well, what is it like?" *11*

He listened attentively to my brief rehearsal of the structure of parts *12* whose names were still unknown to me: the fringed gill-arches and movable operculum; the pores of the head, fleshy lips and lidless eyes; the lateral line, the spinous fins and forked tail; the compressed and arched body. When I finished, he waited as if expecting more, and then, with an air of disappointment:

"You have not looked very carefully; why," he continued more earnestly, *13* "you haven't even seen one of the most conspicuous features of the animal, which is plainly before your eyes as the fish itself; look again, look again!" and he left me to my misery.

I was piqued; I was mortified. Still more of that wretched fish! But *14* now I set myself to my task with a will, and discovered one new thing after another, until I saw how just the Professor's criticism had been. The afternoon passed quickly; and when, towards its close, the Professor inquired:

"Do you see it yet?" *15*

"No," I replied, "I am certain I do not, but I see how little I saw before." *16*

"That is next best," said he, earnestly, "but I won't hear you now; put *17* away your fish and go home; perhaps you will be ready with a better answer in the morning. I will examine you before you look at the fish."

This was disconcerting. Not only must I think of my fish all night, *18* studying, without the object before me, what this unknown but most visible feature might be; but also, without reviewing my discoveries, I must give an exact account of them the next day. I had a bad memory; so I walked home by Charles River in a distracted state, with my two perplexities.

The cordial greeting from the Professor the next morning was reas- *19* suring; here was a man who seemed to be quite as anxious as I that I should see for myself what he saw.

"Do you perhaps mean," I asked, "that the fish has symmetrical sides *20* with paired organs?"

His thoroughly pleased "Of course! Of course!" repaid the wakeful *21* hours of the previous night. After he had discoursed most happily and enthusiastically—as he always did—upon the importance of this point, I ventured to ask what I should do next.

"Oh, look at your fish!" he said, and left me again to my own devices. *22* In a little more than an hour he returned, and heard my new catalogue.

"That is good, that is good!" he repeated; "but that is not all; go on"; *23* and so for three long days he placed that fish before my eyes, forbidding me to look at anything else, or to use any artificial aid. "Look, look, look," was his repeated injunction.

This was the best entomological lesson I ever had—a lesson whose influence has extended to the details of every subsequent study; a legacy the Professor had left to me, as he has left it to so many others, of inestimable value, which we could not buy, with which we cannot part. 24

A year afterward, some of us were amusing ourselves with chalking outlandish beasts on the Museum blackboard. We drew prancing starfishes; frogs in mortal combat; hydra-headed worms, stately crawfishes with gaping mouths and staring eyes. The Professor came in shortly after, and was as amused as any at our experiments. He looked at the fishes. 25

"Haemulons, every one of them," he said; "Mr. _____ drew them." 26

True; and to this day, if I attempt a fish, I can draw nothing but haemulons. 27

The fourth day, a second fish of the same group was placed beside the first, and I was bidden to point out the resemblances and differences between the two; another and another followed, until the entire family lay before me, and a whole legion of jars covered the table and surrounding shelves; the odor had become a pleasant perfume; and even now, the sight of an old, six-inch worm-eaten cork brings fragrant memories. 28

The whole group of haemulons was thus brought in review; and whether engaged upon the dissection of the internal organs, the preparation and examination of the bony framework, or the description of the various parts, Agassiz's training in the method of observing facts and their orderly arrangement was ever accompanied by the urgent exhortation not to be content with them. 29

"Facts are stupid things," he would say, "until brought into connection with some general law." 30

At the end of eight months, it was almost with reluctance that I left these friends and turned to insects; but what I had gained by this outside experience has been of greater value than years of later investigation in my favorite groups. 31

In your journal, write down the meanings of the following words:

- my *antecedents* generally **(1)**
- *Entomology* was a cleaner science than *ichthyology* **(7)**
- dared not show any *aversion* **(7)**
- to *resuscitate* the beast **(8)**
- instruments of all kinds were *interdicted* **(9)**
- movable *operculum* **(12)**
- I was *piqued* **(14)**
- with my two *perplexities* **(18)**
- his repeated *injunction* **(23)**
- *hydra-headed* worms **(25)**
- the urgent *exhortation* **(29)**

QUESTIONS FOR WRITING AND DISCUSSION

1. If you have taken any science classes with laboratory sections, describe any observing techniques you used while completing the lab assignments. What were you asked to observe? What were you asked to record? How were these sessions similar to or different from Scudder's experience? Explain.

2. Follow Professor Agassiz's advice about observing: Without looking again at the essay, record in writing what you found to be the most memorable parts of the essay. What parts seemed most vivid? Explain.

3. Apply Scudder's technique of *repeated observation* to his own essay. Read the essay a second time, carefully, looking for techniques for recording observations. Use a pencil to help you read, by underlining or making brief notes. What do you notice on the *second* reading that you did not see in the first?

4. What is the purpose of this essay? To inform us about fish? To explain how to learn about fish? To persuade us to follow Professor Agassiz's method? To entertain us with college stories? In your estimation what is the primary purpose?

5. Describe the genre and intended audience for this essay. Review the list of genres on page 20. What features of the essay (such as content, dialogue, paragraphing, narrative voice) help indicate the genre of this piece? Who is the intended audience? Which sentences most clearly address the intended audience?

6. "Facts are stupid things," Agassiz says, "until brought into connection with some general law." Reread paragraph 8. What is the "general law" about scientific observation—or, in this case, the *dominant idea*—created by the specific details describing Scudder's first session with his fish? Explain.

7. On the Internet, access a biography of Louis Agassiz at *http://www.ucmp.berkeley.edu/history/agassiz.html*. Does this biography explain why Agassiz was one of the scientists who paved the way for Darwin's discoveries but also attacked Darwin's theory of evolution? Should Agassiz's discoveries be discredited because he did not agree with Darwin?

8. Connect Scudder's techniques to those in the other essays in this chapter. Does Farley Mowat use repeated observation to make an important discovery? In your own essay, how can you use Scudder's or Agassiz's advice to make your descriptions more vivid or insightful?

PROFESSIONAL WRITING

OBSERVING WOLVES

Farley Mowat

Farley Mowat was born in Ontario in 1921 and received a B.A. from the University of Toronto. He has published over fifty books of fiction and nonfiction, including People of the Deer *(1952),* Never Cry Wolf *(1963), and* Woman in the Mists: The Story of Dian Fossey and the Mountain Gorillas of Africa *(1987).* Never Cry Wolf *(1963), from which "Observing Wolves" was taken, describes how the Canadian government sent Mowat to the Keewatin Barren Lands in the Northwest Territories to prove that the wolves were decimating the caribou herds—and thus should be exterminated. After observing wolves for a few short days, however, Mowat realized that "the centuries-old and universally accepted human concept of wolf character was a palpable lie. . . . I made my decision that, from this hour onward, I would go open-minded into the lupine world and learn to see and know the wolves, not for what they were supposed to be, but for what they actually were." In the first scene, Mowat learns how wolves establish territories; in the second, he discovers something about their diet. Mowat also gives names to each wolf that he observes: Angeline is a female wolf, George is her mate, and Uncle Albert is a male attached to the group.*

I

During the next several weeks I put my decision into effect with the thoroughness for which I have always been noted. I went completely to the wolves. To begin with I set up a den of my own as near to the wolves as I could conveniently get without disturbing the even tenor of their lives too much. After all, I *was* a stranger, and an unwolflike one, so I did not feel I should go too far too fast.

Abandoning Mike's cabin (with considerable relief, since as the days warmed up so did the smell) I took a tiny tent and set it up on the shore of the bay immediately opposite to the den esker. I kept my camping gear to the barest minimum—a small primus stove, a stew pot, a teakettle, and a sleeping bag were the essentials. I took no weapons of any kind, although there were times when I regretted this omission, even if only fleetingly. The big telescope was set up in the mouth of the tent in such a way that I could observe the den by day or night without even getting out of my sleeping bag.

During the first few days of my sojourn with the wolves I stayed inside the tent except for brief and necessary visits to the out-of-doors which I always undertook when the wolves were not in sight. The point of this personal concealment was to allow the animals to get used to the tent and to accept it as only another bump on a very bumpy piece of terrain. Later, when the mosquito population reached full flowering, I stayed in the tent practically all of the time unless there was a strong wind blowing, for the most bloodthirsty beasts in the Arctic are not wolves, but the insatiable mosquitoes.

My precautions against disturbing the wolves were superfluous. It had required a week for me to get their measure, but they must have taken mine at our first meeting; and, while there was nothing overtly disdainful in their evident assessment of me, they managed to ignore my presence, and indeed my very existence, with a thoroughness which was somehow disconcerting.

Quite by accident I had pitched my tent within ten yards of one of the major paths used by the wolves when they were going to, or coming from, thought, simply went for a walk to stretch her legs. Usually her peregrinations took her to the point of the bay farthest from my tent where she was hidden from sight by a low gravel ridge; but this time she came my way in full view and so I swung my telescope to keep an eye on her.

She went directly to the rocky foreshore, waded out until the icy water *31* was up to her shoulders, and had a long drink. As she was doing so, a small flock of Old Squaw ducks flew around the point of the Bay and pitched only a hundred yards or so away from her. She raised her head and eyed them speculatively for a moment, then waded back to shore, where she proceeded to act as if she had suddenly become demented.

Yipping like a puppy, she began to chase her tail; to roll over and over *32* among the rocks; to lie on her back; to wave all four feet furiously in the air; and in general to behave as if she were clean out of her mind.

I swung the glasses back to where Albert was sitting amidst a gaggle *33* of pups to see if he, too, had observed this mad display, and, if so, what his reaction to it was. He had seen it all right, in fact he was watching Angeline with keen interest but without the slightest indication of alarm.

By this time Angeline appeared to be in the throes of a manic parox- *34* ysm, leaping wildly into the air and snapping at nothing, the while uttering shrill squeals. It was an awe-inspiring sight, and I realized that Albert and I were not the only ones who were watching it with fascination. The ducks seemed hypnotized by curiosity. So interested were they that they swam in for a closer view of this apparition on the shore. Closer and closer they came, necks outstretched, and gabbling incredulously among themselves. And the closer they came, the crazier grew Angeline's behavior.

When the leading duck was not more than fifteen feet from shore, *35* Angeline gave one gigantic leap towards it. There was a vast splash, a panic-stricken whacking of wings, and then all the ducks were up and away. Angeline had missed a dinner by no more than inches.

This incident was an eye-opener since it suggested a versatility at food- *36* getting which I would hardly have credited to a human being, let alone to a mere wolf. However, Angeline soon demonstrated that the charming of ducks was a mere side line.

Having dried herself with a series of energetic shakes which momen- *37* tarily hid her in a blue mist of water droplets, she padded back across the grassy swale. But now her movements were quite different from what they had been when she passed through the swale on the way to the bay.

Angeline was of a rangy build, anyway, but by stretching herself so that *38* she literally seemed to be walking on tiptoe, and by elevating her neck like a camel, she seemed to gain several inches in height. She began to move infinitely slowly upwind across the swale, and I had the impression that both ears were cocked for the faintest sound, while I could see her nose wrinkling as she sifted the breeze for the most ephemeral scents.

Suddenly she pounced. Flinging herself up on her hind legs like a horse trying to throw its rider, she came down again with driving force, both forelegs held stiffly out in front of her. Instantly her head dropped; she snapped once, swallowed, and returned to her peculiar mincing ballet across the swale. Six times in ten minutes she repeated the straight-armed pounce, and six times she swallowed—without my having caught a glimpse of what it was that she had eaten. The seventh time she missed her aim, spun around, and began snapping frenziedly in a tangle of cotton grasses. This time when she raised her head I saw, quite unmistakably, the tail and hind quarters of a mouse quivering in her jaws. One gulp, and it too was gone. *39*

Although I was much entertained by the spectacle of one of this continent's most powerful carnivores hunting mice, I did not really take it seriously. I thought Angeline was only having fun; snacking, as it were. But when she had eaten some twenty-three mice I began to wonder. Mice are small, but twenty-three of them adds up to a fairsized meal, even for a wolf. *40*

It was only later, by putting two and two together, that I was able to bring myself to an acceptance of the obvious. The wolves of Wolf House Bay, and, by inference at least, all the Barren Land wolves who were raising families outside the summer caribou range, were living largely, if not almost entirely, on mice. *41*

In your journal, write down the meanings of the following words:

- the den *esker* **(2)**
- *superfluous* **(4)**
- somehow *disconcerting* **(4)**
- *preternaturally* **(5)**
- *evince* the slightest interest **(6)**

- *lupine* **(9)**
- *extirpation* **(20)**
- *her peregrinations* **(30)**

QUESTIONS FOR WRITING AND DISCUSSION

1. Describe what you knew about wolves before you read Mowat's description. Which parts of Mowat's description agreed with your preconceptions? Which parts gave you new information or a different opinion?

2. *What* is observed depends on *who* is doing the observing. Describe the narrator's behavior and personality. How do his preconceptions affect what he observes? Should a scientific observer interfere with the lives of the wolves, as the narrator does? What does the narrator learn?

3. Some readers complain that Mowat is not scientific. Mowat's genre, a personal essay, suggests in fact that he is writing a personal observation, not a scientific treatise. For example, compare Mowat's essay with an article published in *Science,* February 6, 2004, entitled "Evolutionary Dynamics of Biological Games," by Martin A. Nowak and Karl Sigmund (full text available at *http://www.sciencemag.org.* The authors begin their abstract with the following two sentences: "Darwinian dynamics based on mutation and selection form the core of mathematical models for adaptation and co-evolution of biological populations. The evolutionary outcome is often not a fitness-maximizing equilibrium but can include oscillations and chaos." Read the opening page or two of this article, and then write a paragraph explaining how Mowat's style and genre is different from the style and genre of this article in *Science.* How does changing a genre affect a writer's purpose?

4. Four keys to effective description are repeated observation, attention to sensory details, noticing changes in the subject or the subject's behavior, and noticing what is not present. Find examples of each of these four strategies in this essay.

5. On the Internet, log on to one of the wolf organization sites such as the International Wolf Center at *http://www.wolf.org*, the North American Wolf Association at *http://www.nawa.org*, or Wolfcountry at *http://www.wolfcountry.net* to check the accuracy of Mowat's essay. For example, the

Wolfcountry site explains that wolves are, as Mowat suggests, very opportunistic in their feeding. Although they will prey on deer, moose, bison, elk, and caribou, they also eat beavers, rabbits, rodents, and wild berries. They are also able to catch fish to supplement their diet. Check the information about wolves on these sites: Are Mowat's conclusions about wolf behavior scientifically accurate? Explain.

6. The photograph below shows a gray wolf feeding on a caribou in Denali National Park, Alaska. Assuming that you were arguing that wolves do reduce caribou herd populations and should be controlled, how useful might this image be in supporting your position? Based on this photograph, what logical conclusions could you reach? What conclusions could you *not* logically draw? Explain.

7. Naturalists have reintroduced wolves into Yellowstone National Park. Nearby ranchers, however, are still fearful that wolves will continue to leave the park and kill their livestock. How would Mowat respond to this debate? Imagine that Mowat has logged on to one of the wolf sites and is going to post a response to one of the ranchers. Write the response that Mowat might post.

Observing: The Writing Process

ASSIGNMENT FOR OBSERVING

Do a piece of writing in which you observe a specific person, place, object, or image. Your goal is to show how specific, observed details create dominant ideas about the person, place, object, or image. Your initial purpose is to use your writing to help you observe, discover, and learn about your subject; your final purpose will be to show your reader what you have seen and learned.

While your main purpose is to observe, you also need to think about a possible audience and genre. Are you writing primarily for yourself, to observe and learn? Are you writing for a specific audience? What genre or form would best suit your purpose and audience: a journal entry, a letter to a friend, a personal essay, an editorial, an article to be published in a particular magazine, or a posting to an Internet forum?

Important: Repeated observation is essential. Choose some *limited* subject—a person or small group of people, a specific place, a single object or animal, or a recurring event—that *you can reobserve over a period of several days during the writing process.*

CHOOSING A SUBJECT

If one of your journal entries suggested an interesting subject, try the collecting and shaping strategies. If none of those exercises caught your interest, consider the following ideas:

- Think about your current classes. Do you have a class with a laboratory—chemistry, physics, biology, engineering, animal science, horticulture, industrial sciences, physical education, social work, drawing, pottery—in which you have to make detailed observations? Use this assignment to help you in one of those classes: Write about what you observe and learn during one of your lab sessions.
- Seek out a new place on campus that is off your usual track. Check the college catalog for ideas about places you haven't yet seen: a theater where

actors are rehearsing, a greenhouse, a physical education class in the martial arts, a studio where artists are working, a computer laboratory, or an animal research center. Or visit a class you wouldn't take for credit. Observe, write, and learn about what's there.

• From a magazine that you read, choose an advertisement or an image to describe. Start by observing the composition or arrangement of the figures and the use of color, lines, balance, and contrast in the advertisement or work of art. *Your goals are to describe this image in detail and to analyze the effectiveness of this image in its rhetorical context.* As part of the rhetorical context, consider the artist or sponsor, the occasion, the purpose and intended audience, the genre, and the cultural context of this image.

As you write on your subject, consider a tentative audience and purpose. Who might want to know what you learn from your observations? What do you need to

"*Write about dogs!*"

explain? What will readers already know? Jot down tentative ideas about your subject, audience, and purpose. Remember, however, that these are not cast in concrete: You may discover some new idea, focus, or angle as you write.

COLLECTING

Once you have chosen a subject from your journal or elsewhere, begin collecting information. Depending on your purpose, your topic, or even your personal learning preferences, some activities will work better than others. However, you should *practice* all of these activities to determine which is most successful for you and most appropriate to your topic. During these collecting activities, go back and *reobserve your subject*. The second or third time you go back, you may see additional details or more actively understand what you're seeing.

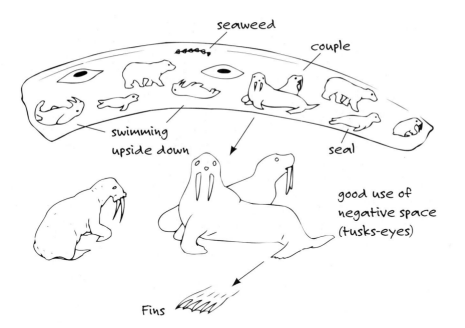

> *We don't take in the world like a camera or a set of recording devices. The mind is an agent, not a passive receiver. . . . The active mind is a composer and everything we respond to, we compose.*
>
> —ANN BERTHOFF,
> AUTHOR AND TEACHER

SKETCHING   Begin by *drawing* what you see. The essayist Samuel Scudder says that pen or pencil can be "the best of eyes." Your drawing doesn't have to be great art to suggest other details, questions, or relationships that may be important. Instead of trying to cover a wide range of objects, try to focus on one limited subject and draw it in detail.

Here's an example. Writing student Brad Parks decided to visit an Eskimo art display at a local gallery. As part of his observing notes, he drew these sketches of Eskimo paintings. As he drew, he made notes in the margins of his sketches and zoomed in for more detail on one pair of walruses.

TAKING DOUBLE-ENTRY NOTES   Taking notes in a double-entry format is a simple but effective system for recording observed details. At the top of the page, write the place and time of your observation and your perspective, role, or point of view. Draw a vertical line down the middle of a page in your journal. On the left-hand side, write down description and sensory details. On the right-hand side, record your reactions, thoughts, ideas, and questions.

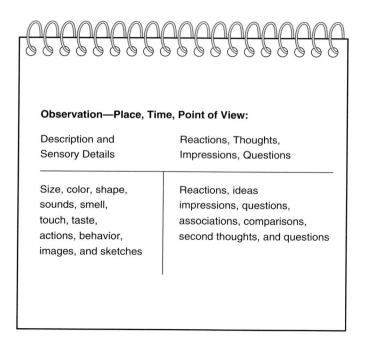

Observation—Place, Time, Point of View:

Description and Sensory Details	Reactions, Thoughts, Impressions, Questions
Size, color, shape, sounds, smell, touch, taste, actions, behavior, images, and sketches	Reactions, ideas impressions, questions, associations, comparisons, second thoughts, and questions

ANSWERING QUESTIONS   To help you describe the person, place, object, or image, write a short response in your journal to each of the following questions:

- What exactly is it? Can you *define* this person, place, object, or image? If it's an object, are its parts related? Who needs it, uses it, or produces it?
- How much could it change and still be recognizable?

- Compare and contrast it. How is it similar to or different from other comparable people, places, things, or images?
- From what points of view is it usually seen? From what point of view is it rarely seen?

FREEWRITING Freewriting means exactly what it says. Write about your subject, nonstop, for five to ten minutes. Sometimes you may have to write, "I can't think of anything" or "This is really stupid," but keep on writing. Let your words and ideas suggest other thoughts and ideas. For observing, the purpose of freewriting is to let your *imagination* work on the subject, usually *after* you have observed and recorded specific details. Freewriting on your subject will also develop more *associations* or *comparisons* for the right-hand side of your double-entry log. It should also help you to identify a dominant idea for your details.

SHAPING

To focus once again on the shaping process, consider your subject, purpose, and audience. Has your purpose changed? Can you narrow your subject to a specific topic? You may know the answers to some questions immediately; others you may not know until after you complete your first draft. Jot down your current responses to the following questions:

- **Subject:** What is your general subject?
- **Specific topic:** What aspect of your subject are you interested in? Try to *narrow* your field or limit your focus.
- **Purpose:** Why is this topic interesting or important to you or to others? From what point of view will you be writing? What is the *dominant idea* you are trying to convey?
- **Audience:** Who are your readers? What are these readers like, and why might they be interested in this topic? How can you direct your description of your subject to your particular audience?
- **Context:** What is the cultural, political, social, or personal context in which this person, object, or image appears? How does that context affect your subject? How does the context affect you?

With answers to these questions in mind, you should experiment with several of the following genre possibilities and organization strategies. These genres and strategies not only will organize your specific examples but also may suggest related ideas to improve your description.

> *"Your audience is one single reader. I have found that sometimes it helps to pick out one person—a real person you know, or an imagined person—and write to that one."*
> —JOHN STEINBECK, NOVELIST

As you practice these strategies, try to *focus* on your subject. In a profile of a person, for example, focus on key facial features or revealing habits or mannerisms. If you're writing about a place or an event, narrow the subject. Describe, for instance, the street at night, a spider spinning a web in a windowsill, a man in a laundromat banging on a change machine, a bird hovering in midair, a photograph, a fish. Write in depth and detail about a *limited* subject.

With a limited subject, a shaping strategy such as spatial order, chronological order, or comparison/contrast will organize all the specific details for your audience. Shaping strategies give you ways of seeing relationships among the many bits of your description and of presenting them in an organized manner for your reader. Seeing these relationships will also help you discover and communicate the *dominant idea* to your reader.

GENRE   As you begin thinking about organizing or shaping your description, consider what genre would work best for your topic. Should you write an essay? Should you write a letter? Might this be part of your Web page or weblog? Would a multigenre or multimedia approach work? Do you want to have text, pictures, graphics, Web links, or added sound? Would text and a paper or digital collage be most effective for your purpose, audience, and occasion?

SPATIAL ORDER   Spatial order is a simple way to organize your descriptive details. Choose some sequence—left to right, right to left, bottom to top—and describe your observed details in that sequence. In the following description of his "trashed" dorm room, Dale Furnish, a student who was the victim of a prank, uses spatial order. The italicized words illustrate the spatial order.

> As I walked in the door, I could hardly believe that this scene of destruction used to be my room. *Along the left-hand wall,* nearly hiding my desk and mirror, was a pile of beer cans and bottles, paper cups, and old crumpled newspapers. The small window *on the far wall* was now covered with the mattress of the bed, and the frame of the bunk bed stood on end. The clothes closet, *to the right of the window,* looked as though it were a giant washing machine which had just gone through spin cycle—clothes were plastered all over, and only four hangers remained, dangling uselessly on the pole. *On the right wall,* where the bed had been, was the real surprise. Tied to the heating pipe was a mangy looking sheep. I swear. It was a real sheep. As I looked at it, it turned to face me and loudly and plaintively said, "Baaaa." *Behind me,* in the hall, everyone began laughing. I didn't know whether to laugh or cry.

CHRONOLOGICAL ORDER   Chronological order is simply the time sequence of your observation. In the following passage, Gregory Allen, writing from his point of view as a five-foot-six-inch guard on a basketball team, describes sights, sounds, and his feelings during a pickup game. The italicized words emphasize the chronological order.

> The game *begins*. The guy checking me is about 6′1″, red hair, freckles, and has no business on the court. He looks slow, so I decide to run him to tire him. I dribble twice, pump fake, and the guy goes for it, thinking that he's going to block this much smaller guy's shot. *Then* I leap, flick my wrist, and the ball glides through the air and flows through the net with a swish as the net turns upside down. I come down and realize that I have been scratched. *Suddenly,* I feel a sharp pain as sweat runs into the small red cut. I wipe the blood on my shorts and *continue playing* the game. *After* that first play, I begin to hear the common song of the game. There's the squeak of the high-top Nike sneakers, the bouncing ball, the shuffle of feet. *Occasionally,* I hear "I'm open!" "Pass the ball!" "Augghh!" And *then,* "Nice play, man!"

COMPARISON/CONTRAST   If what you've observed and written about your subject so far involves seeing similarities or differences, you may be able to use comparison/contrast as a shaping strategy—either for a single paragraph or for a series of paragraphs. The following two paragraphs, for example, are taken from Albert Goldman's biography of Elvis Presley, entitled *Elvis*. In these paragraphs, Goldman's dominant idea depends on the striking contrast between what he finds on the front lawn of Graceland, the rock star's mansion in Memphis, and what he notices when he steps through the front door.

> Prominently displayed on the front lawn is an elaborate creche. The stable is a full-scale adobe house strewn with straw. Life-sized are the figures of Joseph and Mary, the kneeling shepherds and Magi, the lambs and ewes, as well as the winged annunciatory angel hovering over the roof beam. Real, too, is the cradle in which the infant Jesus sleeps.
>
> When you step through the ten-foot oak door and enter the house, you stop and stare in amazement. Having just come from the contemplation of the tenderest scene in the Holy Bible, imagine the shock of finding yourself in a *whorehouse!* Yet there is no other way to describe the drawing room of Graceland except to say that it appears to have been lifted from some turn-of-the-century bordello down in the French Quarter of New Orleans. . . . The room is a gaudy melange of red velour and gilded tassels, Louis XV

furniture and porcelain bric-a-brac, all informed by the kind of taste that de-
lights in a ceramic temple d'amour housing a miniature Venus de Milo with
an electrically simulated waterfall cascading over her naked shoulders.

Examine once again your collecting notes about your subject. If there are striking similarities or differences between the two parts or between various aspects of
your subject, perhaps a comparison or contrast structure will organize your details.

DEFINITION   Definition is the essence of observation. Defining a person, place,
or object requires stating its exact meaning and describing its basic qualities. Literally, a definition sets the boundaries, indicating, for example, how an apple is distinct
from an orange or how a canary is different from a sparrow. *Definition,* however, is a
catchall term for a variety of strategies. It uses classification and comparison as well
as description. It often describes a thing by negation—by saying what it is not. For
example, Sidney Harris, a columnist for many years for the *Chicago Daily News,* once
defined a "jerk" by referring to several types of people ("boob," "fool," "dope," "bore,"
"egotist," "nice person," "clever person") and then compared or contrasted these terms
to show where "jerk" leaves off and "egotist" begins. In the following excerpt, Harris
also defines by negation, saying that a jerk has no grace and is tactless. The result, when
combined with a description of qualities he has observed in jerks, is definition.

> Thinking it over, I decided that a jerk is basically a person without insight.
> He is not necessarily a fool or a dope, because some extremely clever per-
> sons can be jerks. In fact, it has little to do with intelligence as we commonly
> think of it; it is, rather, a kind of subtle but persuasive aroma emanating
> from the inner part of the personality.
>
> I know a college president who can be described only as a jerk. He is
> not an unintelligent man, or unlearned, nor even unschooled in the social
> amenities. Yet he is a jerk *cum laude,* because of a fatal flaw in his nature—
> he is totally incapable of looking into the mirror of his soul and shudder-
> ing at what he sees there.
>
> A jerk, then, is a man (or woman) who is utterly unable to see himself
> as he appears to others. He has no grace, he is tactless without meaning to
> be, he is a bore even to his best friends, he is an egotist without charm. All
> of us are egotists to some extent, but most of us—unlike the jerk—are per-
> fectly and horribly aware of it when we make asses of ourselves. The jerk
> never knows.

At this stage in the writing process, you have already been defining your subject simply by describing it. But you may want to use a deliberately structured definition, as Harris does, to shape your observations.

SIMILE, METAPHOR, AND ANALOGY   Simile, metaphor, and analogy create vivid word pictures or *images* by making *comparisons.* These images may take up only a sentence or two, or they may shape several paragraphs.

- A *simile* is a comparison using *like* or *as:* A is like B. "George eats his food like a vacuum cleaner."
- A *metaphor* is a direct or implied comparison suggesting that A is B: "At the dinner table, George is a vacuum cleaner."
- An *analogy* is an extended simile or metaphor that builds a point-by-point comparison into several sentences, a whole paragraph, or even a series of paragraphs. Writers use analogy to explain a difficult concept, idea, or process by comparing it with something more familiar or easier to understand.

If the audience, for example, knows about engines but has never seen a human heart, a writer might use an analogy to explain that a heart is like a simple engine, complete with chambers or cylinders, intake and exhaust valves, and hoses to carry fuel and exhaust.

As an illustration of simile and metaphor, notice how Joseph Conrad, in the following brief passage from *Heart of Darkness,* begins with a simile and then continues to build on his images throughout the paragraph. Rather than creating a rigid structural shape for his details (as classification or comparison/contrast would do), the images combine and flow like the river he is describing.

> Going up that river was like travelling back to the earliest beginnings of the world, when vegetation rioted on the earth and the big trees were kings. An empty stream, a great silence, an impenetrable forest. The air was warm, thick, heavy, sluggish. There was no joy in the brilliance of sunshine. The long stretches of the waterway ran on, deserted, into the gloom of overshadowed distances. On silvery sand-banks hippos and alligators sunned themselves side by side. The broadening waters flowed through a mob of wooded islands; you lost your way on that river as you would in a desert, and butted all day long against shoals, trying to find the channel, till you thought yourself bewitched and cut off forever from everything you had known once—somewhere—far away—in another existence perhaps.

An analogy helps shape the following paragraph by Carl Sagan, author of *The Dragons of Eden* and *Cosmos.* To help us understand a difficult concept, the immense age of the Earth (and, by comparison, the relatively tiny span of human history),

Sagan compares the lifetime of the universe to something simple and familiar: the calendar of a single year.

> The most instructive way I know to express this cosmic chronology is to imagine the fifteen-billion year lifetime of the universe . . . compressed into the span of a single year. . . . It is disconcerting to find that in such a cosmic year the Earth does not condense out of interstellar matter until early September; dinosaurs emerge on Christmas Eve; flowers arise on December 28th; and men and women originate at 10:30 P.M. on New Year's Eve. All of recorded history occupies the last ten seconds of December 31; and the time from the waning of the Middle Ages to the present occupies little more than one second.

Consider whether a good analogy would help you shape one or more paragraphs in your essay. Ask yourself, "What is the most difficult concept or idea I'm trying to describe?" Is there an extended point-by-point comparison—an analogy—that would clarify it?

TITLE, INTRODUCTION, AND CONCLUSION   Depending on your purpose and audience, you may want a title for what you're writing. At the minimum, titles—like labels—should accurately indicate the contents in the package. In addition, however, good titles capture the reader's interest with some catchy phrasing or imaginative language—something to make the reader want to "buy" the package. Samuel H. Scudder's title is a good label (the essay is about looking at fish) and uses catchy phrasing: "Take This Fish and Look at It." If a title is appropriate for your observation, write out several possibilities in your journal.

The introduction should set up the context for the reader—*who, what, when, where,* and *why*—so that readers can orient themselves. Depending on your audience and purpose, introductions can be very brief, pushing the reader quickly into the scene, or they can take more time, easing readers into the setting. Stephen White, in his essay about Mesa Verde at the end of this chapter, begins mysteriously: "It is difficult for me to say exactly what it was that drew me to this solitary place." White doesn't tell his reader that he's talking about Mesa Verde until the second paragraph.

Conclusions should wrap up the observation, providing a sense of completeness. Conclusions vary, depending upon a writer's purpose and audience, but they tend to be of two types or have two components: a *summary* and a *reference* to the introduction. Mowat uses both components when he concludes his essay. Part II of his essay ends by referring to and then answering the central question of his expedition, that is: How do wolves survive? "The wolves of Wolf House Bay," Mowat tells us, "were living largely, if not almost entirely, on mice."

As you work on shaping strategies and drafting, make notes about possible titles, appropriate introductions, or effective conclusions for your written observations.

DRAFTING

"The idea is to get the pencil moving quickly."
—BERNARD MALAMUD, NOVELIST

REREAD JOURNAL ENTRIES AND NOTES FROM COLLECTING AND SHAPING   Before you start drafting, review your material so you aren't writing cold. Stop and reread everything you've written on your subject. You're not trying to memorize particular sentences or phrases; you're just getting it all fresh in your mind, seeing what you still like and discarding details that are no longer relevant.

REOBSERVE YOUR SUBJECT   If necessary, go back and observe your subject again. One more session may suggest an important detail or idea that will help you get started writing.

REEXAMINE PURPOSE, AUDIENCE, DOMINANT IDEA, AND SHAPE After all your writing and rereading, you may have some new ideas about your purpose, audience, or dominant idea. Take a minute to jot these down in your journal. Remember that your specific details should show the main point or dominant idea, whether you state it explicitly or not.

Next, if the shaping strategies suggested an order for your essay, use it to guide your draft. You may, however, have only your specific details or a general notion of the dominant idea you're trying to communicate to your reader. In that case, you may want to begin writing and work out a shape or outline as you write.

CREATE A DRAFT   With the above notes as a guide, you are ready to start drafting. Work on establishing your ritual: Choose a comfortable, familiar place with the writing tools you like. Make sure you'll have no interruptions. Try to write nonstop. If you can't think of a word, substitute a dash. If you can't remember how to spell a word, don't stop to look it up now—keep writing. Write until you reach what feels like the end. If you do get stuck, reread your last few lines or some of your writing process materials. Then go back and pick up the thread. Don't stop to count words or pages. You should shoot for more material than you need because it's usually easier to cut material later, when you're revising, than to add more if you're short.

REVISING

> *All the stuff you see back there on the floor is writing I did last week that I have to rewrite this week.*
>
> —ERNEST J. GAINES,
> AUTHOR OF
> THE AUTOBIOGRAPHY
> OF MISS JANE PITTMAN

GAINING DISTANCE AND OBJECTIVITY Revising, of course, has been going on since you put your first sentence down on paper. You've changed ideas, thought through your subject again, and observed your person, place, object, or image. After your rough draft is finished, your next step is to revise again to resee the whole thing. But before you do, you need to let it sit at least twenty-four hours, to get away from it for a while, to gain some distance and perspective. Relax. Congratulate yourself.

About the time you try to relax, however, you may get a sudden temptation—even an overwhelming urge—to have someone else read it—immediately! Usually, it's better to resist that urge. Chances are, you want to have someone else read it either because you're bubbling with enthusiasm and you want to share it or because you're certain that it's all garbage and you want to hear the bad news right away. Most readers will not find it either as great as you hope *or* as awful as you fear. As a result, their offhand remarks may seem terribly insensitive or condescending. In a day or so, however, you'll be able to see your writing more objectively: Perhaps it's not great yet, but it's not hopeless, either. At that point, you're ready to get some feedback and start your revisions.

REREADING AND RESPONDING TO YOUR READERS When you've been away from the draft for a while, you are better able to see the whole piece of writing. Start by rereading your own draft and making marginal notes. Don't be distracted by spelling errors or typos; concentrate on the quality of the details and the flow of the sentences. Focus on the overall effect you're creating, see if your organization still makes sense, and check to make sure that all the details support the dominant idea. Now you're ready to get some peer feedback. Depending on the reactions of your readers, you may need to change the point of view, add a few specific examples or some comparisons or images, fix the organization of a paragraph, reorder some details, delete some sentences, or do several of the above. Be prepared, however, to rewrite several paragraphs to help your readers really see what you are describing.

PEER RESPONSE

The instructions below will help you give and receive constructive advice about the rough draft of your observing essay. You may use these guidelines for an in-class workshop, a take-home review, or a computer e-mail response.

Writer: Before you exchange drafts with another reader, write out the following information about your rough draft:

1. What is the dominant impression that you want your description to make? What overall idea or impression do you want your reader to have?

2. What paragraph(s) contains your best and most vivid description? What paragraph(s) still needs some revision?

3. Explain one or two things you would like your reader to comment on as he or she responds to your draft.

Reader: First, without making any marks, read the entire draft from start to finish. As you *reread* the draft, answer the following questions.

1. What *dominant impression* does the draft create? Does the dominant impression you received agree with the writer's own idea? If not, how might the writer better achieve that overall impression?

2. Look at the writer's responses to question 2. Does the writer, in fact, use vivid description in his or her best paragraph(s)? How might the paragraphs that the writer says need revision be improved? Review the six techniques for descriptive writing at the beginning of this chapter. Where or how might the writer improve the *sensory details, images,* descriptions of what is *not there, changes* in the subject, or *point of view?* Offer specific suggestions.

3. Reread the assignment for this essay. Explain how this essay should be revised to more clearly *meet the assignment.* Does the writer understand the *rhetorical situation?* What changes in purpose, audience, genre, or style would help the essay meet the assignment?

4. List the *two most important things* this writer should work on as he or she revises this draft. Explain why these are important.

Guidelines for Revision

- As you revise your essay, keep the following tips and checklist questions in mind:
  - **Reexamine your purpose and audience.** Are you doing what you intended? If your purpose or audience has changed, what other changes do you need to make as you revise?
  - **Pay attention to the advice your readers give you, but don't necessarily make all the changes they suggest.** Ask them *why* something should be changed. Ask them specifically *where* something should be changed.
  - **Consider your genre.** Does your chosen genre still work for your purpose, audience, and context? Would including pictures, visuals, graphics, poetry, or quotations in a multigenre format be more effective?
  - **Consider your point of view.** Would changing to another point of view clarify what you are describing?
  - **Consider your vantage point.** Do you have a bird's-eye view, or are you observing from a low angle? Do you zoom in for a close-up of a person or object? Would a different vantage point fit your purpose and audience?
  - **Make sure you are using sensory details where appropriate.** Remember, you must *show* your reader the details you observe. If necessary, *reobserve* your subject.
  - **Do all your details and examples support your dominant idea?** Reread your draft and omit any irrelevant details.
  - **What is *not* present in your subject that might be important to mention?**
  - **What changes occur in the form or function of your subject?** Where can you describe those changes more vividly?
  - **Make comparisons if they will help you or your reader understand your subject better.** Similes, metaphors, or analogies may describe your subject more vividly.
  - **Does what you are observing belong to a class of similar objects?** Would classification organize your writing?
  - **Be sure to cue or signal your reader with appropriate transition words.** Transitions will improve the coherence or flow of your writing.
    - **Spatial order:** on the left, on the right, next, above, below, higher, lower, farther, next, beyond
    - **Chronological order.** before, earlier, after, afterward, thereafter, then, from then on, the next day, shortly, by that time, immediately, slowly, while, meanwhile, until, now, soon, within an hour, first, later, finally, at last
    - **Comparison/contrast:** on one hand, on the other hand, also, similarly, in addition, likewise, however, but, yet, still, although, even so, nonetheless, in contrast.

“I went for years not finishing anything. Because, of course, when you finish something you can be judged.”
—ERICA JONG, AUTHOR OF FEAR OF FLYING

- **Revise sentences for clarity, conciseness, emphasis, and variety.**
- **When you have revised your essay, edit your writing for correct spelling and appropriate word choice, punctuation, usage, and grammar.**

POSTSCRIPT ON THE WRITING PROCESS

When you've finished writing this assignment, do one final journal entry. Briefly, answer the following questions:

1. What was the hardest part of this writing assignment for you?

2. Put brackets ([ ]) around the paragraph containing your most vivid sensory details. Explain what makes this paragraph so vivid.

3. What exercise, practice, strategy, or workshop was the "breakthrough" for you? What led you to your discovery or dominant idea?

4. State in one sentence your discovery or the dominant idea of your essay.

5. What did you learn about your writing ritual and process? What did you learn about observing? What did you learn about your rhetorical situation?

STUDENT WRITING

PERMANENT TRACINGS

Jennifer Macke

Jennifer Macke, a student in Professor Rachel Henne-Wu's class at Owens Community College in Findlay, Ohio, decided to write her observing essay about a tattoo parlor. She visited the Living Color Tattoo Parlor and took notes on the office, the clientele, the conversations, the artwork of the tattoos, and the owner of the establishment. Ms. Macke wrote that her preconceptions about tattoo parlors were that they were "smoke-filled, dimly lit places" where "undesirables gathered." Gradually, her impressions changed as she saw firsthand the high quality and the remarkable artistry of the tattoos. Reprinted below are some of her original notes, questions and answers, an outline, and the final version of her essay.

Notes on a Visit

—A couple with a young school-aged daughter looks at the artwork on the walls for about 15 minutes before saying anything to the owner. They are looking for a design for the wife for her birthday. They appear to be a typical young couple with a limited amount of money. They ask how much a particular design will be and say they will have to save for it. "How much for this ankle bracelet?" he says. "It'll run you between $45 and $60, depending on how thick you want the rose vine," Gasket says.

—Two Latino men enter the waiting room. One peeks his head into the office and says, "I'm here early for my appointment because I'm not sure exactly what I want. Do you have any books or more pictures I can look through?" Gasket gives him six photo albums full of ideas (designs).

—Five young adult black men enter. They begin browsing through the photos on the wall. There are designs with prices below them so you know what it costs without asking. They too look through the photo albums the Latinos left on the floor. One of the black guys announces, "I'll go first 'cause I want to get it over with." One says, "I'm not going to do this. I can't stand the sound of that needle!" Gasket looks at me and says, "It's amazing how many people just think all you have to do is walk through the door like a walk-in barber shop. They don't know I'm booked for at least a week. During the summer, it's three weeks."

—The phone rings and since his daughter, who normally works there, is gone to visit her mother, he tells me to pick it up. The guy on the other end says, "My uncle wants to know if Jeff's cousin works here?" I relay the message to the owner and he replies, "Yes, that's me." Back on the phone, "He says he's the best in the business. Does he have any time today?" Gasket says, "Here we go again." I tell the guy it will be a week. He says, "OK, I'll call back then." I tell Gasket what he said and he comments, "He'll call back next week, and I'll have to tell him it'll be another week. You would not believe the intelligence level of some people."

—The next girl is going to have lips tattooed on her right hip. She is a petite nurse whom you would never guess would even consider such a thing. Her husband put lipstick on and kissed a napkin which she brought to use for the pattern. Gasket took a photocopy of this and made a transfer from it to use as the template. She dropped her shorts to expose where the art would be placed. She lay down on the table which Gasket explained he had gotten in trade for a tattoo. He also said the stirrups were still in the drawer. The girl smiled and talked the whole time he worked. At one point, he asked her, "Does it hurt?" She said, "No." He said, "I can go deeper!" She said, "Are you supposed to?" He said, laughing, "It's just a joke. If I see someone who's comfortable, I'll ask them this." It only took about 30 minutes to complete this one. You would swear someone just kissed her with bright red lipstick. It's amazing how realistic his work looks.

Questions and Answers

1. "Why do people get tattoos?"

   "A tattoo is a very personal thing. It's an expression of one's self."

2. "Does it hurt to get a tattoo?"

   "It all depends on the placement and the person. Guys tend to be bigger wimps. I'd rather do women any day. The most painful areas are the ankle and higher up on the belly. I've had the pain described as something annoying but not necessarily painful to such a point that they cannot stand it. I've never had anyone pass out, though."

3. "What kind of person gets a tattoo?"

   "There's not one particular type of person who gets a tattoo. I once had a call from some lawyers from Findlay. They wanted to know if they had five or so people who wanted a tattoo, would I come over? I said, yes, and I tattooed six lawyers at a party."

4. "What is the process of getting a tattoo?"

   "Depending if it will be freehand or something the people bring in, it starts with drawing the art. It is drawn either on the person or on carbon paper backwards. The carbon design is transferred to the skin with Speed Stick deodorant. The outline is applied first. As the single needle picks up and sews into the skin, excess ink covers the work area."

   As Gasket works, it's hard to see the actual area he's working on because of the excess ink. When asked how he can work with the excess ink obstructing the guidelines, he says he just knows where the line goes. (I wouldn't.) Once the outline is complete he changes to use a 3 or 4 needle set, depending on the coverage necessary. He colorizes the art, which brings it to life. After it's complete, he puts a thick coat of Bacitracin on and covers it with a gauze bandage. The gauze must remain on for one and a half to two hours.

5. "What is the most common place for a tattoo?"

   "Placement runs in cycles, sometimes the upper arm, sometimes the ankle." While we were talking, a man came in with one on the back of his neck.

6. "How expensive are tattoos?"

The minimum is $30. Depending on how detailed and how big. Gasket has bartered for the tattoos, too.

7. "Do most people get more than one tattoo?"

"I've seen people go through life with only one or maybe two, but it's said when you get your third, you're hooked. You'll be back for more."

8. "Are there health department requirements?"

"At the beginning, the requirements (laws) weren't very strict. I knew I wanted to be supersterile, so I put my needles and equipment through a much stricter procedure. Since then, the health department has taken on my policy and requires everyone to process their stuff like me. They drop in to make sure the laws are being followed."

9. "How many times do you use your needles?" "They are single-application needles, but they still need to be sterilized. People ask me if they can watch their needles being sterilized so they can make sure. I say fine, but it will be two and a half hours until I can work on you."

Outline

Working Thesis: "Gasket's creative artistic ability and perfectionist work ethic make his designs worth sewing into your body for a lifetime."

I. Describe the Tattoo Parlor
   A. Outer area (waiting room)
   B. Inner office

II. Describe the owner
   A. The way he looks
   B. The way he feels about his work

III. Describe the people
   A. People getting a tattoo
   B. People not getting a tattoo

Final Version

PERMANENT TRACINGS

At first glance, the Living Color Tattoo Parlor appears to be just another typical tattoo establishment. You enter through a glass door only to find a waiting room with the decor reminiscent of the 1970s. The dark paneled walls display numerous types of artwork that range from pencil sketching to color Polaroid snapshots of newly completed tattoos. The gold and green davenport looks as if it came from a Saturday morning garage sale. The inner office is celery green with a dental chair and an obstetrics table that the owner bartered for a tattoo (the stirrups are still in the drawer). A filing cabinet, desk, and copy machine make you feel as if you're in a professional office. The sterilizer is in plain sight and is in operation. Bottle after bottle of brightly colored inks are neatly arranged on a tiered wooden stand. The sound of the oscillating fan that cools the client interrupts the buzz of the needle sewing the paint into the client's skin. A freeze-dried turtle is displayed on a table in the office.

I still wondered, though. Could tattoos actually be a form of art?   2

As soon as I could, I asked the owner, a man called Gasket, about his   3
occupation. "I was a suit for fifteen years and now I can work as much as I want. There's always somebody wanting a tattoo or something pierced," Gasket said. He's often asked if he'll scratch out the name of a previous girlfriend, and he always replies that he would never even consider it. "That would be defacement," he said. "When I'm done, the design should look better than when I started." Gasket is not his given name but one he acquired because of his expert repair work on Harley Davidson motorcycles. Gasket is the owner of this establishment, and to look at him, you would never guess he is a college-educated engineer. His long curly, graying hair flows from under his Harley hat, and examples of his handiwork are visible under the rolled up sleeves of his black Harley T-shirt. The harshness of his heavily bearded face is softened by his slate-blue eyes, which mirror his gentle demeanor. If you look past his casual exterior, you will find a code of steel. "At the beginning, the laws weren't very strict. I knew I wanted to be supersterile, so I put my single-use needles and equipment through a much stricter procedure. Since then, the health department has taken on my policy and requires everyone to process their stuff like me," he said.

The appearance of the Living Color Tattoo Parlor may be typical, but   4
two things are distinctly different: the quality and the creativity of the tattoo designs. A young college couple from Toledo was asked why they would drive to Fremont for an appointment. They answered, "Gasket's the best! We wouldn't trust something that's going to be on our body for the rest of our lives to someone other than him."

"I already have two tattoos from you, and I love your work," a middle-   5
aged woman said. Displaying two greeting cards, she asked, "Is it possible to get a combination of these two designs?"

"I can create anything you want," Gasket said.   6

"I'll have to wait a couple of weeks because I'm not working much and   7
my other bills come first," she said.

"Yes, you have to get your priorities straight. When you're ready, I'm   8
here," he said.

Gasket is performing his tattoo magic on a young college female. He's   9
creating a rose with a heart stem wrapping around her belly button, which
is pierced. The girl is nervously seated in the green dental chair, which is
tilted back to flatten the skin surface. First, Gasket draws the sketch on her
belly. He covers his hands with a thin layer of latex once the exact position
and specific details are decided upon. A small device resembling a fountain
pen with a brightly colored motor and a single needle moving at 1,000 rpm
is used to apply the black outline first. As the needle moves up and down,
it picks up a small amount of ink and deposits it just under the surface of
the skin. When asked how he can work with the excess ink obstructing the
guidelines, he simply said he just knows where the line goes. This is a difficult task because unlike a paint-by-number design, the image not only
has to be in his mind but he also has to have the artistic ability to convert
the image to the skin. The girl asks a pain-filled question, "How much
longer?"

"I can stop and let you take a break at any time," Gasket says. His soft   10
tone and slow-paced voice help soothe the girl. "The higher up on the belly,
the more painful," he says. The process of colorizing the tattoo begins once
the outline is complete. This is accomplished with a three- or four-needle
set, depending on the amount of coverage desired. It takes about forty-five
minutes to complete the multicolored masterpiece, which is literally sewn
into her skin. Some of Gasket's designs can be compared to Picasso's brilliantly colored, dreamlike images. Upon completion, the girl is directed to
a full-length mirror to inspect her permanently altered abs.

"It looks fantastic!" she exclaims. "I was a little vague on how I pic-   11
tured it would look, but it looks even better than I had imagined. I'm
thrilled."

Once thought of as green-toned disfigurements that only drunken   12
sailors and lowlife people would don, tattoos are now high fashion. Now it
is possible to see skin art on TV stars, sports superstars, and a multitude of
individuals you might not suspect. The future of this trendy fashion has its
roots firmly planted in today's society. Young people seem to be one of its
biggest supporters.

"I'll go first 'cause I want to get it over with," one young black man   13
states to his four companions.

"I'm not going to do this. I can't stand the sound of that needle!" an-   *14*
other man proclaims.

"It's amazing how many people think all you have to do is just walk   *15*
through the door like a walk-in barber shop. They don't know I'm booked
for at least a week. During the summer, it's three weeks," Gasket claims. He
explains this to the young men, who make appointments. They leave, dis-
appointed.

Gasket's tattoo designs can be compared to the famous fashion de-   *16*
signs by Bob Mackie. Like Mackie's one-of-a-kind designs, they are not
mass-produced, but are hand-sewn for a specific individual. As I left, my
first impression of the Living Color Tattoo Parlor was changed by the incredibly beautiful skin art and the comments of the satisfied clients. For
many, Gasket's artistic ability and perfectionism make his designs worth
sewing into your body for a lifetime.

QUESTIONS FOR WRITING AND DISCUSSION

1. Review the techniques for writing observing papers at the beginning of the chapter. Which paragraph(s) in Macke's essay have the best sensory detail, images, comparisons, and other effective bits of description?
Which paragraphs might use more descriptive detail?

2. Macke describes the office, the owner, the customers, the process of tattooing,
and the prices of a tattoo. Should she also describe several of the tattoos?
Should she describe the colors in a typical tattoo? If she did these descriptions, where might she put them in her essay?

3. Reread Macke's notes of her visit, including her questions and answers. What
interesting ideas and descriptions in her notes might be included in her final
draft? Why might Macke have left these details out? Assume that you are a
peer reader for Macke's essay. Fill out the peer response questions printed earlier in this chapter so you can help her with a revision of her essay.

4. List the three things that you like best about Macke's essay. Which of her
strategies might work for a revision of your own essay? Make a revision plan
for your own essay, based on what you learned from reading "Permanent
Tracings."

STUDENT WRITING

EMPTY WINDOWS

Stephen White

In this essay written for Professor John Boni at Colorado State University, Stephen White describes both what his senses tell him and what he can only imagine about the Anasazi, the ancient Native Americans who more than a thousand years ago built the cliff dwellings at Mesa Verde in southwestern Colorado. Writing about those empty dwellings with their darkened windows, White says, "Perhaps there lurks, behind every blackened window, a certain unexplainable something we can never understand."

1   It is difficult for me to say exactly what it was that drew me to this solitary place and held me here, virtually entranced, the entire day. It's the silence, maybe, or the empty houses perched precariously on the canyon wall below me. Or could it be the knowledge that something seemingly nonexistent does indeed exist?

2   I awoke this morning with a sense of unexplainable anticipation gnawing away at the back of my mind, that this chilly, leaden day at Mesa Verde would bring something new and totally foreign to any of my past experiences. It was a sensation that began to permeate my entire being as I sat crouched before my inadequate campfire, chills running up my spine. Chills which, I am certain, were due not entirely to the dreary gray of a winter "sunrise."

3   It had been my plan to travel the so-called Ruins Road early today and then complete my visit here, but as I stopped along the road and stood scanning the opposite wall of the canyon for ruins, I felt as if some force had seized control of my will. I was compelled to make my way along the rim.

4   Starting out upon the rock, I weaved in and out repeatedly as the gaping emptiness of the canyon and the weathered standstone of the rim battled one another for territory. At last arriving here, where a narrow peninsula of canyon juts far into the stone, I was able to peer back into the darkness of a cave carved midway in the vertical wall opposite, within whose smoke-blackened walls huddle, nearly unnoticeable, the rooms of a small, crumbled ruin.

Cliff Palace at Mesa Verde National Park.

They are a haunting sight, these broken houses, clustered together 5
down in the gloom of the canyon. It presents a complete contrast to the tidy,
excavated ruins I explored yesterday, lost within a cluster of tourists and
guided by a park ranger who expounded constantly upon his wealth of
knowledge of excavation techniques and archaeological dating methods.
The excavated ruins seemed, in comparison, a noisy, almost modern city,
punctuated with the clicking of camera shutters and the bickering of children. Here it is quiet. The silence is broken only by the rush of the wind in
the trees and the trickling of a tiny stream of melting snow springing from
ledge to ledge as it makes its way down over the rock to the bottom of the
canyon. And this small, abandoned village of tiny houses seems almost as
the Indians left it, reduced by the passage of nearly a thousand years to
piles of rubble through which protrude broken red adobe walls surrounding ghostly jet-black openings, undisturbed by modern man.

Those windows seem to stare back at me as my eyes are drawn to them. 6
They're so horribly empty, yet my gaze is fixed, searching for some sign of
the vitality they must surely have known. I yearn for sounds amidst the silence, for images of life as it once was in the bustling and prosperous community of cliff dwellers who lived here so long ago. It must have been a
sunny home when the peaceful, agrarian Anasazi, or ancient ones, as the
Navajo call them, lived and dreamed their lives here, wanting little more

than to continue in their ways and be left alone, only to be driven away in the end by warring people with whom they could not contend.

I long to hear, to see, and to understand, and though I strain all my 7 senses to their limits, my wishes are in vain. I remain alone, confronted only by the void below and the cold stare of those utterly desolate windows. I know only an uneasy sensation that I am not entirely alone, and a quick, chill gust gives birth once again to that restless shiver tracing its path along the length of my spine.

As a gray afternoon fades into a gray evening, I can find neither a true 8 feeling of fear nor one of the quiet serenity one would expect to experience here. It is comforting for me to believe that it was the explorer in me which brought me here, to feel that I was lured to stand above this lonely house by that same drive to find and explore the unknown which motivated the countless others who have come here since seeking knowledge and understanding of the ancient people of the "Green Table." Yet as I begin the journey back to my car and the security of an evening fire, I remain uncomfortably unconvinced.

Perhaps the dreariness of a cloudy day united with my solitude to pave 9 a mental pathway for illusion and mystery. Or perhaps all homes are never truly empty, having known the multitude of experience which is human life. Perhaps there lurks, behind every blackened window, a certain unexplainable something we can never understand. I know only that the Indian has long respected these places and given them wide berth, leaving their sanctity inviolate.

QUESTIONS FOR WRITING AND DISCUSSION

1. Describe a similar experience you have had with an empty room or a vacant house. White says that "perhaps all homes are never truly empty, having known the multitude of experience which is human life." Based on your experience, do you agree with him?

2. Through his description, what did White help you "see" about the Anasazi and their cliff dwellings? What did you learn?

3. Consider once again the basic techniques for observing—using sensory detail, comparisons, and images; describing what is not there; noting changes; and

writing from a clear point of view. Which ones does White use most effec-tively? Cite an example of each technique from his essay.

4. In which paragraphs does White use each of the following shaping strategies: spatial order, chronological order, comparisons or contrasts, and simile, metaphor, or analogy? Which strategies did you find most effective in organ-izing the experience for you as a reader?

5. White's essay illustrates how the *occasion* for writing can figure prominently in a writer's rhetorical situation. What sentences and paragraphs best describe the occasion that motivated him to write? Why is occasion so important to the success of his essay? Explain.

6. Consider the relationship between the photograph of Cliff Palace at Mesa Verde Park and White's essay. Does this image add to the overall effect of the essay? Does it detract from the essay by giving the reader an actual picture rather than an imagined one? Should the image be retained, replaced with another image, or removed altogether? Explain your response.

Edward Hopper was one of the most important American realists in the first half of the twentieth century. Art critic Edward Lucie-Smith has said that Hopper was a "pictorial poet who recorded the starkness and vastness of America." After studying the details and composition of this painting, try the journal exercise on page 125 of this chapter.

Edward Hopper
Ryder's House (1933)
Oil on canvas
Smithsonian American Art Museum

chapter

4 Remembering

You and several coworkers have formed a committee to draft a report for your company's vice president in charge of personnel. You have grievances about workload, pay scale, daily procedures, and the attitudes of supervisors. Your report needs to recommend changes in current policies. The committee decides that each person will contribute part of the report by describing actual incidents that have had negative effects on efficiency and human relations. You decide to describe a day last June when your immediate supervisor expected you to learn a new word-processing system and at the same time meet a 3:00 P.M. deadline for a thirty-seven-page budget analysis..

This morning you accidentally ran into a certain person whom you knew several years ago, and for several hours you've been in a bad mood. You called your best friend, but no one answered the phone. You went to class and then for your usual jog, but you pooped out after only half a mile. You even watched a game show on television in the middle of the afternoon and ate half a bag of potato chips, but you still felt lousy. You yell at the television: "Why do I always react this way when I see that person?" But the television has no reply. So you grab some paper and begin scrawling out every memory you have of your experiences with the person you ran into this morning, hoping to understand your feelings.

For me the initial delight is in the surprise of remembering something I didn't know I knew.

ROBERT FROST, POET

The fact is that there's no understanding the future without the present, and no understanding where we are now without a glance, at least, to where we have been.

—JOYCE MAYNARD, COLUMNIST AND AUTHOR OF LOOKING BACKWARD: A CHRONICLE OF GROWING UP OLD IN THE SIXTIES

THE HUMAN BRAIN IS A PACK RAT: NOTHING IS TOO SMALL, OBSCURE, OR MUNDANE FOR THE BRAIN'S COLLECTION. OFTEN THE BRAIN COLLECTS AND DISCARDS INFORMATION WITHOUT REGARD TO OUR WISHES. OUT OF THE collection may arise, with no warning, the image of windblown whitecaps on a lake you visited more than five years ago, the recipe for Uncle Joe's incomparable chili, or even the right answer to an exam question that you've been staring at for the past fifteen minutes.

Remembering is sometimes easy, sometimes difficult. Often careful concentration yields nothing, while the most trivial occurrence—an old song on a car radio, the acrid smell of diesel exhaust, the face of a stranger—will trigger a flood of recollections. Someone tells a story and you immediately recall incidents, funny or traumatic, from your own life. Some memories, however, are nagging and troublesome, keeping you awake at night, daring you to deal with them. You pick at these memories. Why are they so important? You write about them, usually to probe that mystery of yesterday and today. Sights, sounds, or feelings from the present may draw you to the past, but the past leads, just as surely, back to the present.

Direct observations are important to learning and writing, but so are your memories, experiences, and stories. You may write an autobiographical account of part of your life, or you may recall a brief event, a person, or a place just as an example to illustrate a point. Whatever form your writing from memory takes, however, your initial purpose is to remember experiences so that you can understand yourself and your world. The point is not to write fiction, but to practice drawing on your memories and to write vividly enough about them so that you and others can discover and learn.

The value of remembering lies exactly here: written memories have the power to teach you and, through the *empathy* of your readers, to inform or convince them as well. At first, you may be self-conscious about sharing your personal memories. But as you reveal these experiences, you realize that your story is worth telling—not because you're such an egotist, but because sharing experiences helps everyone learn.

> *Time passes and the past becomes the present. . . . These presences of the past are there in the center of your life today. You thought . . . they had died, but they have just been waiting their chance.*
>
> —CARLOS FUENTES, MEXICAN ESSAYIST AND NOVELIST, AUTHOR OF THE CRYSTAL FRONTIER

Techniques for Writing About Memories

Writing vividly about memories includes all the skills of careful observing, but it adds several additional narrative strategies. Listed below are five techniques that writers use to compose effective remembering essays. As you read the essays that follow in this chapter, notice how each writer uses these techniques. Then, when you write your own remembering essay, use these techniques in your own essay. Remember: Not all writing about memories uses all of these techniques, but one or two of them may transform a lifeless or boring account into an effective narrative.

- **Using *detailed observation* of people, places, and events.** Writing vividly about memories requires many of the skills of careful observation. Give actual dialogue where appropriate.
- **Focusing on *occasion* and *cultural context*.** These two aspects of the rhetorical situation are especially important for remembering essays. First, think about the personal *occasion* that motivated you to write. Second, you may want to include details about the *cultural context* for key events.
- **Creating *specific scenes* set in time and space.** Show your reader the actual events; don't just tell about events; Narrate specific incidents as they actually happened. Avoid monotonously summarizing events or presenting just the conclusions (for instance, "those experiences really changed my life").
- **Noting *changes, contrasts,* or *conflicts*.** Changes in people or places, contrasts between two different memories or between memories of expectations and realities, and conflicts between people or ideas—any of these may lead to the meaning or importance of a remembered person, place, or event.
- **Making *connections* between past events, people, or places and the present.** The main idea of a narrative often grows out of changes and conflicts or arises from the connections you make between past and present.
- **Discovering and focusing on a *main idea*.** A remembering essay is not a random narrative of the writer's favorite memories. A narrative should have a clear main point, focus on a main idea, or make a discovery. The essay should clearly show why the memories are important.

All of these techniques are important, but you should also keep several other points in mind. Normally, you should write in the *first person,* using *I* or *we* throughout the narrative. Although you will usually write in *past tense,* sometimes you may wish to lend immediacy to the events by retelling them in the *present tense,* as if they are happening now. Finally, you may choose straightforward *chronological order,* or you may begin near the end and use a *flashback* to tell the beginning of the story.

The key to effective remembering, however, is to get beyond *generalities and conclusions* about your experiences ("I had a lot of fun—those days really changed my life"). Your goal is to recall *specific incidents set in time and place* that *show* how and why those days changed your life. The specific incidents should show your *main point* or *dominant idea*.

The following passage by Andrea Lee began as a journal entry during a year she spent in Moscow and Leningrad following her graduation from college. She then combined these firsthand observations with her memories and published them in a collection called *Russian Journal.* She uses first person and, frequently, present tense as she describes her reactions to the sights of Moscow. In these paragraphs, she weaves observations and memories together to show her main idea: The contrast between American and Russian advertising helped her understand both the virtues and the faults of American commercialism. (The annotations in the margin illustrate how Lee uses all five remembering techniques.)

Specific scene

In Mayakovsky Square, not far from the Tchaikovsky Concert Hall, a big computerized electric sign sends various messages flashing out into the night. An outline of a taxi in green dots is accompanied by the words: "Take Taxis—All Streets Are Near." This is replaced by multicolored human figures and a sentence urging Soviet citizens to save in State banks. The bright

Detailed observation

patterns and messages come and go, making this one of the most sophisticated examples of advertising in Moscow. Even on chilly nights when I pass through the square, there is often a little group of Russians standing in front of the sign, watching in fascination for five and ten minutes as the colored dots go through their magical changes. The first few times I saw

Connections past and present

this, I chuckled and recalled an old joke about an American town so boring that people went out on weekends to watch the Esso sign.

Contrast
Main idea

Advertising, of course, is the glamorous offspring of capitalism and art: why advertise in a country where there is only one brand, the State brand, of anything, and often not enough even of that? There is nothing here comparable to the glittering overlay of commercialism that Americans, at least, take for granted as part of our cities; nothing like the myriad small seductions of the marketplace, which have led us to expect to be

Detailed observation

enticed. The Soviet political propaganda posters that fill up a small part of the Moscow landscape with their uniformly cold red color schemes and monumental robot-faced figures are so unappealing that they are dismissable.

Connections past and present

I realize now, looking back, that for at least my first month in Moscow, I was filled with an unconscious and devastating disappointment. Hardly realizing it, as I walked around the city, I was looking for the constant sen-

Contrast and change

sory distractions I was accustomed to in America. Like many others my age, I grew up reading billboards and singing advertising jingles; my idea

Main idea

of beauty was shaped—perniciously, I think—by the models with the painted eyes and pounds of shining hair whose beauty was accessible on every television set and street corner.

REMEMBERING PEOPLE

In the following passage from the introduction to *The Way to Rainy Mountain,* N. Scott Momaday remembers his grandmother. While details of place and event are also recreated, the primary focus is on the character of his grandmother as revealed in several *specific,* recurring actions. Momaday does not give us generalities about his feelings (for instance, "I miss my grandmother a lot, especially now that she's gone"); instead, he begins with specific memories of scenes that *show* how he felt.

> Now that I can have her only in memory, I see my grandmother in the several postures that were peculiar to her: standing at the wood stove on a winter morning and turning meat in a great iron skillet; sitting at the south window, bent above her beadwork, and afterwards, when her vision failed, looking down for a long time into the fold of her hands; going out upon a cane, very slowly as she did when the weight of age came upon her; praying. I remember her most often at prayer. She made long, rambling prayers out of suffering and hope, having seen many things. I was never sure that I had the right to hear, so exclusive were they of all mere custom and company. The last time I saw her she prayed standing by the side of her bed at night, naked to the waist, the light of a kerosene lamp moving upon her dark skin. Her long, black hair, always drawn and braided in the day, lay upon her shoulders and against her breasts like a shawl. I do not speak Kiowa, and I never understood her prayers, but there was something inherently sad in the sound, some merest hesitation upon the syllables of sorrow. She began in a high and descending pitch, exhausting her breath to silence; then again and again—and always the same intensity of effort, of something that is, and is not, like urgency in the human voice. Transported so in the dancing light among the shadows of her room, she seemed beyond the reach of time. But that was illusion; I think I knew then that I should not see her again.

> *" A writer is a reader moved to emulation. "*
> —SAUL BELLOW,
> AUTHOR OF
> HENDERSON
> THE RAIN KING

REMEMBERING PLACES

In the following passage from *Farewell to Manzanar,* Jeanne Wakatsuke Houston remembers the place in California where, as Japanese-Americans, her family was imprisoned during World War II. As you read, look for specific details and bits of description that convey her main idea.

In Spanish, Manzanar means "apple orchard." Great stretches of Owens Valley were once green with orchards and alfalfa fields. It has been a desert ever since its water started flowing south into Los Angeles, sometime during the twenties. But a few rows of untended pear and apple trees were still growing there when the camp opened, where a shallow water table had kept them alive. In the spring of 1943 we moved to block 28, right up next to one of the old pear orchards. That's where we stayed until the end of the war, and those trees stand in my memory for the turning of our life in camp, from the outrageous to the tolerable.

Papa pruned and cared for the nearest trees. Late that summer we picked the fruit green and stored it in a root cellar he had dug under our new barracks. At night the wind through the leaves would sound like the surf had sounded in Ocean Park, and while drifting off to sleep, I could almost imagine we were still living by the beach.

REMEMBERING EVENTS

In the following essay, called "The Boy's Desire," Richard Rodriguez recalls a particular event from his childhood that comes to mind when he remembers Christmas. In his memory, he sorts through the rooms in his house on Thirty-ninth Street in

Sacramento, recalling old toys: a secondhand bike, games with dice and spinning dials, a jigsaw puzzle, and a bride doll. In this passage, Rodriguez describes both the effort to remember and the memory itself—the one memory that still "holds color and size and shape." Was it all right, he wonders, that a boy should have wanted a doll for Christmas?

The fog comes to mind. It never rained on Christmas. It was never sharp blue and windy. When I remember Christmas in Sacramento, it is in gray: The valley fog would lift by late morning, the sun boiled haze for a few hours, then the tule fog would rise again when it was time to go into the house.

The haze through which memory must wander is thickened by that fog. The rooms of the house on 39th Street are still and dark in late afternoon, and I open the closet to search for old toys. One year there was a secondhand bike. I do not remember a color. Perhaps it had no color even then. Another year there were boxes of games that rattled their parts—dice and pegs and spinning dials. Or perhaps the rattle is of a jigsaw puzzle that compressed into an image . . . of what? of Paris? a litter of kittens? I cannot remember. Only one memory holds color and size and shape: brown hair, blue eyes, the sweet smell of styrene.

That Christmas I announced I wanted a bride doll. I must have been seven or eight—wise enough to know not to tell anyone at school, but young enough to whine out my petition from early November.

My father's reaction was unhampered by psychology. A shrug—"Una muñeca?"—a doll, why not? Because I knew it was my mother who would choose all the presents, it was she I badgered. I wanted a bride doll! "Is there something else you want?" she wondered. No! I'd make clear with my voice that nothing else would appease me. "We'll see," she'd say, and she never wrote it down on her list.

By early December, wrapped boxes started piling up in my parents' bedroom closet, above my father's important papers and the family album. When no one else was home, I'd drag a chair over and climb up to see . . . Looking for the one. About a week before Christmas, it was there. I was so certain it was mine that I punched my thumb through the wrapping paper and the cellophane window on the box and felt inside—lace, two tiny, thin legs. I got other presents that year, but it was the doll I kept by me. I remember my mother saying I'd have "to share her" with my younger sister—but Helen was four years old, oblivious. The doll was mine. My arms would hold her. She would sleep on my pillow.

And the sky did not fall. The order of the universe did not tremble. In fact, it was right for a change. My family accommodated itself to my request.

> *Some very small incident that takes place today may be the most important event that happens to you this year, but you don't know that when it happens. You don't know it until much later.*
> —TONI MORRISON,
> NOBEL PRIZE-WINNING
> AUTHOR OF BELOVED
> AND SONG OF
> SOLOMON

My brother and sisters played round me with their own toys. I paraded my doll by the hands across the floor.

The other day, when I asked my brother and sisters about the doll, no one remembered. My mother remembers. "Yes," she smiled. "One year there was a doll."

The closet door closes. (The house on 39th Street has been razed for a hospital parking lot.) The fog rises. Distance tempts me to mock the boy and his desire. The fact remains: One Christmas in Sacramento I wanted a bride doll, and I got one.

WARMING UP: JOURNAL EXERCISES

The following topics will help you practice writing about your memories. Read all of the following exercises, and then write on three that interest you the most. If another idea occurs to you, write a free entry about it.

1. Look again at the artwork in the beginning of this chapter, *Ryder's House,* by Edward Hopper. Use your observing skills with this image of the solitary house. Does the picture suggest a warm home, a house from earlier decades, or a house abandoned for years? Then find a picture—or draw one—of the house you spent your childhood in. Is that picture (or your representation) friendly, warm, colorful, and inviting? Is it more austere and old? If you are looking at a picture, does it seem smaller or larger than your memories? Use your pictures as a starting point for a narrative about some important event from your own life that centered on your house.

2. Reread Jeanne Wakatsuke Houston's excerpt from *Farewell to Manzanar* and then re-examine the accompanying image, "Manzanar War Relocation Center." What details of the image's composition stand out? What other elements do you notice? What does the image add to Houston's account? Would a different image be more effective for her excerpt? Why or why not? Explain.

3. Go through old family photographs and find one of yourself, taken at least five years ago. Describe the person in the photograph—what he or she did, thought, said, or hoped. How is that person like or unlike the person you are now?

4. Remember the first job you had. How did you get it, and what did you do? What mistakes did you make? What did you learn? Were there any humorous or serious misunderstandings between you and others?

5. What are your earliest memories? Choose one particular event. How old were you? What was the place? Who were the people around you? What happened? After you write down your earliest memories, call members of your family, if possible, and interview them for their memories of this incident. How does what you actually remember differ from what your family tells you? Revise your first memory to incorporate additional details provided by your family.

6. At some point in the past, you may have faced a conflict between what was expected of you—by parents, friends, family, coach, or employer—and your own personality or abilities. Describe one occasion when these expectations seemed unrealistic or unfair. Was the experience entirely negative or was it, |in the long run, positive?

7. At at least one point in our lives, we have felt like an outsider. In a selection earlier in this chapter, for instance, Richard Rodriguez recalls feelings of being different, rejected, or outcast. Write about an incident when you felt alienated from your family, peers, or social group. Focus on a key scene or scenes that show what happened, why it was important, and how it affects you now.

8. Read Helen Keller's or Mike Rose's essay later in this chapter and write your own literacy narrative. What are your early memories about learning to read and write? At what points did you struggle or fail? When did you most enjoy reading or writing?

PROFESSIONAL WRITING

THE DAY LANGUAGE CAME INTO MY LIFE

Helen Keller

At the age of eighteen months, Helen Keller (1880–1968) lost her sight and hearing as a result of illness. During the next five years of her childhood, Keller became increasingly wild and unruly as she struggled against her dark and silent world. In "The Day Language Came into My Life," Keller remembers how, at age seven, her teacher, Anne Sullivan, arrived and taught her the miracle of language. After learning sign language and Braille, Keller began her formal schooling and—with continued help from Sullivan—eventually graduated with honors from Radcliffe College. In her adult years, Keller became America's best-loved ambassador for the blind and disabled. She met nearly every American president, traveled to dozens of countries to speak on behalf of blind and deaf people, and wrote several books, including The Story of My Life *(1903),* The World I Live In *(1908), and* Midstream: My Later Life *(1930). The story of Anne Sullivan's teaching is told in William Gibson's Pulitzer Prize-winning play,* The Miracle Worker.

Helen Keller with Anne Sullivan

The most important day I remember in all my life is the one on which my *1*
teacher, Anne Mansfield Sullivan, came to me. I am filled with wonder
when I consider the immeasurable contrast between the two lives which it
connects. It was the third of March 1887, three months before I was seven
years old.

On the afternoon of that eventful day, I stood on the porch, dumb, ex- *2*
pectant. I guessed vaguely from my mother's signs and from the hurrying
to and fro in the house that something unusual was about to happen, so I
went to the door and waited on the steps. The afternoon sun penetrated the
mass of honeysuckle that covered the porch and fell on my upturned face.
My fingers lingered almost unconsciously on the familiar leaves and blos-
soms which had just come forth to greet the sweet southern spring. I did
not know what the future held of marvel or surprise for me. Anger and bit-
terness had preyed upon me continually for weeks and a deep languor had
succeeded this passionate struggle.

Have you ever been at sea in a dense fog, when it seemed as if a tan- *3*
gible white darkness shut you in, and the great ship, tense and anxious,
groped her way toward the shore with plummet and sounding-line, and
you waited with beating heart for something to happen? I was like that
ship before my education began, only I was without compass or sounding-
line and had no way of knowing how near the harbor was. "Light! give me
light!" was the wordless cry of my soul, and the light of love shone on me
in that very hour.

I felt approaching footsteps. I stretched out my hand as I supposed to *4*
my mother. Someone took it, and I was caught up and held close in the arms
of her who had come to reveal all things to me, and, more than all things
else, to love me.

The morning after my teacher came she led me into her room and *5*
gave me a doll. The little blind children at the Perkins Institution had sent
it and Laura Bridgman had dressed it; but I did not know this until afterward. When I had played with it a little while, Miss Sullivan slowly spelled
into my hand the word "d-o-l-l." I was at once interested in this finger play
and tried to imitate it. When I finally succeeded in making the letters correctly I was flushed with childish pleasure and pride. Running downstairs
to my mother I held up my hand and made the letters for doll. I did not
know that I was spelling a word or even that words existed; I was simply
making my fingers go in monkeylike imitation. In the days that followed I
learned to spell in this uncomprehending way a great many words, among
them *pin, hat, cup* and a few verbs like *sit, stand* and *walk*. But my teacher

had been with me several weeks before I understood that everything has a name.

One day, while I was playing with my new doll, Miss Sullivan put my big rag doll into my lap also, spelled "d-o-l-l" and tried to make me understand that "d-o-l-l" applied to both. Earlier in the day we had had a tussle over the words "m-u-g" and "w-a-t-e-r." Miss Sullivan had tried to impress it upon me that "m-u-g" is *mug* and that "w-a-t-e-r" is *water*, but I persisted in confounding the two. In despair she had dropped the subject for the time, only to renew it at the first opportunity. I became impatient at her repeated attempts and, seizing the new doll, I dashed it upon the floor. I was keenly delighted when I felt the fragments of the broken doll at my feet. Neither sorrow nor regret followed my passionate outburst. I had not loved the doll. In the still, dark world in which I lived there was no strong sentiment or tenderness. I felt my teacher sweep the fragments to one side of the hearth, and I had a sense of satisfaction that the cause of my discomfort was removed. She brought me my hat, and I knew I was going out into the warm sunshine. This thought, if a wordless sensation may be called a thought, made me hop and skip with pleasure.

We walked down the path to the well-house, attracted by the fragrance of the honeysuckle with which it was covered. Someone was drawing water and my teacher placed my hand under the spout. As the cool stream gushed over one hand she spelled into the other the word *water*, first slowly, then rapidly. I stood still, my whole attention fixed upon the motions of her fingers. Suddenly I felt a misty consciousness as of something forgotten—a thrill of returning thought; and somehow the mystery of language was revealed to me. I knew then that "w-a-t-e-r" meant the wonderful cool something that was flowing over my hand. The living word awakened my soul, gave it light, hope, joy, set it free! There were barriers still, it is true, but barriers that could in time be swept away.

I left the well-house eager to learn. Everything had a name, and each name gave birth to a new thought. As we returned to the house every object which I touched seemed to quiver with life. That was because I saw everything with the strange, new sight that had come to me. On entering the door I remembered the doll I had broken. I felt my way to the hearth and picked up the pieces. I tried vainly to put them together. Then my eyes filled with tears; for I realized what I had done, and for the first time I felt repentance and sorrow.

I learned a great many new words that day. I do not remember what they all were; but I do know that *mother, father, sister, teacher* were among them—words that were to make the world blossom for me, "like Aaron's rod, with flowers." It would have been difficult to find a happier child than I was as I lay in my crib at the close of that eventful day and lived over the joys it had brought me, and for the first time longed for a new day to come.

In your journal, write the meanings of the following words:

- I stood on the porch, *dumb* **(2)**
- a deep *languor* **(2)**
- with *plummet* and *sounding-line* **(3)**
- no strong *sentiment* **(6)**
- like *Aaron's rod* **(9)**

QUESTIONS FOR WRITING AND DISCUSSION

1. Write for five minutes, recalling your earliest memories of reading, speaking, or writing. Focus on one specific incident. How old were you? Where were you? What were you reading or writing?

2. Helen Keller's books have been translated into more than fifty languages. Explain why you believe her story, as illustrated in this essay, has such universal appeal.

3. In paragraph 3, Keller uses an analogy to explain her feelings and her state of mind before language opened her life. Identify the extended comparison. What "difficult concept" does Keller explain through her analogy?

4. In paragraph 8, Keller says, "Everything had a name, and each name gave birth to a new thought." Explain what Keller means by using examples of the names of things from your own life.

5. Contrast Keller's actions and feelings before she discovers language to her actions and feeling afterward. In addition to learning words, how do her feelings and personality change?

6. A century ago, when Helen Keller was learning to read and speak, people who were blind and deaf were classified by the law as "idiots." Describe one

experience you have had with a disabled person. Based on that experience, explain how Americans' attitudes toward people with some disability have (or have not) improved.

7. On the Internet, use a search engine to gather articles on the education of deaf and/or blind children. What technologies are available to help teachers and students? One recent program on ABC's *20/20* featured a computer animation character named Baldi who helps children learn to read lips. Kids wear headphones over an acoustic nerve implant that converts sound into electrical signals that are relayed to the brain. Check out the article entitled "Look Who's Talking" from ABCNEWS.com: PrimeTime: Teaching Deaf Kids to Speak.

PROFESSIONAL WRITING

LIVES ON THE BOUNDARY

Mike Rose

Mike Rose was born to Italian immigrant parents in 1944, and his family moved to Los Angeles, where he attended Our Lady of Mercy, a private Catholic school. He continued his education at Loyola University, graduating in 1966, and went on to earn his Ph.D. from UCLA in 1981. Rose currently teaches at UCLA and is the author of numerous articles and books, including When a Writer Can't Write: Studies in Writer's Block and Other Composing Problems *(1985),* Lives on the Boundary *(1989), and* Possible Lives: The Promise of Public Education in America *(1995). In the following selection, taken from the second chapter of* Lives on the Boundary, *Rose recalls how he was originally misplaced in a high school vocational track and then was shifted to college prep courses. Rose focuses his memories on his fellow students in the voc. ed. track and on one English teacher, Jack MacFarland, who opened his mind to the world of books and ideas and who helped him get to college and live "beyond the limiting boundaries" of his South Los Angeles neighborhood.*

My parents used to say that their son would have the best education they   1
could afford. Maybe I would be a doctor. There was a public school in our
neighborhood and several Catholic schools to the west. They had heard
that quality schooling meant private, Catholic schooling, so they somehow

got the money together to send me to Our Lady of Mercy, fifteen or so miles southwest of Ninety-first and Vermont.

It took two buses to get to Our Lady of Mercy. The first started deep 2 in South Los Angeles and caught me at midpoint. The second drifted through neighborhoods with trees, parks, big lawns, and lots of flowers. The rides were long but were livened up by a group of South L.A. veterans whose parents also thought that Hope had set up shop in the west end of the county. There was Christy Biggars, who, at sixteen, was dealing and was, according to rumor, a pimp as well. There were Bill Cobb and Johnny Gonzales, grease-pencil artists extraordinaire, who left Nembutal-enhanced swirls of "Cobb" and "Johnny" on the corrugated walls of the bus. And then there was Tyrrell Wilson. Tyrrell was the coolest kid I knew. He ran the dozens like a metric half-back, laid down a rap that outrhymed and out-pointed Cobb, whose rap was good but not great—the curse of a moderately soulful kid trapped in white skin. But it was Cobb who would sneak a radio onto the bus, and thus underwrote his patter with Little Richard, Fats Domino, Chuck Berry, the Coasters, and Ernie K. Doe's mother-in-law, an awful woman who was "sent from down below." And so it was that Christy and Cobb and Johnny G. and Tyrrell and I and assorted others picked up along the way passed our days in the back of the bus, a funny mix brought together by geography and parental desire.

Entrance to school brings with it forms and releases and assessments. 3 Mercy relied on a series of tests, mostly the Stanford-Binet, for placement, and somehow the results of my tests got confused with those of another student named Rose. The other Rose apparently didn't do very well, for I was placed in the vocational track, a euphemism for the bottom level. Neither I nor my parents realized what this meant. We had no sense that Business Math, Typing, and English-Level D were dead ends. The current spate of reports on the schools criticizes parents for not involving themselves in the education of their children. But how would someone like Tommy Rose, with his two years of Italian schooling, know what to ask? And what sort of pressure could an exhausted waitress apply? The error went undetected, and I remained in the vocational track for two years. What a place.

Students will float to the mark you set. I and the others in the voca- 4 tional classes were bobbing in pretty shallow water. Vocational education has aimed at increasing the economic opportunities of students who do not do well in our schools. Some serious programs succeed in doing that, and through exceptional teachers—like Mr. Gross in *Horace's Compromise*—students learn to develop hypotheses and troubleshoot, reason through a problem, and communicate effectively—the true job skills. The vocational track, however, is most often a place for those who are just not making it, a dumping ground for the disaffected. There were a few teachers who worked hard at education; young Brother Slattery, for example, combined a stern voice with weekly quizzes to try to pass along to us a skeletal outline of world history. But mostly the teachers had no idea of how to engage the imaginations of us kids who were scuttling along at the bottom of the pond.

But I did learn things about people and eventually came into my own socially. I liked the guys in Voc. Ed. Growing up where I did, I understood and admired physical prowess, and there was an abundance of muscle here. There was Dave Snyder, a sprinter and a half-back of true quality. Dave's ability and his quick wit gave him a natural appeal, and he was welcome in any clique, though he always kept a little independent. It was a testament to his independence that he included me among his friends—I eventually went out for track, but I was no jock. Owing to the Latin alphabet and a dearth of Rs and Ss, Snyder sat behind Rose, and we started exchanging one-liners and became friends.

There was Ted Richard, a much-touted Little League pitcher. He was chunky and had a baby face and came to Our Lady of Mercy as a seasoned street fighter. Ted was quick to laugh and he had a loud, jolly laugh, but when he got angry he'd smile a little smile, the kind that simply raises the corner of the mouth a quarter of an inch. For those who knew, it was an eerie signal. Those who didn't found themselves in big trouble, for Ted was very quick. He loved to carry on what we would come to call philosophical discussions: What is courage? Does God exist? He also loved words, enjoyed picking up big ones like *salubrious* and *equivocal* and using them in our conversations—laughing at himself as the word hit a chuckhole rolling off his tongue. Ted didn't do all that well in school—baseball and parties and testing the courage he'd speculated about took up his time. His textbooks were *Argosy* and *Field and Stream*, whatever newspapers he'd find on the bus stop—from the *Daily Worker* to pornography—conversations with uncles or hobos or businessmen he'd meet in a coffee shop, *The Old Man and the Sea.* With hindsight, I can see that Ted was developing into one of those rough-hewn intellectuals whose sources are a mix of the learned and the apocryphal, whose discussions are both assured and sad.

And then there was Ken Harvey. Ken was good-looking in a puffy way and had a full and oily ducktail and was a car enthusiast . . . a hodad. One day in religion class, he said the sentence that turned out to be one of the share an evening, talk that talk, with Jack MacFarland, the man I most admired at the time. Knowledge was becoming a bonding agent. Within a year or two, the persona of the disaffected hipster would prove too cynical, too alienated to last. But for a time it was new and exciting: It provided a critical perspective on society, and it allowed me to act as though I were living beyond the limiting boundaries of South Vermont.

In your journal, write the meanings of the following words:

- a *euphemism* for the bottom level **(3)**
- picking up big ones like *salubrious* and *equivocal* **(6)**
- a mix of the learned and the *apocryphal* **(6)**
- centerpiece of his *pedagogy* **(10)**
- turning his *incipient* alcoholism to literary ends **(13)**
- beyond Jack MacFarland's *ministrations* **(14)**
- this embrace of the *avant-garde* **(17)**
- new wave *shibboleths* **(17)**
- a *Baedeker* to a vocabulary of ideas **(17)**

QUESTIONS FOR WRITING AND DISCUSSION

1. The title of Mike Rose's book is *Lives on the Boundary.* In this selection, what "boundaries" do the voc. ed. students face? What boundaries does Rose face? Which of these boundaries is Rose able to cross? (How are these boundaries similar to or different from the boundaries you faced growing up?)

2. Effective remembering essays build on detailed descriptions. Review the *observing* techniques from Chapter 3. Of the techniques discussed there (using sensory details and images, describing what is not present, noting changes, writing from a point of view, and focusing on a dominant idea), which does Rose use most effectively? To support your choice(s), find examples from Rose's essay.

3. Review the remembering techniques listed early in this chapter. Which does Rose use most effectively in his essay? Cite examples to support your choice(s). Which techniques might he add to his essay? Where, for example, might Rose use dialogue to recreate a school scene more vividly?

4. In his essay, Rose creates two voices, which represent him as a high school student and as a forty-five-year-old man looking back on his early education. Find examples that illustrate each of these voices. (Should Rose interrupt the narration about his high school years with his older reflections? Why or why not?)

5. Write your own remembering essay describing a particular teacher from high school or college who impressed you or influenced the direction of your life. Recall scenes from this time in your life that illustrate how this teacher changed your life.

6. Although Rose overcame his misplacement in the voc. ed. track, the consequences of standardized tests can be disastrous. What is your experience with state tests, high stakes tests, exit tests, and SAT tests? Have the results accurately indicated your abilities? Do these tests cause more harm than good? Read the essay by Eric Boese. Then check out a Web site, the Fordam Foundation at *http://www.edexcellence.net/topics/standards.html*. Browse through some of the articles. Then write your own essay that draws on your experience with educational testing to recommend changes in testing procedures to the administrators of your high school.

PROFESSIONAL WRITING

BEAUTY: WHEN THE OTHER DANCER IS THE SELF

Alice Walker

The author of the Pulitzer Prize–winning novel The Color Purple *(1983), Alice Walker has written works of fiction and poetry, including* Love and Trouble: Stories of Black Women *(1973),* Meridian *(1976), and* By the Light of My Father's Smile: A Novel *(1998). "Beauty: When the Other Dancer Is the Self" originally appeared in* Ms. *magazine and was revised and published in Walker's collection of essays,* In Search of Our Mother's Gardens *(1983).*

Walker, a former editor of Ms., *refers in this essay to Gloria Steinem and an interview published in* Ms. *entitled "Do You Know This Woman? She Knows You—A Profile of Alice Walker." As you read the essay reprinted here, consider Walker's purpose: Why is she telling us—total strangers—about a highly personal and traumatic event that shaped her life?*

It is a bright summer day in 1947. My father, a fat, funny man with beautiful eyes and a subversive wit, is trying to decide which of his eight children he will take with him to the county fair. My mother, of course, will not go. She is knocked out from getting us ready: I hold my neck stiff against the pressure of her knuckles as she hastily completes the braiding and then beribboning of my hair.   1

My father is the driver for the rich old white lady up the road. Her   2
name is Miss Mey. She owns all the land for miles around, as well as the house in which we live. All I remember about her is that she once offered to pay my mother thirty-five cents for cleaning her house, raking up piles of her magnolia leaves, and washing her family's clothes, and that my mother—she of no money, eight children, and a chronic earache—refused it. But I do not think of this in 1947. I am two-and-a-half years old. I want to go everywhere my daddy goes. I am excited at the prospect of riding in a car. Someone has told me fairs are fun. That there is room in the car for only three of us doesn't faze me at all. Whirling happily in my starchy frock, showing off my biscuit polished patent leather shoes and lavender socks, tossing my head in a way that makes my ribbons bounce, I stand, hands on hips, before my father. "Take me, Daddy," I say with assurance, "I'm the prettiest!"

Later, it does not surprise me to find myself in Miss Mey's shiny black   3
car, sharing the backseat with the other lucky ones. Does not surprise me that I thoroughly enjoy the fair. At home that night I tell all the unlucky ones about the merry-go-round, the man who eats live chickens, and the abundance of Teddy bears, until they say: that's enough, baby Alice. Shut up now, and go to sleep.

It is Easter Sunday, 1950. I am dressed in a green, flocked scalloped-   4
hem dress (handmade by my adoring sister Ruth) that has its own smooth satin petticoat and tiny hot-pink roses tucked into each scallop. My shoes, new T-strap patent leather, again highly biscuit polished. I am six years old and have learned one of the longest Easter speeches to be heard in church that day, totally unlike the speech I said when I was two: "Easter lilies/pure and white/blossom in/the morning light." When I rise to give my speech

I do so on a great wave of love and pride and expectation. People in the church stop rustling their new crinolines. They seem to hold their breath. I can tell they admire my dress, but it is my spirit, bordering on sassiness (womanishness), they secretly applaud.

"That girl's a little *mess*," they whisper to each other, pleased.   5

Naturally I say my speech without stammer or pause, unlike those who   6 stutter, stammer, or, worst of all, forget. This is before the word "beautiful" exists in people's vocabulary, but "Oh, isn't she the *cutest* thing!" frequently floats my way. "And got so much sense!" they gratefully add . . . for which thoughtful addition I thank them to this day.

It was great fun being cute. But then, one day, it ended.   7

I am eight years old and a tomboy. I have a cowboy hat, cowboy boots,   8 checkered shirt and pants, all red. My playmates are my brothers, two and four years older than I. Their colors are black and green, the only difference in the way we are dressed. On Saturday nights we all go to the picture show, even my mother: Westerns are her favorite kind of movie. Back home, "on the ranch," we pretend we are Tom Mix, Hopalong Cassidy, Lash LaRue (we've even named one of our dogs Lash LaRue); we chase each other for hours rustling cattle, being outlaws, delivering damsels from distress. Then my parents decide to buy my brothers guns. These are not "real" guns. They shoot "BBs," copper pellets my brothers say will kill birds. Because I am a girl, I do not get a gun. Instantly I am relegated to the position of Indian. Now there appears a great distance between us. They shoot and shoot at everything with their new guns. I try to keep up with my bow and arrows.

One day while I am standing on top of our makeshift "garage"—pieces   9 of tin nailed across some poles—holding my bow and arrow and looking out toward the fields, I feel an incredible blow in my right eye. I look down just in time to see my brother lower his gun.

Both brothers rush to my side. My eye stings, and I cover it with my   10 hand. "If you tell," they say, "we will get a whipping. You don't want that to happen, do you?" I do not. "Here is a piece of wire," says the older brother, picking it up from the roof; "say you stepped on one end of it and the other flew up and hit you." The pain is beginning to start. "Yes," I say. "Yes, I will say that is what happened." If I do not say this is what happened, I know my brothers will find ways to make me wish I had. But now I will say anything that gets me to my mother.

Confronted by our parents we stick to the lie agreed upon. They place   11 me on a bench on the porch and I close my left eye while they examine the right. There is a tree growing from underneath the porch, that climbs past the railing to the roof. It is the last thing my right eye sees. I watch as its trunk, its branches, and then its leaves are blotted out by the rising blood.

I am in shock. First there is intense fever, which my father tries to 12 break using lily leaves bound around my head. Then there are chills: my mother tries to get me to eat soup. Eventually, I do not know how, my parents learn what has happened. A week after the "accident" they take me to see a doctor. "Why did you wait so long to come?" he asks, looking into my eye and shaking his head. "Eyes are sympathetic," he says. "If one is blind, the other will likely become blind too."

This comment of the doctor's terrifies me. But it is really how I look that 13 bothers me most. Where the BB pellet struck there is a glob of whitish scar tissue, a hideous cataract, on my eye. Now when I stare at people—a favorite pastime, up to now—they will stare back. Not at the "cute" little girl, but at her scar. For six years I do not stare at anyone because I do not raise my head.

Years later, in the throes of a mid-life crisis, I ask my mother and sis- 14 ter whether I changed after the "accident." "No," they say, puzzled. "What do you mean?"

What do I mean? 15

I am eight, and for the first time, doing poorly in school, where I have 16 been something of a whiz since I was four. We have just moved to the place where the "accident" occurred. We do not know any of the people around us because this is a different county. The only time I see the friends I knew is when we go back to our old church. The new school is the former state penitentiary. It is a large stone building, cold and drafty, crammed to over-flowing with boisterous, ill-disciplined children. On the third floor there is a huge circular imprint of some partition that has been torn out.

"What used to be here?" I ask a sullen girl next to me on our way past 17 it to lunch.

"The electric chair," says she. 18

At night I have nightmares about the electric chair, and about all the 19 people reputedly "fried" in it. I am afraid of the school, where all the students seem to be budding criminals.

"What's the matter with your eye?" they ask, critically. 20

When I don't answer (I cannot decide whether it was an "accident" or 21 not), they shove me, insist on a fight.

My brother, the one who created the story about the wire, comes to my 22 rescue. But then brags so much about "protecting" me, I become sick.

After months of torture at the school, my parents decide to send me 23 back to our old community to my old school. I live with my grandparents and the teacher they board. But there is no room for Phoebe, my cat. By the time my grandparents decide there is room, and I ask for my cat, she cannot be found. Miss Yarborough, the boarding teacher, takes me under her wing, and begins to teach me to play the piano. But soon she marries an African—a "prince," she says—and is whisked away to his continent.

At my old school there is at least one teacher who loves me. She is the teacher who "knew me before I was born" and bought my first baby clothes. It is she who makes my life bearable. It is her presence that finally helps me turn on the one child at the school who continually calls me "one-eyed bitch." One day I simply grab him by his coat and beat him until I am satisfied. It is my teacher who tells me my mother is ill. *24*

My mother is lying in bed in the middle of the day, something I have never seen. She is in too much pain to speak. She has an abscess in her ear. I stand looking down on her, knowing that if she dies, I cannot live. She is being treated with warm oils and hot bricks held against her cheek. Finally a doctor comes. But I must go back to my grandparents' house. The weeks pass, but I am hardly aware of it. All I know is that my mother might die, my father is not so jolly, my brothers still have their guns, and I am the one sent away from home. *25*

"You did not change," they say. *26*

Did I imagine the anguish of never looking up? *27*

I am twelve. When relatives come to visit I hide in my room. My cousin Brenda, just my age, whose father works in the post office and whose mother is a nurse, comes to find me. "Hello," she says. And then she asks, looking at my recent school picture which I did not want taken, and on which the "glob" as I think of it is clearly visible, "You still can't see out of that eye?" *28*

"No," I say, and flop back on the bed over my book. *29*

That night, as I do almost every night, I abuse my eye. I rant and rave at it, in front of the mirror. I plead with it to clear up before morning. I tell it I hate and despise it. I do not pray for sight. I pray for beauty. *30*

"You did not change," they say. *31*

I am fourteen and baby-sitting for my brother Bill who lives in Boston. He is my favorite brother and there is a strong bond between us. Understanding my feelings of shame and ugliness, he and his wife take me to a local hospital where the "glob" is removed by a doctor named O. Henry. There is still a small bluish crater where the scar tissue was, but the ugly white stuff is gone. Almost immediately I become a different person from the girl who does not raise her head. Or so I think. Now that I've raised my head, I win the boyfriend of my dreams. Now that I've raised my head, I *32* have plenty of friends. Now that I've raised my head, classwork comes from my lips as faultlessly as Easter speeches did, and I leave high school as valedictorian, most popular student and *queen,* hardly believing my luck. Ironically, the girl who was voted most beautiful in our class (and was) was later shot twice through the chest by a male companion, using a "real" gun, while she was pregnant. But that's another story in itself. Or, is it?

"You did not change," they say.   *33*

It is now thirty years since the "accident." A beautiful journalist comes *34* to visit and to interview me. She is going to write a cover story for her magazine that focuses on my last book. "Decide how you want to look on the cover," she says. "Glamorous, or whatever."

Never mind "glamorous," it is the "whatever" that I hear. Suddenly all *35* I can think of is whether I will get enough sleep the night before the photography session: if I don't, my eye will be tired and wander, as blind eyes will.

At night in bed with my lover I think up reasons why I should not ap- *36* pear on the cover of a magazine. "My meanest critics will say I've sold out," I say. "My family will now realize I write scandalous books."

"But what's the real reason you don't want to do this?" he asks.   *37*

"Because in all probability," I say in a rush, "my eye won't be straight." *38*

"It will be straight enough," he says. Then, "Besides, I thought you'd *39* made your peace with that."

And I suddenly remember that I have.   *40*

I remember: *41*

I am talking to my brother Jimmy, asking if he remembers anything unusual about the day I was shot. He does not know I consider that day the last time my father, with his sweet home remedy of cool lily leaves, "chose" me, and that I suffered and raged inside because of this. "Well," he says, "all I remember is standing by the side of the highway with Daddy, trying to flag down a car. A white man stopped, but when Daddy said he needed somebody to take his little girl to the doctor, he drove off."

I remember: *42*

I am in the desert for the first time. I fall totally in love with it. I am so overwhelmed by its beauty, I confront for the first time, consciously, the meaning of the doctor's words years ago: "Eyes are sympathetic. If one is blind, the other will likely become blind too." I realize I have dashed about the world madly, looking at this, looking at that, storing up images against the fading of the light. But I might have missed seeing the desert! The shock of that possibility—and gratitude for over twenty-five years of sight—

sends me literally to my knees. Poem after poem comes—which is perhaps how poets pray.

On Sight

I am so thankful I have seen
The Desert
And the creatures in the desert
And the desert Itself.
The desert has its own moon
Which I have seen
With my own eye
There is no flag on it.
Trees of the desert have arms
All of which are always up
That is because the moon is up
The sun is up
Also the sky
The stars
Clouds
None with flags.
If there were flags, I doubt
the trees would point.
Would you?

But mostly, I remember this: 43

I am twenty-seven, and my baby daughter is almost three. Since her birth I have worried over her discovery that her mother's eyes are different from other people's. Will she be embarrassed? I wonder. What will she say? Every day she watches a television program called "Big Blue Marble." It begins with a picture of the earth as it appears from the moon. It is bluish, a little battered-looking, but full of light, with whitish clouds swirling around it. Every time I see it I weep with love, as if it is a picture of Grandma's house. One day when I am putting Rebecca down for her nap, she suddenly focuses on my eye. Something inside me cringes, gets ready to try to protect myself. All children are cruel about physical differences, I know from experience, and that they don't always mean to be is another matter. I assume Rebecca will be the same.

But no-o-o-o. She studies my face intently as we stand, her inside and 44 me outside her crib. She even holds my face maternally between her dimpled little hands. Then, looking every bit as serious and lawyerlike as her father, she says, as if it may just possibly have slipped my attention: "Mommy, there's a *world* in your eye." (As in, "Don't be alarmed, or do anything crazy.") And then, gently, but with great interest: "Mommy, where did you *get* that world in your eye?"

For the most part, the pain left then. (So what if my brothers grew up 45 to buy even more powerful pellet guns for their sons and to carry real guns themselves. So what if a young "Morehouse man" once nearly fell off the steps of Trevor Arnett Library because he thought my eyes were blue.) Crying and laughing I ran to the bathroom, while Rebecca mumbled and sang herself off to sleep. Yes indeed, I realized, looking into the mirror. There *was* a world in my eye. And I saw that it was possible to love it; that in fact, for all it had taught me, of shame and anger and inner vision, I *did* love it. Even to see it drifting out of orbit in boredom, or rolling up out of fatigue, not to mention floating back at attention in excitement (bearing witness, a friend has called it), deeply suitable to my personality, and even characteristic of me.

That night I dream I am dancing to Stevie Wonder's song "Always" 46 (the name of the song is really "As," but I hear it as "Always"). As I dance, whirling and joyous, happier than I've ever been in my life, another bright-faced dancer joins me. We dance and kiss each other and hold each other through the night. The other dancer has obviously come through all right, as I have done. She is beautiful, whole and free. And she is also me.

In your journal, write the meanings of the following words:

- a *subversive* wit **(1)**
- rustling their new *crinolines* **(4)**
- Eyes are *sympathetic* **(12)**
- a hideous *cataract* **(13)**
- *boisterous*, ill-disciplined children **(16)**
- bearing *witness* **(45)**

QUESTIONS FOR WRITING AND DISCUSSION

1. Why does Alice Walker share this story with us? What memories from your own life did her story trigger? Write them down.

2. What does Walker discover or learn about herself? As a reader, what did you learn about your own experiences by reading this essay?

3. Reread the essay, looking for examples of the following techniques for writing about memories: (1) using detailed observations; (2) creating specific scenes; (3) noting changes, contrasts, or conflicts; and (4) seeing relationships between past and present. In your opinion, which of these techniques does she use most effectively?

4. What is Walker's main idea in this autobiographical account? State it in your own words. Where in the essay does she state it most explicitly?

5. How many scenes or episodes does Walker recount? List them according to her age at the time. Explain how each episode relates to her main idea.

6. Walker also uses images of sight and blindness to organize her essay. The story begins with a description of a father who has "beautiful eyes" and ends with her dancing in her dream to a song by Stevie Wonder. Catalog the images of sight and blindness from each scene or episode. Explain how, taken together, these images reinforce Walker's main idea.

7. Walker writes her essay in the present tense, and she uses italics not only to emphasize ideas but to indicate the difference between past thoughts and events and the present. List the places where she uses italics. Explain how the italicized passages reinforce her main point.

8. What is the *occasion* in Walker's life that motivates her to write this narrative? Is it told in the story or does it happen in her life after the story concludes? Explain. Where does Walker include details about the social, historical, or cultural *context* for her story? Locate at least three paragraphs that provide details about context. Explain how these details are important for you as a reader in understanding her narrative.

9. Walker writes a multigenre essay, weaving poetry into her narrative essay. What other multigenre elements—such as photographs, drawings, excerpts from journals, or material from scrapbooks—might also be appropriate in your remembering essay? Might you want to do a "multimedia essay" in

which you include not only photographs, images, and childhood artifacts, but also weblog excerpts, streaming video, audio, and hyperlinks?

Remembering: The Writing Process

ASSIGNMENT FOR REMEMBERING

Write an essay about an important person, place, and/or event in your life. Your purpose is to recall and then use specific examples that *recreate* this memory and *show* why it is so important to you.

Think also about your possible audience and genre. Usually the audience for memories, autobiographical essays, and personal essays is fairly general. Since many people are interested in events from our lives, we may not want to restrict our audience too much. You may want to write just for your family or friends, however, or put your memories in the form of a letter you wish to send to a particular person. Also, you may want to think of a particular magazine that frequently publishes personal essays. Nearly every speciality magazine (sports, nature, outdoors, genealogy, cooking, clothing, style) occasionally publishes personal essays with memories that focus on the subject of the publication. Browsing through magazines may give you an idea for an audience and genre that would work for the event you wish to narrate.

> "*Memory is more indelible than ink.*"
>
> —ANITA LOOS,
> AUTHOR OF KISS
> HOLLYWOOD GOODBYE

CHOOSING A SUBJECT

If one of the journal entry exercises suggested a possible subject, try the collecting and shaping strategies below. If none of those exercises led to an interesting subject, consider the following ideas:

- Interview (in person or over the phone) your parents, a brother or sister, or a close friend. What events or experiences do they remember that were important to you?

- Get out a map of your town, city, state, or country and spend a few minutes doing an inventory of places you have been. Make a list of trips you have taken, with dates and years. Which of those places is the most memorable for you?
- Dig out a school yearbook and look through the pictures and the inscriptions that your classmates wrote. Whom do you remember most clearly? What events do you recall most vividly?
- Go to the library and look through news magazines or newspapers from five to ten years ago. What were the most important events of those years? What do you remember about them? Where were you and what were you doing when these events occurred? Which events had the largest impact on your life?
- Choose an important moment in your life, but write from the *point of view* of another person—a friend, family member, or stranger who was present. Let this person narrate the events that happened to you.

Note: Avoid choosing overly emotional topics such as the recent death of a close friend or family member. If you are too close to your subject, responding to your reader's revision suggestions may be difficult. Ask yourself if you can emotionally distance yourself from that subject. If you received a C for that essay, would you feel devastated?

COLLECTING

Once you have chosen a subject for your essay, try the following collecting strategies:

Brainstorming Brainstorming is merely jotting down anything and everything that comes to mind that is remotely connected to your subject: words, phrases, images, or complete thoughts. You can brainstorm by yourself or in groups, with everyone contributing ideas and one person recording them.

Looping Looping is a method of controlled freewriting that generates ideas and provides focus and direction. Begin by freewriting about your subject for eight to ten minutes. Then pause, reread what you have written, and *underline* the most interesting or important idea in what you've written so far. Then, using that sentence or idea as your starting point, write for eight to ten minutes more. Repeat this cycle, or "loop," one more time. Each loop should add ideas and details from some new angle or viewpoint, but overall you will be focusing on the most important ideas that you discover.

Clustering Clustering is merely a visual scheme for brainstorming and free-associating about your topic. It can be especially effective for remembering because it helps you sketch relationships among your topics and subtopics. As you can see from the sample sketch, the sketch that you make of your ideas should help you see relationships between ideas or get a rough idea about an order or shape you may wish to use.

SHAPING

First, reconsider your purpose; perhaps it has become clearer or more definite since you recorded it in your journal entry. In your journal, jot down tentative answers for the following questions. If you don't have an answer, go on to the next question.

- **Subject:** What is your general subject?
- **Specific topic:** What aspect of your subject are you interested in?
- **Purpose:** Why is this topic interesting or important to you or your readers?
- **Main idea:** What might your main idea be?
- **Audience:** For whom are you writing this? What is your reader like, and why might he or she be interested in this topic?
- **Genre:** What genre might help you communicate your purpose and main idea most effectively to your audience? (See suggestions below.)

As you think about ways to organize and shape your essay, reread your assignment and think about your purpose and possible audience. Consider several possible *genres* or combinations of genres that might work. Then, for particular parts or sections of your essay, review the strategies described below. *Chronological order* will shape a major part of your narrative, but think also about using *comparison/contrast* for highlighting past and present or for contrasting two places, two events, or two key people. In addition, *similes, metaphors,* and *analogies* will make your writing more vivid, and paying attention to your *voice* and *tone* can help your achieve your purpose.

Most important, be sure to *narrow* and *focus* your subject. If you're going to write a three-page essay, don't try to cover everything in your life. Focus on one person, one episode, one turning point, one discovery, or one day, and do that in depth and detail.

GENRE   As you collect ideas, draft sample passages, and discuss your assignment with your peers, think about genre alternatives that might be appropriate for your purpose and audience. You may want to write in a traditional narrative format suitable for informal essays, autobiographical passages, or memoirs. You may want to consider multigenre essays in which you include photographs, graphics, drawings, letters, or material from scrapbooks. You may even want to write a multimedia essay in which you include not only photographs and artifacts but also weblog passages, video, audio, and hyperlinks.

CHRONOLOGICAL ORDER   If you are writing about remembered events, you will probably use some form of chronological order. Try making a *chronological list of the major scenes or events*. Then go through the list, deciding what you will emphasize by telling about each item in detail and what you will pass over quickly.

Normally, you will be using a straightforward chronological order, but you may wish to use a flashback, starting in the middle or near the end and then returning to tell the beginning. In his paragraph about a personal relationship, for example, student writer Gregory Hoffman begins the story at the most dramatic point, returns to tell how the relationship began, and then concludes the story.

> Her words hung in the air like iron ghosts. "I'm pregnant," she said as they walked through the park, the snow crackling beneath their feet. Carol was looking down at the ground when she told him, somewhat ashamed, embarrassed, and defiant all at once. Their relationship had only started in September, but both had felt the uneasiness surrounding them for the past months. She could remember the beginning so well and in such favor, now that the future seemed so uncertain. The all-night conversations by the bay window, the rehearsals at the university theater—where he would make her laugh during her only soliloquy, and most of all the Christmas they had spent together in Vermont. No one else had existed for her during those months. Yet now, she felt duped by her affections—as if she had become an absurd representation of a tragic television character. As they approached the lake, he put his arm around her, "Just do what you think is best, babe. I mean, I think you know how I feel." At that moment, she knew it was over. It was no longer "their" decision. His hand touched her cheek in a benedictorial fashion. The rest would only be form now. Exchanging records and clothes with an aside of brief conversation. She would see him again, in the market or at a movie, and they would remember. But like his affection in September, her memory of him would fade until he was too distant to see.

COMPARISON/CONTRAST Although you may be comparing or contrasting people, places, or events from the past, you will probably also be comparing or contrasting the past to the present. You may do that at the beginning, noting how something in the present reminds you of a past person, place, or event. You may do it at the end, as Andrea Lee does in *Russian Journal*. You may do it both at the beginning and at the end, as Richard Rodriguez does in "The Boy's Desire." You may even contrast past and present throughout, as Alice Walker does in "Beauty: When the Other Dancer Is the Self." Comparing or contrasting the past with the present will often clarify your dominant idea.

IMAGE Sometimes a single mental picture or recurring image will shape a paragraph or two in an essay. Consider how novelist George Orwell, in his essay "Shooting an Elephant," uses the image of a puppet or dummy to describe his feeling at a moment when he realized that, against his better judgment, he was going to have to shoot a marauding elephant in order to satisfy a crowd of two thousand Burmese who had gathered to watch him. The italicized words emphasize the recurring image.

> Suddenly I realized that I should have to shoot the elephant after all. The people expected it of me and I had got to do it; I could feel their *two thousand wills pressing me forward,* irresistibly. And it was at this moment, as I stood there with the rifle in my hands, that I first grasped the hollowness, the futility of the white man's dominion in the East. Here was I, the white man with his gun, standing in front of the unarmed native crowd—*seemingly the leading actor* of the piece; but in reality I was only an absurd *puppet pushed to and fro* by the will of those yellow faces behind. I perceived in this moment that when the white man turns tyrant it is his own freedom that he destroys. He becomes a sort of *hollow, posing dummy,* the *conventionalized figure* of a sahib. For it is the condition of his rule that he shall spend his life in trying to impress the "natives" and so in every crisis he has got to do what the "natives" expect of him. He *wears a mask,* and his face grows to fit it. I had got to shoot the elephant. I had committed myself to doing it when I sent for the rifle. *A sahib has got to act like a sahib;* he has got to appear resolute, to know his own mind and do definite things.

VOICE AND TONE   When you have a personal conversation with someone, the way you look and sound—your body type, your voice, your facial expressions and gestures—communicates a sense of personality and attitude, which in turn affects how the other person reacts to what you say. In written language, although you don't have those gestures, expressions, or the actual sound of your voice, you can still create the sense that you are talking directly to your listener.

The term *voice* refers to a writer's personality as revealed through language. Writers may use emotional, colloquial, or conversational language to communicate a sense of personality. Or they may use abstract, impersonal language either to conceal their personalities or to create an air of scientific objectivity.

Tone is a writer's attitude toward the subject. The attitude may be positive or negative. It may be serious, humorous, honest, or ironic; it may be skeptical or accepting; it may be happy, frustrated, or angry. Often voice and tone overlap, and together they help us hear a writer talking to us. In the following passage, we hear student writer Kurt Weekly talking to us directly; we hear a clear, honest voice telling the story. His tone is not defensive or guilty: He openly admits he has a "problem."

> Oh no, not another trash day. Every time I see all those trash containers, plastic garbage bags and junk lined up on the sidewalks, it drives me crazy. It all started when I was sixteen. I had just received my driver's license and

the most beautiful Ford pickup. It was Wednesday as I remember and trash day. I don't know what happened. All of a sudden I was racing down the street swerving to the right, smashing into a large green Hefty trash bag filled with grass clippings. The bag exploded, and grass clippings and trash flew everywhere. It was beautiful and I was hooked. There was no stopping me.

At first I would smash one or two cans on the way to school. Then I just couldn't get enough. I would start going out the night before trash day. I would go down the full length of the street and wipe out every garbage container in sight. I was the terror of the neighborhood. This was not a bad habit to be taken lightly. It was an obsession. I was in trouble. There was no way I could kick this on my own. I needed help.

I received that help. One night after an evening of nonstop can smashing, the Arapahoe County Sheriff Department caught up with me. Not just one or a few but the whole department. They were willing to set me on the right path, and if that didn't work, they were going to send me to jail. It was a long, tough road to rehabilitation, but I did it. Not alone. I had the support of my family and the community.

PERSONA   Related to voice and tone is the *persona*—the "mask" that a writer can put on. Sometimes in telling a story about yourself, you may want to speak in your own "natural" voice. At other times, however, you may change or exaggerate certain characteristics in order to project a character different from your "real" self. Writers, for example, may project themselves as braver and more intelligent than they really are. Or to create a humorous effect, they may create personas who are more foolish or clumsy than they really are. This persona can shape a whole passage. In the following excerpt, James Thurber, a master of autobiographical humor, uses a persona—along with chronological narrative—to shape his account of a frustrating botany class.

> I passed all the other courses that I took at my university, but I could never pass botany. This was because all botany students had to spend several hours a week in a laboratory looking through a microscope at plant cells, and I could never see through a microscope. I never once saw a cell through a microscope. This used to enrage my instructor. He would wander around the laboratory pleased with the progress all the students were making in drawing the involved and, so I am told, interesting structure of flower cells, until he came to me. I would just be standing there. "I can't see anything," I would say. He would begin patiently enough, explaining how anybody can see through a microscope, but he would always end up in a fury claiming that I could too see through a microscope but just pretended that I couldn't. "It takes away from the beauty of flowers anyway," I used to tell

him. "We are not concerned with beauty in this course," he would say. "We are concerned solely with the mechanics of flowers." "Well," I'd say, "I can't see anything." "Try it just once again," he'd say, and I would put my eye to the microscope and see nothing at all, except now and again a nebulous milky substance—a phenomenon of maladjustment. You were supposed to see a vivid, restless clockwork of sharply defined plant cells. "I see what looks like a lot of milk," I would tell him. This, he claimed, was the result of my not having adjusted the microscope properly, so he would readjust it for me, or rather, for himself. And I would look again and see milk. I finally took a deferred pass, as they called it, and waited a year and tried again. (You had to pass one of the biological sciences or you couldn't graduate.) The professor had come back from vacation brown as a berry, bright-eyed, and eager to explain cell-structure again to his classes. "Well," he said to me, cheerily, when we met in the first laboratory hour of the semester, "we're going to see cells this time, aren't we?" "Yes, sir," I said. Students to the right of me and to the left of me and in front of me were seeing cells; what's more, they were quietly drawing pictures of them in their notebooks. Of course, I didn't see anything.

"We'll try it," the professor said to me, grimly, "with every adjustment of the microscope known to man. As God is my witness, I'll arrange this glass so that you see cells through it or I'll give up teaching. In twenty-two years of botany, I—" He cut off abruptly for he was beginning to quiver all over, like Lionel Barrymore, and he genuinely wished to hold onto his temper; his scenes with me had taken a great deal out of him.

So we tried it with every adjustment of the microscope known to man. With only one of them did I see anything but blackness or the familiar lacteal opacity, and that time I saw, to my pleasure and amazement, a variegated constellation of flecks, specks, and dots. These I hastily drew. The instructor, noting my activity, came back from an adjoining desk, a smile on his lips and his eyebrows high in hope. He looked at my cell drawing. "What's that?" he demanded, with a hint of a squeal in his voice. "That's what I saw," I said. "You didn't, you didn't, you didn't!" he screamed, losing control of his temper instantly, and he bent over and squinted into the microscope. His head snapped up. "That's your eye!" he shouted. "You've fixed the lens so that it reflects! You've drawn your eye!"

DIALOGUE   Dialogue, which helps to *recreate* people and events rather than just tell about them, can become a dominant form and thereby shape your writing. Recreating an actual conversation, you could possibly write a whole scene using nothing but dialogue. More often, however, writers use dialogue occasionally for dramatic effect. In the account of his battle with the microscope, for instance, Thurber uses dialogue in the last two paragraphs to dramatize his conclusion:

"We'll try it," the professor said to me, grimly, "with every adjustment of the microscope known to man. As God is my witness, I'll arrange this glass so that you see cells through it or I'll give up teaching. In twenty-two years of teaching botany, I—"... "What's that?" he demanded.... "That's what I saw," I said. "You didn't, you didn't, you didn't!" he screamed.... "You've fixed the lens so that it reflects! You've drawn your eye!"

TITLE, INTRODUCTION, AND CONCLUSION In your journal, sketch out several possible titles you might use. You may want a title that is merely an accurate label, such as *Russian Journal* or "The Boy's Desire," but you may prefer something less direct that gets your reader's attention. For example, for his essay about his hat that appears at the end of this chapter, student writer Todd Petry uses the title "The Wind Catcher." As a reader, what do you think about Alice Walker's title, "Beauty: When the Other Dancer Is the Self"?

Introductions or beginning paragraphs take several shapes. Some writers plunge the reader immediately into the action—as Gregory Hoffman does—and then later fill in the scene and context. Others are more like Kurt Weekly, announcing the subject—trash cans—and then taking the reader from the present to the past and the beginning of the story: "It all started when I was sixteen...." At some point, however, readers do need to know the context—the *who, what, when,* and *where* of your account.

Conclusions are also of several types. In some, writers will return to the present and discuss what they have learned, as Andrea Lee does in *Russian Journal.* Some, like Alice Walker, end with an image or even a dream. Some writers conclude with dramatic moments, or an emotional scene, as student writer Juli Bovard does in the essay "The Red Chevy" that appears at the end of this chapter. But many writers will try to tie the conclusion back to the beginning, as Richard Rodriguez does at the end of "The Boy's Desire": "The closet door closes ... the fog rises." In your journal, experiment with several possibilities until you find one that works for your subject.

> *I start at the beginning, go on to the end, then stop.*
> —GABRIEL GARCÍA MÁRQUEZ,
> AUTHOR OF <u>ONE HUNDRED YEARS OF SOLITUDE</u>

> *I always know the ending; that's where I start.*
> —TONI MORRISON,
> NOBEL PRIZE-WINNING NOVELIST

DRAFTING

When you have experimented with the above shaping strategies, reconsider your purpose, audience, and main idea. Have they changed? In your journal, reexamine the notes you made before trying the shaping activities. If necessary, revise your statements about purpose, audience, or main idea based on what you have actually written.

Working from your journal material and from your collecting and shaping activities, draft your essay. It is important *not* to splice different parts together or just recopy and connect segments, for they may not fit or flow together. Instead, reread what you have written, and then start with a clean sheet of paper. If you're working on a computer file, you can start with your list of events or one of your best shaping strategies and expand that file as you draft. Concentrate on what you want to say and write as quickly as possible.

To avoid interruptions, choose a quiet place to work. Follow your own writing rituals. Try to write nonstop. If you cannot think of the right word, put a line or a dash, but keep on writing. When necessary, go back and reread what you have previously written.

REVISING

Revising begins, of course, when you get your first idea and start collecting and shaping. It continues as you redraft certain sections of your essay and rework your organization. In many classes, you will give and receive advice from the other writers in your class. Use the guidelines below to give constructive advice about a remembering essay draft.

Guidelines for Revision

- **Reexamine your purpose and audience.** Are you doing what you intended?
- **Reconsider the genre you selected.** Is it working for your purpose and audience? Can you add multigenre elements to make your narrative more effective?
- **Revise to make the main idea of your account clearer.** You don't need a "moral" to the story or a bald statement saying, "This is why this person was important." Your reader, however, should know clearly why you wanted to write about the memory that you chose.
- **Revise to clarify the important relationships in your story.** Consider relationships between past and present, between you and the people in your story, between one place and another place, between one event and another event.
- **Close and detailed observation is crucial.** *Show,* don't just tell. Can you use any of the collecting and shaping strategies for observing discussed in Chapter 3?
- **Revise to show crucial changes, contrasts, or conflicts more clearly.** Keller's and Walker's essays, for instance, illustrate how *conflict* and *change* are central to an effective remembering essay. See if their strategies will work in your essay.
- **Have you used a straight chronological order?** If it works, keep it. If not, would another order be better? Should you begin in the middle and do a flashback? Do you want to move back and forth from present to past or stay in the past until the end?

PEER RESPONSE

The instructions below will help you give and receive constructive advice about the rough draft of your remembering essay. You may use these guidelines for an in-class workshop, a take-home review, or a computer e-mail response.

Writer: Before you exchange drafts with another reader, write out the following information about your own rough draft.

1. State the main idea that you hope your essay conveys.
2. Describe the best *one* or *two* key scenes that your narrative creates.
3. Explain one or two problems that you are having with this draft that you want your reader to focus on.

Reader: Without making any comments, read the *entire* draft from start to finish. As you *reread* the draft, answer the following questions.

1. Locate one or two of the *key scenes* in the narrative. Are they clearly set at an identified time and place? Does the writer use vivid description of the place or the people? Does the writer use dialogue? Does the writer include his or her reflections? Which of these areas need the most attention during the writer's revision? Explain.
2. Write out a *time line* for the key events in the narrative. What happened first, second, third, and so forth? Are there places in the narrative where the time line could be clearer? Explain.
3. When you finished reading the draft, *what characters or incidents were you still curious about?* Where did you want more information? What characters or incidents did you want to know more about?
4. What *overall idea* does the narrative convey to you? How does your notion of the main idea compare to the writer's answer to question 1? Explain how the writer might revise the essay to make the main idea clearer.
5. Answer the *writer's questions* in question 3.

After you have some feedback from other readers, you need to distance yourself and objectively reread what you have written. Review the advice you received from your peer readers. Remember, you will get both good and bad advice, so *you* must decide what you think is important or not important. If you are uncertain about advice you received from one of your peers, ask for a third or fourth opinion. In addition, most writing centers will have tutors available who can help you sort through the advice you have received on your draft and figure out a revision plan. Especially for this remembering essay, make sure your memories are recreated on paper. Don't be satisfied with suggesting incidents that merely trigger your own memories: You must *show* people and events vividly for your reader.

If you are using a chronological order, cue your reader by occasionally using transitional words to signal changes: *then, when, first, next, last, before, after, while, as, sooner, later, initially, finally, yesterday, today.*

- **Be clear about point of view.** Are you looking back on the past from a viewpoint in the present? Are you using the point of view of yourself as a child or at some earlier point in your life? Are you using the point of view of another person or object in your story?
- **What are the key images in your account?** Should you add or delete an image to show the experience more vividly?
- **What voice are you using?** Does it support your purpose? If you are using a persona, is it appropriate for your audience and purpose?
- **Revise sentences to improve clarity, conciseness, emphasis, and variety.**
- **Check your dialogue for proper punctuation and indentation.** See the essay by Alice Walker in this chapter for a model.
- **When you are relatively satisfied with your draft, edit for correct spelling, appropriate word choice, punctuation, and grammar.**

POSTSCRIPT ON THE WRITING PROCESS

After you finish writing, revising, and editing your essay, you will want to breathe a sigh of relief and turn it in. But before you do, think about the problems that you solved as you wrote this essay. *Remember:* Your major goal for this course is to learn to write and revise more effectively. To do that, you need to discover and adapt your writing processes so you can anticipate and solve the problems you face as a writer. Take a few minutes to answer the following questions. Be sure to hand in this postscript with your essay.

1. Review your writing process. Which collecting, shaping, and revising strategies helped you remember and describe incidents most quickly and clearly? What problems were you unable to solve?

2. Reread your essay. With a small asterisk [*], identify in the margin of your essay sentences where you used sensory details, dialogue, or images to *show* or recreate the experience for your reader.

3. If you received feedback from your peers, identify one piece of advice that you followed and one bit of advice that you ignored. Explain your decisions.

4. Rereading your essay, what do you like best about it? What parts of your essay need work? What would you change if you had another day to work on this assignment?

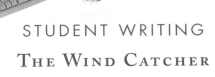

STUDENT WRITING

The Wind Catcher

Todd Petry

*Todd Petry decided to write about his cowboy hat, observing it in the present
and thinking about some of the memories that it brought back. His notes, his first
short draft paragraphs, and his revised version demonstrate how observing and
remembering work together naturally: the details stimulate memories, and memories lead to more specific details.*

NOTES AND DETAILS

DETAILS	MORE SPECIFIC DETAILS
Gray	Dirty, dust coated, rain stained cowdung color
Resistol	The name is stained and blurred
Size 7 3/8	
Diamond shape	Used to be diamond shape, now battered, looks abandoned
4" brim	Front tipped down, curled up in back
1" sweat band	blackish
5 yrs. old	still remember the day I bought it
4x beaver	
What it is not:	it is unlike a hat fresh out of the box
What it compares to:	point of crown like the north star like a pancake with wilted edges battered like General Custer's hat
What I remember:	the day I bought the hat a day at Pray Mesa

First Draft

THE WIND CATCHER

The other day while I was relaxing in my favorite chair and listening to Ian Tyson, I happened to notice my work cowboy hat hanging on the wall. Now I look at that old hat no less than a dozen times a day without too much thought, but on that particular day, my eyes remained fixed on it and my mind went to remembering.

I still remember I had $100 cash in my pocket the day I went hat shopping. The local tack, feed, and western wear CO-OP was my first and only stop. Finding a hat to meet my general specifications was no big deal. I wanted a gray Resistol, size 7 3/8, with a 4-inch brim and diamond-shaped crown. From there on, though, my wants became very particular. I took 30 minutes to find the one that had the right fit, and five times that long to come to terms with the hat shaper. Boy, but I was one proud young fellow the next day when I went to school sporting my new piece of head gear. I've had that wind catcher five years through rough times, but in a way, it really looks better now, without any shape, dirty, and covered with dust and cowdung.

Revised Version

THE WIND CATCHER

The other day, while I was relaxing in my favorite chair and listening to Ian Tyson, I happened to notice my work cowboy hat hanging on the wall. Now, I look at that old hat no less than a dozen times a day without too much thought, but on that particular day, my eyes remained fixed on it and my mind went to remembering. _1_

I was fifteen years old and had $100 cash in my pocket the day I _2_ went hat shopping five years ago. The local tack, feed, and western wear CO-OP was my first and only stop. Finding a hat to meet my general specifications was no big deal. I wanted a gray 4X Resistol, size 7 3/8, with a four-inch brim and diamond-shaped crown. I wanted no flashy feathers or gaudy hatbands, which in my mind were only for pilgrims. From there on, though, my wants became very particular. I took thirty minutes to find the one that had the right fit, and five times that long to come to terms with the hat shaper. Boy, but I was one proud young fellow the next day when I went to school sporting my new piece of head gear.

About that time, Ian Tyson startled me out of my state of reminiscence by singing "Rose in the Rockies," with that voice of his sounding like ten cow elk cooing to their young in the springtime. As I sat there listening to the music and looking at that old hat, I had to chuckle to myself because that wind catcher had sure seen better days. I mean it looked rode hard and put up wet. The gray, which was once as sharp and crisp as a mountain lake, was now faded and dull where the sun had beat down. Where the crown and brim met, the paleness was suddenly transformed into a gritty black which ran the entire circumference of the hat. This black was unlike any paint or color commercially available, being made up of head sweat, dirt, alfalfa dust, and powdered cow manure. Water blemishes from too much rain and snow mottled the brim, adding to the colors' turbidity. Inside the crown and wherever the slope was less than ninety degrees, dust had collected to hide the natural color even more.

After a while, my attention lost interest in the various colors and began to work its way over the hat's shape, which I was once so critical of. General Custer's hat itself could not have looked worse. All signs of uniformity and definite shape had disappeared. The diamond-shaped crown, which was once round and smooth, now bowed out on the sides and had edges as blunt as an orange crate. The point, which once looked like the North Star indicating the direction, now was twisted off balance from excessive right hand use. Remembering last spring, how I threw that hat in the face of an irate mother cow during calving, I had to chuckle again. Throwing that hat kept my horse and me out of trouble but made the "off-balance look" rather permanent. As I looked at the brim, I was reminded of a three-day-old pancake with all its edges wilted. The back of that brim curled upward like a snake ready to strike, and the front had become so narrow and dipped, it looked like something a dentist would use on your teeth.

For probably half an hour, I sat looking at the wear and tear on that ancient hat. Awhile back, I remember, I decided to try to make my old hat socially presentable by having it cleaned and blocked, removing those curls and dips and other signs of use. However, when a hat shop refused to even attempt the task, I figured I'd just leave well enough alone. As I scanned my eyes over the hat, I noticed several other alterations from its original form, such as the absent hat band, which was torn off in the brush on Pray Mesa, and the black thread that drew together the edges of a hole in the crown. However, try as I might, I could not for the life of me see where any character had been lost in the brush, or any flair had been covered with cowdung.

QUESTIONS FOR WRITING AND DISCUSSION

1. Close observation often leads to specific memories. In the opening paragraph of his revised version, Todd Petry says that "on that particular day, my eyes remained fixed on it and my mind went to remembering." He then recalls the time when he was fifteen years old and bought his hat. Identify two other places where observation leads Petry to remember specific scenes from the past.

2. Petry chose "The Wind Catcher" as the title for his essay. Reread the essay and then brainstorm a list of five other titles that might be appropriate for this short essay. Which title do you like best?

3. Where does Petry most clearly express the main idea of his essay? Write out the main idea in your own words.

STUDENT WRITING

THE RED CHEVY

Juli Bovard

In the following essay, Juli Bovard recalls several of the most traumatic days of her life. She remembers not just the day she was raped by an unknown assailant, but the days she had to spend in the police station, the day she confronted her attacker in the courtroom, and the days she spent regaining control of her life. In the end, Bovard helps us understand how she overcame being a rape victim and reclaimed her life.

From the moment the man in the Chevy stopped to offer me a ride on that blistering September afternoon, I knew I was in trouble. Before I could say, 1

"No, but thanks anyway," the man in the passenger side of the car jumped at me, twisted my arm and held a shiny piece of steel to my side. I was pushed into the car and driven 30 miles over the county line. During the ride, I did everything every article or specialist on abduction had advised against: I cried, I babbled, and I lost control. In the end it was all futile. Two hours later—after they dumped me off near my home—I was another statistic. I had been raped, and was now a victim of the brutal, demeaning, sad violent crime of sexual assault. I was officially one of the 1,871 rapes that occur each day in the United States ("Sexual Assault Statistics").

2   Rape not only has physical repercussions, but has an enormous psychological and emotional impact as well. During my "event" as I like to call it, I remembered an initial feeling of shock and numbness, and soon found myself babbling incoherently. I begged my attackers to let me go. I tried to talk my way out of the car. I even tried to beg or bargain my way out. However, the driver was very much in control of the situation, and my weak efforts failed. Eventually my babbling gave way to cold reason, and I became convinced that not only would I be raped, but that I would also die. My life did not pass before me—as is said to happen to dying people. In fact, I did not think of the past at all, but only the future and all the things I had not yet done. I had never ridden a horse other than the ponies at the fair. I had not learned to play golf—though I had intended to—or learned to snow ski down a mountain with my son. There were too many people I had not told how I really felt, too many people to whom I wanted to say good-bye. I seriously doubted I would ever be given another chance.

3   I did not die. In fact, other than a few bruises and scratches from the field grass (where I was forced to lie during my rape), and several cuts on my neck and cheek—left by the brass knuckle style knife, I was remarkably, physically unhurt. The greatest trauma was to my mind. The psychological and emotional wounds in the ensuing months were far worse than the actual sexual assault.

4   Within a week of my report, the man who raped me was arrested and held without bail (he had previously been convicted of attempted rape), his accomplice was not accused since he agreed to turn state's evidence—which means he made a deal to cover himself and agreed to testify against my assailant. What followed these events, I remember, was a long investigation that involved many tedious hours in the police station, and numbing revisits

to the scene of the crime. Through it all I was alone, and I halfheartedly tried to comfort myself for enduring the stress so well. By late October, the month of the preliminary hearing, I had gone back to work, and was back in control of my life—or so I thought. The actual hearing proved me wrong.

Though I do not remember much about the actual courtroom or its proceedings, I will always remember the warmth of the day and the overwhelming odor of my perpetrator's cologne (to this day I become nauseous if I smell the cologne Obsession). Seeing my assailant again had an effect on me that I was not prepared for. I felt the same fear that I had experienced the day of my rape, and for the second time in my life I felt terror so deep it paralyzed me. The pressure from the entire incident finally overwhelmed me, and when I returned home that afternoon I climbed into bed and did not leave it for three days. I spent seventy-two hours staring at the ceiling and vomiting. When I finally emerged from my emotional coma, I could not eat or sleep. Everything seemed unreal and unclear to me. It was weeks before I could focus on everyday tasks, even something as simple as showering.

By the middle of November, I had lost close to fifteen pounds. I had constant diarrhea, my menstrual cycle had stopped, and I was constantly bombarded by anxiety attacks. I could no longer get up each day and go to work and act like nothing had happened. Leaving the house left me with cold sweats, and sleeping through the night became impossible. I became paranoid and despondent. I knew I would have to seek professional help.

Fortunately, through counseling I learned that my reactions were very common, and are shared by most rape victims. Through research, I found that all the feelings I was having were very normal. My fear that the rapist would return was natural, and my inability to face unfamiliar situations or people was a classic symptom. I also learned that the guilt that plagued me, which made me think that somehow I had provoked the rape or "wore" the wrong clothes to entice the rapist, was simply untrue. I was feeling a great amount of shame and embarrassment—a stigma I learned society often places on rape victims. My anger, which was the most natural response, was also the most helpful. When you are angry, you tend to want to fight back. My way of fighting back was to get on with living. Still I asked, "Why me?" I had followed all the rules set by society. I did not walk the streets at night, hang out in bars, or talk to strangers. I was an actively employed member of society. So why me? I found it wasn't just me or something I did. It could have been any woman walking the streets that day, and it went far beyond what I wore or how I walked, something noted author Susan Brownmiller eloquently affirms in her statement that, "any female may become a victim of rape. Factors such as youth, advanced age, physical homeliness and virginal lifestyle do not provide a fool-proof deterrent to render a women impervious to sexual assault" (Brownmiller 348).

Through my experience and in talking with other victims I have learned that rape has no typical "face." Certainly the man who raped me looked normal, (He was not obscene, ugly, or disfigured). He could have been my neighbor, my grocer, or even my boyfriend. Rape victims and its perpetrators are colorless and ageless. There is no stereotypical rapist *or* victim. We can be doctors, lawyers, mothers, or fathers. We are tall, short, fat, and skinny. And, as in most victims' cases, simply in the wrong place at the wrong time.   8

After the question of "why me?" I asked, "WHY, at all?" Why *does* a man rape a woman? Initially I thought it was obvious—for sex. But I was wrong. The motivations of rape include anger, aggression, dominance, hostility, and power, but generally are not usually associated with just the actual act of sex. Quite simply it is violence. Men who rape do so because they are violent and psychotic. There is no other reason, and no valid excuse.   9

In the end, before I was to testify, the man who attacked me changed his plea to guilty. I walked out of the district attorney's office and never asked how many years the rapist would serve in prison. It did not matter. He would be behind bars, but more importantly, I would be free to begin living again. Now, instead of dreading the month of September, I celebrate it. I celebrate the month, in which, instead of just existing, I started living. I was a victim of rape, but through years of counseling and support *I am not a victim any longer.*   10

Works Cited

Brownmiller, Susan. *Against Our Will.* New York: Simon and Schuster, 1975.

"Sexual Assault Statistics." Sexual Assault Site. *Abuse Counseling and Treatment.* 22 Oct. 2000 *http://actabuse.com/SAstatistics.html.*

In your journal, write down the meanings of the following words:

- babbling *incoherently* **(2)**
- the greatest *trauma* **(3)**
- a *stigma* **(7)**
- render a woman *impervious* **(7)**
- they are violent and *psychotic* **(9)**

QUESTIONS FOR WRITING AND DISCUSSION

1. Psychological research has shown that people remember trauma more vividly and with more detail than other events. Has that been true in your experience? Recall two experiences—one happy, one traumatic—and consider whether your experiences support or do not support the research.

2. Remembering essays should have a purpose—that is, they should focus on having a specific effect on their audience. Why is Juli Bovard writing about this experience? What effect does she want to have on her readers? Is she just giving information or does she want to convince us about something? Explain.

3. Review the techniques for writing a remembering essay listed at the beginning of this chapter? Which of these techniques does Bovard use? Where does she use them? Which are, in your opinion, most effective? Why?

4. In addition to remembering specific scenes, Bovard uses some research and explains the causes and effects of the event. Should she have research and cite sources in a narrative essay? Do her explanations and her research help achieve her purpose or do they detract from the story? Support your response by citing specific sentences from her essay.

5. Bovard chose the title "The Red Chevy" for her essay. Brainstorm five other titles she might use for her essay. Compare your ideas with those of your classmates. Did you come up with titles that might be more effective for the purpose of her essay? Explain.

Often called the greatest modern Mexican painter, Diego Rivera is most famous for his mural paintings showing the lives of working people. The journal exercise on page 178 provides ideas for writing and research about Diego Rivera and his paintings.

Diego Rivera
The Flower Carrier (formerly *The Flower Vendor*) (1934)
© Estate of Diego Rivera, Courtesy Banco de Mexico

chapter

5 Reading

As an assignment in class, you are reading and critiquing an article by Deborah Tannen on how men and women respond differently during class conversations. As you read the article, you like the thought-provoking examples, but soon you find yourself becoming frustrated. First, you have trouble locating the main focus of the article, and then you are disturbed by some unsupported assertions that she makes about typical behavior of men and women. Do men really like to argue and dominate class discussions? Do women always benefit from smaller, more intimate group discussions? You reread the article and make notes in the margin. After discussing your reactions with other readers, you write the draft of your summary and response. You argue that readers should expect clearer organization and fewer unsupported assertions about the gender-based differences between men and women.

After discussing stereotyped and sexist images in advertising, you leaf through a copy of a popular magazine. A two-page advertisement for Fila jeans catches your attention. The first page shows a man in jeans and a jeans jacket in the foreground with football players pictured in the background. The caption at the bottom of the page says, "Some like their blues hard." On the facing page is a woman curled up in a chair and wearing her blue jeans. Her background photograph shows a woman clad in a bikini. The caption says, "Some like their blues soft." For your essay, you describe the features of the ad carefully and then offer your own analysis of the sexist features of the images and the language. The language and the imagery of the Fila jeans ad, you argue, stereotype and alienate the sexes by conveying the idea that men and women are not parallel in nature but are fundamentally separate and different.

> **If we think of it, all that a University, or final highest School can do for us, is still but what the first School began doing—teach us to read.**
> —THOMAS CARLYLE, AUTHOR OF <u>ON HEROES AND HERO WORSHIP</u>

> **Reading is not a passive process by which we soak up words and information from the page, but an active process by which we predict, sample, and confirm or correct our hypotheses about the written text.**
> —CONSTANCE WEAVER, AUTHOR OF <u>READING PROCESS AND PRACTICE</u>

A T FIRST GLANCE, A CHAPTER ON READING IN A TEXTBOOK ON WRITING MAY CATCH YOU BY SURPRISE. THIS CHAPTER, HOWEVER, IS NOT ABOUT LEARNING YOUR ABC'S OR ABOUT READING *THE CAT IN THE HAT*. IT IS ABOUT LEARN-ing to read texts actively and critically. It is about learning how to summarize and respond to what you read. It is about using reading—along with observing and remembering—as a source for your writing.

At the beginning of this chapter, we need to define two key terms: *texts* and *reading*. Normally, when you think about a text, you may think of a textbook. A text, however, can be any graphic matter—a textbook, an essay, a poem, a newspaper editorial, a photograph, an image, or an advertisement. Some people expand the definition of texts to include any thing or phenomenon in the world. In this widest sense, the layout of a restaurant, the behavior of children on a playground, or clouds in the sky could be "texts" that can be read.

Similarly, the term *reading* has both narrow and broad senses. In a narrow sense, reading is simply understanding words on a page. But reading has a variety of wider meanings as well. Reading can mean analyzing, as when an architect "reads" blueprints and knows how to construct a roof. Reading can also mean interpreting, as when a sailor "reads" the sky and knows that the day will bring winds and rough weather. Reading can also mean examining images, media, or cultural artifacts and perceiving textual messages of, for example, racism, gender bias, or cultural exploitation. All of these "readings" require close, critical reading of the text and an ability to engage, analyze, probe, respond to, and interpret the text.

In this chapter, you will practice active, critical reading and responding to academic texts and to images. Implied in active, critical reading are both writing about the texts and discussing the texts with other readers. Writing requires reading with your pen in your hand to annotate the texts you read with comments, questions, and observations. You can also write double-entry logs that will help you become an active, critical reader. You may consider reading a solitary activity, but texts appear in social contexts and should be read in social contexts. Active reading, therefore, also involves sharing ideas in small groups, engaging in a class conversation, posting e-mail responses, or writing for an online discussion forum.

This chapter provides guidelines for critical reading, tips for summarizing ideas accurately, and techniques for responding to academic essays, editorials, images, and other texts you will encounter in college, on the job, and in your community.

Techniques for Writing About Reading

- **Using active and responsive reading, writing, and discussing strategies.** Preview the author's background and the writing context. Prewrite about your own experiences with the subject. Read initially for information and enjoyment. As you reread, make annotations, write questions, or do a double-entry log. Discuss the text with other readers.
- **Summarizing the main ideas or features of the text.** A summary should *accurately* and *objectively* represent the key ideas. Summaries cite the author and title, accurately represent the main ideas, quote directly key phrases or sentences, and describe main features of the text.
- **Responding to or critiquing the ideas in the text.** A response should focus on your ideas and reactions. Types of responses include *analysis* of the rhetorical situation, argument, organization, or evidence in the text; *agreement* or *disagreement* with the author/text; or *interpretation* of the text.
- **Supporting the response with evidence.** As supporting evidence for the response, writers should analyze key features of the text, cite evidence from other relevant texts, and/or use examples from personal experience.
- **Combining summary and response into a coherent essay.** Usually, the summary appears first, followed by the reader's response, but be sure to *integrate* the two parts. Focus early on a main idea for your response. Use transitions between the summary and the response.

As you work on these techniques, don't simply read the text, listen to a class discussion, and write out your critique. Instead, annotate the text by circling key ideas and writing your questions and responses in the margin. Continue reading and discussing your ideas after you have written out a draft. Use the interactive powers of reading, writing, and discussing to help you throughout your writing process.

> **"**Reading involves a fair measure of push and shove. You make your mark on a book and it makes its mark on you. Reading is not simply a matter of hanging back and waiting for a piece, or its author, to tell you what the writing has to say.**"**
>
> —DAVID BARTHOLOMAE AND ANTHONY PETROSKY, AUTHORS OF WAYS OF READING

CRITICAL READING STRATEGIES

Critical reading does not mean that you always criticize something or find fault. *Critical reading simply means questioning what you read.* You may end up liking or praising certain features of a text, but you begin by asking questions, by resisting the text, and by demanding that the text be clear, logical, reliable, thoughtful, and honest.

You begin your critical reading by asking questions about every element in the rhetorical situation. Who is the *author*, and what is his or her background or potential bias? What was the *occasion*, and who was the intended *audience?* Is the writer's *purpose* achieved for that occasion and audience? Did the writer understand and fairly represent other writers' positions on this topic? Did the writer understand the *genre* and use it to achieve the purpose? How did the *cultural context* affect the author and the text? How did the context affect you as a reader?

You continue your critical reading by asking about the writer's claim or argument, the representation of the background information, the organization, the logical use of evidence, and the effectiveness of the style, tone, and word choice. You may find these elements effective or ineffective, but you start your critical reading by reading and then rereading, by probing key passages, by looking for gaps or ideas not included, by discussing the text with other readers, by assessing your position as a reader, and by continually making notes and asking questions.

DOUBLE-ENTRY LOG   One of the most effective strategies to promote critical reading is a double-entry log. Draw a line down the middle of a page in your notebook. On the left-hand side, keep a running summary of the main ideas and features that you notice in the text. On the right-hand side, write your questions and reactions.

Author and Title:_____

Summary	Response
Main ideas, key features	Your reactions, comments, and questions

CRITICAL REREADING GUIDE   If your double-entry log did not yield some good ideas, try the ideas and suggestions in this rereading guide. First, read the essay in its entirety. Then, let the following set of questions guide your rereading. The questions on the left-hand side will help you summarize and analyze the text; the questions on the right-hand side will start your critical reading and help focus your response.

DESCRIPTION	RESPONSE
I. Purpose • Describe the author's overall *purpose* (to inform, explain, explore, evaluate, argue, negotiate, or other purpose). • How does the author/text want to affect or change the reader?	• Is the overall purpose clear or muddled? Was the actual purpose different from the stated purpose? • How did the text actually affect you?
II. Audience/Reader • Who is the *intended* audience? • What *assumptions* does the author make about the reader's knowledge or beliefs? • From what *point of view* or *context* is the author writing?	• Are you part of the intended audience? • Does the author misjudge the reader's knowledge or beliefs? • Examine your own personal or cultural bias or point of view. How does that hinder you from being a critical reader of this text?
III. Occasion, Genre, Context • What was the occasion for this text? • What genre is this text? • What is the cultural or historical context for this text?	• What ideas or conversation was taking place on this topic? • Does the author's chosen genre help achieve the purpose for the audience? • What passages show the cultural forces at work on the author and the text?
IV. Thesis and Main Ideas • What key *question* or *problem* does the author/text address? • What is the author's *thesis*? • What *main ideas* support the thesis?	• Where is the thesis stated? • Are the main ideas related to the thesis? • Where do you agree or disagree?

DESCRIPTION	**RESPONSE**
• What are the key passages or key moments in the text?	• Does the essay have contradictions or errors in logic? • What ideas or arguments does the essay omit or ignore? • What experience or prior knowledge do you have about the topic? • What are the implications or consequences of the essay's ideas?

V. Organization and Evidence

• Where does the author *preview* the essay's organization? • How does the author *signal* new sections of the essay? • What kinds of *evidence* does the author use (personal experience, descriptions, statistics, interviews, other authorities, analytical reasoning, or other)?	• At what point could you accurately predict the organization of the essay? • At what points were you confused about the organization? • What evidence was most or least effective? • Where did the author rely on assertions rather than on evidence? • Which of your own personal experiences did you recall as you read the essay?

VI. Language and Style

• What is the author's *tone* (casual, humorous, ironic, angry, preachy, academic, or other)? • Are *sentences* and *vocabulary* easy, average, or difficult? • What key *words* or *images* recur throughout the text?	• Did the tone support or distract from the author's purpose or meaning? • Did the sentences and vocabulary support or distract from the purpose or meaning? • Did recurring words or images relate to or support the purpose or meaning?

Remember that not all these questions will be relevant to any given essay or text, but one or two of these questions may suggest a direction or give a *focus* to your overall response. When one of these questions suggests a focus for your response to the essay, *go back to the text, to other texts, and to your experience* to gather *evidence* and *examples* to support your response.

GUIDELINES FOR CLASS DISCUSSION

Class discussions are an important part of the reading, writing, and discussing process. Often, however, class discussions are not productive because not everyone knows the purpose of the discussion or how to discuss openly and fairly. Following is a suggested list of goals for class discussion. Read them carefully. *Make notes about any suggestions, revisions, or additions for your class.* Your class will then review these goals and agree to adopt, modify, or revise them for your own class discussions for the remainder of the semester.

Discussion Goals

1. To understand and *accurately represent* the views of the author(s) of an essay. The first discussion goal should be to summarize the author's views fairly.
2. To understand how the views and arguments of individual authors *relate* to each other. Comparing and contrasting different authors' views help clarify each author's argument.
3. To encourage all members of the class to articulate their *understanding* of each essay and their *response* to the ideas in each essay. Class discussions should promote multiple responses rather than focus on a single "right" interpretation or response.
4. To hear class members' responses in an *open forum*. All points of view must be recognized. *Discussions in class should focus on ideas and arguments, not on individual class members.* Class members may attack ideas but not people.
5. To relate class discussions to the *assigned reading/writing task*. What effective writing strategies are illustrated in the essay the class is discussing? How can class members use any of these strategies in writing their own essays?

Summarizing and Responding to an Essay

Following is an essay by Barbara Ehrenreich, "Teach Diversity—with a Smile." First, write for five minutes on the suggested Prereading Journal Entry that precedes the essay. The purpose of the journal entry is to allow you to collect your thoughts about the subject *before* you read Ehrenreich's essay. You will be a much more responsive reader if you reflect on your experiences and articulate your opinions *before* you are influenced by the author and her text. If possible, discuss your experiences and opinions with your classmates after you write your entry but before you read the essay. Next, read the introductory note about Barbara Ehrenreich to understand her background and the context for the essay. Finally, practice active reading techniques as you read. Read first for information and enjoyment. Then, reread with a pen in your hand. Either write your comments and questions directly in the text or do a double-entry log, summarizing the main ideas on one side of a piece of paper and writing your questions and reactions on the other.

PREREADING JOURNAL ENTRY

Describe the ethnic groups of people who live in your neighborhood or who attended your previous school. List all the groups you can recall. Then choose one of the following terms and briefly explain what it means: *diversity, multiculturalism,* or *political correctness.* Finally, describe one personal experience that taught you something about diversity or political correctness. What was the experience and how did you react?

PROFESSIONAL WRITING

TEACH DIVERSITY—WITH A SMILE

Barbara Ehrenreich

Barbara Ehrenreich was born in Butte, Montana, in 1941 and received a B.A. degree from Reed College and a Ph.D. from Rockefeller University. She has been a health policy adviser and a professor of health sciences, but since 1974, she has spent most of her time writing books and articles about socialist and feminist issues. She has received a Ford Foundation award and a Guggenheim fellowship for her writings, which include The Worst Years of Our Lives: Irreverent Notes from a Decade of Greed *(1990),* The Snarling Citizen: Essays *(1995), and* Nickel and Dimed: On (Not) Getting by in America *(2001). Her articles and essays have appeared in* Esquire, Mother Jones, Ms., New Republic, The New York Times Magazine, *and* Time. *The following essay on cultural diversity appeared in* Time *magazine.*

Something had to replace the threat of communism, and at last a workable   *1*
substitute is at hand. "Multiculturalism," as the new menace is known, has

been denounced in the media recently as the new McCarthyism, the new fundamentalism, even the new totalitarianism—take your choice. According to its critics, who include a flock of tenured conservative scholars, multiculturalism aims to toss out what it sees as the Eurocentric bias in education and replace Plato with Ntozake Shange and traditional math with the Yoruba number system. And that's just the beginning. The Jacobins of the multiculturalist movement, who are described derisively as P.C., or politically correct, are said to have launched a campus reign of terror against those who slip and innocently say "freshman" instead of "freshperson," "Indian" instead of "Native American" or, may the Goddess forgive them, "disabled" instead of "differently abled."

So you can see what is at stake here: freedom of speech, freedom of thought, Western civilization and a great many professorial egos. But before we get carried away by the mounting backlash against multiculturalism, we ought to reflect for a moment on the system that the P.C. people aim to replace. I know all about it; in fact it's just about all I *do* know, since I—along with so many educated white people of my generation—was a victim of monoculturalism. 2

American history, as it was taught to us, began with Columbus's "discovery" of an apparently unnamed, unpeopled America, and moved on to the Pilgrims serving pumpkin pie to a handful of grateful red-skinned folks. College expanded our horizons with courses called Humanities or sometimes Civ, which introduced us to a line of thought that started with Homer, worked its way through Rabelais and reached a poignant climax in the pensées of Matthew Arnold. Graduate students wrote dissertations on what long-dead men had thought of Chaucer's verse or Shakespeare's dramas; foreign languages meant French or German. If there had been high technology in ancient China, kingdoms in black Africa or women anywhere, at any time, doing anything worth noticing, we did not know it, nor did anyone think to tell us. 3

Our families and neighborhoods reinforced the dogma of monoculturalism. In our heads, most of us '50s teenagers carried around a social map that was about as useful as the chart that guided Columbus to the "Indies." There were "Negroes," "whites" and "Orientals," the latter meaning Chinese and "Japs." Of religions, only three were known—Protestant, Catholic and Jewish—and not much was known about the last two types. The only remaining human categories were husbands and wives, and that was all the diversity the monocultural world could handle. Gays, lesbians, Buddhists, Muslims, Malaysians, Mormons, etc. were simply off the map. 4

So I applaud—with one hand, anyway—the multiculturalist goal of preparing us all for a wider world. The other hand is tapping its fingers 5 impatiently, because the critics are right about one thing: when advocates of multiculturalism adopt the haughty stance of political correctness, they quickly descend to silliness or worse. It's obnoxious, for example, to rely on university administrations to enforce P.C. standards of verbal inoffensiveness. Racist, sexist and homophobic thoughts cannot, alas, be abolished by fiat but only by the time-honored methods of persuasion, education and exposure to the other guy's—or, excuse me, woman's—point of view.

And it's silly to mistake verbal purification for genuine social reform. 6 Even after all women are "Ms." and all people are "he or she," women will still earn only 65¢ for every dollar earned by men. Minorities by any other name, such as "people of color," will still bear a hugely disproportionate burden of poverty and discrimination. Disabilities are not just "different abilities" when there are not enough ramps for wheelchairs, signers for the deaf or special classes for the "specially" endowed. With all due respect for the new politesse, actions still speak louder than fashionable phrases.

But the worst thing about the P.C. people is that they are such poor ad- 7 vocates for the multicultural cause. No one was ever won over to a broader, more inclusive view of life by being bullied or relentlessly "corrected." Tell a 19-year-old white male that he can't say "girl" when he means "teen-age woman," and he will most likely snicker. This may be the reason why, despite the conservative alarms, P.C.-ness remains a relatively tiny trend. Most campuses have more serious and ancient problems: faculties still top-heavy with white males of the monocultural persuasion; fraternities that harass minorities and women; date rape; alcohol abuse; and tuition that excludes all but the upper fringe of the middle class.

So both sides would be well advised to lighten up. The conservatives 8 ought to realize that criticisms of the great books approach to learning do not amount to totalitarianism. And the advocates of multiculturalism need to regain the sense of humor that enabled their predecessors in the struggle to coin the term P.C. years ago—not in arrogance but in self-mockery.

Beyond that, both sides should realize that the beneficiaries of multi- 9 culturalism are not only the "oppressed peoples" on the standard P.C. list (minorities, gays, etc.). The "unenlightened"—the victims of monoculturalism—are oppressed too, or at least deprived. Our educations, whether at Yale or at State U, were narrow and parochial and left us ill-equipped to navigate a society that truly is multicultural and is becoming more so every day. The culture that we studied was, in fact, *one* culture and, from a world perspective, all too limited and ingrown. Diversity is challenging, but those of us who have seen the alternative know it is also richer, livelier and ultimately more fun.

SUMMARIZING

" *Inferences about the writer's intentions appear to be an essential building block—one that readers actively use to construct a meaningful text.* **"**

—LINDA FLOWER,
AUTHOR OF
"THE CONSTRUCTION
OF PURPOSE"

The purpose of a summary is to give a reader a condensed and objective account of the main ideas and features of a text. Usually, a summary has between one and three paragraphs or one hundred to three hundred words, depending on the length and complexity of the original essay and the intended audience and purpose. Typically, a summary will do the following:

- **Cite the author and title of the text.** In some cases, the place of publication or the context for the essay may also be included.
- **Indicate the main ideas of the text.** Accurately representing the main ideas (while omitting the less important details) is the major goal of a summary.
- **Use direct quotation of key words, phrases, or sentences.** *Quote* the text directly for a few key ideas; *paraphrase* the other important ideas (that is, express the ideas in your own words).
- **Include author tags.** ("According to Ehrenreich" or "as Ehrenreich explains") to remind the reader that you are summarizing the author and the text, not giving your own ideas. *Note:* Instead of repeating "Ehrenreich says," choose verbs that more accurately represent the purpose or tone of the original passage: "Ehrenreich argues," "Ehrenreich explains," "Ehrenreich warns," "Ehrenreich asks," "Ehrenreich advises."
- **Avoid summarizing specific examples or data** unless they help illustrate the thesis or main idea of the text.
- **Report the main ideas as objectively as possible.** Represent the author and text as accurately and faithfully as possible. Do not include your reactions; save them for your response.

SUMMARY OF "TEACH DIVERSITY— WITH A SMILE"

Following is a summary of Ehrenreich's essay. Do *not* read this summary, however, until you have tried to write your own. After you have made notes and written a draft for your own summary, you will more clearly understand the key features of a summary. *Note:* There are many ways to write a good summary. If your summary conveys the main ideas and has the features described previously, it may be just as good as the following example. (Key features of a summary are annotated in the margin.)

Title and author

Main idea

Paraphrase

Context for essay

Author tag

Direct quotations

Main idea

Paraphrase

Author tag

Main idea

Paraphrase

In "Teach Diversity—with a Smile," journalist Barbara Ehrenreich explains the current conflict between people who would like to replace our Eurocentric bias in education with a multicultural approach and those critics and conservative scholars who are leading the backlash against multiculturalism and "political correctness." Writing for [readers of *Time* magazine] Ehrenreich uses her own experience growing up in the 1950s to explain that her narrow education left her a "victim of monoculturalism," ill-equipped to cope with America's growing cultural diversity. Ehrenreich applauds multiculturalism's goal of preparing people for a culturally diverse world, but she is impatient at the "haughty stance" of the P.C. people because they mistake "verbal purification for genuine social reform" and they arrogantly bully people and "correct" their language. Since actions speak louder than words, Ehrenreich argues, the multiculturalists should focus more on genuine social reform—paying equal salaries to men and women, creating access for people with disabilities, and reducing date rape and alcohol abuse. The solution to the problem, according to Ehrenreich, is for both sides to "lighten up." The conservatives should recognize that criticizing the great books of Western civilization is not totalitarian, and the multiculturalists should be less arrogant and regain their sense of humor.

RESPONDING

A response requires your reaction and interpretation. Your own perspective—your experiences, beliefs, and attitudes—will guide your particular response. Your response, as the Viuti cartoon illustrates, may be totally different from another reader's response, but that does not necessarily make yours better or worse. Good responses say what you think, but then they *show why* you think so. They show the relationships between your opinions and the text, between the text and your experience, and between this text and other texts.

Depending on its purpose and intended audience, a response to a text can take several directions. Responses may focus on one or more of the following strategies. Consider your purpose and audience or check your assignment to see which type(s) you should emphasize.

> *"Reading the world always precedes reading the word, and reading the word implies continually reading the world."*
>
> —PAULO FREIRE,
> AUTHOR OF LITERACY:
> READING THE WORD
> AND THE WORLD

VIUTI
Buenos Aires
ARGENTINA

Cartoonists & Writers Syndicate

VIUTI

Types of Responses

- **Analyzing the effectiveness of the text.** In this case, the response analyzes key features such as the clarity of the main idea, the rhetorical situation, the organization of the argument, the logical reasoning of an argument, the quality of the supporting evidence, and/or the effectiveness of the author's style, tone, and voice.
- **Agreeing and/or disagreeing with the ideas in the text.** Often responders react to the ideas or the argument of the essay. In this case, the responders show why they agree and/or disagree with what the author/text says.
- **Interpreting and reflecting on the text.** The responder explains key passages or examines the underlying assumptions or the implications of the ideas. Often, the responder reflects on how his or her own experiences, attitudes, and observations relate to the text.

Analyzing, agreeing/disagreeing, and interpreting are all slightly different directions that a response may take. But regardless of the direction, responses must be supported by evidence, examples, facts, and details. A responder cannot simply offer an opinion or agree or disagree. Good responses draw on several kinds of supporting evidence.

Kinds of Evidence

- **Personal experience.** Responders may use *examples* from their personal experiences to show why they interpreted the text as they did, why they agreed or disagreed, or why they reacted to the ideas as they did.
- **Evidence from the text.** Responders should cite *specific phrases* or sentences from the text to support their explanation of a section, their analysis of the effectiveness of a passage, or their agreement or disagreement with a key point.
- **Evidence from other texts.** If appropriate, responders may bring in ideas and information from other relevant essays, articles, books, or graphic material.

Not all responses use all three kinds of supporting evidence, but all responses *must* have sufficient examples to support the responder's ideas, reactions, and opinions. Responders should not merely state their opinions. They must give evidence to *show* how and why they read the text as they did.

One final—and crucial—point about responses: A response should make a coherent, overall main point. It should not be just a laundry list of reactions, likes, and dislikes. Sometimes the main point is that the text is not convincing because it lacks evidence. Sometimes the overall point is that the text makes an original statement even though it is difficult to read. Perhaps the basic point is that the author/text stimulates the reader to reflect on his or her experience. Every response should focus on a coherent main idea.

RESPONSE TO "TEACH DIVERSITY—WITH A SMILE"

Following is one possible response to Ehrenreich's essay. Before you read this response, however, write out your own reactions. You need to decide what you think before other responses influence your reading. There are, of course, many different but legitimate responses to any given essay. As you read this response, note the marginal annotations indicating the different types of responses and the different kinds of evidence this writer uses.

What I like best about Barbara Ehrenreich's article is her effective use of personal experience to clarify the issues on both sides of the multicultural-ism debate. However, her conclusion, that we should "lighten up" and accept diversity because it's "more fun," weakens her argument by ignoring the social inequalities at the heart of the debate. The issue in this debate, I believe, is not just enjoying diversity, which is easy to do, but changing cultural conditions, which is much more difficult.

Analyzing effectiveness of text

Responder's main point

Ehrenreich effectively uses her own experiences—and her common sense—to let us see both the virtues and the excesses of multiculturalism. When she explains that her monocultural education gave her a social map that was "about as useful as the chart that guided Columbus to the 'Indies,'" she helps us understand how vital multicultural studies are in a society that is more like a glass mosaic than a melting pot. Interestingly, even her vocabulary reveals—perhaps unconsciously—her Western bias: *Jacobins, pensées, fiat,* and *politesse* are all words that reveal her Eurocentric education. When Ehrenreich shifts to discussing the P.C. movement, her common-sense approach to the silliness of excessive social correctness ("the other guy's—or, excuse me, woman's—point of view") makes us as readers more willing to accept her compromise position.

Evidence from text

Evidence from text

My own experience with multiculturalism certainly parallels Ehrenreich's impatience with the "haughty stance" of the P.C. people. Of course, we should avoid racist and sexist terms and use our increased sensitivity to language to reduce discrimination. But my own backlash began several years ago when a friend said I shouldn't use the word *girl.* I said, "You mean, not ever? Not even for a ten-year-old female child?" She replied that the word had been so abused by people referring to a "woman" as a "girl" that the word *girl* now carried too many sexist connotations. Although I understood my friend's point, it seems that *girl* should still be a perfectly good word for a female child under the age of twelve. Which reminds me of a book I saw recently, *The Official Politically Correct Dictionary.* It is loaded with examples of political correctness out of control: Don't say *bald,* say *hair disadvantaged.* Don't use the word *pet,* say *nonhuman companion.* Don't call someone *old,* say that they are *chronologically gifted.*

Reflecting on the text

Personal experience

Evidence from other texts

Ehrenreich does recommend keeping a sense of humor about the P.C. movement, but the conclusion to her essay weakens her argument. Instead of focusing on her earlier point that "it's silly to mistake verbal purification for genuine social reform," she advises both sides to lighten up and have fun with the diversity around us. Instead, I wanted her to conclude by reinforcing her point that "actions still speak louder than fashionable phrases."

Analyzing effectiveness of text

Changing the realities of illiteracy, poverty, alcohol abuse, and sexual harassment should be the focus of the multiculturalists. Of course, changing language is crucial to changing the world, but the language revolution has already happened—or at least begun. Ehrenreich's article would be more effective, I believe, if she concluded her essay with a call for both sides to help change cultural conditions rather than with a reference to the silly debate about what to call a teenage woman.

Responder's main point

SUMMARIZING AND RESPONDING TO IMAGES

Images, which include works of art, photographs, advertisements, graphics, and video, should be approached like essays or articles—with just a few key differences. In your summary, refer to the author and title if the work has a title. Then, instead of citing the thesis and main ideas, indicate which images provide the central focus of the composition. If the visual includes written text, as in many advertisements, cite key words and phrases that explain the central image or images. Use author tags if the author, creator, or sponsoring agency is known; otherwise, refer to the product or service in the advertisement or the subject of the photograph. As you describe the image, your goal is to be both accurate and detailed. Note key features of the composition such as color, shading, size, balance, background, use of diagonals, perspective, and point of view. Also note relationships among the objects and figures.

Your response, then, "reads" the image in its rhetorical context. For rhetorical context, remember that you are considering author, occasion, genre, audience, purpose, and cultural context. You may, for example, focus on how purpose, genre, audience, and context come together to convey a message or create an argument. You may consider how effectively the image achieves its purpose or does not meet some ideal purpose. You may agree or disagree with the message or argument implied in the image. Finally, you may interpret or reflect on the image or examine its underlying cultural assumptions, implications, or consequences. (For additional ideas, see the Tips on Analyzing Images.)

Your supporting evidence your response should rely heavily on the details of composition of the image, but you may also talk about your own experiences (as appropriate) or cite what other commentators on this image or on this genre have said. Remember, though, that your response must make a coherent, overall main point.

The following two student essays read and respond to advertisements. The first, "Beauty and Violence," by Adam Forest, responds to a TIGI Bed Head promotional

TIPS FOR ANALYZING IMAGES

As you analyze images, pay attention to the following visual elements. How do these elements contribute to the overall impact of the message?

Composition

To analyze the composition of an image, consider the following "Wh" questions:

- Who or what is pictured in the main figure?
- What is in the background?
- What is the relationship between the main figure and the background?
- When was the image painted or photographed?
- Where or in what cultural/environmental context is the image placed?
- What is absent or missing from the main figure or background?
- What message does the image convey?
- Why or for what purpose was the image created?

Focal Point

- What point or image first draws your attention?
- Is this focal point centered or offset?
- Do diagonal lines draw you to or away from the focal point?
- What is the relationship between the focal point, the main figure, and the background?
- How does the focal point relate to the message of the image?

Color, Shape, Contrast, Light, and Shadow

- How do colors and shapes reinforce the message of the image?
- How are contrast, light, and shadow used to emphasize the message?
- How do patterns or repetitions of color, shape, or contrast reinforce the message?

Narrative

- What story or narrative does the image suggest?
- Do the central figures represent the main characters in a narrative?
- Do certain objects act as symbols or metaphors?
- How do these story values support the central message?

video. The annotations in the margin illustrate how Adam Forest follows the above guidelines for his summary and response. The second essay, "Some Don't Like Their Blues at All," by Karyn M. Lewis, responds to a magazine ad for Fila jeans. In both essays, the writers summarize and describe the advertisement before they analyze and interpret the text for key messages.

STUDENT WRITING

BEAUTY AND VIOLENCE

Adam Forest

Author or sponsoring agency: TIGI

"Real people, real life, real products." This catchy new motto from the Bed Head 2000 line of TIGI hair and makeup products is missing only two words: "Real Violence." 1

Thesis or main idea of response

The most dangerous social trends are those that subconsciously shift the way society thinks about itself. A recent disturbing trend has been the glorification of violence toward both men and women, predominantly through the television and movie industry. Riding the societal surge of this trend comes an emerging, possibly more frightening one—the beautification of violence. It is a trend aimed solely at uniquely susceptible, unassuming young women. 2

Audience: women

Description of key images and details

I recently had the opportunity to watch the TIGI Bed Head 2000 promotional video: it was gut-wrenching. It literally depicted a decapitated woman's head being bludgeoned by an invisible presence. Her eyes jerking wildly about in fear, lips twitching, she shook her head back and forth while her face was brutally beaten. Her lipstick was smeared across her face to look like spilt blood, greenish-purple bruise-like blotches appearing on her cheeks and eye sockets, her mouth letting go an occasional silent scream while still shaking her head "no." This continued until her face was entirely covered by a multicolored smear of makeup and her head dropped dead to the side, only to start the process all over again. Amid the sickening array flashed hip techno music and pictures of colorful beauty products accompanied by words such as "Fat Lip," "Get-Whipped" and "Dominatrix," topped off by the final catch phrase, "Makeup of the Future." 3

Description of text or audio

"Shock fashion" is a new but sickening genre

The scene presents an interesting metaphor: Women are indeed being bludgeoned by the currently surfacing shock "fashion" trends in American culture. 4

This video is obviously an extreme example of the trend, but less blatant techniques grounded in the same principle are more prevalent and dif- 5 ficult to spot, therefore making them more dangerous as well. I recall having to stare at a poster of a model in a hair salon before ultimately realizing that her eyeliner had been applied to make her look as though she had been socked in the face.

Media and fashion have a profound influence on how humans think and behave through the creation of gradual shifts in societal trends. While violent television advertisements and "beauty" products such as "Fat-Lip" lipliner may not appear to directly affect the specific actions of individuals, by gradually causing the abused and battered look among women to be socially accepted as sexy, they can have a substantial impact on how men and women think about themselves and each other, consequently causing violence to skyrocket. And the movement has no conceivable end. Sadly, one would not be hard-pressed to find a blatant example of media perpetuated violence toward women other than the TIGI video. The disconcerting part is that this has been going on for years.

Being able to consciously recognize the problem is only part of the solution. Many people do not understand the difference between being a nonsexist and an anti-sexist individual. While someone who is nonsexist merely does nothing to further the problem, an anti-sexist takes an active stance against it.

A great example of an anti-sexist individual in our community is Phyllis Thode, president of Headlines Salon of the Rockies. Having formerly supported TIGI products, she, too, saw their new promotional video. Afterward she wrote to the president of TIGI, announcing that Headlines would not sell many of its new line of products. She stated, "I am concerned that it is targeting a very narrow market with a strong emphasis on the youth" and "I feel that I need to evaluate my relationship with TIGI. I am not interested in 'Getting Whipped' this Christmas." Right on, Phyllis.

With a sexual assault occurring every 45 seconds in America and one in four Colorado women having been the victim of rape or attempted rape, sexual violence is a more serious problem than is often realized. With current media and fashion trends pointing American society in a dangerous direction, it will take a culture comprised of socially aware, anti-sexist men and women to counter the movement. I sincerely hope we can meet the challenge.

Example of another relevant visual image

6

Cultural consequences of these violent images

7

8

Citing other writers who have also objected to this trend toward violence

9

Conclusion: Americans must become aware of the consequences of violence toward women in "shock fashion" ads.

STUDENT WRITING

SOME DON'T LIKE THEIR BLUES AT ALL

Karyn M. Lewis

He strides toward us in navy and white, his body muscled and heavy-   1
set, one arm holding his casually flung jeans jacket over his shoulder. A
man in his prime, with just the right combination of macho and sartorial
flair.

He is also black.   2

She is curled and giggling upon a chair, her hair loose and flowing   3
around her shoulders, leaning forward innocently—the very picture of a
blossoming, navy flower.

She is white.   4

They are each pictured on a magazine page of their own, situated op-   5
posite each other in a complementary two-page spread. They are stationed
in front of a muted photograph which serves as a background for each one.
They both merit their own captions: bold indigo letters presiding over them
in the outer corners of each page.

His says: SOME LIKE THEIR BLUES HARD.   6

Hers says: SOME LIKE THEIR BLUES SOFT.   7

His background depicts a thrusting struggle between a quarterback   8
and a leaping defender, a scene of arrested violence and high tension.

Her background is a lounging, bikini-clad goddess, who looks at the   9
camera with intriguing, calm passion. She raises her hand to rest behind her
head in a languid gesture as she tries to incite passion within the viewer.

At the bottom of the page blazes the proud emblem of the company   10
that came up with this ad: FILA JEANS.

This advertisement blatantly uses stereotypes of men and women to sell   11
its product. It caters to our need to fit into the roles that society has deemed
right for the individual sexes ever since patriarchal rule rose up and replaced
the primitive worship of a mother goddess and the reverence for women.
These stereotypes handed down to us throughout the centuries spell out to
us that men are violence and power incarnate, and that the manly attitude

has no room for weakness or softness of nature. And we find our role model of women in the compliant and eager female who obeys her man in all things, who must not say no to a male, and who is not very bright—someone who flutters her eyelashes, giggles a lot, and uses tears to get her way.

This ad tells us, by offering the image of a hard, masculine male, who *12* is deified in violence, that he is the role model men should aspire to, and that for women, their ideal is weak but sexual, innocent and at the same time old enough to have sex. In viewing this ad, we see our aspirations clothed in Fila jeans, and to be like them, we must buy the clothes pictured here. This ad also suggests that a man can become hard and powerful (or at least look it) dressed in these jeans; a woman can become sexually intense and desirable dressed in Fila's clothing.

The words of the captions tantalize with their sexual innuendo. The *13* phrase "Some like their blues hard" hints at male sexual prowess. Most men and women in this country are obsessed with males' need to prove their virility, and Fila plays on this obsession. Females too have their own stereotype of what constitutes their sexuality. "Some like their blues soft" exemplifies this ideal: A woman should be soft and yielding. Her soft, sensuous body parts, which so excite her partners, have been transformed into her personal qualities. By using the term *soft,* Fila immediately links the girl with her sexuality and sexual organs.

We are shown by the models' postures that men and women are (ac- *14* cording to Fila) fundamentally different and total antonyms of one another. He is standing and walking with purpose; she sits, laughing trivially at the camera. Even the background hints at separation of the sexes.

The football players on the man's page are arranged in a diagonal line *15* which starts at the upper left-hand corner and runs to the opposite corner, which is the center of the ad. On her page, the enchanting nymph in the bathing suit runs on a diagonal, beginning where his ends, and traveling up to the upper right-hand corner of her page. These two photos in effect create a *V,* which both links the two models and suggests movement away from one another. Another good example of their autonomy from one another is their skin color. He is a black man, she's white. Black is the opposite color of white on an artist's color wheel and palette and symbolizes dynamically opposed forces: good and evil, night and day, man and woman. This ad hits us with the idea that men and women are not parallel in nature to one another but are fundamentally different in all things. It alienates the sexes from each other. Opposites may attract, but there is no room for understanding a nature completely alien to your own.

So in viewing this ad, and reading its captions, the consumer is left   *16*
with the view that a woman must be "soft" and sensual, a male's sexual
dream, and must somehow still retain her innocence after having sex. She
must be weak, the opposite of the violence which contrasts with her on the
opposite page. The men looking at this ad read the message that they are
supposed to be well-dressed and powerful and possess a strength that borders on violence. As we are told by the caption, men should be "hard." Fur-
thermore, men and women are opposite creatures, as different as two sides
of a coin.

This ad is supposed to cause us to want to meet these requirements, but   *17*
it fills me with a deep-rooted disgust that we perpetuate the myth that men
are unyielding creatures of iron and women are silly bits of fluff. The ad generates no good role models to aspire to, where men and women are equal
beings, and both can show compassion and still be strong. Fila may like
their blues hard and soft, but I don't like their blues at all.

WARMING UP: JOURNAL EXERCISES

The following topics will help you practice your reading and responding.

1. Find an advertisement in a magazine and do a summary/interpretation, fol-
    lowing the model provided by Karyn Lewis. First, describe the advertise-
    ment carefully so your readers can visualize its graphic features. Quote
    directly any key parts of the ad copy or language. Then offer your response
    to this ad. You may wish to analyze the effectiveness of the ad and/or offer
    your interpretation of its cultural significance.

2. Study the painting by Diego Rivera, *The Flower Carrier*, at the beginning of
    this chapter. Use the tips for analyzing images on page 173 in this chapter to
    describe the key features of this image. Then use your search engine or li-
    brary databases to find out information about the work of Diego Rivera.
    What are major themes in his art? What is his attitude toward workers and
    how is that reflected in this portrait? How does Rivera's style and message
    compare to a similar image by Dorothea Lange in Chapter 7?

3. If you have a community-service learning project in your class, go to your
    agency or organization and collect texts, images, and brochures that advertise

the organization or explain its mission. Choose one or two documents and write a summary and response addressed both to your classmates and to the organization itself. Consider the rhetorical context of these documents (author, purpose, audience, occasion, genre, and cultural context) as you explain why they are or are not effective or appropriate and/or how you interpret the assumptions and implications contained in these texts or images. Your goal is to provide constructive suggestions about ways to revise or improve these texts.

4.   Study the print by Maurits Escher reproduced here. How many different ways of perceiving this picture can you see? Describe each perspective. How is "reading" this picture similar to reading a printed text? How is it different?

Day and Night by M.C. Escher. © 1997 Cordon Art-Baarn-Holland. All rights reserved.

5.   Because previewing material is an important part of active reading, most recent psychology and social science textbooks use previewing or prereading strategies at the beginning of each new chapter. Find one chapter in a textbook that uses these previewing techniques. How does the author preview the material? Does the preview help you understand the material in the chapter?

6.   Reading the following paragraph illustrates how our prior experience can combine with our predictions to make meaning. The following passage describes a common procedure in our lives. Read the passage. Can you identify the procedure?

> The procedure is actually quite simple. First, you arrange things into different groups. Of course, one pile may be sufficient depending on how much there is to do. If you have to go somewhere else because of

lack of facilities, that is the next step; otherwise you are pretty well set. It is important not to overdo things. That is, it is better to do too few things at once than too many. In the short run this may not seem important, but complications can easily arise. A mistake can be expensive as well. At first, the whole procedure will seem complicated. Soon, however, it will become just another facet of life. It is difficult to foresee any end to the necessity for this task in the immediate future, but then one can never tell. After the procedure is completed, one arranges the materials into different groups again. Then they can be put into their appropriate places. Eventually, they will be used once more, and the whole cycle will then have to be repeated. However, that is part of life.

As you read, record your guesses. What words helped to orient you? Where did you make wrong guesses? Discuss your reactions in class.

7. Reprinted below is a letter written by Margaret Atwood, which appeared in *The Nation*. The editors of *The Nation* had asked several foreign writers and political commentators to "share their reflections" about the debate concerning America's foreign policy. An award-winning Canadian novelist, Margaret Atwood has written many volumes of poetry and short fiction as well as over a dozen novels, including *Surfacing* (1973), *The Handmaid's Tale* (1986), and *Oryx and Crake* (2003). Read her "Letter to America," and then write your own summary and response to her ideas.

LETTER TO AMERICA
Margaret Atwood

Dear America:

This is a difficult letter to write, because I'm no longer sure who you are. Some of you may be having the same trouble.

I thought I knew you: We'd become well acquainted over the past fifty-five years. You were the Mickey Mouse and Donald Duck comic books I read in the late 1940s. You were the radio shows—Jack Benny, Our Miss Brooks. You were the music I sang and danced to: the Andrews Sisters, Ella Fitzgerald, the Platters, Elvis. You were a ton of fun.

You wrote some of my favorite books. You created Huckleberry Finn, and Hawkeye, and Beth and Jo in *Little Women*, courageous in their different ways. Later, you were my beloved Thoreau, father of environmentalism, witness to individual conscience; and Walt Whitman, singer of the great Republic; and Emily Dickinson, keeper of the private soul. You were Hammett and Chandler, heroic walkers of mean streets; even later, you were the amazing trio, Hemingway, Fitzgerald and Faulkner, who traced the dark labyrinths of your hidden heart. You were Sinclair Lewis and Arthur Miller, who, with their own American idealism, went after the sham in you, because they thought you could do better.

You were Marlon Brando in *On the Waterfront,* you were Humphrey Bogart in *Key Largo,* you were Lillian Gish in *Night of the Hunter.* You stood up for freedom, honesty and justice; you protected the innocent. I believed most of that. I think you did, too. It seemed true at the time.

You put God on the money, though, even then. You had a way of thinking that the things of Caesar were the same as the things of God: That gave you self-confidence. You have always wanted to be a city upon a hill, a light to all nations, and for a while you were. Give me your tired, your poor, you sang, and for a while you meant it.

We've always been close, you and us. History, that old entangler, has twisted us together since the early seventeenth century. Some of us used to be you; some of us want to be you; some of you used to be us. You are not only our neighbors: In many cases—mine, for instance—you are also our blood relations, our colleagues and our personal friends. But although we've had a ringside seat, we've never understood you completely, up here north of the 49th parallel. We're like Romanized Gauls—look like Romans, dress like Romans, but aren't Romans—peering over the wall at the real Romans. What are they doing? Why? What are they doing now? Why is the haruspex eyeballing the sheep's liver? Why is the soothsayer wholesaling the Bewares?

Perhaps that's been my difficulty in writing you this letter. I'm not sure I know what's really going on. Anyway, you have a huge posse of experienced entrail-sifters who do nothing but analyze your every vein and lobe. What can I tell you about yourself that you don't already know?

This might be the reason for my hesitation: embarrassment, brought on by a becoming modesty. But it is more likely to be embarrassment of another sort. When my grandmother—from a New England background—was confronted with an unsavory topic, she would change the subject and gaze out the window. And that is my own inclination: Keep your mouth shut, mind your own business.

But I'll take the plunge, because your business is no longer merely your business. To paraphrase Marley's Ghost, who figured it out too late, mankind is your business. And vice versa: When the Jolly Green Giant goes on the rampage, many lesser plants and animals get trampled underfoot. As for us, you're our biggest trading partner: We know perfectly well that if you go down the plug-hole, we're going with you. We have every reason to wish you well.

I won't go into the reasons why I think your recent Iraqi adventures have been—taking the long view—an ill-advised tactical error. By the time you read this, Baghdad may or may not be a pancake, and many more sheep entrails will have been examined. Let's talk, then, not about what you're doing to other people but about what you're doing to yourselves.

You're gutting the Constitution. Already your home can be entered without your knowledge or permission, you can be snatched away and incarcerated without cause, your mail can be spied on, your private records searched. Why isn't this a recipe for widespread business theft, political intimidation and fraud? I know you've been told that all this is for your own safety and protection, but think about it for a minute. Anyway, when did you get so scared? You didn't used to be easily frightened.

You're running up a record level of debt. Keep spending at this rate and pretty soon you won't be able to afford any big military adventures. Either that or you'll go the way of the USSR: lots of tanks, but no air conditioning. That will make folks very cross. They'll be even crosser when they can't take a shower because your shortsighted bulldozing of environmental protections has dirtied most of the water and dried up the rest. Then things will get hot and dirty indeed.

You're torching the American economy. How soon before the answer to that will be not to produce anything yourselves but to grab stuff other people produce, at gunboat-diplomacy prices? Is the world going to consist of a few mega-rich King Midases, with the rest being serfs, both inside and outside your country? Will the biggest business sector in the United States be the prison system? Let's hope not.

If you proceed much further down the slippery slope, people around the world will stop admiring the good things about you. They'll decide that your city upon the hill is a slum and your democracy is a sham, and therefore you have no business trying to impose your sullied vision on them. They'll think you've abandoned the rule of law. They'll think you've fouled your own nest.

The British used to have a myth about King Arthur. He wasn't dead, but sleeping in a cave, it was said: and in the country's hour of greatest peril, he would return. You too have great spirits of the past you may call upon: men and women of courage, of conscience, of prescience. Summon them now, to stand with you, to inspire you, to defend the best in you. You need them.

PROFESSIONAL WRITING

Vows

Christopher Caldwell

A senior editor at The Weekly Standard, *Christopher Caldwell is a prolific journalist and a regular contributor to dozens of newspapers and magazines, including the* Financial Times, *the* New York Times, *the* Wall Street Journal, Commentary, *the* National Review, *and the* Washington Post. *When he is not writing about cultural and political relationships between Europe and the United States, he reviews popular and controversial books. In this book review, Caldwall summarizes and responds to the arguments in Jonathan Rauch's recent book,* Gay Marriage: Why It Is Good for Gays, Good for Straights, and Good for America *(2004). As you read his review, consider your own views about same-sex marriage but also evaluate Caldwell's response. Does Caldwell's summary represent Rauch's arguments clearly? Does his response include analysis of Rauch's argument, points where he agrees or disagrees with Rauch, and/or interpretations or examination of the implications of Rauch's ideas?*

The average American views same-sex marriage as a bad idea whose time   *1*
has come. Solid majorities—generally around two-thirds—oppose it. But now that Vermont has introduced "civil unions" for gays, Belgium and the

Netherlands have legalized gay marriages and courts have mandated them in both Ontario and Massachusetts, stopping gay marriage appears to require measures (like an amendment to the Constitution) more reactionary than Americans will countenance. What opponents of single-sex marriage have failed miserably to do is enunciate a rationale for blocking it that the country can rally behind.

There's a reason for that, according to the veteran Washington journalist Jonathan Rauch. Most arguments against gay marriage, he writes in a closely argued new polemic, are "overblown, at best, often just fanciful, and sometimes hypocritical." Worse, they ignore the possibility that gays, once admitted to marriage, would have a stake in defending its traditions.

Some people may support same-sex marriage only as a roundabout means to recognition for gays. Not Rauch. Gay himself, he seeks it because he wants to get married, and thinks everyone should. His idea of marriage is old-school, even sentimental. ("I mean two souls bonded in each other's eyes and together clasped to their community's bosom.") Of those gays who fear that marriage will force them to trade in a libertine lifestyle for a bourgeois heterosexual one, Rauch says, "I believe that they are largely right, and that gay integration into the mainstream would be, on balance, a good thing."

Marriage has a "special power" to bind people into communities and into other families, Rauch thinks. Its two primary purposes are setting young adults into a web of commitments and providing caregivers to the old and infirm. Since homosexuals can and do carry out the responsibilities of marriage, they deserve to accede to its rights. A marriage regime that excludes homosexuals "no longer accords with liberal justice or the meaning of marriage as it is practiced today." Neither, Rauch writes, do Vermont-style civil unions (which he calls "marriage-lite") and corporate partnership plans (which he thinks should be abolished the moment gay marriage is passed). These not only keep gays stranded on a different plane of citizenship but also threaten to undermine marriage for straights. Should a legal challenge make them universally available, they will compete with the marriages they're meant to defend.

So while traditionalists complain that marriage is embattled, and while gay activists complain that marriage is unfair, Rauch insists that marriage is embattled because it's unfair. When gays can marry, they will appear in a new light—as allies, not interlopers; relations between gays and straights will improve, because what makes homosexuals appear most "grotesque and threatening" is not their sexual orientation but the outlawry against convention to which the unavailability of marriage consigns them. For Rauch, the best way to defend marriage is by letting gays in, not keeping them out.

But even if gays deserve the right to marry, can they be given their due   6
without altering marriage? Over the course of several chapters, Rauch holds up to close examination some key arguments used to defend the marital status quo. There is, for instance, what he calls the "Anything Goes" argument, which holds that if gay marriage is allowed, then polygamists and incestuous pairs will demand marriage under the same logic. Rauch's reply is that incestuous marriage "is an option no one needs and no one even seems to want," and that Americans will easily recognize that polygamy does considerably more damage to a liberal-democratic order than his own preferred policy of "one person, one spouse" possibly could. To the "Men Behaving Badly" argument—that what "settles" men is not the institution of marriage but the need to negotiate a modus vivendi with women—he narrows the discussion to adultery and finds the jury still out. Even if gay men are more likely to cheat on their partners than heterosexuals, Rauch points out, there would be a clear net gain to society in having them disciplined into discretion by a marital vow.

Rauch's points do not close any arguments. Strands of two large American religions, Islam and Mormonism, will surely demand polygamy once gay marriage passes; and the question of whether women help settle men might look different if Rauch used the lens of, say, substance abuse or violence. But his discussion is enough to reassure anyone not already dug in against gay marriage. Even more important, it puts on display his arguing style, an appealing combination of prosecutorial logic and gentlemanly forbearance. Rauch strains to find merit even in the positions of intemperate talk-show hosts. He neither twists words nor tweaks statistics. He takes pains not to leave angles unexamined.

And yet he commits an important error of emphasis, which is not fatal   8
to his case for gay marriage but damages his case that gay marriage can be traditional marriage. It concerns the importance of childbearing. "I hope I won't be accused of saying that children are a trivial reason for marriage," he says early in the book. "They just cannot be the only reason." It is true that marriage has historically served many purposes. But alongside that of providing a nonanarchic context for producing children, they all look like moons against Jupiter. Rauch hates this argument. He finds it "incoherent, incorrect and antimarriage." He is happy to speak of the welfare of children, but skirts the production of children, dismissing it as a "sex-centered view."

Rauch is not being prudish, only unreasonable. "If the possibility of   9
procreation is what gives meaning to marriage," he writes, "then a post-
menopausal woman who applies for a marriage license should be turned
away at the courthouse door. What's more, she should be hooted at and
condemned for breaking the crucial link between marriage and procreation." Not necessarily. The state's reluctance to engage in purposeless
Maoist persecution of the infertile does not mean the state has no interest
in fertility. (And, in fact, traditional marriage has been consistently heart-
less towards infertile heterosexuals, particularly women.)

Rauch believes the argument-from-procreation is made in bigoted bad   10
faith. "Well, there is one thing no homosexual couple can do, and that is to
procreate," he writes. "So gay-marriage opponents come back time and
again, at the outset and then as a last resort, to the claim that marriage is
inseparable from procreation." That word "So" contains an accusation. And
it is not a slip, for Rauch writes elsewhere, "With the rise of the gay-
marriage debate, another view has come to the fore: marriage is about children." Rauch has this exactly backward. Far from being a recent pretext, the
idea that marriage is about producing children is an ancient understanding,
and a steadily weakening one.

Those who make this argument today are guilty only of failing to re-   11
examine ideas that have passed down from earlier understandings of marriage. That is why they claim to be defending "tradition." Traditional society
never had any reason to marry gays, even in periods of relative tolerance, because it never had any need for homosexual sex. Nor does it today. What
has happened to render gay marriage suddenly more logical is society's waning need for married people's sex. Sex, childbearing and childrearing—
which marriage once bound as tightly as an atomic nucleus—have been
disaggregated. This has happened partly through law (on divorce and adoption), partly through technology (contraception, abortion and artificial in-
semination), partly through convention (cohabitation) and partly through
knowledge (on the innateness of homosexuality, for instance).

Rauch may have too high an opinion of the sort of marital club that   12
would have gays as members. It seems unlikely that marriage could simultaneously be flexible enough to admit homosexuals and rigid enough to
offer them the same protection and rights (and discipline) it offered heterosexuals in the old days. But it seems even less likely that, as Rauch hopes,
the gay-marriage movement will be able to shore up an institution that has
for decades been undermined legally, socially, medically, theologically, philo-
sophically, psychologically and politically. Gays will soon accede to marriage,

but only because marriage is losing its old set of purposes and is becoming, irrevocably, something else.

In your journal, write the meaning of each of the following words:

- new *polemic* (**2**)
- a *libertine* lifestyle (**3**)
- deserve to *accede* to its rights (**4**)
- as allies, not *interlopers* (**5**)
- *incestuous* marriage (**6**)
- negotiate a *modus vivendi* with women (**6**)
- disciplined into *discretion* (**6**)
- providing a *nonanarchic* context (**8**)
- made in *bigoted* bad faith (**10**)
- have been *disaggregated* (**11**)
- on the *innateness* of homosexuality (**11**)

QUESTIONS FOR WRITING AND DISCUSSION

1. Analyze yourself as a reader and responder to arguments about same-sex marriage. First, consider your own background and beliefs. What are your parents' religious, political, and cultural beliefs on this issue, and how do your beliefs differ? What experiences have shaped your beliefs on this issue? Second, would you describe yourself as a person in favor of same-sex marriage, a person in favor of a compromise position such as civil unions, a person in favor of having individual states decide the issue rather than favoring a constitutional amendment, or a person who is, as Caldwell says, "already dug in against gay marriage?"

2. Based on your answer to question 1, how has your reading of this article and your previous reading and conversation on this topic altered your beliefs?

What passages in this article provided new ideas, arguments, or issues that you had not previously considered? How did they affect your position?

3.   Review the strategies for summary given earlier in the chapter. Which of those strategies (cite author and title, accurately represent main ideas, use direct quotation for key ideas, include author tags, and report ideas objectively) does Caldwell model? Find at least one example from his review illustrating each of those techniques.

4.   After reviewing the chapter's discussion of types of responses and kinds of evidence, comment on Caldwell's response to Rauch's argument. Find two examples where Caldwell analyzes the effectiveness of Rauch's argument. Find two passages where Caldwell either agrees or disagrees with Rauch. Find at least one passage where Caldwell offers an interpretation or reflects on the implications of Rauch's argument. Based on your analysis, how effective is Caldwell's response to Rauch? Explain.

5.   The cultural context and the ongoing conversation surrounding a topic are important parts of the rhetorical situation surrounding any controversial topic. Use your library's online full-text databases (such as EBSCO or Lexis Nexis) to find at least three other reviews of Jonathan Rauch's book. What other ideas or arguments from Rauch's book do those reviewers cite that Caldwell omits? Examine the responses of the reviewers. How are their responses similar to or different from Caldwell's? Illustrate those similarities or differences by citing at least two examples from each of the other reviews. Are the responses more conservative or more liberal than Caldwell's? How do those responses reflect the policies of the magazines or newspapers in which they appear?

PROFESSIONAL WRITING

ATLAS SHRUGS

Nicholas Lemann

A prolific and acclaimed journalist and national correspondent to the Atlantic Monthly, *Nicholas Lemann has written on social issues, culture, history, and contemporary politics in magazines such as* The New Republic, The Nation, The New Yorker, Washington Monthly, Time, *and* Newsweek. *His recent books include* The Promised Land: The Great Black Migration and How It Changed America *(1991) and* The Big Test: The Secret History of the American Meritocracy *(1999). In the following* New Yorker *essay, Lemann introduces the reader to the "new geography" or "critical geography" through several texts which he summarizes and then comments on. He focuses on two works of critical geography: J. B. Harley's* The New Nature of Maps *and Susan Schulten's* The Geographical Imagination in America, 1880–1950. *According to Lemann, these authors argue that maps are more than innocent directions indicating how to get from Point A to Point B; they are, in fact, "social constructions," "polemics," and "texts of power."*

After the Second World War, most of the Ivy League universities abol- 1
ished their departments of geography, and the subject inexorably began to slip, at least in the mind of the general public, into the realm of junior-high-school memorization of placenames and climatic zones. (The advent, whenever it was, of Geography, the annoying word game that children insist on playing during road trips, didn't elevate the image of the discipline, either.) But geography is back. In the past couple of decades, a group of mostly British, mostly left-wing scholars—David Harvey, David Woodward, J. B. Harley, and others—have created a field known, variously, as "critical geography" and "the new geography." They have taken up residence in the remaining university geography departments in this country, and have started turning out protégés and publications, promoting a new, more cunning way of looking at maps.

When you think about it, geography is a rich subject. Much of the 2
politics and economics of the world revolves around the question of who controls what space, and to what end. This was plainly true during the Age of Exploration that we all learned about—though we may have been so intent on remembering the difference between Vasco da Gama and Vasco Núñez de Balboa that we didn't notice—and it's still true today, in the age of the global economy and metropolitan sprawl. Here in the United States, the idea of the vanished frontier, a pure geographical construct, has shaped our understanding of ourselves for a century.

One of the main subspecialties of critical geography is critical cartog- 3
raphy, the study of maps and mapmaking. We're accustomed to thinking of maps as useful objects, whose purpose is to direct us from one location to another, or, in the case of old maps, as fanciful arrangements of bright-colored ink on paper, most evocative for what they get wrong. Clearly, though, maps have played an enormous part in shaping the nonphysical

world. States, nations, empires, even continents are not natural geographic features, and their existence would be impossible without maps. The mapping of the world has been one of the monumental human endeavors.

Now playing at the New York Public Library is a charming exhibition, assembled by Alice Hudson, the chief of the library's Map Division, called "Heading West: Mapping the Territory." The show, a cartographic record of the American West, is made up of selections from the library's collection of half a million maps: "This is the old geography," Hudson told me the other day, when she walked me through the show. She pointed to a Union Pacific Railway map from 1881, on which somebody had scribbled a couple of sentences, probably from a telegraphed message, and drawn fresh lines showing the latest extension of a rail line. What could be more straightforward and practical than that? The show has an aesthetic aspect, too. Hudson obviously loves the craftsmanship of cartography, and she has found some wonderful specimens. Geological and botanical maps from the period of initial Western exploration are composed and colored (usually by nameless government bureaucrats) with a startling intensity and grace. The star of the show—Hudson's big rediscovery—is the incredibly detailed, meticulously shaded engraving work of Frederick Von Egloffstein, a nineteenth-century Prussian émigré who produced both maps and views of the West. His drawing of the rim of the Grand Canyon, for example, makes it easy to strip away the many coats of tourist culture and imagine how forbidding and awful it must once have appeared.

At the same time, historical maps are necessarily suffused with the agendas, beyond accuracy and elegance, of their makers: maps serve interests. The earliest maps exhibited in "Heading West," which date from before 1700, hopefully depict the Americas as an island or, at least, a raggedy blob that ships might cruise past on their way to trade in Asia. Almost immediately after the West was accurately mapped, the familiar ruler lines and colors of political division appear; very soon after that the property grids and rail lines of commerce are evident; and, finally, the maps acquire an exaggerated pictorial style associated with the promotion of tourism and residential real estate. Put into historical perspective, every map on display communicates a sense not just of a piece of land but also of the apportionment of money and power in the world at a particular moment.

The father of critical cartography, and therefore of the idea that a map should be understood as more than just a set of directions, was J. B. Harley, a map historian who died ten years ago. Harley spent most of his life in England and, in middle age, moved to the University of Wisconsin-

Milwaukee, where he helped launch an ambitious publishing series called the History of Cartography. This spring, Johns Hopkins is bringing out a collection of his essays, *The New Nature of Maps.* It is a curious book, which manages to make the case both for and (unwittingly) against critical cartography. Harley seems to have been one of those academics whose careers are spent reconnoitring the lower slopes of a magnum opus—in his case, a book to be called "The Map as Ideology"—without ever writing it. His oeuvre thus consists of essays that display great erudition but make quick, darting points rather than full, sustained arguments. Harley was a follower of Michel Foucault, who held that all knowledge is a form of power. Rummaging through the history of mapmaking, Harley has found enough material to bear out Foucault's idea, at least in the realm of cartography.

Before mass production, only the powerful had access to maps. Much   7 early mapping was done by people who had job titles like Geographer to the King. (Even now, a large share of mapping, including American mapping, is done by governments.) Maps were a way of locating resources, so that the map-holding few could get their hands on them, and of establishing control over land. As Harley points out in one of his essays, old maps of England often demarcate the estates of noblemen as if they were natural features of the environment, and relegate the places where everybody else lives to (one of his favorite words) "silences." Cartouches, those small emblems drawn in the margins of old maps and now a godsend to critical cartographers, showed heraldic crests. "There are no map signs for poverty or squalor, and the bland washes of the map colorer denote a green and pleasant land," Harley notes, with characteristic grim satisfaction. The soil in the British Empire was not in fact colored pink, except on maps, but the uniform color there helped fix the empire in people's minds as an organic whole. ("The way things were going nothing was pink on the map any more," a character in Barbara Pym's declinist novel *Quartet in Autumn* reflects.)

As Harley's colleague J. H. Andrews puts it in his introduction to *The*   8 *New Nature of Maps,* Harley "gathered ideas from (to quote one of his own lists) "information-theory, linguistics, semiotics, structuralism, phenomenology, developmental theory, hermeneutics, iconology, Marxism, and ideology." Despite, or perhaps because of the capacious intellectual toolkit at his disposal, Harley is deeply unwilling to admit that most maps are used by most people for simple directional purposes. To him, a map is a "social construction," a "thick text," a "redescription of reality," a "silent arbiter of power," "a polemic," a "manifesto for a set of beliefs about the world," or a "text of power." Even the official state highway map of North Carolina, he insists, is "making other dialogical assertions behind its mask of innocence and transparence," by which he means that its emphasis on superhighways subjects other aspects of the Tarheel State to those dreaded "silences." As Jeremy Black, another critical cartographer, writes in his own, somewhat disjointed new collection of essays, "Maps and Politics" (Chicago), the work of Harley and his followers is flawed by an impulse to "search for conspiracy" and "a tendency to state the obvious."

The work of the Harley school, once encountered, makes it impossible to look at maps in a completely straightforward way ever again. Instead, the urge to decode arises every time you come across one (and, once you stop taking maps for granted, it's amazing how often you do). The question is whether the habit of reading maps as sociopolitical artifacts can generate something more complicated and coherent than mordantly ironic observations about the subtexts of specific maps—the scholarly equivalent of the running commentary that knowing college kids produce as they sprawl on couches and watch old television shows. *9*

Another new book on maps, "The Geographical Imagination in America, 1880–1950" (Chicago), by Susan Schulten, steps up to the challenge of producing a full-length work about the political economy of mapmaking. Schulten, a historian at the University of Denver who has a basically Harleyan consciousness ("Maps are arguments that mediate our understanding of the world," she writes), has done an enormous amount of research and put together an ambitious history of the rise of popular cartography in the United States. *10*

This country, Schulten says, was the birthplace of maps and geography for the masses. Published maps were traditionally made by the copper-engraving process, which yields fine but expensive work. The advent of the much cheaper, though less elegant, wax-engraving process, in the mid-nineteenth century, made it possible to publish maps for a popular audience. American map publishers—in particular, Rand McNally, of Chicago, whose archives Schulten has perused extensively—used wax engraving to develop a distinctively American style of map, loud and commercial, crammed with as many place-names as possible, in thick type, and garishly colored state by state. Nineteenth-century American commercial mapmakers were pathologically particular in their treatment of the United States and pathologically general in their treatment of the rest of the world. "Most of the civilized people of the world belong to the white race, though in some countries the *11* people of that race are half-civilized," reported Rand McNally's "Elementary Geography," a textbook published in 1894 for the booming public-school geography-class market. "The savages belong to the red, brown, and black races. Most people of the yellow race are half-civilized, but you will read some day of the yellow people of Japan."

With the Spanish-American War and the rise of American imperialism, Americans began to focus much more seriously on faraway places. Schulten is not exactly soft on imperialism, but she presents it as a developmental step in geography, objectionable on its own but less so if seen as a station on the way to true understanding: better to think of the world as an arena for commercial exploitation than not to think about it at all. Schulten explores this phase through the magazine *National Geographic*, which became prominent in the first two decades of the twentieth century. Like Rand McNally, *National Geographic* is a peculiarly American institution, part public agency (with its official expeditions and articles by government authorities), part academic journal (published by a society of experts), and part high-minded mass entertainment (naked photographs of dusky maidens). During and after the Spanish-American War, it published many articles about the new little siblings in the American family, Cuba and the Philippines, as a way not so much of justifying our foreign policy as of making people feel comfortable with the idea of being linked to such exotic locales. *National Geographic* reassured us by presenting them as charming and folkish, rather than as threatening; its central editorial goal, as the magazine's brilliant editor, Gilbert Grosvenor, put it later in a letter to one of his contributors, was to provide "mental relaxation without emotional stimulus."

Unlike Harley, Schulten seems to have gone native in the course, of her research. To her, the leading mapmakers are more than just one-dimensional avatars of entrenched power, and she is sympathetic to them when, by her lights, they are trying to behave well. The last part of her book presents the mid-twentieth century as the dawn of a golden age of geographic understanding. The American map industry, having advanced from race-and-climate-are-destiny theories to an interest in faraway places as potential areas of economic exploitation, awoke to questions about the good of all people, not just Americans. Several weeks after Pearl Harbor, Franklin Roosevelt gave a radio address urging people to go out and buy a world map, and an awful lot of them did. Sales of geographic material soared during the war years. *National Geographic* and then Rand McNally abandoned their habit of filling every available bit of map surface with place-names, and adopted a suaver, more European style of presentation. Commercial aviation led to maps that showed the world from a point above the North Pole, with the Arctic Ocean as the "new Mediterranean." Rand McNally replaced its old Imperial Atlas with an elaborately produced Cosmopolitan Atlas.

During the Second World War, Schulten reports, practically cheering, *14* even the Mercator projection—which had dominated world mapping since it was devised, in 1569—finally fell out of favor. Mayor LaGuardia personally banned its use in New York City public schools in 1943, perhaps afraid that another generation of schoolchildren would grow up thinking that Greenland was the size of South America. *National Geographic* now uses the oval Robinson projection, and when you move out of the mass market in a leftward direction you encounter the Peters projection, developed in 1967, which makes the Third World look bigger than the First and the Second—and thus "embodies the map as redistributive polemic," according to Jeremy Black. At the end of Schulten's story, she finds a mapmaker she feels comfortable lionizing: Richard Edes Harrison, whose maps offered gorgeous, sweeping views of the globe from unfamiliar angles—they look like the photographs that astronauts take. Many of them were produced at the height of the war, and they implicitly communicate internationalist editorial messages (e.g., the United States is highly vulnerable to attack from all sides). Harrison, Schulten notes approvingly, understood "that all cartography was inherently argumentative, and all maps inherently suggestive."

"The Geographical Imagination" is Schulten's first book. A more ex- *15* perienced author might have been able to produce out of all the institutional specifics a magisterial narrative that began at the beginning and ended at the end. Instead, each chapter is a mini-monograph, and the weight of detail about the different geographic institutions can become oppressive. Schulten has clearly demonstrated that mapping is a subject that can support sustained historical inquiry. What she hasn't demonstrated is that it can also support intellection richer and more interesting than the two or three fairly straightforward changes she manages to ring on the basic idea of critical cartography.

Critical cartography is propelled by an odd mixture of cynicism and ide- *16* alism. After having expertly seen through the bad faith of mapmakers up to this point, writers in the field usually express the hope that future mapmakers, elevated by self-awareness and progressive principles, can produce maps that will be as benevolent as past maps have been baneful. They are reformers at heart. J. B. Harley, rather than wanting mapmaking to free it-self of the indicia of power relations, merely wanted it to be more in line with his politics. His collection of essays winds up with a call for cartographers to endorse "principles of social justice" in order to produce "a socially re-sponsible representation of the world." It is a hope that Susan Schulten seems to share.

Could this really happen? One of the critical cartographers' strongest 17
points is that maps, like every human endeavor, are saturated with tempo-ral, social, political, and economic contexts that their makers can't tran-scend. Imagine if the Peters projection had been developed in 1569 and the Mercator four centuries later. Would history really have unfolded dif-ferently? And, if so, how, exactly? Critical cartography is persuasive in ar-guing that maps are more than straightforward collections of geographic data—"constitutive, not representative," as Jeremy Black puts it. What is not so persuasive is the idea that enlightened mapmakers could somehow break out of the perspectival prison in which we are all consigned to dwell, and direct us to a better world.

In your journal, write the meaning of each of the following words:

- turning out *protégés* (1)
- a *cartographic* record (4)
- of a *magnum opus* (6)
- his *oeuvre* (6)
- display great *erudition* (6)
- often *demarcate* the estates (7)
- including . . . *semiotics* . . . *phenomenology* . . . *hermeneutics* (8)
- *mordantly* ironic observations (9)
- arguments that *mediate* our understanding (10)
- *avatars* of entrenched power (13)

- map as *redistributive polemic* **(14)**
- the *indicia* of power relations **(16)**
- *constitutive,* not representative **(17)**

QUESTIONS FOR WRITING AND DISCUSSION

1. Take an inventory of the maps in your possession. Locate maps from your car, in magazines, or in an atlas. What features do these maps highlight? What geographical or cultural features do they ignore? What power constructions can you find on these maps? Do they confirm or refute the arguments of the authors Lemann summarizes?

2. Audience is a key component of the rhetorical situation. Lemann's essay was published in *The New Yorker,* whose readers are sophisticated but not necessarily experts in "the new geography." Where does Lemann give enough background information for his readers? Cite several specific passages. Where might Lemann give clearer explanations or a more accessible summary and response? Explain.

3. List the texts and authors that Lemann comments on. Does he spend more time summarizing each text or more time responding? Would less summary and more response make his essay more or less effective for you or for his audience? Explain.

4. In paragraph 17, Lemann quotes Jeremy Black as saying that maps are "more than straightforward collections of geographic data," that they are "constitutive, not representative." What does Black mean when he says that maps are "constitutive, not representative?" Is he right? Can't a map just be a set of directions showing how to get from Point A to Point B? Do all maps contain, as Lemann suggests, "social, political, and economic contexts that their makers can't transcend?"

5. On the Internet, find another review of J. B. Harley's book. Check Lexis-Nexis, for example, at *http://web.lexis-nexis/universe* and search in the news for a review of *The Nature of Maps* by Nick Saunders in the *New Scientist,* July 7, 2001. Does Saunders give a clear summary of Harley's argument? Is it more or less informative than Lemann's essay? Explain.

6. Reproduced on the following page is a map of the United States showing the expanding territories with their dates of acquisition. Moving from east to west, the map gives the following labels to each of the territories: Porto Rico

Ceded by Spain 1899; Territory of the Original Thirteen States as recognized by Great Britain in 1783; Ceded by Spain in 1819 [Florida]: Province of Louisiana Ceded by France in 1803; Texas annexed in 1845; Ceded by Mexico in 1848; Oregon Territory Discovered and Settled. British Claims Extinguished 1848; and Hawaii (Sandwich Islands) Annexed 1895. Explain how this map and the labels suggest social, political, and economic contexts of this period of expansion. Does this map and the labels support Harley's belief that a map is a social construction, a rediscription of reality, or a manifesto for a set of beliefs about the world? Explain.

Reading and Writing Processes

ASSIGNMENT FOR READING/WRITING

Write an essay that summarizes and then responds to one or more essays, articles, or advertisements. As you review your particular assignment, make sure you understand what text or texts you should respond to, how long your summary and response should be, and what type(s) of responses you should focus on.

Your purpose for this assignment is to represent the text(s) accurately and faithfully in your summary and to explain and support your response. Taken together, your summary and response should be a coherent essay, with a main idea and connections between summary and response. Assume that your audience is other members of the class, including the instructor, with whom you are sharing your reading.

Your instructor's assignment should indicate your audience and appropriate genres. You need to know your intended audience in order to decide and what kinds of evidence will make your analysis and response convincing and how detailed your summary should be. If your audience is not familiar with your text, for example, you'll need a more detailed summary. Typically, responses take the form of an essay, but a letter to the editor may be appropriate (see Adam Forest's "Beauty and Violence," which was originally published as an editorial in a daily newspaper).

CHOOSING A SUBJECT

Suggested processes, activities, and strategies for reading and writing will be illustrated in response to the following essay by Dudley Erskine Devlin.

PROFESSIONAL WRITING

TEACHING TOLERANCE IN AMERICA

Dudley Erskine Devlin

Dudley Erskine Devlin was born in Syracuse, New York, and attended the University of Kansas. Originally trained as a scientist, he currently teaches English at Colorado State University and writes columns and editorials on contemporary problems. The targets for his editorials are often the large and complicated issues of the day, such as education, violence, health care, and the media. "My first goal as a writer," Devlin said in a recent interview, "is to provoke response. If just one reader is angry enough to write me a letter of response, then my time is not wasted." As you read Devlin's essay, note places where you agree or disagree with his ideas. How would you respond to Devlin's argument?

In the past few years, American high schools have struggled with a variety of forces that have threatened to tear them apart: reduced funding, increased class sizes, fewer music and art classes, violence in schools, and racial and class divisions among students. Although educational reform in America tends to focus on curriculum issues, class sizes, and security issues, one lesson seems increasingly hard to teach—helping students appreciate and welcome differences in culture, racial heritage, and personal identity. Despite the emphasis on increasing respect and tolerance in schools, teenagers still bring the social and racial divisions found in society at large back into the halls of high schools across America. Social cliques based on race, gender, athletic prowess, income, social class, dress, and even body piercings still define the culture at most schools. 1

America, we fervently believe, is still the land of opportunity, the land where we can be judged on our merits and achievements, not on stereotypes 2 or preconceptions or prejudices. Yet the social clique is based on the notion that one group imagines it is superior to another and thus can ridicule, taunt, or even bully another group. And nowhere does the social clique have more devastating and long-lasting effects than in our high schools.

High school cliques, which reproduce the class divisions found in so- *3* ciety, originate from three distinct sources: racial differences, gender differences, and social differences. Racial problems in high schools need no explanation. Every high school in America has racial problems that have led to continuing conflicts. A reporter visiting one typical suburban high school found that each ethnic group—Hispanics, whites, blacks, Asians—had a place where they gathered between classes and after school. Although individual members in an ethnic group gain security from being in the group, they make outsiders—people who do not belong to their racial group—feel insecure and often threatened. As one student put it, "The problem is that some people think they are better than others. So they make disparaging remarks about one another, creating tension and conflict in the school."

The ongoing gender problems in America's high schools are men- *4* tioned—if at all—on the back pages of newspapers, as if the sexist treatment of girls is a normal and inconsequential behavior. Nan Stein, author of *Classrooms and Courtrooms: Facing Sexual Harassment in K-12 Schools*, recounts numerous incidents where school administrations overlook student-on-student sexual harassment. In a recent interview with *Harvard Educational Letter*, Stein recalled a case in which "15 boys harassed this one girl verbally, mooing like cows whenever they saw her and talking about the size of her breasts. They did this outside of school, in school, on the way to school. Other kids heard it and saw it. Teachers and custodians told the administrator, who kept saying, 'It's not a big deal.'" When the case involves males of status, the chances are even more likely that school administrators will look the other way. Ignoring the flagrant behavior of the popular students happens at every school in America—despite a recent Supreme Court ruling that now holds schools liable in such cases of sexual harassment.

Finally, the differences in social classes among the various cliques— *5* most notably between the jocks and the geeks, between the powerful and the weak—is a continuing source of conflict. As one student put it, "If you're not a jock in this school . . . you're not part of it." The outsiders, geeks, and gays are ridiculed by everyone and harassed, bullied, and picked on by the jocks and by other members of the elite social class. Bullying is sometimes connected to cliques and gangs, and it affects both boys and girls. Allan Beane, author of *The Bully Free Classroom,* writes that he has "heard from so many adults who are still very angry and hurt from when they were mistreated in school." Frequently school bullies are boys—and the ridicule and intimidation they inflict has played a role, Beane says, in "almost all of the school shootings that have outraged the nation in the past two years." Hara Marano, an editor for *Psychology Today,* points out that girls, too, engage in physical aggression even though they are "more apt to be masters of indirect bullying, spreading lies and rumors and destroying reputations." The result is that about one in seven schoolchildren is either a bully or a victim of bullying.

6   How do we solve these problems? First we need to eliminate those liberal solutions that simply aren't working—thus releasing funds for more effective deterrents. Many schools, for example, have introduced diversity issues into English and social studies classes, and some schools even have sensitivity training classes that seek to "instill respect for others and training students how to speak up when they hear insulting or intimidating comments." However, most students react negatively to such classes. In a recent report, one student said that he really didn't like having notions of tolerance and acceptance drilled into him: "It's like shoving something down our throats." Besides, we want students to be able to express their feelings—if more students were like John Rocker of the Atlanta Braves, then we would have more of these problems out in the open.

7   There are, however, some real and sensible solutions that could solve the intolerance problem in our high schools. For years, parents and educators have recommended that schools adopt uniforms, so that every student wears the same clothing to school. Already, many schools ban specific colors or types of hats, shirts, or jewelry. We need uniforms not just to eliminate gangs, but to reduce the visual cues that enable one group to maintain social power. And we need to enforce those dress rules with a zero tolerance policy. Second, schools need to make single-sex classes a standard practice. Not only do boys and girls learn better in single-sex environments, but the segregated classes will reduce the differences and thus reduce conflicts. Finally, schools need to improve security—both to protect students from the outside and to protect students from each other. Schools need more video cameras, drug sniffing dogs, and spot checks of cars and lockers. Governor Jesse Ventura had an excellent idea when he suggested that every school needs to have teachers with paramilitary and anti-riot training. Last but not least, students need to wear picture ID tags hung on ribbons around their necks—so videotapes can easily identify any troublemakers.

The class system that is created and perpetuated by student cliques is   *8* the most important problem in our high schools today. In any high school on any day, we see the strong picking on the weak, the bullies intimidating the outcasts, and the jocks and the social elite dominating everyone else. Only when we apply our zero tolerance policy to the dress code, the gender makeup of our classes, and the security of our schools will students learn how to treat all people and social classes with acceptance and tolerance.

COLLECTING

Once a text or texts have been selected or assigned for your summary and response, try the following reading, writing, and discussing activities.

PREREADING JOURNAL ENTRY

In your journal, write what you already know about the subject of the essay. The following questions will help you to recall your prior experiences and think about your own opinions before you read the essay. The purpose of this entry is to think about your own experiences and opinions *before* you are influenced by the arguments of the essay.

- What classes or programs at your high school were designed to improve tolerance of social differences among students? Did they increase or decrease tolerance for social, sexual, or racial difference among students at your school?

- Were cliques a big problem at your school? Did your high school have bullies who picked on other students? Were the jocks or the upper-class students given preferential treatment?

- What measures to increase security, reduce potential violence, and increase tolerance had your high school taken in the last few years? Were these changes necessary? Did they improve the quality of your education? Did they make you feel more secure at school?

TEXT ANNOTATION   Most experts on reading and writing agree that you will learn more and remember more if you actually write out your comments, questions, and reactions in the margins of the text you are reading. Writing your responses helps you begin a conversation with the text. Reproduced below are one reader's marginal responses to paragraph 7 of Devlin's essay.

Second, schools need to make single-sex classes a (standard practice.) Not only do

Why not have them optional for some subjects?

boys and girls learn better in single-sex environments, but the segregated classes

will reduce the differences and thus reduce conflicts. Finally, schools need to

In the real world men and women work together, so why not start now?

improve security—both to protect students from the outside and to protect

students from each other. Schools need more video cameras, drug sniffing dogs,

A few cameras will provide security, but spot checks invade our privacy.

and spot checks of cars and lockers. Governor Jesse Ventura had an excellent idea

when he suggested that every school needs to have teachers with paramilitary and

What? Schools are not wrestling arenas and we don't have riots.

anti-riot training. Last but not least, students need to wear picture ID tags hung

on ribbons around their necks—so videotapes can easily identify any trouble-

Students should not be treated like jail inmates!

makers.

READING LOG   A reading log, like text annotation, encourages you to interact with the author/text and write your comments and questions as you read. While text annotation helps you identify specific places in the text for commentary, a reading log encourages you to write out longer, more thoughtful responses. In a reading log, you can keep a record of your thoughts *while you read* and *reread* the text. Often, reading-log entries help you focus on a key idea to develop later in your response.

Below is one reader's response to Devlin's ideas about single-sex classes and bullying.

> I attended a private elementary school and junior high where a school uniform was required and some of the classes were single-sex. Personally, I can say that the uniform did not make a bit of difference where bullying was an issue. Kids still made fun of other kids no matter what they were wearing. The real reason that kids make fun of others is because of social differences and because they themselves do not want to be picked on, so they deflect the attention onto others.

It is true that bullying is carried on with people throughout life, which is why there should be no tolerance at all for teasing. For example, I was talking with a very good friend of mine who told me that he is still haunted by memories of when children would call him a "fag" on the playground. This has affected him for a long time, and he is still fearful of admitting his homosexuality because he feels as if he is letting the bullies win and proving that they were right.

SHAPING

Summaries and responses have several possible shapes, depending on the writer's purpose and intended audience. Keep in mind, however, that in a summary/response essay or critique, *the summary and the response should be unified by the writer's overall response.* The summary and the response may be organized or drafted separately, but

---

AVOIDING PLAGIARISM

Plagiarism is knowingly and deliberately using the language, ideas, or visual materials from another person or text without acknowledging that person or source. Use the following guidelines to avoid plagiarism.

- Do not use language, ideas, or graphics from any essay, text, or visual image that you find online, in the library, or from commercial sources without acknowledging the source.
- Do not use language, ideas, or visual images from any other student's essay without acknowledging the source.

Students who deliberately plagiarize typically fail the course and face disciplinary action by the university.

Sometimes, however, students plagiarize out of carelessness or inadequately citing words, specific languages, ideas, or visual images. You can avoid this *inadvertent* plagiarism by learning how to quote accurately from your sources, how to paraphrase using your own words, and how to cite your sources accurately. In this chapter, you will learn how to quote accurately, to paraphrase without plagiarizing, and to use author tags to indicate your sources. In addition, Chapter 6, "Investigating," and Chapter 12, "Writing a Research Paper," have examples illustrating how to do in-text citation and how to do a Works Cited page.

The best way to avoid inadvertent plagiarism is to ask your instructor how to document a source you are using. Your instructor will help you with conventions of direct quotation, paraphrasing, and in-text reference or citation.

they are still parts of one essay, focused on the writer's most important or overall response.

SUMMARY SHAPING

Summaries should convey the main ideas, the essential argument, or the key features of a text. The purpose should be to represent the author's/text's ideas as accurately and as faithfully as possible. Summaries rely on description, paraphrase, and direct quotation. Below are definitions and examples for each of these terms.

DESCRIPTION   The summary should *describe* the main features of an essay, including the author and title, the context or place of publication of the essay (if appropriate), the essay's thesis or main argument, and any key text features, such as sections, chapters, or important graphic material.

> In the article "Teaching Tolerance in America," Dudley Erskine Devlin reports some disturbing issues concerning America's high schools. Devlin states that intimidation, through dress, social cliques, gender, and race, is causing tension and danger in high schools today. According to Devlin, sexual harassment is allowed and condoned, and that in some cases jocks bully geeks and racial and social groups intimidate one another. As a solution, Devlin suggests that schools enforce strict, zero-tolerance dress codes, segregate the sexes in classes, increase security through surveillance cameras and drug-sniffing dogs, and require students to wear photo IDs.

PARAPHRASE   A paraphrase restates a passage or text in different words. The purpose of a paraphrase is to recast the author's/text's words in your own language. A good paraphrase retains the original meaning without plagiarizing from the original text.

> **Original:** High school cliques, which reproduce the class divisions found in society, originate from three distinct sources: racial differences, gender differences, and social differences.
>
> **Paraphrase:** Peer groups in high school mirror society's class distinctions, which stem from differences in race, gender, and social status.
>
> **Plagiarism:** Peer groups in high school *reproduce the class divisions found in society* and come *from three distinct sources: race, gender, and social differences.* [This is plagiarism because the writer uses exact phrases (see italics) from the original without using quotation marks.]

DIRECT QUOTATION   Often, summaries directly quote a few key phrases or sentences from the source. *Remember: Any words or phrases within the quotation marks must be accurate, word-for-word transcriptions of the original.* Guidelines for direct quotation and examples are as follows. Use direct quotations sparingly to convey the key points in the essay:

> Devlin focuses on what he believes is the school system's largest problem today, the issue of "helping students appreciate and welcome differences in culture, racial heritage, and personal identity."

Use direct quotations when the author's phrasing is more memorable, more concise, or more accurate than your paraphrase might be:

> Devlin claims that teenagers "still bring the social and racial divisions found in society at large back into the halls of high schools across America."

Use direct quotations for key words or phrases that indicate the author's attitude, tone, or stance:

> According to Devlin, we should "eliminate those liberal solutions that simply aren't working" in order to fund his solutions.

Don't quote long sentences. Condense the original sentence to the most important phrases. Use just a short phrase from a sentence or use an ellipsis (three spaced periods . . .) to indicate words that you have omitted.

> **Original:** Although educational reform in America tends to focus on curriculum issues, class sizes, and security issues, one lesson seems increasingly hard to teach—helping students appreciate and welcome differences in culture, racial heritage, and personal identity.

> **Condensed Quotation:** Educational reform, according to Devlin, should focus less on curriculum issues and class sizes and more on helping students "appreciate . . . differences in culture, racial heritage, and personal identity."

SAMPLE SUMMARIES

Following are summaries of Devlin's essay written by two different readers. Notice that while both convey the main ideas of the essay by using description, paraphrase, and direct quotation, they are not identical. Check each summary to see how well it meets these guidelines:

- Cite the author and title of the text.
- Indicate the main ideas of the text.
- Use direct quotation of key words, phrases, or sentences.
- Include author tags.
- Do not summarize most examples or data.
- Be as accurate, fair, and objective as possible.

Summary 1

Dudley Erskine Devlin's essay "Teaching Tolerance in America" addresses several hot topics concerning the American public school system. Devlin focuses on what he believes is the school system's largest problem today, the issue of "helping students appreciate and welcome differences in culture, racial heritage, and personal identity." According to Devlin, the root of the problem lies within the social clique, particularly the social cliques found inside the halls of your local high school. According to Devlin, these cliques originate from three different sources: social, racial, and gender differences. Devlin suggests that we solve the problems these cliques create by eliminating "those liberal solutions that simply aren't working—thus releasing funds for more effective deterrents." Devlin's solutions to eradicate the intolerance are to impose dress codes or uniforms, to create single-sex classrooms, and to markedly increase security at every high school.

Summary 2

The idea of social reform in education has been a pressing issue given the increase in youth violence in high schools across America. In Dudley Erskine Devlin's article "Teaching Tolerance in America," he outlines some of the problems in schools caused by members of cliques and bullies who feed on the "racial differences, gender differences, and social differences" found in society at large. Devlin's argument then moves on to attack the "liberal solutions" (such as introducing diversity issues in classes) and proposes to replace them with "more effective deterrents" such as instituting single-sex classes, school uniforms, picture IDs, and heightened security measures. This zero-tolerance policy, Devlin believes, will teach students how to accept diversity and "appreciate and welcome differences in culture, racial heritage, and personal identity."

RESPONSE SHAPING

Strategies for organizing a response depend on the purpose of the response. Typically, responses include one or more of the following three purposes:

- Analyzing the effectiveness of the text.
- Agreeing and/or disagreeing with the ideas in the text.
- Interpreting and reflecting on the text.

As the following explanations illustrate, each of these types of responses requires supporting evidence from the text, from other texts, and/or from the writer's own experience.

ANALYZING   Analysis requires dividing a whole into its parts in order to better understand the whole. In order to analyze a text for its effectiveness, start by examining key parts or features of the text, such as the purpose, the intended audience, the thesis and main ideas, the organization and evidence, and the language and style. Notice how the following paragraph analyzes Devlin's illogical argument.

> Devlin's essay has some clear problems with the logic of his argument. The title of his essay is "Teaching Tolerance in America," but his solutions contradict his stated purpose. Devlin's proposal to tighten security in our high schools is not going to teach tolerance in high schools across America. As a teenager in a post-Columbine era, I can tell you that ID card checks, patrolling security officers, and hall monitors do not create an atmosphere conducive to teaching tolerance. Students who are treated like prisoners in a maximum security ward do not feel increased warm wishes to faculty and administrators nor are they more likely to tolerate differences in their classmates. Being watched like a hawk by a hall monitor does nothing to make a person more socially outgoing or more tolerant of difference. These security measures will increase fear during the school hours and not encourage tolerance once students leave the school grounds. In short, Devlin's solutions do not, in fact, solve the problems with tolerance created by racial, gender, or social differences.

AGREEING/DISAGREEING   Often, a response to a text focuses on agreeing and/or disagreeing with its major ideas. Responses may agree completely, disagree completely, or agree with some points but disagree with others. Responses that agree with some ideas but disagree with others are often more effective because they show that the responder sees both strengths and weaknesses in an argument. In the following paragraphs, notice how the responder agrees and disagrees and then supports each judgment with evidence.

> About Devlin's recommendation that schools can "reduce conflicts" and teach tolerance by creating single-sex classrooms, I have mixed feelings. From my own personal experience, I agree that single-sex classes can have benefits. Perhaps I am biased, but attending an all-girls high school was very beneficial for me and many of my classmates. Although I have always been a very outgoing individual, I watched many of my friends grow from timid, shy freshmen to independent, strong women. Furthermore, I was never sexually harassed by a classmate, nor did I hear of any of the kinds of harassment Devlin mentions. On the other hand, however, I must disagree with Devlin that single-sex classes are a long-term solution. In the real world, women and men constantly interact, so they need to learn how to positively interact as girls and boys in school. Students need to be comfortable and learn to work with the opposite sex in preparation for college and the workplace. Although my high school gave me academic confidence, it did not really prepare me for the diverse world I met once I went to college. Single-sex classrooms may just postpone learning about tolerance and difference rather than actually teaching it.

INTERPRETING AND REFLECTING   Many responses contain interpretations of passages that might be read from different points of view or reflections on the assumptions or implications of an idea. An interpretation says, "Here is what the text says, but let me explain what it means, what assumptions the argument carries, or what the implications might be." Here is a paragraph from an interpretive response to Devlin's essay.

> If we stop a moment and reflect on the purpose of schools, we realize that schools should be a place where learning and growth can take place. All of Devlin's solutions, however, are designed to increase security and control rather than actually teach tolerance. Perhaps Devlin has modeled his "final solution" on prisons, where students as inmates would have no rights, no privacy, no room to express either tolerance or hatred. Rather than place students in a maximum security prison, we should return to the more liberal approach of teaching tolerance and understanding—the very solution that Devlin initially rejects. While the simple method of teaching about cultural,

social, and ethnic differences does not guarantee a conflict-free school environment, it does ensure that students have the opportunity to embrace rather than just accept differences. The forced tolerance that Devlin recommends through dress codes and maximum security measures ultimately discourages students from using their schools to actively examine and freely embrace the differences among their peers.

OUTLINES FOR SUMMARY/RESPONSE ESSAYS

Three common outlines for summary/response essays are as follows. Select or modify one of these outlines to fit your audience, purpose, and kind of response. Typically, a summary/response takes the following form:

 I. Introduction to text(s)

 II. Summary of text(s)

 III. Response(s)

   A. Point 1

   B. Point 2

   C. Point 3, etc.

 IV. Conclusion

A second kind of outline focuses initially on key ideas or issues and then examines the text or texts for their contribution to these key ideas. This outline begins with the issues, then summarizes the text(s), and then moves to the reader's responses:

 I. Introduction to key issues

 II. Summary of relevant text(s)

 III. Response(s)

   A. Point 1

   B. Point 2

   C. Point 3, etc.

 IV. Conclusion

A third outline integrates the summary and the response. It begins by introducing the issue and/or the text, gives a brief overall idea of the text, but then summarizes and responds point by point.

I.   Introduction to issues and/or text(s)

II.   Summary of text's Point 1/response to Point 1

III. Summary of text's Point 2/response to Point 2

IV. Summary of text's Point 3/response to Point 3, etc.

V.   Conclusion

DRAFTING

If you have been reading actively, you have been writing throughout the reading/ writing/discussing process. At some point, however, you will gather your best ideas, have a rough direction or outline in mind, and begin writing a draft. Some writers like to have their examples and evidence ready when they begin drafting. Many writers have outlines in their heads or on paper. Perhaps you like to put your rough outline on the computer and then just expand each section as you write. Finally, most writers like to skim the text and *reread their notes* immediately before they start their drafts, just to make sure everything is fresh in their minds.

Once you start drafting, keep interruptions to a minimum. Because focus and concentration are important to good writing, try to keep writing as long as possible. If you come to a spot where you need an example that you don't have at your fingertips, just put in parentheses—(put the example about cosmetics and animal abuse here)—and keep on writing. Concentrate on making all your separate responses add up to a focused, overall response.

REVISING

Revision means, literally, *reseeing.* Revising requires rereading the text and rewriting your summary and response. While revision begins as you read and reread the text, it continues until—and sometimes after—you turn in a paper or send it to its intended audience.

A major step in your revision is receiving responses from peer readers and deciding on a revision plan, based on the feedback. Use the following guidelines as you read your peers' papers and respond to their advice.

Guidelines for Revision

- **Review the purpose and audience for your assignment.** Is your draft addressed to the appropriate audience? Does it fulfill its intended purpose?

PEER RESPONSE

The instructions below will help you give and receive constructive advice about the rough draft of your summary/response essay. You may use these guidelines for an in-class workshop, a take-home review, or a computer e-mail response.

Writer: Before you exchange drafts with another reader, write out the following information about your own rough draft:

1. On your draft, *label* the parts that are summary and the parts that are your own response.
2. *Underline* the sentence(s) that signal to the reader that you are shifting from objective summary to personal response.
3. Indicate your purpose, intended audience, and any special genre features such as graphs or images.
4. Explain *one or two problems* that you are having with this draft that you want your reader to comment on.

Reader: Without making any comments, read the *entire* draft from start to finish. As you *reread* the draft, answer the following questions.

1. Review the guidelines for writing summaries. Has the writer remained *objective* in his or her summary? Does the summary *omit* any key ideas? Does the writer use *author tags* frequently and accurately? Can you clearly understand the main ideas of the article? Is the summary written in language appropriate for the intended audience? Do any added images or graphic material support the writer's purpose?
2. Review the guidelines for writing responses. What type(s) of response is the writer using? In the margin, label the types. What kinds of evidence does the writer use in support of his or her response? In the margin, label the kinds of supporting evidence. Is this response addressed appropriately to the audience?
3. In your own words, state the main idea or the focus that organizes the writer's response.
4. Write out your own reactions to the writer's response. Where do you disagree with the writer's analysis or interpretation? Explain.
5. Answer the writer's questions in number 4, above.

- **Reconsider the genre you selected.** Is the genre you selected (essay, letter, letter to the editor) still working for your audience and purpose? Are there multigenre elements you could add to make your summary and response more effective?

- **Continue to use your active reading/writing/discussing activities as you revise your draft.** If you are uncertain about parts of your summary or response, reread the text, check your notes, or discuss your draft with a classmate.

- **Reread your summary for key features.** Make sure your summary indicates author and title, cites main ideas, uses an occasional direct quotation, and includes author tags. Check your summary for accuracy and objectivity.

- **Check paraphrases and direct quotations.** If you are paraphrasing (without quotation marks), you should put the author's ideas into your own language. If you are quoting directly, make sure the words within the quotation marks are accurate, word-for-word transcriptions.

- **Review the purpose of your response.** Are you analyzing, agreeing/disagreeing, interpreting, or some combination of all three? Do your types of responses fit the assignment or address your intended audience and satisfy your purpose?

- **Amplify your supporting evidence.** Summary/response drafts often need additional, relevant evidence. Be sure you use sufficient personal experience, evidence from the text, or examples from other texts to support your response.

- **Focus on a clear, overall response.** Your responses should all add up to a focused, overall reaction. Delete or revise any passages that do not maintain your focus.

- **Revise sentences to improve clarity, conciseness, emphasis, and variety.** (See Handbook.)

- **Edit your final version.** Use the spell check on your computer. Have a friend help proofread. Check the Handbook for suspected problems in usage, grammar, and punctuation.

POSTSCRIPT ON THE WRITING PROCESS

1. As you finish your essay, what questions do you still have about how to summarize? What questions do you have about writing a good response?

2. Which paragraphs in your response contain your most effective supporting evidence? What kinds of evidence (analysis of the text, evidence from other texts, or personal experience) did you use?

3. What sentences in your response contain your overall reaction to the text?

4. If you had one more day to work on your essay, what would you change? Why?

5. Review the guidelines for critical reading at the beginning of this chapter. Which of those strategies was most successful for you? What did you learn about active, critical reading that you applied to the writing of your response? Cite one passage that illustrates what you learned about critical reading.

STUDENT WRITING

LETTER TO MARGARET ATWOOD

Dean C. Swift

After reading Margaret Atwood's "Letter to America," which is reprinted earlier in this chapter, Dean Swift decided to write a letter of response to Ms. Atwood. In his letter, he focuses particularly on Ms. Atwood's rosy picture of America's past and her claim that America is no longer a "city on a hill," but instead a country where a war with Iraq, problems with erosion of constitutional rights, and looming economic problems have threatened America's standing in the world. In his letter of response, Swift argues that the America in the past faced significant problems with civil rights, with assassinations of our great leaders, and with a severe economic depression. Before you read Swift's response, however, be sure to read Atwood's letter and form your own opinion.

1763 Fox Wood Ct.
Rockford, IL 61106
March 11, 2004

Ms. Margaret Atwood
C/o Editors, The Nation
33 Irving Place
New York, New York 10003

Dear Ms. Atwood:

I am writing in response to your "Letter to America." Although I do   *1*
not agree totally with everything you say in the letter, I do agree that

you can get a much better sense of your country through the eyes of another. There are many things we do not see or realize as Americans until we look at America from the outside. We get tunnel vision. Yet when reading your letter and hearing your description of the America you "once knew," I believe you also have tunnel vision. Throughout the letter you seem to compare the negative things about America today to all the positive things of the past. You fail to mention any negative aspects of America during those days. Maybe you should take a look at someone else's view on America today versus America in the past.

You started your letter by relating the America you once knew to its popular culture. For one thing, I don't really think that is an appropriate subject on which to judge a country. There are more important aspects to our history than what the hit movies and songs were. But on that subject, of course it has changed—that was fifty years ago! You can't expect all the music and books to be the same; we are a completely different generation. Now we have our Dave Mathews Band and our Jennifer Lopez—we go to the movies to see *Lord of the Rings*. What is wrong with that? You've drawn us a picture that the America you once knew was flawless. Why don't you try to tell that to the African Americans living in this country back at that time? Would they really believe that America was so much better back then? I'll guarantee that if you were to ask Rosa Parks today whether America has changed for the better or worse, she would go on for hours on how great this country has become. African Americans have been used as slaves, abused, discriminated against, and even tortured to death for hundreds of years until the later 1950s and '60s. Violent race riots and disturbing demonstrations took place during the Civil Rights Movement. Didn't it bother you that women didn't have equal rights until 1964? How was that such a perfect country when people were being discriminated against and in some cases beaten, simply because of their race or gender?

Our economy now and the debt we have gotten ourselves into is frustrating to everyone, but what about the economy in the past? Were there no problems with it in the 1930s during the Great Depression? I understand that you feel there are many corrupt things in our country today, but it is no more corrupt than it was in the past. Our country has been going to war as far back as our history dates. What about all the assassinations that took place back then? Your generation lost some great people. Throughout America's history, these tragedies have taken place: the assassination of President Lincoln and President Kennedy, Martin Luther King, Jr., Senator Robert Kennedy—yet these disturbing events don't seem to have left an impression on you.

On the subject of gutting the constitution, it's hard to draw a clear line as to where I stand on that issue. On the one hand, according to our amendments, it is wrong for the government to be able to do such things as tap phone lines, enter a home without a warrant, and incarcerate suspects without cause. These are our rights as Americans. But is this invasion of our privacy really wrong? Why should this bother us unless we are on the guilty side or under suspicion of a crime? I know I don't have anything to hide myself. Although everyone in the U.S. should be entitled to certain privacy rights, isn't it in our best interest—for safety purposes—to go sacrifice some rights in order to gain better knowledge and leads on subjects such as terrorism, gang violence, drug deals, and other serious matters? From my point of view, I believe that the Patriot Act is good for our country, and for our own safety. If you have nothing to hide, then why worry—if you are guilty or have information on something serious, then it should be in our best interest to apprehend the suspects or information by any means possible.

4

You say that our "city upon a hill" is slipping to the slums, but I say you are far from the truth. Though we have fallen in some ways, we have also risen in many. Look at all the technological and medical advances we have made. Our efforts to improve equal rights among all people have clearly improved since your time. We are still a great country. To be sure, there are flaws along the way, but that doesn't change for any country, at any time in history. I felt you were a little narrow minded in your judgment about how America has changed since the time period you grew up in. From generation to generation, people will always have different views on other time periods. I think you should try to open your mind and see that there were many flaws in your time also, and that although there are still many today, we have changed many things for the better. America is still that city upon a hill.

5

Sincerely,

Dean C. Swift

QUESTIONS FOR WRITING AND DISCUSSION

1. Reread Margaret Atwood's "Letter to America" reprinted earlier in this chapter. Write your own summary of her main ideas. Then reread Dean Swift's essay. Which of her points or arguments does he mention and respond to? Which ones does he ignore? Would he have a more effective letter if he responded to all of her points? Why or why not?

2. Dean Swift chose to use the genre of a letter to respond to Atwood's own letter. How are the stylistic conventions of a letter different from the conventions of an academic essay? How would Swift's response be different if he were writing a letter to the editor of *The Nation?* Does Swift use the more informal conventions of a letter to make his point in a more effective or personal way? Explain.

3. Responses typically analyze the logic and presentation of the argument, agree or disagree with the main ideas, and/or offer an interpretation or an examination of assumptions and implications behind an argument. Which of these does Swift do most effectively? Where could he add more supporting analysis, evidence, or interpretation? Should he use more of his own personal experience? Explain, referring to specific paragraphs in his essay.

STUDENT WRITING

TWO RESPONSES TO DEBORAH TANNEN

Jennifer Koester and Sonja H. Browe

The two essays reprinted here were written in response to an essay by Deborah Tannen, "How Male and Female Students Use Language Differently," which appears in Chapter 7. Jennifer Koester and Sonja H. Browe have opposite responses to Tannen's essay. Jennifer Koester, a political science major at Colorado State University, argues that Tannen's essay is effective because she uses sufficient evidence and organizes her essay clearly. On the other hand, Sonja Browe, an English education major at the University of Wyoming, writes an essay that is critical of Deborah Tannen's focus and supporting evidence. Be sure to read Tannen's essay and decide for yourself before you read the following essays.

A RESPONSE
TO DEBORAH TANNEN'S ESSAY
Jennifer Koester

Deborah Tannen's "How Male and Female Students Use Language Differently" addresses how male and female conversational styles influence classroom discussions. Tannen asserts that women speak less than men in class because often the structure of discussion is more "congenial" to men's style of conversing.

Tannen looks at three differences between the sexes that shape classroom interaction: classroom setting, debate format, and contrasting attitudes toward classroom discussion. First, Tannen says that during childhood, men "are expected to seize center stage: by exhibiting their skill, displaying their knowledge, and challenging and resisting challenge." Thus, as adults, men are more comfortable than women when speaking in front of a large group of strangers. On the other hand, women are more comfortable in small groups.

Second, men are more comfortable with the debate format. Tannen asserts that many classrooms use the format of putting forth ideas followed by "argument and challenge." This too coincides with men's conversational experiences. However, Tannen asserts that women tend to "resist discussion they perceive as hostile."

Third, men feel it is their duty to think of things to say and to voice them. On the other hand, women often regulate their participation and hold back to avoid dominating discussion.

Tannen concludes that educators can no longer use just one format to facilitate classroom discussion. Tannen sees small groups as necessary for any "non-seminar" class along with discussion of differing styles of participation as solutions to the participation gap between the sexes.

Three things work together to make Deborah Tannen's essay "How Male and Female Students Use Language Differently" effective: the qualifications of her argument, the evidence used, and the parallel format of comparison/contrast.

First, Tannen's efforts to qualify her argument prevent her from committing logical errors. In the first paragraphs of her essay, she states, "This is not to say that all men talk in class, nor that no women do. It is simply that a greater percentage of discussion time is taken by men's voices." By acknowledging exceptions to her claim, Tannen avoids the mistake of oversimplification. She also strengthens her argument because this qualification tells the reader that she is aware of the complexity of this issue. *7*

Later, Tannen uses another qualification. She says, "No one's conversational style is absolute; everyone's style changes in response to the context and others' styles." Not only does this qualification avoid a logical fallacy, but it also strengthens Tannen's argument that classroom discussion must have several formats. By acknowledging that patterns of participation can change with the setting, Tannen avoids oversimplifying the issue and adds to her argument for classroom variety. *8*

Second, Tannen's evidence places a convincing argument before her reader. In the beginning of her essay, Tannen states that a greater percentage of discussion time in class is taken by men and that those women who attend single-sex schools tend to do better later in life. These two pieces of evidence present the reader with Tannen's jumping-off point. These statistics are what Tannen wants to change. *9*

In addition, Tannen effectively uses anecdotal evidence. She presents the reader with stories from her colleagues and her own research. These stories are taken from the classroom, a place which her audience, as educators, are familiar with. Her anecdotal evidence is persuasive because it appeals to the common sense and personal experiences of the audience. While some might question the lack of hard statistics throughout the essay, the anecdotal evidence serves Tannen best because it reminds her audience of educators of their own experiences. When she reminds the audience of their experiences, she is able to make them see her logic. *10*

Third, the parallel format of comparison/contrast between the genders highlights for the reader Tannen's main points. Each time Tannen mentions the reactions of one gender, she follows with the reaction of the other gender. For example, Tannen states, "So one reason men speak in class more than women is that many of them find the 'public' classroom setting more conducive to speaking, whereas most women are more comfortable speaking in private to a small group of people they know well." Here, Tannen places the tendencies of men and of women together, thus preventing the reader from having to constantly refer back to another section of the essay. *11*

In an earlier example, Tannen discusses men's comfort with the debate   *12*
format in class discussion. The majority of that paragraph relates why men
feel comfortable with that format. After explaining this idea, Tannen then
tells the reader how women feel about the debate structure. Because how
men and women feel about the debate format is placed within a paragraph,
the readers easily see the difference between the genders. Tannen's use of
the parallel format in the above examples and the rest of the essay provides
a clear explanation of the differences in men's and women's interactions in
the classroom.

Tannen writes her essay effectively. She makes the essay convincing by   *13*
qualifying her claims about gender participation. This strengthens her argument that just as the classroom is diverse, so should the format be diverse.
Her supporting evidence is convincing because it comes from Tannen's own
experience, reminds the audience of its own experiences, and appeals to the
audience's common sense. Finally, her parallel format for discussing the
differences between men and women enhances the reader's understanding.
Overall, Tannen's essay is effective because she qualifies her argument, uses
convincing evidence, and makes clear how men and women use language
differently through a parallel comparison/contrast format.

IS DEBORAH TANNEN
CONVINCING?

Sonja H. Browe

In her article entitled "How Male and Female Students Use Language Dif-   *1*
ferently," Deborah Tannen explores the issue of gender as it affects the way
we use language to communicate. Specifically, she discusses how differences in the way males and females are socialized to use language affect
their classroom interactions. She explains that as females are growing up,
they learn to use language to talk to friends, and to tell secrets. She states
that for females, it is the "telling of secrets, the fact and the way they talk
to each other, that makes them best friends." Boys, on the other hand, are
"expected to use language to seize center stage: by exhibiting their skill,
displaying their knowledge, and challenging and resisting challenge."

According to Tannen, these differences make classroom language use   *2*
more conducive to the way males were taught to use language. Tannen suggests that speaking in front of groups and the debatelike formats used in
many classrooms are more easily handled by male students.

Finally, Tannen describes an experiment she conducted in her own 3 classroom which allowed students to evaluate their own conversation transcripts. From this experience, she deduced that small-group interaction is essential in the classroom because it gives students who don't participate in whole-class settings the opportunity for conversation and interaction.

Though Tannen's research is a worthwhile consideration and provides 4 information which could be of great interest to educators, this particular article lacks credibility and is unfocused. The points she is trying to make get lost in a world of unsupported assertions, and she strays from her main focus, leaving the reader hanging and confused.

Tannen does take some time at the beginning of her article to establish 5 her authority on linguistic analysis, but we may still hold her accountable for supporting her assertions with evidence. However, Tannen makes sweeping declarations throughout the essay, expecting the reader to simply accept them as fact. For example, when discussing the practice of the teacher playing devil's advocate and debating with the students, she states that "many, if not most women would shrink from such a challenge, experiencing it as public humiliation." Following such an assertion, we expect to see some evidence. Whom did Tannen talk to? What did they say? What percentage of women felt this way? This sort of evidence is completely lacking, so that what Tannen states as fact appears more like conjecture.

Tannen makes another such unsupported pronouncement when she 6 discusses the debatelike formats used in many classrooms. She explains that this type of classroom interaction is in opposition to the way that females, in contrast to males, approach learning. She states that "it is not that females don't fight, but that they don't fight for fun. They don't ritualize opposition." Again, where is Tannen's evidence to support such a claim?

When Tannen does bother to support her assertions, her evidence is 7 trite and unconvincing. For example, she reviews Walter Ong's work on the pursuit of knowledge, in which he suggested that "ritual opposition . . . is fundamental to the way males approach almost any activity." Tannen supports this claim of Ong's in parentheses, saying, "Consider, for example, the little boy who shows he likes a little girl by pulling her braids and shoving her." This statement may serve as an example but is not enough to convince the reader that ritual opposition is fundamental to the way males approach "almost any activity."

Other evidence which Tannen uses to support her declarations comes 8 in the form of conversations she has had with colleagues on these issues.

Again, though these may provide examples, they do not represent a broad enough database to support her claims.

Finally, Tannen takes three pages of her article to describe in detail an experiment she conducted in her classroom. Though the information she collected from this experiment was interesting, it strayed from the main point of the essay. Originally, Tannen's article was directed specifically at gender differences in communication. In this classroom activity, she looked at language-use differences in general, including cultural differences. She states that some people may be more comfortable in classes where you are expected to raise your hand to speak, while others prefer to be able to talk freely. She makes no mention of gender in regard to this issue.

Finally, at the close of her essay, where we can expect to get the thrust of her argument or at least some sort of summary statement which ties into her main thesis, Tannen states that her experience in her classroom convinced her that "small-group interaction should be a part of any classroom" and that "having students become observers of their own interaction is a crucial part of their education." Again, these are interesting points, but they stray quite a bit from the original intention of the article.

In this article, Tannen discusses important issues of which those of us who will be interacting with students in the classroom should be aware. However, her article loses a great deal of its impact because she does not stay focused on her original thesis and fails to support her ideas with convincing evidence.

QUESTIONS FOR WRITING AND DISCUSSION

1. Do your own double-entry log for Tannen's essay (see Chapter 7). On the left-hand side of a piece of paper, record Tannen's main points. On the right-hand side, write your own questions and reactions. Compare your notes to Koester's and Browe's responses. Whose response most closely matches your own? Where or how does your response differ from each?

2. Review the critical reading strategies at the beginning of this chapter (see page 173). Identify specific places in both Koester's and Browe's essays where they analyze elements of the rhetorical situation—such as purpose, audience, or context. Where do they analyze the effectiveness of the organization, use

of evidence, or the style? Based on your analyses of both essays, which writer does a better job of critically reading Tannen's essay? Explain your choice.

3. Responses to texts may analyze the effectiveness of the text, agree or disagree with the ideas in the text, and/or interpret or reflect on the text. What kinds of responses do Koester and Browe give? Would a different kind of response work better for either writer? Why or why not?

4. Koester focuses on three writing strategies that Tannen uses to make her essay more effective. What are they? What weaknesses of Tannen's essay does Koester ignore or downplay?

5. Browe's response focuses on two criticisms of Tannen's essay. What are they? In which paragraphs does Browe develop each criticism? What strengths of Tannen's essay does Browe ignore or downplay?

6. Neither Browe nor Koester uses personal experience as supporting evidence. Think of one experience that you have had in a specific class illustrating the conversational preferences of men and women. Write out that specific example. Could either Browe or Koester use such a specific example. Could either Browe or Koester use such a specific example? Where might each writer use it in her response?

7. Reread the essays by Tannen, Koester, and Browe. Review your reactions with your classmates. Then write your own summary and response. In your response, mention both the strengths and the weaknesses of Tannen's article. Then indicate whether or not you found Tannen's essay, in general, thought-provoking or convincing.

At the time of this painting, scientific discoveries in mathematics, navigation, and astronomy in Europe were laying the groundwork for modern science. The globe at which the astronomer gazes was modeled on one made by Jococus Hondius in 1600. Vermeer himself is credited with using a *camera obscura,* a precursor of the modern camera, to help generate the optical effects of his paintings. As a possible topic for investigation, the journal entry on page 242 invites you to compare this painting with recent images from the NASA Web site.

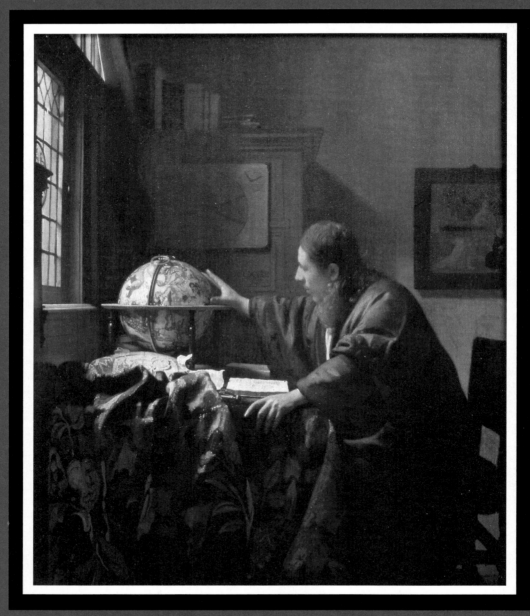

Jan Vermeer Van Delft, (1632-1675)
The Astronomer (1668)
Oil on canvas, 31.5 x 45.5 cm
Louvre, Department des Peintures, Paris, France
Photograph © Erich Lessing, Art Resource, NY

6 Investigating

While watching joggers running in the park one day, you notice their straining muscles, their labored breathing, and the grimaces etched on their faces. Why, you wonder, do people go through the pain of running? Does it have a physical or a psychological benefit? Or can it even become an addiction for those people who *have* to run every day? You decide to investigate this question in runners' magazines and professional journals and then interview a few serious runners to determine their motives and the effects that running has on them, both physically and psychologically. The results of your report, you hope, will prove interesting to those who run as well as to those who merely watch others run.

Your boss at the local self-service gas station wants to expand the station's range of convenience items. Currently, you sell only snacks, such as soda pop, candy, and ice cream. Your boss asks you to find out what is sold at other gas station convenience stores. Next, she wants you to design a survey for your customers, asking which items they would like to have the station carry. After tabulating questionnaires from thirty-five customers, you write a short report for the boss outlining what the competition stocks, how you designed your questionnaire, and what the responses from your customers indicate.

When you stop learning, stop listening, stop looking and asking questions, always new questions, then it is time to die.
—LILLIAN SMITH, CIVIL RIGHTS ACTIVIST, JOURNALIST, AUTHOR OF <u>KILLERS OF THE DREAM</u>

As the free press develops, the paramount point is whether the journalist, like the scientist or scholar, puts truth in the first place or in the second.
—WALTER LIPPMANN, JOURNALIST AND AUTHOR

INVESTIGATING BEGINS WITH QUESTIONS. WHAT CAUSES THE GREENHOUSE EFFECT? WHEN WILL THE WORLD BEGIN TO RUN OUT OF OIL? HOW DOES ILLITERACY AFFECT A PERSON'S LIFE? HOW WAS THE WORLD WIDE WEB created? How does rape affect the lives of women in America? How do colleges recruit applicants? What can you find out about a famous person's personality, background, and achievements? At what age do children first acquire simple mathematical abilities? Why are sunsets yellow, then orange, red, and finally purple?

Investigating also carries an assumption that probing for answers to such questions—by observing and remembering, researching sources, interviewing key people, or conducting surveys—will uncover truths not generally known or accepted. As you dig for information, you learn *who, what, where,* and *when.* You may even learn *how* and *why.*

The purpose of investigating is to uncover or discover facts, opinions, information, and reactions and then to report that information to other people who want to know. Although no writing is ever free from cultural or personal bias, a report strives to be as neutral and objective as possible. It may summarize other people's judgments, but it does not consciously editorialize. It may represent opposing viewpoints or arguments, but it does not argue for one side or the other. A report attempts to be a window on the world, allowing readers to see the information for themselves.

> *Curiosity is my natural state and has led me headlong into every worthwhile experience . . . I have ever had.*
> —ALICE WALKER,
> AUTHOR OF
> THE COLOR PURPLE

Techniques for Investigative Writing

Investigative writing begins with asking questions and finding informed sources: published material, knowledgeable people, or both. In most cases, collecting information in an investigation requires the ability to use a library and then to summarize, paraphrase, and quote key ideas accurately from other people's writing. In addition, personal interviews are often helpful or necessary. For an investigation, you might talk to an expert or an authority, an eyewitness or participant in an event, or even the subject of a personality profile. Finally, you may wish to survey the general public to determine opinions, trends, or reactions. Once you have collected your information, you must then present your findings in a written form suitable for your audience, with clear references in the text to your sources of information.

Investigative writing uses the following techniques:

- **Beginning with an interesting title and a catchy lead sentence or paragraph.** The first few sentences arouse your readers' *interest* and focus their attention on the subject.
- **Giving background information by answering relevant who, what, when, where, and why questions.** Answering the *reporter's "Wh" questions* ensures that readers have sufficient information to understand your report.
- **Stating the main idea, question, or focus of the investigation.** The purpose of a report is to convey information as *clearly* as possible. Readers shouldn't have to guess the main idea.
- **Summarizing or quoting information from written or oral sources; citing sources in the text.** Quote *accurately* any statistics, data, or sentences from your sources. Cite authors and titles.
- **Following appropriate genre conventions.** A news report, a profile, an interview, and an investigative report require different form and style conventions. Learn the key features of the particular genre you are working with.
- **Writing in a readable and interesting style appropriate for the intended audience.** Clear, direct, and readable language is essential in a report. Use graphs and charts as appropriate.

The following reports illustrate several types of investigative writing: the *summary* of a single book or article, the *investigation* of a controversial issue (using multiple sources), and the *profile* of a person. These types may overlap (the investigation of a controversial issue may contain a personality profile, for instance), and all three types may use summaries of written material, questionnaires, and interviews. While some investigative reports are brief, intended to be only short news items, others are full-length features.

The intended audience for each report is often determined by the publication in which the report appears: *Psychology Today* assumes that its readers are interested in personality and behavior; *Discover* magazine is for readers interested in popular science; readers of *Ms.* magazine expect coverage of contemporary issues concerning women.

SUMMARY OF A BOOK OR ARTICLE

The following report from *Psychology Today*, by journalist Jeff Meer, summarizes information taken from an article by Charlene L. Muehlenhard and Melaney A. Linton that appeared in the *Journal of Counseling Psychology*. Although the *Psychology*

Today report summarizes only that one article, it demonstrates several key features of an investigative report.

PROFESSIONAL WRITING

DATE RAPE: FAMILIAR STRANGERS

Attention-getting title

Lead-in paragraph

By now, everyone knows the scenario. Boy meets girl, they go to a party, get drunk, return to his apartment, and he forces her to have sex.   1

Focus of investigation or report

Most people assume that date rape occurs on a first or second date between relative strangers. But new research supports a different conclusion: The individuals involved generally know each other fairly well.   2

Who, what, where questions answered

Psychologist Charlene L. Muehlenhard and undergraduate Melaney A. Linton asked more than 600 college men and women about their most recent dates, as well as their worst experience with "sexual aggression"—any time a woman was forced to participate in acts, ranging from kissing to intercourse, against her will. More than three quarters of the women and more than half of the men admitted to having an experience with sexual aggression on a date, either in high school or in college. And nearly 15 percent of the women and 7 percent of the men said they had intercourse against the woman's will.   3

Summary of results

Summary of results

The researchers found that when a man initiated the date, drove to and from and paid for the date, sexual aggression was more likely. They also found that if both people got drunk (at a party, for example) and "parked," or found themselves in the man's dorm room or apartment, the date was more likely to end with the woman being forced to perform against her wishes. Men and women who thought of themselves as having traditional values and those who were more accepting of violence were also more likely to have been involved in date rape.   4

Summary of results

Quotation

But contrary to what one might expect, date rape and sexual aggression were much more likely to happen between partners who knew each other. On average, students said they had known the partner almost a year before the incident. "If women were more aware of this, they might be less surprised and more prepared to deal with sexual aggression by someone they know well," Muehlenhard says.   5

She points out that communication is often a big problem on dates during which there is sexual aggression. Both men and women reported that the man had felt "led on" during such dates. Men said that women desired more sexual contact on these dates than had others on previous dates. Women said that they had desired less sexual contact than usual.

6   *Summary*

Muehlenhard believes that a direct approach, such as a woman saying "I don't want to do anything more than kiss," might clear up confusion better than simply saying "No."

7   *Quotation*

A BRIEF REPORT WITH GRAPHICS

The following passage illustrates the genre of the brief report with graphics that was popularized by *USA Today*. Abigail Sullivan Moore's report, which appeared in the Education Life section of the *New York Times*, illustrates how a simple graphic can enhance the impact of a report.

PROFESSIONAL WRITING

GIMME AN A (I INSIST!)

Abigail Sullivan Moore

Grade inflation seems to be reaching record levels at the nation's high schools, according to a new survey of incoming freshmen at more than 400 colleges and universities. Almost half reported an A average in high school, up from 18 percent in 1968. "Something is amiss," says Linda J. Sax, who directed the survey of 276,000 students for the Higher Education Research Institute at the University of California at Los Angeles. At the same time, she says, "students are studying, but not as often as they were."

Based on conversations with educators, Dr. Sax believes that parents and pupils are pushing teachers for higher grades amid the intense competition for desirable colleges. Also, she says: "What I'm hearing is that

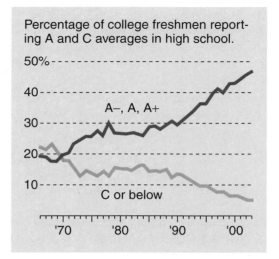

Percentage of college freshmen reporting A and C averages in high school.

teachers feel a pressure to not shatter students' self-esteem. Teachers are caught up in this web of pressure."

A study by the College Board released in January confirms the findings: high school seniors' grades have climbed but SAT scores remain nearly unchanged. Wayne J. Camara, the board's vice president for research and development, says the trend started to accelerate in the early 90's, when "more and more middle-income families had much more awareness of college, and at the same time there was more discretionary income" to pay for the expensive, hard-to-get-into institutions. He predicts a correction is due. "Everyone can't get A's," he says.

INVESTIGATION USING MULTIPLE SOURCES

Most investigative reports draw on multiple sources: books, articles, research reports, and interviews. Some interviews are conducted in person, but also interviews on the phone or via e-mail are common. The following article, "That Parent-Child Conversation Is Becoming Instant, and Online," by John Schwartz, appeared in the *New York Times* on January 3, 2004. As you read this report, first notice its genre features: short paragraphs, catchy quotations, and focus on contemporary features of instant messaging rather than an in depth, academic analysis. After you read the article, go back and reread, looking for all the sources Schwartz uses and cites. Schwartz cites over a dozen different sources—can you identify all of them and guess how he gathered his information?

PROFESSIONAL WRITING

THAT PARENT-CHILD CONVERSATION IS BECOMING INSTANT, AND ONLINE

John Schwartz

Nina Gordon types out an instant message and sends it. The data travels some 500 miles, from the computer in her living room in Queens to America Online's servers in Northern Virginia, and then to her son Schuyler's computer, which just happens to be in the next room—about 20 feet away from where she is sitting.   *1*

you hungry for dinner?

After a little online banter over dining options, her son, a 17-year-old with a wicked sense of humor and no shortage of attitude, sends his request: *2*

an insty pizza and a beer
   don't push your luck, comes the reply.

Instant messaging, long a part of teenagers' lives, is working its way into the broader fabric of the American family. The technology "has really grown up in the last 18 months," said Michael Gartenberg, vice president and research director at Jupiter Research. "It's certainly not just for kids anymore."   *3*

Almost three-quarters of all teenagers with online access use instant messaging and about half of all adults have tried the services, surveys show. Adults, who generally began using the services from AOL, Microsoft and Yahoo! to stay in touch with co-workers during the day, Mr. Gartenberg   *4* said, are saying "this stuff I'm using for work is actually useful in my personal life as well."

Use among adults has grown to include friends and far-flung family members, particularly children away at college. AOL, which provides the most popular service, reports that more than one billion instant messages each day flow through its networks.   5

And now, as families own more than one computer, the machines spread beyond the den and home networks relying on wireless connections become increasingly popular, instant messaging is taking root within the home itself.   6

Although it might seem lazy or silly to send electronic messages instead of getting out of a chair and walking into the next room, some psychologists say that the role of the technology within families can be remarkably positive. In many cases, they say, the messages are helping to break down the interpersonal barriers that often prevent open communication.   7

"Conversation between parents and teenagers could be highly emotional and not necessarily productive," said Elisheva F. Gross, a psychology researcher at the Children's Digital Media Center at the University of California at Los Angeles. When young people are online, however, "it's their turf," she said. "It may be a way for parents to communicate in a language and in a space that their children are more comfortable with."   8

Teenagers already use online communications to take on difficult topics with one another, said Katelyn McKenna, a research assistant professor in psychology at New York University. Preliminary results from a study she conducted last year, she said, suggest that "they are able to talk with one another about issues that bother them more readily online than when they are talking face to face."   9

Lissa Parsonnet said that her daughter, Dorrie, is sometimes more open to talking with her and her husband online about difficult subjects, like conflicts with friends, than in person.   10

"She talks to us as if we're people, not parents," she said.   11

Ms. Parsonnet, a psychotherapist, said that the online back channel strips away some of the parts of face-to-face communication that complicate matters: "They don't see your face turning red," she said. "They don't see you turning cross—all the things that will shut them up immediately."   12

Both instant messages and e-mail messages can help smooth things over after a fight, said Nora Gross, a 17-year-old in Manhattan who said that electronic communications had helped strengthen her relationship   13 with her father. "I can remember a few times when we've had little blowups and sent apology letters over e-mail," she said. "We're both writers, so I guess it's easier for us to put our feelings into words through text."

While even quicker than e-mail, instant messages also have the advantage of not actually being instant, Ms. Parsonnet said, because the medium at least gives the user time to compose his or her thoughts and comments before hitting the button.   *14*

"You know all the times you wish you'd counted to 10 before you said something?" she said with a laugh. With instant messages, she said, "you have a built-in counting-to-10."   *15*

For users, instant-messaging software typically displays, in a small box on the computer screen, a "buddy list" of friends who are online at any given moment. Most instant messaging conversations are one-to-one, but it also possible to include several people in a group discussion—and to carry on multiple sessions with several people at once.   *16*

Ms. Parsonnet said that the instant messaging habit began naturally with Dorrie. One night, she wanted to ask Dorrie a question, but "I didn't want to go chasing her around the house." She didn't have to wander around the family's Short Hills, N.J., home, though, because "I could hear her instant message thing bleeping."   *17*

She signed on, saw that Dorrie was indeed online, and sent a note. "It was so easy," she recalled.   *18*

That ease of use is essential for adopting any new technology, said Michael Osterman, an industry analyst who studies the instant messaging market. The concept should even seem familiar to the many baby boomers who grew up in post-World War II suburban houses with built-in home intercom systems. But families rarely used the clunky devices to talk from room to room, he noted.   *19*

Instant messaging puts a much simpler, more effective intercom system at every set of fingertips. "It's an old idea that's been made practical," he said. "Instead of yelling downstairs, 'Hey, is there any fried chicken left?' You can I.M. downstairs.'"   *20*

Using instant messages to reach out to adolescents fits into the broad structure of experimentation and adaptation that family therapists generally recommend, said A. Rae Simpson, program director for parenting education and research at the M.I.T. Center for Work, Family & Personal Life in Cambridge, Mass.   *21*

"People who are having difficulty communicating with each other write   *22*
to each other," Ms. Simpson said, similar to the way that many parents and
adolescents find they can talk more freely in the car than at home because
they are not looking directly at each other. "It takes the intensity out of the
eye-to-eye contact."

The uses of instant messages in the home can be banal, playful or pro-   *23*
found. Lily Mandlin, 15, who lives with her mother and two siblings in a
four-bedroom apartment on Manhattan's Upper West Side, said that an
instant message is sometimes the best way to get her older brother to turn
down his stereo.

"A little ping on the computer actually gets to him a lot quicker than   *24*
screaming, 'Turn the music down!'" she said.

Mr. Gartenberg, the industry analyst, said, "there has been more than   *25*
one time when I have been checking something late at night and discovered one of the kids was logged on. And I said, 'What are you doing? Go
to bed!'"

Sometimes the messages are more, well, adult. Ms. Gordon, the Queens   *26*
mother, said that when she and her husband first got laptop computers
with wireless cards, they would even send messages to each other as they
worked at home, sitting across from each other in bed.

What messages would they send back and forth when they were sit-   *27*
ting so close?

"Use your imagination," she said. "Sparks flying across the wireless net-   *28*
work, so to speak!"

Kathy Grace, a Web site designer in Austin, said that she is more   *29*
likely to send instant messages to her husband, Dennis, than to her daughter Ariel, because "we're on different systems." Ariel is on AOL; Ms.
Grace and her husband favor Microsoft Messenger, which he uses at
work.

Husband and wife will pop a message back and forth while she is work-   *30*
ing on the laptop at the dining room table and he is using the bedroom
PC, even though the house is small, Ms. Grace said. "We keep the bedroom
doors closed, and it's easier than shouting," she said.

For all the advantages many families and experts see in instant mes-   *31*
saging, some adolescents say that they simply do not want their parents on
their buddy list.

"People can be easily misunderstood online," one teenager, who asked   *32*
that her name not be used, wrote in an I.M. interview. "I am not as re-

© Randy Glasbergen. www.glasbergen.com

**"Dear Andy: How have you been?
Your mother and I are fine. We miss you.
Please sign off your computer and come
downstairs for something to eat. Love, Dad."**

served when I talk to people online than in real life, so really, it would just exacerbate whatever problem was there."

Back at the Gordon home, the chatter is often just for the fun of word- *33*
play—and that, too, can strengthen the bond between generations.

It is another night, another dinner. Takeout seafood. *34*

want another clam? Nina Gordon asks her son, eating in the next room.

i havent started the crab yet, he replies. A pun-fest ensues.

don't be crabby, she writes.

don't be coy, he replies.

never, she counters. oy, not coy.

While instant messages and e-mail may helpfully supplement face-to- *35*
face discussion, experts warn that it should not be relied on as the principal means of communication.

"The question is whether you can use it constructively, to bring it back *36*
to the face to face," said Sherry Turkle, director of the Initiative on Technology and Self at the Massachusetts Institute of Technology. If the conversation is strictly virtual, she said, "it's not so different from saying, 'I have
a wonderful epistolary relationship with my husband, who I can't stand.'"

PROFILE OF A PERSON

The following passage is a profile of a person—a biographical sketch intended to give a sense of the person's appearance, behavior, character, and accomplishments. The paragraphs are part of a profile, "Rick Steves's Not-So-Lonely Planet," by Sara Corbett, that appeared in the *New York Times Magazine*. The passage gives the first five paragraphs of the profile.

The guy is just another tourist. Or that's how it appears, anyway, to Cristina, the prim Portuguese woman holding down the front desk at the Residencia Roma, a spartan three-star hotel on a quiet side street in Lisbon. No two tourists are the same, of course, but there is something familiar, even iconic, in this man's eager-beaver smile, his unstylish windbreaker and leather walking shoes, his broken-spined guidebook to Spain and Portugal. Like most Americans, he doesn't pretend to speak anything but English. He inquires about rates—60 euros for a double—then asks to see a room. Cristina shrugs, hands the man a key and waves him toward a set of stairs leading up into the hotel's interior, unaware that she has just set a dervish loose in her establishment.

Safely beyond her gaze, Rick Steves accelerates up the stairs and rockets down a dim hallway, quickly shedding all pretense of leisure. This is what he calls a "blitz," a 10-minute undercover rampage during which he will poke mattresses and inspect toilet seats, prowling the hotel like an unleashed hound. Earlier in the day, as we ate breakfast together, Steves had spelled out his plan for seeing Lisbon. "We'll just blitz the Bairro Alto and the castle, then the restaurants," he said, spooning yogurt into his mouth at double the pace most of us think of as normal. "And after that, we'll blitz the museums." With this, he peered under the breakfast table at my feet, adding, "I hope those shoes are comfortable."

Dashing through the Residencia Roma qualifies as an unscheduled side blitz, but its small sign caught Steves's eye as he passed by on the street, and he couldn't resist taking a look. This is often how it goes with Steves, who has written 27 eponymous guidebooks to Europe, stars in a public-television travelogue series called "Rick Steves' Europe" and also runs Europe Through the Back Door, a $20-million-a-year tour business he started in his hometown of Edmonds, Wash. At the age of 49, he is a methodical, even obsessive, planner, but he remains a sucker for a worthy diversion. In many respects, this is the root of Steves's character: a fastidious mind coupled with an explorer's sense of whimsy. After 30 years of professional travel, he has built a fortune from veering off course, discovering and expertly promoting what he calls the "backdoors" to Europe—the alleyway pension, the forgotten Alpine village, the poorly lighted restaurant with the souvlaki to die for.

On camera and off, Steves comes across as a perambulating, mildly mischievous Mister Rogers, relentlessly chipper and almost painfully square, delivering feel-good messages about travel with an earnestness that could be mistaken for naïveté. "This is fun!" he bubbles when he is having fun. "Wouldya look at that?" he exclaims, happening upon a pretty view or a pigeon-covered plaza.

This enthusiasm has found a fertile audience, even in an era when many Americans have grown more afraid of traveling abroad. Last year, as the United Nations chafed at the U.S. decision to invade Iraq, as American tourists reportedly received extra-snarly treatment in France and orange alerts crawled across the bottom of the CNN screen, Rick Steves still managed to sell more than 600,000 guidebooks and sign up some 5,000 people for his company's bus tours. For the last three years, Steves' guide to Italy has outsold those from Frommer's, Fodor's and Lonely Planet; several of his foreign phrase books—which include translations like "If you don't slow this taxi down, I will throw up"—have become more popular than Berlitz.

EXTENDED INTERVIEW

Extended interviews with newsmakers, writers, and celebrities are a common genre in newspapers and magazines. The following is an interview with demographer Harold Hodgkinson, author of many books and articles, including "Educational Demographics: What Teachers Should Know," which appeared in *Educational Leadership* in 2001. Interviewing Hodgkinson is Karen Arenson, an education reporter for *The New York Times*. Arenson has written articles on education fund raising, honors programs, award-winning teachers, and illegal immigrants at CUNY. In the following interview, which appeared in *The New York Times* in August, 2001, Arenson asks Hodgkinson to explain how population trends are affecting America's colleges and universities. Hodgkinson reports that poor children are still underrepresented in colleges while the number of older, nontraditional students has continued to increase. As you read this interview, consider how Arenson directs the interview to provide information to her audience, which consists of teachers and administrators as well as immigrant and non-traditional students.

READING STATISTICAL TEA LEAVES

Harold Hodgkinson likes to say that "demography is destiny." As a demographer focused on education, he has looked at how births, ethnic backgrounds, family income and other factors shape education. He is convinced that careful scrutiny of such data can lead to better education policy. A former dean at Simmons and Bard colleges, Dr. Hodgkinson led the National Institute of Education under President Gerald R. Ford. Since 1987, he has directed the Center for Demographic Policy at the Institute for Educational Leadership in Washington.

What is the most important demographic trend affecting higher education?

The No. 1 demographic change is probably the increase in ethnic diversity in America. If you look 20 years out, 63 percent of the new population growth in the United States will be Hispanic and Asian. And virtually all of the diversity in America is concentrated in 10 states. Hispanics are now the largest minority group in the United States, and 34 percent of them live in California, 19 percent in Texas, 10 percent in New York and 7 percent in Florida. All of the other states are under 5 percent. Of the Asian population in America, nearly half live in three metropolitan areas, San Francisco, Los Angeles and New York. And 75 percent of the black population is in the Southeast and the Mississippi Delta.

What does that mean for colleges?

There is a move afoot to have every college be a mirror of the national population distribution. Given that 80 percent of kids going to college do so in their own state, looking like the country as a whole becomes a challenge in a state where minorities are 10 percent of the population. It also raises the issue of whether you should have the same proportion of minority faculty. The recruitment of minority faculty becomes a real crisis, because graduate schools are not turning out that many minority Ph.D.'s. One area where there will be a real problem is in developing new teachers. There has been a fairly pervasive decline in the number of blacks and Hispanics majoring in education—a decline of about 30 percent.

You say you like demographics because population trends are predictable. Have there been any surprises in the last 20 years?

There was only one surprise: the percentage of children living below the poverty line.

The strong economy pushed it down somewhat in recent years, but for decades the number was about 20 percent of American children. Any lessons there for colleges and universities?

For the lowest 20 percent, the amount of household income required to send children to college has increased, while their income has not increased at all. Tuition as a proportion of income has risen. But as we look at programs to help the poor, we have to remember that they are not all minorities. We tend to associate poverty mostly with minorities. But the largest number of poor children are white. Of the 14 million poor children in 1999, 8.9 million were white, 4 million were black and 3.9 million were Hispanic. But the children in poverty represented 16 percent of all white children, 37 percent of all black children and 36 percent of Hispanic children.

What are some of the other demographic trends?

People are moving much more frequently. About 43 million Americans move every year. That means people are changing jobs, and employers need to know who they are and what they can do. So they need a piece of paper—a college diploma or a certificate stating their skills. That is putting pressure on universities and colleges for those pieces of paper to mean the same thing. But there is almost no way you can guarantee that they do. It will only be a matter of time before states require tests to show what students have learned in college. But that would be terrible.

Did anyone predict there would be so many adult students?

Nobody in 1980 assumed that the number of adults going to college would be so high today. Of the 15 million students in college, almost half of them are adults with kids and jobs. The Joe College stereotype—the 18-to-22-year-old full-time student in residence on a campus—accounts for only 20 percent of the 15 million students.

Has the increase in older students run its course, or do you think it will continue?

I think it will continue. A lot of people are beginning to come back to higher education for a capstone experience in their 40's, 50's and 60's. Not for a better job, but for a vindication of their life. I was speaking at a commencement a few months ago and an older man walked across the stage to receive his doctoral degree. Someone shouted out, "Way to go, grandpa." I just love it. There is no reason to think that higher education was designed solely for the post-pubescent adolescent.

What does that mean for colleges faced with serving such students?

Older students have different needs. A whole lot of 30- and 40-year-olds have been out of education a long time. They may have a lot of innate smarts, but they don't remember the quadratic equation. So a lot of remedial education is to get 40-year-olds to remember how to write a good theme, and that is fine.

Many of the immigrants who come to the United States count on higher education to help them make it. How well does it work for them?

American higher education performs a unique function. No other country takes such a diverse group of people and turns them into the middle class. In the 1900's, it worked for Italians, Germans, French and English-speaking immigrants. Now it is working for Koreans and the Hmong. It is even working for the black population that is already here. Twenty percent of black households now have a higher income than the average for white households. That's never been true before. The mobility machine is clicking along like it should. We're very cynical, especially about our education system. But we need some appreciation for the kind of miracle we accomplish that doesn't happen in other countries—it's all due to our system of education.

So is college really available to all?

The percentage of college students who are minorities is virtually the same in every state as the percentage of high school students who are minorities. In California, for example, 54 percent of high school graduates are minorities, while 53 percent of college students are minorities. In Minnesota, 10 percent of high school graduates are minorities, while 9 percent of college students are minorities.

If you had a billion dollars to invest in education, how would you spend it?

I would spend most of it on the years before college, not on colleges. Money spent on Head Start and Trio and other precollege programs saves lots of money later on. To remediate someone at age 20 when their last 14 years were misused is really a chore. It can be done. But it is not efficient. College is really the icing on the cake.

WARMING UP: JOURNAL EXERCISES

The following exercises will help you practice investigative writing. Read all of the following exercises and then, in your journal, write on the three that interest you most. One of these exercises may suggest an idea for your investigating essay.

1. Write an "authority" list of topics about which you have some information or experience. Consider your hobbies, academic interests, job skills, community experiences, or other experience with art, music, sports, travel, films, and so forth. Jot down a few sentences about three or four possible topics. Then go to the Internet and use your favorite search engine to continue investigating these topics. When you are finished browsing, write out the key questions you could answer about each of these topics.

2. Page through the notebooks and texts from another course you are currently taking. What subjects mentioned in class or referred to in the text might you investigate? Make a list of topics for investigation that would help you in that course. During that class, jot down any other suggestions that occur to you. While the topics should not be assignments for essays already assigned in that course, they could relate to relevant background reading.

3. Next semester, you will be taking a course in your major field, but you aren't sure which professor you should pick. To investigate the differences among the teachers, interview several students who have taken this course from different professors. Prepare questions that encourage factual responses: How many papers or tests does the teacher require? What is the grade distribution? What textbook was required? What was the reading or homework load? What were typical lecture topics? Was the teacher available outside class?

4. As a member of the student governing board, your job is to solicit student opinions about some aspect of campus life that needs improving. Choose a subject such as dorms, classes, the library, parking, student clubs, the film or fine art series, or recreational opportunities. Then choose a question to focus your investigation and write a one-page questionnaire that you might distribute to students. (See the section on writing questionnaires in this chapter.)

5. Watch an investigative news show such as *60 Minutes or Nightline,* taking notes about the interviewer's techniques. Is there a sequence to the questions—say, from gentle and polite to critical or controversial? What information does the interviewer have *before* the interview? Can you tell

which questions are planned or scripted and which are spontaneous? After taking notes on a show, explain what you think are the *three* most important tips for successful interviewing.

6.   Interview a classmate for a 200- to 250-word "personality profile." Your object is to profile this person and one of his or her major interests. First, in your daybook, prepare questions you need to ask for biographical information. Then, in an eight- to ten-minute interview, ask questions about the person and about several topics from that person's "authority" list. After the interview, take two or three minutes to review your notes. At home, write up the results of your interview, which will appear in your local or campus newspaper.

7.   In early 2004, NASA landed two rovers, *Opportunity* and *Spirit,* on the surface of Mars. Below is an image from the NASA Web site. Observe the

Image available at: *http://www.dfrc.nasa.gov/Newsroom/X-Press/images/072503/EC03016606.jpg*

details of this image. Consider the rhetorical context: authoring agency, purpose, occasion, audience, composition, and cultural context. Then compare this image with the painting by Vermeer van Delft, *The Astronomer,* which appears at the beginning of this chapter. Using the Internet and your library's online databases, investigate the scientific, artistic, and/or cultural backgrounds of both of these images. What did scientists know about astronomy and our solar system when Vermeer painted his picture in 1668? What do we know—or not know—today? Use your research to start your own investigative article about some aspect of astronomy and space exploration then and now.

8. Read the following article by Elizabeth Larson, *Surfin' the Louvre.* Use her model to write your own investigating essay comparing online learning with a traditional textbook-based course. Choose a course you are taking or have recently taken, and then find and report on key Web sites that enable you to learn about your subject without going to a single class, reading a textbook, or taking an exam.

PROFESSIONAL WRITING

SURFIN' THE LOUVRE

Elizabeth Larsen

I first studied art history the old-fashioned way: scribbling notes in a dark auditorium as a parade of yellowing slides whizzed past in an overwhelming progression from ancient Greece to Andy Warhol. Four years and tens of thousands of dollars later, I had traveled from the ruins of Tikal in Guatemala to a tiny Giotto-decorated chapel in Padua to Rodin's Paris atelier without ever leaving my college's urban campus.

Today it's possible to get a similar education—minus the sometimes inspired (and sometimes not-so-inspired) comments of a professor—on the Internet. In the past few years, virtually every museum of note has established a presence on the World Wide Web. While some sites still stick to the basics (cost of admission, hours, information about the permanent collection and current exhibits), more and more institutions are following the lead of the Fine Arts Museums of San Francisco (*www.thinker.org/*

index.shtml) which is using the Web to promote its new commitment to "behave more like a resource and less like a repository." Currently the site houses over 65,000 images—from Mary Cassatt's *Woman Bathing* to more than 3,000 examples of Japanese ukiyo-e printmaking—with plans to double that number as the museum digitizes its entire collection.

That's a heck of a lot more reproductions than you'll find in that chiropractically unfriendly art history text, H. W. Janson's *History of Art.* Inspired by the sheer volume of images available on FAMSF's "Imagebase," I decided to try my hand at digitally designing my own art education.

My self-directed syllabus started in Spain at the new Guggenheim Museum in Bilbao (*www.bm30.es/guggenheim*), the recently opened critic's darling designed by maverick California architect Frank Gehry. As befits a museum where the architecture is as much a piece of art history as the works it houses, much of the site is devoted to Gehry's oddly gorgeous design, which looks like a cross between a medieval fortress and a bouquet of flowers sculpted in titanium. But there's a lot of other great stuff as well, including reproductions of the museum's most famous acquisitions—like Richard Serra's *Snake,* an appropriately jarring-yet-graceful panel of curving steel set smack dab in the middle of a gallery.

Eager to see more, I moved on to the Museums page of the World Wide Web Virtual Library (*www.comlab.ox.ac.uk/archive/other/museums .html*). A clearinghouse of links to museums, the site is most helpful for those who want to search according to the countries the museums are in. I started in Italy, which I soon discovered doesn't include that country-within-a-country, the Vatican (*www.christusrex.org/www1citta/O-Citta.html*). At the Uffizi Gallery in Florence (*www.italink.com/eng/egui/hogui.html*), I checked out a number of Renaissance heavy hitters, including Botticelli's *The Birth of Venus* and Paolo Ucello's *Battle of San Romano.* To get more of a feeling for Florentine art as it exists on the streets and in the churches of Florence, I used the Florence Art Guide to take me all over the city, from the Ponte Vecchio to the Piazzale Michelangelo.

My next stop was Paris, where my first visit was to—where else?—the Louvre (*www.mistral.culture.fr/Louvre/Louvrea.html*), where I lingered over a Watteau and a Poussin before getting absorbed in the history of the building. From there it was an easy trek to the countryside and the Giverny home page (*www.giverny.org/index.html*) to check out the gardens that inspired Monet.

From Giverny I hopped over to Greece and the Hellenic Ministry of Culture's Guide to Athens (*www.culture.gr/maps/sterea/attiki/athens.html*) where I gazed out over the Acropolis. Then I spent the rest of the afternoon in Japan at the Kyoto National Museum (*www.kyohaku.go.jp/*), where I studied up on the intricacies of Chinese and Japanese lacquerware.

I know I'm starting to sound pretty starry-eyed about my cyber-education, so I'll temper my enthusiasm with a few caveats. From the vantage point of my office chair, I obviously wasn't able to glean insights from the people standing next to me as I contemplated de Kooning's *Woman I.* But I don't require that every symphony I listen to be live, and I'm equally comfortable with the trade-offs inherent in a digital visual experience. Especially since I won't need to worry about those threatening form letters from the bursar's office.

PROFESSIONAL WRITING

PLOTTING A NET GAIN

Connie Koenenn

In this profile of sociologist and computer guru Sherry Turkle, Los Angeles Times staff writer Connie Koenenn gives her readers information on Turkle's book, Life on the Screen: Identity in the Age of the Internet, *as well as a perspectives on Turkle's private life. In writing this profile, notice how Koenenn interweaves material from interviews with Turkle, quotations and information from Turkle's book, information from a radio interview, and personal observations about Turkle's lifestyle.*

Microsoft Chairman Bill Gates looks at the Internet and sees a transformation in the way we get information. MIT sociologist Sherry Turkle looks at the Internet and sees a transformation in the way we view ourselves.   1

Despite all the hype and babble about the information super-highway, Turkle says, most people actually have underestimated the coming knowledge revolution. When we log onto a bulletin board, chat room, forum or other cyberspace sites, she says, we are entering a world of possibility. There, we can change our name, our appearance, even our sex, and test ourselves   2 in that different persona. "We can easily move through multiple identities," Turkle says, "and we can embrace—or be trapped by—cyberspace as a way of life."

This is the theme of her new book, *Life on the Screen: Identity in the Age of the Internet* (Simon & Schuster). It's based on her studies, which started 20 years ago when she noticed the way MIT students used computer language ("Let's debug this relationship") in everyday life. *3*

And although Turkle has been tracking the emerging computer culture for two decades, the exploding popularity of the Internet world has turned a new spotlight on her. *Newsweek* magazine listed her among "50 for the Future" for 1995 and *Time* dubbed her the "Margaret Mead of Silicone." *4*

"Sherry Turkle is an important thinker and very perspicacious—she was way ahead of the curve," says Constance Hale, associate managing editor of *Wired* magazine, which is excerpting Turkle's book in its January issue. "Her book is groundbreaking. Her theory—that the computer isn't a tool but that it is giving you access to parts of yourself that you didn't have before—is revolutionary." *5*

Like Gates, Turkle says we are on the brink of a revolution, now that computers inhabit life at every turn. But while Gates' new book, *The Road Ahead* (Viking), focuses on the outward shapes of the computers and software (such as a wallet PC), Turkle is more concerned with the loosening of the boundaries between people and their computers. "If you want to call this an 'information revolution,' you can," she said on a recent visit to Los Angeles. "I think it is more than that." *6*

Turkle, 47, who was wearing a trim black pantsuit and carrying an immense leather handbag, had just been a guest on Michael Jackson's CABC-AM (790) talk show. The discussion had turned to such new phenomena as "cyber-infidelity." Turkle had mentioned a wife who decided her husband's online affair was better than his looking around for real-life women. *7*

That brought up the question of what constitutes infidelity in a world where nothing is physical. "I think when you can connect via the computer, you can adopt a persona somewhat different than the one you ordinarily have," she told the radio audience. "People feel that the anonymity and distance allow them to experience different aspects of themselves." *8*

Later, she elaborates. In person, Turkle is an engaging conversationalist, jumping from thought to thought with energy and humor. "People can experience other aspects of themselves online," she says. "I have seen it happen!" *9*

She has seen how people, talking online in a low-risk setting, have slowly developed social skills or been able to discuss physical problems, such as *10* weight or disabilities, that they previously repressed. She has watched men and women gradually move from virtual online worlds into real relationships ("Rush Limbaugh met his wife on CompuServe," she says).

Turkle put six years into writing *Life on the Screen*. Despite its catchy *11* title and rich use of case studies, the heavily footnoted book, interweaving psychological and social analysis with an overview of intelligent machine development, is not light reading. "The meaning of the computer presence in people's lives is very different from what most expected in the late 1970s," Turkle writes. "One way to describe what has happened is to say we are moving from a modernist culture of calculation toward a postmodernist culture of simulation." In short, computers have moved from machines that do things for us (our tax returns or spreadsheets) to machines that do things to us, such as provide experiences that will affect our social and emotional life.

Describing e-mail as a "return to conversation over the backyard fence," *12* Turkle notes that in the Massachusetts Institute of Technology Media Lab, where she works, she can log on any morning and scroll through the staff messages. "Someone has died, someone has a baby, someone has won an award—it's like a small-town newspaper."

Now, her interest is turning to families. She recently interviewed a *13* woman whose son, just off to college, was studying for his first physics test. The woman had gotten America Online so they could keep in touch, and when she sent her first e-mail message, he replied, "Mom, you did it right!" She had insomnia and got up about 5 A.M. and, on an impulse, sent him another message. When he answered immediately, she realized he was very nervous about the test and had been studying all night. So she sent him a reassuring message that his parents will love him however he does on tests. "Here was a socially acceptable way to talk. She would never have called him at 5 in the morning, but this allows him to be in control, which is what kids that age need to be," Turkle says.

Computers were not on the agenda when Turkle graduated in 1976 *14* from Harvard with a double doctorate in sociology and personality psychology. She had spent a year in France analyzing how Freudian thought had been rejected and then accepted by the French; her first book, *Psychoanalytic Politics: Jacques Lacan & Freud's French Revolution*, has been reissued (Guilford Press, 1992).

"I thought I would have a career studying how complicated ideas come *15* into everyday life. I didn't anticipate the next set of ideas I would look at would be from computer science," Turkle says.

She was hired because MIT wanted somebody who studied the cul- *16* tural diffusion of scientific ideas. As technophobe Turkle began listening to the computer-savvy students, she realized they were using computer ideas (instead of "Freudian slip," they would say "information-processing error") to describe their lives. "It was like a 'Eureka!' experience to me," she says.

Beginning in her own backyard, Turkle organized pizza parties for stu- *17* dents playing MUDS (Multi-User Domains), the intricate online games in which participants can alter their real-life identities to improvise elaborate melodramas. She interviewed them at length about their experiences in the fantasies that grew out of the Dungeons and Dragons fantasy games of the early 1970s. She also studied children who were being introduced to computer toys. More recently, she began monitoring Internet chat and bulletin boards.

"I just kept studying people and machines," says Turkle, who has *18* steadily written articles for academic journals about the computer culture—about women and computers, physicists and computers, children and computers. Ten years ago she wrote *The Second Self: Computers and the Human Spirit* (Simon & Schuster).

Turkle estimates that she has interviewed more than 1,000 people. *19* Mitchel Resnick, a colleague at the MIT Media Lab, admires Turkle's ability to get people to open up in interviews. "She can make people feel comfortable sharing their deepest feelings," he says. "I think often they have been transformed by these [online] experiences and most people don't understand that world."

Although Turkle may meet her subjects online, she insists on inter- *20* viewing them in person, usually in her MIT office. She doesn't even have a computer there—it's reserved for seeing RL (real life) students and colleagues, she explains.

She is, however, surrounded by computers at home. Turkle is married *21* to consultant Ralph Willard, and they have a daughter, 4. Her routine in their Boston home is to wake up at 6 A.M. and devote two hours to e-mail, sitting at her Macintosh with a Powerbook nearby to receive faxes. "I have a little computer for my daughter and a palmtop I travel with. I don't watch TV and I write very few letters anymore—I spend a fair amount of time Internet-surfing."

And although she signs on daily to a huge amount of e-mail, she says *22* it is worth it. She recently heard from an old high school friend who had seen an article about her in a Boston paper. He had thought about contacting her previously, but with e-mail it was too easy to pass up, he said. She was delighted. "To me, making possible that kind of connection with your past, with people all over the world, is so precious. I am willing to bite the bullet and sort through all the e-mail."

And although she acknowledges a darker side of cyberspace (people can *23* get stuck in the selves they have created on the screen, or hurt by an online relationship that turns out to be fraudulent, she says), Turkle has great hopes for the emerging computer culture.

"Here's the good news," she says briskly. "Being online can help you de- *24* velop parts of yourself that have been underdeveloped and it can help your personal growth. Here's the bad news: Some people find themselves just acting out the same problems they have in real life in virtual life. If they've been hostile, they become the 'flamers' on the Internet, using the anonymity to act out their hangups."

She doesn't like the question, "Is cyberspace good or bad?" The point *25* is, it is, she says. "It's going to demand ongoing conversations about the new definition of work, of marriage, of sexuality, of child care, of every aspect of our lives."

She thus welcomes the fuss over pornography on the Internet as a sig- *26* nal that we are living in a very different time. "It's setting the stage for that longer-term reflection. It's important to keep in mind that we are not going to sort this out in the next two months or two years."

In your journal, write the meanings of the following words:

- *Margaret Mead* of Silicone **(4)**
- very *perspicacious* **(5)**
- *postmodernist* culture **(11)**
- cultural *diffusion* of scientific ideas **(16)**
- *technophobe* Turkle **(16)**
- *Freudian slip* **(16)**

QUESTIONS FOR WRITING AND DISCUSSION

1. Investigative essays focus on answering at least one key question. The question for Connie Koenenn's article might be "Who is Sherry Turkle and what does she think about the Internet?" Reread the article, focusing on Koenenn's answer to the second part of that question. Find at least three specific passages that reveal what Turkle finds important about the Internet.

2. Typically, profiles have certain identifying features, such as physical description, personal quotations, and informal observations as well as comments about professional achievements, articles or books written, awards received, and plans for the future. Reread Koenenn's profile, "Plotting a Net Gain," and list all the features that you find. When you finish your list, write a paragraph that describes the profile as a genre.

3. Reread Koenenn's article, looking for evidences of the sources she used in writing this essay. Next to major paragraphs, indicate the probable source of the quotations, facts, or information. Does Koenenn rely most on quotations and information from a personal interview, on information from Turkle's books, on outside biographical information, on additional third-party interviews, on transcripts of a radio interview, or on other sources? Write a list of the kinds of sources Koenenn probably used.

4. Write your own investigative profile about a person from your school, an employee at your place of work, or a member of your family. Schedule an interview to find out about this person. Use your own observations. Interview other people about their acquaintance with this person. Read anything this person may have written. Assume that your profile will appear in a local or campus newspaper.

5. Sherry Turkle continues to be interviewed about her views on how computers and the Internet are changing and—especially—how they are changing us. Use Lexis-Nexis or Electric Library to find recent full-text articles on Sherry Turkle. In one interview published in *Fortune* magazine, Turkle had the following comments: "The Internet is a place of experimentation on your identity—in positive as well as negative ways." "The more complicated computer networks get, the more people use them as models for their own minds." "It's going to create a crisis about the simulated and the real. The notion of what it is to live in a culture of simulation . . . is going to become more and more

[important]." What new information can you find about how computers are changing our identity, our culture, and our sense of what is real and what is only simulated?

PROFESSIONAL WRITING

THE END OF CHEAP OIL

Tim Appenzeller

According to this report published in National Geographic *magazine, the world will reach its peak of oil production sometime in the next decade—and from then on, world demand will exceed production. Tim Appenzeller, an editor at* U.S. News & World Report, *has written and edited articles about biology, astronomy, and physics in a variety of other publications, including* Scientific American, The Sciences, *and* Science. *In "The End of Cheap Oil," Appenzeller begins by describing his visit to a drilling platform called the* Discover Enterprise *located in the Gulf of Mexico, some 120 miles southeast of New Orleans. Although technology has created breakthroughs in drilling in the Gulf—and elsewhere in the world—the peak of oil production will likely occur in the next few years. Appenzeller describes the state of oil exploration in the North Sea of Europe, Alaska, Venezuela, Russia, and Canada before concluding with predictions from experts about the timing of the oil peak. The following article and accompanying graphic illustrations, excerpted from a thirty-page* National Geographic *spread, illustrates the key features of an investigative report.*

Below more than a mile of ocean and three more of mud and rock, the 1 prize is waiting. At the surface a massive drilling vessel called the *Discoverer Enterprise* strains to reach it. It's the spring of 2003, and for more than two months now the *Enterprise* has been holding steady over a spot 120 miles southeast of New Orleans in the Gulf of Mexico. The ship is driving a well toward an estimated one billion barrels of oil below the seafloor—the biggest oil field discovered in United States territory in three decades.

The 835-foot *Enterprise* shudders every few minutes as its thrusters 2 put out a burst of power to fight the strong current. The PA system crackles, warning of small amounts of gas bubbling from the deep Earth. And in the shadow of the 23-story-tall derrick, engineers and managers gather in worried knots. "We've got an unstable hole," laments Bill Kirton, who's overseeing the project for the oil giant BP.

The drill, suspended from the *Enterprise*'s derrick through a swimming-pool-size gap in the hull, has penetrated 17,000 feet below the sea-floor. Instead of boring straight down, it has swerved more than a mile sideways, around a massive plume of rock salt. But now, with 2,000 feet to go, progress is stalled. Water has begun seeping into the well from the surrounding rock, and the engineers are determined to stem its spread before drilling farther. Otherwise, the trickle of water could turn into an uncontrolled surge of crude. "There's a lot of oil down there wanting to come out," says Cecil Cheshier, a drilling supervisor, after struggling all night with the unruly hole. "You can cut corners and take chances—but that could cost you a lawsuit or cause a spill into the Gulf of Mexico, and then deepwater drilling gets shut down."   *3*

The troubled well is just one of 25 that BP plans to drill in the giant field, called Thunder Horse, which sprawls over 54 square miles of seafloor. The entire project, including a floating platform half again as wide as a football field that will collect the oil from individual wells and pipe it to shore starting next year, will cost four billion dollars. But if the wells live up to expectations, each will eventually gush tens of thousands of barrels a day. "That's like a well in Saudi Arabia," says Cheshier. "We hardly get those in the U.S. anymore."   *4*

You wouldn't know it from the hulking SUVs and traffic-clogged freeways of the United States, but we're in the twilight of plentiful oil. There's no global shortage yet; far from it. The world can still produce so much crude that the current price of about $30 for a 42-gallon barrel would plummet if the Organization of the Petroleum Exporting Countries (OPEC) did not limit production. This abundance of oil means, for now, that oil is cheap. In the United States, where gasoline taxes average 43 cents a gallon (instead of dollars, as in Europe and Japan), a gallon of gasoline can be cheaper than a bottle of water—making it too cheap for most people to bother conserving. While oil demand is up everywhere, the U.S. remains the king of consumers, slurping up a quarter of the world's oil—about three gallons a person every day—even though it has just 5 percent of the population.   *5*

Yet as the *Enterprise* drillers know, slaking the world's oil thirst is harder than it used to be. The old sources can't be counted on anymore. On land the lower 48 states of the U.S. are tapped out, producing less than half the oil they did at their peak in 1970. Production from the North Slope of   *6*

Alaska and the North Sea of Europe, burgeoning oil regions 20 years ago, is in decline. Unrest in Venezuela and Nigeria threatens the flow of oil. The Middle East remains the mother lode of crude, but war and instability underscore the perils of depending on that region.

7   And so oil companies are searching for new supplies and braving high costs, both human and economic. Making gambles like Thunder Horse and venturing into West Africa and Russia, they are still finding oil in quantities to gladden a Hummer owner's heart. But in the end the quest for more cheap oil will prove a losing game: Not just because oil consumption imposes severe costs on the environment, health, and taxpayers, but also because the world's oil addiction is hastening a day of reckoning.

8   Humanity's way of life is on a collision course with geology—with the stark fact that the Earth holds a finite supply of oil. The flood of crude from fields around the world will ultimately top out, then dwindle. It could be 5 years from now or 30: No one knows for sure, and geologists and economists are embroiled in debate about just when the "oil peak" will be upon us. But few doubt that it is coming. "In our lifetime," says economist Robert K. Kaufmann of Boston University, who is 46, "we will have to deal with a peak in the supply of cheap oil."

9   The peak will be a watershed moment, marking the change from an increasing supply of cheap oil to a dwindling supply of expensive oil. Some experts foresee dire consequences: shortages, price spikes, economic disruption, and a desperate push to wrest oil from "unconventional" sources such as tar sands, oil shale, or coal. Others think that by curbing our oil use and developing sustainable alternatives now, we can delay the peak and wean ourselves more easily when the inevitable happens. "There are many things you can do to ease the transition," says Alfred Cavallo, an energy consultant in Princeton, New Jersey. "And you can have a very nice life on a sustainable system. Of course, not everyone is going to be driving SUVs."

10   The stuff we pump into our gas tanks is a freak of geology, the product of a series of lucky breaks over millions of years. The first break came in a life-rich ancient sea: Sediments buried the organic material raining down onto the seafloor faster than it could decay. The next break: Eons later the seafloor sediments ended up at just the right depth—generally between 7,500 and 15,000 feet—for heat and pressure to slow-cook the organic material into oil. Then the oil collected in a "trap" of porous sandstone or limestone, and an impermeable cap of shale or salt kept it from escaping.

Any gap in this lucky chain of happenstance means a dry hole today. The   *11*
luck held often enough that the world can now feed a daily oil habit of nearly
80 million barrels. In the
U.S. about two-thirds of the
oil goes to make fuel for
cars, trucks, and planes. But
the synthetic fabrics in our
wardrobe and the plastics in
just about everything we
touch started out as oil too.
We can also thank oil and
its cousin, natural gas, for
the cheap and plentiful food
at the supermarket, grown
with the help of hydrocar-
bon-based fertilizers and
pesticides. As Daniel Yergin
writes in his oil history *The
Prize*, we live in "the Age of
Hydrocarbon Man."

"IN OUR LIFETIME," SAYS ECONOMIST ROBERT KAUFMANN, "WE WILL HAVE TO DEAL WITH A PEAK IN THE SUPPLY OF CHEAP OIL." THAT PEAK WILL BE A WATERSHED MOMENT.

Around the world Hy-
drocarbon Man is getting thirstier. In the U.S., where oil consumption is expected to grow nearly 50 percent in 20 years, carmakers are touting
horsepower as they did in the muscle-car 1960s. SUVs and minivans are dis-
placing thriftier sedans and wagons as the standard family car. Even the tax
code encourages consumption, offering people who buy the biggest SUVs
for business use a deduction of up to $100,000. Since 1988 the average gas
mileage of U.S. passenger vehicles has fallen, while the world has burned up
more than a third of a trillion barrels of irreplaceable oil.

China, too, is learning to drink deep. A decade ago the world's most   *13*
populous nation sipped oil, its streets choked with bicycles rather than motorized traffic. But last year newly prosperous professionals snapped up over
two million cars—up 70 percent over 2002. China may have already
leapfrogged Japan to become the world's second largest oil user. By 2025
China could be using ten million barrels a day, most of which will come
from outside its own borders.

That's a predicament familiar to the U.S., where the roots of oil de-   *14*
pendence deepened in the spring of 1971. Through 1970 the U.S. produced
more than two-thirds of the oil it needed. An agency called the Texas Rail-

road Commission held down oil production to avoid overwhelming the market, keeping prices stable. By that spring, though, the giant, seemingly inexhaustible fields of Texas had reached their limits. The commission announced it would allow full-throttle production, but even so imports began rising—and the Texas fields just couldn't produce any faster.

That became painfully clear two years later, when Arab leaders clamped *15* an oil embargo on the U.S. in retaliation for Washington's support of Israel in the 1973 Mideast war. Fields at home could not make up the difference. Gas lines grew and prices soared, giving most Americans their first lesson in the fragility of oil supplies.

The speed limit was dropped to 55 miles an hour to save fuel, and sales *16* of thrifty Japanese and European cars surged. The 1978 revolution in Iran cut off that country's oil exports and triggered a second oil shock. By 1981 crude oil prices had risen above $70 a barrel in today's dollars, and U.S. oil consumption had dropped by nearly 15 percent from its 1978 peak. Higher prices also spurred the development of new fields outside the Persian Gulf: on Alaska's North Slope and in Mexico and the North Sea.

The new fields increased the world's oil supply, and by the inevitable *17* logic of the market, more supply and less demand led to a price collapse. By the mid-1980s oil was selling for less than $25 a barrel in today's dollars. OPEC's grip weakened, its share of the oil on the world market falling from 55 percent to 30 percent. And even though supply disruptions in Venezuela, Nigeria, and Iraq have pushed up prices, "the stuff is still dirt cheap," says Cavallo. It's so cheap that U.S. consumption has climbed 25 percent since the mid-1980s, to its highest level ever. Imports have surged to 54 percent of the country's oil needs. And the best hope for slowing the U.S. rise in dependence on imported oil lies far out at sea.

To reach the deep waters of the Gulf of Mexico, where the tireless *18* drillers aboard the *Enterprise* are wrestling with the balky well, you board a helicopter in the coastal flatlands of Louisiana and fly south, over the small oil platforms that have colonized the green shallows of the Gulf in the past 30 to 40 years. Like the fields on the U.S. mainland, they are in their twilight, their oil production slipping year by year.

The platforms thin out and vanish by the time the ocean turns the *19* blue of deep water, an hour from shore. Soon, another platform emerges from the haze. Called Marlin, it rides the waves on stout orange pontoons, its bright gas flare streaming in the breeze. Marlin is where BP engineers first learned to tap the Gulf's deepwater riches. Discovered in 1993, the Marlin field is now in full-scale production.

THE U.S. USES MORE, PRODUCES LESS, AND RELIES ON IMPORTS

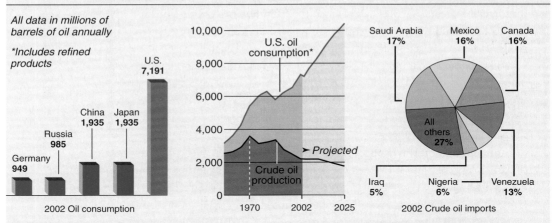

All data in millions of barrels of oil annually

*Includes refined products

U.S.
7,191

China
1,935

Japan
1,935

Russia
985

Germany
949

2002 Oil consumption

10,000

8,000

6,000

4,000

2,000

0

U.S. oil consumption*

➤ Projected

Crude oil production

1970   2002   2025

Saudi Arabia
17%

Mexico
16%

Canada
16%

All others
27%

Iraq
5%

Nigeria
6%

Venezuela
13%

2002 Crude oil imports

The gap in the U.S. between the production of crude oil and the consumption of all the products made from it has been widening steadily since the 1970s. As a result the U.S. imports crude from dozens of countries, Saudi Arabia first among them. The U.S. will likely become more dependent on Middle East supplies in the future.

CHARTS BY 5W INFOGRAPHICS: ENERGY INFORMATION ADMINISTRATION

All in all, oil experts estimate that the deep waters of the Gulf of Mexico   20
will yield more than 25 billion barrels of oil. That's twice as much as in Alaska's giant Prudhoe Bay field, and far more than in any untapped U.S. prospect, including the controversial Arctic National Wildlife Refuge. "There's a major consensus that there's more oil there than you'd ever find in ANWR," says Anderson. With the boost from deepwater wells, offshore oil should increase from a third of U.S. oil production now to more than 40 percent by 2008, before tapering off. But it will still barely ease the American thirst for oil.

In Kazakhstan, another frontier in the oil scramble, the crude itself is   21
literally corrosive. The Central Asian land east of the Caspian Sea boasts the biggest single discovery in 30 years: a vast geologic trap extending beneath the Caspian, called the Kashagan field, that could yield seven billion to thirteen billion barrels as it's developed. But it won't be easy. Its oil is under high pressure and laced with poisonous hydrogen sulfide, which requires special equipment and handling. And the field lies in the northern Caspian, a stronghold of the endangered beluga sturgeon, in waters too shallow for ordinary ships and oil platforms.

In the 1990s the first glimpse of fields like Kashagan spurred talk that   22
the Caspian might be a new Middle East, with reserves of hundreds of billions of barrels. But the promising geologic structures did not always hold

oil. More sober assessments now put the Caspian's promise at 17 billion to 33 billion barrels.

The real challenge to the Middle East's oil dominance comes from *23* elsewhere in the old Soviet Union: the boggy, cold forest of western Siberia. Once the bulwark of the Soviet oil industry, Siberia declined in the early 1990s as its wells and infrastructure fell into disrepair. Many analysts believed Siberia's oil was played out. Now it's making a comeback.

Russia passed Saudi Arabia in 2003 as the world's biggest producer. And, *24* says Matt Sagers, a Russia expert at Cambridge Energy Research Associates, "for Russia it's still up, up, and away." That's because the rough-and-tumble private companies that grabbed the Soviet fields at fire-sale prices in the early 1990s have gotten serious about modernizing them. Enlisting Western specialists, the companies resurveyed the fields with up-to-date seismic technology to determine where the oil was hiding and how best to get it out. They shut down unpromising wells and coaxed more out of others by hydraulic fracturing: driving high-pressure fluids down the wells to break up the rock and open new escape routes for the crude. "We went in and developed the fields the way ExxonMobil or ChevronTexaco would have done and are getting [production] increases of 20 percent a year," says Ray Leonard, an American oilman and a vice president of Yukos, one of Russia's two largest oil companies.

Leonard puts Russian reserves at around 100 billion barrels. Other experts *25* say the companies haven't explored enough to know. Either way, even Russia has its limits, as Leonard acknowledges. He thinks Russia's oil output will crest in 10 to 15 years, putting OPEC firmly in control of prices again. "Around the middle of the next decade, the price of oil is going to go up and stay up," he says. If it does, an unusual kind of oil that exists far from the Middle East will become more alluring.

You can get a glimpse of it just north of Fort McMurray, a former fur- *26* trading outpost in the Canadian province of Alberta. Just where the highway crosses the Athabasca River, veins of black, tarry sand streak the riverbanks. On a hot day tar sand is sticky and smells like fresh asphalt— the smell of money the locals call it. No wonder they're smug. The tar-sand deposits here and elsewhere in Alberta hold the equivalent of more than 1.6 trillion barrels of oil—an amount that may exceed the world's remaining reserves of ordinary crude. But this is no ordinary crude. In fact, it's a residue created when conventional oil escaped from its birthplace deep in the Earth's crust and was degraded into tar by groundwater and bacteria.

Most of the tar sand lies too deep or in deposits too sparse to be ex- *27* ploited. But oil-sand companies got a boost in the 1990s as technology improved and Canada cut the first few years of the royalties that companies were required to pay. The Alberta government reckons that 174 billion barrels could now be tapped economically. Last year the U.S. Department of Energy agreed and included that number in Canada's proven reserves. The move catapulted Canada to second place in the ranking of oil-rich states, right behind Saudi Arabia—and ahead of Iraq, Iran, and Kuwait.

But standing at the edge of a 200-foot-deep pit where giant electric- 28 and diesel-powered shovels devour beds of oil sand, Shell Canada Senior Vice President Neil Camarta acknowledges that there's a big difference between the oil-sand riches and free-flowing crude. "It's not like the oil in Saudi Arabia. You see all the work we have to do; it doesn't just jump out of the ground." Shell's is one of three big operations that together wring more than 600,000 barrels of oil a day from the Athabasca sands. Every step of the way takes brute force.

The sand has to be strip-mined, two tons of it for each barrel of oil. 29 Dump trucks the size of mini-mansions haul 400 tons in a single load, in beds heated during the subarctic winters so the sand doesn't freeze into a giant blob. Next to the mine, the sand goes into the equivalent of giant washing machines, where torrents of warm water and solvent rinse out the tar, or bitumen, leaving wet sand that is dumped in tailing ponds.

Even then the bitumen is not ready to be piped off to a refinery like 30 ordinary crude. To turn it back into crude oil, the operations either cook it in cokers, where temperatures of 900°F break up the giant tar molecules, or heat it to lower temperatures and churn it with hydrogen gas and a catalyst. The result is a clean, low-sulfur crude—"beautiful stuff," says Camarta.

But producing it is not so pretty, he acknowledges. "This really is a 31 big, big project," Camarta says of Shell's four-billion-dollar mine and plant, which opened last year. "It has a big footprint too, and we don't hide that— a big environmental and a big social imprint."

Unless oil prices collapse, the destruction is likely to continue. With tar- 32 sand production costs down to about ten dollars a barrel, the operations expect to make a handsome profit. Existing mines are expanding, and more companies are jumping in. Some are starting to exploit tar sands too deep to be mined, by forcing high-pressure steam down wells to melt out the bitumen. Production could reach two million barrels a day in a decade, according to the Alberta government.

That may be a comfort when the other up-and-coming oil fields of 33 today start to dwindle, from the Gulf of Mexico to Russia. But the tar sands won't be enough to stave off new dependence on the volatile Middle East.

The U.S. government's Energy Information Administration projects that in 20 years, the Persian Gulf will supply between one-half and two-thirds of the oil on the world market—the same percentage as before the 1973 embargo. Fifty years later, in other words, the Middle East will have regained all its old power over oil—and the U.S. government knows it. Whether or not Washington's war in Iraq was directly motivated by oil, American planners clearly hoped it would lay the groundwork for a stable, democratic Middle East—which, among other benefits, would in Washington's view put the world's oil supply in more trustworthy hands.

Yet the real threat to the world economy 20 years from now may not *34* be the policies of the Middle East. It may be a global shortage of conventional oil. These days a raging debate divides oil experts, with prophets of imminent shortage pitted against believers in at least a couple more decades of abundance. Pessimists note that oil prospectors had their best luck in the early 1960s, and that discoveries have slowed since then. They conclude that little conventional oil is left to be found and that the oil peak could be upon us by 2010. Optimists call that a naive extrapolation, which overlooks the economic and political factors that drive the search for oil. "People who are predicting an imminent peak are simply wrong," says Boston University's Kaufmann. The United States Geological Survey (USGS) concluded in a 2000 study that there's at least 50 percent more oil left than the pessimists believe, much of it in the Middle East. New technologies will wring additional supplies from existing fields, the USGS predicts, and vast new reserves remain to be found. Many economists agree, saying discoveries have fallen off simply because countries awash in oil like Iraq, Iran, and Saudi Arabia have had no incentive to drill for more. "If I'm an OPEC producer, with lots of spare capacity, why would I waste money looking for more reserves?" asks Kaufmann.

But in the end, "you're talking about a few years one way or another," *35* says Cavallo, the Princeton consultant. Thomas Ahlbrandt, the geologist who led the USGS study, says that even the larger reserves he envisions can't sustain the world's growing thirst for oil indefinitely. "Oil and gas are limited," he says flatly. "My personal feeling is, we have a concern in the next couple of decades."

Either way, the crude won't suddenly dry up: Old oil fields don't die, *36* they slowly fade away. But the world will face shortages more lasting than any 1970s oil shock—and some stark choices. Should we increase production from the Canadian tar sands and similar "heavy oil" deposits in Venezuela? Try to exploit the American West's vast deposits of oil shale

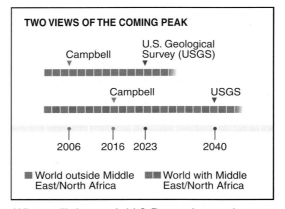

TWO VIEWS OF THE COMING PEAK

Campbell

U.S. Geological Survey (USGS)

Campbell

USGS

2006   2016 2023   2040

■ World outside Middle East/North Africa   ■■ World with Middle East/North Africa

When will the peak hit? Depends on who you ask. David Greene of Oak Ridge National Laboratory analyzed oil production rates based on a variety of supply estimates. His interpretation of data from U.K.-based Colin Campbell offers a grim picture (above): World production will most likely peak about 2016, and outside the Middle East around 2006. Using data from the U.S. Geological Survey, Greene presents a brighter picture, with world production most likely to peak around 2040. Greene notes, however, that his study has built-in optimism, since it doesn't factor in political or environmental constraints on production. Some experts, in fact, think the peak is already here. The timing rests largely on the actions of Middle East producers and on moves to conserve and to develop unconventional sources. Either way, time is short.

and other organic-rich rock that yields oil when roasted? Both options carry heavy environmental costs. Or should we pin our hopes on finding new supplies of natural gas, extracting fuel from plant material, or building solar, wind, or nuclear plants to make hydrogen for fuel-cell vehicles? There are no easy options, and all will take time to explore.

Aboard the *Enterprise* drill ship in the deep Gulf, engineers and roughnecks are doing their best to postpone the day of reckoning. By the summer of 2003 they had brought the well under control and finished it, 15 million dollars over budget and a month behind schedule. "We did fight that

37

well for a little while," says BP's Kirton wryly. Now they've moved on to other holes, laboring on a drilling floor slick with fluids while the ship battles the current and the bit gnaws through salt, shale, and sandstone toward the geologic legacy that fuels our way of life.

But at least some of the ingenuity and toil that goes into getting oil *38* needs to go toward limiting our thirst for it. "People should be doing something now to reduce oil dependence and not waiting for Mother Nature to slap them in the face," says Cavallo.

With every visit to the gas pump, after all, the end of cheap oil draws *39* closer.

In your journal, write the meaning of each of the following words:

- *burgeoning* oil regions **(6)**
- foresee *dire* consequences **(9)**
- an oil *embargo* on the U.S. **(15)**
- up-to-date *seismic* technology **(24)**
- by hydraulic *fracturing* **(24)**
- dependence on the *volatile* Middle East **(33)**
- prophets of *imminent* shortage **(34)**
- the geologic *legacy* that fuels our way of life **(37)**

QUESTIONS FOR WRITING AND DISCUSSION

1. In small groups in your class—or on your class computer forum—interview other members of your class about their attitudes toward oil and energy alternatives. Write out several questions to ask, such as "How many miles do you commute to school or work? What gas mileage does your automobile get? Do you use public transportation? Should the government permit more arctic or offshore oil drilling? What changes in your life would reduce your consumption of natural gas or oil? Should the federal government raise fuel taxes on gasoline to support alternative forms of public transportation?"

Choose three or four questions, compile the responses, and be ready to report your findings to the class.

2. Investigating essays should begin with a lead paragraph or two that arouse the reader's interest and then give background information that answers relevant *who, what, when, where,* and *why* questions. Reread the opening paragraphs of Appenzeller's essay. Does he get your attention with his lead-in? Does he provide sufficient background information? Would another example from the article more dramatically set the stage for his investigation? Why or why not?

3. An investigative report is a particular genre used by media journalists. Investigative reports often have the following genre features: (a) on-the-scene reporting of sensory details, principal characters, and quotations; (b) a representation of ideas from a range of experts and authorities in the field; (c) the inclusion of accurate background or historical research on the question or problem; (d) a sense of story, of building drama, as the report unfolds; and (e) a style that appeals to the target audience. Reread the article and locate examples of each of these genre features. Based on your critical reading, how well does Appenzeller meet the requirements of the investigative report genre? Explain.

4. In his article, Appenzeller cites a dozen authorities or petroleum industry workers, usually giving their job title. Make a list of these citations in the article. How would you guess, from the article, that he obtained these quotations—from personal interviews, e-mail or telephone interviews, or as citations from publications? What is the advantage, in terms of readability and impact on the target audience, of using quotations obtained on the actual scene? Explain.

5. Investigative reporting, as a job or career, has its good and bad moments. Read some notes from the field made by Tim Appenzeller while he was on assignment in Alaska recently. The notes are available at *http://magma .nationalgeographic.com/ngm/0402/feature5/assignment1.html*. Read other field notes by writers and photographers at this site. If you have any experience with reporting for a school or local newspaper, do these accounts tell what reporting is really like?

6. Use your library databases and the Internet to research what other authorities are saying about the date of the oil production peak. What are the credentials of the authors that you find? Are they scientists, geologists, executives at an oil company, politicians, consumers, citizens affected by environmental degradation, or other journalists? What is their potential bias or point of view? How reliable is each source? (For help in judging the reliability of a library or Internet source, see Chapter 12.)

7. In paragraph 36, Appenzeller lists the alternative fuels or sources of energy that we should be developing: natural gas, fuel from plant material, solar and wind power, nuclear energy, and fuel-cell technology. Investigate the state of several of these options. Which are showing the most signs of promise? Which, in your judgment, offer the most hope for reducing dependence on oil supplies? Write your response in the form of a letter to the editor of a local or school newspaper.

PROFESSIONAL WRITING

The Homeless and Their Children

Jonathan Kozol

In his most famous book, Illiterate America *(1985), Jonathan Kozol says that because more than one-third of America's adults are at least partially illiterate, we should organize a massive government and volunteer army to liberate people imprisoned by illiteracy. More recently, Kozol has written about children in underclass America in* Amazing Grace: The Lives of Children and the Conscience of a Nation *(1996) and* Ordinary Resurrections *(2000). In "The Homeless and Their Children," taken from* Rachel and Her Children *(1988), Kozol investigates individual cases of poverty in a New York City welfare hotel. Although welfare laws have changed and the Martinique Hotel has since been renovated, Kozol's investigative report accurately chronicles the effects of illiteracy on the lives of the poor. Kozol uses his own observations and interview transcripts to demonstrate vividly the connection between illiteracy and poverty. However, instead of arguing indignantly for literacy programs to save the lives of the poor and illiterate, Kozol simply reports the case of a single illiterate woman trying to raise her four children. The woman he calls Laura cannot decipher labels on products at the grocery store, cannot read notices from the welfare office, and cannot understand letters from the hospital warning of her children's lead poisoning.*

The Martinique Hotel, at Sixth Avenue and Thirty-second Street, is one of the largest hotels for homeless people in New York City. When I visited it, in December of 1985, nearly four hundred homeless families, including   *1* some twelve hundred children, were lodged in the hotel, by arrangement with the city's Human Resources Administration. One of the residents I spoke to at some length was an energetic, intelligent woman I'll call Kim. During one of our conversations, she mentioned a woman on the seventh floor who had seemingly begun to find her situation intolerable. Kim described this woman as "a broken stick," and offered to arrange for us to meet.

The woman—I will call her Laura, but her name, certain other names, and certain details have been changed—is so fragile that I find it hard to start a conversation when we are introduced, a few nights later. Before I begin, she asks if I will read her a letter from the hospital. The oldest of her four children, a seven-year-old boy named Matthew, has been sick for several weeks. He was tested for lead poisoning in November, and the letter she hands me, from Roosevelt Hospital, says that the child has a dangerous lead level. She is told to bring him back for treatment. She received the letter some weeks ago. It has been buried in a pile of other documents that she cannot read. 2

Although Laura cannot read, she knows enough about the dangers of lead to grasp the darker implications of this information. The crumbling plaster in the Martinique Hotel is covered with sweet-tasting paint, and children eat or chew chips of the paint as it flakes off the walls. Some of the paint contains lead. Children with lead poisoning may suffer loss of coordination or undergo convulsions. The consequences of lead poisoning may be temporary or long lasting. They may appear at once or not for several years. This final point is what instills so much uneasiness; even months of observation cannot calm a parent's fear. 3

Lead poisoning, then, is Laura's first concern, but she has other problems. The bathroom plumbing has overflowed and left a pool of sewage on the floor. A radiator valve is broken, and every now and then releases a spray of scalding steam at the eye level of a child. A crib provided by the hotel appears to be unstable. A screw that holds two of its sides together is missing. When I test the crib with my hand, it starts to sway. There are four beds in the room, and they are dangerous, too. They have metal frames with unprotected corners, and the mattresses do not fit the frames; at one corner or another, metal is exposed. If a child has the energy or the playfulness to jump or turn a somersault or wrestle with a friend, and if he falls and strikes his head against the metal corner, the consequences can be serious. The week before, a child on the 4 fourteenth floor fell in just this way, cut his forehead, and required stitches. Most of these matters have been brought to the attention of the hotel management; in Laura's case, complaints have brought no visible results.

All of this would be enough to make life difficult for an illiterate young   5
woman in New York, but Laura has one other urgent matter on her hands. It appears that she has failed to answer a request for information from her welfare office, and, for reasons that she doesn't understand, she did not receive her benefits this week. The timing is bad; it's a weekend. The city operates a crisis center in the Martinique, where residents can go for food and other help, but today the crisis center is not open, so there's nobody around to tide her over with emergency supplies. Laura's children have been eating cheese and bread and peanut butter for two days. "Those on welfare," the Community Service Society of New York said in a report published in 1984, may be suddenly removed from welfare rolls "for reasons unrelated to their actual need," or even to eligibility standards. Welfare workers in New York City call this practice "churning." Laura and her children are being churned.

The room is lighted by fluorescent tubes in a ceiling fixture. They cast   6
a stark light on four walls of greenish paint smeared over with sludge draining from someone's plumbing on the floor above. In the room are two boys with dark and hollowed eyes and an infant girl. A third boy is outside and joins us later. The children have the washed-out look of the children Walker Evans photographed for "Let Us Now Praise Famous Men." Besides the four beds and the crib, the room contains two chairs, a refrigerator, and a television set, which doesn't work. A metal hanger serves as an antenna, but there is no picture on the screen. Instead, there is a storm of falling flakes and unclear lines. I wonder why Laura keeps it on. There are no table lamps to soften the fluorescent glare, no books, no decorations. Laura tells me that her father is of Panamanian birth but that she went to school in New York City. Spanish is her first language. I don't speak Spanish well. We talk in English.

"I cannot read," Laura says. "I buy the New York *Post* to read the pic-   7
tures. In the grocery, I know what to buy because I see the pictures."

What of no-name products—generic brands, whose labels have no   8
pictures but which could save her a great deal of money?

"If there are no pictures, I don't buy it," she says. "I want to buy pan-   9
cakes, I ask the lady, 'Where's the pancakes?' So they tell me."

She points to the boys and says, "He's two. He's five. Matthew's seven. *10* My daughter is four months. She has this rash." She shows me ugly skin eruptions on the baby's neck and jaw. "The carpets, they was filthy from the stuff, the leaks that come down on the wall. All my kids have rashes, but the worst she has it. There was pus all over. Somewhere here I have a letter from the nurse." She shuffles around but cannot find the letter. "She got something underneath the skin. Something that bites. The only way you can get rid of it is with a cream."

She finds the letter. The little girl has scabies. *11*

Laura continues, "I have been living here two years. Before I came *12* here, I was in a house we had to leave. There was rats. Big ones, they crawl on us. The rats, they come at night. They come into our house, run over my son's legs. The windows were broken. It was winter. Snow, it used to come inside. My mother lived with us before. Now she's staying at my grandma's house. My grandma's dying in the bed. She's sixty-five. My mother comes here once a week to do the groceries. Tomorrow she comes. Then she goes back to help my grandma.

"I know my name, and I can write my name, my children's names. To *13* read, I cannot do it. Medicines, I don't know the instructions. I was living here when I was pregnant with Corinne. No, I didn't see no doctor. I was hungry. What I ate was rice and beans, potato chips and soda. Up to now this week we don't have food. People ask me, 'Can you help? Do you got this? Do you got that?' I don't like to tell them no. If I have something, I give it. This week, I don't got. I can read baby books—like that, a little bit. If I could read, I would read newspapers. I would like to know what's going on. Matthew, he tells me I am stupid. 'You can't read.' You know, because he wants to read. He don't understand what something is. I tell him, 'I don't know it. I don't understand.' People laugh. You feel embarrassed. On the street. Or in the store." She weeps. "There's nothing here."

Laura sweeps one hand in a wide arc, but I can't tell whether she means *14* the gesture to take in the room or something more. Then she makes her meaning clear: "Everything I had, they put it on the sidewalk when I was evicted. I don't know if that's the law. Things like that—what is the law, what isn't? I can't read it, so I didn't understand. I lost everything I had. I sign papers. Somebody could come and take my children. They could come. "Sign this. Sign that.' I don't know what it says. Adoption papers—I don't know. This here paper that I got I couldn't understand."

She hands me another letter. This one is from the management of the *15* hotel: "This notice is to inform you that your rent is due today. I would appreciate your cooperation in seeing to it that you go to your center today." Another form that she hands me asks her to fill out the names and the ages of her children.

"Papers, documents—people give it to me. I don't know it: I don't un- 16 derstand." She pauses, and then says, "I'm a Catholic. Yes—I go two weeks ago to church. This lady say they have these little books that learn me how to spell. You see the letters. Put them together. I would like to read. I go to St. Francis' Church. Go inside and kneel—I pray. I don't talk to the priest. I done so many things—you know, bad things. I buy a bottle of wine. A bottle of beer. That costs a dollar. I don't want to say to God. I get a hundred and seventy-three dollars restaurant allowance. With that money I buy clothes. Food stamps, I get two hundred dollars. That's for groceries. Subway tokens I take out ten dollars. Washing machine, I do downstairs. Twenty-five dollars to dry and wash. Five dollars to buy soap. Thirty dollars twice a month."

Another woman at the Martinique calculates her laundry costs at my 17 request, and they come out to nearly the same figure. These may be the standard rates for a midtown site. The difficulty of getting out and traveling to find lower prices, whether for laundromats or for groceries, cannot be overstated. Families at the Martinique are trapped in a commercial district.

I ask Laura who stays with the children when she does her chores. 18

"My mother keeps the children when I do the wash," she replies. "If she 19 can't, I ask somebody on the floor. 'Give me three dollars. I watch your kids.' For free? Nothing. Everything for money. Everybody's poor."

Extending a hand, she says, "This is the radiator. Something's wrong." 20 She shows me where the steam sprays out. I test it with my hand. "Sometimes it stops. The children get too close. Then it starts—like that! Leak is coming from upstairs down." I see the dark muck on the wall. "The window is broke. Lights broke." She points to the fluorescent tubes. They flicker on and off. "I ask them, 'Please, why don't you give me ordinary lights?' They don't do nothing. So it been two weeks. I go downstairs. They say they coming up. They never come. So I complain again. Mr. Tuccelli—Salvatore Tuccelli, the manager of the Martinique—said to come here to his office. Desks and decorations and a lot of pictures. It's above the lobby. So the manager was there. Mr. Tuccelli sat back in his chair. He had a gun. He had it here under his waist. You know, under his belt. I said, 'Don't show it to me if you isn't going to use it.' I can't tell what kind of gun it was. He had it in his waist. 'You are showing me the gun so I will be afraid.' If he was only going to show it, I would not be scared. If he's going to use it, I get scared.

"So he says, 'You people bring us trouble.' I said, 'Why you give my son 21 lead poison and you didn't care? My child is lead-poisoned.' He said, 'I don't want to hear of this again.' What I answer him is this: 'Listen. People like you live in nice apartments. You got a home. You got TV. You got a family. You got children in a school that learn them. They don't got lead poison.'"

"I don't know the reason for the guards. They let the junkies into the 22 hotel. When my mother comes, I have to sign. If it's a family living good, they make it hard. If it's the drug dealers, they come in. Why they let the junkies in but keep away your mother? The guards, you see them taking women in the corner. You go down twelve-thirty in the night, they're in the corner with the girls. This is true. I seen it."

She continues, "How I know about the lead is this: Matthew sits there 23 and he reaches his fingers in the plaster and he put it in his mouth. So I ask him, 'Was you eating it?' He says, 'Don't hit me. Yes, I was.' So then I took him to the clinic and they took the blood. I don't know if something happen to him later on. I don't know if it affects him. When he's older . . ."

I ask Laura why she goes to church. 24

"I figure: Go to church. Pray God. Ask Him to help. I go on my 25 knees. I ask Him from my heart. 'Jesus Christ, come help me, please. Why do you leave me here?' When I'm lying down at night, I ask, 'Why people got to live like this?' On the street, the people stare at you when you go out of the hotel. People look. They think, I wonder how they live in there. Sometimes I walk out this door. Garbage all over in the stairs. When it's hot, a lot of bugs around the trash. Sometimes there are fires in the trash. I got no fire escape. You have to get out through the hall. I got no sprinkler. Smoke detector doesn't work. When I cook and food is burning, it don't ring. If I smoke, it starts to ring. I look up. I say, 'Why you don't work? When I need you, you don't work. I'm gonna knock you down.' I did!" She laughs.

There is a sprinkler system in the corridor. In 1987, the hotel man- 26 agement informed residents that the fire-alarm system was "inoperable."

I ask Laura if the older children are enrolled in school. Nodding at 27 Michael, her middle son, she says, "This one doesn't go to school. He's five. I need to call tomorrow. Get a quarter. Then you get some papers. Then you got to sign those papers. Then he can start school.

"For this room I pay fifteen hundred dollars for two weeks. I don't pay. 28 The welfare pays. I got to go and get it." The room, although it is undivided, was originally a two-room suite and is being rented at the two-room rate. "They send me this. I'm suppose to sign. I don't know what it is. Lots of things you suppose to sign. I sign it but I don't know what it is."

While we are talking, Matthew comes in and sits beside his mother. *29* He lowers his eyes when I shake his hand.

Laura goes on, "Looking for a house, I got to do it." She explains that *30* she's required to give evidence that she is searching for a place to live. "I can't read, so I can't use the paper. I get dressed. I put my makeup on. If I go like this, they look afraid. They say, 'They going to destroy the house!' You got to dress the children and look nice. Owners don't want homeless. Don't want welfare. Don't want kids. What I think? If they pay one thousand and five hundred dollars every two weeks, why not pay five hundred dollars for a good apartment?"

She hands me another paper. "Can you tell me what is this?" *31*

It's a second letter from the hospital, telling her to bring her son for *32* treatment.

She says, "Every day, my son this week, last week was vomiting. Every *33* time he eat his food, he throw it right back out. I got to take him to the clinic.

"Christmas, they don't got. For my daughter I ask a Cabbage Patch. For *34* my boys I ask for toys. I got them stockings." She shows me four cotton stockings tacked to the wall with nothing in them. "They say, 'Mommy, there's no toys.' I say not to worry. 'You are going to get something.' But they don't. They don't get nothing. I could not afford. No, this isn't my TV. Somebody lended it to me. Christmas tree I can't afford. Christmas I don't spend it happy. I am thinking of the kids. What we do on Christmas is we spend it laying on the bed. If I go outside, I feel a little better. When I'm here, I see those walls, the bed, and I feel sad. If I had my own apartment, maybe there would be another room. Somewhere to walk. Walk back and forth."

I ask her, "How do you relax?" *35*

"If I want to rest, relax, I turn out the light and lie down on the bed," *36* she says. "When I met his father, I was seventeen." She says she knew him before she was homeless, when she lived in Brooklyn with her mother. He was working at a pizza parlor near her mother's home. "One night, he bought me liquor. I had never tasted. So he took me to this hallway. Then my mother say that what I did is wrong. So I say that I already did it. So you have to live with what you did. I had the baby. No. I did not want to have abortion. The baby's father I still see. When he has a job, he brings me food. In the summer, he worked in a flower store. He would bring me flowers. Now he don't have any job. So he don't bring me flowers."

She sweeps her hand in a broad arc and says again, "Nothing here. I feel *37* embarrassed for the room. Flowers, things like that, you don't got. Pretty things you don't got. Nothing like that. No."

In the window is a spindly geranium plant. It has no flowers, but some *38* of the leaves are green. Before I go, we stand beside the window. Blowing snow hits the panes and blurs the dirt.

"Some of the rooms high up, they got a view," Laura says. "You see the *39* Empire State."

I've noticed this—seen the building from a window. It towers high *40* above the Martinique.

"I talk to this plant. I tell him, 'Grow! Give me one flower!' He don't *41* do it." Then, in an afterthought, "No pets. No. You don't got. Animals. They don't allow."

It occurs to me that this is one of the few places I have been except a *42* hospital or a reform school where there are hundreds of children and virtually no pets. A few people keep cats illegally.

"I wish I had a dog," Laura says. "Brown dog. Something to hug." *43*

In your journal, write the meanings of the following words:

- the darker *implications* **(3)**
- call this practice "*churning*" **(5)**
- ugly skin *eruptions* **(10)**
- girl has *scabies* **(11)**

QUESTIONS FOR WRITING AND DISCUSSION

1. Describe your intellectual and emotional reaction to Kozol's article. What information about the lives of the poor and illiterate did you already know? What information surprised you? How did Kozol's essay make you feel about this problem?

2. The purpose of an investigative report is to give information without editorializing or arguing for or against a solution. In which paragraphs does Kozol remain most objective and unemotional? Which passages reveal Kozol's sympathy for Laura's situation? Does he avoid editorializing?

3. Reread the essay, marking those places where Laura's illiteracy causes her problems. Based on your notes, explain how her illiteracy (rather than her poverty) causes or magnifies her problems.

4. Describe the investigative techniques that Kozol probably used to write his essay. In addition to his interviews with Laura, what were his other probable sources of information?

5. According to the information provided by Kozol, what support does the welfare system provide Laura and her children? How does the welfare system encourage Laura to improve her life? List three changes that you believe the welfare system should make to solve Laura's problems and make her more self-sufficient.

6. On your next trip to the grocery store, see which products would appeal to an illiterate person. List the items (and their prices) that you might buy based on the pictures on the labels. Write a paragraph describing your findings. Is Kozol correct in assuming that Laura pays too much for her groceries?

7. Jonathan Kozol's latest investigative book, *Ordinary Resurrections* (2000), is a postscript to his earlier works such as *Savage Inequalities: Children in America's Schools* (1992) and *Amazing Grace: The Lives of Children and the Conscience of a Nation* (1995). Use the Internet to access full-text reviews of *Ordinary Resurrections*. On Amazon.com, you will find interesting but mostly positive comments—Amazon is, after all, in the business of selling books. A review in *Newsweek* by Ellis Cose is also positive, but check out Sol Stern's review, "America's Most Influential—And Wrongest—School Reformer," available in full text from Lexis-Nexis. Stern claims, for example, that "Kozol's mistaken but hugely influential diagnosis leads education advocates to keep proposing still more of the wrong cure [giving resources to these schools], while the real causes of school failure—the monopoly public education system, the teachers' unions, and the ed schools—go on wreaking their damage unimpeded, and inner-city schools keep on failing." Read all of Stern's review. Do you agree or disagree with Stern's analysis? Explain.

Investigating: The Writing Process

ASSIGNMENT FOR INVESTIGATING

Choose a subject to investigate: one aspect of a current social or political policy, a scientific discovery or principle, a historical event, a profile of a controversial public figure, or perhaps just an ordinary event, person, process, or place that you find interesting. Your initial purpose should be to discover or learn about your subject. Then, with a specific audience in mind, report your findings. A report presents the information that you find; it should not argue for or against any idea or plan. With the final copy of your investigative report, you must turn in photocopies of any sources you have summarized or cited, notes from your interview(s), and/or copies of questionnaires that you used.

Selecting your audience and genre is especially important for your investigating piece. If an audience is not specified in your assignment, check out newspapers, magazines, websites for appropriate audiences and genres. You may want to do an investigating essay, but perhaps a pamphlet, website, or letter would be more effective. Limiting your audience and selecting a possible newspaper, journal, magazine, forum, or Web site will help you focus your information. Where possible, think globally but focus locally—what global topic has local implications that you can investigate, and what local publication might be interested in your essay?

CHOOSING A SUBJECT

If one of your journal topics does not suggest a subject for your investigation, consider the following ideas. If you have a subject, go on to the collecting and shaping strategies.

- Choose some idea, principle, process, or theory discussed in a class that you are currently taking. In biology, you might focus on the Krebs cycle; in art, investigate the Dutch school of painters; or in education, investigate community literacy programs. In physics, research low-temperature conductivity or hydrogen fuels, or in astronomy, investigate competing theories about the formation of the universe. Begin by interviewing a professor, graduate students, or classmates about how to research the history, development, or personalities behind this idea. With information from the interview, continue your investigation in the library and online. As you read, focus your question to one narrow or specific area.

- Investigate and report on a campus or community service organization. Choose any academic, minority, cultural, or community organization. Visit the office. Interview an official. Read the organization's literature. Talk to students or community members who have used the service. Check the library for background information. Find people who are dissatisfied with or critical of the organization. Select an audience who might use this service or who might be interested in volunteering for the organization, and report the relevant *who, what, when, where, why,* and/or *how* information.

- At your workplace, investigate how something does or does not work, research how the business (or your part of the business) is organized, do a profile of a coworker, or survey your customers to find out what they like best or least about your store or company.

- For practice, investigate one of the following questions on the Internet and/or in the library (be prepared to explain your answers to your class members): How can you minimize jet lag? Can aspirin prevent heart attacks? How expensive is television advertising? What is a wind tunnel used for? Why is the Antarctic ice shelf melting? How do endorphins work? What is a melanoma? What causes seasonal affective disorder? How does a "Zamboni" work? What effects does Megan's law have? Do Americans spend more money on cosmetics than on education? What are the newest ways to repair torn ACLs (anterior cruciate ligaments) in your knee? What is computer morphing, and how does it work?

- Investigate an academic major, a career, or a job you are interested in. List some of the *who, what, when, where,* and *why* questions you want to answer. Who is interested in this major? What background or courses are required? What is the pay scale or opportunities for advancement? What appeals to you about this major or job? What are the disadvantages of this major or career? Research your major or career on the Internet and in the library. Plan to interview an adviser, a friend who majors in the field, or a person who works at that job. Be prepared to report your findings to your classmates.

COLLECTING

The collecting strategies discussed in Chapters 3, 4, and 5 (brainstorming, clustering, looping, mapping, sketching, reading, summarizing, taking double-entry notes) may be useful as you collect ideas. Other strategies particularly useful for investi-

---

COMMUNITY SERVICE LEARNING

If you have a service-learning project connected with your writing course, below is some background information that will help you understand your project.

Definition Community-service learning is simply a mutually beneficial partnership with a community agency.

Goals Teachers, students, and the partnering agency work together to set mutual goals promoting both civic action and academic learning. The agency receives your assistance with projects involving planning, writing, and communicating. You receive valuable experience related to your writing class goals: working and writing collaboratively, assessing and addressing agency needs, and getting practice with real-world writing situations, tasks, and genres.

Requirements Most service-learning projects require both a certain number of hours of service and a portfolio of pieces of writing *about* the agency, *for* the agency, and *with* the agency. A major requirement of service-learning projects is a reflective account about your participation, about the agency and its mission, and about what you have learned.

Writing Situations and Genres Depending on the goals and mission of the agency, you may write any combination of the following genres or kinds of writing: journal writing, online discussion forums, observation of the agency, profile of the agency, research, needs assessment, audience analysis, interviews, pamphlets, Web site design, public service announcements, feature articles, and impact assessment.

Benefits The agency benefits from your help with its ongoing projects (but remember that it also gives its time to help you learn). You benefit from getting to write in real-world situations—not just for your teacher and classmates. You also gain civic and crosscultural awareness, experience in working and writing collaboratively, increased problem-solving skills, contacts for possible job or career choices, and personal satisfaction for helping with a worthy civic cause.

> ** *Had I known the answer to any of these questions, I would never have needed to write.* **
>
> —JOAN DIDION,
> ESSAYIST
> AND NOVELIST

gating are suggested here. Try each of the following collecting strategies for your subject.

ASKING QUESTIONS   Asking the *right questions* is crucial to investigative writing. Sets of questions (often called *heuristics*) will help you narrow and focus your subject and tailor your approach to the expectations or needs of your audience. You don't know what information you need to collect until you know what questions your investigation needs to answer.

1.   The "reporter's" or the familiar "Wh" questions are one basic heuristic: Who? What? When? Where? Why?

Asking these questions of a topic ensures that you're not leaving out any crucial information. If, for example, you are investigating recreational opportunities in your city or on campus, you might ask the following questions to focus your investigation (remember to ask the *negative* version of each question, too):

- *Whom* is the recreation for?
- *Who* runs the programs?
- *Who* is excluded from the programs?
- *Who* pays for the programs?
- *What* is the program?
- *What* sports are included in the program?
- *What* sports are not included?
- *What* is the budget for these programs?
- *When* are these opportunities available or not available?
- *Where* do the activities take place?
- *Where* are they restricted?
- *Why* are these programs offered?
- *Why* are certain activities not offered?
- *Why* have activities been changed?

These questions might lead you to focus your investigation on the scheduling, on why soccer has been excluded, or on why participants are charged a fee for one class or program but not for another.

2. The classical "topics" provide a second set of questions for an investigation.

Definition:	What is it?
Comparison:	What is it like or unlike?
Relationship:	What caused it? What are its consequences?
Testimony:	What has been said or written about it?

These questions can be used in conjunction with the reporter's questions to focus an investigation. Applied to the topic on recreational opportunities, the questions might be as follows:

Definition:	What activities exist? How can the activities be described, classified, or analyzed?
Comparison:	What are similarities to or differences from other programs?
Relationship:	What caused these programs to be offered? What causes people to use or avoid these activities? What are the consequences of these programs?
Testimony:	What do students think about these activities? What do administrators think? What have other schools done?

THE FAR SIDE® By GARY LARSON

What does research show?

What proverbs or common sayings apply here?

These two sets of questions will *expand* your information, helping you collect facts, data, examples, and ideas—probably more than you can use in a short essay. Once you have all of this information, you can then *narrow* your topic.

Using Written and Electronic Sources

- **When printed copies are not available directly from your computer access, make photocopies of relevant articles.** The small amount of money you spend on copies will enable you to reread articles if necessary, quote or paraphrase from them accurately, and cite them accurately as references. (The money you spend is also excellent antifrustration insurance, in case you return to the library stacks and discover that someone else has checked out your magazine or book.) On your photocopies, be sure to write *source information:* magazine or book title, author, publisher, date and place of publication, volume, and page numbers. For this investigative report, remember that you must turn in photocopies of any pages of articles or books you use.
- **Make notes and summaries from your photocopied sources.** As you collect information from photocopied sources, jot down key facts, ideas, and direct

Research Tips ⬤ GO

As you work on your investigating essay, use the following research strategies.

Library Orientation Every library is different, so be sure to take your library's tour and find out how the online catalog searches and databases work. Knowing which databases to use and how to effectively use their search strategies makes your research quicker and more effective.

Internet Searches Use Internet search engines, such as Google, Yahoo! or Altavista, primarily for introductory or background information. Remember that the sites you find online may not be as reliable as information you find through your library's academic databases.

Evaluate Your Sources For all your Internet and library database sources, be sure to carefully evaluate the reliability, accuracy, and bias of your sources. Is the author of the text or Web site an authority on the subject? What is the author's connection to the subject, point of view, or bias? Has the text been published by a reputable magazine, or is it a self-published Web site?

Talk to Your Reference Librarian An informal interview with a reference librarian may be the most important ten minutes you spend doing research. Start by telling the librarian about your assignment—the topic and issue you're investigating—and then ask which databases, sources, or reference guides might be most helpful. Remember, there are no stupid questions in a library. Everyone has to learn how electronic databases work.

Include Field Research Field research, including personal observations, interviews, and questionnaires, can be effective in almost every research project. An interview with a campus or community expert on your topic may be a great place to start. A questionnaire for other students or potential readers may give you a better sense of what your audience knows or does not know about your topic and what points of view they have on the issue.

quotations. For every note you take, record the author, title, publishing information, and page numbers. You may *paraphrase* another writer's ideas, examples, sentences, or short passages by writing them in your own words. Use *direct quotation* when words or phrases in a source are more striking than your paraphrase might be. You may edit a direct quotation by (1) deleting any irrelevant or unnecessary words or phrases by using ellipsis points (three spaced periods) to indicate the deleted words and by (2) inserting your own

words in square brackets [] if you need to clarify a quoted passage. Otherwise, the words within the quotation marks must accurately reproduce the
original: No altered spellings, changed words, or rephrasings are allowed.

- **Avoid plagiarism.** Use quotation marks whenever you quote more than a
word or two from your source. Paraphrase in your own words rather than
stringing together phrases and sentences written by someone else. Give
credit for ideas, facts, and language by citing your sources. In informal investigative writing, you may simply mention the author and title of written
sources, citing page numbers of direct quotations in parentheses. (All formal research papers and some investigative essays cite sources in full in a
"Works Cited" section at the end. See Chapter 12, "Writing a Research
Paper," for more details.)

SUMMARIZING   As explained in Chapter 5, a *summary* is a concise explanation
of the main and supporting ideas in a passage, report, essay, book, or speech. It is usually written in the present tense. It identifies the author and title of the source; it may
refer to the context or the actual place where the study took place; it contains the passage's main ideas; and it may quote directly a few forceful or concise sentences or
phrases. It will not usually cite the author's examples. A *paraphrase* usually expresses
all the information in the passage—including examples—in your own words. Summary, paraphrase, and direct quotation often occur together as you use sources. (See
Chapter 5 for more details.)

CITING SOURCES IN YOUR TEXT   As you collect information, you should
note authors, titles of books or magazines, dates of publication, publishers, and page
numbers to give proper credit to your sources. For some journalistic writing, you
may need to cite only the author, the title of your source, or both:

> According to Constance Hale, associate managing editor of *Wired* maga-
> zine, "Sherry Turkle . . . was way ahead of the curve" **(2).**

> *Newsweek* magazine listed Sherry Turkle among their "50 for the Future" **(2).**

For a more formal, academic context, the MLA (Modern Language Association) requires that the author and page numbers be given, in parentheses, at the end
of the sentence—for example "(Turkle 24–25)":

> A key point in *Life on the Screen: Identity in the Age of the Internet* is that we
> can "embrace—or be trapped by—cyberspace as a way of life" (Turkle 25).

If you refer to the author in the sentence that contains the citation, indicate just the page numbers in parentheses.

In her book, *Life on the Screen: Identity in the Age of the Internet,* Turkle argues that we can "embrace—or be trapped by—cyberspace as a way of life" (25).

For additional information on formal, in-text citation, consult Chapter 12, "Writing a Research Paper."

DOING FIELD RESEARCH

Field research is essential for many kinds of investigative reports. Typically, field research—as opposed to library research—involves first-hand observations, interviews, and questionnaires. For observing strategies, see Chapter 3, "Observing." Using interviews and writing questionnaires are discussed below.

INTERVIEWING   After you have done some initial research, interviews are a logical next step. Remember that the more you know about the subject (and the person you're interviewing), the more productive the interview will be. In planning an interview, keep the following steps in mind:

1. Make an *appointment* with the person you wish to interview. Although you may feel hesitant or shy about calling or e-mailing someone for an interview, remember that most people are flattered that someone else is interested in them and wants to hear their opinions or learn about their areas of expertise.

2. Make a *list of questions,* in an appropriate *sequence,* that you can ask during the interview. The interview itself will generate additional topics, but your list will jog your memory if the interview gets off the track. Begin with relatively objective or factual questions and work your way, gradually, to the more subjective questions or controversial issues. Try to phrase your questions so that they require more than a yes or no answer.

3. Begin the interview by introducing yourself and describing *your* investigation. Keep your biases or opinions out of the questions. Be sure to *listen* carefully and ask follow-up questions: "What information do you have on that? What do the statistical studies suggest? In your opinion, do these data show any trends? What memorable experiences have you had relating to this topic?"

Like a dog with a good bone, a reporter doesn't drop a topic until the meat's all gone.

4. During the interview, *take notes,* and, if appropriate, use a tape recorder to ensure accuracy. Don't hesitate to ask your interviewee to repeat or clarify a statement. Remember: People want you to get the facts right and quote them accurately. Especially if you're doing a personality profile, describe notable features of your interviewee: hair color, facial features, stature, dress, gestures, and nervous habits, as well as details about the room or surroundings. Finally, don't forget to ask your interviewee for additional leads or sources. At the conclusion of the interview, express your thanks and ask if you can check with him or her later, perhaps by e-mail, for additional details or facts.

5. Immediately after the interview, go over your notes. If you recorded the interview, listen to the tape and transcribe important responses. List other questions you may still have.

WRITING QUESTIONNAIRES   Questionnaires are useful when you need to know the attitudes, preferences, or opinions of a large group of people. If you are surveying customers in your business, you may discover that 39 percent of those surveyed would prefer that your business stay open an additional hour, from 5 P.M. to 6 P.M. If you are surveying students to determine their knowledge of geography, you might discover that only 8 percent can correctly locate Beirut on a map of the Middle East. The accuracy and usefulness of a survey depend on the kinds of questions you ask, on the number of people you survey, and on the sample of people you select to respond to your questionnaire.

Open questions are easy to ask, but the answers can be difficult to interpret. For example, if you want to survey customers at a department store where you work, you might ask questions requiring a short written response:

- What is your opinion of the service provided by clerks at Macy's?
- What would make your shopping experience at Macy's more enjoyable?

While these questions may give you interesting—and often reliable—responses, the results may be difficult to tabulate. Open questions are often valuable in initial surveys because they can help you to determine specific areas or topics for further investigation.

Closed questions are more typical than open questions in surveys. They limit the responses so that you can focus on a particular topic and accurately tabulate the responses. Following are several types of closed questions:

- *Yes/no questions:* Have you shopped at Macy's in the last three months?
  - _____ Yes
  - _____ No
- *Multiple choice:* How far did you travel to come to Macy's?
  - _____ 0–5 miles
  - _____ 5–10 miles
  - _____ 10–15 miles
  - _____ Over 15 miles
- How would you characterize the salespeople at Macy's?
  - _____ Exceptionally helpful
  - _____ Helpful
  - _____ Indifferent
  - _____ Occasionally rude
  - _____ Usually rude
- *Checklists:* Which departments at Macy's do you usually visit?
  - _____ Women's Wear
  - _____ Sporting Goods
  - _____ Children's Wear
  - _____ Lingerie
  - _____ Men's Wear
  - _____ Household Goods
- *Ranking lists:* Rank the *times* you prefer to shop (1 indicates most convenient time, 2 indicates slightly less convenient, and so on).
  - _____ 9 A.M.–11 A.M.
  - _____ 11 A.M.–1 P.M.
  - _____ 1 P.M.–4 P.M.
  - _____ 4 P.M.–8 P.M.

As you design, administer, and use your questionnaire, keep the following tips in mind:

- Limit and focus your questions so that respondents can fill out the questionnaire quickly.
- Avoid loaded or biased questions. For example, don't ask, "How do you like the high-quality merchandise in Macy's sports department?"
- At the top of your questionnaire, write one or two sentences describing your study and thanking participants.
- Pretest your questionnaire by giving it to a few people. Based on their oral and written responses, focus and clarify your questions.

- Use a large sample group. Thirty responses will give you more accurate information about consumer attitudes than will three responses.
- Make your sample as *random* or as evenly representative as possible. Don't survey customers on only one floor, in only one department, or at only one time of day.
- Be sure to include a copy of your questionnaire with your article or essay.

Note: If you intend to do a formal study using questionnaires, check your library for additional sources to help you design and administer statistically reliable surveys.

SHAPING

As you begin shaping your material, reconsider your purpose and audience. Limit your subject to create a *narrowed* and *focused* topic. Don't try to cover everything; focus on *the most interesting questions and information*. Take the time to write out a statement of your topic, key questions, purpose, and audience. Then try the following strategies.

INVERTED PYRAMID   A common form for reports, especially in journalism, is the *inverted pyramid*. The writer begins with a succinct but arresting title, opens the story with a sentence or short paragraph that answers the reporter's "Wh" questions, and then fills in the background information and details in order of importance, from the *most important* to the *least important*.

> **❝** *But for whom have I tried so steadfastly to communicate? Who have I worried over in this writing? Who is my audience?* **❞**
>
> —CHERRIE MORAGA,
> SOCIAL CRITIC
> AND POET

"Wh" question lead: Who, What, When, Where, Why
Most important information and details

Important information and details

Least important information and details

Writers use the inverted pyramid when concrete information and the convenience of the reader are most important. The advantage of the inverted pyramid is that a hurried reader can quickly gather the most important information and determine whether the rest of the story is worth reading. The disadvantage is that some details or information may be scattered or presented out of clear sequence. In investigative writing, therefore, writers often supplement the inverted pyramid with other forms of development: chronological order, definition, classification, or comparison/contrast.

CHRONOLOGICAL ORDER   Often, writers present their information in the order in which they discovered it, enabling the reader to follow the research as if it were a narrative or a story. In this format, the writer presents the steps of the investigation, from the earliest incidents, to the discoveries along the way, to the final pieces of information.

Elizabeth Larsen, for example, uses chronological order to make a story out of her report on websites in art history. The following sentences—most of them appearing at the beginning of paragraphs—illustrate how she uses time signals ("first," "today," "started," "my next stop," and "then") to create an interesting story about surfing the Web.

> I first studied art history the old-fashioned way: scribbling notes in a dark auditorium . . .

> Inspired by the sheer volume of images available . . . I decided to try my hand at digitally designing my own art education.

> My self-directed syllabus started in Spain . . .

> Eager to see more, I moved on to the Museums page of the World Wide Web Virtual Library.

> I started in Italy, which I soon discovered doesn't include . . . the Vatican.

> My next stop was Paris, where my first visit was to . . . the Louvre.

> From Giverny I hopped over to Greece . . .

As these sentences illustrate, chronological order can transform a potentially boring list of websites into an interesting narrative journey through the information.

DEFINITION   Definitions are central to investigating and reporting, whether they shape only a sentence or two or several paragraphs. In her article on Sherry Turkle, Connie Koenenn uses an informal definition of MUDS in order to shape one paragraph. Her definition helps us understand how the Internet can alter our real-life identity:

> Beginning in her own backyard, Turkle organized pizza parties for students playing MUDS (Multi-User-Domains), the intricate online games in which participants can alter their real-life identities to improvise elaborate melo-dramas.

COMPARISON AND CONTRAST   Comparison and contrast are as essential to investigating and reporting as they are to observing and remembering. In "Surfin' the Louvre," Elizabeth Larson organizes her essay around a comparison between her traditional campus art course and her online education. Jonathan Kozol, in "The Homeless and Their Children," concludes his investigative report about Laura and her children with a comparison to other places where children have no pets: "It occurs to me that this is one of the few places I have been except a hospital or a reform school where there are hundreds of children and virtually no pets."

ADDITIONAL SHAPING STRATEGIES   Other shaping strategies, discussed in previous chapters, may be useful for your investigation, too. *Classifying people, places,* or *things* may help organize your investigation. *Simile, metaphor,* or *analogy* may develop and shape parts of your article. Even in investigative reporting, writers may create an identifiable *persona* or adopt a humorous tone. In the example report given earlier in this chapter, Jeff Meer assumes a reporter's objective persona and uses a serious, straightforward tone. In contrast, Elizabeth Larsen, in "Surfin' the Louvre," establishes a friendly and humorous tone: "That's a heck of a lot more reproductions than you'll find in that chiropractically unfriendly art history text, H.W. Janson's *History of Art.*" Larsen demonstrates that even journalistic writing can have a sense of fun.

TITLE, INTRODUCTION, AND CONCLUSION   Especially in an investigative report, a catchy title is important to help get your readers' interest and attention. Jot down several ideas for titles now and add to that list *after* you've drafted your essay.

   In your introductory paragraph(s), answering the "Wh" questions will help focus your investigation. Or you may wish to use a short *narrative,* as Larsen does in

"Surfin' the Louvre." Other types of lead-ins, such as a short *description*, a *question*, a *statement of a problem*, a *startling fact* or *statistic*, or an arresting *quotation*, may get the reader's interest and focus on the main idea you wish to investigate. (See Chapter 7 for additional examples of lead-ins.)

The conclusion should resolve the question or questions posed in the investigation, summarize the most important information (useful primarily for long or complicated reports), and give the reader a sense of completion, often by picking up an idea, fact, quotation, narrative, or bit of description used in the introduction.

Some writers like to have a title and know how they're going to start a piece of writing before they begin drafting. However, if you can't think of the perfect title or introduction, begin drafting, and continue working on the title, the introduction, and the conclusion after the first draft.

DRAFTING

Before you begin a first draft, reconsider your purpose in writing and further focus your questions, sense of audience, and shaping strategies.

The actual drafting of an investigative essay requires that you have all your facts, statistics, quotations, summaries, notes from interviews, or results of surveys ready to use. Organize your notes, decide on an overall shaping strategy, or write a sketch outline. In investigative writing, a primary danger is postponing writing too long in the mistaken belief that if you read just one more article or interview just one more person, you'll get the information you need. At some point, usually *before* you feel ready, you must begin writing. (Professional writers rarely feel they know enough about their subject, but deadlines require them to begin.) Your main problem, you'll quickly discover, will be having too much to say rather than not enough. If you have too much, go back to your focusing questions and see whether you can narrow your topic further.

> *"All good writing is swimming under water and holding your breath."*
> —F. SCOTT FITZGERALD, AUTHOR OF THE GREAT GATSBY

REVISING

After you have drafted your essay, you may wish to get some feedback from your peers about your work in progress. The peer response guidelines below will help you to review your goals for this investigative assignment and to construct a revision plan. When you read other students' drafts or ideas, be as constructively critical as

PEER RESPONSE

The instructions that follow will help you give and receive constructive advice about the rough draft of your investigating essay. You may use these guidelines for an in-class workshop, a take-home review, or a computer e-mail response.

Writer: Before you exchange drafts with another reader, write out the following on your essay draft or in an e-mail message:

1. **Purpose** Briefly, describe your purpose and intended audience. For your audience, write out the title of a newspaper or magazine that might print your investigative report.
2. **Revision plans** Obviously, your draft is just a draft. What still needs work as you continue revising? Explain. (You don't want your reader to critique problems you are already intending to fix.)
3. **Questions** Write out one or two questions that you still have about your draft. What questions would you like your reader to answer?

Reader: First, read the entire draft from start to finish. As you reread the draft, answer the following questions:

1. **Purpose** Remember that the purpose of this essay is to accurately and objectively report information, not argue or editorialize. Does this writer go beyond reporting to editorializing or arguing? If so, point out specific sentences that need revision.
2. **Evidence** List the kinds of evidence the writer uses. What additional kinds of sources might the writer use: an additional interview? a source on the Web? personal observation? other print sources? a survey? Make a specific suggestion about additional, appropriate sources.
3. **Key investigative question** When you read the essay, the key question should become apparent. Write it out. If there are places in the essay that don't relate to that key question, should they be omitted? Explain. Are there other aspects of the key question that the writer should address? Explain.
4. **Reader's response** An investigative essay should satisfy your curiosity about the topic. What did you want to learn about the topic that the essay did not answer? Write out any questions that you would like the writer to answer as he or she revises the essay.
5. **Answer the writer's questions in number 3.**

possible. Think carefully about the assignment. Be honest about your own reactions as a reader. What would make the draft better?

Guidelines for Revision

As you add, delete, substitute, or rearrange materials, keep the following tips in mind:

- **Reexamine your purpose and audience.** Are you doing what you intended? You should be *reporting* your findings; you should *not* be arguing for or against any idea.
- **Is the genre of your report responsive to audience needs and expectations?** Use samples of other writing for your audience (from newspapers, magazines, or journals) as models. Would visuals be appropriate or effective in your essay?
- **Can you add any of your own observations or experiences to the investigation?** Remember that your own perceptions and experiences as a reporter are also relevant data.
- **Review the reporter's "Wh" questions.** Are you providing your readers with relevant information *early* in the report and also catching their interest with a key statistic, fact, quotation, example, question, description, or short narrative?
- **Recheck your summaries, paraphrases, or direct quotations.** Are they accurate, and have you cited these sources in your text?
- **Use signals, cues, and transitions to indicate your shaping strategies.** *Chronological order:* before, then, afterward, next, soon, later, finally, at last *Comparison/contrast:* likewise, similarly, however, yet, even so, in contrast *Analysis:* first, next, third, fourth, finally.
- **Revise sentences for directness, clarity, and conciseness.** Avoid unnecessary passive voice.
- **Edit your report for appropriate word choice, usage, and grammar.** Check your writing for problems in spelling and punctuation.

POSTSCRIPT ON THE WRITING PROCESS

While the process of writing an investigative essay is still fresh in your mind, answer the following questions in your journal.

1. What sources of information (articles, books, interviews, surveys) were most helpful in your investigation? Explain.

We are all apprentices at a craft where no one ever becomes a master.

—ERNEST HEMINGWAY, NOVELIST

2. Most researchers discover that the more they learn, the more they still need to know about their subjects. If you had more time to work on this essay, which sources would you investigate further?

3. What was the most difficult problem you had to solve during your collecting, shaping, drafting, and revising? What helped you most as you tried to solve this problem (further reading, additional writing, advice from peers)? Explain.

4. What was the single most important thing you learned about investigating as you wrote this paper?

5. What do you like best about the final version of your investigative report?

STUDENT WRITING

THE HOLLYWOOD INDIAN

Lauren Strain

As the granddaughter of a Cherokee Indian, Lauren Strain decided to investigate how Native Americans have been portrayed in Hollywood films. How accurately have films such as Dances with Wolves, The Last of the Mohicans, *and Disney's* Pocahontas *portrayed American Indians? What stereotypes are presented in these films? Which Native American actors have helped change these stereotypes? In order to answer these questions, Strain watched old films, interviewed her grandfather, and researched several popular films about American Indians.*

Investigating Paper Proposal

Being a quarter Indian, I have grown up with only a few Indian images in my life. Those images come from my grandfather, a Cherokee, and from the Indians in movies and on television. I have always been curious about Hollywood's portrayal of Indians. My grandfather, being adopted, did not grow up with any traditional Indian beliefs or values, so I heard of none. So I wonder if my perceptions about Indian culture and value systems are correct. I would like to look into that more for my paper.

Using sources from movies, TV, photos and articles, I would like to go into the Native American resource center and speak to a full-blood Indian who has experienced some of the traditional ways and values. Using my grandfather as a resource will also be an option. I would like to ask him how he felt seeing the images of Indians on television, and if he thought that they truly reflected how he saw himself as an Indian.

I would start out my paper with the perception of Tonto in *The Lone Ranger*. Using Sherman Alexie's story, *The Lone Ranger and Tonto Fistfight in Heaven* as one view of Tonto, I would continue with written accounts of the actor who played Tonto in the TV show. Next, I would look at Hollywood's perceptions of Indians on reservations. I could use *Smoke Signals* and other movies for those images. I will also look for movie reviews in journals in the library's database for any articles on Indians in Hollywood. I will finish my paper with the perception of the traditional "soak" Indian in Hollywood—I mean when Indians had just been taken over by the white man. For this I will use old westerns and the written and visual accounts of the movies *Dances with Wolves* and *The Last of the Mohicans*.

I am looking forward to this assignment, although it will be challenging to collect all of the information. It will, however, give me the chance to talk with other Indians and perhaps I will be able to grow as a person as well as a Cherokee Indian. I will also have a reason to ask my grandfather all of the questions that I have had for him ever since I was a child. I would like to direct this paper to all white and red people to help them see that although many of us believe almost everything we see on television and in movies, some of that information might be false. It will be a journey to find out what is true and what is false about some of the first people to inhabit America.

Outline: The Hollywood Indian

I. Introduce Topic
  A. How are Indians portrayed in Hollywood?
  B. Grandfather Cherokee and how I grew up with the TV and movie Indians as my models.
  C. Introduce movies like *Dances with Wolves* and *The Last of the Mohicans.*

II. Movie portrayal of Native Americans
  A. The accurate portrayal and inaccurate portrayal of *Dances with Wolves.*
  B. *The Last of the Mohicans*—are they really gone?
  C. *Pocahontas*—an inaccurate portrayal of true women?

The Hollywood Indian

I am the granddaughter of an adopted Cherokee who grew up knowing only the ways of the white man. Not knowing much about the traditional American Indian, my only perceptions of them were through movies and Hollywood. Now that I am older, I stop and ask myself: What is the perception of Indians in Hollywood movies? Some of the most popular movies portraying Indians came out in my younger years (late 1980's early 1990's). I remember sneaking in to watch *Dances with Wolves* with my parents in the movie theater, which is a source of my perceptions of Indians. I even watched *Last of the Mohicans* in my freshman history class. Not only do I wonder how accurate movies like these are, I am very curious about the actors who play the Indians. During this research I want to answer certain questions. Are recent movies historically correct and do they eliminate stereotypes that people have given to Native Americans? What Native American actors have helped to portray their people accurately? And lastly, how has history helped to portray Native Americans better?

Three films that, despite historical inaccuracies, helped to popularize the life and culture of Native Americans were *Dances with Wolves, Last of the Mohicans,* and *Pocahontas. Dances with Wolves* has been the most critically acclaimed movie that portrays the "correct" Indian. When asking my grandfather about whether or not he thought this movie was a correct portrayal, he said, "Yes, except for one thing." He told me that at the end of the movie, you see a winter camp deep in the mountains. The Indians would never keep their camp that deep in the mountains during the winter; they would move on to a warmer place. This was a detail that I had never known about. In Armando J. Prats' essay about the comparison between the two cinematic versions of *Dances with Wolves,* he states that there was a normal film version shown in the theaters and the one released in a TV miniseries that added scenes. He brings up a very valid point: even though, in this movie, the Indians are portrayed in a valid way, the story's main character is a white man. This title is even the white man's given Indian name (6). Watching the movie myself, I noticed that the portrayal of the Sioux Indians was very human and realistic to tradition. The film showed strong bonds between family and tribesmen. I too—as well as many others I know—also have strong bonds with family and friends. The Indian characters even had a sense of humor, which also helped me connect to them easier.

The movie *Last of the Mohicans* is also a very realistic film but it has   3 some historical misrepresentations. It takes place during the French and Indian War in 1757. This movie was shown to me in my freshman history class to illustrate brutalities of the war itself. Those details of the movie were portrayed very clearly. In one scene, an Indian from the Mohawk tribe eats the heart of a British general. I am not quite sure whether or not this type of brutality actually happened but I do know that scalpings were regular occurrences during the French and Indian War. Just like humans today, people kill people in savage ways. And although there are many accurate historical details about the war itself, like the Mohegan tribe helping out the settlers in Canada, there are misrepresentations about the details concerning the Mohegan tribe.

One plot point that is incorrect is that the Mohegan tribe is extinct,   4 as the movie suggests. Melissa Sayet, in her essay "The Lasting of the Mohegans," tells us "[I am] a Mohegan Indian, alive and well in 1993" (55). The Mohegan tribe still exists, although it is very small, in Uncasville, Connecticut. The small tribe has a church, museum and an all-Indian run institution that has existed for sixty-two years to help show their history. Sayet tells us that the media is responsible for putting the thought into people's heads that the tribe has been dead for a long time. The myth was actually created by Lydia Howard Sigourney. Sayet writes, "It seems that it was far easier for Lydia to romanticize dead Mohegan's than to deal with the realities of alcoholism and poverty among living ones" (56). A well-known poet that knew of the Mohegan tribe, Sigourney wrote of their extinction anyway.

An additional inaccuracy in *The Last of the Mohicans,* although it may be small, is that the spelling of the tribe's name is different in the movie compared to the spelling that the tribe uses (Mohican vs. Mohegan). According to Sayet, this was because of the miscommunication between the tribe and Europeans during first contact. The Mohegan tribe did not have an alphabet to help convey the correct spelling (56). Another reason for the misspelling is the fact that there are two tribes with the same name spelled differently. One tribe comes from Connecticut and the other from the Hudson Valley in New York. The author of *The Last of the Mohicans* just accidentally switched the names unknowingly, according to the First Nations Web Site (*First Nations*). 5

When I watched the movie, I saw the romantic reasons for saying that the tribe was extinct at the end. The Mohegan men were very stoic, smart, athletic and heroic. I have never met a Mohegan Indian, so I am not sure how they carry themselves. I do know that not all the Indians were known heroes. It was hard not to fall in love with these characters, though. The movie was designed to pull at your heart. In the end, when the character Changachook, the father of Uncas and the second-to-last Mohegan, tells us he is the only remaining Mohegan, it is very convincing and sad. This is how Hollywood wants us to feel. If movies did not leave people with any type of feeling, whether humor, sadness or happiness, then there would be no reason to watch. 6

In contrast to the more accurate portrayals of Native Americans in *Dances with Wolves* and *Last of the Mohicans,* a third poplar Native American film, *Pocahontas,* is very inaccurate historically speaking. Disney's version of *Pocahontas* focuses on a very historic American Indian. This movie is very factually inaccurate, however. The Indians were portrayed as very peaceful and loving in this film. Pocahontas is an Indian princess who falls in love with the handsome John Smith, an English soldier looking for land in the New World. She ends up saving his life, and he asks her to come with him back to England to be his wife. She declines his offer, saying she could never leave her family and her land. 7

The true story of Pocahontas is different in many ways. The age of the character in the Disney movie seems to be in her early twenties. The real Pocahontas was sixteen years old. She did save the life of John Smith, but she fell in love with his friend, John Rolfe. She also ended up leaving America and going to England to marry him. Shortly upon her arrival, she died of smallpox. Although the film is historically inaccurate, telling children 8 the real story of Pocahontas would not have been a wise decision on the part of Disney. They like to show a happy story that promotes values. A sixteen-year-old girl marrying an older man is not a common thing these days. Plus, the main character never dies in Disney movies. I can see why Disney changed the story. They did, however, keep the happy and peaceful image of the Indians, thus promoting them; but they didn't tell the story in a historically correct manner.

The second question that I had was who were/are the Native American actors who have helped Hollywood portray a historically unstereotypical Indian? Three of the most recognized Indian actors in Hollywood who have portrayed historically accurate Indian characters are Graham Green, Russell Means, and Chief Dan George.   9

Graham Green is best known for his portrayal of Kicking Bird in *Dances with Wolves*. He received an Academy Award Nomination for best supporting actor for that role. Green is also a well-known draftsman, steel worker, civil technologist, and sound engineer. He graduated from a Native American theater school, where his comedy skills shined (*Graham Green*).   10

We see Green's comic acting shine through in the movie *Maverick*. In this movie, his character, Joseph, is earning money for his tribe by running around in war paint and having his tribe beat their drums for a European who wants to experience the "real west." When we see him encounter the European, he begins to speak the man's native language. When the European tells Joseph to speak as they do in the movies, Joseph says "How, white man," a stereotypical greeting. Joseph tells his friend Maverick how stupid he feels acting as if he is foolish and savage when in fact we see he is a very intellectual person (*Maverick*). I believe that Graham Green chose this role because he was able to show people how inaccurate and stupid the stereotypical Indian can be, when in reality Indians can be intellectual, caring people.   11

Russell Means is known more for his work outside Hollywood, but he is still praised for the roles he has taken in movies. He has been involved in civil rights for Native Americans since the 1960s. He has also done work with the United Nations for over twelve years. His most recent spot in the public eye was not in *a* movie, but rather in the demonstration against Columbus Day celebrations. Means got involved in acting in 1991. His most recognizable role was in *Last of the Mohicans*, where he plays the eldest Mohegan, a wise and brave man. His character was the leader of the   12 family of Mohegans in this movie and he never strayed and helped to keep the spirit of the tribe alive when it was "lost" with the passing of his son.

Chief Dan George (1899–1981) also helped to show film viewers that *13* American Indians were intelligent and civilized and not the typical savages. George was the chief of the Salish Band in the Burrard Inlet, in British Columbia, Canada. He was a very gifted actor and the author of many books, such as *My Heart Soars* and *My Spirit Soars.* George was also nominated for an Academy Award for his role in *Little Big Man.* He was also in the TV miniseries "Centennial" (*Chief Dan George*).

In the movie *The Outlaw Josey Wales,* Chief Dan George's character, *14* Lone Watie, explains to Josey Wales how he was part of the tribe the white man called "the civilized tribe," or the Cherokee. His character is wearing a top hat and a suit when we first see him in the film. He tells Wales that he dressed up as Abe Lincoln to impress Lincoln when he met him. Later we see Watie burning his clothes, wearing less casual traveling garments. He tells Wales how he forgot things and lost his way when he became "civilized" (*The Outlaw Josie Wales*). The clothes Chief Dan George wore in that movie were very symbolic in the story that he told. Although these were the words of a fictional character, I believe that they helped reflect the struggle of a Native American to be accepted as "civilized." Because of Hollywood, these struggles and lifestyles were able to get out to movie watchers.

The final question I was curious about was when and if historical *15* events helped to change the portrayal of Native Americans in Hollywood. The change from the savage enemy Indian came with World War II because the Nazis became the enemy rather then Native Americans. Angela Aleiss writes, "Previous images of menacing warriors who blocked Westward expansion gradually began to fade into one in which Indians stood as allies—rather than enemies—alongside America's frontier heroes" (25). Most movies changed stereotypes, but there were still some that had inaccurate portrayals like *Geronimo* (1939) and *They Died With Their Boots On* (1941).

In addition to the change brought on by World War II, Aleiss tells us *16* that there were three other contributions. The first one was to keep the relations between America, the United Kingdom, and Canada on good terms. Puritanical leaders wanted a good portrayal of Americans with other races. The second contribution, Alesiss says, is "the pro-interventionist politics of Hollywood studios [that] helped to create a mindset that would reshape the Indians image at least two years before America's entry into the war" (26).

Hollywood executives were trying to rid the movie industry of fascist ideals. The final element was that the image of the ally Indian was not a fad, but rather a gateway for other Western movie themes.

My grandfather grew up next to a reservation before World War II, so   *17* I asked him in my interview how Native Americans reacted to the westerns depicting them as the enemy. He told me that most of them went to the movies for the cartoons before the movie itself. "They did not show any emotional reaction to it," he said. I found it interesting that they would even go to the movies at all. When telling my grandfather this, he told me that, "It was a way for the Indians to break into the western culture." That helped me to understand their reasons for going.

When conducting my survey of students in my class, three out of ten   *18* thought that movies still portray Indians in a stereotypically savage manner. Two of them thought that Hollywood was doing a good job in the portrayal of the "correct" Native American. One person wrote, "Hollywood is more worried about offending anybody who is not white. Because people today are very sensitive, everyone, including Hollywood, watches what they say and do."

Throughout my research, I have found that Native Americans are   *19* portrayed in a very positive light. The negative stereotypical Indian has slowly faded with images of "the true west." Although there are still few exceptions, one aspect that I see in movies with Native Americans is historical details being left out. For example, the Mohegan tribe still existing and the movie *Last of the Mohicans* portraying their extinction. Also, the Indians in the last scene of *Dances with Wolves,* who use an incorrect stopping ground during the winter. I believe that Hollywood is concerned about offending Native Americans, but historical context comes into play in what they write and put in movies. Hollywood has a duty to add accurate historical context to the films; movies are taken very seriously in today's culture. Children learn from what they see in movies and on TV. But should Hollywood risk a good story just for entertainment value? I believe that the film industry can mix fact and fiction while still pulling off a good story. They should learn the correct history of America and all its people.

Works Cited

Aleiss, Angela. "Prelude to World War II: Racial Unity and the Hollywood Indian." *Journal of American Culture* 18 (Summer 1995): 25–34.

Chief Dan George. Indigenous Peoples' Literature. 14 Dec. 1998. 7 May 2001 <*http://www.indians.org/welker/dangeorg.htm*>.

First Nations. Ed. Jordan S. Dill. 2000. 23 Apr. 2001 <*http://www.dickshovel .com/www.html*>.

Graham Green. Home page. 16 Jan. 2000. 6 May 2001 <*http://www.geocities.com/ Hollywood/guild/9621/grahamgreen.html*>.

The Last of the Mohicans. Dir. Michael Mann. Perf. Russell Means and Daniel Day-Lewis. Twentieth Century Fox, 1992.

Maverick. Dir. Richard Donner. Perf. Graham Green and Mel Gibson. Warner Brothers, 1994.

The Outlaw Josey Wales. Dir. Clint Eastwood. Perf. Clint Eastwood and Chief Dan George. Warner Brothers, 1976.

Prats, Armando J. "The Image of the Other and the Other 'Dances with Wolves': The Refigured Indian and the Textual Supplement." *Journal of Film and Video* 50.1 (Spring 1998): 3–19.

Sayet, Melissa F. "The Lasting of the Mohegan." *Essence* 23.11 (March 1993): 55–57.

Strain, Jack. Phone interview. 11 April 2001.

Strain, Lauren. Personal survey. 3 May 2001.

In your journal, write down the meanings of the following words:

- some historical *misrepresentations* **(3)**
- the *romantic* reasons **(6)**
- *pro-interventionist* politics of Hollywood studios **(18)**
- rid the movie industry of *fascist* ideals **(18)**

QUESTIONS FOR WRITING AND DISCUSSION

1. Make a list of films you have seen that have Native Americans characters. Choose two of those films—one older, one more recent. Which characters in both films seemed most realistic and which most stereotypical? Describe the changes you notice between these two films' representations of Native American culture, language, politics, or heritage.

2. At the end of her essay, Strain says that Hollywood can "mix fact and fiction" while still creating a good story. Would you agree with that statement, or do you think historical accuracy should come first and entertainment values second? Choose a film about Native Americans—or any ethnic group—and explain what that film loses or gains by placing entertainment values over historical and cultural accuracy (or, conversely, by giving historical/cultural accuracy much more importance than entertainment values).

3. Strain conducts both a short survey and an interview which she reports on at the end of her paper. Assume you are in a peer-response group, giving her feedback on her essay. Would you advise her to integrate the information in paragraphs 17 and 18 earlier in her essay rather than tacking them on at the end? Where might that information fit? (How do you plan to integrate any interview or survey information in your own essay?)

4. Read the essay by Margaret Lazarus in Chapter 8, entitled "All's Not Well in Land of 'The Lion King.'" Rent *Pocahontas* from a video store and watch it. Are there racist or sexist scenes or images in Disney's version of *Pocahontas?* Does the film ultimately promote Native American cultural values or mainstream white American values? Explain.

STUDENT WRITING

MY FRIEND MICHELLE, AN ALCOHOLIC

Bridgid Stone

Bridgid Stone, a student at Southeast Missouri State University, decided to write her investigative essay on alcoholism. In the library, she was able to find quite a lot of information and statistics about alcohol. In her friend, Michelle, she had a living example of the consequences of alcohol abuse. The question, however, was how to combine the two. As you read her essay, notice how she interweaves description and dialogue with facts and statistics.

Five million teenagers are problem drinkers, according to *Group* magazine's article "Sex, Drugs, and Alcohol." One of these five million teenagers is my friend, Michelle.

1

"I can't wait to go out tonight and get drunk," Michelle announces as *2* she walks into my dorm room. I just sigh and shake my head. Michelle has been drunk every night since Wednesday. In the last three days, she has been to more fraternity parties than classes.

We leave a few hours later for a Sig Tau party. Even though I have *3* been attending these parties for weeks now, the amount of alcohol present still amazes me. Almost everyone is walking around with a twelve-pack of beer. Others are carrying fifths of vodka or Jack Daniels whiskey. As cited in *Fraternities and Sororities on Contemporary College Campuses,* 73 percent of fraternity advisers believe that alcohol is a problem in fraternities. I wish the other 27 percent could be here now. Fraternities are synonymous with drinking.

Michelle and I both have innocent-looking squeeze bottles, but inside *4* are very stiff screwdrivers. They probably have more vodka than orange juice. Michelle finishes her drink before I am halfway through mine. So she finishes off mine, too, before disappearing into the throng of people at the party. The next time I see her, she is holding a beer in each hand. Her speech is slurred, and she can barely stand up on her own.

We head back to the dorm when Michelle starts vomiting. Once we *5* are in her room, I help her undress and put her to bed.

"Bridgid, I am so sorry," Michelle cries, "I promise never to drink *6* again."

"Okay, just get some sleep," I tell her as I leave. *7*

It's Thursday night and Michelle is ready to party again. *8*

"I haven't been to my Friday 8:00 class in a month. Do you think I *9* should just stay up all night after the party and go to class drunk? Or should I just not go to class and sleep in?" Michelle asks.

"Don't go out and get drunk. Stay home tonight and get up and go to *10* your classes tomorrow," I advise.

"I am just going to sleep in," Michelle informs me as she leaves for the *11* party.

Like Michelle, an estimated 4.6 million adolescents experience nega- *12* tive consequences of alcohol abuse, such as poor school performance. This was reported in a survey conducted by NIAAA for a United States Con- gressional report.

Early Friday morning, I get a phone call from the on-duty resident *13* adviser. Michelle has passed out in the lobby of the Towers Complex. She couldn't remember her phone number or even what floor she lived on, but

I had written my phone number on Michelle's hand, so she could call me if she got into any trouble. The R.A. had seen my number and decided to call, since Michelle was too drunk to dial the four digits.

"Could you please escort your friend up to your room?" the R.A. asks. *14* She doesn't sound very happy.

"Sure, I will be down in a few minutes," I promise. It takes me and an- *15* other girl from our floor to get Michelle onto the elevator. She keeps lying down or passing out. Thirty minutes later, we get Michelle into bed. She is mumbling incoherently, and she reeks of alcohol. Needless to say, Michelle doesn't make it to her 8:00 A.M. class, again.

Saturday afternoon, I confront Michelle about the Thursday night *16* incident. This is rather hard to do, since she doesn't remember any of it.

"I just drink to loosen up. I'm much more fun if I've been drinking," *17* Michelle tells me.

"You are not much fun when you are puking or passing out," I reply. *18* A desire to loosen up is one of the main reasons that teenagers drink, re- ports *Group* magazine. Other reasons include a need to escape and to rebel.

"I have to release steam every once in a while," she argues. "School is *19* really stressing me out."

"Michelle, you don't even go to class," I tell her. *20*

"Everyone else drinks!" she says. "Why are you picking on me?" She *21* stomps out of my room.

Michelle was partially correct, though, when she stated, "Everyone else *22* drinks." As reported in *Alcohol and Youth,* more than 80 percent of all col- lege students surveyed had been drinking in the previous month. But this doesn't mean that what Michelle is doing is any less serious. In all proba- bility, Michelle is an alcoholic.

A test that is often used to determine if someone has a drinking prob- *23* lem can be found in *Getting Them Sober,* by Toby Rice Andrews. There are twenty questions on the test. A "yes" answer to two of the questions indi- cates a possible drinking problem. Questions include: "Do you miss time from school or work due to drinking?" "Do you drink to escape from wor- ries or troubles?" "Do you drink because you are shy?" "Have you ever had a memory loss due to drinking?" Michelle would probably have answered "yes" to all of the above questions.

I moved out of the dorm at the beginning of the second semester, so I *24* haven't seen much of Michelle. The last time I saw her was about three weeks ago. She had gotten arrested while in New Orleans for spring break. Apparently, Michelle had been out drinking and eventually had been arrested for public drunkenness.

"It wasn't that bad," she told me. "I don't even remember being in the jail cell. I was pretty trashed." 25

Works Cited

Andrews, Toby Rice. *Getting Them Sober.* South Plainfield, N.J.: Bridge Publishing, 1980.

Barnes, Grace. *Alcohol and Youth.* Westport, Conn.: Greenwood Press, 1982.

Pruett, Harold, and Vivian Brown. *Crisis Intervention and Prevention.* San Francisco: Jossey-Bass Inc., 1987.

"Sex, Drugs, and Alcohol." *Group* February 1992: 17–20.

Van Pelt, Rich. *Intensive Care.* Grand Rapids, Mich.: Zondervan Publishing House, 1988.

Winston, Roger, William Nettles III, and John Opper, Jr. *Fraternities and Sororities on Contemporary College Campuses.* San Francisco: Jossey-Bass Inc., 1987.

QUESTIONS FOR WRITING AND DISCUSSION

1. Investigative reports should provide information without editorializing or arguing for or against one perspective or another. Even though Stone is writing about her friend, Michelle, does she sympathize with Michelle or make excuses for her? Does she censure Michelle for her behavior? How effectively does Stone maintain a reporter's distance as she describes Michelle's behavior and presents statistics and other background information? Explain, referring to specific passages in the essay.

2. Who is Stone's audience for her essay? Where would you recommend that Stone send her essay for possible publication? List two possible publication sources (magazines or newspapers), and explain your choices.

3. If Stone were revising her essay, what advice would you give her about balancing statistics and personal experience? Should she have more statistics? Should she have more narrative? Refer to specific paragraphs and examples in your response.

4. Stone's use of the present tense adds dramatic impact to her essay. Reread her essay, noticing where she uses the present tense and where she shifts to the

past tense. Where was the use of the present tense most effective? Did her tense shifting confuse you at any point? Where?

5.   Compare Stone's essay with Kozol's essay earlier in this chapter. What reporting strategies does Stone adapt from Kozol? How are their reporting strategies different? Explain your response by referring to specific passages from each author.

A prolific painter of portraits before and after the French Revolution, Elisabeth Vigée-Lebrun specialized in paintings of the rich and famous of her time. Shortly after completing this portrait, Vigée-Lebrun escaped from France and lived in exile for over a decade. The journal question on page 316 asks you to compare her work with a photograph by Dorthea Lange made in California in 1936 of a migrant mother and her children.

Marie Louise Elisabeth Vigée-Lebrun (1755-1842)
Marie Antoinette and her Children (1787)
Oil on canvas, 9' 1/4" × 7' 5/8"
Musée National du Château de Versailles et de Trianom, © Photo RMN-Gerard Blot

chapter

7 Explaining

You have decided to quit your present job, so you write a note to your boss giving thirty days' notice. During your last few weeks at work, your boss asks you to write a three-page job description to help orient the person who will replace you. The job description should include a list of your current duties as well as advice to your replacement on how to execute them most efficiently. To write the description, you record your daily activities, look back through your calendar, comb through your records, and brainstorm a list of everything you do. As you write up the description, you include specific examples and illustrations of your typical responsibilities.

As a gymnast and dancer, you gradually become obsessed with losing weight. You start skipping meals, purging the little food you do eat, and lying about your eating habits to your parents. Before long, you weigh less than seventy pounds, and your physician diagnoses your condition: anorexia nervosa. With advice from your physician and counseling from a psychologist, you gradually begin to control your disorder. To explain to others what anorexia is, how it is caused, and what its effects are, you write an essay in which you explain your ordeal, alerting other readers to the potential dangers of uncontrolled dieting.

> *Become aware of the two-sided nature of your mental make-up: one thinks in terms of he connectedness of things, the other thinks in terms of parts and sequences.*
>
> —GABRIELE LUSSER RICO,
> AUTHOR OF WRITING THE NATURAL WAY

> *What [a writer] knows is almost always a matter of the relationships he establishes, between example and generalization, between one part of a narrative and the next, between the idea and the counter idea that the writer sees is also relevant.*
>
> —ROGER SALE,
> AUTHOR OF ON WRITING

EXPLAINING AND DEMONSTRATING RELATIONSHIPS IS A FREQUENT PURPOSE FOR WRITING. EXPLAINING GOES BEYOND INVESTIGATING THE FACTS AND REPORTING INFORMATION; IT ANALYZES THE COMPONENT PARTS OF A SUB-ject and then shows how the parts fit in relation to one another. Its goal is to clarify for a particular group of readers *what* something is, *how* it happened or should happen, and/or *why* it happens.

Explaining begins with assessing the rhetorical situation: the writer, the occasion, the intended purpose and audience, the genre, and the cultural context. As you begin thinking about a subject, topic, or issue to explain, keep in mind your own interests, the expectations of your audience, the possible genre you might choose to help achieve your purpose (essay, article, pamphlet, multigenre essay, Web site), and finally the cultural or social context in which you are writing or in which your writing might be read.

Explaining any idea, concept, process, or effect requires analysis. Analysis starts with dividing a thing or phenomenon into its various parts. Then, once you explain the various parts, you put them back together (synthesis) to explain their relationship or how they work together.

Explaining how to learn to play the piano, for example, begins with an analysis of the parts of the learning process: playing scales, learning chords, getting instruction from a teacher, sight reading, and performing in recitals. Explaining why two automobiles collided at an intersection begins with an analysis of the contributing factors: the nature of the intersection, the number of cars involved, the condition of the drivers, and the condition of each vehicle. Then you bring the parts together and show their *relationships:* you show how practicing scales on the piano fits into the process of learning to play the piano; you demonstrate why one small factor—such as a faulty turn signal—combined with other factors to cause an automobile accident.

The emphasis you give to the *analysis* of the object or phenomenon and the time you spend explaining *relationships* of the parts depends on your purpose, subject, and audience. If you want to explain how a flower reproduces, for example, you may begin by identifying the important parts, such as the pistil and stamen, that most readers need to know about before they can understand the reproductive process. However, if you are explaining the process to a botany major who already knows the parts of a flower, you might spend more time discussing the key operations in pollination or the reasons why some flowers cross-pollinate and others do not. In any effective explanation, analyzing parts and showing relationships must work together for that particular group of readers.

Because its purpose is to teach the reader, *expository writing,* or writing to explain, should be as clear as possible. Explanations, however, are more than organized pieces of information. Expository writing contains information that is focused by your point of view, by your experience, and by your reasoning powers. Thus, your explanation of a thing or phenomenon makes a point or has a thesis: This is the *right* way to define *happiness.* This is how one *should* bake lasagne or do a calculus problem. These are the *most important* reasons why the senator from New York was elected. To make your explanation clear, you show what you mean by using specific support: facts, data, examples, illustrations, statistics, comparisons, analogies, and images. Your thesis is a *general* assertion about the relationships of the *specific* parts. The support helps your reader identify the parts and see the relationships. Expository writing teaches the reader by alternating between generalizations and specific examples.

Techniques for Explaining

> **"***The main thing I try to do is write as clearly as I can.***"**
> —E. B. WHITE,
> JOURNALIST AND
> COAUTHOR OF
> ELEMENTS OF STYLE

Explaining requires first that you assess your rhetorical situation. Your purpose must work for a particular audience, genre, and context. You may revise some of these aspects of the rhetorical situation as you draw on your own observations and memories about your topic. As you research your topic, conduct an interview, or do a survey, keep thinking about issues of audience, genre, and context. Below are techniques for writing clear explanations.

- **Considering (and reconsidering) your purpose, audience, genre, and social context.** As you change your audience or your genre, for example, you must change how you explain something as well as how much and what kind of evidence and support you use.
- **Getting the reader's attention and stating the thesis.** Devise an accurate but interesting *title.* Use an attention-getting *lead-in.* State the *thesis* clearly.
- **Defining key terms and describing *what* something is.** Analyze and *define* by describing, comparing, classifying, and giving examples.
- **Identifying the steps in a process and showing *how* each step relates to the overall process.** Describe how something should be done or how something typically happens.

- **Describing causes and effects and showing *why* certain causes lead to specific effects.** Analyze how several causes lead to a single effect, or show how a single cause leads to multiple effects.
- **Supporting explanations with specific evidence.** Use descriptions, examples, comparisons, analogies, images, facts, data, or statistics to *show* what, how, or why.

In *Spirit of the Valley: Androgyny and Chinese Thought,* psychologist Sukie Colgrave illustrates many of these techniques as she explains an important concept from psychology: the phenomenon of *projection.* Colgrave explains how we "project" attributes missing in our own personality onto another person—especially someone we love:

Explaining what: Definition example

A one-sided development of either the masculine or feminine principles has [an] unfortunate consequence for our psychological and intellectual health: it encourages the phenomenon termed "projection." This is the process by which we project onto other people, things, or ideologies, those aspects of ourselves which we have not, for whatever reason, acknowledged or developed. The most familiar example of this is the obsession which usually accompanies being "in love." A person whose feminine side is unrealised will often "fall in love" with the feminine which she or he "sees" in another person, and similarly with the masculine. The experience of being "in love" is one of powerful dependency. As long as the projection appears to fit its object nothing awakens the person to the reality of the projection. But sooner or later the lover usually becomes aware of certain discrepancies between her or his desires and the person chosen to satisfy them. Resentment, disappointment, anger and rejection rapidly follow, and often the relationship disintegrates. . . . But if we can explore our own psyches we may discover what it is we were demanding from our lover and start to develop it in ourselves. The moment this happens we begin to see other people a little more clearly. We are freed from some of our needs to make others what we want them to be, and can begin to love them more for what they are.

Explaining why: Effects of projection

Explaining how: the process of freeing ourselves from dependency

EXPLAINING *WHAT*

Explaining *what* something is or means requires showing the relationship between it and the *class* of beings, objects, or concepts to which it belongs. *Formal definition,* which is often essential in explaining, has three parts: the thing or term to be defined, the class, and the distinguishing characteristics of the thing or term. The thing being defined can be concrete, such as a turkey, or abstract, such as democracy.

THING OR TERM	CLASS	DISTINGUISHING CHARACTERISTICS
A turkey is a	bird	that has brownish plumage and a bare, wattled head and neck; it is widely domesticated for food.
Democracy is	government	by the people, exercised directly or through elected representatives.

Frequently, writers use *extended definitions* when they need to give more than a mere formal definition. An extended definition may explain the word's etymology or historical roots, describe sensory characteristics of something (how it looks, feels, sounds, tastes, smells), identify its parts, indicate how something is used, explain what it is not, provide an example of it, and/or note similarities or differences between this term and other words or things.

The following extended definition of democracy, written for an audience of college students to appear in a textbook, begins with the etymology of the word and then explains—using analysis, comparison, example, and description—what democracy is and what it is not:

Since democracy is government of the people, by the people, and for the people, a democratic form of government is not fixed or static. Democracy is dynamic; it adapts to the wishes and needs of the people. The term *democracy* derives from the Greek word *demos,* meaning "the common people," and *-kratia,* meaning "strength or power" used to govern or rule. Democracy is based on the notion that a majority of people creates laws and then everyone agrees to abide by those laws in the interest of the common good. In a democracy, people are not ruled by a king, a dictator, or a small group of powerful individuals. Instead, people elect officials who use the power temporarily granted to them to govern the society. For example, the people may agree that their government should raise money for defense, so the officials levy taxes to support an army. If enough people decide, however, that taxes for defense are too high, then they request that their elected officials change the laws or they elect new officials. The essence of democracy lies in its responsiveness: Democracy is a form of government in which laws and lawmakers change as the will of the majority changes.	*Formal definition* *Description: What democracy is* *Etymology: Analysis of the word's roots* *Comparison: What democracy is not* *Example* *Formal definition*

Figurative expressions—vivid word pictures using similes, metaphors, or analogies—can also explain what something is. During World War II, for example, the Writer's War Board asked E. B. White (author of *Charlotte's Web* and many *New Yorker* magazine essays, as well as other works) to provide an explanation of democracy. Instead of giving a formal definition or etymology, White responded with a series of imaginative comparisons showing the *relationship* between various parts of American culture and the concept of democracy:

> Surely the Board knows what democracy is. It is the line that forms on the right. It is the don't in Don't Shove. It is the hole in the stuffed shirt through which the sawdust slowly trickles; it is the dent in the high hat. Democracy is the recurrent suspicion that more than half of the people are right more than half of the time. It is the feeling of privacy in the voting booths, the feeling of communion in the libraries, the feeling of vitality everywhere. Democracy is the score at the beginning of the ninth. It is an idea which hasn't been disproved yet, a song the words of which have not gone bad. It's the mustard on the hot dog and the cream in the rationed coffee. Democracy is a request from a War Board, in the middle of a morning in the middle of a war, wanting to know what democracy is.

Often, we think that explanations of technical subjects must be academic and complex, but sometimes writers about technical subjects use images and metaphors to get their point across. In the following definition of Web robots—so-called "bots," Andrew Leonard, writing for a contemporary audience in *Wired* magazine, enlivens his explanation by personifying these software programs:

> Web robots—spiders, wanderers, and worms. Cancelbots, Lazarus, and Automoose. Chatterbots, soft bots, userbots, taskbots, knowbots, and mailbots. . . . In current online parlance, the word "bot" pops up everywhere, flung around carelessly to describe just about any kind of computer program—a logon script, a spellchecker—that performs a task on a network. Strictly speaking, all bots are "autonomous"—able to react to their environments and make decisions without prompting from their creators; while the master or mistress is brewing coffee, the bot is off retrieving Web documents, exploring a MUD, or combatting Usenet spam. . . . Even more important than function is behavior—bona fide bots are programs with

personality. Real bots talk, make jokes, have feelings—even if those feelings are nothing more than cleverly conceived algorithms.

EXPLAINING *HOW*

Explaining *how* something should be done or how something happens is usually called *process analysis*. One kind of process analysis is the "how-to" explanation: how to cook a turkey, how to tune an engine, how to get a job. Such recipes or directions are *prescriptive:* You typically explain how something *should* be done. In a second kind of process analysis, you explain how something happens or is typically done—without being directive or prescriptive. In a *descriptive* process analysis, you explain how some natural or social process typically happens: how cells split during mitosis, how hailstones form in a cloud, how students react to the pressure of examinations, or how political candidates create their public images. In both prescriptive and descriptive explanations, however, you are analyzing a *process*—dividing the sequence into its parts or steps—and then showing how the parts contribute to the whole process.

Cookbooks, automobile-repair manuals, instructions for assembling toys or appliances, and self-improvement books are all examples of *prescriptive* process analysis. Writers of recipes, for example, begin with analyses of the ingredients and the steps in preparing the food. Then they carefully explain how the steps are related, how to avoid problems, and how to serve mouth-watering concoctions. Farley Mowat, naturalist and author of *Never Cry Wolf,* gives his readers the following detailed—and humorous—recipe for creamed mouse. Mowat became interested in this recipe when he decided to test the nutritional content of the wolf's diet. "In the event that any of my readers may be interested in personally exploiting this hitherto overlooked source of excellent animal protein," Mowat writes, "I give the recipe in full":

Souris à la Crème

INGREDIENTS:

One dozen fat mice	Salt and pepper	One cup white flour
Cloves	One piece sowbelly	Ethyl alcohol

Skin and gut the mice, but do not remove the heads; wash, then place in a pot with enough alcohol to cover the carcasses. Allow to marinate for about two hours. Cut sowbelly into small cubes and fry slowly until most of the fat has been rendered. Now remove the carcasses from the alcohol and roll them in a mixture of salt, pepper and flour; then place in frying pan and sauté for about five minutes (being careful not to allow the pan to get too hot, or the delicate meat will dry out and become tough and stringy). Now add a cup of alcohol and six or eight cloves. Cover the pan and allow to simmer slowly for fifteen minutes. The cream sauce can be made according to any standard recipe. When the sauce is ready, drench the carcasses with it, cover and allow to rest in a warm place for ten minutes before serving.

Explaining *how* something happens or is typically done involves a *descriptive* process analysis. It requires showing the chronological relationship between one idea, event, or phenomenon and the next—and it depends on close observation. In *The Lives of a Cell,* biologist and physician Lewis Thomas explains that ants are like humans: while they are individuals, they can also act together to create a social organism. Although exactly how ants communicate remains a mystery, Thomas explains how they combine to form a thinking, working organism:

[Ants] seem to live two kinds of lives: they are individuals, going about the day's business without much evidence of thought for tomorrow, and they are at the same time component parts, cellular elements, in the huge, writhing, ruminating organism of the Hill, the nest, the hive. . . .

A solitary ant, afield, cannot be considered to have much of anything on his mind; indeed, with only a few neurons strung together by fibers, he can't be imagined to have a mind at all, much less a thought. He is more like a ganglion on legs. Four ants together, or ten, encircling a dead moth on a path, begin to look more like an idea. They fumble and shove, gradually moving the food toward the Hill, but as though by blind chance. It is only when you watch the dense mass of thousands of ants, crowded together around the Hill, blackening the ground, that you begin to see the whole beast, and now you observe it thinking, planning, calculating. It is an intelligence, a kind of live computer, with crawling bits for its wits.

At a stage in the construction, twigs of a certain size are needed, and all the members forage obsessively for twigs of just this size. Later, when outer walls are to be finished, thatched, the size must change, and as though given new orders by telephone, all the workers shift the search to the new twigs. If you disturb the arrangement of a part of the Hill, hundreds of ants will set it vibrating, shifting, until it is put right again. Distant sources of food are somehow sensed, and long lines, like tentacles, reach out over the ground, up over walls, behind boulders, to fetch it in.

EXPLAINING *WHY*

"Why?" may be the question most commonly asked by human beings. We are fascinated by the reasons for everything that we experience in life. We ask questions about natural phenomena: Why is the sky blue? Why does a teakettle whistle? Why do some materials act as superconductors? We also find human attitudes and behavior intriguing: Why is chocolate so popular? Why do some people hit small leather balls with big sticks and then run around a field stomping on little white pillows? Why are America's family farms economically depressed? Why did the United States go to war in Iraq? Why is the Internet so popular?

Explaining *why* something occurs can be the most fascinating—and difficult—kind of expository writing. Answering the question "why" usually requires analyzing *cause-and-effect relationships.* The causes, however, may be too complex or intangible to identify precisely. We are on comparatively secure ground when we ask *why* about physical phenomena that can be weighed, measured, and replicated under laboratory conditions. Under those conditions, we can determine cause and effect with precision.

Fire, for example, has three *necessary* and *sufficient* causes: combustible material, oxygen, and ignition temperature. Without *each* of these causes, fire will not occur (each cause is "necessary"); taken together, these three causes are *enough* to cause fire (all three together are "sufficient"). In this case, the cause-and-effect relationship can be illustrated by an equation:

CAUSE 1	+	CAUSE 2	+	CAUSE 3	=	EFFECT
(combustible material)		(oxygen)		(ignition temperature)		(fire)

Analyzing both necessary and sufficient causes is essential to explaining an effect. You may say, for example, that wind shear (an abrupt downdraft in a storm) "caused" an airplane crash. In fact, wind shear may have *contributed* (been necessary) to the crash but was not by itself the total (sufficient) cause of the crash: an airplane with enough power may be able to overcome wind shear forces in certain circumstances. An explanation of the crash is not complete until you analyze the full range of necessary *and* sufficient causes, which may include wind shear, lack of power, mechanical failure, and even pilot error.

Sometimes, explanations for physical phenomena are beyond our analytical powers. Astrophysicists, for example, have good theoretical reasons for believing that black holes cause gigantic gravitational whirlpools in outer space, but they have difficulty explaining why black holes exist—or whether they exist at all.

In the realm of human cause and effect, determining causes and effects can be as tricky as explaining why black holes exist. Why, for example, do some children learn math easily while others fail? What effect does failing at math have on a child? What are necessary and sufficient causes for divorce? What are the effects of divorce on parents and children? Although you may not be able to explain all the causes or effects of something, you should not be satisfied until you have considered a wide range of possible causes and effects. Even then, you need to qualify or modify your statements, using such words as *might, usually, often, seldom, many,* or *most,* and then giving as much support and evidence as you can.

In the following paragraphs, Jonathan Kozol, a critic of America's educational system and author of *Illiterate America,* explains the multiple effects of a single cause: illiteracy. Kozol supports his explanation by citing specific ways that illiteracy affects the lives of people:

Illiterates cannot read the menu in a restaurant.

They cannot read the cost of items on the menu in the window of the restaurant before they enter.

Illiterates cannot read the letters that their children bring home from their teachers. They cannot study school department circulars that tell them of the courses that their children must be taking if they hope to pass the SAT exams. They cannot help with homework. They cannot write a letter to the teacher. They are afraid to visit in the classroom. They do not want to humiliate their child or themselves. . . .

Many illiterates cannot read the admonition on a pack of cigarettes. Neither the Surgeon General's warning nor its reproduction on the package can alert them to the risks. Although most people learn by word of mouth that smoking is related to a number of grave physical disorders, they do not get the chance to read the detailed stories which can document this danger with the vividness that turns concern into determination to resist. They can see the handsome cowboy or the slim Virginia lady lighting up a filter cigarette; they cannot heed the words that tell them that this product is (not "may be") dangerous to their health. Sixty million men and women are condemned to be the unalerted, high-risk candidates for cancer. . . .

Illiterates cannot travel freely. When they attempt to do so, they encounter risks that few of us can dream of. They cannot read traffic signs and, while they often learn to recognize and to decipher symbols, they cannot manage street names which they haven't seen before. The same is true for bus and subway stops. While ingenuity can sometimes help a man or woman to discern directions from familiar landmarks, buildings, cemeteries, churches, and the like, most illiterates are virtually immobilized. They seldom wander past the streets and neighborhoods they know. Geographical paralysis becomes a bitter metaphor for their entire existence. They are immobilized in almost every sense we can imagine. They can't move up. They can't move out. They cannot see beyond.

WARMING UP: JOURNAL EXERCISES

The following exercises will help you practice writing explanations. Read all of the following exercises and then write on the three that interest you most. If another idea occurs to you, write about it.

1. Write a one-paragraph explanation of an idea, term, or concept that you have discussed in a class that you are currently taking. From biology, for example, you might define *photosynthesis* or *gene splicing*. From psychology, you might define *psychosis* or *projection*. From computer studies, you might define *cyberspace* or *morphing*. First, identify someone who might need to know about this subject. Then give a definition and an illustration. Finally, describe how the term was discovered or invented, what its effects or applications are, and/or how it works.

2. Imitating E. B. White's short "definition" of democracy, use imaginative comparisons to write a short definition—serious or humorous—of one of the following words: *freedom, adolescence, mathematics, politicians, parents, misery, higher education, luck,* or a word of your own choice.

3. Novelist Ernest Hemingway once defined courage as "grace under pressure." Using this definition, explain how you or someone you know showed this kind of courage in a difficult situation.

4. When asked what jazz is, Louis Armstrong replied, "Man, if you gotta ask you'll never know." If you know quite a bit about jazz, explain what Armstrong meant. Or choose a familiar subject to which the same remark might apply. What can be "explained" about that subject, and what cannot?

5. Choose a skill that you've acquired (for example, playing a musical instrument, operating a machine, playing a sport, drawing, counseling others, driving in rush-hour traffic, dieting) and explain to a novice how he or she can acquire that skill. Reread what you've written. Then write another version addressed to an expert. What parts can you leave out? What must you add?

6. Sometimes writers use standard definitions to explain a key term, but sometimes they need to *resist* conventional definition in order to make a point. LaMer Steptoe, an eleventh-grader in West Philadelphia, was faced with a form requiring her to check her racial identity. Like many Americans of multicultural heritage, she decided not to check one box. In the following paragraphs, reprinted from National Public Radio's *All Things Considered,* Ms. Steptoe explains how she decided to (re)define herself. As you read her response, consider how you might need to resist a conventional definition in your own explaining essay.

Multiracialness

Caucasian, African-American, Latin American, Asian-American. Check one. I look black, so I'll pick that one. But, no, wait, if I pick that, I'll be denying the other sides of my family. So I'll pick white. But I'm not white or black, I'm both, and part Native American, too. It's confusing when you have to pick which race to identify with, especially when you have family who, on one side, ask, "Why do you talk like a white girl?" when, in the eyes of the other side of your family, your behind is black.

I never met my dad's mom, my grandmother, Maybelle Dawson Boyd Steptoe, and my father never knew his father. But my aunts or uncles or cousins all think of me as black or white. I mean, I'm not the lightest-skinned person, but my cousins down South swear I'm white. It bothers them, and that bothers me, how people could care so much about your skin color.

My mother's mother, Sylvia Gabriel, lives in Connecticut, near where my aunt, uncle and cousins on that side of the family live. Now, they're white, and where my grandma lives, there are very few black people or people of color. And when we visit, people look at us a lot, staring like, "What is that woman doing with those people?" It shocks the heck out of them when my brother and I call her Grandma.

My mother's side is Italian. I really didn't get any Italian culture except for the food. My father was raised much differently from my mother. My father is superstitious; he believes that a child should know his or her place and not speak unless spoken to. My father is very much into both his African-American and Native American heritage.

Multiracialness is a very tricky subject for my father. He'll tell people that I'm Native, African-American and Caucasian American, but at the same time he'll say things like, "Listen to jazz, listen to your cultural music." He says, "LaMer, look in the mirror. You're black. Ask any white person: they'll say you're black." He doesn't get it. I really would rather be colorless than to pick a race. I like other music, not just black music.

The term African-American bugs me. I'm not African. I'm American as a hot dog. We should have friends who are yellow, red, blue, black, purple, gay, religious, bisexual, trilingual, whatever, so you don't have a stereotypical view. I've met mean people and nice people of all different backgrounds. At my school, I grew up with all these kids, and I didn't look at them as white or Jewish or heterosexual; I looked at them as, "Oh, she's funny, he's sweet."

I know what box I'm going to choose. I pick D for none of the above, because my race is human.

Lange, Dorothea, photographer, "Migrant Agricultural Worker's Family." February 1936. America from the Great Depression to World War II: Black-and-White Photographs from the FSA-OWI, 1935–1945, Library of Congress.

7. Use your explaining skills to analyze visual images. For example, the work of art that opens this chapter is Elisabeth Vigée-Lebrun's 1788 portrait of Marie Antoinette and her Children. Use your browser to search for information about Marie Antoinette, her role in the French Revolution, and the career of Vigée-Lebrun. Then study the photograph on the previous page of a migrant woman and her children, taken in California in 1936. Do some Internet research on Dorothea Lange and her series of photographs of migrant workers in California. Write an essay comparing and contrasting the artists (Elisabeth Vigée-Lebrun and Dorothea Lange), the composition of these two images, and/or the social/cultural conditions surrounding each image. Assume that your audience is a group of your peers in your composition class.

PROFESSIONAL WRITING

MISS CLAIROL'S "DOES SHE . . . OR DOESN'T SHE?": HOW TO ADVERTISE A DANGEROUS PRODUCT

James B. Twitchell

A longtime professor of English at the University of Florida, James B. Twitchell has written a dozen books on a variety of academic and cultural topics. His recent books on advertising and popular culture include Carnival Culture: The Trashing of Taste in America *(1992),* Adcult USA: The Triumph of Advertising in American Culture *(1996), and* Living It Up: Our Love Affair with Luxury *(2002). In "Miss Clairol's 'Does She . . . Or Doesn't She?'" taken from* Twenty Ads That Shook the World *(2000), Twitchell examines the Miss Clairol advertising campaign, which was designed by Shirley Polykoff. Twitchell explains how Polykoff's ads, which ran for nearly twenty years, revolutionized the hair-coloring industry. Part of the success of the ad was in the catchy title, Twitchell notes, but equally important were the children in the ads and the follow-up phrase, "Hair color so natural, only her hairdresser knows for sure." (Before you read Twitchell's essay, however, look at several of Polykoff's Clairol ads by searching Shirley Polykoff on Google.)*

Two types of product are difficult to advertise: the very common and the very radical. Common products, called "parity products," need contrived distinctions to set them apart. You announce them as "New and Improved, Bigger and Better." But singular products need the illusion of acceptability. They have to appear as if they were *not* new and big, but old and small.

So, in the 1950s, new objects like television sets were designed to look like furniture so that they would look "at home" in your living room. Meanwhile, accepted objects like automobiles were growing massive tail fins to make them seem bigger and better, new and improved.

Although hair coloring is now very common (about half of all American women between the ages of thirteen and seventy color their hair, and about one in eight American males between thirteen and seventy does the same), such was certainly not the case generations ago. The only women who regularly dyed their hair were actresses like Jean Harlow, and "fast women," most especially prostitutes. The only man who dyed his hair was Gorgeous George, the professional wrestler. He was also the only man to use perfume.

In the twentieth century, prostitutes have had a central role in developing cosmetics. For them, sexiness is an occupational necessity, and hence anything that makes them look young, flushed, and fertile is quickly assimilated. Creating a full-lipped, big-eyed, and rosy-cheeked image is the basis of the lipstick, eye shadow, mascara, and rouge industries. While fashion may come *down* from the couturiers, face paint comes *up* from the street. Yesterday's painted woman is today's fashion plate.

In the 1950s, just as Betty Friedan was sitting down to write *The Feminine Mystique,* there were three things a lady should not do. She should not smoke in public, she should not wear long pants (unless under an overcoat), and she should not color her hair. Better she should pull out each gray strand by its root than risk association with those who bleached or, worse, dyed their hair.

This was the cultural context into which Lawrence M. Gelb, a chemical broker and enthusiastic entrepreneur, presented his product to Foote, Cone & Belding. Gelb had purchased the rights to a French hair-coloring process called Clairol. The process was unique in that unlike other available hair-coloring products, which coated the hair, Clairol actually penetrated the hair shaft, producing softer, more natural tones. Moreover, it contained a foamy shampoo base and mild oils that cleaned and conditioned the hair.

When the product was first introduced during World War II, the application process took five different steps and lasted a few hours. The users were urban and wealthy. In 1950, after seven years of research and development, Gelb once again took the beauty industry by storm. He introduced the new Miss Clairol Hair Color Bath, a single-step hair-coloring process.

This product, unlike any haircolor previously available, lightened, dark- *8* ened, or changed a woman's natural haircolor by coloring and shampooing hair in one simple step that took only twenty minutes. Color results were more natural than anything you could find at the corner beauty parlor. It was hard to believe. Miss Clairol was so technologically advanced that demonstrations had to be done onstage at the International Beauty Show, using buckets of water, to prove to the industry that it was not a hoax. This breakthrough was almost too revolutionary to sell.

In fact, within six months of Miss Clairol's introduction, the number *9* of women who visited the salon for permanent hair-coloring services increased by more than 500 percent! The women still didn't think they could do it themselves. And *Good Housekeeping* magazine rejected hair-color advertising because they too didn't believe the product would work. The magazine waited for three years before finally reversing its decision, accepting the ads, and awarding Miss Clairol's new product the "Good Housekeeping Seal of Approval."

FC&B passed the "Yes you *can* do it at home" assignment to Shirley *10* Polykoff, a zesty and genial first-generation American in her late twenties. She was, as she herself was the first to admit, a little unsophisticated, but her colleagues thought she understood how women would respond to abrupt change. Polykoff understood emotion, all right, and she also knew that you could be outrageous if you did it in the right context. You can be very naughty if you are first perceived as being nice. Or, in her words, "Think it out square, say it with flair." And it is just this reconciliation of opposites that informs her most famous ad.

She knew this almost from the start. On July 9, 1955, Polykoff wrote *11* to the head art director that she had three campaigns for Miss Clairol Hair Color Bath. The first shows the same model in each ad, but with slightly different hair color. The second exhorts "Tear up those baby pictures! You're a redhead now," and plays on the American desire to refashion the self by rewriting history. These two ideas were, as she says, "knock-downs" en route to what she really wanted. In her autobiography, appropriately titled *Does She . . . Or Doesn't She?: And How She Did It,* Polykoff explains the third execution, the one that will work:

#3. Now here's the one I really want. If I can get it sold to the client. Listen to this: "*Does she . . . or doesn't she?*" (No, I'm not kidding. Didn't you ever hear of the arresting question?) Followed by: "*Only her mother knows for sure!*" or "*So natural, only her mother knows for sure!*"

I may not do the mother part, though as far as I'm concerned mother is the ultimate authority. However, if Clairol goes retail, they may have a problem of offending beauty salons, where they are presently doing all of their business. So I may change the word "mother" to "hairdresser." This could be awfully good business—turning the hairdresser into a color expert. Besides, it reinforces the claim of naturalness, and not so incidentally, glamorizes the salon.

The psychology is obvious. I know from myself. If anyone admires my hair, I'd rather die than admit I dye. And since I feel so strongly that the average woman is me, this great stress on naturalness is important [Polykoff 1975, 28–29].

While her headline is naughty, the picture is nice and natural. Exactly *12* what "Does She . . . or Doesn't She" do? To men the answer was clearly sexual, but to women it certainly was not. The male editors of *Life* magazine balked about running this headline until they did a survey and found out women were not filling in the ellipsis the way they were.

Women, as Polykoff knew, were finding different meaning because *13* they were actually looking at the model and her child. For them the picture was not presexual but postsexual, not inviting male attention but expressing satisfaction with the result. Miss Clairol is a mother, not a love interest.

If that is so, then the product must be misnamed: it should be *Mrs.* *14* Clairol. Remember, this was the mid-1950s, when illegitimacy was a powerful taboo. Out-of-wedlock children were still called bastards, not love children. This ad was far more dangerous than anything Benetton or Calvin Klein has ever imagined.

The naught/nice conundrum was further intensified *and* diffused by *15* some of the ads featuring a wedding ring on the model's left hand. Although FC&B experimented with models purporting to be secretaries, schoolteachers, and the like, the motif of mother and child was always constant.

So what was the answer to what she does or doesn't do? To women, *16* what she did had to do with visiting the hairdresser. Of course, men couldn't understand. This was the world before unisex hair care. Men still went to barber shops. This was the same pre-feminist generation in which the solitary headline "Modess . . . because" worked magic selling female sanitary products. The ellipsis masked a knowing implication that excluded men. That was part of its attraction. Women know, men don't. This you-just-don't-get-it motif was to become a central marketing strategy as the women's movement was aided *and* exploited by Madison Avenue nichemeisters.

Polykoff had to be ambiguous for another reason. As she notes in her memo, Clairol did not want to be obvious about what they were doing to their primary customer—the beauty shop. Remember that the initial product entailed five different steps performed by the hairdresser, and lasted hours. Many women were still using hairdressers for something they could now do by themselves. It did not take a detective to see that the company was trying to run around the beauty shop and sell to the end-user. So the ad again has it both ways. The hairdresser is invoked as the expert—only he knows *for sure*—but the process of coloring your hair can be done without his expensive assistance. [17]

The copy block on the left of the finished ad reasserts this intimacy, only now it is not the hairdresser speaking, but another woman who has used the product. The emphasis is always on *returning* to young and radiant hair, hair you used to have, hair, in fact, that glistens exactly like your current companion's—your child's hair. [18]

The copy block on the right is all business and was never changed during the campaign. The process of coloring is always referred to as "automatic color tinting." *Automatic* was to the fifties what *plastic* became to the sixties, and what *networking* is today. Just as your food was kept automatically fresh in the refrigerator, your car had an automatic transmission, your house had an automatic thermostat, your dishes and clothes were automatically cleaned and dried, so, too, your hair had automatic tinting. [19]

However, what is really automatic about hair coloring is that once you start, you won't stop. Hair grows, roots show, buy more product . . . automatically. The genius of Gillette was not just that they sold the "safety razor" (they could give the razor away), but that they also sold the concept of being *clean-shaven.* Clean-shaven means that you use their blade every day, so, of course, you always need more blades. Clairol made "roots showing" into what Gillette had made "five o'clock shadow." [20]

As was to become typical in hair-coloring ads, the age of the model was *21*
a good ten years younger than the typical product user. The model is in her
early thirties (witness the age of the child), too young to have gray hair.

This aspirational motif was picked up later for other Clairol products: *22*
"If I've only one life . . . let me live it as a blonde!" "Every woman should
be a redhead . . . at least once in her life!" "What would your husband say
if suddenly you looked 10 years younger?" "Is it true blondes have more
fun?" "What does he look at second?" And, of course, "The closer he gets
the better you look!"

But these slogans for different brand extensions only work because *23*
Miss Clairol had done her job. She made hair coloring possible, she made
hair coloring acceptable, she made at-home hair coloring—dare I say it—
empowering. She made the unique into the commonplace. By the 1980s,
the hairdresser problem had been long forgotten and the follow-up lines
read, "Hair color so natural, they'll never know for sure."

The Clairol theme propelled sales 413 percent higher in six years and *24*
influenced nearly 50 percent of all adult women to tint their tresses. Ironically, Miss Clairol, bought out by Bristol-Myers in 1959, also politely
opened the door to her competitors, L'Oreal and Revlon.

Thanks to Clairol, hair coloring has become a very attractive business *25*
indeed. The key ingredients are just a few pennies' worth of peroxide, am-
monia, and pigment. In a pretty package at the drugstore it sells for four to
ten dollars per application. To put it mildly, the cost-revenue spread is what
is really enticing. Gross profits of 70 percent are standard. As is common
in the beauty industry, advertising and promotion cost far more than the
product.

If you want to see how well this Clairol campaign did, just look at how *26*
L'Oreal sells its version of hair dye. In L'Oreal's pitch, a rapturous beauty
proudly proclaims that her coloring costs more, but that "I'm worth it." In
a generation, hair coloring has gone from a surreptitious whisper (Does she
. . . ?) to a heroic trumpet (You better believe I do!). The user may be dangerous, the product certainly isn't. L'Oreal now dominates the worldwide
market.

But by taking control of how the new woman presented herself, Miss *27*
Clairol did indeed make it possible to come a long way, baby. In a current
ad for Miss Clairol's descendant Nice 'n' Easy, the pixieish Julia Louis-
Dreyfus, from *Seinfeld,* shows us how the unique and dangerous has become common and tame. In her Elaine persona, she interrupts a wedding,

telling the bride, "Even if your marriage doesn't last, your haircolor will." The guests are not shocked; they nod understandingly.

In your journal, write down the meanings of the following words:

- is quickly *assimilated* **(4)**
- from the *couturiers* **(4)**
- enthusiastic *entrepreneur* **(6)**
- *reconciliation* of opposites **(10)**
- filling in the *ellipsis* **(12)**
- models *purporting* to be secretaries **(15)**
- the *motif* of mother and child **(15)**
- had to be *ambiguous* **(17)**

QUESTIONS FOR WRITING AND DISCUSSION

1. Recall the first time you colored your hair—or cut or styled it in a particular way. What was your attitude toward making a change? Did you change because of influences from peers, family, friends, advertisements, or other social pressure? What was the effect of the change—on your attitude, personality, or relationships with others?

2. A key part to any successful advertising campaign is understanding the rhetorical situation: the product, the purpose and audience, the occasion, the selected text and images, and the cultural context. First consider the cultural context. Twitchell subtitles his essay, "How to Advertise a Dangerous Product." According to Twitchell, what was culturally "dangerous" about a haircoloring product at that time? What specifically were the dangers? How did Shirley Polykoff's Miss Clairol ads diffuse each of those dangers?

3. Understanding and successfully appealing to the audience is a second key part of any successful text or advertisement. Who was the audience or audiences

for the Clairol advertisements? Cite particular paragraphs where Twitchell explains how the Clairol advertisements anticipated and successfully managed the problem of audience.

4. Key word choices (diction) played an important role in the success of the Clairol advertisements. Find three examples from the essay that show how Polykoff used—or didn't use—a key word in order to make the advertisement more successful.

5. Explaining essays should have a lead-in that captures the reader's attention, a thesis that focuses the essay's main points, and a conclusion that captures and reemphasizes the thesis and brings closure to the essay—often by picking up an idea introduced earlier in the essay. Review Twitchell's lead-in, thesis, and conclusion. By yourself or in a small group, choose one of these three elements and revise it to make it more effective.

6. In paragraph 15, Twitchell briefly mentions the "motif of mother and child" that appears in every Miss Clairol advertisement. On the Internet or on your library's databases, research cultural images of mother and child. Start by examining traditional Christian imagery. Consider the painting of Marie Antoinette at the beginning of this chapter and Dorothea Lange's famous photograph of a migrant mother. How does the mother–child imagery work in those pictures to make them more effective? (What is the political or cultural goal of both pictures?) Then, working in a small group in your class, develop Twitchell's idea about the motif of mother and child. Why is this image culturally so important? Why was it rhetorically so important in the Miss Clairol advertisements?

PROFESSIONAL WRITING

HOW MALE AND FEMALE STUDENTS USE LANGUAGE DIFFERENTLY

Deborah Tannen

Everyone knows that men and women communicate differently, but Deborah Tannen, a linguist at Georgetown University, has spent her career studying how and why their conversational styles are different. Tannen's books include Conversational Style: Analyzing Talk Among Friends *(1984), her best-selling* You Just Don't Understand: Women and Men in Conversation *(1990), and* I Only Say This Because I Love You *(2001). In the following article from* The Chronicle of Higher Education, *Tannen applies her knowledge of conversational styles to the classroom. How do men and women communicate differently in the classroom? What teaching styles best promote open communication and learning for both sexes? As you read her essay, think about your own classes. Do the men in your classes talk more than the women? Do men like to argue in large groups, while women prefer conversations in small groups? How clearly— and convincingly—does Tannen explain discussion preferences and their effects in the classroom?*

When I researched and wrote my latest book, *You Just Don't Understand: Women and Men in Conversation,* the furthest thing from my mind was reevaluating my teaching strategies. But that has been one of the direct benefits of having written the book.

The primary focus of my linguistic research always has been the language of everyday conversation. One facet of this is conversational style: how different regional, ethnic, and class backgrounds, as well as age and gender, result in different ways of using language to communicate. *You Just Don't Understand* is about the conversational styles of women and men. As I gained more insight into typically male and female ways of using language, I began to suspect some of the causes of the troubling facts that women who go to single-sex schools do better in later life, and that when young women sit next to young men in classrooms, the males talk more. This is not to say that all men talk in class, nor that no women do. It is simply that a greater percentage of discussion time is taken by men's voices.

The research of sociologists and anthropologists such as Janet Lever, Marjorie Harness Goodwin, and Donna Eder has shown that girls and boys learn to use language differently in their sex-separate peer groups. Typically, a girl has a best friend with whom she sits and talks, frequently telling secrets. It's the telling of secrets, the fact and the way that they talk to each other, that makes them best friends. For boys, activities are central: their best friends are the ones they do things with. Boys also tend to play in larger groups that are hierarchical. High-status boys give orders and push low-status boys around. So boys are expected to use language to seize center stage: by exhibiting their skill, displaying their knowledge, and challenging and resisting challenges.

These patterns have stunning implications for classroom interaction. *4* Most faculty members assume that participating in class discussion is a necessary part of successful performance. Yet speaking in a classroom is more congenial to boys' language experience than to girls', since it entails putting oneself forward in front of a large group of people, many of whom are strangers and at least one of whom is sure to judge speakers' knowledge and intelligence by their verbal display.

Another aspect of many classrooms that makes them more hospitable *5* to most men than to most women is the use of debate-like formats as a learning tool. Our educational system, as Walter Ong argues persuasively in his book *Fighting for Life* (Cornell University Press, 1981), is fundamentally male in that the pursuit of knowledge is believed to be achieved by ritual opposition: public display followed by argument and challenge. Father Ong demonstrates that ritual opposition—what he calls "adversativeness" or "agonism"—is fundamental to the way most males approach almost any activity. (Consider, for example, the little boy who shows he likes a little girl by pulling her braids and shoving her.) But ritual opposition is antithetical to the way most females learn and like to interact. It is not that females don't fight, but that they don't fight for fun. They don't *ritualize* opposition.

Anthropologists working in widely disparate parts of the world *6* have found contrasting verbal rituals for women and men. Women in completely unrelated cultures (for example, Greece and Bali) engage in ritual laments: spontaneously produced rhyming couplets that express their pain, for example, over the loss of loved ones. Men do not take part in laments. They have their own, very different verbal ritual: a contest, a war of words in which they vie with each other to devise clever insults.

When discussing these phenomena with a colleague, I commented *7* that I see these two styles in American conversation: many women bond by talking about troubles, and many men bond by exchanging playful insults and put-downs, and other sorts of verbal sparring. He exclaimed: "I never thought of this, but that's the way I teach: I have students read an article, and then I invite them to tear it apart. After we've torn it to shreds, we talk about how to build a better model."

This contrasts sharply with the way I teach: I open the discussion of *8* readings by asking, "What did you find useful in this? What can we use in our own theory building and our own methods?" I note what I see as weaknesses in the author's approach, but I also point out that the writer's discipline and purposes might be different from ours. Finally, I offer personal anecdotes illustrating the phenomena under discussion and praise students' anecdotes as well as their critical acumen.

These different teaching styles must make our classrooms wildly different places and hospitable to different students. Male students are more likely to be comfortable attacking the readings and might find the inclusion of personal anecdotes irrelevant and "soft." Women are more likely to resist discussion they perceive as hostile, and, indeed, it is women in my classes who are most likely to offer personal anecdotes.

A colleague who read my book commented that he had always taken for granted that the best way to deal with students' comments is to challenge them; this, he felt it was self-evident, sharpens their minds and helps them develop debating skills. But he had noticed that women were relatively silent in his classes, so he decided to try beginning discussion with relatively open-ended questions and letting comments go unchallenged. He found, to his amazement and satisfaction, that more women began to speak up.

Though some of the women in his class clearly liked this better, perhaps some of the men liked it less. One young man in my class wrote in a questionnaire about a history professor who gave students questions to think about and called on people to answer them: "He would then play devil's advocate . . . *i.e.,* he debated us. . . . That class *really* sharpened me intellectually. . . . We as students do need to know how to defend ourselves." This young man valued the experience of being attacked and challenged publicly. Many, if not most, women would shrink from such "challenge," experiencing it as public humiliation.

A professor at Hamilton College told me of a young man who was upset because he felt his class presentation had been a failure. The professor was puzzled because he had observed that class members had listened attentively and agreed with the student's observations. It turned out that it was this very agreement that the student interpreted as failure: since no one had engaged his ideas by arguing with him, he felt they had found them unworthy of attention.

So one reason men speak in class more than women is that many of them find the "public" classroom setting more conducive to speaking, whereas most women are more comfortable speaking in private to a small group of people they know well. A second reason is that men are more likely to be comfortable with the debate-like form that discussion may take. Yet another reason is the different attitudes toward speaking in class that typify women and men.

Students who speak frequently in class, many of whom are men, assume *14* that it is their job to think of contributions and try to get the floor to express them. But many women monitor their participation not only to get the floor but to avoid getting it. Women students in my class tell me that if they have spoken up once or twice, they hold back for the rest of the class because they don't want to dominate. If they have spoken a lot one week, they will remain silent the next. These different ethics of participation are, of course, unstated, so those who speak freely assume that those who remain silent have nothing to say, and those who are reining themselves in assume that the big talkers are selfish and hoggish.

When I looked around my classes, I could see these differing ethics and *15* habits at work. For example, my graduate class in analyzing conversation had twenty students, eleven women and nine men. Of the men, four were foreign students: two Japanese, one Chinese, and one Syrian. With the exception of the three Asian men, all the men spoke in class at least occasionally. The biggest talker in the class was a woman, but there were also five women who never spoke at all, only one of whom was Japanese. I decided to try something different.

I broke the class into small groups to discuss the issues raised in the *16* readings and to analyze their own conversational transcripts. I devised three ways of dividing the students into groups: one by the degree program they were in, one by gender, and one by conversational style, as closely as I could guess it. This meant that when the class was grouped according to conversational style, I put Asian students together, fast talkers together, and quiet students together. The class split into groups six times during the semester, so they met in each grouping twice. I told students to regard the groups as examples of interactional data and to note the different ways they participated in the different groups. Toward the end of the term, I gave them a questionnaire asking about their class and group participation.

I could see plainly from my observation of the groups at work that *17* women who never opened their mouths in class were talking away in the small groups. In fact, the Japanese woman commented that she found it particularly hard to contribute to the all-woman group she was in because "I was overwhelmed by how talkative the female students were in the female-only group." This is particularly revealing because it highlights that the same person who can be "oppressed" into silence in one context can become the talkative "oppressor" in another. No one's conversational style is absolute; everyone's style changes in response to the context and others' styles.

Some of the students (seven) said they preferred the same-gender *18* groups; others preferred the same-style groups. In answer to the question "Would you have liked to speak in class more than you did?" six of the seven who said yes were women; the one man was Japanese. Most startlingly, this response did not come only from quiet women; it came from women who had indicated they had spoken in class never, rarely, sometimes, and often. Of the eleven students who said the amount they had spoken was fine, seven were men. Of the four women who checked "fine," two added qualifications indicating it wasn't completely fine: One wrote in "maybe more," and one wrote, "I have an urge to participate but often feel I should have something more interesting/relevant/wonderful/intelligent to say!!"

I counted my experiment a success. Everyone in the class found the *19* small groups interesting, and no one indicated he or she would have preferred that the class not break into groups. Perhaps most instructive, however, was the fact that the experience of breaking into groups, and of talking about participation in class, raised everyone's awareness about classroom participation. After we had talked about it, some of the quietest women in the class made a few voluntary contributions, though sometimes I had to ensure their participation by interrupting the students who were exuberantly speaking out.

Americans are often proud that they discount the significance of cul- *20* tural differences: "We are all individuals," many people boast. Ignoring such issues as gender and ethnicity becomes a source of pride: "I treat everyone the same." But treating people the same is not equal treatment if they are not the same.

The classroom is a different environment for those who feel comfort- *21* able putting themselves forward in a group than it is for those who find the prospect of doing so chastening, or even terrifying. When a professor asks, "Are there any questions?" students who can formulate statements the fastest have the greatest opportunity to respond. Those who need significant time to do so have not really been given a chance at all, since by the time they are ready to speak, someone else has the floor.

In a class where some students speak out without raising hands, *22* those who feel they must raise their hands and wait to be recognized do not have equal opportunity to speak. Telling them to feel free to jump in will not make them feel free; one's sense of timing, of one's rights and obligations in a classroom, are automatic, learned over years of interaction. They may be changed over time, with motivation and effort, but they cannot be changed on the spot. And everyone assumes his or her own way is best. When I asked my students how the class could be changed to make it easier for them to speak more, the most talkative woman said she would prefer it if no one had to raise hands, and a foreign student said he wished people would raise their hands and wait to be recognized.

My experience in this class has convinced me that small-group inter- 23 action should be part of any class that is not a small seminar. I also am convinced that having the students become observers of their own interaction is a crucial part of their education. Talking about ways of talking in class makes students aware that their ways of talking affect other students, that the motivations they impute to others may not truly reflect others' motives, and that the behaviors they assume to be self-evidently right are not universal norms.

The goal of complete equal opportunity in class may not be attainable, 24 but realizing that one monolithic classroom-participation structure is not equal opportunity is itself a powerful motivation to find more-diverse methods to serve diverse students—and every classroom is diverse.

In your journal, write the meanings of the following words:

- ritual opposition is *antithetical* (**5**)
- personal *anecdotes* (**8**)
- *conducive* to speaking (**13**)
- *ethics* of participation (**14**)
- *monolithic* classroom-participation structure (**24**)

QUESTIONS FOR WRITING AND DISCUSSION

1. Reread Tannen's essay, noting places where your experiences as a student match or do not match her observations. In what contexts were your experiences similar to or different from Tannen's? Explain what might account for the different observations.

2. In her essay, Tannen states and then continues to restate her thesis. Reread her essay, underlining all the sentences that seem to state or rephrase her main idea. Do her restatements of the main idea make her essay clearer? Explain.

3. Explaining essays may explain *what* (describe and define), explain *how* (process analysis), and/or explain *why* (causal analysis). Find one example of each of these strategies in Tannen's essay. Which of these three is the dominant shaping strategy? Support your answer with references to specific sentences or paragraphs.

4. Effective explaining essays must have supporting evidence—specific examples, facts, quotations, testimony from experts, statistics, and so on. Choose four consecutive paragraphs from Tannen's essay and list the kinds of supporting evidence she uses. Based on your inventory, rate her supporting evidence as weak, average, or strong. Explain your choice.

5. Does the style of Tannen's essay support her thesis that men and women have different ways of communicating? Does Tannen, in fact, use a "woman's style" of writing that is similar to women's conversational style? Examine Tannen's tone (her attitude toward her subject and audience), her voice (the projection of her personality in her language), and her supporting evidence (her use of facts and statistics or anecdotal, contextual evidence). Cite specific passages to support your analysis.

6. In another class where students discuss frequently, sit in the back row where you can observe the participation of men and women. First, record the number of men and the number of women in the class. Then, during one class period, record the following: (a) When the teacher calls on a student, record whether the student is male or female; (b) when a student talks without raising his or her hand, record whether the student is male or female; and (c) when students speak in class, record how long they talk and whether they are male or female. Once you have collected and analyzed your data, explain whether they seem to support or refute Tannen's claims.

7. On the Internet, visit Deborah Tannen's home page at *http://www.georgetown.edu/faculty/tannend*. Click on the link "Interviews with Deborah Tannen." How do her responses during these interviews shed light on the conversational styles of men and women? What points does she make that might apply to how men and women communicate and learn differently in the classroom?

Explaining: The Writing Process

ASSIGNMENT FOR EXPLAINING

After assessing your rhetorical situation, *explain* what something means or is, *how* it should be done or *how* it occurs, and/or *why* something occurs. Your purpose is to explain something as clearly as possible for your audience by analyzing, showing relationships, and demonstrating with examples, facts, illustrations, data, or other information.

With a topic in mind, think about your audience and a possible genre. As in your investigating paper, the amount and kind of detail you need depend on how much your readers are likely to know about your topic. What do they already know? What have you discovered in your research that will help explain the topic for them? Is an essay the most appropriate genre, or would an article, editorial, Internet posting, pamphlet, or letter be more effective?

CHOOSING A SUBJECT

If one of your journal entries suggested a possible subject, go on to the collecting and shaping strategies. If you still need an interesting subject, consider the following suggestions:

- Reread your authority list or the most interesting journal entries from previous chapters. Do they contain ideas that you might define or explain, processes suitable for how-to explanations, or causes or effects that you could analyze and explain for a certain audience?
- Reread your notes from another class in which you have an upcoming examination. Select some topic, idea, principle, process, famous person, or event from the text or your notes. Investigate other texts, popular magazines, or journals for information on that topic. If appropriate, interview someone or conduct a survey. Explain this principle or process to a member of your writing class.

> *"You can write about anything, and if you write well enough, even the reader with no intrinsic interest in the subject will become involved."*
>
> —TRACY KIDDER, NOVELIST

- If you are doing a community-service-learning project, consider a writing project explaining the agency's mission to the public or to a potential donor. You might also write an article for a local or campus newspaper explaining some aspect of their service or a recent contribution the agency has made to the community.
- Consider writing an artistic, cultural, historical, or social explanation of a particular visual image or a set of visual images. One excellent Web site for famous photographs is the Pulitzer site at *http://www.gallerym.com/pulitzerphotos.htm*. Decide on a particular audience, genre, and context appropriate for the photograph.
- Choose some current controversy to explain. Instead of arguing for one side or the other, however, explain the different points of view in this controversy. Who are the leading figures or groups representing each of several different positions? Choose a particular audience, genre, and context, and explain what each of these people or groups have to gain or lose and how their personal investments in the topic determine their position.

COLLECTING

QUESTIONS   Once you have a tentative subject and audience in mind, consider which of the following will be your primary focus (all three may be relevant):

- *What* something means or is
- *How* something occurs or is done (or should be done)
- *Why* something occurs or what its effects are

To explain *what* something is, jot down answers to each of the following questions. The more you can write on each question, the more details you'll have for your topic.

- What are its class and distinguishing characteristics?
- What is its etymology?
- How can you describe it?
- What examples can you give?
- What are its parts or its functions?
- What is it similar to? What is it *not?*
- What figurative comparisons apply?
- How can it be classified?
- Which of the above is most useful to your audience?

To explain *how* something occurs or is done, answer the following questions:

- What are the component parts or steps in the whole process?
- What is the exact sequence of steps or events?
- Are several of the steps or events related?
- If steps or events were omitted, would the outcome change?
- Which steps or events are most crucial?
- Which steps or events does your audience most need to know?

To explain *why* something occurs or what its effects are, consider the following issues:

- Which are the necessary or sufficient causes?
- Which causes are remote in time, and which are immediate?
- What is the order or sequence of the causes? Do the causes occur simultaneously?
- What are the effects? Do they occur in a sequence or simultaneously?
- Do the causes and effects occur in a "chain reaction"?
- Is there an action or situation that would have prevented the effect?
- Are there comparable things or events that have similar causes or effects?
- Which causes or effects need special clarification for your audience?

BRANCHING Often, *branching* can help you visually analyze your subject. Start with your topic and then subdivide each idea into its component parts. The resulting analysis will not only help generate ideas but may also suggest ways to shape an essay:

Branching can also take the form of a tree, with a main trunk for the subject and separate branches for each subtopic. For an essay on effective job hunting, information might be diagrammed this way:

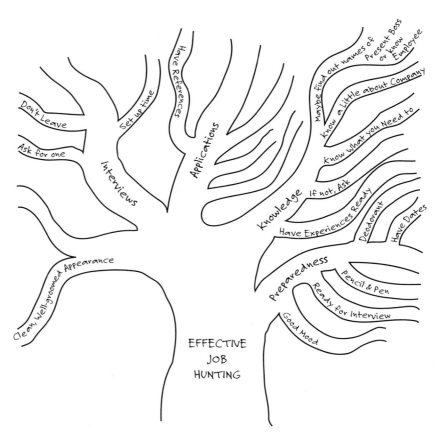

OBSERVING   If you can observe your subject, try drawing it, describing it, or taking careful notes. Which senses can you use to describe it—sight, sound, touch, smell, taste? If it is a scientific experiment that you can reproduce or a social situation you can reconstruct, go through it again and observe carefully. As you observe it, put yourself in your readers' shoes: what do you need to explain it to them?

REMEMBERING   Your own experience and memory are essential for explaining. *Freewriting, looping,* and *clustering* may all generate detailed information, good examples, and interesting perspectives that will make your explanation clearer and move vivid. (See Chapter 4 for an explanation of looping and clustering.)

Research Tips GO

Review your topic for research possibilities. Four research strategies are direct *observation*, use of *memories* and personal experience, *field research* (including interviews and surveys), and *library/Internet research*. (See Chapter 6 for interview and survey techniques. See Chapter 12 on using and documenting sources.) Tips to remember: Make *photocopies* of all the sources that you plan to cite in your essay. When you make copies, be sure to *write all relevant information* on the photocopies, such as author, date, publisher, place of publication, journal title, and volume numbers. When you cite sources in the text, be sure to *introduce* your sources. Make sure your direct quotations are *accurate* word-for-word transcriptions.

READING　When you find written texts about your subject, be sure to use your active reading strategies. You may need only a few sources if you reread them carefully. Write out a short summary for each source. Respond to each source by analyzing its effectiveness, agreeing or disagreeing with its ideas, or interpreting the text. The quality of your understanding is more important than the sheer number of sources you cite.

INVESTIGATING　Use sources available in the library, textbooks containing relevant information, or interviews with teachers, participants, or experts. Interview your classmates about their own subjects for this assignment: someone else's subject may trigger an idea that you can write about or may suggest a fresh approach to the subject that you have already chosen.

SHAPING

As you collect information and generate ideas from your collecting activities, be sure to *narrow* and *focus* your subject into a topic suitable for a short essay. You will not be able to cover everything you've read, thought, or experienced about your subject. Choose the most interesting ideas—for you and for your audience—and shape, order, and clarify those ideas.

AUDIENCE AND GENRE　As you consider ways to organize and shape your explaining essay, think about a possible audience and genre. An essay directed at a general audience composed of peers like your classmates is just one possibility. A letter

> *Readers may be strangers who have no immediate reason to care about your writing. They want order, clarity, and stimulation.*
>
> —ELIZABETH COWAN NEELD, TEACHER AND AUTHOR

to the editor, a pamphlet for a community agency, a job analysis for your employer, an article for a local or school newspaper, a posting or response to a listserve, or an essay for students in your major are other possibilities. Once you have a tentative audience and genre, you'll have a better idea about how to organize your explanation. Reread your assignment for specific suggestions and guidelines about audience and genre.

DEFINITION AND CLASSIFICATION   An essay explaining *what* something means or is can be shaped by using a variety of definition strategies or by classifying the subject.

Definition itself is not a single organizing strategy; it supports a variety of strategies that may be useful in shaping your essay: description, analysis of parts or function, comparison/contrast, development by examples, or figures of speech such as simile, metaphor, and analogy.

Classification, on the other hand, is a single strategy that can organize a paragraph or even a whole essay quickly. Observers of human behavior, for example, love to use classification. Grocery shoppers might be classified by types: racers (the ones who seem to have just won forty-five seconds of free shopping and run down the aisles filling their carts as fast as possible), talkers (the ones whose phone must be out of order because they stand in the aisles gossiping forever), penny-pinchers (who always have their calculators out and read the unit price labels for everything), party shoppers (who camp out in the junk food aisles, filling their carts with potato chips, dip, candy, peanuts, and drink mixers), and dawdlers (who leave their carts crosswise in the aisles while they read twenty-nine different soup can labels). You can write a sentence or two about each type or devote a whole paragraph to explaining a single type.

EXAMPLE   Development by example can effectively illustrate what something is or means, but it can also help explain how or why something happens. Usually, an example describes a specific incident, located at a certain place and occurring at a particular time, that *shows* or *demonstrates* the main idea. In the following paragraph from *Mediaspeak,* Donna Woolfolk Cross explains what effects soap operas can have on addicted viewers. This paragraph is developed by several examples—some described in detail, others referred to briefly:

> Dedicated watchers of soap operas often confuse fact with fiction. . . . Stars of soap operas tell hair-raising stories of their encounters with fans suffering from this affliction. Susan Lucci, who plays the promiscuous Erica Kane on "All My Children," tells of a time she was riding in a parade: "We were

in a crowd of about 250,000 traveling in an antique open car moving
ver-r-ry slowly. At that time in the series I was involved with a character
named Nick. Some man broke through, came right up to the car and said
to me, 'Why don't you give me a little bit of what you've been giving Nick?'
"The man hung onto the car, menacingly, until she was rescued by the police. Another time, when she was in church, the reverent silence was broken by a woman's astonished remark, "Oh, my god, Erica prays!" Margaret
Mason, who plays the villainous Lisa Anderson in "Days of Our Lives,"
was accosted by a woman who poured a carton of milk all over her in the
supermarket. And once a woman actually tried to force her car off the Ventura Freeway.

VOICE AND TONE   Writers also use voice and tone to shape and control whole
passages, often in combination with other shaping strategies. In the following paragraph, Toni Bambara, author of *The Salt Eaters* and numerous short stories, explains
what being a writer is all about. This paragraph is shaped both by a single extended
example and by Bambara's voice talking directly to the reader:

> When I replay the tapes on file in my head, tapes of speeches I've given at
> writing conferences over the years, I invariably hear myself saying—"A
> writer, like any other cultural worker, like any other member of the com-
> munity, ought to try to put her/his skills in the service of the community."
> Some years ago when I returned south, my picture in the paper prompted
> several neighbors to come visit. "You a writer? What all you write?" Before
> I could begin the catalogue, one old gent interrupted with—"Ya know Miz
> Mary down the block? She need a writer to help her send off a letter to her
> grandson overseas." So I began a career as the neighborhood scribe—let-
> ters to relatives, snarling letters to the traffic chief about the promised stop
> sign, nasty letters to the utilities, angry letters to the principal about that
> confederate flag hanging in front of the school, contracts to transfer a truck
> from seller to buyer, etc. While my efforts have been graciously appreciated
> in the form of sweet potato dumplings, herb teas, hair braiding, and the
> like, there is still much room for improvement—"For a writer, honey, you've
> got a mighty bad hand. Didn't they teach penmanship at that college?" An-
> other example, I guess, of words setting things in motion. What goes
> around, comes around, as the elders say.

CHRONOLOGICAL ORDER AND PROCESS ANALYSIS   Writers use
chronological order in expository writing to help explain how to do something or how

TIPS FOR INTEGRATING IMAGES

For your explaining essay, you may wish to integrate images (photographs, images, graphics, or charts), and you may wish to work with your document design. To integrate images with your text, first consider your rhetorical situation.

- **What is your purpose?** Does the visual contribute to your thesis or main idea, or is it just a distraction?
- **Who is your audience?** Is the image appropriate for your target audience? Would it make your document more appealing or attractive? Would it offend them? Would it amuse them? Would it make your point in a way that words could not?
- **What is your intended genre?** Look at other examples of your genre. Find several examples of the kind of essay, pamphlet, Web page, article, advertisement, brochure, laboratory report, letter, or flyer. How do they use images or graphics?
- **What is the social/cultural context of your text?** Consider whether the subject, topic, or issue you are discussing could or should be illustrated with an image or a certain document design.

Use search engines and library sources to find a variety of images relevant to your topic. Start with an image search on Google or Yahoo!, but don't forget that your library has a wealth of online image databases. If you're looking for paintings or fine art, check Web sites for museums around the world. Having several potential images enables you to choose the one most effective for your rhetorical situation.

Finally, don't forget about your document design. Start with your purpose, audience, and genre. Consider how the genre you have selected uses the following document features.

- **Columns** Would a text with two columns work for your purpose?
- **Margins and white space** Avoid overcrowding words, images, and graphics on a page. Use margins and white space to emphasize key parts of your text.
- **Fonts** Use a font appropriate to your purpose, genre, and audience. Times New Roman and Palatino Linotype are widely accepted, but do you need **Franklin Gothic Demi** for particular parts of your text? For special situations, perhaps consider a script face such as Felt Tip or a bolder face such as **TRADE GOTHIC**. If appropriate for your purpose, genre, and audience, play around with the available fonts on your computer.
- **Sidebars** If appropriate for your text, use a sidebar for text emphasis or to add related information.

Is the image appropriate for your target audience? Does the image contribute to your thesis?

something is typically done. In her essay "Anorexia Nervosa," student writer Nancie Brosseau uses transitional words to signal the various stages of anorexia. In the following sentences, taken from the third paragraph of her essay, the *italicized* words mark the chronological stages of her anorexia:

> Several serious health problems bombarded me, and it's a wonder I'm still alive. . . . *As my weight plummeted*, my circulation grew *increasingly worse*. . . . My hair *started* to fall out, and my whole body took on a very skeletal appearance. . . . I would force myself to vomit *as soon as possible* if I was forced to eat. The enamel on my teeth *started to be eaten away* by the acid in the vomit, and my lips cracked and bled regularly. I *stopped* menstruating completely because I was not producing enough estrogen. . . . *One time*, while executing a chain of back handsprings, I broke all five fingers on one hand and three on the other because my bones had become so brittle. . . . I chose to see a psychologist, and she helped me sort out the emotional aspects of anorexia, *which in turn* solved the physical problems.

CAUSAL ANALYSIS   In order to explain *why* something happens or what the effects of something are, writers often use one of the following three patterns of cause and effect to shape their material:

Cause 1 + Cause 2 + Cause 3 . . . + Cause n → Effect

In the case of fire, for example, we know that three causes lead to a single effect. These causes do not occur in any special sequence; they must all be present at the same time. For historical events, however, we usually list causes in chronological order.

Sometimes one cause has several effects. In that case, we reverse the pattern:

Cause → Effect 1 + Effect 2 + Effect 3 . . . + Effect n

For example, an explanation of the collapse of the economy following the stock market crash of 1929 might follow this pattern. The crash (itself a symptom of other causes) led to a depreciated economy, widespread unemployment, bankruptcy for thousands of businesses, foreclosures on farms, and so forth. An essay on the effects of the crash might devote one or two paragraphs to each effect.

In the third pattern, causes and effects form a pattern of chain reactions. One cause leads to an effect that then becomes the cause of another effect, and so on:

Cause 1 → Effect 1 (Cause 2) → Effect 2 (Cause 3) → Effect 3

We could analyze events in the Middle East during and after the Iraq War as a series of actions and reactions in which each effect becomes the cause of the next effect in the chain of car bombings, air raids, terrorist hijackings, and kidnappings. An essay on the chain reaction of events in the Middle East might have a paragraph or two on each of the links in this chain.

INTRODUCTIONS AND LEAD-INS   Often, the first sentences of the introductory paragraph of an essay are the hardest to write. You want to get your reader's attention and focus on the main idea of your essay, but you don't want to begin, boringly, with your thesis statement. Below are several kinds of opening sentences designed to grab your reader's interest. Consider your topic—see if one of these strategies will work for you.

A Personal Example

I knew my dieting had gotten out of hand, but when I could actually see the movement of my heart beating beneath my clothes, I knew I was in trouble.

—"Anorexia Nervosa," Nancie Brosseau

A Description of a Person or Place

He strides toward us in navy and white, his body muscled and heavyset, one arm holding his casually flung jeans jacket over his shoulder. A man in his prime, with just the right combination of macho and sartorial flair.

—"Some Don't Like Their Blues at All," Karyn M. Lewis

It's still there, the Chinese school on Yale Street where my brother and I used to go. Despite the new coat of paint and the high wire fence, the school I knew ten years ago remains remarkably, stoically the same.

—"The Struggle to Be an All-American Girl," Elizabeth Wong

An Example from a Case Study

Susan Smith has everything going for her. A self-described workaholic, she runs a Cambridge, Massachusetts, real estate consulting company with her husband Charles and still finds time to cuddle and nurture their two young kids, David, 7, and Stacey, 6. What few people know is that Susan, 44, needs a little chemical help to be a supermom: she has been taking the antidepressant Prozac for five years.

—"The Personality Pill," Anastasia Toufexis

A Startling Statement, Fact, or Statistic

Embalming is indeed a most extraordinary procedure, and one must wonder at the docility of Americans who each year pay hundreds of millions of dollars for its perpetuation, blissfully ignorant of what it is all about, what is done, how it is done.

—"To Dispel Fears of Live Burial," Jessica Mitford

A Statement from a Book

The American novelist John Barth, in his early novel *The Floating Opera*, remarks that ordinary, day-to-day life often presents us with embarrassingly obvious, totally unsubtle patterns of symbolism and meaning—life in the midst of death, innocence vindicated, youth versus age, etc.

—"I'm O.K., but You're Not," Robert Zoellner

A Striking Question or Questions

Do non-human animals have rights? Should we humans feel morally bound to exercise consideration for the lives and well-being of individual members of other animal species? If so, how much consideration, and by what logic?

—"Animal Rights and Beyond," David Quammen

A Common Error or Mistaken Judgment

There was a time when, in my search for essences, I concluded that the canyonland country has no heart. I was wrong. The canyonlands did have a heart, a living heart, and that heart was Glen Canyon and the golden, flowing Colorado River.

—"The Damnation of a Canyon," Edward Abbey

Combined Strategies

Last December a man named Robert Lee Willie, who had been convicted of raping and murdering an 18-year-old woman, was executed in the Louisiana state prison. In a statement issued several minutes before his death, Mr. Willie said: "Killing people is wrong. . . . It makes no difference whether it's citizens, countries, or governments. Killing is wrong."

—"Death and Justice," Edward Koch

LEAD-IN, THESIS, AND ESSAY MAP   The introduction to an explaining essay—whether one paragraph or several—usually contains the following features:

- **Lead-in:** Some example, description, startling statement, statistic, short narrative, allusion, or quotation to get the reader's interest *and* focus on the topic you will explain.
- **Thesis:** Statement of the main idea; a "promise" to the reader that the essay fulfills.
- **Essay map:** A sentence, or part of a sentence, that *lists* (in the order in which the essay discusses them) the main subtopics for the essay.

In her essay on anorexia nervosa at the end of this chapter, Nancie Brosseau's introductory paragraph has all three features:

Lead-in: Startling statement

Description

Statistics

Thesis

Essay map

I knew my dieting had gotten out of hand, but when I could actually see the movement of my heart beating beneath my clothes, I knew I was in trouble. At first, the family doctor reassured my parents that my rapid weight loss was a "temporary phase among teenage girls." However, when I, at fourteen years old and five feet tall, weighed in at sixty-three pounds, my doctor changed his diagnosis from "temporary phase" to "anorexia nervosa." Anorexia nervosa is the process of self-starvation that affects over 100,000 young girls each year. Almost 6,000 of these girls die every year. Anorexia nervosa is a self-mutilating disease that affects its victim both physically and emotionally.

The essay map is contained in the phrase "both physically and emotionally": The first half of the essay discusses the physical effects of anorexia nervosa; the second half explains the emotional effects. Like a road map, the essay map helps the reader anticipate what topics the writer will explain.

PARAGRAPH TRANSITIONS AND HOOKS   Transition words and paragraph hooks are audience cues that help the reader shift from one paragraph to the next. These connections between paragraphs help the reader see the relationships of the various parts. Transition words—*first, second, next, another, last, finally,* and so forth—signal your reader that a new idea or a new part of the idea is coming up. In addition to transition words, writers often tie paragraphs together by using a key word or idea from a previous paragraph in the first sentence of the following paragraph to "hook" the paragraphs together. The following paragraphs from James Twitchell's "Miss Clairol's 'Does She . . . Or Doesn't She?'" illustrate how transition words and paragraph hooks work together to create smooth connections between paragraphs.

As was to become typical in hair-coloring ads, the age of the model was a good ten years younger than the typical product user. The model is in her early thirties (witness the age of the child), too young to have gray hair.

This (inspirational motif) was picked up later for other Clairol products: "If I've only one life . . . let me live it as a blonde!" "Every woman should be a redhead . . . at least once in her life!" "What would your husband say if suddenly you looked 10 years younger?" "Is it true blondes have more fun?" "What does he look at second?" And, of course, "The closer he gets, the better you look!"

But (these slogans) for different brand extensions only work because Miss Clairol had done her job. She made hair coloring possible, she made hair coloring acceptable, she made at-home hair coloring—dare I say it—empowering. She made the unique into the commonplace. By the 1980s, the hairdresser problem had been long forgotten and the follow-up lines read, "Hair color no natural, they'll never know for sure."

Hook: "aspirational motif"

Transition: "But"

Hook: "these slogans"

BODY PARAGRAPHS Body paragraphs in expository writing are the main paragraphs in an essay, excluding any introductory, concluding, or transition paragraphs. They often contain the following features:

- **Topic sentence:** To promote clarity and precision, writers often use topic sentences to announce the main ideas of paragraphs. The main idea should be clearly related to the writer's thesis. A topic sentence usually occurs early in the paragraph (first or second sentence) or at the end of the paragraph.
- **Unity:** To avoid confusing readers, writers focus on a single idea for each paragraph. Writing unified paragraphs helps writers—and their readers—concentrate on one point at a time.
- **Coherence:** To make their writing flow smoothly from one sentence to the next, writers supplement their shaping strategies with coherence devices: repeated key words, pronouns referring to key nouns, and transition words.

The following body paragraphs from James Twitchell's "Miss Clairol's 'Does She . . . Or Doesn't She?'" illustrates these features. The second sentence in the first paragraph is the *topic sentence* for the first paragraph—and the second paragraph as well. That topic sentence focuses our attention on the process of "automatic color tinting." These two paragraphs have *unity* because they keep the focus on the "automatic" process of hair tinting. The two paragraphs also achieve *coherence* through the use of transitions and repeated key words and ideas.

Topic sentence

Coherence & repeated key words

Transitions

The copy block on the right is all business and was never changed during the campaign. *The process of coloring is always referred to as "automatic color tinting." Automatic* was to the fifties what *plastic* became to the sixties, and what *networking* is today. Just as your food was kept automatically fresh in the refrigerator, your car had an automatic transmission, your house had an automatic thermostat, your dishes and clothes were automatically cleaned and dried, so, too, your hair had automatic tinting.

However, what is really automatic about hair coloring is that once you start, you won't stop. Hair grows, roots show, buy more product . . . automatically. The genius of Gillette was not just that they sold the "safety razor" (they could give the razor away), *but that they also sold* the concept of being *clean-shaven.* Clean-shaven means that you use their blade every day, so, of course, you always need more blades. Clairol made "roots showing" into what Gillette had made "five o'clock shadow."

DRAFTING

Before you begin drafting, reconsider your purpose and audience. What you explain depends on what your audience needs to know or what would demonstrate or show your point most effectively.

As you work from an outline or from an organizing strategy, remember that all three questions—*what, how,* and *why*—are interrelated. If you are writing about causes, for example, an explanation of *what* the topic is and *how* the causes function may also be necessary to explain your subject clearly. As you write, balance your sense of plan and organization with a willingness to pursue ideas that you discover as you write. While you need to have a plan, you should be ready to change course if you discover a more interesting idea or angle.

REVISING

As you revise your explaining essay, concentrate on making yourself perfectly clear, on illustrating with examples where your reader might be confused, and on signaling the relationship of the parts of your essay to your reader.

Guidelines for Revision

- **Review your purpose, audience, and genre.** Is your purpose clear to your target audience? Should you modify your chosen genre to appeal to your audience?

PEER RESPONSE

The instructions that follow will help you give and receive constructive advice about the rough draft of your explaining essay. You may use these guidelines for an in-class workshop, a take-home review, or a computer e-mail response.

Writer: Before you exchange drafts with another reader, write out the following on your essay draft:

1. **Purpose** Briefly, describe your purpose, genre, and intended audience.
2. **Revision plans** What do you still intend to work on as you revise your draft?
3. **Questions** Write out one or two questions that you still have about your draft. What questions would you like your reader to answer?

Reader: First, read the entire draft from start to finish. As you reread the draft, answer the following questions:

1. **Clarity** What passages were clearest? Where were you most confused? Refer to specific sentences or passages to support your response. How and where could the writer make the draft clearer?
2. **Evidence** Where does the writer have good supporting evidence (specific examples, facts, analysis, statistics, interview results, or citations from sources)? Where does the writer need additional evidence? Refer to specific sentences or passages to support your response.
3. **Organization** Summarize or briefly outline the main ideas of the essay. Where was the organization most clear? Where were you confused? Refer to specific passages as you suggest ways to improve the draft.
4. **Purpose** Underline sentences that express the purpose or contain the thesis of the essay. Does your understanding of the essay's purpose match the writer's statement about purpose? Explain. How might the writer clarify the thesis?
5. **Reader's response** Overall, describe what you liked best about the draft. Then identify one major area that the writer should focus on during the revision. Does your suggestion match the writer's revision plans? Explain. Answer the writer's own question or questions about the draft.

- **Review possibilities for visuals or graphics.** What additions or changes to images might be appropriate for your purpose, genre, or audience?
- **Compare your thesis sentence with what you say in your conclusion.** You may have a clearer statement of your thesis near the end of your paper. Revise your original thesis sentence to make it clearer, more focused, or more in line with what your essay actually says.
- **Explaining means *showing* and *demonstrating* relationships.** Be sure to follow general statements with *specific examples, details, facts, statistics, memories, dialogues,* or other *illustrations.*
- **In a formal definition, be sure to include the class of objects or concepts to which the term belongs.** Avoid ungrammatical writing, such as "Photosynthesis is *when* plants absorb oxygen" or "The lymphatic system is *where* the body removes bacteria and transports fatty cells."
- **Avoid introducing definitions with "Webster says. . . ."** Instead, read definitions from several dictionaries and give the best or most appropriate definition.
- **Remember that you can modify the dictionary definition of a term or concept to fit your particular context.** For example, to you, *heroism* may mean having the courage to *say* what you believe, not just to endanger your life through selfless actions.
- **Don't mix categories when you are classifying objects or ideas.** If you are classifying houses *by floor design* (ranch, bilevel, split-level, two-story), don't bring in other categories, such as passive-solar, which could be incorporated into any of those designs.
- **In explaining *how* something occurs or should be done, be sure to indicate to your audience which steps are *most important.***
- **In cause-and-effect explanations, avoid post hoc fallacies.** This term comes from the Latin phrase *post hoc, ergo propter hoc:* "After this, therefore because of this." For example, just because Event B occurred after Event A, it does not follow, necessarily, that A caused B. If, for example, statistics show that traffic fatalities in your state actually declined after the speed limit on interstate highways was increased, you should not conclude that higher speeds actually caused the reduction in fatalities. Other causes—increased radar patrols, stiffer drunk-driving penalties, or more rigorous vehicle-maintenance laws—may have been responsible for the reduction.
- **As you revise to sharpen your meaning or make your organization clearer, use appropriate transitional words and phrases to signal the *relationships among the various parts of your subject.***

—To signal relation in time: before, meanwhile, later, soon, at last, earlier, thereafter, afterward, by that time, from then on, first, next, now, presently, shortly, immediately, finally

—To signal similarity: likewise, similarly, once again, once more

—To signal difference: but, yet, however, although, whereas, though, even so, nonetheless, still, on the other hand, on the contrary

—To signal consequences: as a result, consequently, therefore, hence, for this reason

POSTSCRIPT ON THE WRITING PROCESS

Before you hand in your essay, reflect on your writing and learning process. In your journal, spend a few minutes answering the following questions:

1. Describe the purpose and intended audience for your essay.

2. What was the best workshop advice that you received? What did you revise in your draft because of that advice? What piece of advice did you ignore? Why?

3. What caused you the most difficulty with this essay? How did you solve the problem—or attempt to solve it? With what parts are you still least satisfied?

4. What are the best parts of your paper? Refer to specific paragraphs—what do you like most about them?

5. If you added visual images or special document-design features to your essay, explain how they supported your purpose or rhetorical goals.

6. What was the most important thing you learned about writing or your writing process as you wrote this paper?

STUDENT WRITING

ENGLISH ONLY

Christine Bishop

Christine Bishop decided to write on "English Only" as one of her semester portfolio topics. She had become interested in the topic in a previous year when she went to a speech tournament that debated the English-only issue. She wrote the following essay as the first step in her semester portfolio project. Following this explaining essay, she wrote a persuasive essay, arguing against English-only legislation. For this initial essay, however, she focused on reading key articles about English only, exploring the issues in each article, and explaining key arguments on both sides. Her goal was not to argue for one side or the other, but to explore the issues and explain the arguments on both sides of the English-only debate. As you read her essay, see if she explains the major arguments for both sides in a clear and balanced manner.

Prewriting for Topic Proposal

The English-only issue is a very controversial issue. Some say America should adopt an official language policy. Others think that this is a very racist idea. I have been reviewing reports of a recent vote on making Puerto Rico a state. Part of the legislation centered on making the people of Puerto Rico (which is predominantly Spanish-speaking) adopt English as their official language. Supporters of this bill claim that it is necessary that the Puerto Ricans learn English to become Americanized. Other people feel this will take away their language rights. Some people speculate that the English-only movement is a xenophobic reaction to the 1960 immigration amendments. These amendments made it illegal to restrict citizenship to America based on race. With this new amendment, there has been an influx in immigrants from diverse places. This influx of people could lead to xenophobia (fear of strangers or foreigners). I feel this speculation may be true. In 1912, when New Mexico became a state, it was allowed to keep Spanish as its official language provided that English was also an official language. Why such a radical change in policy when Puerto Rico applies to be a state? Is America afraid that it will lose its identity to non-English-speaking people? America started out as a conglomerate of immigrants who did not all speak the same language. What now?

I would like to explore this topic more. The two main positions on English-only legislation are as follows:

1. English needs to be the official language of the United States because we need one unifying language. Without English-only laws, immigrants will not learn English and will not contribute to society.

2. It is unfair to expect current citizens in the United States to learn English. Making English official will make people not learn other languages.

I know some about this subject, but I haven't done much research on my own. The questions I have are whether I could tie this into racism and whether I will be able to get enough information in the library and on the Internet.

First Draft

The issue has been raised that the United States needs to make English the official language of the nation. Currently, the Senate is reviewing a proposal to require Puerto Rico to adopt English as its official language before considering it for statehood. While everyone agrees that it is important for all Americans to speak English, there is disagreement as to whether the government should adopt an official language policy. Those who support an official language policy (such as Richard Rodriguez) believe that without a policy, immigrants to America will not learn English. Those who do not support this policy believe that there is enough pressure on immigrants, and that they have enough desire to learn English quickly on their own. Some who oppose an official English policy believe that this policy will alienate immigrants and that Americans who support this policy are having a xenophobic reaction to recent immigrants from more diverse cultures initiated by 1960s immigration laws. I would like to explain exactly what these opposing positions are, using essays written by Richard Rodriguez, Samuel Hayakawa, James Crawford, and James Fallows.

As a champion of English-only legislation, Richard Rodriguez believes that without the government to push them into learning English, immigrants will not learn the language. In "Aria: A Memoir of a Bilingual Childhood," Mr. Rodriguez states, "What I did not believe was that I could speak a single public language. . . . It would have pleased me to hear my teachers address me in Spanish. . . . But I would have delayed—for how long postponed?—having to learn the language of public society [English]." Although Rodriguez was born in the United States, being the son of migrant workers, he had not been exposed to English until he had entered school. Without the church (he attended a Catholic school) to force him to learn English, he believes he would never have learned to speak English. Like all people on both sides of the issue, Rodriguez believes that it is necessary to speak English to succeed in the United States. Because Rodriguez was not motivated to speak English as a child, he feels that it is imperative for the government to push immigrants to learn English by making English the official language of the United States. People opposing English being the official language believe immigrants desire to learn English.

Both James Fallows, in "Viva Bilingualism," and James Crawford, author of *Hold Your Tongue: Bilingualism and the Politics of English Only,* oppose English-only legislation. Fallows, an English-speaking American who lived in Japan, feels that his experiences are contradictory to these beliefs.

While living in Japan—a country that "makes many more accommodations to the English language than America does to Spanish"—Fallows found that most English-speaking people learned Japanese in order to participate in society. In America, Fallows thinks the incentives for immigrants to learn English are greater. The only way to get any kind of white-collar job or to attend college, according to Fallows, is through learning English. English is how communities in America are built.

Other English-only supporters, like former Senator Samuel Hayakawa, feel that a common language in the United States would better unite Americans. Hayakawa uses the example of Chinese- and Japanese-Americans, who didn't get along during World War II. Now they have begun to form Asian-American groups. Hayakawa believes this is the result of having learned English. Hayakawa states, "A common tongue encourages trust while reducing racial hostility and bigotry." Hayakawa believes that unless the United States implements an English-only policy, we will head the way of Quebec or India—"a chaotic mess which has led to countless problems in the government's efforts to manage the nation's business." According to Hayakawa, this problem is already apparent. He blames the 50 percent dropout rate among Hispanic students on the current bilingual policy.

People who do not support English-only, like James Crawford, do not believe that the differences in language will cause chaos. They further believe that an official English policy will separate Americans. In his book, James Crawford quotes Raul Yazquirre, President of the National Council of La Raza, as saying: "U.S. English is to Hispanics as the Ku Klux Klan is to blacks." Crawford says that this is the consensus among Latino leaders. Crawford goes on to say that Latino leaders believe English only "is a Xenophobic, intolerant act."

Because I believe that Rodriguez's experience might be unique and that there are many other people's experiences pointing the other way—including my own—I think Hayakawa's argument may be shaky. Possibly, Crawford and Fallows, because of their experience, may be correct. Crawford has spent ten years researching the issue, which gives his argument credibility. I think that although it is quite debatable, the new push for English as an official language may be due to a backlash against the recent influx of more diverse groups into the United States. But determining exactly how government laws might affect the motivation of immigrants to learn English is difficult. We seem to have different personal testimonies:

Hayakawa and Rodriguez think an English-only policy will encourage immigrants to learn English; Fallows and Crawford think immigrants already have enough incentives to learn English.

Final Draft

ENGLISH ONLY

English-only laws have been in the news again, with a recent debate in the Senate over a requirement that Puerto Rico adopt English as its official language before being allowed to become a state (Gugliotta 1). In the United States, English-only laws currently exist in twenty-three states—having passed recently in Alaska and Missouri—but they suffered a setback in Arizona, where the United States Supreme Court upheld a decision that struck down an Arizona law that passed originally in 1988 (Denniston 1). Basically, English-only laws such as Arizona's state that "this state and all political subdivisions of this state shall act in English and no other language" (Denniston 2). While everyone agrees that it is important for all Americans to speak English, there is disagreement as to whether state governments should adopt an official language policy.   1

The debate over "English only" continues as groups such as U.S. English try to promote language laws in every state. Those who support an official language policy believe that without a policy, immigrants will not learn English. Those who oppose an official English policy believe that English-only laws alienate immigrants and that Americans who support these laws are having a xenophobic reaction to the flood of recent immigrants from more diverse cultures. In order to explain what this debate is about and what the major issues are on both sides, I will look primarily at four authors who have written about English-only laws. Two writers who support English only are the late Senator Samuel Hayakawa and Richard Rodriguez, author of *Hunger of Memory*. Two authors who oppose English only are James Fallows, Washington editor of *Atlantic* magazine, and James Crawford, author of *Hold Your Tongue: Bilingualism and the Politics of English Only*.   2

Those who support an English-only policy feel that it will encourage immigrants and non-English-speaking Americans to speak English. In his essay, "Bilingualism in America: English Should Be the *Only* Language," Hayakawa uses the example of Chinese- and Japanese-Americans, who didn't get along during World War II. Now they have begun to form Asian-   3

American groups (252). Hayakawa believes this is the result of having learned English. Hayakawa states, "A common tongue encourages trust while reducing racial hostility and bigotry" (252). Hayakawa, one of the original founders of U.S. English, believes that unless the United States implements an English-only policy, we will head the way of Quebec or India: India's "ten official languages" have created a situation that is "a chaotic mess which has led to countless problems in the government's efforts to manage the nation's business" (253). According to Hayakawa, the problem in the United States is already apparent. He blames the 50 percent dropout rate among Hispanic students on the current bilingual policy (254). Writers such as Hayakawa forecast a Tower of Babel. They believe that unless we adopt an English-only policy, immigrants will not learn English and U.S. citizens will not be able to communicate with each other. Of course, Hayakawa's analogy with Quebec and India may be difficult to support, because immigrants to the United States have always learned English, whereas in Quebec and India, people have always spoken different languages.

As a champion of English-only legislation, Richard Rodriguez, like   *4*
the late Senator Hayakawa, believes that without the government to push immigrants into learning English, they will not learn English. In "Aria: A Memoir of a Bilingual Childhood," Rodriguez states, "What I needed to learn in school was that I had the right, and the obligation, to speak the public language. . . . It would have pleased me to hear my teachers address me in Spanish. . . . But I would have delayed—postponed for how long?—having to learn the language of public society" (270). Although Rodriguez was born in the United States, the son of migrant workers, he was not exposed to English until he entered school. Without his Catholic schoolteachers' forcing him to learn English, Rodriguez believes that he would never have learned to speak the public language (271). Like people on both sides of the English-only issue, Rodriguez believes that to succeed in the United States, it is necessary to be proficient in English. Because Rodriguez was not motivated to speak English as a child, he feels that it is imperative for the government to push immigrants to learn English by making English the official language of the United States.

In addition, the website for U.S. English agrees with Hayakawa and   *5*
Rodriguez that without English-only legislation, immigrants will "fail to learn English and separate into linguistic enclaves. This division of the United States into separate language groups contributes to racial and eth-

nic conflicts" (U.S. English 1). This is, of course, a controversial position because many other people believe that immigrants have plenty of incentive to learn English on their own, and those people have history to cite as evidence.

On the other side of the English-only debate, James Fallows, a Washington editor of *Atlantic* magazine and author of "Viva Bilingualism," believes that there are enough incentives for immigrants to learn English without adding pressure to the situation. Fallows, an English-speaking American who lived in Japan, feels that his experiences show that English-only laws are unnecessary. When living in Japan, a country that "makes many more accommodations to the English language than America does to Spanish," Fallows found that he, as well as most English-speaking people, needed to learn Japanese to participate in society (262). In America, Fallows thinks the incentives for immigrants to learn English are greater. The only way to get a white-collar job or to attend college, according to Fallows, is to learn English. As Fallows puts it, in America, you can't take the SATs in Spanish or even watch *David Letterman* (262).

Writers such as James Fallows who do not support an English-only policy do not believe that the differences in language will cause chaos. However, some believe that an official English-only policy will actually separate Americans. James Crawford, author of *Hold Your Tongue: Bilingualism and the Politics of English Only,* argues that English-only laws are racist and xenophobic. Crawford quotes Raul Yazguierre, President of the National Council of La Raza, as saying, "U.S. English is to Hispanics as the Ku Klux Klan is to blacks" (1). Crawford says that this is the consensus among Latino leaders. Crawford goes on to say that Latino leaders believe English only is a xenophobic, intolerant act (1). When Spanish leaders are saying that English only is similar to something extreme like the KKK, something has to be wrong. That Latino leaders link English only to the KKK, coupled with the fact that immigrants have always learned English on their own, seems to be compelling evidence that many people think English-only laws are unnecessary and possibly destructive.

If there is any middle ground in this debate, I find it difficult to explain. Often, arguments on both sides seem to come down to personal experiences. Rodriguez thinks his experiences show that there should be the pressure of English-only laws; Fallows's experiences in Japan persuade him that there are already sufficient pressures to encourage immigrants to learn English. Hayakawa does point to real problems in countries such as Canada and India, but his statistics may be shaky. Hayakawa quotes Hispanics as having a 50 percent dropout rate, saying that this could be due to the lack of English proficiency, and then later states that 90 percent of the Hispanics in the United States are fluent in English (254,255). These two statements are contradictory and weaken Hayakawa's position. Crawford and Fallows, because of their experience, do have legitimate points. Crawford spent ten years of research on the issue, which adds to his credibility. In addition, Fallows has personal experience similar to my own. When I was living in a foreign country, I felt continual pressure to learn the language spoken in my host country, and because I did not have my family around, I couldn't hide from the new language and culture.

It is difficult to determine the long-term effects of English-only legislation. I haven't found any evidence that the laws in twenty-three states have increased the number of immigrants who speak English, but I have found evidence that the debate about these laws can be heated and divisive. Although this issue is certainly debatable, I believe that the new push for English as an official language may be due to a backlash against the recent influx of more diverse groups into the United States. If state governments continue to support that backlash, it may further alienate our new citizens. On the other hand, many immigrants don't learn English very quickly, and they survive in linguistic enclaves, separated by language barriers from mainstream American culture. Possibly the economic pressures of earning a living will have a far greater effect on encouraging immigrants to learn English than any official English laws. If the momentum for English-only laws persists in state legislatures, we will continue to see arguments from both sides used in the debate.

Works Cited

Crawford, James. *Hold Your Tongue: Bilingualism and the Politics of English Only.* Reading, MA: Addison Wesley, 1992. 24 Sept. 1998. *http://ourworld.compuserve.com/homepages/JWCRAWFORD/home.html.*

Denniston, Lyle. "English-Only Measure Dealt Blow." *Baltimore Sun.* 12 Jan. 1998. 11 Jan. 1999. *http://www.sunspot.net/cgibin/editorial.*

Fallows, James. "Viva Bilingualism." *Exploring Language.* Ed. Gary Goshgarian. 8th ed. New York: Addison Wesley Longman, 1998. 259–63.

Gugliotta, Guy. "House Passes Puerto Rico Bill." *Washington Post Online.* 5 March 1998. 24 Sept. 1998. *http://ourworld.compuserve.com/homepages/JWCRAWFORD/WPOST4.html.*

Hayakawa, S. I. "Bilingualism in America: English Should Be the *Only* Language." *Exploring Language*. Ed. Gary Goshgarian. 8th ed. New York: Addison Wesley Longman, 1998. 251–56.

Rodriguez, Richard. "Aria: A Memoir of a Bilingual Childhood." *Exploring Language*. Ed. Gary Goshgarian. 8th ed. New York: Addison Wesley Longman, 1998. 266–75.

U.S. English Page. 13 Jan. 1999. *http://www.us-english.org/why.htm.*

QUESTIONS FOR WRITING AND DISCUSSION

1. Compare Bishop's first and revised drafts. What information and explanations did she add in the revised version? How did she reorganize her essay for the revised version? Explain.

2. Bishop's purpose in this first essay for her portfolio was to explore the arguments on each side of the English-only debate and then explain these arguments to her reader. She did *not* want to argue for or against English only until the final essay in her portfolio. What paragraphs does she devote to the advocates of the English-only movement? What paragraphs explain the arguments of those who oppose English only. Does she balance the arguments without taking sides herself? Explain.

3. Explaining essays should define key terms, concepts, or ideas. What terms or ideas does Bishop explain or define? Are there other terms or ideas that she needed to define? Explain.

4. Assume that Bishop wants your advice about how to revise her essay into an argumentative essay, arguing against English-only legislation. Consult the Guidelines for Revision in this chapter. What audience or publication might she choose? In terms of revising the genre, should she write an editorial in a newspaper or a longer essay that might be published in a magazine? Are there additional cultural viewpoints she might consider to make her argument effective for her audience? Would more background information or definitions be helpful? Write out your recommendations.

STUDENT WRITING

ANOREXIA NERVOSA

Nancie Brosseau

In her essay on anorexia nervosa, Nancie Brosseau writes from her own experience, explaining what anorexia nervosa is and what its effects are. Her essay succeeds not only because it is organized clearly, but also because it is so vivid and memorable. Relying on specific details, her explanation shows the effects of anorexia on her life.

I knew my dieting had gotten out of hand, but when I could actually see the movement of my heart beating beneath my clothes, I knew I was in trouble. At first, the family doctor reassured my parents that my rapid weight loss was a "temporary phase among teenage girls." However, when I, at fourteen years old and five feet tall, weighed in at sixty-three pounds, my doctor changed his diagnosis from "temporary phase" to "anorexia nervosa." Anorexia nervosa is the process of self-starvation that affects over 100,000 young girls each year. Almost 6,000 of these girls die every year. Anorexia nervosa is a self-mutilating disease that affects its victim both physically and emotionally.

As both a gymnast and a dancer, I was constantly surrounded by lithe, muscular people, all of them extremely conscious about their weight. Although I wasn't overweight to begin with, I thought that if I lost five to ten pounds I would look, feel, dance, and tumble better. I figured the quickest way to accomplish this was by drastically limiting my intake of food. By doing this, I lost ten pounds in one week and gained the approval of my peers. Soon, I could no longer control myself, and ten pounds turned into twenty, twenty into forty, and so on, until I finally ended up weighing fifty-eight pounds.

Several serious health problems bombarded me, and it's a wonder I'm still alive. Because my body was receiving no nourishment at all, my muscles and essential organs, including my heart, liver, kidneys, and intestines, started to compensate by slowly disintegrating. My body was feeding on itself! As my weight plummeted, my circulation grew increasingly worse. My hands, feet, lips, and ears took on a bluish-purple tint, and I was constantly freezing cold. My hair started to fall out and my whole body took on a very skeletal appearance. My eyes appeared to have sunken into my face, and my forehead, cheekbones, and chin protruded sharply. My wrists were the largest part of my entire arm, as were my knees the widest part of my legs. My pants rubbed my hips raw because I had to wear my belts at their tightest notch to keep them up. I would force myself to vomit as soon as possible if I was forced to eat. The enamel on my teeth started to be eaten away by the acid in the vomit, and my lips cracked and bled regularly. I stopped menstruating completely because I was not producing enough estrogen. Instead of improving my skills as a dancer and a gymnast, I drastically reduced them because I was so weak. One time, while executing a chain of back handsprings, I broke all five fingers on one hand and three on the other because my bones had become so brittle. My doctor realized the serious danger I was in and told me I either had to see a psychologist or be put in the hospital. I chose to see a psychologist, and she helped me sort out the emotional aspects of anorexia, which in turn solved the physical problems.

The emotional problems associated with anorexia nervosa are equally *4* disastrous to the victim's health. Self-deception, lying, and depression are three examples of the emotions and actions an anorexic often experiences. During my entire bout with anorexia, I deceived myself into thinking I had complete control over my body. Hunger pains became a pleasant feeling, and sore muscles from overexercising just proved to me that I still needed to lose more weight. When my psychologist showed me pictures of girls that were of normal weight for my age group, they honestly looked obese to me. I truly believed that even the smallest amount of food would make me extremely fat.

Another problem, lying, occurred most often when my parents tried to *5* force me to eat. Because I was at the gym until around eight o'clock every night, I told my mother not to save me dinner. I would come home and make a sandwich and feed it to my dog. I lied to my parents every day about eating lunch at school. For example, I would bring a sack lunch and sell it to someone and use the money to buy diet pills. I always told my parents that I ate my own lunch. I lied to my doctor when he asked if I was taking an appetite suppressant. I had to cover one lie with another to keep from being found out, although it was obvious that I was not eating by looking at me.

Still another emotion I felt, as a result of my anorexia, was severe de-   6
pression. It seemed that, no matter how hard I tried, I kept growing fatter.
Of course, I was getting thinner all the time, but I couldn't see that. One
time, I licked a postage stamp to put on a letter and immediately remembered that there was 1/4 of a calorie in the glue on the stamp. I punished
myself by doing 100 extra situps every night for one week. I pinched my skin
until it bruised as I lay awake at night because I was so ashamed of the way
I thought I looked. I doomed myself to a life of obesity. I would often slip
into a mood my psychologist described as a "blue funk." That is, I would
become so depressed, I seriously considered committing suicide. The emotional instabilities associated with anorexia nervosa can be fatal.

Through psychological and physical treatment, I was able to overcome   7
anorexia nervosa. I still have a few complications today due to anorexia,
such as dysmenorrhea (severe menstrual cramps) and the tendency to fast.
However, these problems are minute compared to the problems I would
have had if I hadn't received immediate help. Separately, the physical and
emotional problems that anorexia nervosa creates can greatly harm its victim. However, when the two are teamed together, the results are deadly.

QUESTIONS FOR WRITING AND DISCUSSION

1. Without looking back at this essay, jot down the specific examples
    that you found most memorable. How would you describe these
    examples: tedious and commonplace, eye-opening, shocking, upsetting, per-
    suasive? Explain.

2. Identify the thesis statement and essay map. Referring to paragraph numbers,
    show how the essay map sets up the organization of the essay.

3. Reread the opening sentences of each body paragraph. Identify one opening
    sentence that creates a smooth transition from the previous paragraph. Iden-
    tify one opening sentence in which the transition could be smoother. Revise
    this sentence to improve the transition with a paragraph hook.

4. In this essay, Brosseau defines anorexia nervosa, explains its physical and
    emotional effects (and hints at its causes), and analyzes the process of the dis-
    order, from its inception to its cure. Identify passages that illustrate each of
    these strategies: definition, cause-and-effect analysis, and process analysis.

5. A recent study by Judith Rabek-Wagener and her colleagues has shown that the "mass marketing of body images through print media and television and advertising" has helped cause nearly 65 percent of young women and 35 percent of young men to "experience significant dissatisfaction with their body size, shape, condition, or appearance." For the complete article, see "The Effect of Media Analysis on . . . Body Image Among College Students" in the *Journal of American College Health,* August 1, 1998. Read the research on the connection between the media and eating disorders and then write your own essay explaining the causes of eating disorders or the effects that the media have on college students' self-images.

Spanish writer Ramon Gomez de la Serna (1888–1963), the subject of this painting by Diego Rivera, was a prolific and creative novelist, biographer, and critic. The journal exercise on page 375 invites you to compare the style of this painting with Rivera's style in *The Flower Carrier* on page 156.

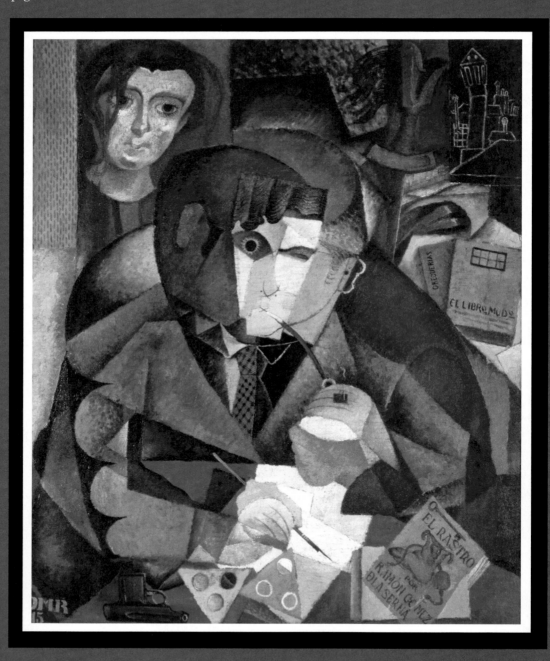

Diego Rivera (1886–1957)
Portrait of Ramon Gomez de la Serna
Oil on canvas
Private Collection, Christie's Images

chapter

8 Evaluating

During your fall semester library-orientation tour, you discover a small office tucked away in the corner of the library building: the interlibrary loan office. Because you occasionally need to see articles and books that your library does not have, you decide to investigate the interlibrary loan service and evaluate the helpfulness of the staff as well as the convenience, speed, and cost of obtaining materials. As part of your evaluation, you interview the office coordinator as well as several teachers and students who have used the service. Their responses—combined with your own observations—indicate that although an interlibrary loan can sometimes take a couple of weeks, the loan office gets high marks for its service. The staff is always helpful and patient, the service is easily accessible through electronic mail, and the cost of books and articles is surprisingly low.

In a letter to your parents, you explain that you are considering transferring to a different school for the following year. You have some misgivings about your decision to change, but after listing your criteria and ranking them in order from most to least important, you are convinced that you're making the right choice. In the letter, you explain your decision, based on your criteria, and ask that your parents continue to support your education

> *When we evaluate, we have in mind ... an ideal of what a good thing—pianist, painting, or professor—should be and do, and we apply that ideal to the individual instance before us.*
>
> —JEANNE FAHNESTOCK AND MARIE SECOR,
> AUTHORS OF A RHETORIC OF ARGUMENT

> *Purpose and craftsmanship—ends and means—these are the keys to your judgment.*
>
> —MARYA MANNES,
> JOURNALIST AND SOCIAL COMMENTATOR

ARDLY A DAY PASSES THAT WE DO NOT EXPRESS OUR LIKES OR DISLIKES. WE CONSTANTLY PASS JUDGMENT ON PEOPLE, PLACES, OBJECTS, EVENTS, IDEAS, AND POLICIES. "SUE IS A WONDERFUL PERSON." "THE FOOD IN THIS cafeteria is horrible." "That movie we saw Saturday night ought to get an Oscar nomination for best picture." "Going to war with Iraq was the wrong response to international terrorism." "The Atkins diet is nothing more than a passing fad." In addition to our own reactions, we are constantly exposed to the opinions of our friends, family members, teachers, and business associates. The media also barrage us with claims about products, famous personalities, and candidates for political office.

A claim or opinion, however, is not an *evaluation*. Your reaction to a person, a sports event, a meal, a movie, or a public policy becomes an evaluation *only* when you support your value judgment with clear standards and specific evidence. Your goal in evaluating something is not only to express your viewpoint, but also to *persuade* others to accept your judgment. You convince your readers by indicating the standards for your judgment and then supporting it with evidence: "The food in this cafeteria is horrible [your claim]. I know that not all cafeteria food tastes great, but it should at least be sanitary [one standard of judgment]. Yesterday, I had to dig a piece of green mold out of the meat loaf, and just as I stuck my fork into the green salad, a large black roach ran out [evidence]."

Most people interested in a subject agree that certain standards are important, for example, that a cafeteria be clean and pest-free. The standards that you share with your audience are the *criteria* for your evaluation. You convince your readers that something is good or bad, ugly or beautiful, tasty or nauseating by analyzing your subject in terms of your criteria. For each separate criterion, you support your judgment with specific *evidence:* descriptions, statistics, testimony, or examples from your personal experience. If your readers agree that your standards or criteria are appropriate, and if you supply detailed evidence, your readers should be convinced. They will take your evaluation seriously—and think twice about eating at that roach-infested cafeteria.

Techniques for Writing Evaluations

The most common genre for evaluations is the review. Most frequently, we read reviews of films, books, restaurants, commercial products, public performances, and works of art. Reviews vary widely depending on the topic, the place of publication, and the social context. Some reviews seem to be little more than thinly disguised promotions, while other reviews are thorough, complex, and highly critical. For any substantive evaluation, the review must set standards of judgment, rely on fair criteria, balance positive and negative evaluations, and provide sufficient evidence to persuade its readers. Use the following techniques as you write your evaluation.

> *It is as hard to find a neutral critic as it is a neutral country in a time of war.*
> —KATHERINE ANNE PORTER,
> NOVELIST AND SHORT STORY WRITER

- **Assessing the rhetorical situation.** What is the social occasion and context for your review? Find examples of the genre you propose to write—where are these reviews typically published? Who is the audience, and what do they already believe or know about the topic?
- **Stating an *overall claim* about your subject.** This statement serves as the *thesis* for your evaluation.
- **Describing the person, place, object, text, event, service, or performance being evaluated.** Readers need basic information—*who, what, when,* and *where*—to form a clear judgment.
- **Clarifying the *criteria* for your evaluation.** A criterion is a standard of judgment that most people interested in your subject agree is important. A criterion serves as a yardstick against which you measure your subject.
- **Stating a *judgment* for each criterion.** The overall claim is based on your judgment of each separate criterion. Include both positive *and* negative judgments.
- **Supporting each judgment with *evidence*.** Support can include detailed description, facts, examples, testimony, or statistics.
- **Balancing your evaluation with both positive and negative judgments about your subject.** Evaluations that are all positive are merely advertisements; evaluations that are entirely negative may seem too harsh or mean-spirited.

In the following evaluation of a Chinese restaurant in Washington, D.C., journalist and critic Phyllis C. Richman illustrates the main features of an evaluation:

Hunan Dynasty

215 Pennsylvania Ave. SE. 546–6161

Information and description

Open daily 11 A.M. to 3 P.M. for lunch, 3 P.M. to 10 P.M. for dinner, until 11 P.M. on Friday and Saturday.

Reservations suggested for large parties.

Prices for lunch: appetizers $2 to $4.50, entrees $4.75 to $6.50. For dinner: appetizers $1 to $13.95 (combination platter), entrees $6.75 to $18.

Complete dinner with wine or beer, tax, and tip about $20 a person.

Description

Chinese restaurants in America were once places one went just to eat. Now one goes to dine. There are now waiters in black tie, cloths on the tables and space between those tables, art on the walls and decoratively carved vegetables on the plate—elegance has become routine in Chinese restaurants. What's more, in Chinese restaurants the ingredients are fresh (have you ever found frozen broccoli in a Chinese kitchen?), and the cooking almost never sinks below decent. . . . And it is usually moderately priced. In other words, if you're among unfamiliar restaurants and looking for good value, Chinese restaurants now are routinely better than ever.

Overall claim

The Hunan Dynasty is an example of what makes Chinese restaurants such reliable choices. A great restaurant? It is not. A good value? Definitely. A restaurant to fit nearly any diner's need? Probably.

Criterion #1: Nice setting
Judgment: Attractive
Evidence

First, it is attractive. There are no silk tassels, blaring red lacquer or Formica tables; instead there are white tablecloths and subtle glass etchings. It is a dining room—or dining rooms, for the vastness has been carved into smaller spaces—of gracefulness and lavish space.

Criterion #2: Good service

Judgment: Often expert

Evidence

Second, service is a strong priority. The waiters look and act polished, and serve with flourishes from the carving of a Peking duck to the portioning of dishes among the diners. I have found some glitches—a forgotten appetizer, a recommendation of two dishes that turned out nearly identical—but most often the service has been expert. . . .

Criterion #3: Good main dishes

Judgment: Good but not memorable

Evidence

As for the main dishes, don't take the "hot and spicy" asterisks too seriously, for this kitchen is not out to offer you a test of fire. The peppers are there, but not in great number. And, like the appetizers, the main dishes are generally good but not often memorable. Fried dishes—and an inordinate number of them seem to be fried—are crunchy and not greasy. Vegetables are bright and crisp. Eggplant with hot garlic sauce is properly unctuous; Peking duck is as fat-free and crackly-skinned as you could hope (though pancakes were rubbery). And seafoods—shrimp, scallops, lobster—are tenderly cooked, though they are not the most full-flavored examples of those ingredients.

I have found only one dismal main dish in a fairly broad sampling: lemon chicken had no redeeming feature in its doughy, greasy, overcooked and underseasoned presentation. Otherwise, not much goes wrong. Crispy shrimp with walnuts might be preferable stir-fried rather than batter-fried, but the tomato-red sauce and crunchy walnuts made a good dish. Orange beef could use more seasoning but the coating was nicely crusty and the meat tender. . . .

So with the opening of the Hunan Dynasty, Washington did not add a stellar Chinese restaurant to its repertoire, but that is not necessarily what the city needed anyway. Hunan Dynasty is a top-flight neighborhood restaurant—with good food, caring service and very fair prices—that is attractive enough to set a mood for celebration and easygoing enough for an uncomplicated dinner with the family after work.

Criterion #3 cont.

Judgment: Sometimes bad

Evidence

Overall claim restated

EVALUATING COMMERCIAL PRODUCTS OR SERVICES

Writers frequently evaluate commercial products or services. Consumer magazines test and rate every imaginable product or service—from cars and dishwashers to peanut butter and brokerage houses. Guidebooks evaluate tourist spots, restaurants, colleges, and hunting lodges. Specialty magazines, such as *Modern Photography, Road and Track, Skiing,* and *Wired,* often rate products and services of interest to their readers. To qualify as evaluation—and not just advertising—the authors and the publishers must maintain an independent status, uninfluenced by the manufacturers of the products or services they are judging.

Consider, first, the following "evaluation" of a wine, found on a bottle of Cabernet Sauvignon:

> This Cabernet Sauvignon is a dry, robust, and complex wine whose hearty character is balanced by an unusual softness.

This "evaluative" language is so vague and esoteric that it may mean very little to the average consumer who just wants some wine with dinner. *Dry:* How can a liquid be dry? *Robust:* Does this refer to physique? *Soft:* Wine is not a pillow, though it might put you to sleep. *Complex:* Are they describing a wine or conducting a psychological analysis? While an independent evaluator may legitimately use these terms for knowledgeable wine drinkers, this particular description suggests that the wine is absolutely everything the buyer would like it to be—dry yet robust, hearty but at the same time soft. Apparently, the writer's purpose here is not to evaluate a product but to flatter readers who imagine themselves connoisseurs of wine.

Now consider the following evaluation of the gas/electric hybrid car, the Toyota Prius. In the following excerpt from *Consumer Reports,* the editors compare the Prius with the Honda Civic Hybrid in terms of fuel economy, clean emissions, size, and engine technology. In this report, notice also document design and graphics features, including the ratings graph and a sidebar on "The Hybrid Report Card."

The Hybrid Grows Up

Achieving 44 mpg overall in our tests and with near-zero emissions, according to the California Air Resources Board, the redesigned Toyota Prius hybrid car scored well enough in our testing to be named our Top Pick in the Green Car category in the April Auto issue. Its gas mileage is the highest we've recorded in a five-passenger vehicle.

The Prius also outscored the 4 midsized family sedans here and finished sixth out of the 15 similarly priced sedans we've tested (see the Ratings on the next page).

If fuel economy and clean emissions are a priority, the Prius's attributes in these areas combined with its roomy interior, five-passenger seating, and hatchback versatility make it a good alternative to many conventional small or midsized sedans.

However, if you want an excellent all-around family sedan regardless of fuel economy, there are several models, such as the four-cylinder versions of the Honda Accord, Toyota Camry, Mazda6, and Nissan Altima,

---

close**up**   THE HYBRID REPORT CARD

Hybrid technology is still new, so some long-term questions remain unanswered. Here are some of the considerations regarding hybrid vehicles.

Price. Hybrids typically cost more than similarly sized and equipped conventional cars. The new Prius, however, has reduced the difference.

Reliability. Reliability for the previous Prius and the Honda Civic Hybrid have been excellent, according to our subscribers survey.

Fuel savings. Fuel costs should be about half what they are for comparable cars. At $1.50 per gallon, cars in this class burn about $1,000 worth of fuel in 15,000 miles. At that rate, the Prius would save about $500 per year.

Depreciation. The previous Prius is holding its value fairly well. After three years it loses about 42 percent of its initial value, compared with about 45 percent of the average car.

Battery pack. Hybrids haven't been around long enough for us to collect data on battery-pack reliability, but the Prius's battery pack is guaranteed for 8 years/100,000 miles (10 years/150,000 in states with California emission rules). Toyota estimates that the replacement cost for the battery pack would be about $3,000 to $3,500 if it's not covered by the warranty. But the company expects the price to drop significantly in coming years.

Ratings family cars

Excellent Very good Good Fair Poor

In performance order. Red check (✔) indicates a recommended model.
Blue key number indicates a Quick Pick.

		Make & model	Is this issue	Overall score					Price as tested	Reliability
				P	F	G	VG	E		
✔	1	**Honda Accord** Ex (4-cyl.)							$23,290	◖
	2	**Volkswagen Passat** GLS (4-cyl.)							25,030	◑
✔	3	**Toyota Camry** LE (4-cyl.)							20,690	◉
✔	4	**Mazda6** i (4-cyl.)							22,635	◉
	5	**Chevrolet Malibu** LS (V6)							22,820	New
✔	6	**Toyota Prius**	●						22,052	◉
	7	**Chevrolet Malibu** (4-cyl.)	●						20,930	New
✔	8	**Nissan Altima** 2.5 S							22,540	◖
✔	9	**Hyundai Sonata** GLS (V6)							19,439	○
	10	**Mitsubishi Galant** ES (4-cyl.)	●						20,342	New
	11	**Kia Optima** EX (V6)							20,930	NA
✔	12	**Crystler Sebring** LX (V6)							21,700	○
✔	13	**Suzuki Verona** LX	●						18,649	New
	14	**Saturn L300** (4-cyl.)							16,995	○
	15	**Dodge Stratus** SXT (4-cyl.)	●						20,620	○

that are similarly priced and have scored better overall in our tests. The overall fuel economy of those four vehicles ranged from 22 to 24 mpg.

A hybrid vehicle couples an electric motor with a gasoline engine to boost fuel economy and provide cleaner emissions. The Prius uses a 76-hp, 1.5-liter gas engine and a 67-hp electric motor. In contrast to dedicated electric vehicles, hybrids do not need to be plugged in for recharging; the batteries recharge as the car is being driven.

This version of the Prius uses Toyota's second-generation hybrid technology. The car is a significant improvement over the first version, with more interior space, quicker acceleration, better gas mileage, and cleaner emissions, all for about the same price. With optional side and head-protection air bags, our Prius stickered at $22,052. In contrast to the Honda Civic Hybrid sedan, which got 36 mpg overall and uses a smaller electric motor to provide a power boost for the gas engine, the Prius can operate on electric or gasoline power or both, depending on the driving conditions. Overall the scores for the Prius and Civic Hybrid are very close.

EVALUATING WORKS OF ART

Evaluations of commercial products and services tend to emphasize usefulness, practicality, convenience, and cost. Evaluations of works of art, on the other hand, focus on form, color, texture, design, balance, image, or theme. Even the phrase "appreciating a work of art" suggests that we are making a value judgment, though usually not one based on money. Through evaluation, writers teach us to appreciate all kinds of art: paintings, sculpture, photographs, buildings, antique cars or furniture, novels, short stories, essays, poems, and tapestries. A Dior fashion, a quilt, a silverware pattern, even an old pair of jeans might be evaluated primarily on aesthetic rather than practical grounds.

In the following selection, art critic Mark Stevens evaluates Francisco Goya's painting *Tre Maggio* (The Third of May), which is reprinted here. This painting depicts the execution of Spanish hostages by Napoleon's forces, in retaliation for an

Francisco de Goya, *Los fusilamientos del 3 de Mayo, 1808* (1814). Oil on canvas, 8′6″ × 11′4″. © MUSEO NACIONAL DEL PRADO MADRID.

attack by a mob on the previous day. As Stevens explains, Goya does not portray the doomed hostages as heroic martyrs; instead, he tries to show the horrors of war and death. In doing that, Stevens believes, Goya "told the truth: what happened on the third of May was a butchering."

> The iconography, the color and light, the composition—all contribute to the power of this picture. Its most impressive aspect, in my view, is that Goya . . . transformed the conventions of hope into those of despair. This makes the horror all the greater, for we can see what we have lost, in addition to what we have. In the background, for example, the spire of the church is a dark, dim reminder, certainly not a cause for hope. The cruelty of the execution, which takes place in a melodramatic light, reminds us of acts of martyrdom—but without the traditional promise of heavenly reward.
>
> Of course, the outstretched arms of the central figure also recall the Crucifixion, and the man's hands bear stigmata. However, the traditional religious gesture of acceptance—the outstretched arms of Christ—has here been turned into an expression of outrage, terror and meaninglessness. What is the victim saying? There is nothing he can say, for his situation is one in which neither faith nor reason matter. His outflung arms

(Detail) Francisco de Goya, *Los fusilamientos del 3 de Mayo, 1808* (1814). Oil on canvas, 8′6″ × 11′4″. © MUSEO NACIONAL DEL PRADO MADRID.

are mirrored by those of the corpse in the foreground: such is the promise of resurrection. The corpse itself is perhaps the most truthful ever painted, for it exhibits the unbearable banality, the crumpled emptiness of death.

The men around the central victim display a variety of other reactions to their fate, none noble. One looks heavenward, but his expression is groveling. The praying man cannot raise his eyes. A third hides his face, as do the victims who await execution. Goya's use of light enhances their horror. The light contains no spiritual overtone, but rather emanates from a common lantern; an intense glow is cast on the small, grisly scene, but it cannot pierce the dark reaches. This light—glaring, without delicacy, lurid, almost artificial—seems peculiarly modern. . . .

In addition to his brilliant use of light and shade, which isolates the central figure, Goya used several other formal devices to make his point. He employed sweeping diagonal lines to scissor the picture into sharp, claustrophobic spaces. He foreshortened the corpse, so that the body seems to draw toward the viewer. (It almost looks as though the dead man is bidding the viewer welcome.) Otherwise, Goya has positioned the figures so that the viewer, curiously, is placed on the side of the executioners. You and I, observing, are implicated in mankind's folly.

EVALUATING PERFORMANCES

Evaluating live, recorded, or filmed performances of people in sports, dance, drama, debate, public meetings or lectures, and music may involve practical criteria, such as the prices of tickets to sports events or rock concerts. However, there are also aesthetic criteria that apply to people and their performances. In film evaluations, for example, the usual criteria are good acting and directing, an entertaining or believable story or plot, memorable characters, dramatic special effects, and so forth.

In the following evaluation of *The Lord of the Rings: The Return of the King,* Richard Alleva, writing in *Commonweal* magazine shortly before *The Lord of the Rings* received eleven Academy Awards, compares the trilogy of books to the film version and then evaluates features of the film's narrative, acting, imagery, gender issues, humor, and themes. Typical of the genre of film review, Alleva balances description of the film with evaluation of the film's strengths and weaknesses.

PROFESSIONAL WRITING

PETER JACKSON'S SORCERY

Richard Alleva

Peter Jackson's three-part film of *The Lord of the Rings* (LOTR) may or
may not please votaries of J.R.R. Tolkien's prose epic, but it is a godsend to
anyone like me. I love the book's "northness," its landscape of towering
forests and monster-housing caves, and the creatures that inhabit that landscape; my problem is with the prose that conveys this world. Though
Tolkien could write well—witness the charming prose of *The Hobbit* and
the incisiveness of his scholarly essays—LOTR the novel contains too many
sentences like this one: "The onslaught of Mordor broke like a wave on the
beleaguered hills, voices roaring like a tide amid the wreck and crash of
arms." The author certainly can't be accused of mixing his metaphors but
this is too much of a wet thing. LOTR is lengthy, and a lengthy book needs
fresher language than Tolkien could provide.

In the film adaptation, of course, the prose is gone, and Middle-earth
floods into movie theaters by way of gorgeous photography and the latest
digital tricks. For some, the movie will seem a desecration precisely because
it is so visually forceful. You thought you knew what the wizard Gandalf
looked like as he took shape within your mind as you read? Well, gaze on
Sir Ian McKellen for just five seconds and kiss your inner-eye wizard good-
bye. This movie isn't merely an adaptation; it's a coup d'etat. It overthrows
our reading responses with a giant's sneer and brushes aside our psychological collaboration with the author. So, caveat lector.

Rather than write a formal movie review, I'm just going to walk around
the film trilogy (*The Fellowship of the Ring, The Two Towers,* and *The Return
of the King*) and point out interesting features, just as I would walk around
a hydroelectric dam or a new skyscraper. Do these comparisons imply something inhuman, or at least grandiose about this movie? Perhaps, but like
Gandalf, let us not be petty in the face of a monster.

Narrative: Tolkien's book wasn't just a literary endeavor but a huge
verbal Lego project that he assembled in his study with the quiet fa-
naticism of a child putting together a toy monster or a train station. He
gorged the reader on Middle-earth genealogy, flora and fauna, weather,

culture, hobbit music, dwarf etiquette, elf ethics, giant cookery, etc., etc., and the whole project spilled over into Tolkien's Silmarillion, a prequel set in the same universe as LOTR. Fiction or mythic anthropology? Narrative propulsion was the goal for the moviemakers, not mythic saturation. I'm not surprised that Miranda Otto (who plays the human princess Eowyn) remarked, "I don't like to think of *Rings* as a fantasy, and, actually, Pete [Jackson] wanted to shoot it like a historical [piece]." Indeed, the whole thing comes across very much like one of those medieval adventure stories you saw in your youth—*Prince Valiant, The Black Shield of Falworth*—only much, much bigger and much, much better.

Nonreaders of LOTR may occasionally be puzzled, however. As in the book (albeit one of its appendixes), Aragorn marries the elf princess Arwen, but does the human princess Eowyn get a consolation prize? During my first viewing of *Return of the King,* I blinked and missed the split-second shot of Eowyn and Prince Faramir standing together like a loving couple. I caught it the second time around, yes, but surely this is compression taken too far. And what is the meaning of the crystal ball-like object that the hobbit Pippin finds and that Gandalf treats with trepidation? I found the brief verbal explanation incomprehensible, but readers will know that several of these orbs are used by the arch-fiend Sauron both to spy and to impose false predictions upon gullible creatures such as the steward of the human kingdom of Gondor (the royal line of heirs has been broken—hence the need for the king to return), who comes across on screen as an unmotivated psychopath rather than a man deceived. This is a compression that distorts. Nevertheless, the scriptwriters, Jackson, Fran Walsh, and Philippa Boyens, must be praised for generally keeping a lengthy movie both richly textured and sleek.

Acting: With dozens of roles so well cast and acted, one hardly knows whom to single out. For that very reason let me bypass the usual accolade-gatherers (McKellen, Sean Astin, Elijah Wood) and draw attention to players who might be overlooked. Because she is so beautiful, Liv Tyler has always been scanted as an actress. But in *The Two Towers,* Arwen's scene with her father (who is trying to dissuade her from loving a mortal) is made truly poignant by Tyler's acting, and she achieves this while speaking a language that doesn't really exist (though Elvish sounds like Welsh). Not for nothing do acting teachers make

5

6

their students study subtext so that the phone book may be recited as if it were Shakespeare.

King Theoden of Rohan is such a sere figure that Bernard Hill's underplaying may be overshadowed by the more flamboyant performances, but if you watch him closely you'll find a fascinating portrayal of a man temperamentally drawn to despair yet determined to fight the good fight. *7*

There really is an actor at the core of Gollum and he's called Andy Serkis. Peter Jackson's special-effects house, Weta Digital, took Serkis's performance, caught by motion-capture cameras, and overlaid the computer-generated monster we see on Serkis's movements. And whatever sound engineering did to the actor's voice, there is a human note somewhere in there. Gollum comes across as a Dostoyevsky character who's been given a makeover by the Brothers Grimm, and Serkis surely deserves some credit for that kernel of complexity. *8*

Imagery: Yes, the computer-generated work is impressive, occasionally overwhelming. Still, some of the most memorable shots are simply good camera setups of actors delivering the emotional goods, just as in nonfantasy movies: Merry the hobbit riding to war while seated in front of Eowyn, his face alight with the discovery of a new way of being in the world; Aragorn (now the returned king), exhausted before the final battle, suddenly smiling at his troops and quietly uttering the mildest of war cries: "For Frodo." *9*

But there are too many camera arcs over rolling plains as the Fellowship theme swells up on the soundtrack. And if I ever have to look at another troupe of horsemen clattering through castle gates, I may throw myself over the nearest battlement. *10*

Feminism: It's not that the film invented the warrior princesses, Eowyn and Arwen. They're in the book too, but Tolkien always seemed a little theoretical in his presentation of women. Here the actresses playing them make them specific, mercurial, and commanding. When Eowyn confronts the Lord of the Nazgûl, he who cannot be killed by any man, with the fact that "I am no man," and then thrusts her sword in his face, I could feel battalions of women cheering her on. I cheered too. *11*

Humor: We can feel a fatherly smile pervading the books, but the movie grins. The body-count rivalry between good guys Gimli the dwarf and Legolas the elf is typical of boys' adventure tales but it leads *12* up to, "That still counts as only one!" which, in context (Legolas has miraculously taken down a gigantic mammoth-like beast carrying scads of enemies), is one of the funniest movie lines of the decade. There is also dry wit, as when (in *Towers*) Aragorn impulsively embraces an elf general for coming to the rescue, and the fastidious warrior registers fleeting repugnance at being hugged by a—ugh!—human.

Themes (spoilers follow): The literary LOTR contains many themes   13
but I venture that the leading one is the necessity to cling stubbornly and absolutely to virtue (no matter how modest) in the face of absolute evil. (This is what makes Tolkien basically conservative. Liberals don't believe in absolute evil.) The movie's climax is the same as the book's: Frodo's failure to throw the ring into the fires of Mount Doom shows that he lacks absolute devotion to virtue, but this very human failure is rescued by Gollum's greedy intervention. Ironically, good comes out of evil; fate is stronger than character.

However, because the movie's script and Sean Astin's wonderfully un-   14
fissured performance spotlight Sam's absolute devotion to Frodo, the preclimactic scene in which Sam carries Frodo up Mount Doom conveys an emotional charge that the morally messy climax doesn't. So Sam emerges as the true hero of the film trilogy, and the most important virtue, it seems, is the capacity for friendship, not the more general devotion to abstract virtue.

Though the creator of Middle-earth feared and hated many aspects   15
of technology, the technology of the movies has treated Tolkien with respect. Peter Jackson, master of technomagic and generalissimo of a thousand technicians and actors, has made of Tolkien's deliberately archaic epic a fresh, bracing revel.

WARMING UP: JOURNAL EXERCISES

The following exercises will help you practice writing evaluations. Read all of the following exercises and then write on the three that interest you most. If another idea occurs to you, write about it:

1. Choose the best of the courses that you are currently taking. To persuade a friend to take it, evaluate the course, the teacher, or both. What criteria and evidence would you select to persuade your friend?

2. Evaluate an object related to one of your hobbies or special interests—stereo or video equipment, water or snow skis, a cooking appliance or utensil, diving or hiking equipment, photography or art equipment, ranching or farming apparatus, fishing rods or reels, some part of a car, or computers. Write an evaluation of that object following the format used by *Consumer Reports.*

3. Evaluate a TV show that you find particularly irritating, boring, or insipid, but that you find yourself watching occasionally anyway. Watch the show, taking notes about scenes, characters, dialogue, and plot. Write a critique of the show for other students in this class.

4. To gather some information for yourself about a possible job or career, interview a person in your prospective field about his or her job or profession. Focus your questions on the person's opinions and judgments about this career. What criteria does this person use to judge it? What other jobs serve as a good basis for comparison? What details from this person's daily routine support his or her judgments?

5. At your place of work, evaluate one of your products or services. Write down the criteria and evidence that your business might use to determine whether it is a "good" product or service. Then list the criteria and evidence that your customers or patrons probably use. Are these two sets of criteria and evidence identical? Explain.

6. Choose a piece of modern art (painting, drawing, poster, sculpture, ceramics, and so forth). Describe and evaluate it for an audience that is indifferent or possibly even hostile to contemporary art. Explain why your readers should appreciate this particular art object.

7. Reexamine the painting of Ramon Gomez de la Serna by Diego Rivera that appears at the beginning of this chapter. Describe the people, objects, use of color, and perspective in this painting. Then compare this painting with the painting of *The Flower Carrier,* also by Diego Rivera, on page 156. Compare these two paintings in order to evaluate which is the better, more interesting, or more effective painting. Consider their styles (realism versus cubism), dynamic use of color, effective arrangement and perspective, interesting subject matter, effective theme, and so forth. Do some research on the Web about Diego Rivera's paintings. Use your evaluation and research to explain, in two or three paragraphs, which is the most interesting or effective painting.

8. The following two articles present other alternatives for writing reviews. In the first example, Margaret Lazarus writes a cultural critique of Walt Disney's *The Lion King.* Instead of the typical review that evaluates the plot,

acting, and cinematography, Lazarus focuses on the cultural stereotyping contained in a film targeted at children. Read her review and decide if you find her evaluation persuasive. In the second short review, David Sedaris, author of the best-selling *Me Talk Pretty One Day*, uses humor to evaluate one of the "precious little bistros" that have sprung up in New York. Sedaris provides an excellent model of how to use a personal narrative and humor to create a memorable review.

PROFESSIONAL WRITING

ALL'S NOT WELL IN LAND OF "THE LION KING"

Margaret Lazarus

It's official: Walt Disney's *The Lion King* is breaking box-office records. Unfortunately, it's not breaking any stereotypes.

My sons, along with millions of other kids around the world, joyously awaited *The Lion King*. I was intrigued because this time Disney appeared to be skipping the old folk-tales with their traditional and primal undercurrents.

I hoped Disney had grown weary of reinforcing women's subordinate status by screening fables about a beauty who tames an angry male beast or a mermaid who gives up her glorious voice and splits her body to be with a prince.

So off we went to the movies, figuring we would enjoy an original, well-animated story about animals on the African plain. Even before the title sequence, however, I started to shudder.

Picture this (and I apologize for spilling the plot): The golden-maned—that is, good—lion is presenting his first born male child to his subjects. All the animals in the kingdom, known as Pride Lands, are paying tribute to the infant son that will someday be their king. These royal subjects are basically lion food—zebras, monkeys, birds, etc.—and they all live together in supposed harmony in the "circle of life."

Outside the kingdom, in a dark, gloomy, and impoverished elephant graveyard, are the hyenas. They live dismally jammed together among bones and litter. The hyenas are dark—mostly black—and they are nasty, menacing the little lion prince when he wanders into their territory.

One of their voices is done by Whoopie Goldberg, in a clearly inner-city dialect. If this is not the ghetto, I don't know what is.

All is not perfect inside Pride Lands, however. The king's evil brother Scar has no lionesses or cubs. Scar has a black mane, and speaks in an effeminate, limp-pawed, British style done by Jeremy Irons—seemingly a gay caricature.

Scar conspires with the hyenas to kill the king and send the prince into exile. In exchange for their support, Scar allows the hyenas to live in Pride Lands. But property values soon crash: The hyenas overpopulate, kill all the game, and litter the once-green land with bones.

Already Disney has gays and blacks ruining the "natural order," and the stereotypes keep rolling. The lionesses never question whether they should be serving Scar and the hyenas—they just worry a lot. They are mistreated, but instead of fighting back these powerful hunters passively await salvation. (Even my 7-year-old wondered why the young, strong lioness didn't get rid of Scar.)

The circle of life is broken; disaster awaits everyone. But then the first-born male returns to reclaim power. The royal heir kills the gay usurper, and sends the hyenas back to the dark, gloomy, bone-filled ghetto. Order is restored and the message is clear: Only those born to privilege can bring about change.

This is not a story about animals—we know animals don't behave like this. This is a metaphor for society that originated in the minds of Disney's creators. These bigoted images and attitudes will lodge deeply in children's consciousness.

I'm not sure I always understand the law of the Hollywood jungle, but my boys definitely don't. Scared and frightened by *The Lion King,* they were also riveted, and deeply affected. But entranced by the "Disney magic," they and millions of other children were given hidden messages that can only do them—and us—harm.

PROFESSIONAL WRITING

TODAY'S SPECIAL

David Sedaris

It is his birthday, and Hugh and I are seated in a New York restaurant, awaiting the arrival of our fifteen-word entrées. He looks very nice, dressed in the suit and sweater that have always belonged to him. As for me, I own only my shoes, pants, shirt, and tie. My jacket belongs to the restaurant and was offered as a loan by the maître d', who apparently thought I would feel more comfortable dressed to lead a high-school marching band.

I'm worrying the thick gold braids decorating my sleeves when the waiter presents us with what he calls "a little something to amuse the palette." Roughly the size and color of a Band-Aid, the amusement floats on a shallow, muddy puddle of sauce and is topped with a sprig of greenery.

"And this would be . . . what, exactly?" Hugh asks.

"This," the waiter announces, "is our raw Atlantic sword-fish served in a dark chocolate gravy and garnished with fresh mint."

"Not again," I say. "Can't you guys come up with something a little less conventional?"

"Love your jacket," the waiter whispers.

As a rule, I'm no great fan of eating out in New York restaurants. It's hard to love a place that's outlawed smoking but finds it perfectly acceptable to serve raw fish in a bath of chocolate. There are no normal restaurants left, at least in our neighborhood. The diners have all been taken over by precious little bistros boasting a menu of indigenous American cuisine. They call these meals "traditional," yet they're rarely the American dishes I remember. The patty melt has been pushed aside in favor of the herb-encrusted medallions of baby artichoke hearts, which never leave me thinking, Oh, right, those! I wonder if they're as good as the ones my mom used to make.

Part of the problem is that we live in the wrong part of town. SoHo is not a macaroni salad kind of place. This is where the world's brightest young talents come to braise carmelized racks of corn-fed songbirds or offer up their famous knuckle of flash-seared crappie served with a collar of chided ginger and cornered by a tribe of kiln-roasted Chilean toadstools, teased with a warm spray of clarified musk oil. Even when they promise something simple, they've got to tart it up—the meatloaf has been poached in seawater, or there are figs in the tuna salad. If cooking is an art, I think we're in our Dada phase.

I've never thought of myself as a particularly finicky eater, but it's hard to be a good sport when each dish seems to include no fewer than a dozen ingredients, one of which I'm bound to dislike. I'd order the skirt steak with a medley of suffocated peaches, but I'm put off by the aspirin sauce. The sea scallops look good until I'm told they're served in a broth of malt liquor and mummified litchi nuts. What I really want is a cigarette, and I'm always searching the menu in the hope that some courageous young chef has finally recognized tobacco as a vegetable. Bake it, steam it, grill it, or stuff it into littleneck clams, I just need something familiar that I can hold on to.

When the waiter brings our entrées, I have no idea which plate might be mine. In yesterday's restaurants it was possible both to visualize and to recognize your meal. There were always subtle differences, but for the most part, a lamb chop tended to maintain its basic shape. That is to say that it looked choplike. It had a handle made of bone and a teardrop of meat hugged by a thin rind of fat. Apparently, though, that was too predictable. Order the modern lamb chop, and it's likely to look no different than your companion's order of shackled pompano. The current food is always arranged into a senseless, vertical tower. No longer content to recline, it now reaches for the sky, much like the high-rise buildings lining our city streets. It's as if the plates were valuable parcels of land and the chef had purchased one small lot and unlimited air rights. Hugh's saffron linguini resembles a miniature turban, topped with architectural spires of shrimp. It stands there in the center while the rest of the vast, empty plate looks as though it's been leased out as a possible parking lot. I had ordered the steak, which, bowing to the same minimalist fashion, is served without the bone, the thin slices of beef stacked to resemble a funeral pyre. The potatoes I'd been expecting have apparently either been clarified to an essence or were used to stoke the grill.

"Maybe," Hugh says, "they're inside your tower of meat."

This is what we have been reduced to. Hugh blows the yucca pollen off his blackened shrimp while I push back the sleeves of my borrowed sport coat and search the meat tower for my promised potatoes.

"There they are, right there." Hugh uses his fork to point out what could easily be mistaken for five cavity-riddled molars. The dark spots must be my vegetable.

Because I am both a glutton and a masochist, my standard complaint, "That was so bad," is always followed by "And there was so little of it!"

Our plates are cleared, and we are presented with dessert menus. I learn that spiced ham is no longer considered just a luncheon meat and that even back issues of *Smithsonian* can be turned into sorbets.

"I just couldn't," I say to the waiter when he recommends the white chocolate and wild loganberry couscous.

"If we're counting calories, I could have the chef serve it without the crème fraîche."

"No," I say. "Really, I just couldn't."

We ask for the check, explaining that we have a movie to catch. It's only a ten-minute walk to the theater, but I'm antsy because I'd like to get something to eat before the show. They'll have loads of food at the concession stand, but I don't believe in mixing meat with my movies. Luckily there's a hot dog cart not too far out of our way.

Friends always say, "How can you eat those? I read in the paper that they're made from hog's lips."

"And . . . ?"

"And hearts and eyelids."

That, to my mind, is only three ingredients and constitutes a refreshing change of pace. I order mine with nothing but mustard, and am thrilled to watch the vendor present my hot dog in a horizontal position. So simple and timeless that I can recognize it, immediately, as food.

PROFESSIONAL WRITING

PRIME TIME ART?

Kathyrn Hughes and Ben Rogers

In the following exchange of letters, British critics Kathyrn Hughes and Ben Rogers debate the merits of the award-winning American television series ER. *Kathyrn Hughes is the author of* George Eliot: The Last Victorian *(1999) and Ben Rogers has published* A. J. Ayer: A Life *(1999). The following exchange appeared originally in* Prospect *magazine and was reprinted in* Utne.

Following the film debate format popularized by Siskel and Ebert, Hughes and Rogers debate, through letters, whether ER *deserves to be called art. Both critics attempt to define "art" and then to show why* ER *does or does not meet this demanding criterion. As you follow their conversation, decide which—if either—critic is more persuasive. Are there other criteria you use to judge television programs that they don't consider?*

Dear Kathryn,

Wednesday nights (when *ER* is on) begin with skepticism and end in rapture. I can't believe that the program is going to meet my art-critical standards, but it does. The traumas and dramas, the jokes and intimacies of County General Hospital emergency room—the ER in question—sweep me up. The series knows its limitations, but it is art of a very high order indeed.

I don't have to take sides in the elite versus popular culture wars to champion *ER.* It is enough to draw attention to its excellence. It has evolved a distinctive aesthetic, a distinctive feel and vision. It moves through a wide array of moods—from farce to romance, from pathos to high drama. Sometimes it is clever—witness the allusions to *Reservoir Dogs* in the episode directed by Quentin Tarantino. It flirts with kitsch, it dabbles in parody, but it knows when to stop.

Characters like Romano or Jerry may come close to caricature, but art has a place for this—and here they are brilliantly done. And the central characters, with their all too human foibles, their imperfect beauty and life-saving zeal, draw us in. The minor characters, too, are invariably played by the strong character actors so common in the United States. *ER* takes us out of ourselves and, like the best fiction, gives us contact with a heightened reality.

You have written about George Eliot, and I would hesitate to compare *ER* to her infinitely subtle novels. Yet the series has some of the qualities of the 19th-century novel. Both have dramatic plots, comic minor characters, and keen social observation; and both are marked by moral seriousness. Didn't Dickens' novels first appear in serial form? If *ER* is sometimes sentimental, wasn't he?

America is a funny place. It can be the crass, corrupt, and unfeeling country depicted by Tom Wolfe in *The Bonfire of the Vanities,* where rich and poor live in separate worlds. But it also remains in many respects the most democratic of countries. Status counts for little. This is the aspect of American life expressed in *ER*. It depicts men and women, black and white, working together; and it sets out quite consciously to drive home certain lessons—about health and violence, but also about fairness and respect. In the United States, where broadcasting has become ghettoized, it is almost the only show watched by blacks and whites. Blacks don't watch *Friends*, whites don't watch *Moesha*, but both tune in to *ER*.

The interesting question is not whether *ER* is art—obviously it is—but how it comes to be such old-fashioned art. We are told that we live in postmodern times. The real has given way to the simulated, grand narrative to little stories. *ER*, though, does not fit this scheme. Its leading characters labor together united by an old-fashioned work ethic. In the emergency room all the divisions of American society are overcome. Doubtless Dr. Anspaugh takes home rather more than Nurse Hathaway, but we aren't reminded of that. Socialist artists— Charlie Chaplin, the painters Férnand Leger and Diego Rivera— would have understood *ER*.

Of course art does not have to serve progressive causes. But it adds to its power when it does. George Eliot's novels condemn the subjection of women and Jews, they take aim at religious cant, moral hypocrisy, and commercial greed. In the end, *Middlemarch* and *ER* move us in much the same way.

Yours, Ben

Dear Ben,

I share your disbelieving rapture that television could ever get this good, but is *ER* art? Well, no. It's a magnificent achievement, but it does not do the specific and important work of art. Unlike George Eliot's novels, which you cite as a paradigm, *ER* neither extends nor explores the limits of its own genre. When Eliot put the "working day world" into her novels, she was doing something revolutionary. But when the producers of *ER* chose to set their drama in the workplace, they were staying firmly within the parameters set by Steven Bochco in the mid-1980s with *Hill Street Blues* and *L.A. Law*. With good reason: setting a series in an office or police station provides a central, socially stratified setting from which story lines can be compactly generated. And using an accident and emergency setting is hardly breaking new ground.

You say that *ER* is "old-fashioned art" and that its emphasis on shared endeavor and grand narrative represents a heroic rebuttal of postmodernism, with its small. whiny stories (were you thinking of *Ally McBeal?*). But *ER* places itself entirely in relation to other television narratives, and spends too much time playing postmodern games. Take that Tarantino episode. The allusions to *Reservoir Dogs* (itself generated from a web of references to other movies) undercut what little relationship *ER* had with social reality. The sight of Dr. Lewis and Nurse Hathaway in wraparound shades broke a trust in the story-telling process that took several episodes to repair.

I agree that if Dickens were around today he'd be writing TV drama. As you say, *ER* is stuffed with the kinds of caricatures he liked. Kerry Weaver's tics—the unexplained crutch, the management-speak—is a prime example. But Dickens, like the directors of *ER,* was not producing art. George Eliot, by contrast, was—and the proof lies in the absence of stereotypes in her work. Even her minor characters have lives that seem to have begun before the novels open and continue long after they have ended.

By contrast, when the characters in *ER* are taken out of context, they crumble into dust. Remember the episode when Peter Benton went to work in the Deep South? Or what about the two hours we were forced to watch Mark Greene return to his hometown and look after his ailing mother?

Another mark of Eliot's artistry is that she didn't create idealizations either. She demanded that people look like people, with potato heads, bad skin, and odd sniffs. You say that the main characters have an "imperfect beauty." But I can't see much that is imperfect about them. They look like a team of gods and goddesses descended from the sky, who have decided for some reason to don surgical gloves. *ER* scarcely pushes back the boundaries of what television drama demands aesthetically of its main players.

Art is often ugly, usually difficult, sometimes boring. It doesn't care   *13*
whether it pleases, and indeed it would rather not. It refuses to give up
its meaning without a fight, and insists that we work hard to make some
sense of what is going on. *ER* is brilliant television, but it doesn't have
the power to make up the world in a new way. I love it, but it isn't art.

Yours, Kathryn

Dear Kathryn,

You say that I offer George Eliot as a paradigm. Nothing could be   *14*
further from the case. You evidently see her as such, which is why you
can't bring yourself to acknowledge *ER*'s claim to art. But to do so is
to take a very narrow—even, I am afraid, stuffy—view of art.

Art comes in many forms. Sometimes it is a collective endeavor (the   *15*
Gothic cathedrals), sometimes intensely individual (Gaudí's *Sagrada
Familia*). It can appeal to a small group (Schoenberg) or to a whole
people (Greek tragedy, Elizabethan drama). You say art is "usually difficult, sometimes boring." But it is, just as often, easy (Oscar Wilde's
plays), and sometimes thrilling—*ER*. When you refer to "the specific
and important work" art does, I hear echoes of all those guardians of
high art, sure on *a priori* grounds that art cannot be too popular and
cannot exist in a modern medium.

You are forcing "art" into a narrow mold, implying that it needs to   *16*
"break with tradition" or at least "explore and extend the limits of its
own boundaries." But you underestimate the role tradition, convention, and genre play in art. You complain that the producers of *ER* set
their drama in the workplace, like other shows, but was Shakespeare
less of a poet because he "stayed firmly within the parameters" of the
sonnet?

In any case, *ER* does "extend' and "explore" its own genre. Look at its   *17*
lead characters. They come in as types, as they tend to in any narrative: Elizabeth Corday the troubled English-woman; Benton the
angry, driven African American; Carter the dissatisfied WASP. In
time, however, these labels fall aside to reveal real people. And because it is a series, they are given time to breathe. You say that Eliot's
characters have lives seemingly real enough to exist outside her novels. It seems to me that *ER*'s characters have just this "real" quality.
Art has to meet certain standards—it has to be technically expert, rel-

atively self-aware, enduring in its appeal. But it does not have to have all the qualities you think it requires.

Yours, Ben

P.S.: The idea that Dickens was not a serious artist is absurd. You were joking, I presume?

18

Dear Ben,

You've got me wrong. I can't abide the sniffy attitude that just because something is popular or pleasurable it must be second-rate. As someone who started her working life on the fashion pages of a glossy magazine, I know what it feels like to be the casualty of other people's intellectual insecurity. Women, I recall, were the worst offenders.

19

So I was delighted when in the early 1980s the cultural studies revolution transformed the way in which we were allowed to think about, and admit to liking, popular culture.

20

But now, like most insurrectionaries, I wonder if the revolution hasn't gone too far. I gave up glossy magazines, retrained, and now teach university students. The 20-year-olds I meet in the seminar room have received their entire education in the postmodern age. I am shocked by how little discomfort they can bear in confronting a difficult text. I long ago gave up expecting all but the very keenest (often mature) students to get through *Middlemarch.* Mostly they watch it on video and hope for the best. I am besieged for advice about which courses involve the least reading.

21

So you see why I am edgy about elevating *ER* to art. It bothers me that a work as comfortable, regressive even, as *ER* should be given the status you claim for it. For if *ER* is allowed to bask in this central cultural space, then what place is there for the difficult, uncomfortable, or downright odd piece of work?

22

I do not, as you suggest, assume that anything that appears in a "modern medium" cannot be art. There is, in fact, an American import (now canceled in the U.S.) that might qualify as art. *Homicide: Life on the Street* is on the face of it a formulaic cop show. But it does things that *ER* only pretends to do—it makes the everyday and the real its subject matter. *Homicide* once did a whole episode on what happened

23

when the station lavatory flooded. The main characters spent their time tip-toeing on planks, trying not to gag. That, it seems to me, is taking risks. That, indeed, is art.

Yours, Kathryn

VOCABULARY

In your journal, write the meanings of the following words:

- a distinctive *aesthetic* (**2**)
- it flirts with *kitsch,* it dabbles in *parody* (**2**)
- close to *caricature* (**3**)
- in *serial* form (**4**)
- serve *progressive* causes (**7**)
- cite as a *paradigm* (**8**)
- its own *genre* (**8**)
- the *allusions* (**9**)
- on *a priori* grounds (**15**)
- firmly within the *parameters* (**16**)

QUESTIONS FOR WRITING AND DISCUSSION

1. What is your favorite or least favorite television program? What criteria would you use to explain why it is or is not a great program—filming, acting, story line, relevant social themes, entertainment value, and so on? Using these criteria, explain why you would or would not recommend it to your friends.

2. In his letters to Kathyrn, Ben claims that *ER* is "art of a very high order." How does he define art? What are his main criteria? What evidence from *ER* does Ben cite to support his criteria?

3. In her responses to Ben, Kathyrn claims that *ER* is "a magnificent achievement," but it is not art. How is her definition of art different from Ben's? What are her main criteria? What evidence from *ER* does she give to support her claim?

4. Because Kathyrn and Ben carry out their discussion of *ER* through multiple letters, they are each able to respond to the other—creating an argument in dialogue form. Where do you see each writer responding specifically to the other? Where do they make their argument clearer? Where do they give ground or negotiate their positions? Finally, is their dialogue format more interesting than reading a review of *ER* by a single author? Explain.

5. The authors are writing for the British magazine *Prospect*. Where is their English point of view expressed most clearly? Since the essay was reprinted in *Utne* magazine, do you think the authors' debate is just as interesting for American readers? Why or why not?

6. On the Internet, visit the alt.tv.er Web pages at *http://www.digiserve.com/er*. The editor, Mike Sugimoto, posts regular responses to episodes of *ER*. Originally a fan of *ER,* his later reviews complain about the degenerating quality of the show: "Recent episodes have been unraveling in front of my eyes faster than a cheap sweater. Asking me to believe that these formerly realistic people are now acting like . . . well, aliens . . . is a little much. It's very much like going to a circus, watching a puppet show, and being acutely aware of the presence of strings. You can see them bouncing around. Which is fine if you're watching Punch and Judy in the park. It's not very good when you're watching what is supposedly a realistic TV drama." For commentary on recent *ER* shows, go to Television Without Pity, a Yahoo!-sponsored site, at *http://www.televisionwithoutpity.com*. Visit one of these sites—or similar ones—and read responses to *ER* episodes. Then write your own evaluation of a particular episode of *ER*, responding to Ben, Kathryn, or any of the online commentators you read.

WATCHING THE EYEWITLESS NEWS

Elayne Rapping

Culture critic Elayne Rapping is a professor of communications at Adelphi University and is the author of several books, including The Looking Glass World of Nonfiction TV *(1987),* Mediations: Forays into the Culture and Gender Wars *(1994), and* The Culture of Recovery: Making Sense of the Self-Help Movement in Women's Lives *(1996). She has also published dozens of articles about a variety of social, cultural, and media-related issues. "Watching the Eyewitless News," which originally appeared as a column in* The Progressive, *evaluates the local "Eyewitness" news programs featured daily in regional television markets.*

Jimmy Cagney, the ultimate street-smart wise guy, used to snap, "Whadya hear? Whadya know?" in the days of black-and-white movies and READ ALL ABOUT IT! headlines. But that was then and this is now. Today, when gangsta rap has replaced gangster movies, and television has replaced newsprint as the primary source of information (for two-thirds of us, the *only* source), Cagney's famous question is not only antiquated, it is beside the point. What we hear when we consume "the news" has only the most marginal relationship to what we *know* about anything. 1

I'm not referring here to CNN or the "evening news" on the national broadcast networks. I'm referring here to what passes for news in the homes and minds of the vast majority of Americans today: The Eyewitless, Happy Talk local newscasts that run in many cities for as much as an hour and a half to two hours a day, on as many as seven or eight different channels. 2

The rise of local news, the infotainment monster that ate the news industry, is a long and painful story about a key battle-front in the endless media war between capitalism and democracy, between the drive for profits and the constitutional responsibility of those licensed to use the airwaves to serve the public interest. We know who's winning, of course. The game was rigged from the start. . . . 3

Local news as we know it was invented in 1970, the brainchild of a marketing research whiz hired by the industry to raise ratings by finding out 4 what audiences "wanted to see." The Jeffersonian notion that public media should cover what citizens "need to know" was not a big consideration. Nor was it a concern to respect the audience's intelligence or diversity.

The researchers offered a limited, embarrassingly vapid list of choices   5
of formats and subjects, while ignoring the possibility that different groups might want different kinds of information and analysis. More annoying still, they ignored the possibility that individual viewers, of all kinds, might want and need different things at different times for different reasons. Nope, said the marketing whizzes, this master model of "The News" will buy us the most overall-ratings bang per buck. Wrap it up and send it out.

And it worked. Their invention has conquered the TV world. The set,   6
the news lineups, the anchors, the weather maps, the sports features—all developed for a New York City market—quickly became a universal formula, sent out to every network affiliate and independent station in America, complete with fill-in-the-blanks guidelines for adaptation to any community, no matter how large or small, urban or rural. Local news today is the single most profitable form of nonfiction television programming in the country and, for most stations, the only thing they actually produce. Everything else comes from the networks. As time went by, this tendency toward cookie-cutter formulas, exported far and wide from a central media source, reached ever more depressing depths. The trend has led to ever more nationally produced, generic features exported to local stations to be passed off as "local."

So today we have a phenomenon euphemistically called "local news,"   7
although it is anything but, filled with images of a pseudo-community called "America," which is actually closer to Disney World in its representation of American life. But why should that surprise us, in a national landscape now filled, from coast to coast, with identical, mass-produced shopping malls that pass for town marketplaces, and hotels and airports that pass for village inns? In postmodern America, after all, this kind of brand-name synthetic familiarity appears to be the only thing that holds us—a nation of endlessly uprooted and mobile strangers—together.

When you turn on the news, whether at home or in an airport or Holiday Inn in some totally strange locale, you see a predictable, comforting   8
spectacle. The town or city in question, whether Manhattan or Moose Hill, Montana, is presided over by a group of attractive, charming, well-dressed performers—whose agents, salaries, and movements up and down the ladder of media success, gauged by the size of the "market" they infiltrate, are chronicled each week in *Variety*. They seem to care endlessly for each other

and us. "Tsk, tsk," they cluck at news of yet another gang rampage or Congressional scandal. "Ooh," they sigh, at news of earthquakes and plane crashes, far and near.

If it bleeds, it leads is the motto of the commercial news industry and   *9* local news. Its endless series of fires, shootouts, collapsing buildings, and babies beaten or abandoned or bitten by wild dogs is the state-of-the-art showcase for the industry. As Don Henley once put it, in a scathing song about the local news phenomenon, "It's interesting when people die." And it's especially interesting when they die in bizarre or inhuman situations, when their loved ones are on camera to moan and wail, when a lot of them die at once. And since so much of our news is indeed personally terrifying and depressing, we need to have it delivered as cleverly and carefully as possible. And so we have the always smiling, always sympathetic, always confidently upbeat news teams to sugarcoat the bad news.

Not that local news ignores the politically important stories. Well, not   *10* entirely anyway. When wars are declared or covered, when elections are won or lost, when federal budgets and plant closings do away with jobs and services or threaten to put more and more of us in jail, for less and less cause, the local news teams are there to calm our jagged nerves and reassure us that we needn't worry.

This reassurance is sometimes subtle. National news items typically   *11* take up less than two minutes of a half-hour segment. And what's said and seen in that brief interlude is hardly enlightening. On the contrary, the hole for "hard news" is generally filled with sound bites and head shots, packaged and processed by the networks, from news conferences with the handful of movers and shakers considered "newsworthy"—the President and his key henchmen and adversaries, mostly.

But even local issues of serious import are given short shrift on these   *12* newscasts. Hard news affecting local communities takes up only a minute or two more airtime than national events. And local teams are obsessed with "man-on-the-street" spot interviews. Neighbors on local TV are forever gasping and wailing the most clichéd of reflex responses to actual local horrors, whether personal or social.

"It's so horrible," they say over and over again, like wind-up dolls with   *13* a limited repertoire of three-word phrases, when asked about a local disaster. And when the crisis affects them directly—a school budget cut or neighborhood hospital closing, for example—their on-air responses are equally vapid. "I don't know what we're going to do without any teachers or books," they say with puzzled, frenzied expressions as they try desperately to articulate some coherent reply to a complex issue they've just heard about.

"Glad you brought that up, Jim. The latest research on polls has turned up some interesting variables. It turns out, for example, that people will tell you any old thing that pops into their heads."

14   I am not suggesting that the news should not feature community residents' views and experiences. Of course it should. But the local news teams' way of presenting such community responses is deliberately demeaning and fatuous. No one could say much worth saying in such a format. And if someone managed to come up with something serious and intelligent, rest assured it would be cut in favor of a more sensational, emotional response.

15   But real news, even about cats in trees or babies in wells, is hardly what takes up the most airtime. "Don't bother too much about that stuff," say the guys and gals in the anchor chairs. Here's Goofy Gil with the weather, or Snappy Sam with the sports—the two features which, on every local newscast, are given the longest time slots and the most elaborate and expensive props. The number and ornateness of the weather maps on local news, and the endlessly amazing developments in special-effects technology to observe climate changes and movements of impending "fronts" is truly mind-boggling.

16   Who needs this stuff? But we're forgetting that this is not the question to ask. "Who wants it?" is the criterion for news producers, and it is, understandably, the weather and sports that most people, most of the time, are

likely to sit still for. If local news is meant to be a facsimile of a sunny Disneyesque community of happy, cozy campers, in which the bothersome bad guys and events of the day are quickly dealt with so that community harmony may once more reign, at least for the moment—and that *is* the intended fantasy—then what better, safer, kind of information than weather reports. Historically, after all, the weather is the standard small-talk item for people wishing to be pleasant and make contact without getting into anything controversial or heavy. It is the only kind of news we can all share in—no matter what our race, class, gender, or political differences—as members of a common community.

The researchers are not entirely wrong, after all, about what people in 17 this kind of society want. They do want comfort, reassurance, and a community where they belong and feel safe. And why shouldn't they? They find precious little of those things in the streets and buildings they traverse and inhabit in their daily lives. In my urban neighborhood, parents warn children never to make eye contact with anyone on the street or subway; never to speak to anyone, even in case of tragedy or emergency; never to look at or listen to the pathetic souls who regularly beg for money or ramble incoherently in the hope that someone, anyone, will take pity and respond.

Remember when California was God's country, the Promised Land of 18 Milk and Honey, to which people migrated for clean air, good jobs, and single-dwelling homes? Try to find these things in overpopulated, polluted, socially vexed and violent LA today. . . . But if we can't all dream of moving to sunny California anymore, there's always TV, where something resembling that innocent dream still exists. Eyewitness News and its various clones allow us to believe, just for a moment, that there really is a Santa Claus, a Mary Poppins, a Good Samaritan giving away fortunes to the needy, a spirit of Christmas Past to convert the most cold-hearted of corporate Scrooges. Indeed, this kind of "good news" is another staple of the genre. Charities, celebrations, instances of extraordinary good luck or good works by or for local residents are ever-present on local newscasts. Every day, in the midst of even the most dreadful and depressing news, there are legions of friends and neighbors to mourn and console each other, offering aid, bringing soup and casseroles to the victims of natural and manmade disasters, stringing lights and hanging balloons for festive neighborhood gatherings.

The news teams themselves often play this role for us. They march at 19 the head of holiday parades and shake hands and kiss babies at openings of malls and industrial parks. They are the neighbors—often thought of as friends by the loneliest among us—we wish we had in real life, there to do the right thing on every occasion. That is their primary function. They are not trained in journalism. They often cannot pronounce the local names and foreign words they read from teleprompters. But they sure can smile. . . .

Sociologist Joshua Gamson has suggested, in an insightful essay, that *20* there is a lesson to be learned from the enormous popularity of tabloid television—a category in which I would certainly include local news. The lesson is not that people are stupid, venal, "addicted," or otherwise blameworthy for their fascinated interest in junk TV. On the contrary, it is those responsible for the quality of our public life who are more deserving of such terms of contempt and opprobrium. For it is, says Gamson, "Only when people perceive public life as inconsequential, as not their own, [that] they readily accept the invitation to turn news into play." And people most certainly do perceive public life as inconsequential and worse these days, whether outside their doors or in Washington or on Wall Street.

Only I don't think it is primarily the desire to "play" that drives peo- *21* ple in droves to local newscasts, or even the trashier tabloid shows like *Hard Copy*. What people are getting from local newscasts—and here the researchers were right on the money, literally—is indeed what they want, in the most profound and sad sense of that phrase. They are getting what they always sought in fantasy and fiction, from *The Wizard of Oz* to *As the World Turns*. They are getting, for a brief moment, a utopian fantasy of a better, kinder, more decent and meaningful world than the one that entraps them.

It is not only that public life is inconsequential, after all. It is, far more *22* tragically, that public and private life today are increasingly unjust, inhumane, painful, even hopeless, materially and spiritually, for many of us. And there is no relief in sight except, ironically, on the local newscasts that are a respite from reality. Only, unlike the utopian villages of soap opera and fairy tale, these "imagined communities" are supposed to be, pretend to be, real and true. And for that reason they are more troubling than the trashiest or silliest of pop-culture fictions.

In your journal, write down the meanings of the following words:

- is not only *antiquated* **(1)**
- *euphemistically* called "local news" **(7)**
- are given short *shrift* **(12)**
- a limited *repertoire* **(13)**
- equally *vapid* **(13)**
- demeaning and *fatuous* **(14)**
- be a *facsimile* **(16)**
- a *utopian* fantasy **(21)**

QUESTIONS FOR WRITING AND DISCUSSION

1. When you finish reading Elayne Rapping's essay, write out your personal responses. Did you agree or disagree with her analysis? Did you find her essay humorous or were you angry at her pronouncements? Were her judgments believable? Did her judgments fit with your own experiences watching your local news programs? Write out your reactions as fully as possible.

2. Reread Rapping's essay, identifying the criteria behind her judgments. In this case, criteria are statements describing what an ideal news program should be; for example, "Good news programs should provide what the people need, not necessarily what they want." Find and list as many of these criteria as you can. Then make a three-column log for this essay, indicating the judgment that Rapping makes about each criterion and the supporting evidence that she provides.

3. Referring to the three-column log from question 2, above, assess Rapping's use of supporting evidence—specific examples from local news shows illustrating her point. Which of Rapping's judgments have supporting evidence? Which are merely unsupported assertions? Based on your analysis, do you think Rapping has written an effective evaluative essay? Explain.

4. Examine the cartoon by Charles Saxon included in this essay. Is this cartoon an effective visual for Rapping's essay? What makes it effective and appropriate? Why might it not be effective? Would another visual be more effective? Explain. (*Note:* This cartoon did not appear in the original version of Rapping's essay.)

5. Observe a local news program. If possible, videotape the program. As you replay your videotape, list each segment of the news: local events, national news, weather, sports, business news, international news, medical and health issues, and so forth. Note any transitional sections (segues) that contain small talk among the anchors. Next to each segment, record the length of time. Next, indicate your opinion about quality or depth of coverage. Finally, record any evidence about the newscasters' personalities, on-camera style, or journalistic ability. Based on your observations and evidence, write an essay responding to Elayne Rapping. How accurately do her observations apply to the case you have observed? What other general conclusions about Rapping's article or about local news programs might you make?

6. Using Rapping's method of cultural analysis, observe and then analyze/evaluate a particular social, cultural, or media-related event. You might choose hall or club meetings at your university, lecture or lab classes, sports events, class registration rituals, TV sitcoms, Internet home pages—the list is bounded only by your imagination. (Be sure to focus on only one particular kind of cultural event or media program.) Your purpose is both to evaluate these cultural "events" and to explain why the cultural event itself is or is not constructed to avoid limited, stereotypical visions of reality or of people.

7. A study by the Kaiser Family Foundation and the Center for Media and Public Affairs found that "the five most common topics in local TV news coverage are crime (20 percent of news items), weather (11 percent), accidents and disasters (9 percent), human interest stories (7 percent), and health stories (7 percent), with all other topics ranking below the top five." "Local TV news wouldn't cover crime as much as it does if the public didn't reward such coverage with high ratings," according to Drew Altman, President of the Kaiser Family Foundation. "But," he continues, "does anyone seriously believe that crime is twice as important as any other issue that the public needs to learn about from local television news?" On the Internet, access Academic Search Premier and search for recent articles on "network news" and "local news." How do the findings described above or in the articles you locate compare with Rapping's argument? Write your own analysis of local or network TV news using the sources you find.

Evaluating: The Writing Process

ASSIGNMENT FOR EVALUATING

With a specific audience in mind, evaluate a product or service, a work of art, or a performance. Choose a subject that is *reobservable*—that you can revisit or review as you write your essay. Select criteria appropriate for your subject and audience. Collect evidence to support or determine a judgment for each criterion.

The review is the most common genre for evaluating pieces, but "reviews" cover a wide range of documents. Some film reviews are academic and critical while others merely indicate the major plot line without much evaluation. Similarly, some reviews of performances or products are short, informal, and intended mainly as information and entertainment for the reader. After you choose your topic, then be sure to consider the requirements or expectations of your audience. Are they expecting merely to be informed or entertained, or do they want the thorough and critical evaluation described in this chapter?

CHOOSING A SUBJECT

If you have already settled on a possible subject, try the following collecting and shaping strategies. If you have not found a subject, consider these ideas:

- Evaluating requires some expertise about a particular person, performance, place, object, or service. You generate expertise not only through experience but also through writing, reading, and rewriting. Review your authority list from Chapter 6. Which of those subjects could you evaluate? Reread your journal entries on observing and investigating. Did you observe or investigate some person, place, or thing that you could write about again, this time for the purpose of evaluating it?

- Comparing and contrasting lead naturally to evaluation. For example, compare two places you've lived, two friends, or two jobs. Compare two newspapers for their coverage of international news, local features, sports, or business. Compare two famous people from the same profession. Compare your expectations about a person, place, or event with the reality. The purpose of your comparison is to determine, for a specific audience, which is "better," based on the criteria you select and the evidence you find.

- Evaluating a possible career choice can help you choose courses, think about possible summer jobs, and prepare for job interviews. Begin by describing several jobs that fit your particular career goals. Then go to several of the following Web sites and gather information.

  http://www.monster.com   *http://www.bestjobsusa.com*
  http://www.careers.com   *http://www.fortune.com*
  http://www.careers.yahoo.com   *http://www.getthatgig.com*

  Choose the career criteria that are most important for you, such as job satisfaction, location, benefits, salary, education requirements, and so forth. Decide which criteria are most important for **you.** Is job satisfaction more important than pay or location? Choose your criteria and rank them in order of importance. Then write an evaluation of one or two jobs that you find described on the Internet or in your local newspaper.

- Community service-learning projects often require an assessment at the end of the period of service. These reflective evaluations start with the goals of the agency, the goals of your class project, and your goals as a learner as the major criteria. Then you gather evidence to see how well the actual experiences and projects met these overall project goals. Sometimes participants use short evaluation questionnaires to get feedback at the midpoint and then again at the end of the project. If you are participating in a community service-learning project, check with your teacher or coordinator about how to write this assessment.

COLLECTING

Once you have a tentative subject and audience in mind, ask the following questions to focus your collecting activities:

- Can you narrow, restrict, or define your subject to focus your paper?
- What *criteria* will you use to evaluate your subject?
- What *evidence* might you gather? As you collect evidence, focus on three questions:
- What *comparisons* can you make between your subject and similar subjects?
- What are the *uses* or *consequences* of this subject?

- What *experiments* or *authorities* might you cite for support?
- What initial *judgments* are you going to make?

OBSERVING   Observation and description of your subject are crucial to a clear evaluation. In most cases, your audience will need to know *what* your subject is before they can understand your evaluation.

- Examine a place or object repeatedly, looking at it from different points of view. Take notes. Describe it. Draw it, if appropriate. Analyze its component parts. List its uses. To which senses does it appeal—sight, sound, touch, smell, taste? If you are comparing your subject to other similar subjects, observe them carefully. Remember: The second or third time you observe your subject, you will see even more key details.
- If you are evaluating a person, collect information about this person's life, interests, abilities, accomplishments, and plans for the future. If you are able to observe the person directly, describe his or her physical features, write down what he or she says, and describe the person's environment.
- If you are evaluating a performance or an event, a tape recording or videotape can be extremely useful. If possible, choose a concert, film, or play on tape so that you can stop and review it if and when necessary. If a tape recording or videotape is not available, attend the performance or event twice.

Making notes in a *three-column log* is an excellent collecting strategy for evaluations. Using the following example from Phyllis Richman's evaluation of the Hunan Dynasty restaurant, list the criteria, evidence, and judgments for your subject:

Subject: Hunan Dynasty Restaurant

Criteria	Evidence	Judgment
Attractive setting	No blaring red-lacquer tables	Graceful
	White tablecloths	
	Subtle glass etchings	
Good service	Waiters serve with flourishes	Often expert
	Some glitches, such as forgotten appetizer	

REMEMBERING   You are already an authority on many subjects, and your personal experiences may help you evaluate your subject. Try *freewriting, looping, branching,* or *clustering* your subject to help you remember relevant events, impressions, and information. In evaluating appliances for consumer magazines, for example, reporters often use products over a period of months, recording data, impressions, and experiences. Those experiences and memories are then used to support criteria and judgments. Evaluating a film often requires remembering similar films that you have liked or disliked. An evaluation of a great athlete may include your memories of previous performances. A vivid narrative of those memories can help convince an audience that a performance is good or bad.

READING Some of the ideas and evidence for your evaluation may come from reading descriptions of your subject, other evaluations of your subject, or the testimony of experts. Be sure you read these texts critically: Who is the intended audience for the text? What evidence does the text give? What is the author's bias? What are other points of view? Read your potential sources critically.

INVESTIGATING All evaluations involve some degree of formal or informal investigation as you probe the characteristics of your subject and seek evidence to support your judgments.

Using the Library or the Internet Check the library and Internet resources for information on your subject, for ideas about how to design and conduct an evaluation of that subject, for possible criteria, for data in evaluations already performed, and for a sense of different possible audiences. In its evaluation of chocolate chip cookies, for example, *Consumer Reports* suggests criteria and outlines procedures. The magazine rated some two dozen popular store-bought brands, as well as four "boutique" or freshly baked varieties, on "strength of chocolate flavor and aroma, cookie and chip texture, and freedom from sensory defects." When the magazine's evaluators faced a problem sampling the fresh cookies in the lab, they decided to move the lab: "We ended up loading a station wagon with scoresheet, pencils, clipboards, water containers, cups, napkins . . . and setting off on a tasting safari to shopping malls."

Gathering Field Data You may want to supplement your personal evaluation with a sample of other people's opinions by using *questionnaires* or *interviews.* (See Chapter 6.) If you are rating a film, for example, you might give people leaving the theater a very brief *questionnaire,* asking for their responses on key criteria relating to the movie that they just saw. If you are rating a class, you might want to *interview* several students in the class to support your claim that the class was either effective or ineffective. The interviews might also give you some specific examples: descriptions of experiences that you can then use as evidence to support your own judgments.

SHAPING

While the shaping strategies that you have used in previous essays may be helpful, the strategies that follow are particularly appropriate for shaping evaluations.

AUDIENCE AND GENRE   As you consider ways to organize and shape your explaining essay, think about your probable audience and genre. Reviews vary greatly in length, critical depth, complexity, and reader appeal. Think about your own purpose and goal; find several magazines, newspapers, or Web sites that publish the kind of review you would like to write, and use the best ones as genre models—not as blueprints—to guide your own writing.

ANALYSIS BY CRITERIA   Often, evaluations are organized by criteria. You decide which criteria are appropriate for the subject and audience, and then you use those criteria to outline the essay. Your first few paragraphs of introduction establish your thesis or overall claim and then give background information: what the subject is, why you are evaluating it, what the competition is, and how you gathered your data. Then you order the criteria according to some plan: chronological order, spatial order, order of importance, or another logical sequence. Phyllis Richman's evaluation of the Hunan Dynasty restaurant follows the criteria pattern:

- **Introductory paragraphs:** *information* about the restaurant (location, hours, prices), general *description* of Chinese restaurants today, and *overall claim:* The Hunan Dynasty is reliable, a good value, and versatile.
- **Criterion #1/judgment:** Good restaurants should have an attractive setting and atmosphere/Hunan Dynasty is attractive.
- **Criterion #2/judgment:** Good restaurants should give strong priority to service/Hunan Dynasty has, despite an occasional glitch, expert service.
- **Criterion #3/judgment:** Restaurants that serve moderately priced food should have quality main dishes/Main dishes at Hunan Dynasty are generally good but not often memorable. (*Note:* The most important criterion—the quality of the main dishes—is saved for last.)
- **Concluding paragraphs:** Hunan Dynasty is a top-flight neighborhood restaurant.

COMPARISON AND CONTRAST   Many evaluations compare two subjects in order to demonstrate why one is preferable to another. Books, films, restaurants, courses, music, writers, scientists, historical events, sports—all can be evaluated by means of comparison and contrast. In evaluating two Asian restaurants, for example, student writer Chris Cameron uses a comparison-and-contrast structure to shape her essay. In the following body paragraph from her essay, Cameron compares two restaurants, the Unicorn and the Yakitori, on the basis of her first criterion—an atmosphere that seems authentically Asian:

> Of the two restaurants, we preferred the authentic atmosphere of the Unicorn to the cultural confusion at the Yakitori. On first impression, the Yakitori looked like a converted truck stop, sparsely decorated with a few bamboo slats and Japanese print fabric hanging in slices as Bruce Springsteen wailed loudly in the ears of the customers. The feeling at the Unicorn was quite the opposite as we entered a room that seemed transported from Chinatown. The whole room had a red tint from the light shining through the flowered curtains, and the place looked truly authentic, from the Chinese patterned rug on the wall to the elaborate dragon on the ceiling. Soft oriental music played as the customers sipped tea from small porcelain cups and ate fortune cookies.

Cameron used the following *alternating* comparison-and-contrast shape for her whole essay:

- Introductory paragraph(s)
- **Thesis:** Although several friends recommended the Yakitori, we preferred the Unicorn for its more authentic atmosphere, courteous service, and well-prepared food.
- **Authentic atmosphere:** Yakitori versus Unicorn
- **Courteous service:** Yakitori versus Unicorn
- **Well-prepared food:** Yakitori versus Unicorn
- Concluding paragraph(s)

On the other hand, Cameron might have used a *block* comparison-and-contrast structure. In this organizational pattern, the outline would be as follows:

- Introductory paragraph(s)
- **Thesis:** Although several friends recommended the Yakitori, we preferred the Unicorn for its more authentic atmosphere, courteous service, and well-prepared food.
- **The Yakitori:** atmosphere, service, and food
- **The Unicorn:** atmosphere, service, and food as compared to the Yakitori's
- Concluding paragraph(s)

CHRONOLOGICAL ORDER Writers often use chronological order, especially in reviewing a book or a film, to shape parts of their evaluations. Film reviewers rely on chronological order to sketch the main outlines of the plot as they comment on the quality of the acting, directing, or cinematography. At the end of this chapter, for example, Kent Y'Blood's review of the film *The Big Chill* uses chronological order to organize the middle paragraphs of his essay.

CAUSAL ANALYSIS Analyzing the *causes* or *effects* of a place, object, event, or policy can shape an entire evaluation. Evaluations of works of art or performances, for example, often measure the *effect* on the viewers or audience. Mark Stevens, for example, claims that Goya's painting has several definite effects on the viewer; those specific effects become the evidence that supports the claim:

- **Criterion #1/judgment:** The iconography, or use of symbols, contributes to the powerful effect of this picture on the viewer.
  Evidence: The church as a symbol of hopefulness contrasts with the cruelty of the execution. The spire on the church emphasizes for the viewer how powerless the Church is to save the victims.
- **Criterion #2/judgment:** The use of light contributes to the powerful effect of the picture on the viewer.
  Evidence: The light casts an intense glow on the scene, and its glaring, lurid, and artificial qualities create the same effect on the viewer that modern art sometimes does.
- **Criterion #3/judgment:** The composition or use of formal devices contributes to the powerful effect of the picture on the viewer.
  Evidence: The diagonal lines scissor the picture into spaces that give the viewer a claustrophobic feeling. The corpse is foreshortened, so that it looks as though the dead man is bidding the viewer welcome.

> **" *I have to stop being afraid of being wrong; I can't wait until everything is perfect before the work comes out. I don't have that kind of time.* "**
> —SHERLEY ANNE WILLIAMS, NOVELIST AND CRITIC

TITLE, INTRODUCTION, AND CONCLUSION Titles of evaluative writing tend to be short and succinct, stating what product, service, work of art, or performance you are evaluating ("The Big Chill" or "Watching the Eyewitless News") or suggesting a key question or conclusion in the evaluation ("Borrowers Can Be Choosy").

Introductory paragraphs provide background information and description and usually give an overall claim or thesis. In some cases, however, the overall claim comes last, in a concluding "Recommendations" section or in a final summary paragraph. If the overall claim appears in the opening paragraphs, the concluding paragraph may simply review the strengths or weaknesses or may just advise the reader: This *is* or *is not* worth seeing, reading, watching, doing, or buying.

Research Tips GO

Before you draft your evaluating essay, stop for a moment and *evaluate your sources* of information and opinion. If you are citing ideas or information from library articles—or especially from the Internet—be skeptical. How reliable is your source? What do you know about your source's reliability or editorial slant? Does the author have a particular bias? Be sure to *qualify* any biased or absolute statements you use from your sources. (See Chapter 12 for additional ideas on evaluating written sources.)

If you cite observations or field sources (interviews, surveys), evaluate the information you collected. Does it reflect only one point of view? How is it biased? Are your responses in surveys limited in number or point of view? Remember: You may use sources that reflect a limited perspective, but *be sure to alert your readers to those limitations.* For example, you might say, "Obviously, these reactions represent only four viewers who saw this film, but . . ." or "Of course, the administrator wanted to defend this student program when he said . . ."

DRAFTING

With your criteria in front of you, your data or evidence at hand, and a general plan or sketch outline in mind, begin writing your draft. As you write, focus on your audience. If your evaluation needs to be short, you may have to use only those criteria that will appeal most effectively to your audience. As you write, check occasionally to be sure that you are including your key criteria. While some parts of the essay may seem forced or awkward as you write, other parts will grow and expand as you get your thoughts on paper. As in other papers, don't stop to check spelling or worry about an occasional awkward sentence. If you stop and can't get going, reread what you have written, look over your notes or sketch outline, and pick up the thread again.

> *"I have rewritten—often several times—every word I have ever published. My pencils outlast their erasers."*
> —VLADIMIR NABOKOV, NOVELIST

REVISING

Remember that revision is not just changing a word here and there or correcting occasional spelling errors. Make your evaluation more effective for your reader by including more specific evidence, changing the order of your paragraphs to make them clearer, cutting out an unimportant point, or adding a point that one of your readers suggests.

PEER RESPONSE

The instructions that follow will help you give and receive constructive advice about the rough draft of your evaluating essay. You may use these guidelines for an in-class workshop, a take-home review, or an e-mail computer response.

Writer: Before you exchange drafts, write out the following information about your essay draft:

1. **Purpose, audience, and genre.** Briefly, describe your overall purpose, your genre, and your intended audience. Do you plan to incorporate visuals? If so, where?
2. **Revision plans.** What do you know you still need to work on as you revise your draft?
3. **Questions.** Write out one or two questions about your draft that you would like your reader to answer.

Reader: Before you answer the following questions, read the entire draft from start to finish. As you *reread* the draft, to the following:

1. Underline the sentence(s) that state the writer's *overall claim* about the subject.
2. In the margin, put large brackets [ ] around paragraphs that *describe* what the writer is evaluating.
3. On a separate piece of paper or at the end of the writer's essay, make a *three-column log* indicating the writer's criteria, evidence, and judgments. (Does the log include both positive and negative judgments?)
4. Identify with an asterisk (*) any passages in which the writer needs more *evidence* to support the judgments.
5. Write out one *criterion* that is missing or that is not appropriate for the given subject.
6. Assess how well the writer explains the purpose and addresses the intended audience. Do you agree with the writer about his or her revision plans? Finally, answer the writer's questions.

Writer: As you read your peer reviewer's notes and comments, do the following:

1. Consider your peer reviewer's comments and notes. Has your reviewer correctly identified your overall claim? Do you need to add more description of your subject? Does the reviewer's three-column log look like yours? Do you need to revise your criteria or add additional evidence? Do you balance positive and negative judgments?
2. Based on your review, draw up a *revision plan*. Write out the three most important things you need to do as you revise your essay.

Guidelines for Revision

During your revision, keep the following points in mind:

- **Review your purpose, audience, and genre.** Is your purpose clear to your target audience? Should you modify your chosen genre to appeal to your audience?

- **Review possibilities for visuals or graphics.** What additions or changes to images might be appropriate for your purpose, genre, or audience?

- **Criteria are *standards of value*.** They contain categories and judgments, as in "good fuel economy," "good reliability," or "powerful use of light and shade in a painting." Some categories, such as "price," have clearly implied judgments ("low price"), but make sure that your criteria refer implicitly or explicitly to a standard of value.

- **Examine your criteria from your audience's point of view.** Which criteria are most important in evaluating your subject? Will your readers agree that the criteria you select are indeed the most important ones? Will changing the order in which you present your criteria make your evaluation more convincing?

- **Include both positive and negative evaluations of your subject.** If all of your judgments are positive, your evaluation will sound like an advertisement. If all of your judgments are negative, your readers may think you are too critical.

- **Be sure to include supporting evidence for each criterion.** Without any data or support, your evaluation will be just an opinion that will not persuade your reader.

- **Avoid overgeneralizing in your claims.** If you are evaluating only three software programs, you cannot say that Lotus 1-2-3 is the best business program around. You can say only that it is the best among the group or the best in the particular class that you measured.

- **Unless your goal is humor or irony, compare subjects that belong in the same class.** Comparing a Ford Focus to a BMW is absurd because they are not similar cars in terms of cost, design, or purpose.

- **If you need additional evidence to persuade your readers, review the questions at the beginning of the "Collecting" section of this chapter.** Have you addressed all the key questions listed there?

- **If you are citing other people's data or quoting sources, check to make sure your summaries and data are accurate.**

- ***Signal* the major divisions in your evaluation to your reader using clear transitions, key words, and paragraph hooks.** At the beginning of new paragraphs or sections in your essay, let your reader know where you are going.

- **Revise sentences for directness and clarity.**
- **Edit your evaluation for correct spelling, appropriate word choice, punctuation, usage, and grammar.**

POSTSCRIPT ON THE WRITING PROCESS

When you finish writing your essay, answer the following questions:

1. Who is the intended audience for your evaluation? Write out one sentence from your essay in which you appeal to or address this audience.

2. Describe the main problem that you had writing this essay, such as finding a topic, collecting evidence, or writing or revising the draft.

3. What parts or paragraphs of your essay do you like best? Indicate the words, phrases, or sentences that make it effective. What do you like about them?

4. Explain what helped you most with your revision: advice from your peers, conference with the teacher, advice from a writing center tutor, rereading your draft several times, or some other source.

5. Write out one question that you still have about the assignment or about your writing and revising process.

STUDENT WRITING

BORROWERS CAN BE CHOOSY

Linda Meininger

Linda Meininger wrote her evaluation essay on the Interlibrary Loan Office at her campus library. Her purpose was to advise her readers—other students— about the usefulness of the interlibrary loan service. In order to gather information for her essay, she visited the office, learned how to access an interlibrary loan with her computer, interviewed the coordinator of the office, and surveyed nine people who had used the library service. Overall, she discovered that the interlibrary loan office provided a surprisingly convenient, helpful, and inexpensive service. Included here are the following writing-process materials: a draft of her interview and survey questions, a three-column log, her first rough draft, questions for a conference with her instructor, and her final draft.

Draft of Interview and Survey Questions

Interview Questions for Interlibrary Loan Office (ILL) Coordinator

1. Have you surveyed your clients to get their impressions about the service? Results? Favorable—why? Unfavorable—why? Valid or not—why?

2. How do you and your employees rate your service?

3. Do you offer any special services for your clients?

4. Have you received any recognition for your work in the ILL?

5. What institutions lend documents to our library?

6. How convenient do you make it for clients to use your services?

Survey Questions

1. Were you satisfied with the interlibrary loan service you received? Why? Why not?

2. How often do you use the service?

3. How much lead time did you allow for your request?

4. What was your area of research?

5. What type of materials did you request? Periodicals? Books? Documents? Theses?

6. What was the cost of using the service?

Draft of Three-Column Log

Claim: The Interlibrary Loan Office runs a well-organized and efficient operation.

Audience: Students.

Purpose: To evaluate the service and encourage students to use it.

CRITERIA	EVIDENCE	JUDGMENT
1. Timely delivery of materials	Survey results	Mixed
2. Helpful service	Personal experience	Positive
3. Convenience for users	Survey	Positive
4. Scope of libraries available	Interview and brochure	Positive
5. Reasonable cost	Survey and interview	Positive

First Rough Draft

Are you someone who has searched endlessly through the library's computer database or the card catalog only to have that elusive title never appear? Go directly to Room 210, Morgan Library, and collect an Interlibrary Loan request card, or if that's too far to walk, place your order via e-mail from your PC.   *1*

How useful can this service be to you? Stay tuned and I'll show you everything you need to know about Morgan Library Interlibrary Loan (ILL). In evaluating this service, available to all who are affiliated with CSU as a student or employee, I will be looking at the following criteria: convenience and ease of use; timely arrival of materials requested; cooperation and assistance from the ILL staff; and reasonable fees for use of loaned materials.   *2*

Jane Smith of the ILL department informed me that request cards can be found in many locations in the library. These color-coded cards are used to request documents, periodicals, theses, or books. The color of the card corresponds to the type of material. Requests may be left at any of the reference desks, or you may drop off your request in person in Room 210 of the library, Monday through Friday.   *3*

Students and employees with a PC and a modem may request materials from their office or home. According to Jane Smith, electronic access was developed in-house by the ILL department. A new service has also been established, called the Library Retrieval and Delivery Service (LRDS). This is available to disabled students on campus. Requests may be made by the computer or manually.   *4*

Jane Smith of the ILL office informed me that normal turnaround for requests is 24 hours. That translates to one day from the time the requests leave the ILL office for another lending institution. Unless . . . it's spring semester. Then, look out! Deadlines for theses and research are closing in and everyone is in need of the materials yesterday. Then the turnaround time is a week. Most likely materials will not arrive until the end of the school year. Requests in spring semester jump to 300–400 per day compared to a norm of approximately 200 daily.   *5*

I would say that being able to fill 300 requests for material is efficient by my standards. Jane was delighted to inform me that Morgan Library was chosen most efficient in the state by other ILLs in Colorado. I think that could be comparable to a Good Housekeeping Seal of Approval or a five-star rating by AAA.   *6*

When I visited the ILL office I discovered a staff willing to answer my questions and with a sense of humor. They made me feel comfortable   *7* and at ease. One of the brochures I picked up was a pamphlet with their job descriptions: Queen of the World, Resident Geek, ILL's Mouthpiece, Double Agent, ILL's Movie Star and answer to Greta Garbo, and Leading (Lending) Lady. The pamphlet shows me that these people like what they do and can laugh at themselves and their idiosyncrasies. I believe this impression is relayed to their patrons.

Conference Questions

1. Are the criteria I have sufficient? Should I have chosen more of the criteria from my log? Or other criteria from my list?

2. My development needs improvement. I need more evidence to substantiate my criteria. What if I didn't secure the surveys necessary (ten) to be fairly objective?

3. Should I introduce my criteria in a subtle manner or just come right out and state them?

4. After class today, I felt that I needed to state judgments for each of my criteria, although they could change after the survey results.

5. Does it sound like I'm writing to a student audience?

Revised Version
BORROWERS CAN BE CHOOSY

Are you someone who has searched endlessly through the library's computer *1* listing, the card catalog, or even the stacks, only to have that elusive title never appear? Don't give up. Go directly to Room 210, Morgan Library, and collect an Interlibrary Loan request card. If that's too far to walk, just place your order via e-mail with your PC, a modem, and some communications software.

This service can be useful to you during your four-year educational *2* experience at Colorado State University. So stay tuned, and I'll review four characteristics of Morgan Library Interlibrary Loan (ILL). In evaluating this service, which is available to all CSU students, faculty, or staff, I will be looking at the following criteria: convenience and ease of use, timely arrival of materials requested, reasonable fees for materials, and cooperation and assistance from the ILL staff. To gain evidence about the performance of this department, I interviewed the staff, observed their operation, and conducted a survey of CSU students, faculty, and employees (see Appendix for results of survey). Out of nine survey respondents, the level of usage varied from four one-time users to two weekly users.

The convenience and ease of using the interlibrary loan service was definitely a high point. Jane Smith of the ILL department informed me that request cards have been placed in many locations in the library for convenient access. These color-coded cards are used to request documents, periodicals, theses, or books. The color of the card corresponds to the type of material requested. Cards may be left at any of the reference desks, or you may drop off your request in person in Room 210 of the library, just off to your left at the top of the stairs, Monday through Friday, 8:00 A.M.–5:00 P.M.   3

The addition of computer access to interlibrary loans also adds to the ease of requesting materials. At the present time, students, faculty, and employees with a PC and a modem may request materials from their office or home. According to Ms. Smith, electronic access was developed in-house by the ILL department, making their service available 24 hours per day. Julie Wessling, coordinator of the Interlibrary Loan department, said, "About one third of our users request their specific information via our electronic service."   4

The ILL has also established another convenient new service, called Library Retrieval and Delivery Service (LRDS). This is available to disabled students on campus and other off-campus users. Requests may be made by computer or by using the request cards. Delivery or notice of nonavailability of materials will be made within 48 hours to three sites on campus: Braiden Hall, the RDS Office in 116 Student Services Building, and the ILL office. There is also dial-up access to the library's computer listings. This service is especially valuable to off-campus users or students with mobility problems. The ILL staff retrieves requests, most of which—according to Ms. Wessling—are in the CSU stacks, and then delivers them to one of the collection sites for pickup by the patron.   5

Overall, I found the request forms and located the ILL office without any problem, and according to nine out of the nine people surveyed, the ILL service was "easy to use and locate." Judy Lira, a Rocky Mountain High School media specialist, faxes her requests and feels that the technology is a service to the staff and students at her school. Bonnie Mueller, a Morgan Library cataloguing employee, uses LAN to order materials, and she states, "It's wonderful!" While I was in the ILL office, a student was filling out request cards. I tried to enlist her aid for my survey, but she declined, saying that this was her first time using the Interlibrary Loan service. However, she did have one comment for me: "They [the ILL office] need to make us [students] more aware of this." It appears that the convenient access to the ILL system makes it an asset to CSU students and to the local schools.   6

I wished to experiment personally with the ILL to evaluate the timely   *7*
arrival of requests, but Ms. Smith explained to me that it would be impossible to receive anything within the time frame I was allotted to finish this
essay. Therefore, I will be relying on the experiences and testimony of others.

The normal processing turnaround time for requests, Ms. Smith informed   *8*
me, is 24 hours. That means that it takes one day from the time the request is
made by the borrower to the time it leaves the ILL office for another lending
institution. Unless . . . it's spring semester. Then look out! Deadlines for theses and research papers are closing in, and students and faculty need their
materials yesterday. Ms. Smith related the story of a student who recently
came in on a Wednesday and wanted the item by Monday. She had to tell him,
"Sorry, it's not possible, especially now." She said at this time of the year—
spring semester—the processing time is approximately one week, and that's just
until the request leaves the CSU ILL office. Most likely, materials will not
arrive until April or the end of the school year. Normal arrival time seems
to vary between ten days and two weeks, according to survey results. Requests at spring semester jump to 300–400 per day, and these requests include not only the CSU customers, but the borrowers from other institutions
who are requesting materials from Morgan Library, reported Ms. Wessling.

The normal processing time can be speeded up, however, in some cases.   *9*
Ms. Wessling explained that "the use of e-mail allows us to locate and help
process customers' requests faster. This allows the student or professor to receive the information more quickly. The only thing holding the process back
is the time it takes to get the specific request in the mail." Also, articles from
periodicals or a document can be sent electronically or by fax. When materials are needed in a hurry, a RUSH may be affixed to the card and a last usable
date recorded. This will bring the request to the attention of the office, and they
will give it priority to try to locate a copy at a nearby library for pickup by the
client. Of the nine people I surveyed, six reported that their materials arrived
within 24 hours to two weeks, but one person reported that it took eight
weeks and didn't arrive in time to be of use. He allowed two weeks of lead time,
but he ordered the material in April. Another person stated that she had to wait
over six weeks for materials to arrive. Her materials were "very difficult to locate." My accounting professor, Dr. Middlemist, usually allows a two-week lead
time when ordering and said that the "time taken to arrive depended on where
the materials were coming from." Dr. Middlemist stated that she uses the
service 10–12 times per year, maybe more, depending on what her needs are.

By my standards, being able to fill 300 requests for materials is efficient.   *10*
In addition, Ms. Smith was delighted to inform me that Morgan Library

was chosen most efficient by other ILLs in Colorado and will be "looked over" by a team from the state so that their efficient and innovative ideas may be used in other libraries. I think that could be comparable to a Good Housekeeping Seal of Approval or a four-star rating by AAA.

While the timely arrival of materials was a problem, especially in the 11 spring semester, the cost of materials received was very reasonable. For most requests, there is no charge for the service. I found that only on the journal request card was there a line item for maximum cost. This is in the event that there could be photocopying charges. Eight of my nine respondents said they received their materials (books, theses, and journals) free of charge, and the other paid a reasonable fee for Xeroxing one time. It is through the lending and borrowing reciprocal agreement between libraries that the ILL service can be offered at no cost or low cost to the user.

Perhaps the strongest feature of the ILL service was the willingness of 12 the staff to help patrons, answer questions, and keep their sense of humor. They made me feel comfortable and at ease. One of the brochures I picked up was a pamphlet with their job descriptions: Queen of the World, Resident Geek, ILL's Mouthpiece, Double Agent, ILL's Movie Star and Answer to Greta Garbo, and Leading (Lending) Lady. This pamphlet shows that these people like what they do and can laugh at themselves and their idiosyncrasies. Something else Ms. Smith said really sticks in my mind. She said, "I think we're the only department in the whole library where everyone really likes what they do." I believe this impression is relayed to the patrons. My survey results concurred with this, as seven respondents felt that the staff was friendly and helpful. One dissenting student felt that the office could have presented the information she needed over the phone, saving her a trip to the library. The other person felt there wasn't any follow-up on a trace request to see if a book had been lost. Morgan Library has lost this patron to another library. Some of the positive comments received were as follows: "The ILL personnel went out of their way to help me." "What I needed was extremely obscure, and they got most of it." "They found a German book in Berlin, and they Xeroxed it and sent the whole thing FREE!"

As a result of my investigation and evaluation of the ILL office, I hope 13 I have occasion to use their service in the future. I know from my conversations with the staff and other users of ILL that the service and staff are reliable and willing to assist at any time (during office hours, of course). The cost is well within the reach of all patrons, and we have two methods of booking our requests: manually on cards and electronically by computer. So the next time you need an item that the CSU library doesn't own, remember that you do have another resource available at your fingertips: Morgan Library's Interlibrary Loan.

Works Cited

Interlibrary Loan. Fort Collins: Colorado State University, 1992.

It's Here! Fort Collins: Colorado State University, 1992.

Libraries Retrieval and Delivery Service. Fort Collins: Colorado State University, 1992.

Morgan Library Interlibrary Loan Survey. Personal Survey. 2 March 1992.

Self-Guided Tour of Morgan Library. Fort Collins: Colorado State University, 1992.

Smith, Jane. Personal Interview. 27 Feb. and 2 March 1992.

Wessling, Julie. Personal Interview. 2 March 1992.

APPENDIX

MORGAN LIBRARY INTERLIBRARY LOAN SURVEY

The following survey was completed by nine students and faculty members. Responses follow each question.

1. What was the subject area of the materials requested?

Accounting—1	Ben Jonson—17th C writer & critic—1
Agriculture—1	Cognitive development—1
Ancient Roman Art—1	Popular fiction—1
Anthropology—1	Travelogues—1800s—1
Archaeology—1	Various subjects—1

2. What type of material did you request?

Book—7	Journal—6
Thesis—1	Documents—0

3. How much lead time did you allow the Interlibrary Loan office to secure your materials?

   No deadline—5

   24 hours—1

   1 week—1

   2 weeks—2

4. At what time of the year did you request materials?

Fall semester	Specify month	3 in Oct, Nov, and Dec
Spring semester	Specify month	1—Jan, 4—Feb & Mar, 2—April, 1—May

5. Did your materials arrive in a timely manner? How much time did it take?

24 hours—1	Very quickly—1
1 week—1	Not more than $1\frac{1}{2}$–2 months—1
8 weeks—1	Over 3 weeks—1
Typically timely—1	10 days—1

6. Were you satisfied with the service you received? Why? Why not?

No, not friendly, no follow-up if lost—1

Yes, friendly and helpful—1

Yes—2

Yes, very satisfied—1

Very, needed extremely obscure stuff & got most of it—1

Extremely satisfied, wonderful to have access to otherwise unreachable materials—1

No problem with service or individuals, satisfied—1

Friendly—1

7. How often do you use the service?

1 time—3	Weekly—1
2 times/year—1	One semester a lot of times—1
10–12 times/year—1	
Goes to Boulder-CU library—1	
2–3 times/week avg., usually turns in requests in batches—1	

8. Was there a charge for your requested materials? If so, did you feel the charge was reasonable or not? How much was it?

No charge—8

Xeroxing charge, reasonable—1

9. Was the staff of the Interlibrary Loan office helpful? Friendly? Did it give out-of-the-ordinary service?

Not friendly, not helpful, no out-of-ordinary service—1

Could have presented info over phone, save trip to library—1

Staff went out of their way to help—1

Worked hard on obscure stuff—1

Always do their best—1

Very friendly—3   Friendly & helpful—3
Regular service—1   Fax requests—1

10. Did you feel that the service was convenient to use (e.g., easy to order materials and pick them up, forms to be filled out, the open hours of the office)?

Easy to use—2   Very—2   Yes—2
Used LAN—1

Yes, feels guilty about amt. of paper involved in all of the requests—1

Fax technology availability real service to students & staff—1

11. From which institution did you receive your materials?

Northwestern—1

Dartmouth—1

Berlin—1

Denver Public Library—1

Oklahoma State University—1

CU-Boulder—1

Don't know—2

QUESTIONS FOR WRITING AND DISCUSSION

1. Evaluate Meininger's final draft, using the peer response guidelines in this chapter. What are the strengths and weaknesses of her essay? Now read Meininger's first rough draft. Which areas did she improve most in her revision?

2. Based on her final draft, make a revised version of Meininger's three-column log. Write out each criterion, the main supporting evidence for that criterion, and the judgment. Indicate the paragraphs (by number) that Meininger devotes to each of her criteria.

3. In her postscript, Meininger wrote, "I revised my criteria and rearranged them in a different order after we talked in class. I didn't want to have my weakest criteria last." Compare her criteria (see her three-column log) with her revised draft. Explain how her additions, deletions, and reordering improved her criteria—and her essay.

4. Reread the questionnaire in Meininger's Appendix. How might she improve that questionnaire? What questions might she add or delete? How might she rephrase the questions?

5. Brainstorm a list of other campus services or organizations that you could evaluate. Choose one of those services or organizations and write a three-column log, indicating the subject, the audience, the criteria, and the possible kinds of evidence that you might collect for your essay.

STUDENT WRITING

THE BIG CHILL

Kent Y'Blood

In his review of The Big Chill, *Kent Y'Blood writes a compact evaluation of the film for a campus newspaper audience. Film review writers often need to walk a tightrope: They should give the basic information about key characters and plot—without revealing too much about the story; they should analyze and evaluate the film—without so much analysis that the reader is bored. As you read the essay, decide how successful Y'Blood is at both informing and entertaining the reader.*

The Big Chill is an actors' film in the very best sense. It's no easy task to cre-   1
ate eight major characters we can care about immediately without resorting to some form of cinematic stereotyping, but director Lawrence Kasdan does it. We meet eight individuals whose stories of fading youthful optimism are familiar in many ways. These characters are not mere representatives of those stories but living, breathing people in a psychological comedy.

And what a dark comedy it is. Death pervades every scene, and not   2
just the death of The Movement, or the death of Revolutionary Ideals, or the death of The Spirit of a Generation. Those generalizations have little place here. *The Big Chill* is about a real, particular death: that of Alex Marshall, permanent dropout, college friend of Sam, Sarah, Michael, Nick, Harold, Meg, and Karen. He committed suicide in Harold and Sarah's house, where he was staying with his young girlfriend, Chloe. The old

friends, who haven't seen much of each other in years, regroup for his funeral and all decide to spend a weekend at Harold and Sarah's house in Georgia to try to sort out their confusion over Alex's act.

At the beginning of the film, Kasdan packs plenty of character infor- *3* mation into a relatively short space so that we get to know the people well. As they make their various ways to the funeral, spread out across the country as they are, we begin to learn about them. Sam (Tom Berenger) lines up four miniature vodka bottles on his airplane tray and charms the stewardess out of just one more. Nick (William Hurt) empties out a collection of pills on the seat of his Porsche, downs a couple, and the car roars out ahead of the camera. We get glimpses of the other characters intercut with shots of a man dressing in a pinstripe suit and white shirt, all to the tune of Marvin Gaye's "I Heard It Through the Grapevine." Kasdan ends this scene with a shocker. As a sewn-up wrist is slipped beneath a white cuff, we realize it was Alex's corpse we saw being dressed. This combination of expository information with emotionally powerful action is superb movie making, and Kasdan does not let down after the promise of this opening sequence.

At the funeral itself, we learn more about the principals. Michael (Jeff *4* Goldblum) obviously wants more than comfort from Chloe (Meg Tilly). Harold (Kevin Kline) intones a eulogy and breaks down as he remembers, "There was something about Alex that was too good for this world." His wife, Sarah (Glenn Close), weeps but holds together admirably. Throughout the film, all the characters are true to our first impressions of them but are not mechanically programmed to act predictably. They can still surprise us, and they all do. Later, when the characters get assigned their bedrooms, we get a glimpse of their luggage. Knowing who brings the economy-size bottle of Maalox, who the TV script and a volume of Kafka, and who has many pairs of designer men's underwear just adds that much more to our sense of who each of these people is. It is a weekend of talk, but the talk is supplemented by what we've observed about these people, so the dialogue doesn't have to carry all the weight in the film.

When they do talk, the chat is brilliant. Their sentiment is constantly *5* undercut by jokes that don't weaken their emotions, just complicate them. When Beth rises to play Alex's favorite song on the organ at the funeral (Rolling Stones' "You Can't Always Get What You Want"), it is simultaneously funny and heartbreaking. The friends collectively try to work out how they failed Alex, how they failed their younger selves by becoming successful and rich, and how the people they were became the people they are.

The Big Chill is beautifully edited and masterfully acted and has a script 6 that has more depth than anything I've seen in a long time. The film directly confronts such tough themes as the endurance of friendship, the question of suicide, isolation, meaninglessness—and all to the '60s music of the Temptations, Smokey Robinson, and the Rascals. That's what I call a good movie.

QUESTIONS FOR WRITING AND DISCUSSION

1. Profile yourself as a typical reader of this review: Give your age, note whether you frequently go to movies, describe the kinds of films you enjoy, describe your attitude toward music or events from the sixties, and indicate whether or not you have seen *The Big Chill*. With these notes, come to class prepared to discuss whether or not Y'Blood's review succeeded. Did it make you want to see the movie? If you've seen the film already, was his evaluation convincing? Was it entertaining?

2. Y'Blood's writing-process materials are not reproduced here, but how do you suppose that he collected all the information and supporting evidence for his review? Describe a plausible sequence for his collecting activities.

3. In his review, Y'Blood emphasizes Lawrence Kasdan's skills in directing this film. However, if he had chosen to focus on one particular actor's performance (for example, William Hurt's performance as Nick) or on the relationship of the songs to the story, how would that have changed the review? For practice, rewrite the opening paragraph of this review, focusing either on one principal actor or on the sixties songs.

4. Kent Y'Blood's review, while clearly written, does not discuss any of the film's weaknesses. Does his review sound too positive or too much like an advertisement or blurb for the film? How do you think Y'Blood should have handled this problem? Should he have found some weaknesses in the film to make his evaluation more credible? Explain.

5. Y'Blood's review was written for a campus newspaper. His assignment (the occasion for the review) was to review classic films that college students might want to watch. Where might Y'Blood appeal to this audience more directly? Should he make references to other classic films that college students watch on video or DVD? What other revisions might make his essay more effective for his purpose, the occasion, and his audience? Explain.

Vermeer's painting of a young woman engaged in the delicate craft of lacemaking appears to celebrate the virtue of skill and work. Notice the nearly photographic reproduction of the details of lacemaking in this painting. A journal entry on page 428 asks you to compare Vermeer's image with a contemporary photograph of a young boy in Cholomo, Honduras, stitching softballs to be sold in the United States.

Jan Vermeer van Delft
The Lacemaker (1670)
Oil on canvas transferred to panel
Musee du Louvre, Paris

chapter

9 Problem Solving

In your writing class, you read a conversation between two minority women about racial tensions in African-American and Asian-American communities. The problems, you realize, are continuing and widespread. Publicized instances include a boycott by blacks of Korean shops in New York City and the looting of Korean stores during the Los Angeles riots. As a member of the American-Korean community, you decide to propose three solutions to promote education and understanding. First, encourage the American-Korean media to educate Koreans about cultural differences. Next, ask Korean-American churches to cooperate with churches in African-American communities. Finally, appeal to Korean businesspeople to invest in the black communities where they work. Communities, you argue, cannot wait for local or federal governments to solve these problems. They must take the initiative and work cooperatively to solve their problems.

Trying to take notes in your Psych I lecture class—along with 250 other students—you realize that you are completely lost and confused. So you raise your hand to ask a question, but the professor keeps on talking, throwing out more new terms and examples. You look at your neighbor, who just shrugs and keeps on writing. After class, when you think about how hard you've worked to pay your tuition, you realize that you deserve better classes for your money. The problem, you decide, is in the large lecture format—there are just too many students for the teacher to answer questions and explain difficult concepts. So you decide to write a letter to the head of the psychology department (with a copy to the dean of arts and sciences) outlining your problems with this class and proposing that Psychology I be taught in classes no larger than fifty. Where the administrators get additional teachers, you decide, is their responsibility. You argue that, as administrators, it is their duty to give quality education the highest priority.

> *This country has more problems than it should tolerate and more solutions than it uses.*
> —RALPH NADER,
> CONSUMER RIGHTS ADVOCATE AND PRESIDENTIAL CANDIDATE

> *Whenever life doesn't seem to give an answer, we create one.*
> —LORRAINE HANSBERRY
> AUTHOR OF A RAISIN IN THE SUN

WE DON'T HAVE TO LOOK DILIGENTLY TO LOCATE PROBLEMS IN OUR LIVES. THEY HAVE A HABIT OF SEEKING US OUT. IT SEEMS THAT IF SOMETHING CAN GO WRONG, IT WILL. COUNTRIES ARE FIGHTING each other, the environment is polluted, prejudice is still rampant, television shows are too violent, sports are corrupted by drugs and money, education is too impersonal, and people drive so recklessly that you take your life in your hands every time you go across town. Everywhere we look, someone else creates problems for us—from minor bureaucratic hassles to serious or life-threatening situations. (On rare occasions, of course, we're part of the problem ourselves.)

Once we identify a potential problem, we must critically question and investigate the issue. Just because we think something is a problem does not mean that other people in other social, political, or cultural contexts will agree that it is a problem. For example, let's critically analyze what appears to be a straightforward issue: grade inflation. First, notice the language used to describe the issue. In this case, the word *inflation* suggests a negative bias; we are predisposed to think that any "inflation" is a bad thing. Next, we need to know who is involved in this issue and who has the most to gain or lose by its existence. What different positions are students, teachers, parents, school administrators, admissions officers at colleges, and companies who hire applicants likely to take on this issue? Some of these groups may see grade inflation as a serious problem, while others may not agree that it is a problem or that it even exists. Finally, we must gather the "facts" about grade inflation and the various definitions commonly used to describe it. There are statistics both proving and disproving that grade inflation exists and a variety of definitions for grade inflation.

Once you can identify something that is actually a problem for a specific group of people, the difficult part is to propose a solution and then persuade others that your solution will in fact solve the problem—without creating new problems and without costing too much. Because your proposal may ask readers to take some action, vote in a certain way, or actually work to implement your proposal, you must make sure that your readers vividly perceive the problem and agree that your plan outlines the most logical and feasible solution.

Techniques for Problem Solving

Problem solving requires all your skills as a writer. You need to observe carefully to see if a problem exists. You may need to remember experiences that illustrate the seriousness of the problem. You need to read and investigate which solutions have worked or have not worked. You often have to explain what the problem is and why or how your proposal would remedy the situation. You may need to evaluate both the problem and alternative solutions. To help you identify the problem and convince your readers of the soundness of your proposal, keep the following techniques in mind:

- **Critically analyzing the political, social, and cultural context.** When, where, and why do some people perceive this issue as a problem? What groups of people are affected, and what do they have to gain or lose? Who would be most affected by a particular solution?
- **Identifying and understanding your *audience*.** If you want something done, fixed, changed, improved, subsidized, banned, reorganized, or made legal or illegal, make sure that you are writing to the appropriate audience.
- **Demonstrating that a *problem exists*.** Some problems are so obvious that your readers will readily acknowledge them: high crime rates, conflicts in Africa and the Middle East, air pollution in industrialized nations, and drug and alcohol abuse. Often, however, you must first convince your audience that a problem exists: Are food preservatives really a serious problem, or would eliminating them cause even more problems?
- **Proposing a *solution* that will solve the problem.** After convincing your readers that a serious problem exists, you must then propose a remedy, plan, or course of action that will eliminate or reduce the problem.
- **Persuading your readers that your *proposal will work*,** that it is *feasible,* or that it is better than the *alternative solutions*. You convince your readers by supporting your proposal with *reasons* and *evidence*.

As you start your problem-solving paper, concentrate on ways to *narrow and focus* your topic. When you think about possible topics, follow the advice of environmentalists: "Think Globally, Act Locally." Rather than talk about education or drugs or crime or pollution on a national scale, find out how your community or campus is dealing with a problem. A local focus will help narrow your topic—and provide possibilities for using firsthand observations, personal experience, and interviews.

> *"You see things; and you say, "Why?" But I dream things that never were; and I say, "Why not?""*
>
> —GEORGE BERNARD SHAW, DRAMATIST

DEMONSTRATING THAT A PROBLEM EXISTS

A proposal begins with a description of a problem. Demonstrating that the problem exists (and is serious) will make your readers more receptive to your plan for a solution. The following selection from Frank Trippett's *Time* magazine essay "A Red Light for Scofflaws" identifies a problem and provides sufficient examples to demonstrate that scofflawry is pervasive and serious enough to warrant attention. Even if we haven't been personally attacked while driving the Houston or Miami or Los Angeles freeways, Trippett convinces us that *scofflawry*—deliberately disobeying ("scoffing at") laws—is serious. His vivid description makes us aware of the problem:

Demonstrating that a problem exists

Law and order is the longest-running and probably the best-loved political issue in U.S. history. Yet it is painfully apparent that millions of Americans who would never think of themselves as lawbreakers, let alone criminals, are taking increasing liberties with the legal codes that are designed to protect and nourish their society. Indeed, there are moments today—amid outlaw litter, tax cheating, illicit noise, and motorized anarchy—when it seems as though the scofflaw represents the wave of the future.

Evidence: Authority

Harvard sociologist David Riesman suspects that a majority of Americans have blithely taken to committing supposedly minor derelictions as a matter of course. Already, Riesman says, the ethic of U.S. society is in danger of becoming this: "You're a fool if you obey the rules."

Evidence: Examples

The dangers of scofflawry vary wildly. The person who illegally spits on the sidewalk remains disgusting, but clearly poses less risk to others than the company that illegally buries hazardous chemical waste in an unauthorized location. The fare beater on the subway presents less threat to life than the landlord who ignores fire safety statutes. The most immediately and measurably dangerous scofflawry, however, also happens to be the most visible. The culprit is the American driver, whose lawless activities today add up to a colossal public nuisance. The hazards range from routine double parking that jams city streets to the drunk driving that kills some 25,000 people and injures at least 650,000 others yearly.

Evidence: Statistics

The most flagrant scofflaw of them all is the red-light runner. The flouting of stop signals has got so bad in Boston that residents tell an anecdote about a cabby who insists that red lights are "just for decoration." The power of the stoplight to control traffic seems to be waning everywhere. In Los Angeles, red-light running has become perhaps the city's most common traffic violation. In New York City, going through an intersection is like Russian roulette. Admits Police Commissioner Robert J. McGuire: "Today it's a 50–50 toss-up as to whether people will stop for a red light." Meanwhile, his own police largely ignore the lawbreaking.

Evidence: Authority

The prospect of the collapse of public manners is not merely a matter of etiquette. Society's first concern will remain major crime, but a foretaste of the seriousness of incivility is suggested by what has been happening in Houston. Drivers on Houston freeways have been showing an increasing tendency to replace the rules of the road with violent outbreaks. Items from the Houston police department's new statistical category—freeway traffic violence: (1) Driver flashes high-beam lights at car that cut in front of him, whose occupants then hurl a beer can at his windshield, kick out his tail lights, slug him eight stitches worth. (2) Dump-truck driver annoyed by delay batters trunk of stalled car ahead and its driver with steel bolt. (3) Hurrying driver of 18-wheel truck deliberately rear-ends car whose driver was trying to stay within 55 m.p.h. limit.

Evidence: Examples

PROPOSING A SOLUTION AND CONVINCING YOUR READERS

Once you have vividly described the problem, you are ready to propose a solution and persuade your readers. In the following selection from his book *Fist Stick Knife Gun,* Geoffrey Canada proposes ways to create a safer world for our children. Geoffrey Canada is president and CEO of Harlem's Rheedlen Center for Children and Families, an organization that serves at-risk inner-city children. As you read Canada's proposal, notice how he narrows the problem to saving the lives of inner-city children. When he makes a recommendation, he talks about the advantages of his solution, but he talks about *feasibility problems* and real drawbacks. At several points, he gives *reasons* why we must change and supports his reasons with *evidence* from statistics and from his own personal experience.

If I could get the mayors, the governors, and the president to look into the eyes of the 5-year-olds of this nation, dressed in old raggedy clothes, whose jacket zippers are broken but whose dreams are still alive, they would know what I know—that children need people to fight for them. To stand with them on the most dangerous streets, in the dirtiest hallways, in their darkest hours. We as a country have been too willing to take from our weakest when times get hard. People who allow this to happen must be educated, must be challenged, must be turned around.

Personal experience

If we are to save our children we must become people they will look up to. We must stand up and be visible heroes. I want people to understand the

Proposal

crisis and I want people to act: Either we address the murder and mayhem in our country or we simply won't be able to continue to have the kind of democratic society that we as Americans cherish. Violence is not just a problem of the inner cities or of the minorities in this country. This is a national crisis and the nation must mobilize differently if we are to solve it.

Part of what we must do is change the way we think about violence. Trying to catch and punish people after they have committed a violent act won't deter violence in the least. In life on the street, it's better to go to jail than be killed, better to act quickly and decisively even if you risk being caught.

Specific recommendations

There are, however, things that governments could and should do right away to begin to end the violence on our streets. They include the following:

Specific details

Create a peace officer corps. Peace officers would not be police; they would not carry guns and would not be charged with making arrests. Instead they would be local men and women hired to work with children in their own neighborhoods. They would try to settle "beefs" and mediate disputes. They would not be the eyes and ears of the regular police force. Their job would be to try to get these young people jobs, to get them back into school, and, most importantly, to be at the emergency rooms and funerals where young people come together to grieve and plot revenge, in order to keep them from killing one another.

Recommendation

Reduce the demand for drugs. Any real effort at diverting the next generation of kids from selling drugs must include plans to find employment for these children when they become teenagers. While that will require a significant expenditure of public funds, the savings from reduced hospitalization and reduced incarceration will more than offset the costs of employment....

Recommendation

Reduce the amount of violence on television and in the movies. Violence in the media is ever more graphic, and the justification for acting violently is deeply implanted in young people's minds. The movie industry promotes the message that power is determined not merely by carrying a gun, but by carrying a big gun that is an automatic and has a big clip containing many bullets.

Reason + evidence

What about rap music, and especially "gangsta rap"? It is my opinion that people have concentrated too much attention on this one source of media violence. Many rap songs are positive, and some are neither positive nor negative—just kids telling their stories. But there are some rap singers who have decided that their niche in the music industry will be the most violent and vile. I would love to see the record industry show some restraint in limiting these rappers' access to fame and fortune.

Reduce and regulate the possession of handguns. I believe all handgun sales should be banned in this country. Recognizing, however, that other Americans may not be ready to accept a ban on handguns, I believe there are still some things we must do.

Recommendation

Licensing. Every person who wants to buy a handgun should have to pass both a written test and a field test. The cost for these new procedures should be paid by those who make, sell, and buy handguns. . . .

Recommendation

Gun buy-backs. The federal government, which recently passed a $32 billion crime bill, needs to invest billions of dollars over the next ten years buying guns back from citizens. We now have more than 200 million guns in circulation in our country. A properly cared-for gun can last for decades. There is no way we can deal with handgun violence until we reduce the number of guns currently in circulation. We know that young people won't give up their guns readily, but we have to keep in mind that this is a long-term problem. We have to begin to plan now to get the guns currently in the hands of children out of circulation permanently.

Recommendation

Statistics

The truth of the matter is that reducing the escalating violence will be complicated and costly. If we were fighting an outside enemy that was killing our children at a rate of more than 5,000 a year, we would spare no expense. What happens when the enemy is us? What happens when those Americans' children are mostly black and brown? Do we still have the will to invest the time and resources in saving their lives? The answer must be yes, because the impact and fear of violence has over-run the boundaries of our ghettos and has both its hands firmly around the neck of our whole country. And while you may not yet have been visited by the spectre of death and fear of this new national cancer, just give it time. Sooner or later, unless we act, you will. We all will.

Response to feasibility problems

Evidence

Statistics

Call to action

WARMING UP: JOURNAL EXERCISES

The following exercises will help you practice problem solving. Read all of the following exercises and then write on one or two that interest you most. If another idea occurs to you, write about it.

1. Wishful-thinking department: Assume that you are a member of the student government, and your organization has $10,000 to spend on a campus improvement project. Think of some campus problem that needs solving. Describe why it is a problem. Then outline your plan for a solution, indicating how you would spend the money to help solve the problem.

> *"A good solution solves more than one problem, and it does not make new problems. I am talking about health as opposed to almost any cure, coherence of pattern as opposed to almost any solution produced piecemeal or in isolation."*
>
> —WENDELL BERRY,
> AUTHOR OF THE GIFT
> OF THE GOOD LAND

2. Reread Frank Trippett's analysis of the scofflaw problem. Write a letter to the city council recommending a solution to one of the problems that Trippett identifies—a solution that the city council has the power to implement.

3. Eldridge Cleaver once said, "You're either part of the solution or part of the problem." Examine one of your activities or pastimes—sports, shopping, cruising, eating, drinking, or even studying. How does what you do possibly create a problem from someone else's point of view? Explain.

4. "Let the buyer beware" is a time-honored maxim for all consumers. Unless you are vigilant, you can easily be ripped off. Write a letter to the Better Business Bureau explaining some consumer problem or rip-off that you've recently experienced and suggest a solution that will prevent others from being exploited.

5. The following visual, with an accompanying paragraph, appears on the United Nations Children's Fund (UNICEF) Web site at *http://www.unicef.org*. Analyze the effectiveness of the image and text in demonstrating the problem of child labor. What details in the picture support the argument that child labor is a problem we must solve?

> *"God, give us grace to accept with serenity the things that cannot be changed, courage to change the things which should be changed, and the wisdom to distinguish the one from the other."*
>
> —REINHOLD
> NIEBUHR,
> AUTHOR AND
> THEOLOGIAN

A small boy sleeps at the table where he was making softballs in the village of Cholomo, Honduras.

Some people say that boycotts—that is, refusing to buy goods made by children—will help put an end to child labour. But boycotts can also hurt working children and their families, as the children lose their jobs, and then their families have even less money to live on. If employers provided parents with jobs at a living wage, fewer children would be forced to go to work. (UNICEF/89-0052/Vauclair)

6. Changing the rules of some sports might make them more enjoyable, less violent, or fairer: moving the three-point line farther out, introducing the 30-second clock in NCAA basketball, using TV instant replays in professional and college football and basketball, imposing stiffer fines for brawls in hockey games, requiring boxers to wear padded helmets, giving equal pay and media coverage to women's sports. Choose a sport you enjoy as a participant or observer, identify and explain the problem you want to solve, and justify your solution in a letter to the editors of *Sports Illustrated.*

7. After studying the text and image in question 6, reexamine the Vermeer painting, *The Lacemaker,* which appears at the beginning of this chapter. Art critic Mark Harden says the following about this painting: "Contemporary Dutch painting portrayed industriousness as an allegory of domestic virtue. While the inclusion of the prayer book pays fealty to this theme, it is a secondary concern to the depiction of the handicraft of lacemaking, and in the highest sense, the creative act itself." Compare and contrast the Vermeer painting with the UNICEF photograph in terms of the details of composition, the work being done, the social class and age of the central figures, and the cultural/social context of the two images. Why does one image seem to suggest a social problem while the other appears to depict a social virtue?

8. Read the following short essay on grade inflation, which appeared in the *New York Times Magazine* in May 2004. Michael Bérubé, the Paterno Family professor of literature at Pennsylvania State University, proposes a solution to grade inflation based on scoring systems used in figure skating and gymnastics. Using the guidelines for problem solving given at the beginning of this chapter, write a journal entry evaluating the effectiveness of Bérubé's analysis of the problem and his proposal for his audience of *New York Times* readers.

How to End Grade Inflation: A Modest Proposal

Michael Bérubé

Last month, Princeton University announced it would combat grade inflation by proposing that A-minuses, A's and A-pluses be awarded to no more than the top 35 percent of students in any course. For those of us in higher education, the news has come as a shock, almost as if Princeton had declared that spring in central New Jersey would begin promptly on March 21, with pleasant temperatures in the 60s and 70s through the end of the semester. For until now, grade inflation was like the weather: it got worse every year, or at least everyone said so, and yet hardly anybody did anything about it.

There is nothing inherently wrong with grade inflation. Imagine a system of scoring on a scale from 1 to 6 in which everyone gets a 5 and above, or a scale of 1 to 10 in which the lowest posted score is around 8.5. Such are the worlds of figure skating and gymnastics. If colleges employed similar scoring systems, the class valedictorian would come in with a 4.0, followed closely by hundreds of students above 3.95, trailed by the class clown at 3.4.

Critics would argue that we must be perilously close to such a system right now. Several years ago, Harvard awarded "honors" to 90 percent of its graduates. For its part, Princeton has disclosed that A's have been given 47 percent of the time in recent years, up from 31 percent in the mid-1970s. Perhaps grade inflation is most severe at the most elite colleges, where everyone is so far above average that the rules of the Caucus Race in "Alice in Wonderland" apply: everybody has won, and all must have prizes. At the school where I teach, Penn State, grade inflation over the same period has not been nearly so drastic. In the spring semester of 1975, the average G.P.A. was 2.86; in 2001 it had risen to only 3.02.

Still, we don't grade all that toughly. English departments have basically worked on the A/B binary system for some time: A's and A-minuses for the best students, B's for everyone else and C's, D's and F's for students who miss half the classes or threaten their teachers with bodily harm. At Penn State, A's accounted for 47 percent of the grades in English in 2002. The numbers are similar for sociology, comparative literature and psychology—and indeed for the College of Liberal Arts as a whole. The sciences and engineering, notoriously, are stingier.

What to do? If we so desired, we could recalibrate grades at Penn State, at Princeton or at any college in the country. The principle is simple enough, and it's crucial to every diving competition: we would merely need to account for each course's degree of difficulty.

Every professor, and every department, produces an average grade—an average for the professor over her career and an average for the discipline over the decades. And if colleges really wanted to clamp down on grade inflation, they could whisk it away statistically, simply by factoring those averages into each student's G.P.A. Imagine that G.P.A.'s were calculated on a scale of 10 with the average grade, be it a B-minus or an A-minus, counted as a 5. The B-plus in chemical engineering, where the average grade is, say, C-plus, would be rewarded accordingly and assigned a value of 8; the B-plus in psychology, where the average grade might be just over B-plus, would be graded like an easy dive, adequately executed, and given a 4.7.

After all, colleges keep all the necessary statistics—by year, by course and by department. We know perfectly well which courses require a forward somersault with two and a half twists from the pike position for an A, and which courses will give B's for cannonballs. We could even encourage professors and entire departments to increase their prestige by lowering their average grade and thereby increasing their "degree of difficulty." Students who earn A's in difficult courses would benefit—as would students who earn B's.

Incorporating "degree of difficulty" into students' G.P.A.'s would turn campuses upside down; it would eliminate faculty capriciousness precisely by factoring it in; and it would involve nothing more than using the numbers we already have at our disposal. It would be confusing as hell. But it would yield a world in which the average grade was never anything more or less than the middle of the scale.

PROFESSIONAL WRITING

SOLVING FOR PATTERN

Wendell Berry

A native of Kentucky and professor of English at the University of Kentucky, Wendell Berry is a prolific writer of poetry, fiction, and nonfiction. He is most noted for his essays and books on agricultural and ecological topics, including The Unforeseen Wilderness: An Essay on Kentucky's Red River Gorge *(1971),* The Unsettling of America: Culture and Agriculture *(1977),* The Gift of Good Land *(1981),* Home Economics *(1987), and* What Are People For? *(1990). In this selection from "Solving for Pattern," which appears in* The Gift of Good Land, *while Berry talks about solving specific problems in farming and agriculture, he focuses on the nature of problem solving itself. Although too many farm "solutions" (larger tractors, feed lots, overuse of fertilizers and pesticides) solve one problem, they create a host of destructive side effects. Good solutions, Berry argues, do not address problems in isolation. Good solutions must promote the harmony, health, and quality of the whole system.*

Our dilemma in agriculture now is that the industrial methods that have so   *1* spectacularly solved some of the problems of food production have been accompanied by "side effects" so damaging as to threaten the survival of farming. Perhaps the best clue to the nature and the gravity of this dilemma is that it is not limited to agriculture. My immediate concern here is with the irony of agricultural methods that destroy, first, the health of the soil and, finally, the health of human communities. But I could just as easily be talking about sanitation systems that pollute, school systems that graduate illiterate students, medical cures that cause disease, or nuclear armaments that explode in the midst of the people they are meant to protect. This is a kind of surprise that is characteristic of our time: The cure proves incurable; security results in the evacuation of a neighborhood or a town. It is only when it is understood that our agricultural dilemma is characteristic not of our agriculture but of our time that we can begin to understand why these surprises happen, and to work out standards of judgment that may prevent them.

To the problems of farming, then, as to other problems of our time, there appear to be three kinds of solutions: *2*

There is, first, the solution that causes a ramifying series of new problems, the only limiting criterion being, apparently, that the new problems should arise beyond the purview of the expertise that produced the solution—as, in agriculture, industrial solutions to the problem of production have invariably caused problems of maintenance, conservation, economics, community health, etc., etc. *3*

If, for example, beef cattle are fed in large feed lots, within the boundaries of the feeding operation itself a certain factorylike order and efficiency can be achieved. But even within those boundaries that mechanical order immediately produces biological disorder, for we know that health problems and dependence on drugs will be greater among cattle so confined than among cattle on pasture. *4*

And beyond those boundaries, the problems multiply. Pen feeding of cattle in large numbers involves, first, a manure-removal problem, which becomes at some point a health problem for the animals themselves, for the local watershed, and for the adjoining ecosystems and human communities. If the manure is disposed of without returning it to the soil that produced the feed, a serious problem of soil fertility is involved. But we know too that large concentrations of animals in feed lots in one place tend to be associated with, and to promote, large cash-grain monocultures in other places. These monocultures tend to be accompanied by a whole set of specifically agricultural problems: soil erosion, soil compaction, epidemic infestations of pests, weeds, and disease. But they are also accompanied by a set *5* of agricultural-economic problems (dependence on purchased technology; dependence on purchased fuels, fertilizers, and poisons; dependence on credit)—and by a set of community problems, beginning with depopulation and the removal of sources, services, and markets to more and more distant towns. And these are, so to speak, only the first circle of the bad effects of a bad solution. With a little care, their branchings can be traced on into nature, into the life of the cities, and into the cultural and economic life of the nation.

The second kind of solution is that which immediately worsens the 6 problem it is intended to solve, causing a hellish symbiosis in which problem and solution reciprocally enlarge one another in a sequence that, so far as its own logic is concerned, is limitless—as when the problem of soil compaction is "solved" by a bigger tractor, which further compacts the soil, which makes a need for a still bigger tractor, and so on and on. There is an identical symbiosis between coal-fired power plants and air conditioners. It is characteristic of such solutions that no one prospers by them but the suppliers of fuel and equipment.

These two kinds of solutions are obviously bad. They always serve one 7 good at the expense of another or of several others, and I believe that if all their effects were ever to be accounted for they would be seen to involve, too frequently if not invariably, a net loss to nature, agriculture, and the human commonwealth.

Such solutions always involve a definition of the problem that is either 8 false or so narrow as to be virtually false. To define an agricultural problem as if it were solely a problem of agriculture—or solely a problem of production or technology or economics—is simply to misunderstand the problem, either inadvertently or deliberately, either for profit or because of a prevalent fashion of thought. The whole problem must be solved, not just some handily identifiable and simplifiable aspect of it.

Both kinds of bad solutions leave their problems unsolved. Bigger trac- 9 tors do not solve the problem of soil compaction any more than air conditioners solve the problem of air pollution. Nor does the large confinement-feeding operation solve the problem of food production; it is, rather, a way calculated to allow large-scale ambition and greed to profit from food production.

The real problem of food production occurs within a complex, mutu- 10 ally influential relationship of soil, plants, animals, and people. A real solution to that problem will therefore be ecologically, agriculturally, and culturally healthful.

Perhaps it is not until health is set down as the aim that we come in   11
sight of the third kind of solution: that which causes a ramifying series of
solutions—as when meat animals are fed on the farm where the feed is
raised, and where the feed is raised to be fed to the animals that are on the
farm. Even so rudimentary a description implies a concern for pattern, for
quality, which necessarily complicates the concern for production. The
farmer has put plants and animals into a relationship of mutual dependence,
and must perforce be concerned for balance or symmetry, a reciprocating
connection in the pattern of the farm that is biological, not industrial, and
that involves solutions to problems of fertility, soil husbandry, economics,
sanitation—the whole complex of problems whose proper solutions add up
to health: the health of the soil, of plants and animals, of farm and farmer,
of farm family and farm community, all involved in the same internested,
interlocking pattern—or pattern of patterns.

A bad solution is bad, then, because it acts destructively upon the larger   12
patterns in which it is contained. It acts destructively upon those patterns,
most likely, because it is formed in ignorance or disregard of them. A bad
solution solves for a single purpose or goal, such as increased production.
And it is typical of such solutions that they achieve stupendous increases
in production at exorbitant biological and social costs.

A good solution is good because it is in harmony with those larger pat-   13
terns—and this harmony will, I think, be found to have the nature of analogy. A bad solution acts within the larger pattern the way a disease or
addiction acts within the body. A good solution acts within the larger pattern the way a healthy organ acts within the body. But it must at once be
understood that a healthy organ does not—as the mechanistic or industrial mind would like to say—"give" health to the body, is not exploited for
the body's health, but is a part of its health. The health of organ and organism is the same, just as the health of organism and ecosystem is the
same. And these structures of organ, organism, and ecosystem belong to a
series of analogical integrities that begins with the organelle and ends with
the biosphere.

In your journal, write the meanings of the following words:

- *ramifying* series of new problems **(3)**
- *purview* of the expertise **(3)**
- hellish *symbiosis* **(6)**
- soil *husbandry* **(11)**
- *analogical* integrities **(13)**
- begins with the *organelle* **(13)**

QUESTIONS FOR WRITING AND DISCUSSION

1. Reread your response to the freewriting exercise at the beginning of this chapter. What campus problem did you describe, and what was your solution? Now, assume that you are Wendell Berry. Write one paragraph of Berry's response to your solution. Specifically, consider how well your solution meets Berry's goal of solving for the harmony, health, and quality of the whole college or university system.

2. Berry's essay explains three kinds of solutions. What are these three types of solutions, and what makes the third kind the best?

3. In paragraph 1, Berry says that he "could just as easily be talking about sanitation systems that pollute, school systems that graduate illiterate students, [or] medical cures that cause disease." Choose one of these problems (or another common problem) and explain how Berry would analyze the problem.

4. Berry clarifies his explanation for his reader by using audience cues (transitions, paragraph hooks, and topic sentences) at the beginning of paragraphs. Choose any three successive paragraphs (for example, paragraphs 3, 4, and 5) and identify any words or phrases that (a) make a transition from the previous paragraph or idea and (b) announce or preview the subject of the new paragraph. Make a sketch outline of Berry's essay.

5. An analogy is a comparison between two things or processes in which a simple or familiar thing helps to explain a complex or unfamiliar thing. Thus, we can explain how the human heart works by drawing an analogy with a simple mechanical pump. In paragraph 13, Berry says that a "bad solution acts

within the larger pattern the way a disease or addiction acts within the body." Explain Berry's analogy. Then apply this analogy to one specific problem that you have discussed in class. Does Berry's organic analogy make sense in that particular case? Why or why not?

6. Apply Berry's ideas about "solving for pattern" to the following essay by Deborah Tannen. How well do her arguments and solutions address the overall harmony, health, and quality of the system?

7. On the Internet, investigate what organic farming is and how food products get to be labeled "organic." Start with a site such as the Organic Farming Research Foundation at *http://www.ofrf.org* and find out answers to your questions. Does eating organic foods help solve problems in farming? Does it create other problems— higher prices, shorter shelf life, less efficient production—that the organic farmer or the consumer needs to consider?

PROFESSIONAL WRITING

THE ARGUMENT CULTURE

Deborah Tannen

A professor of linguistics at Georgetown University, Deborah Tannen is also a best-selling author of many books on discourse and gender, including You Just Don't Understand: Women and Men in Conversation *(1990),* Talking from 9 to 5 *(1994),* The Argument Culture: Moving from Debate to Dialogue *(1998), and* I Only Say This Because I Love You *(2001). Throughout her career, Tannen has focused on how men and women have different conversational habits and assumptions, whether they talk on the job or at home. In the following essay, taken from* The Argument Culture, *Tannen tries to convince her readers that adversarial debates—which typically represent only two sides of an issue and thus promote antagonism— create problems in communication. As a culture, Tannen believes, we would be much more successful if we didn't always think of argument as a war or a fight but as a dialogue among a variety of different positions. As you read her essay, does Tannen persuade you that our "argument culture" really is a problem and that her solutions will help solve that problem?*

Balance. Debate. Listening to both sides. Who could question these noble   *1*
American traditions? Yet today, these principles have been distorted.

Without thinking, we have plunged headfirst into what I call the "argument culture."

The argument culture urges us to approach the world, and the people 2 in it, in an adversarial frame of mind. It rests on the assumption that opposition is the best way to get anything done: The best way to discuss an idea is to set up a debate; the best way to cover news is to find spokespeople who express the most extreme, polarized views and present them as "both sides"; the best way to settle disputes is litigation that pits one party against the other; the best way to begin an essay is to attack someone; and the best way to show you're really thinking is to criticize.

More and more, our public interactions have become like arguing with 3 a spouse. Conflict can't be avoided in our public lives any more than we can avoid conflict with people we love. One of the great strengths of our society is that we can express these conflicts openly. But just as spouses have to learn ways of settling their differences without inflicting real damage, so we, as a society, have to find constructive ways of resolving disputes and differences.

The war on drugs, the war on cancer, the battle of the sexes, politi- 4 cians' turf battles—in the argument culture, war metaphors pervade our talk and shape our thinking. The cover headlines of both *Time* and *Newsweek* one recent week are a case in point: "The Secret Sex Wars," proclaims *Newsweek*. "Starr at War," declares *Time*. Nearly everything is framed as a battle or game in which winning or losing is the main concern.

The argument culture pervades every aspect of our lives today. Issues 5 from global warming to abortion are depicted as two-sided arguments, when in fact most Americans' views lie somewhere in the middle. Partisanship makes gridlock in Washington the norm. Even in our personal relationships, a "let it all hang out" philosophy emphasizes people expressing their anger without giving them constructive ways of settling differences.

Sometimes You Have to Fight

There are times when it is necessary and right to fight—to defend your 6 country or yourself, to argue for your rights or against offensive or dangerous ideas or actions. What's wrong with the argument culture is the ubiquity, the knee-jerk nature of approaching any issue, problem or public person in an adversarial way.

Our determination to pursue truth by setting up a fight between two 7 sides leads us to assume that every issue has two sides—no more, no less.

But if you always assume there must be an "other side," you may end up scouring the margins of science or the fringes of lunacy to find it.

This accounts, in part, for the bizarre phenomenon of Holocaust de-   8
nial. Deniers, as Emory University professor Deborah Lipstadt shows, have been successful in gaining TV air time and campus newspaper coverage by masquerading as "the other side" in a "debate." Continual reference to "the other side" results in a conviction that everything has another side—and people begin to doubt the existence of any facts at all.

The power of words to shape perception has been proved by researchers   9
in controlled experiments. Psychologists Elizabeth Loftus and John Palmer, for example, found that the terms in which people are asked to recall some-thing affect what they recall. The researchers showed subjects a film of two cars colliding, then asked how fast the cars were going; one week later they asked whether there had been any broken glass. Some subjects were asked, "How fast were the cars going when they bumped into each other?" Oth-ers were asked, "How fast were the cars going when they smashed into each other?"

Those who read the question with "smashed" tended to "remember"   10
that the cars were going faster. They were also more likely to "remember" having seen broken glass. (There wasn't any.) This is how language works.

"What about here? This looks like a good spot for an argument."

It invisibly molds our way of thinking about people, actions and the world around us.

In the argument culture, "critical" thinking is synonymous with criti- *11* cizing. In many classrooms, students are encouraged to read someone's life work, then rip it to shreds.

When debates and fighting predominate, those who enjoy verbal spar- *12* ring are likely to take part—by calling in to talk shows or writing letters to the editor. Those who aren't comfortable with oppositional discourse are likely to opt out.

How High-Tech Communication Pulls Us Apart

One of the most effective ways to defuse antagonism between two groups *13* is to provide a forum for individuals from those groups to get to know each other personally. What is happening in our lives, however, is just the op- posite. More and more of our communication is not face to face, and not with people we know. The proliferation and increasing portability of tech- nology isolates people in a bubble.

Along with the voices of family members and friends, phone lines bring *14* into our homes the annoying voices of solicitors who want to sell some- thing—generally at dinnertime. (My father-in-law startles phone solici- tors by saying, "We're eating dinner, but I'll call you back. What's your home phone number?" To the nonplused caller, he explains, "Well, you're calling me at home; I thought I'd call you at home, too.")

It is common for families to have more than one TV, so the adults can *15* watch what they like in one room and the kids can watch their choice in another—or maybe each child has a private TV.

E-mail, and now the Internet, are creating networks of human con- *16* nection unthinkable even a few years ago. Though e-mail has enhanced communication with family and friends, it also ratchets up the anonymity of both sender and receiver, resulting in stranger-to-stranger "flaming."

"Road rage" shows how dangerous the argument culture—and espe- *17* cially today's technologically enhanced aggression—can be. Two men who engage in a shouting match may not come to blows, but if they express their anger while driving down a public highway, the risk to themselves and others soars.

The Argument Culture Shapes Who We Are

The argument culture has a defining impact on our lives and on our *18* culture.

- **It makes us distort facts,** as in the Nancy Kerrigan-Tonya Harding story. After the original attack on Kerrigan's knee, news stories focused on the rivalry between the two skaters instead of portraying Kerrigan as the victim of an attack. Just last month, *Time* magazine called the event a "contretemps" between Kerrigan and Harding. And a recent joint TV interview of the two skaters reinforced that skewed image by putting the two on equal footing, rather than as victim and accused.

- **It makes us waste valuable time,** as in the case of scientist Robert Gallo, who co-discovered the AIDS virus. Gallo was the object of a groundless four-year investigation into allegations he had stolen the virus from another scientist. He was ultimately exonerated, but the toll was enormous. Never mind that, in his words, "These were the most painful and horrible years of my life." Gallo spent four years fighting accusations instead of fighting AIDS.

- **It limits our thinking.** Headlines are intentionally devised to attract attention, but the language of extremes actually shapes, and misshapes, the way we think about things. Military metaphors train us to think about, and see, everything in terms of fighting, conflict and war. Adversarial rhetoric is a kind of verbal inflation—a rhetorical boy-who-cried-wolf.

- **It encourages us to lie.** If you fight to win, the temptation is great to deny facts that support your opponent's views and say only what supports your side. It encourages people to misrepresent and, in the extreme, to lie.

End the Argument Culture by Looking at All Sides

How can we overcome our classically American habit of seeing issues in absolutes? We must expand our notion of "debate" to include more dialogue. To do this, we can make special efforts not to think in twos. Mary Catherine Bateson, an anthropologist at Virginia's George Mason University, makes a point of having her class compare three cultures, not two. Then, students are more likely to think about each on its own terms, rather than as opposites. 19

In the public arena, television and radio producers can try to avoid, whenever possible, structuring public discussions as debates. This means avoiding the format of having two guests discuss an issue. Invite three 20 guests—or one. Perhaps it is time to re-examine the assumption that audiences always prefer a fight.

Instead of asking, "What's the other side?" we might ask, "What are *21* the other sides?" Instead of insisting on hearing "both sides," let's insist on hearing "all sides."

We need to find metaphors other than sports and war. Smashing heads *22* does not open minds. We need to use our imaginations and ingenuity to find different ways to seek truth and gain knowledge through intellectual interchange, and add them to our arsenal—or, should I say, to the ingredients for our stew. It will take creativity for each of us to find ways to change the argument culture to a dialogue culture. It's an effort we have to make, because our public and private lives are at stake.

VOCABULARY

In your journal, write down the meanings of the following words:

- in an *adversarial* frame of mind **(2)**
- the *ubiquity* **(6)**
- *synonymous* with criticizing **(11)**
- with *oppositional* discourse **(12)**
- the *proliferation* **(13)**
- a *contretemps* between Kerrigan and Harding **(18)**
- he was ultimately *exonerated* **(18)**
- imaginations and *ingenuity* **(22)**

QUESTIONS FOR WRITING AND DISCUSSION

1. List three controversial topics currently in the news. Then choose one of those topics and explain the two "sides" of this argument. Now, imagine a third point of view. How is it different from the first two positions? Does coming up with a third position help you think creatively about how to resolve this dispute? Explain.

2. As she writes her essay, Tannen initially outlines the nature of the problem with the "argument culture" before she gives her solution. Which paragraphs most clearly demonstrate the problem? Which paragraphs explain her solution? Does she ignore any aspects of the problem? Would her solution really solve the problem she describes? Why or why not?

3. Critically analyzing the social, political, or cultural context is an important strategy for solving a problem. Where does Tannen explain the context(s) for the problem? Where does she argue that her solution will help resolve social, political, or cultural problems? Are there contexts where her solution might not work? Explain.

4. Read Tannen's advice in the final four paragraphs of her essay. Does she follow her own advice in writing this essay? Which pieces of advice does she follow and which does she ignore? Cite examples from the essay to support your analysis. Would her essay be more effective if she followed her own advice? Explain.

5. As a professor of linguistics, Tannen can write in a formal, academic style, but she can also write in an informal style for general audiences. In this essay, is Tannen writing for academics or for anyone interested in culture and communication? Find examples of Tannen's "academic" style as well as her informal style. Does she successfully integrate the two or is she too informal or too academic? Explain.

6. According to Tannen, the language we choose and the metaphors we use affect our perceptions of the world. Where does Tannen discuss how words or metaphors shape our perceptions? What examples does she give? In her own argument, does Tannen herself avoid language or metaphors referring to war, violence, or conflict?

7. The *New Yorker* cartoon by BEK, "This looks like a good spot for an argument," did not originally appear with Tannen's essay. Evaluate the appropriateness of this visual image for Tannen's essay. Does the cartoon support Tannen's thesis? Does it contribute to the essay's appeal, or does it distract from Tannen's argument? Citing details from the cartoon and passages from Tannen's essay, explain your response.

8. On the Internet, log on to the Web site of a national news magazine such as *Newsweek* or *Utne* magazine and read their e-mail letters in response to an essay on a controversial topic such as stem cell research, global warming, public transportation, educational testing, and so forth. Read several letters or responses. Can you find at least *three* positions on that issue—rather than just

the standard "pro" and "con"? Explain the controversial topic and then write out at least three different positions or points of view which you discover in the responses.

Problem Solving: The Writing Process

ASSIGNMENT FOR PROBLEM SOLVING

Select a problem that you believe needs a solution. Narrow and focus the problem and choose an appropriate audience. Describe the problem and, if necessary, demonstrate for your audience that it needs a solution. State your solution, and justify it with reasons and evidence. Where appropriate, weigh alternative solutions, examine the feasibility of your own solution, and answer objections to your solution.

The problem-solving assignment leads naturally to the genre of a proposal. Some proposals are long, formal documents addressed to knowledgeable readers, while others are short and informal, intended more for general audiences. Review your assignment and your intended audience to help determine the amount of analysis and research you need for your essay.

CHOOSING A SUBJECT

If one of your journal entries suggests a possible subject, try the collecting and shaping strategies below. If none of these leads to a workable subject, consider the following suggestions:

- Evaluating leads naturally into problem solving. Reread your journal entries and topic ideas for "evaluating." If your evaluation of your subject was negative, consider what would make your evaluation more positive. Based on your evaluation, write a proposal, addressed to the proper audience, explaining the problem and offering your solution.
- Organized groups are already trying to solve a number of national and international problems: homelessness, illegal aliens, the slaughter of whales, acid

rain, abuse of animals in scientific experiments, drug and alcohol abuse, toxic-waste disposal, and so forth. Read several current articles on one of these topics. Then narrow the problem to one aspect that students or residents of your town could help to resolve. Write an essay outlining the problem and proposing some *specific and limited* actions that citizens could take.

"I can't think of anything I have no problem with."

© The New Yorker Collection (1987) (Stevenson) from cartoonbank.com. All Rights Reserved.

- An important part of any community-service-learning project is collaborating with the agency to assess problems and propose possible solutions. If you have a community-service-learning project in one of your classes, work collaboratively with the agency to assess the community's and/or the agency's needs as well as the knowledge and skills you might bring to the agency to contribute to a possible solution. Working with the agency, decide on a purpose, audience, and genre for your proposal.
- Every day, the news media features images that seem to suggest a problem that needs a solution. Choose one image that you have found in the media and investigate the issue. What problem does the image suggest? What does your research and investigation reveal about the rhetorical situation and cultural context surrounding this image and this issue? Choose a possible audience, genre, and context, and write your own problem-solving essay based on the issue raised by this image.

COLLECTING

With a possible subject and audience in mind, write out answers for each of the following topics. Remember that not all of these approaches will apply to your subject; some topics will suggest very little, while others may prompt you to generate ideas or specific examples appropriate to your problem and solution. A hypothetical problem—large classes that hinder learning—illustrates how these topics may help you focus on your subject and collect relevant ideas and information.

IDENTIFY AND FOCUS ON THE SPECIFIC PROBLEM Answer the first four "Wh" questions:

> **Who:** A Psychology I professor; the Psychology Department
>
> **What:** Psychology I class
>
> **When:** Spring semester (the structure of this class may be slightly different from previous semesters)
>
> **Where:** University of Illinois (large lecture classes at one school may be different from those at another)

You may want to generalize about large lecture classes everywhere, but begin by identifying the specific problem at hand.

DEMONSTRATE THAT THE PROBLEM NEEDS A SOLUTION Map out the *effects* of a problem. (See the diagram.)

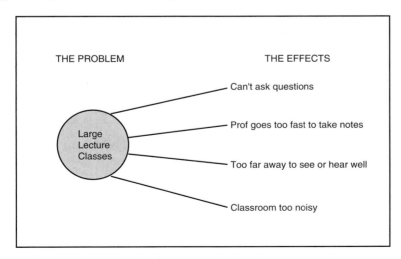

THE PROBLEM

THE EFFECTS

Large Lecture Classes

Can't ask questions

Prof goes too fast to take notes

Too far away to see or hear well

Classroom too noisy

You may want to map out both *short-term effects* and *long-term effects.* Over the short term, large lecture classes prevent you from asking questions; over the long term, you may do poorly on examinations, get a lower grade in the class, lose interest in the subject, be unable to cope with your own and others' psychological problems, or end up in a different career or job.

DISCOVER POSSIBLE SOLUTIONS   One strategy is to map out the history or the causes of the problem. If you can discover what caused the problem in the first place, you may have a possible solution. (See the diagram.)

A second strategy takes the imaginative approach. Brainstorm hypothetical cases by asking, "What if . . ."

"What if students petitioned the president of the university to abolish all lecture classes with enrollments over 100 students?" Would that work?

"What if students invited the professor to answer questions at a weekly study session?" Would the professor attend? Would students attend?

"What if students taught each other in a psychology class?" How would that work?

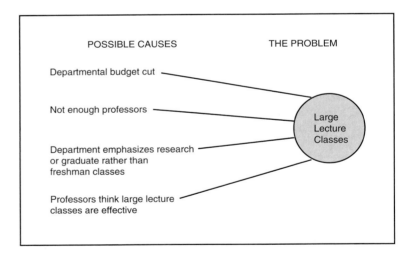

EVALUATE POSSIBLE SOLUTIONS   Apply the "If . . . then . . ." test on each possible solution: Consider whether each proposal would:

A. actually solve the problem;

B. meet certain criteria, such as cost-effectiveness, practicality, ethicality, legality;

C. not create new problems.

"*If* classes were smaller, *then* students would learn more":

If classes were smaller, students might learn more, but a small class size does not necessarily guarantee greater learning.

Although students might learn more, do smaller classes meet other criteria? While they are legal and ethical, are they practical and cost-effective?

Would smaller classes create new problems? Smaller classes might mean fewer upper-level course offerings. Is that a serious new problem?

CONVINCE YOUR READERS   Support your proposed solutions by stating *reasons* and finding supporting *evidence:*

Reason: Smaller classes are worth the additional expense because students actually engage the material rather than just memorizing for exams.

Evidence: Data from studies comparing large and small classes; personal testimony by students, interviews, or questionnaires; testimony or evidence from authorities on teaching.

ANSWER POSSIBLE OBJECTIONS TO YOUR PROPOSAL   Every solution has a down side or possible drawbacks. You need to respond to the most important objections.

List Drawbacks

Small classes cost more.

Small classes might reduce course offerings.

Small classes might mean less money for research.

List Your Responses

Good education does cost more. The University of Illinois has a reputation as an excellent undergraduate institution, and small classes would help it maintain quality education.

Perhaps some classes with low demand could be cut, but the necessary funds should not be taken out of upper-division classes for psychology majors or research projects.

LIST POSSIBLE STEPS FOR IMPLEMENTATION   If appropriate, indicate the key steps or chronological sequence of your proposal:

1. Poll students and teachers in large lecture classes to confirm that the problem warrants attention.

2. Gather evidence from other colleges or universities to show how they reduced class sizes.

3. Present results of polls and other evidence to the state legislature to request more funds.

OBSERVING As you gather evidence and examples, use your observation skills. If the problem is large lecture classes, attend classes and *observe* the behavior of students and professors. Are students distracted by noise? Can they ask questions? Does the professor talk too softly to be heard in the back row? Remember that *repeated* observation is essential. If necessary, observe your subject over a period of several days or weeks.

REMEMBERING Use *freewriting*, *looping*, or *clustering* to help you remember examples from your experience of the problem or of possible solutions. Brainstorm or freewrite about previous class sessions in Psychology I. Do looping or mapping on other small-enrollment classes: What made these classes effective or ineffective? What teaching strategies, projects, or small-group activities were possible in these classes that would not be possible in a class of 250 students?

READING AND INVESTIGATING *Use the library* to find books or articles about the particular problem. Other writers have no doubt offered solutions to your prob-

> ❝*The best time for planning . . . is when you're doing the dishes.*❞
>
> —AGATHA CHRISTIE, MYSTERY WRITER

Research Tips

As you begin researching your problem, don't spend all your time on the Internet or on the library's databases. Remember to interview people who may know about your problem. Use your investigating skills to locate local authorities and interview them in person, via e-mail, or on the telephone (see Chaper 6). Find out what other people think about this problem. How do they explain or define the problem? What are they already doing to solve the problem? Why are current solutions not working or not working effectively enough? Interview a teacher who knows about the problem, a student who has firsthand experience with the problem, an owner of a local business, or the coordinator of a community service or agency. Combining your online and library research with interviews makes your research more interesting, more local and current, and more effective.

lem that you could consider. Articles may even suggest objections to your proposed solution that you need to answer.

Interview participants or authorities on the problem. The professor who is teaching your Psychology I class may have some ideas about a solution. Administration—department chairs, deans, even the president—may agree to answer your questions and react to your possible solutions.

Design a questionnaire that addresses aspects of your problem. Responses to questionnaires provide evidence that a problem is serious, immediate, and in need of a solution. If the results of a questionnaire show that 175 of the 200 people in Psychology I who returned it favor smaller sections, you can include those data in your letter to the head of the department and the dean of the college.

SHAPING

GENRES FOR PROBLEM SOLVING   Initially, you must consider possible genres appropriate for your issue and your particular rhetorical situation. Typical genres used for proposals include articles in magazines, letters to the editor, academic essays, self-help essays, political essays, and business proposals. Depending on the genre and audience you choose, proposals often do the following:

- Identify, analyze, and demonstrate the problem.
- Describe and evaluate alternative solutions.
- Make proposals.
- Give reasons and evidence to support the proposal.
- Answer objections; discuss feasibility problems.
- Indicate implementation and call for action.

Of course, not all problem-solving essays have all six elements. Some do not discuss feasibility in detail or do not describe and evaluate alternative solutions. Michael Bérubé's proposal to end grade inflation, for example, presents only one possible solution and acknowledges that the feasibility problems might be confusing. Reconsidering your rhetorical situation and genre helps you decide how to shape your proposal.

OUTLINES FOR PROBLEM SOLVING   The following patterns indicate four possible ways to organize a problem-solving essay. One of these patterns may help you organize your proposal:

Problem-Solving Pattern

    I. Introduction

   II. The problem: Identify and demonstrate

  III. The solution(s)

  IV. Answering possible objections, costs, drawbacks

   V. Conclusion: Implementation plan; call to action

Point-by-Point Pattern

    I. Introduction

   II. The overall problem: Identify and demonstrate

  III. One part of the problem, solution, evidence, answers to possible objections, feasibility

  IV. Second part of the problem, solution, evidence, answers to possible objections, feasibility

   V. Third part of the problem, solution, evidence, and so on

  VI. Conclusion: Implementation; call to action

Alternative Pattern

    I. Introduction

   II. The problem: Identify and demonstrate

  III. Alternative Solution 1; why it's not satisfactory

  IV. Alternative Solution 2; why it's not satisfactory

   V. Alternative Solution 3; why it works best: Evidence, objections, feasibility

  VI. Conclusion: Implementation; call to action

Step-by-Step Pattern

    I. Introduction

   II. The problem: Identify and demonstrate

  III. Plan for implementing the solution or how solution has worked in the past:

      A. Step 1: Reasons and evidence showing why this step is necessary and feasible

      B. Step 2: Reasons and evidence showing why this step is necessary and feasible

  C. Step 3: Reasons and evidence showing why this step is necessary and feasible

IV. Conclusion

CAUSAL ANALYSIS Causal analysis can be used to organize some paragraphs of a proposal. In arguing the benefits or advantages of a proposed solution, you are actually explaining the *effects* of your solution.

- The effects or advantages of smaller class sections in Psychology I would be greater student participation, fewer distractions, more discussion during lectures, and more individual or small-group learning.
- Shortening the work week to thirty-two hours would increase the number of jobs, reduce tensions for working parents, and give employees time to learn new skills.
- Eliminating steroid use among NFL athletes would reduce the impact of collisions and enable players to recover from injuries faster. Long-term effects of eliminating steroids would be to reduce incidence of cancers and urinary-tract problems.

In each of these cases, each effect or advantage can become a separate point and, sometimes, a separate body paragraph.

CRITERIA ANALYSIS In some cases, the *criteria* for a good solution are quite clear. For example, cost-effectiveness, feasibility, and worker morale might be important criteria for a business-related proposal. If you work in a fast-food restaurant and are concerned about the increasing number of crimes, for example, you might propose that your manager add a video surveillance system. In order to overcome the manager's resistance to spending the needed funds, you could defend your proposal (and answer possible objections) by discussing relevant criteria.

  Proposal: To reduce theft and protect the employees of the restaurant by installing a video surveillance system.

- **Cost-effectiveness.** Citing evidence from other stores that have video cameras, you could prove that the equipment would pay for itself in less than a year. In addition, you could argue that if the life of just one employee—or possibly one manager—were saved, the cost would be worth it.
- **Feasibility.** Installing a security system would not require any extensive remodeling or any significant training time for employees to learn how to operate the system.

> **"Vigorous writing is concise."**
> —WILLIAM STRUNK, JR.,
> AUTHOR AND TEACHER

Writer: Provide the following information about your essay before you exchange drafts with a peer reader.

1. a. Audience and genre
   b. Statement of problem and context of problem
   c. Possible or alternative solutions
   d. Your recommended solution(s)
2. Write out one or two questions about your draft that you want your reader to answer.

Reader: Read the writer's entire draft. As you *reread* the draft, do the following:

1. Without looking at the writer's responses, describe (a) the essay's intended audience, (b) the main problem that the essay identifies, (c) the possible or alternative solutions, and (d) the writer's recommended solution. What feasibility problems or additional solutions should the writer consider? Why?
2. Indicate one paragraph in which the writer's evidence is strong. Then find one paragraph in which the writer needs more evidence. What additional *kinds* of evidence (personal experience, testimony from authorities, statistics, specific examples, etc.) might the writer use in this paragraph? Explain.
3. Number the paragraphs in the writer's essay and then describe, briefly, the purpose or main idea of each paragraph: paragraph 1 introduces the problem, paragraph 2 gives the writer's personal experience with the problem, and so on. When you finish, explain how the writer might improve the organization of the essay.
4. List the three most important things that the writer should focus on during revision.
5. Respond to the writer's questions in number 2.

Writer: When your essay is returned, read the comments by your peer reader(s) and do the following:

1. Compare your description of the audience, the problem, and the solutions with your reader's description. Where there are differences, try to clarify your essay.
2. Reconsider and revise your recommended solution(s).
3. What additional kinds of evidence will make your recommendations stronger?
4. Make a revision plan. List, in order, the three most important things that you need to do as you revise your essay.

- **Employee morale.** The benefits to employee morale would be significant: Workers would feel more secure, they would feel that the management cares about them, and they would work more productively.

CHRONOLOGICAL ORDER   If your proposal stresses the means of implementing your solution to a problem, you may organize several paragraphs or even an entire essay using a chronological order or step-by-step pattern.

A proposal to improve the reading skills of children might be justified by a series of coordinated steps, beginning by organizing seminars for teachers and PTA meetings to discuss possible solutions; establishing minimal reading requirements in grades K–6 that teachers and parents agree on; offering reading prizes; and organizing media coverage of students who participate in reading programs.

DRAFTING

Using your examples, recorded observations, reading, interviews, results from questionnaires, or your own experience, make a sketch outline and begin writing. As you write, let your own proposal and your intended audience guide you. In your first draft, get as much as possible on paper. Don't worry about spelling or awkward sentences. If you hit a snag, stop and read what you have written so far or reread your collecting and shaping notes.

REVISING

When you have a completed draft and are ready to start revising your essay, get another member of your class to read and respond to your essay. Use the peer response guidelines that follow to get—and give—constructive advice on your draft.

Use the following revising guidelines to identify areas for improving your draft. Even at this point, don't hesitate to collect additional information, if necessary, or reorganize your material. If a reader makes suggestions, reread your draft to see if those changes will improve your essay.

Guidelines for Revision

- **Review your rhetorical situation.** How can you revise your selected genre to make it more effectively communicate your purpose to your intended audience?

- **Review to make sure you critically analyze the problem.** Don't just assume that everyone will agree with your definition or representation of the problem. Investigate and describe the groups of people who are affected by the problem.
- **Have a classmate or someone who might understand your audience read your draft and play devil's advocate.** Have your reader pretend to be hostile to your solution and ask questions about alternative solutions or weaknesses in your own solution. Revise your proposal so that it answers any important objections.
- **Review your proposal for key elements.** If you are missing one of the following, would adding it make your proposal more effective for your audience? *Remember:* Proposals do not necessarily have to have all of these elements.

  Develop the items that are most applicable to your proposal.
  Show that a problem exists and needs attention.
  Evaluate alternative solutions.
  Propose your solution.
  Show that your solution meets certain criteria: feasibility, cost-effectiveness, legality.
  Answer possible objections.
  Suggest implementation or call for action.
- **Be sure that you *show* what you mean, using specific examples, facts, details, statistics, quotations from interviews or articles.** Don't rely on general assertions.
- **Signal the major parts of your proposal with key words and transitions.**
- **Avoid the following errors in logic and generalization.**
  Don't commit an "either-or" fallacy. For example, don't say that "*either* we reduce class sizes *or* students will drop out of the university." There are more than two possible alternatives.
  Don't commit an "ad hominem" fallacy by arguing "to the man" or "to the woman" rather than to the issue. Don't say, for example, that Deborah Tannen is wrong about argument because she is just another pushy woman who should stick to teaching linguistics.
  Test your proposal for "If . . . then . . ." statements. Does it really follow that "if we reduce class size, teaching will be more effective"?
  Avoid overgeneralizing your solution. If all your research applies to solving problems in large lecture classes in psychology, don't assume that your solution will apply to, say, classes in physics or physical education.

- **If you are citing data or quoting sources, make sure that your material is accurately cited.**
- **Read your proposal aloud for flabby, wordy, or awkward sentences.** Revise your sentences for clarity, precision, and forcefulness.
- **Edit your proposal for spelling, appropriate word choice, punctuation, usage, mechanics, and grammar.** Remember that, in part, your form and audience help determine what are appropriate usage and mechanics.

POSTSCRIPT ON THE WRITING PROCESS

Before you turn in your essay, answer the following questions in your journal.

1. As you worked on your essay, what elements of the rhetorical situation did you revise? How did you change the purpose, audience, or genre elements as you drafted your essay? Cite specific sentences or paragraphs from your essay as examples.

2. List the skills you used in writing this paper: observing people, places, or events; remembering personal experience; using questionnaires and interviews; reading written material; explaining ideas; evaluating solutions. Which of these skills was most useful to you in writing this essay?

3. What was your most difficult problem to solve while writing this paper? Were you able to solve it yourself, or did your readers suggest a solution?

4. In one sentence, describe the most important thing you learned about writing while working on this essay.

5. What were the most successful parts of your essay?

STUDENT WRITING

NO PARKING

Kristy Busch, Steve Krause, and Keith Wright

Kristy Busch, Steve Krause, and Keith Wright worked together on a proposal to solve the parking problem at their university. They met several times to discuss the topic, select questions for the survey and interview, divide the research responsibilities, and determine who was going to draft each section. They agreed that Keith Wright would interview the director of parking management, and that Kristy Busch and Steve Krause would survey students about the parking problem. After they collected their information, Wright drafted a first version of the section on the multilevel garage, Busch worked on the shuttle bus proposal, and Krause wrote out the introduction and the rezoning proposal. Then they worked together to combine and revise their drafts, adding new information, reorganizing the paragraphs, and editing the final draft. Shown below are the questions for the interview, the results of the survey, the first draft of the introduction and rezoning proposal, and the revised draft of the entire proposal.

Interview

Interview Questions for Wes Westfall, Director of Parking Management

1. Do you perceive a serious parking problem at CSU?

2. Do you think that students' arguments about lack of "X" parking spaces along the dorms on the north side of the campus are valid?

3. How many stickers for each zone are issued each year? Do these numbers fluctuate?

4. Are you in favor of building a multilevel parking facility?
   Where would you build such a structure?
   What would it cost? Is it feasible?
   How long would it take to build?

5. Have you considered a shuttle bus system between Moby Gym and the central campus?
   What would it cost? Is it feasible?

6. Is rezoning possible? Is it currently under consideration? Would it solve the problem? Is it feasible? What would it cost?

Parking Survey Results

1. Do you drive to CSU?
   Yes: 36
   Occasionally: 53
   No: 11

2. Does CSU need more parking for students?
   Yes: 62
   No: 38

3. Would rezoning close-in lots to eliminate dorm parking help?
   Yes: 78
   No: 22

4. Class (Fr., Soph., Jr., Sr., Other)
   Fr: 33
   Soph: 20
   Jr: 22
   Sr: 13
   Other: 12

First Draft

If you drive to CSU, you may already know how hard it can be to find a parking place. If not, then now would be a good time to make the changes necessary to accommodate more cars (before you start driving). Not only is the parking inadequate for the number of cars, but it is also poorly organized and poorly distributed among the groups who use it. A very common occurrence is being forced to park very far from the building where you need to go. Not only students are affected; faculty, staff, and visitors also have problems finding somewhere to park. For a visitor, this is very distressing and certainly doesn't present an attractive first impression of CSU. It is clear that something will have to be done; what is unclear is exactly what would be the most practical and cost-effective solution. First, and probably the most effective for the immediate future, would be to rezone the existing parking to better accommodate the users. A shuttle bus system could also be used; however, this could be costly and would have to be used a lot to make it a practical investment. The ominous "multilevel parking facility" is a drastic last measure that we would have a lot of trouble paying for. [add closing sentence]

The most cost-effective and probably the most immediately effective would be a partial rezoning of existing parking. This year, the office of parking management sold 7,641 parking stickers for an available 6,238 spaces, a difference of 1,703. This means that there are a lot more stickers than places to park. Granted, all these people do not drive at the same time, but enough do to cause a problem. In a poll taken this March, 78 percent of the people said that they would like to see the parking rezoned. In rezoning, we should first look at the parking areas which are not full and determine why and then shift the zones in a way in which they will help. For example, the western sections of the "Z" lot at Moby Gym could be changed to "X" for those dorm dwellers. Then the close-in lots could be changed to "Z" for the commuting students. Or we could eliminate the metered parking and put "Z" parking in its place. Rezoning the lots would seem to be the easiest solution to the problem, but it cannot be permanent, since if this school survives it will inevitably grow.

Revised Version
No Parking

On Monday morning, Jennifer Martin left her apartment at 8:30 to drive   *1*
to the Colorado State University campus, hoping to arrive on time for a test in her 9 A.M. sociology class. When she arrived at the student parking lot west of Aylesworth Hall, there were no parking spots. So she began cruising up and down the lot, hoping that someone would soon pull out. As she drove slowly up and down the lanes, she muttered to herself and clenched her hands on the steering wheel. She did have a permit to park in the lot, but there were obviously more permits than spaces. About five minutes before class, a car pulled out of a place at the far end of the lot. She accelerated down the next lane, driving as fast as she could without running over other students, but just as she arrived, a green Ford Focus cut in front of her and darted into the vacant space. She honked her horn and waved her fist, but the person quickly got out of the car and walked away. At this point, she realized that she had no choice. She wheeled into the area marked for motorcycles, parked her car, and raced for class. She was angry because she knew she was going to get a ticket even though she had a legal permit.

If you drive to the CSU campus for classes, you have probably had a   *2*
similar experience. But students are not the only ones who have parking problems on campus: Faculty, staff, and visitors also have problems finding places to park. Especially for visitors, the overcrowded conditions don't present an attractive first impression of the campus. Clearly, something has

to be done to improve parking facilities. After studying the problem, interviewing the director of parking management, and polling 100 students, we believe that there are three alternatives that the CSU administration should consider: building a multilevel parking facility, starting a shuttle bus from remote lots, and rezoning the existing parking lots to better serve the users.

A first possible solution to CSU's parking problem would be to build *3* a multilevel parking facility. This sounds like a promising idea because it would allow more students, faculty, and staff to park over the same amount of ground space. CSU could build this facility at any of several locations. One place is on the west side of the Morgan Library, where the "A" parking zone—for faculty—is now. This location would provide parking convenient to classes, faculty offices, and the library. A second site would be the open parking lot west of Moby Gym. Although this location is farther from classes, it would also be used during basketball games and concerts. A third location might be the large parking lot north of the Student Center. This, too, like the library lot, would be close to classrooms and faculty offices.

While these sites are all promising, we discovered that a multilevel *4* parking facility has some serious drawbacks. Wes Westfall, manager of CSU parking, explained that there are several problems with these garages that most people don't consider. A first drawback to the parking garage is the expense. Westfall said that a multilevel garage would cost a minimum of $6,000 per parking space, raising the price of a parking permit from $30 to over $300. And that would be for a sticky piece of paper that still wouldn't guarantee a parking space for every car. Perhaps the president of the university could pay $300 a year, but most students can barely afford $30.

A second drawback to a parking garage is that it doesn't last forever, *5* and the maintenance costs can be considerable. Mr. Westfall has some frightening photographs of sections of strong, stable-looking concrete that has collapsed for no visible reason at all. One picture shows a whole garage leveled as though a good-sized bomb had hit it—nothing was left standing except for a pillar here and there. Unless garages are carefully maintained, Westfall stated, they may not last over twenty years. The problem, he explained, lies in the rebar (steel rods inside the concrete) that reinforces the concrete. Gas, oil, and antifreeze from cars are gradually absorbed into the concrete, a condition causing the rebarb to deteriorate and weaken the whole structure. The only way to check for this kind of damage, Westfall noted, is to use an expensive concrete X-ray machine. So even the maintenance of a garage can be an expensive proposition.

The third and most serious problem, Westfall claims, is security. Parking garages can become just another place for sexual assault, drug trafficking, vandalism, and theft. Westfall commented that most garages have a monitor system and guards, but those precautions are not totally effective. By the time the guard detects a theft over the security system and arrives at the location, the thief has usually fled. In addition, any security system adds to the already high costs of a parking facility. Clearly, the problems connected with a multilevel garage make it a last resort for solving the parking problems on campus.

A second alternative for solving the parking problems on the CSU campus is to use a bus shuttle service from the outlying "Z" lot at Moby Gym to the central campus. Many of the students who responded to our survey said that the lots on the perimeter of the campus were nearly empty, but they were too far away from the library and the classrooms. The shuttle would solve this problem by taking the following route: Beginning at the Lory Student Center, the bus would head west down North Drive (along the residence halls) to the Moby Gym lot and then stop and pick up drivers at both the north and the south ends of the lot. It would then turn south onto Shields at the stoplight and turn east on South Drive, returning to central campus. This system would allow easier access to the core of the campus and, in return, put to full use the 539 parking spaces available in the Moby Gym parking lot. Of course, the shuttle, driver, and maintenance would cost money, so this solution would require a commitment from the university administration.

The most cost-effective solution would be a partial rezoning of the parking lots. This past year, the office of parking management sold 7,461 parking stickers for an available 6,238 spaces, a difference of 1,403. This means that they sold 1,403 more stickers than there are places to park. Not all people need to park at the same time, but enough do to cause a problem. Of the 100 students that we polled, 78 percent said that they would like to see the central campus lots rezoned. In this scheme, students parking their cars for long periods of time would use the outlying lots, and commuting students, faculty, and staff would use the closer lots. For example, if we changed the western section of the outlying "Z" lot to "X" for those students living in the dorms, the parking spaces near the dorms along South Drive could be made available to those who have to drive every day to campus to attend classes. Such rezoning seems to be the easiest and least expensive solution.

One main obstacle to overcoming CSU's parking problem is money. A multilevel parking facility would accommodate more cars per acre of ground space, yet it is the most expensive solution. The shuttle bus system—which could still be implemented—is more economical, but it would require raising additional revenue, most likely by raising the price of parking stickers. We certainly recommend that the university try a shuttle system on an experimental basis to determine the exact costs and to see whether the number of riders justifies the expense. Rezoning the lots, however, is clearly the least complicated and most economical solution. Signs could be changed during the summer months, and new maps and brochures printed in time for the beginning of fall semester. Our group proposes that the university rezone the lots at the end of this academic year and start planning for a shuttle bus and a garage to meet the need in future years. With more careful management of the close-in lots, the new parking stickers might be more than just a hunting license. A person with a permit might actually be able to arrive at a lot at 8:45 and still make that nine o'clock class.

QUESTIONS FOR WRITING AND DISCUSSION

1. After reading the revised version, look again at the questions for the interview and the survey. How would you advise the authors to modify either set of questions? What questions would you add? What questions would you change or delete? Explain.

2. Compare the introduction in the first draft with the introduction in the revised version. Which is more effective? Jot down an idea for a third introduction that the authors might consider.

3. Reread the revised version and *outline* the major parts of the proposal. Then compare that outline with the authors' initial outline, given here:

   I. Introduction

   II. Rezoning proposal

   III. Shuttle bus proposal

   IV. Multilevel garage proposal

   V. Conclusion

   Do you think that their revised plan for organizing the paper was an improvement? Explain.

4. Who is the intended audience for this proposal? What revisions would make this proposal appeal even more strongly to that audience? (During the

planning stages of this essay, the authors decided to send this proposal to Wes Westfall, director of parking management. How do you think Westfall would react to this proposal as it stands?)

STUDENT WRITING

New Regulations and You

Jessica Cook

For her problem-solving essay, Jessica Cook decided to write about current solutions for solving a recent outbreak of mad cow disease. Her purpose was "to persuade cattle ranchers that the new regulations and changes in policy that arose in the wake of the discovery of mad cow disease (BSE) in the U.S. are necessary and can even be beneficial." Her audience was beef producers and ranchers, and she choose Beef *magazine as a target publication. After reviewing current issues of* Beef *magazine, she modeled her essay on the genre features of their articles: a personal voice combined with current research, short paragraphs with headings and bullets, a two-column format, and graphics to illustrate her point. Cook also wrote a Works Cited page, but did not use in-text citation because that was not the format used by* Beef *magazine. As you read her essay, decide how successful she is at arguing for the recommended policies, addressing her target audience, and meeting the genre requirements.*

New Regulations and You

When I was growing up, my mother always told me that I was just one small pebble on a very large beach, meaning that I was just an insignificant part of the world, and as a single person, I couldn't bring about any huge changes.

It may sound demeaning, but the truth is, most people will never change the world.

However, after seeing how much of an impact one dairy cow in Washington can have on American agriculture and world trade, I am beginning to think my mother might have been wrong.

In case you hadn't already guessed, the infamous cow I am referring to is the Holstein that tested positive for mad cow disease, or bovine spongiform encephalopathy (BSE), on December 23, 2003.

According to a special report in *Cattle-Fax*, this discovery caused nearly all of our trading partners to ban the import of U.S. beef, a plunge in beef prices, and a recall of 10,400 pounds of beef associated with the cow. Consumer confidence in beef and bovine-derived products also plummeted. In addition, this cow spawned several new government-issued regulations and changes to procedures.

The New Rules

In two articles in the *New York Times*, Denise Grady and Donald G. McNeil, Jr., the two writers following mad cow disease, discuss the new regulations, including bans on the following:

- Feeding cattle blood to calves as a milk replacer
- Allowing chicken litter—feathers, spilled feed, bedding, and feces—in cattle feed
- Using the same equipment that makes feed containing bone meal for making cattle feed
- Allowing dead or downer cattle to be used for human food or products, including dietary supplements, cosmetics or soups
- Feeding "plate waste" or table scraps to cattle
- Air-injection stunning

Also, carcasses that are tested for BSE must be held until the results are known.

Even more changes are being considered for the future, including testing more cattle, mandatory identification and tracking systems, and banning all animal protein from cattle feed.

What This Means to You

By now, beef producers have realized how these new rules will affect them, and most have already implemented the government-mandated changes.

Although many producers share the opinion that these new regulations just increase the time, effort and money it takes to produce beef, I disagree.

I believe that the new regulations and changes in policy that arose in the wake of the discovery of BSE in the U.S. are necessary and can even be beneficial to the cattle industry.

Although I realize that these changes will be expensive and tedious to implement, I believe that the advantages will outweigh the disadvantages.

These regulations will increase food safety, open opportunities in niche markets, facilitate exportation, and boost consumer confidence and demand.

Because I was raised in a small town by the name of Burns, Wyoming, and grew up in an agricultural community, I know what it takes to produce our nation's food supply. I am familiar with the "blood, sweat and tears" that go hand-in-hand with raising cattle, or any other species of livestock.

The Downside

Anyone who has been around agriculture and cattle knows that the new regulations will be expensive and time consuming to implement, and I acknowledge this.

Many ranchers feel that changing the way things have always been done is pointless; the current methods were passed down from our successful elders, and "if it isn't broke, why fix it?" Another argument against the new rules is that changing the way a ranch operates takes an exorbitant effort.

A group of government officials, many of whom have no idea what goes into raising cattle, have made several new rules that ranchers must follow. As Wes Ishmael phrased it in the February 1, 2004, issue of *Beef* magazine, "How many laws would a lawmaker make if a lawmaker could make laws without pause or cause?"

Despite all of those negative side effects, there are some redeeming features to the new regulations.

Increased Food Safety

Although the beef industry is quick to claim that the beef supply is safe (after all, there has only been one case of mad cow disease out of the nearly 36 million cattle slaughtered per year in the U.S.), there is evidence to the contrary.

Dave Louthan (as recorded by McNeil of the *New York Times*), the man who killed the infected cow at the slaughterhouse in Moses Lake, WA, warns of the danger.

Louthan claims that the infected cow was not a downer when it was killed, which contradicts the official reports from the federal Department of Agriculture, and would thus make the discovery of it just a fluke. Because the guidelines only mandate testing for downer cattle, this could mean BSE-infected cattle are slipping through the testing procedures and into the food chain.

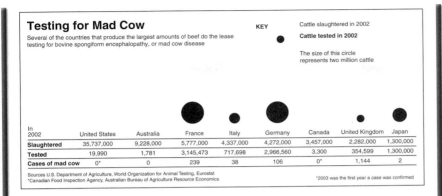

Testing for Mad Cow

Several of the countries that produce the largest amounts of beef do the lease testing for bovine spongiform encephalopathy, or mad cow disease

KEY

Cattle slaughtered in 2002

Cattle tested in 2002

The size of this circle represents two million cattle

In 2002	United States	Australia	France	Italy	Germany	Canada	United Kingdom	Japan
Slaughtered	35,737,000	9,228,000	5,777,000	4,337,000	4,272,000	3,457,000	2,282,000	1,300,000
Tested	19,990	1,781	3,145,473	717,698	2,966,560	3,300	354,599	1,300,000
Cases of mad cow	0*	0	239	38	106	0*	1,144	2

Sources U.S. Department of Agriculture, World Organization for Animal Testing, Eurostat
*Canadian Food Inspection Agency, Australian Bureau of Agriculture Resource Economics

*2003 was the first year a case was confirmed

According to another of McNeil's articles, last year only about 20,000 cattle were tested for BSE, which is only 0.06% of those slaughtered. New testing protocol calls for doubling the number tested, which is an improvement that's worth is easily demonstrated.

Even if only one cow slips by the testing, which is statistically insignificant, I sure don't want to be the person innocently consuming that meat and risking a fatal disease. Do you want to be the rancher responsible for creating another disaster because you didn't implement the changes to move your enterprise into the future?

Louthan also claims that the carcass splitting process is unsafe as well. When the carcass is split the blade cleaves the spinal column while jets of water blast away the fat and bone dust.

The "slurry" containing spinal column matter, a portion of the carcass that can transmit BSE, "runs all over the beef." Obviously, this poses a risk, and if a way to change this process is feasible, it should be implemented.

Niche Market Opportunities

Another potential benefit of the new regulations is the opportunity to move into niche markets. Currently, raising beef is a commodity market, where one rancher's beef is basically the same as the next rancher's.

There have been some recent changes to help ranchers differentiate their products, like the Certified Angus Beef campaign.

In theory, the kind of packaging and label on a product shouldn't play a part in consumer's decisions, yet in reality, it does. In the text book *Scientific Farm Animal Production,* Drs. Taylor and Field, professors at Colorado State University, state that the five main factors used to determine value of meat products are palatability, fat composition, presentation, price, and convenience.

As the producers who can place the sticker that says "Certified Angus Beef" on their packages in the supermarket have found out, making your product just a little different so that it stands out from the crowd can be an effective marketing technique.

Although labeling of products, mandatory identification, and traceability are not yet required, I believe that the implementation of these procedures now —before they are deemed necessary—could benefit a producer in the same way.

According to Dr. Field during a lecture in Introduction to Animal Science, some Japanese producers can already testify to its effectiveness.

One ranch decided to raise all of its beef cattle from birth to slaughter on their family-owned ranch, and advertise their beef in that way. They stated that all of their beef was raised solely on that farm. Consumers liked knowing that they only had to trust one ranch instead of several places and businesses.

Another ranch put a picture of their family on the beef packaging, making it more personal. When the consumers saw the nice, honest-looking family on the package of steak, it made them choose it over the standard package beside it.

When marketing beef, producers must consider opportunities like these in order to move into niche markets and leave the commodity market in the past. Implementing things like identification and traceability before they are required can give producers a jump on the market and a chance to become more profitable.

Exportation

As American agriculturalists, we know the importance of exportation. When BSE was discovered, our export markets were drastically affected.

According to an article from Mexico City on AOLNews, "U.S. beef exports came to a virtual halt after the Dec. 23 announcement that mad cow had been found." This is a major concern; last year alone, the U.S. exported $3.8 billion worth of beef products.

Many of the new regulations were essential in convincing our major trading partners, namely Mexico, Japan and South Korea, into reopening borders.

In a market where we are such a big player, we cannot afford to allow the borders to remain closed for long. Some of the regulations that might seem like they go beyond what is actually necessary for food safety are vital in meeting the requirements of other countries.

Consumer Confidence

Boosting consumer confidence is the most important advantage of the new rules and regulations. In a consumer-driven market, the importance of consumer confidence in the product cannot be overstated.

If confidence sinks, so will demand and prices. However, if we come up with a way to buoy their belief in the product, we can save the market from disaster during the mad cow crisis.

Many of the new regulations serve this purpose. While some of the rules may seem like they are more restricting than absolutely necessary for food safety, if they put the consumer's mind as ease, then they are indispensable.

For example, consider the rule that bans feeding cow blood to calves as a milk replacer. So far, there has been no conclusive evidence that BSE can be transmitted through blood, but once the topic had been brought up and consumers heard about this common practice, measures had to be taken.

Grady writes in the *New York Times*, consumers "imagine bucolic scenes of nursing calves and cows munching on grass."

Realistically, this isn't productive, but we must cater to the more delicate nature of consumers wherever possible to insure that they will buy the product.

According to one of Dr. Field's lectures in my animal science class, when you are producing a product for consumers, you have to produce it in a way that consumers want to buy it, not just in a way that you want to produce it.

An example of this is producing a product in a way that is inexpensive and easy, but yields a poor quality product that won't sell or bring a good price, so you are better off not producing anything at all.

If you produce *for* the consumers, giving them what they want, it will be worth the extra effort and money required.

That is why the new regulations are crucial. They force producers to yield to consumer desires on specific things, increasing the consumer's confidence in the product and therefore the demand for the product.

Why the Government?

Finally, I would like to discuss why it actually makes sense that the government is making these rules, when they really don't know much about cows. From their city dwellings, government officials might not know the exact nutrients that a lactating cow requires, but they have a much more comprehensive understanding of the economics of production.

They have the knowledge of other countries requirements and what is necessary to facilitate exportation. They understand the effects that the rules will have on consumer confidence and demand. Government officials also have scientific information that isn't available to the general public to help them make their decisions.

And the last critical piece to the puzzle is the fact that they don't have a vested interest. They can attempt to satisfy all groups without favoring any.

The Decision

It's incredible to think that all of these issues stemmed from one cow, one incidence of a disease. However, now that it has occurred, we must accept and flow with the changes if we hope to be productive in the future.

The government's regulations have already been passed and ranchers are forced to comply. Although the changes will be expensive and a pain-in-the-round to implement they do have benefits.

It is up to each rancher to decide if they will plant their feet in resistance, hoping to hold on to the ways of the past, or embrace the changes and the increased food safety, niche market opportunities, export markets, and boosted consumer confidence that they will bring. If ranchers choose the latter, they will have the opportunity to profit and grow with the future of beef and make their product stand out from the rest of the herd.

Before you make your decision about how to react to these new regulations, consider all of the benefits. I'm sure they will tip the scale in favor of being proactive and optimistic.

Works Cited

Field, Thomas G., and Robert E. Taylor. *Scientific Farm Animal Production.* Ed. Debbie Yarnell. 8th ed. Upper Saddle River, NJ: Pearson, 2003.

Grady, Denise. "Mad Cow Quandary: Making Animal Feed." *New York Times* 6 Feb. 2004: A20.

Grady, Denise, and Donald G. McNeil, Jr. "Rules Issued on Animal Feed and Use of Disabled Cattle." *New York Times* 27 Jan. 2004: A12.

Ismael, Wes. "Raining Regulations." *Beef.* Feb. 2004. 3 Mar. 2004 <*http://beef-mag .com/ar/beef_raining_regulations/index.htm*>.

McNeil, Donald G, Jr. "Doubling Tests for Mad Cow Doesn't Quiet Program Critics." *New York Times* 9 Feb. 2004: A8.

McNeil, Donald G, Jr. "Man Who Killed the Mad Cow Has Questions of His Own." *New York Times* 3 Feb. 2004: D2.

"Mexico to Ban U. S. Beef Until Mad Cow Controlled." *Reuters.* 10 Feb. 2004. 10 Feb 2004 <*http:aolsvc.news.aol.com/news/*>.

"Time for Perspective." *Cattle-Fax.* 36 (2004): 1.

QUESTIONS FOR WRITING AND DISCUSSION

1. In her essay, Cook takes a slightly different approach to her problem-solving essay. Instead of trying to prove that a problem exists, she assumes that her readers are aware of the problem and argues for accepting a solution already in place. List the reasons she gives in arguing that the advantages of this policy outweigh the disadvantages. What evidence or support does she provide for each reason? Will the readers of *Beef* magazine find her reasons and evidence persuasive? Why or why not?

2. In addressing her target audience, Cook uses a personal voice and an appeal to character (*ethos*). Voice is the personality of the writer as revealed through her language and personal experience. The appeal to character or *ethos* (see Chapter 10, p. 480) is based on the writer's character as honest, fair-minded, ethical, and knowledgeable about the key issues. Find examples in which Cook uses a personal voice and makes appeals based on her character. For each example, evaluate the effectiveness of her appeal. Overall, does her personal approach make her argument more effective or less effective for her target audience? Explain.

3. In the library, find a copy of *Beef* magazine and read one or two sample articles. What are the key genre features of articles that appear in this magazine? Pay attention to audience, reference to sources, voice, style, article length, use of pictures and graphics, organization and use of headings, and paragraph length. Then find examples where Cook successfully models these genre features. Are there genre features that Cook does not imitate? Explain why you believe that Cook has or has not effectively modeled the genre features of her target publication.

4. For your own problem-solving essay, choose a target magazine or newspaper where you might publish your essay. Analyze the genre features of articles that appear in that publication. Write out your own plan for revising your essay to meet the requirements of that publication. Specifically, list and explain the genre features that you would include in your essay.

For twelve swelteringly hot days in July 1925, the famous Scopes "Monkey Trial" in Dayton, Tennessee, tested a state law banning the teaching of evolution. The original debate between Clarence Darrow and William Jennings Bryan is recreated in this film version of the play *Inherit the Wind*. Written arguments sometimes recreate the pro–con debate style of a trial, but frequently, they represent multiple points of view, just as parents, teachers, administrators, and students might gather to recommend policy changes at a school or citizens get together to solve problems in the community. This chapter encourages you to imagine multiple images for written argument as you adapt to different audiences, genres, and social contexts.

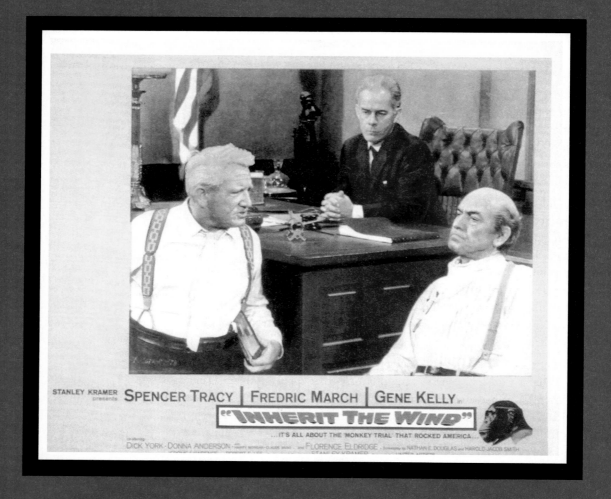

Jerome Lawrence and Robert E. Lee
Inherit the Wind (1960)
Stanley Kramer, Director

10 Arguing

As a recent high school graduate, you decide to write about the increasing number of standardized tests currently required of primary and secondary school students. The question you want to investigate is whether schools are teaching students important skills and making them better members of society or whether schools are just teaching them how to do well on tests. After reading current articles on standardized tests and interviewing your classmates, you decide to write to politicians who are in favor of standardized tests and argue that, while the tests should not be thrown out, they should be changed in order to solve several serious problems they have created for students, teachers, and parents.

After being cited for not wearing a seat belt while operating a motor vehicle, you decide that your rights have been violated. In order to write a convincing argument to your representative that seat belt laws are unfair, you research current articles about the law and interview a law professor on the issue. You decide to claim that the seat belt laws should be repealed because they are a fundamental violation of individual liberty. You believe that the opposing argument—that seat belts save lives and reduce insurance rates for everyone—is not relevant to the issue of individual liberty. Because your representative has supported seat belt laws, you present both sides of the issue but stress the arguments supporting your viewpoint.

> *"Give me liberty to know, to utter, and to argue freely according to conscience, above all liberties."*
> —JOHN MILTON, POET

> *"Freedom of speech is established to achieve its essential purpose only when different opinions are expounded in the same hall to the same audience. . . . The opposition is indispensable."*
> —WALTER LIPPMANN, JOURNALIST

W HEN PEOPLE ARGUE WITH EACH OTHER, THEY OFTEN BECOME HIGHLY EMOTIONAL OR CONFRONTATIONAL. REMEMBER THE LAST HEATED AR-GUMENT YOU HAD WITH A FRIEND OR FAMILY MEMBER: AT THE END OF the argument, one person stomped out of the room, slammed the door, and didn't speak to the other for days. In the aftermath of such a scene, you felt angry at the other person and angry at yourself. Nothing was accomplished. Neither of you came close to achieving what you wanted when you began the argument. Rather than understanding each other's point of view and working out your differences, you effectively closed the lines of communication.

When writers construct arguments, however, they try to avoid the emotional outbursts that often turn arguments into displays of temper. Strong feelings may energize an argument—few of us make the effort to argue without emotional investment in the subject—but written argument stresses a fair presentation of opposing or alternative arguments. Because written arguments are public, they take on a civilized manner. They implicitly say, "Let's be reasonable about this. Let's look at the evidence on all sides. Before we argue for our position, let's put all the reasons and evidence on the table so everyone involved can see what's at stake."

As writers construct written arguments, they carefully consider the rhetorical situation:

- What is the social or cultural context for this issue?
- Where might this written argument appear or be published?
- Who is the audience, and what do they already know or believe?
- Do readers hold an opposing or alternative viewpoint, or are they more neutral and likely to listen to both sides before deciding what to believe?

A written argument creates an atmosphere of reason, which encourages readers to examine their own views clearly and dispassionately. When successful, such argument convinces rather than alienates an audience. It changes people's minds or persuades them to adopt a recommended course of action.

> *All writing . . .*
> *is propaganda for*
> *something.*
> —ELIZABETH DREW,
> WRITER AND CRITIC

Techniques for Writing: Argument

A written argument is similar to a public debate—between attorneys in a court of law or between members of Congress who represent different political parties. It begins with a debatable issue: Is this a good bill? Should we vote for it? In such debates, one person argues for a position or proposal, while the other argues against it. The onlookers (the judge, the members of Congress, the jury, or the public) then decide what to believe or what to do. The chapter opening art, which shows a scene from *Inherit the Wind*, pictures the debate about evolution between Clarence Darrow and William Jennings Bryan during the 1925 Scopes trial. The judge in the picture makes sure the trial follows certain rules, and the audience (not in the picture) decides what or whom to believe.

Written argument, however, is not identical to a debate. *In a written argument, the writer must play all the different roles.* The writer is first of all the person arguing for the claim. But the writer must also represent what the opposition might say. In addition, the writer must think like the judge and make sure the argument follows appropriate rules. Perhaps certain arguments and evidence are inadmissible or inappropriate in this case. Finally, the writer often anticipates the responses of the audience and responds to them as well.

Written argument, then, represents several different points of view, responds to them reasonably and fairly, and gives reasons and evidence that support the writer's claim. An effective written argument uses the following techniques:

- **Analyzing the *rhetorical situation*.** Reviewing your purpose, audience, occasion, genre, and cultural context helps you understand how to write your essay. Pay particular attention to your *audience*. Knowing what your audience already knows and believes helps you convince or persuade them.
- **Focusing on a *debatable* proposition or claim.** This claim becomes your thesis.
- **Representing and evaluating the *opposing points of view* on the issue fairly and accurately.** The key to a successful arguing paper is anticipating and responding to the most important opposing positions.
- **Arguing reasonably *against opposing arguments* and *for your claim*.** State and refute opposing arguments. Present the best arguments supporting your claim. Argue reasonably and fairly.
- **Supporting your claims with *sufficient* evidence.** Use firsthand observations; examples from personal experience; statistics, facts, and quotations from your reading; and results of surveys and interviews.

In an article entitled "Active and Passive Euthanasia," James Rachels claims that active euthanasia may be defensible for patients with incurable and painful diseases. The following paragraphs from that article illustrate the key features of argument:

The distinction between active and passive euthanasia is thought to be crucial for medical ethics. The idea is that it is permissible, at least in some

Opposing position

Claim

Audience

Argument for claim

Example

cases, to withhold treatment and allow a patient to die, but it is never permissible to take any direct action designed to kill the patient. This doctrine seems to be accepted by most doctors. . . .

However, a strong case can be made against this doctrine. In what follows I will set out some of the relevant arguments, and urge doctors to reconsider their views on this matter.

To begin with a familiar type of situation, a patient who is dying of incurable cancer of the throat is in terrible pain, which can no longer be satisfactorily alleviated. He is certain to die within a few days, even if present treatment is continued, but he does not want to go on living for those days, since the pain is unbearable. So he asks the doctor for an end to it, and his family joins in the request.

Example

Argument against opposition

Suppose the doctor agrees to withhold treatment, as the conventional doctrine says he may. The justification for his doing so is that the patient is in terrible agony, and since he is going to die anyway, it would be wrong to prolong his suffering needlessly. But now notice this. If one simply withholds treatment, it may take the patient longer to die, and so he may suffer more than he would if more direct action were taken and a lethal injection given. This fact provides strong reason for thinking that, once the initial decision not to prolong his agony has been made, active euthanasia is actually preferable to passive euthanasia, rather than the reverse. To say otherwise is to endorse the option that leads to more suffering rather than less, and is contrary to the humanitarian impulse that prompts the decision not to prolong his life in the first place.

CLAIMS FOR WRITTEN ARGUMENT

The thesis of your argument is a *debatable claim*. Opinions on both sides of the issue must have some merit. Claims for a written argument usually fall into one of four categories: claims of fact, claims about cause and effect, claims about value, and claims about solutions and policies. A claim may occasionally fall into several categories or may even overlap categories.

CLAIMS OF FACT OR DEFINITION   These claims are about facts that are not easily determined or about definitions that are debatable. If I claim that a Lhasa apso was an ancient Chinese ruler, you can check a dictionary and find out that I am wrong. A Lhasa apso is, in fact, a small Tibetan dog. There is no argument. But people do disagree about some supposed "facts": Are polygraph tests accurate? Do grades measure achievement? People also disagree about definitions: Gender discrimination exists in the marketplace, but is it "serious"? What is discrimination, anyway? And what constitutes "serious" discrimination? Does the fact that women currently earn only seventy-three cents for every dollar that men earn qualify as serious discrimination?

In an excerpt from a *Newsweek* column entitled "A Case of Severe Bias," Patricia Raybon makes claims of both fact and definition when she argues that the news media's portrayal of black America is inaccurate, biased, and stereotyped:

> This is who I am not. I am not a crack addict. I am not a welfare mother. I am not illiterate. I am not a prostitute. I have never been in jail. My children are not in gangs. My husband doesn't beat me. My home is not a tenement. None of these things defines who I am, nor do they describe the other black people I've known and worked with and loved and befriended over these 40 years of my life.
>
> Nor does it describe most of black America, period.
>
> Yet in the eyes of the American news media, this is what black America is: poor, criminal, addicted and dysfunctional. Indeed, media coverage of black America is so one-sided, so imbalanced that the most victimized and hurting segment of the black community—a small segment, at best— is presented not as the exception but as the norm. It is an insidious practice, all the uglier for its blatancy.
>
> In recent months, oftentimes in this very magazine, I have observed a steady offering of media reports on crack babies, gang warfare, violent youth, poverty and homelessness—and in most cases, the people featured in the photos and stories were black. At the same time, articles that discuss other aspects of American life—from home buying to medicine to technology to nutrition—rarely, if ever, show blacks playing a positive role, or for that matter, any role at all.
>
> Day after day, week after week, this message—that black America is dysfunctional and unwhole—gets transmitted across the American landscape. Sadly, as a result, America never learns the truth about what is actually a wonderful, vibrant, creative community of people.

CLAIMS ABOUT CAUSE AND EFFECT

- Testing in the schools improves the quality of education.
- Secondhand smoke causes lung cancer.
- Capital punishment does not deter violent crime.

Unlike the claim that grades affect admission to college—which few people would deny—the above claims about cause and effect are debatable. Most states require tests in order to evaluate individual schools. But do these tests ultimately improve students' education, or do they just make students better test-takers? The claim that secondhand smoke causes cancer is behind the rush to make all public and commercial spaces smoke-free. But what scientific evidence demonstrates a cause-and-effect link? Finally, the deterring effect of capital punishment is still an arguable proposition with reasonable arguments on both sides.

In a selection from her book *The Plug-In Drug: Television, Children, and the Family,* Marie Winn argues that television has a negative effect on family life. In her opening paragraphs, she sets forth both sides of the controversy and then argues that the overall effect is negative:

> Television's contribution to family life has been an equivocal one. For while it has, indeed, kept the members of the family from dispersing, it has not served to bring them *together*. By its domination of the time families spend together, it destroys the special quality that depends to a great extent on what a family does, what special rituals, games, recurrent jokes, familiar songs, and shared activities it accumulates.
>
> "Like the sorcerer of old," writes Urie Bronfenbrenner, "the television set casts its magic spell, freezing speech and action, turning the living into silent statues so long as the enchantment lasts. The primary danger of the television screen lies not so much in the behavior it produces—although there is danger there—as in the behavior it prevents: the talks, the games, the family festivities and arguments through which much of the child's learning takes place and through which his character is formed. Turning on the television set can turn off the process that transforms children into people."
>
> Yet parents have accepted a television-dominated family life so completely that they cannot see how the medium is involved in whatever problems they might be having.

CLAIMS ABOUT VALUE

- Boxing is a dehumanizing sport.
- Internet pornography degrades children's sense of human dignity.
- Toni Morrison is a great American novelist.

Claims about value typically lead to evaluative essays. All the strategies discussed in Chapter 8 apply here, with the additional requirement that you must anticipate and respond to alternate or opposing arguments. The essay that claims that boxing is dehumanizing must respond to the argument that boxing is merely another form of competition that promotes athletic excellence. The claim that pornography degrades children's sense of dignity must respond to the claim that restricting free speech on the Internet would cause greater harm. Arguing that Morrison is a great American novelist requires setting criteria for great American novels and then responding to critics who argue that Morrison's work does not reach those standards.

In "College Is a Waste of Time and Money," teacher and journalist Caroline Bird argues that many students go to college simply because it is the "thing to do." For those students, Bird claims, college is not a good idea:

> Nowadays, says one sociologist, you don't have to have a reason for going to college; it's an institution. His definition of an institution is an arrangement everyone accepts without question; the burden of proof is not on why you go, but why anyone thinks there might be a reason for not going. The implication is that an 18-year-old . . . should listen to those who know best and go to college.
>
> I don't agree. I believe that college has to be judged not on what other people think is good for students, but on how good it feels to the students themselves.
>
> I believe that people have an inside view of what's good for them. If a child doesn't want to go to school some morning, better let him stay at home, at least until you find out why. Maybe he knows something you don't. It's the same with college. If high-school graduates don't want to go, or if they don't want to go right away, they may perceive more clearly than their elders that college is not for them. It is no longer obvious that adolescents are best off studying a core curriculum that was constructed when all educated men could agree on what made them educated, or that professors, advisors, or parents can be of any particular help to young people in choosing a major or a career. High-school graduates see college graduates driving cabs and decide it's not worth going. College students find no intellectual stimulation in their studies and drop out.

CLAIMS ABOUT SOLUTIONS OR POLICIES

- Pornography on the Internet should be censored.
- The penalty for drunk driving should be a mandatory jail sentence and loss of driver's license.
- To reduce exploitation and sensationalism, the news media should not be allowed to interview victims of crime or disaster.

Claims about solutions or policies sometimes occur *along with* claims of fact or definition, cause and effect, or value. Because grades do not measure achievement (argue that this is a fact), they should be abolished (argue for this policy). Boxing is a dehumanizing sport (argue this claim of value); therefore, boxing should be banned (argue for this solution). Claims about solutions or policies involve all the strategies used for problem solving (see Chapter 9), but with special emphasis on countering opposing arguments: "Although advocates of freedom of speech suggest that we cannot suppress pornography on the Internet, in fact, we already have self-monitoring devices in other media that could help reduce pornography on the Internet."

In *When Society Becomes an Addict,* psychotherapist Anne Wilson Schaef argues that our society has become an "Addictive System" that has many characteristics in common with alcoholism and other addictions. Advertising becomes addictive, causing us to behave dishonestly; the social pressure to be "nice" can become addictive, causing us to lie to ourselves. Schaef argues that the solution for our social addictions begins when we face the reality of our dependency:

> We cannot recover from an addiction unless we first admit that we have it. Naming our reality is essential to recovery. Unless we admit that we are indeed functioning in an addictive process in an Addictive System, we shall never have the option of recovery. Once we name something, we own it. . . . Remember, to name the system as addict is not to condemn it: it is to offer it the possibility of recovery.
>
> Paradoxically, the only way to reclaim our personal power is by admitting our powerlessness. The first part of Step One of the AA [Alcoholics Anonymous] Twelve-Step Program reads, "We admitted we were powerless over alcohol." It is important to recognize that admitting to powerlessness over an addiction is not the same as admitting powerlessness as a person. In fact, it can be very powerful to recognize the futility of the illusion of control.

APPEALS FOR WRITTEN ARGUMENT

"Mere knowledge of the truth will not give you the art of persuasion."
—PLATO,
PHAEDRUS

To support claims and respond to opposing arguments, writers use *appeals* to the audience. Argument uses three important types of appeals: to *reason* (logic and evidence support the claim), to *character* (the writer's good character itself supports the claim), and to *emotion* (the writer's expression of feelings about the issue may support the claim). Effective arguments emphasize the appeal to reason but may also appeal to character or emotion.

APPEAL TO REASON   An appeal to reason depends most frequently on *inductive logic,* which is sometimes called the *scientific method.* Inductive logic draws a general conclusion from personal observation or experience, specific facts, reports, statistics, testimony of authorities, and other bits of data.

Experience is the best teacher, we always say, and experience teaches inductively. Suppose, using biologist Thomas Huxley's famous example, you pick a green apple from a tree and take a bite. Halfway through the bite you discover that the apple is sour and quickly spit it out. But, you think, perhaps the next green apple will be ripe and will taste better. You pick a second green apple, take a bite, and realize that it is just as sour as the first. However, you know that some apples—like the Granny Smith—look green even when they're ripe, so you take a bite out of a third apple. It is also sour. You're beginning to draw a conclusion. In fact, if you taste a fourth or fifth apple, other people may begin to question your intelligence. How many green apples from this tree must you taste before you get the idea that all of these green apples are sour?

Experience, however, may lead to wrong conclusions. You've tasted enough of these apples to convince *you* that all these apples are sour, but will others think that these apples are sour? Perhaps you have funny taste buds. You may need to ask several friends to taste the apples. Or perhaps you are dealing with a slightly weird tree—in fact, some apple trees are hybrids, with several different kinds of apples grafted onto one tree. Before you draw a conclusion, you may need to consult an expert in order to be certain that your tree is a standard, single-variety apple tree. If your friends and the expert also agree that all of these green apples are sour, you may use your experience *and* their testimony to reach a conclusion—and to provide evidence to make your argument more convincing to others.

In inductive logic, a reasonable conclusion is based on a *sufficient* quantity of accurate and reliable evidence that is selected in a *random* manner to reduce human bias or to take into account variation in the sample. The definition of *sufficient* varies, but generally the number must be large enough to convince your audience that your sample fairly represents the whole subject.

Let's take an example to illustrate inductive reasoning. Suppose you ask a student, one of fifty in a Psychology I class, a question of value: "Is Professor X a good teacher?" If this student says, "Professor X is the worst teacher I've ever had!" what conclusion can you draw? If you avoid taking the class based on a sample of one, you may miss an excellent class. So you decide to gather a *sufficient sample* by polling twenty of the fifty students in the class. But which twenty do you interview? If you ask the first student for a list of students, you may receive the names of twenty other students who also hate the professor. To reduce human or accidental bias, then, you choose a random method for collecting your evidence: As the students leave the class, you give a questionnaire to two out of every five students. If they all fill out the questionnaires, you probably have a *sufficient* and *random* sample.

Finally, if the responses to your questionnaire show that fifteen out of twenty students rate Professor X as an excellent teacher, what *valid conclusion* should you draw? You should not say, categorically, "X is an excellent teacher." Your conclusion must be restricted by your evidence and the method of gathering it: "Seventy-five percent of the students polled in Psychology I believe that Professor X is an excellent teacher."

Most arguments use a shorthand version of the inductive method of reasoning. A writer makes a claim and then supports it with *reasons* and representative *examples* or *data:*

Claim: Professor X is an excellent psychology teacher.

Reason #1: Professor X is an excellent teacher because she gives stimulating lectures that students rarely miss.

Evidence: Sixty percent of the students polled said that they rarely missed a lecture. Three students cited Professor X's lecture on "assertiveness" as the best lecture they'd ever heard.

Reason #2: Professor X is an excellent teacher because she gives tests that encourage learning rather than sheer memorization.

Evidence: Seventy percent of the students polled said that Professor X's essay tests required thinking and learning rather than memorization. One student said that Professor X's tests always made her think about what she'd read. Another student said he always liked to discuss Professor X's test questions with his classmates and friends.

APPEAL TO CHARACTER   An appeal based on your good character as a writer can also be important in argument. (The appeal to character is frequently called the *ethical appeal* because readers make a value judgment about the writer's character.) In a written argument, you show your audience—through your reasonable persona, voice, and tone—that you are a person who abides by moral standards that your audience shares: You have a good reputation, you are honest and trustworthy, and you argue "fairly."

A person's reputation often affects how we react to a claim, but *the argument itself* should also establish the writer's trustworthiness. You don't have to be a Mahatma Gandhi or a Mother Teresa to generate a strong ethical appeal for your claim. Even if your readers have never heard your name before, they will feel confident about your character if you are knowledgeable about your subject, present the pros and cons fairly, and support your own claim with sufficient, reliable evidence.

If your readers have reason to suspect your motives or think that you may have something personal to gain from your argument, you may need to bend over backward to be fair. If you do have something to gain, lay your cards on the table. Declare your vested interest but explain, for example, how your solution would benefit everyone equally. Similarly, don't try to cover up or distort the opponents' arguments; acknowledge the opposition's strong arguments and refute the weak ones.

At the most basic level, your interest in the topic and willingness to work hard can improve your ethical appeal. Readers can sense when a writer cares about his or her subject, when a writer knows something about the topic, about the rhetorical or cultural context, and about the various viewpoints on a topic. Show your readers that you care about the subject, and they will find your arguments more convincing:

- Show you care by using sufficient details and specific, vivid examples.
- Show you care by including any relevant personal experience you have on the topic.
- Show you care by including other people's ideas and points of view and by responding to their views with fairness and tact.
- Show you care by organizing your essay so your main points are easy to find and transitions between ideas are clear and logical.
- Show you care by revising and proofreading your essay.

Readers know when writers care about their subjects, and they are more willing to listen to new ideas when the writer has worked hard and is personally invested in the topic.

APPEAL TO EMOTION   Appeals to emotion can be tricky because, as we have seen, when emotions come in through the door, reasonableness may fly out the window. Argument emphasizes reason, not emotion. We know, for example, how advertising plays on emotions, by means of loaded or exaggerated language or through images of famous or sexy people. Emotional appeals designed to *deceive* or *frighten* people or to *misrepresent* the virtues of a person, place, or object have no place in rational argument. But emotional appeals that illustrate a truth or movingly depict a reality are legitimate and effective means of convincing readers.

COMBINED APPEALS   Appeals may be used in combination. Writers may appeal to reason and, at the same time, establish trustworthy characters and use legitimate emotional appeals. The following excerpt from Martin Luther King, Jr.'s "Letter from Birmingham Jail" illustrates all three appeals. He appeals to reason, arguing that, historically, civil rights reforms are rarely made without political pressure. He establishes his integrity and good character by treating the opposition (in this case, the Birmingham clergy) with respect and by showing moderation and restraint. Finally, he uses emotional appeals, describing his six-year-old daughter in tears and recalling his own humiliation at being refused a place to sleep. King uses these emotional appeals legitimately; he is not misrepresenting reality or trying to deceive his readers.

Appeal to character and appeal to reason

Appeal to reason

Evidence

One of the basic points in [the statement by the Birmingham clergy] is that the action that I and my associates have taken in Birmingham is untimely. Some have asked: "Why didn't you give the new city administration time to act?" The only answer that I can give to this query is that the new Birmingham administration must be prodded about as much as the outgoing one, before it will act. We are sadly mistaken if we feel that the election of Albert Boutwell as mayor will bring the millennium to Birmingham. While Mr. Boutwell is a much more gentle person than Mr. Connor, they are both segregationists, dedicated to the maintenance of the status quo. I have hoped that Mr. Boutwell will be reasonable enough to see the futility of massive resistance to desegregation. But he will not see this without pressure from devotees of civil rights. My friends, I must say to you that we have not made a single gain in civil rights without determined legal and nonviolent pressure. Lamentably, it is an historical fact that privileged groups seldom give up their privileges voluntarily. Individuals may see the moral light and voluntarily give up their unjust posture; but, as Reinhold Niebuhr has reminded us, groups tend to be more immoral than individuals.

Appeal to character and reason

We know through painful experience that freedom is never voluntarily given by the oppressor; it must be demanded by the oppressed. Frankly, I have yet to engage in a direct-action campaign that was "well timed" in the view of those who have not suffered unduly from the disease of segregation. For years now I have heard the word "Wait!" It rings in the ear of every Negro with piercing familiarity. This "Wait" has almost always meant "Never." We must come to see, with one of our distinguished jurists, that "justice too long delayed is justice denied."

Appeal to emotion

Evidence

We have waited for more than 340 years for our constitutional and God-given rights. . . . Perhaps it is easy for those who have never felt the stinging darts of segregation to say, "Wait." But when you have seen vicious mobs lynch your mothers and fathers at will and drown your sisters and brothers at whim; when you have seen hate-filled policemen curse, kick, and even kill your black brothers and sisters; when you see the vast majority of your twenty million Negro brothers smothering in an airtight cage of poverty in the midst of an affluent society; when you suddenly find your tongue twisted and your speech stammering as you seek to explain to your six-year-old daughter why she can't go to the public amusement park that has just been advertised on television, and see tears welling up in her eyes when she is told that Funtown is closed to colored children. . .when you take a cross-country drive and find it necessary to sleep night after night in the uncomfortable corners of your automobile because no motel will accept you; when you are humiliated day in and day out by nagging signs reading "white" and "colored"; when your first name becomes "nigger," your middle name becomes "boy" (however old you are) and your last name becomes "John". . .—then you will understand why we find it difficult to wait. There comes a time when the cup of endurance runs over, and men are no longer willing to be plunged into the abyss of despair. I hope, sirs, you can understand our legitimate and unavoidable impatience.

Appeal to emotion

Evidence

Appeal to emotion

Evidence

Appeal to character

ROGERIAN ARGUMENT

Traditional argument assumes that people are most readily convinced or persuaded by a confrontational "debate" on the issue. In a traditional argument, the writer argues reasonably and fairly, but the argument becomes a kind of struggle or "war" as the writer attempts to "defeat" the arguments of the opposition. The purpose of a traditional argument is thus to convince an undecided audience that the writer has "won a fight" and emerged "victorious" over the opposition.

In fact, however, there are many situations in which a less confrontational and less adversarial approach to argument is more effective. Particularly when the issues are highly charged or when the audience that we are trying to persuade is the opposition, writers may more effectively use negotiation rather than confrontation. *Rogerian argument*—named after psychologist Carl Rogers—is a kind of negotiated argument where understanding and compromise replace the traditional, adversarial approach. Rogerian, or *nonthreatening,* argument opens the lines of communication by reducing conflict. When people's beliefs are attacked, they instinctively become defensive and strike back. As a result, the argument becomes polarized: The writer argues for a claim, the reader digs in to defend his or her position, and no one budges.

Crucial to Rogerian argument is the fact that convictions and beliefs are not abstract but reside in people. If people are to agree, they must be sensitive to each other's beliefs. Rogerian argument, therefore, contains a clear appeal to character. While Rogerian argument uses reason and logic, its primary goal is not to "win" the argument but to open the lines of communication. To do that, the writer must be sympathetic to different points of view and willing to modify his or her claims in response to people who hold different viewpoints. Once the reader sees that the writer is open to change, the reader may become more flexible.

Once both sides are more flexible, a compromise position or solution becomes possible. As Rogers says, "This procedure gradually achieves a mutual communication. Mutual communication tends to be pointed toward solving a problem rather than toward attacking a person or group." Rogerian argument, then, imitates not a courtroom debate but the mutual communication that may take place between two people. Whereas traditional argument intends to change the actions or the beliefs of the opposition, Rogerian argument works toward changes *in both sides* as a means of establishing common ground and reaching a solution.

If you choose Rogerian argument, remember that you must actually be willing to change your beliefs. Often, in fact, when you need to use Rogerian argument most, you may be least inclined to use it—simply because you are inflexible on an issue. If you are unwilling to modify your own position, your reader will probably sense your basic insincerity and realize that you are just playing a trick of rhetoric.

Rogerian argument is appropriate in a variety of sensitive or highly controversial situations. You may want to choose Rogerian argument if you are an employer requesting union members to accept a pay cut in order to help the company avoid bankruptcy. Similarly, if you argue to husbands that they should assume responsibility for half the housework, or if you argue to Anglo-Americans that Spanish language and culture should play a larger role in public education, you may want to use a Rogerian strategy. By showing that you empathize with the opposition's position and are willing to compromise, you create a climate for mutual communication.

Rogerian argument makes a claim, considers the opposition, and presents evidence to support your claim, but in addition, it avoids threatening or adversarial language and promotes mutual communication and learning. A Rogerian argument uses the following strategies:

- **Avoiding** *a confrontational stance.* Confrontation threatens your audience and increases their defensiveness. Threat hinders communication.
- **Presenting** your *character* as someone who understands and can empathize with the opposition. Show that you understand by restating the opposing position accurately.
- **Establishing** *common ground* with the opposition. Indicate the beliefs and values that you share.
- **Being willing** *to change your views.* Show where your position is not reasonable and could be modified.
- **Directing your argument** toward *a compromise or workable solution.*

Note: An argument does not have to be either entirely adversarial or entirely Rogerian. You may use Rogerian techniques for the most sensitive points in an argument that is otherwise traditional or confrontational.

In his essay "Animal Rights Versus Human Health," biology professor Albert Rosenfeld illustrates several features of Rogerian argument. Rosenfeld argues that animals should be used for medical experiments, but he is aware that the issues are emotional and that his audience is likely to be antagonistic. In these paragraphs, Rosenfeld avoids threatening language, represents the opposition fairly, grants that he is guilty of *speciesism,* and says that he sympathizes with the demand to look for alternatives. He indicates that his position is flexible: Most researchers, he says, are delighted when they can use alternatives. He grants that there is some room for compromise, but he is firm in his position that some animal experimentation is necessary for advancements in medicine.

It is fair to say that millions of animals—probably more rats and mice than any other species—are subjected to experiments that cause them pain, discomfort, and distress, sometimes lots of it over long periods of time.... All new forms of medication or surgery are tried out on animals first. Every new substance that is released into the environment, or put on the market, is tested on animals....

States opposing position fairly and sympathetically

In 1975, Australian philosopher Peter Singer wrote his influential book called *Animal Liberation,* in which he accuses us all of "speciesism"—as reprehensible, to him, as racism or sexism. He freely describes the "pain and suffering" inflicted in the "tyranny of human over nonhuman animals" and sharply challenges our biblical license to exercise "dominion over the fish of the sea, and over the fowl of the air, and over every living thing that moveth upon the Earth."

States opposing position fairly

Well, certainly we are guilty of speciesism. We do act as if we had dominion over other living creatures. But domination also entails some custodial responsibility. And the questions continue to be raised: Do we have the right to abuse animals? To eat them? To hunt them for sport? To keep them imprisoned in zoos—or, for that matter, in our households? Especially to do experiments on these creatures who can't fight back?

Acknowledges common ground

Sympathetic to opposing position

Hardly any advance in either human or veterinary medicine—cure, vaccine, operation, drug, therapy—has come about without experiments on animals.... I certainly sympathize with the demand that we look for ways to get the information we want without using animals. Most investigators are delighted when they can get their data by means of tissue cultures or computer simulations. But as we look for alternative ways to get information, do we meanwhile just do without?

Suggests compromise position

THE TOULMIN METHOD OF ARGUMENT

In *The Uses of Argument* (1958), British philosopher Stephen Toulmin argued against applying formal logic and the concepts of deduction and induction to written arguments. Instead, he suggested, the laws of logic are not universal but depend upon the knowledge of each specific field. Thus, the rules for argument vary from economics to philosophy or from political science to biology. What counts as evidence and a good argument is not the same in human nutrition as it is in literature. The following six concepts that Toulmin identified are not universal rules but merely guidelines that can be helpful as we analyze the logic of an argument:

- **Data:** The evidence gathered to support a particular claim.
- **Claim:** The overall thesis the writer hopes to prove. This thesis may be a claim of fact or definition, of cause and effect, of value, or of policy.
- **Warrant:** The statement that explains why or how the data support the writer's claim.
- **Backing:** The additional logic or reasoning that, when necessary, supports the warrant.
- **Qualifier:** The short phrases that limit the scope of the claim, such as "typically," "usually," or "on the whole."
- **Exceptions:** Those particular situations in which the writer does not or would not insist on the claim.

We can illustrate each of these six concepts using Cathleen A. Cleaver's argument against Internet pornography in her essay, "The Internet: A Clear and Present Danger?" that appears later in this chapter. The relationship of the data, warrant, and claim may be illustrated in the following diagram:

Data: Pornographic images on the Internet bombard children with images that dehumanize women and degrade human dignity.

Claim: [Therefore] the government should regulate Internet pornography.

Warrant: [Since] government regulation is an effective way to reduce children's exposure to pornographic images.

Backing: Government regulation already exists in print, radio, and television media, so it should be extended to the Internet.

Qualifier: *In most cases,* the government should regulate pornography on the Internet. (Cleaver does not actually use a qualifier for her claim. This is a qualifier she might use.)

Exceptions: Government regulations must protect children, but *where children are not involved, regulation may not be as urgent.* (Cleaver implies this exception, since she focuses her argument only on pornography's effect on children.)

Applying the Toulmin model of argument to written texts can help us as readers and writers if we follow a few guidelines. First, the Toulmin model is especially helpful as we critically read texts for their logical strengths and weaknesses. As we become better critical readers, we are likely to make our own arguments more logical and thus more persuasive. Second, as we critically read texts, not all of us find the same warrant statements, because there can be several ways of explaining a logical connection between the data and the stated claim. Third, applying the Toulmin model and using warrants, backing, qualifiers, and exceptions becomes more important when our readers are likely to disagree with the claim. Just as Rogerian argument tries to reduce conflict in adversarial situations through mutual communication and a strong appeal to character, the Toulmin model helps communicate in adversarial contexts by being especially reasonable and logical. If our readers already agree that pornography on the Internet is a bad thing, we need to give only a few examples and go straight to our claim. But if readers are members of the ACLU or have a strong belief in free speech on the Internet, we need to qualify our claim and make our warrants—the connections between the data and the claim—as explicit and logical as possible. We may also need to state backing for the warrant and note the exceptions where we don't want to press our case. The more antagonistic our readers are, the more we need to be as logical as possible. The Toulmin model is just one approach that can help bolster the logic of our argument.

WARMING UP: JOURNAL EXERCISES

The following exercises will help you practice arguing. Read all of the following exercises and then write on the three that interest you most. If another idea occurs to you, write about it.

1. From the following list of "should" statements, choose one that relates to your experience and freewrite for ten minutes. When you finish your freewriting, state a claim and list arguments on both sides of the issue.

ANALYZING STATISTICS

Whether you are evaluating statistical sources in an essay that you are reading or choosing statistical data to use as evidence for a claim in your own essay, use the following questions to help you determine the relevance, validity, and bias of the statistics.

- Who is the author or the group responsible for gathering or presenting the information? Do they have a bias or point of view?
- What is the date of the study or survey? Are the data still relevant?
- For a survey or poll, what is the sample size (number of respondents) and sample selection (demographic group selected)? Is the sample large enough to give reliable results? Is the group randomly selected? Are certain key groups not included?
- Analyze the wording of the questions asked in the poll or survey. Are the questions relatively neutral? Do the questions lead respondents to a certain conclusion?
- Are the conclusions drawn justified by the data? Are the conclusions exaggerated or overgeneralized?

> *A society which is clamoring for choice [is] filled with many articulate groups, each arguing its own brand of salvation.*
>
> —MARGARET MEAD,
> ANTHROPOLOGIST

- Bicyclists should be subject to regular traffic laws, including DWI.
- The sale of all handguns should be illegal.
- NCAA football should have playoffs.
- High-quality child care should be available to all working parents at public expense.
- Computer literacy courses should be required at the college level.
- Police should live in the neighborhoods they serve.
- Fraternities and sororities should be forbidden to serve alcoholic beverages.
- Students should work for one year between high school and college.
- Businesses should be required to provide free health insurance for all employees.
- Nonmajor courses should be graded pass/fail.
- After committing three felonies, criminals should receive mandatory life sentences.

2. Controversial subjects depend as much on the audience as they do on the issue itself. Make a quick list of things you do every day: the kind of clothes you wear, the food you eat, the books you read, the friends you have, the ideas you discuss. For one of these activities, imagine people who might find what you do immoral, illogical, unjust, or unhealthy. What claim might they make about your activity? What reasons or evidence might they use to argue that your activity should be abolished, outlawed, or changed? Write for five minutes arguing *their* point of view.

3. Television and television advertising are often the subject of much criticism, such as in Marie Winn's excerpt from "The Plug-In Drug." Write a letter to Marie Winn, to your local or college newspaper, or to members of the PTA in your city defending the *positive* effects or value of television. Cite one particular program or commercial as an example.

4. Grades are important, but in some courses, they get in the way of learning. Choose an actual course that you have taken and write an open letter to the school administration, arguing for credit/no-credit grading in that particular course. Assume that you intend to submit your letter to the campus newspaper.

5. News items often contain incidents that spark arguments about morality or justice. Choose a recent controversial news story and write out the arguments for or against the action taken in the case.

6. Read the following essay by Ellen Goodman that was written in response to the photograph showing the signing of the Partial Birth Abortion Ban Act. After reading the article and studying the photograph, write a paragraph identifying each element of the rhetorical situation (writer, purpose, audience, genre, occasion, and cultural/political context). Identify particular passages in Goodman's essay that refer to the photograph. (Since photographs both represent and misrepresent the truth, explain both what the picture shows and what it neglects to show.) Then write a second paragraph explaining why you agree or disagree with Goodman's thesis.

PROFESSIONAL WRITING

OUT OF THE PICTURE
ON THE ABORTION BAN

Ellen Goodman

Maybe this picture isn't worth a thousand words. That honor probably be- 1
longs to the flight deck portrait of the president under the sign. "Mission
Accomplished." Maybe the presidential photo op now flying around the
Internet and soon to be available on your local T-shirt is only worth 750
words.

The picture shows the president surrounded by an all-male chorus line 2
of legislators as he signs the first ban on an abortion procedure. It's a single-
sex class photo of men making laws governing something they will never
have: a womb.

This was not just a strategic misstep, a rare Karl Rove lapse. It per- 3
fectly reflected the truth of the so-called partial-birth abortion law. What's
wrong with this picture? The legislators had indeed erased women. They
used the law as if it were Photoshop software, to crop out real women with
real problems.

4

Indeed, just days after the shutter snapped, three separate courts ordered a temporary halt to the ban on these very grounds: It doesn't have any exemption for the health of a women.

This is what brings me back, kicking and screaming, to the subject of 5 abortion. I don't want to write about this. Like most Americans, I want the abortion debate to end. I want abortion to be safe and rare. That's safe and rare. And early.

Over the years, I've rejoiced at sonograms and picked names 6 for what we call a baby when it's wanted and a fetus when it isn't. I'm aware that medicine has put the moment of viability on a collision course with the moment of legal abortion. And I am also aware that not every pregnancy goes well, that sometimes families face terrible, traumatic choices.

Sixty-eight percent of Americans have been convinced by a public re- 7 lations coup that this new law bans only a fringe and outrageous procedure. But the refusal to include an exception for the health of a pregnant woman takes this from the fringe to the heart of the debate. It's a deliberate, willful first strike at some of the most vulnerable women, those who need medical help the most.

The moment the anti-abortion leaders invented the term "partial-birth 8 abortion," they made women invisible. The cartoon figures shown at congressional debates were, literally, drawings of a headless womb holding a perfect Gerber baby of some six or more months.

As Priscilla Smith, legal director of the Center for Reproductive Rights, 9 said, "they turned the argument from the right of a woman to have an abortion to the reasons women have abortions." And then they declared those reasons to be frivolous.

The headless womb belonged to a generic woman who, as one oppo- 10 nent said, would get an abortion to fit into a prom dress. She would carry a pregnancy for months and then casually flip a coin between birth and an abortion "inches from life."

Time and again, abortion-rights supporters said they too would vote 11 for the ban if opponents recognized that some pregnancies go terribly awry for the fetus or the woman and that some doctors found this procedure safest. But anti-abortion forces simply declared—against the evidence of the AMA or the American College of Obstetrics and Gynecology—that it was never medically necessary.

Some years ago, when President Clinton vetoed a similar bill, he was 12 surrounded by women. These women had been through pregnancies that came with words like hydrocephalus and polyhydramnia, and came with risks like hysterectomies. But the men around Bush see a health exception as a giant loophole. They believe a woman would leap through this loophole to get to the prom.

Behind this is simply a mistrust of women as moral decision-makers. *13* A mistrust so profound that their health is now in the hands of the courts. Not long ago, the Supreme Court ruled by exactly one vote that a law similar to this one violated the Constitution.

This should be a wake-up call to young women, because it's their health *14* at risk, their role as moral decision-makers disparaged.

The most reliable supporters of abortion rights today are women over *15* 50. It is, ironically, post menopausal women who still lead the struggle to keep abortion legal for younger women. Everyone will tell you that the younger generation simply doesn't remember a time when abortion was illegal. They can't believe that it will ever be illegal again. How many believe they could be among those who need it?

Days before signing this ban, the president tried to reassure voters that *16* it wasn't the time to "totally ban abortions." But young women should put this picture up on their desktops. The folks in that photo op don't trust you. They don't even see you.

PROFESSIONAL WRITING

THE INTERNET: A CLEAR AND PRESENT DANGER?

Cathleen A. Cleaver

Cathleen Cleaver is a former director of legal studies at the Family Research Council, an organization based in Washington, D.C. She has published extensively on issues relating to children and the Internet, in newspaper and magazines such as USA Today, Newsday, *and the* Congressional Quarterly Researcher. *The following essay was originally a speech given at Boston Uni-*

versity as part of a College of Communication Great Debate. In this speech, she argues that some industry and government regulation of the Internet is necessary.

- Someone breaks through your firewall and steals proprietary information from your computer systems. You find out and contact a lawyer who says, "Man, you shouldn't have had your stuff online." The thief becomes a millionaire using your ideas, and you go broke, if laws against copyright violation don't protect material on the Internet.   *1*

- You visit the Antiques Anonymous Web site and decide to pay their hefty subscription fee for a year's worth of exclusive estate sale previews in their private online monthly magazine. They never deliver and, in fact, never intended to—they don't even have a magazine. You have no recourse, if laws against fraud don't apply to online transactions.   *2*

- Bob Guccione decides to branch out into the lucrative child porn market and creates a Teen Hustler Web site featuring nude adolescents and preteens. You find out and complain, but nothing can be done, if child pornography distribution laws don't apply to computer transmissions.   *3*

- A major computer software vendor who dominates the market develops his popular office software so that it works only with his browser. You're a small browser manufacturer who is completely squeezed out of the market, but you have to find a new line of work, if antitrust laws don't apply online.   *4*

- Finally, a pedophile e-mails your son, misrepresenting himself as a twelve-year-old named Jenny. They develop an online relationship and one day arrange to meet after school, where he intends to rape your son. Thankfully, you learn in advance about the meeting and go there yourself, where you find a forty-year-old man instead of Jenny. You flee to the police, who'll tell you there's nothing they can do, if child-stalking laws don't apply to the Internet.   *5*

The awesome advances in interactive telecommunication that we've witnessed in just the last few years have changed the way in which many Americans communicate and interact. No one can doubt that the Internet is a technological revolution of enormous proportion, with outstanding possibilities for human advancement.   *6*

As lead speaker for the affirmative, I'm asked to argue that the Internet poses a "clear and present danger," but the Internet, as a whole, isn't dangerous. In fact, it continues to be a positive and highly beneficial tool, which will undoubtedly improve education, information exchange, and commerce in years to come. In other words, the Internet will enrich many aspects of our daily life. Thus, instead of defending this rather apocalyptic view of the Internet, I'll attempt to explain why some industry and government regulation of certain aspects of the Internet is necessary—or, stated another way, why people who use the Internet should not be exempt from many of the laws and regulations that govern their conduct elsewhere. My opening illustrations were meant to give examples of some illegal conduct which should not become legal simply because someone uses the Internet. In looking at whether Internet regulation is a good idea, I believe we should consider whether regulation is in the public interest. In order to do that, we have to ask the question: Who is the public? More specifically, does the "public" whose interests we care about tonight include children? *7*

Children and the Internet

Dave Barry describes the Internet as a "worldwide network of university, government, business, and private computer systems, run by a thirteen-year-old named Jason." This description draws a smile precisely because we acknowledge the highly advanced computer literacy of our children. Most children demonstrate computer proficiency that far surpasses that of their parents, and many parents know only what their children have taught them about the Internet, which gives new relevance to Wordsworth's insight: "The child is father of the man." In fact, one could go so far as to say that the Internet is as accessible to many children as it is inaccessible to many adults. This technological evolution is new in many ways, not the least of which is its accessibility to children, wholly independent of their parents. *8*

When considering what's in the public interest, we must consider the whole public, including children, as individual participants in this new medium. *9*

Pornography and the Internet

This new medium is unique in another way. It provides, through a single avenue, the full spectrum of pornographic depictions, from the more familiar convenience store fare to pornography of such violence and depravity that it surpasses the worst excesses of the normal human imagination. Sites displaying this material are easily accessible, making pornography far more freely available via the Internet than from any other communications *10* medium in the United States. Pornography is the third largest sector of sales on the Internet, generating $1 billion annually. There are an estimated seventy-two thousand pornographic sites on the World Wide Web alone, with approximately thirty-nine new explicit sex sites every day. Indeed, the *Washington Post* has called the Internet the largest pornography store in the history of mankind.

There is little restriction of pornography-related activity in cyberspace. *11* While there are some porn-related laws, the specter of those laws does not loom large in cyberspace. There's an implicit license there that exists nowhere else with regard to pornography—an environment where people are free to exploit others for profit and be virtually untroubled by legal deterrent. Indeed, if we consider cyberspace to be a little world of its own, it's the type of world for which groups like the ACLU have long fought but, so far, fought in vain.

I believe it will not remain this way, but until it changes, we should *12* take the opportunity to see what this world looks like, if for no other reason than to reassure ourselves that our decades-old decisions to control pornography were good ones.

With a few clicks of the mouse, anyone, any child, can get graphic and *13* often violent sexual images—the kind of stuff it used to be difficult to find without exceptional effort and some significant personal risk. Anyone with a computer and a modem can set up public sites featuring the perversion of their choice, whether it's mutilation of female genitals, eroticized urination and defecation, bestiality, or sites featuring depictions of incest. These pictures can be sold for profit, they can be sent to harass others, or posted to shock people. Anyone can describe the fantasy rape and murder of a specific person and display it for all to read. Anyone can meet children in chat rooms or via e-mail and send them pornography and find out where they live. An adult who signs onto an AOL chat room as a thirteen-year-old girl is hit on thirty times within the first half hour.

All this can be done from the seclusion of the home, with the feeling *14* of near anonymity and with the comfort of knowing that there's little risk of legal sanction.

The phenomenon of this kind of pornography finding such a welcome *15* home in this new medium presents abundant opportunities for social commentary. What does Internet pornography tell us about human sexuality? Photographs, videos, and virtual games that depict rape and the dehumanization of women in sexual scenes send powerful messages about human dignity and equality. Much of the pornography freely available without restriction on the Internet celebrates unhealthy and antisocial kinds of sexual activity, such as sadomasochism, abuse, and degradation. Of course, by its very nature, pornography encourages voyeurism.

Beyond the troubling social aspects of unrestricted porn, we face the 16 reality that children are accessing it and that predators are accessing children. We have got to start considering what kind of society we'll have when the next generation learns about human sexuality from what the Internet teaches. What does unrestricted Internet pornography teach children about relationships, about the equality of women? What does it teach little girls about themselves and their worth?

Opponents of restrictions are fond of saying that it's up to the parents 17 to deal with the issue of children's exposure. Well, of course it is, but placing the burden solely on parents is illogical and ineffective. It's far easier for a distributor of pornography to control his material than it is for parents, who must, with the help of software, search for and find the pornographic sites, which change daily, and then attempt to block them. Any pornographer who wants to can easily subvert these efforts, and a recent Internet posting from a teenager wanting to know how to disable the filtering software on his computer received several effective answers. Moreover, it goes without saying that the most sophisticated software can only be effective where it's installed, and children will have access to many computers that don't have filtering software, such as those in libraries, schools, and at neighbors' houses.

Internet Transactions Should Not be Exempt

Opponents of legal restrictions often argue simply that the laws just cannot 18 apply in this new medium, but the argument that old laws can't apply to changing technology just doesn't hold. We saw this argument last in the early' 80s with the advent of the videotape. Then, certain groups tried to argue that, since you can't view videotapes without a VCR, you can't make the sale of child porn videos illegal, because, after all, they're just plastic boxes with magnetic tape inside. Technological change mandates legal change only insofar as it affects the justification for a law. It just doesn't make sense that the government may take steps to restrict illegal material in *every* medium—video, television, radio, the private telephone, *and* print—but that it may do nothing where people distribute the material by the Internet. While old laws might need redefinition, the old principles generally stand firm.

The question of enforcement usually is raised here, and it often comes 19 in the form of: "How are you going to stop people from doing it?" Well, no law stops people from doing things—a red light at an intersection doesn't force you to stop but tells you that you should stop and that there could be legal consequences if you don't. Not everyone who runs a red light is caught, but that doesn't mean the law is futile. The same concept holds true for Internet laws. Government efforts to temper harmful conduct online will never be perfect, but that doesn't mean they shouldn't undertake the effort at all.

There's clearly a role for industry to play here. Search engines don't *20* have to run ads for porn sites or prioritize search results to highlight porn. One new search engine even has sex as the default search term. Internet service providers can do something about unsolicited e-mail with hotlinks to porn, and they can and should carefully monitor any chat rooms designed for kids.

Some charge that industry standards or regulations that restrict ex- *21* plicit pornography will hinder the development of Internet technology. But that is to say that its advancement depends upon unrestricted exhibition of this material, and this cannot be true. The Internet does not belong to pornographers, and it's clearly in the public interest to see that they don't usurp this great new technology. We don't live in a perfect society, and the Internet is merely a reflection of the larger social community. Without some mitigating influences, the strong will exploit the weak, whether a Bill Gates or a child predator.

Conclusion: Technology Must Serve Man

To argue that the strength of the Internet is chaos or that our liberty depends *22* upon chaos is to misunderstand not only the Internet but also the fundamental nature of our liberty. It's an illusion to claim social or moral neutrality in the application of technology, even if its development may be neutral. It can be a valuable resource only when placed at the service of humanity and when it promotes our integral development for the benefit of all.

Guiding principles simply cannot be inferred from mere technical ef- *23* ficiency or from the usefulness accruing to some at the expense of others. Technology by its very nature requires unconditional respect for the fundamental interests of society.

Internet technology must be at the service of humanity and of our in- *24* alienable rights. It must respect the prerogatives of a civil society, among which is the protection of children.

In your journal, write the meanings of the following words:

- steals *proprietary* information **(1)**
- rather *apocalyptic* view **(7)**
- legal *deterrent* **(11)**
- don't have *filtering* software **(17)**
- the law is *futile* **(19)**
- cannot be *inferred* **(23)**
- usefulness *accruing* to some **(23)**
- respect the *prerogatives* **(24)**

QUESTIONS FOR WRITING AND DISCUSSION

1. Before you read or reread Cleaver's essay, write down your own thoughts and experiences about pornography on the Internet. Have you run into sites that you find offensive? Should access to such sites be made more difficult? Do you think children should be protected from accessing such sites—either by accident or on purpose? What do you think are the best method(s) for such regulation: Internet software programs, parental regulation, governmental regulation? Explain.

2. Cleaver begins her essay with several scenarios describing potential abuses and crimes that occur online. Did you find these scenarios effective as a lead-in to her argument? Did they help you focus on her thesis? Should she use fewer scenarios? Why do you think she used all of these examples when only two dealt with child pornography on the Internet?

3. The rhetorical occasion for Cleaver's argument is a debate sponsored by the College of Communication at Boston University. In her essay, can you find evidences (word choice, vocabulary, sentence length, tone, use of evidence, use of appeals) that suggest that her original *genre* was a speech and that her *audience* was college students, college faculty, and members of the community? Cite evidence from the essay showing where Cleaver uses debate elements appropriate for this genre and makes appeals to this audience.

4. Cleaver states her case for government regulation of pornography on the Internet, but who is against regulation, and what are their arguments? What ar-

guments opposing Internet regulation does Cleaver cite? (Are there other opposing arguments that Cleaver does not consider?) How well does Cleaver answer these opposing arguments?

5. Arguing essays make appeals to reason, to character, and to emotion. Find examples of each type of appeal in Cleaver's essay. Which type of appeal does she use most frequently? Which appeals are most or least effective? Does she rely too much on her emotional appeals (see paragraph 13, for example)? For her audience and her context (a debate), should she bolster her rational appeals with more evidence and statistics? Why or why not?

6. Imagine that you are at this debate on the Internet and that your side believes that there should be no or very little regulation of the Internet. What arguments might you make in response to Cleaver? Make a list of the possible pro–con arguments on this topic and explain which ones you will focus on as you respond to Cleaver.

PROFESSIONAL WRITING

THE DAMNATION OF A CANYON

Edward Abbey

"In wildness is the preservation of the world." Henry David Thoreau's words *serve to introduce Edward Abbey's own nature ethic. Beginning with the classic* Desert Solitaire *(1968) and including* The Monkey Wrench Gang *(1975),* Abbey's Road *(1979), and* Down the River *(1982), Abbey's writings celebrate the American West, its deserts, canyons, mountains, and rivers. But always in full view are Abbey's villains in the black hats: Industrialists, Bureaucrats, and Developers. And Dammers. In this selection, taken from* Beyond the Wall *(1984), Abbey contrasts the Eden that was Glen Canyon with the stagnant, lifeless waters of Lake Powell. Abbey's argument is shaped by a clear outline—his claim, his refutation of the opposing view, his analysis of consequences, and his solution— and also by Abbey's insistent, cranky, and passionate voice, which echoes throughout the essay.*

There was a time when, in my search for essences, I concluded that the   *1*
canyonland country has no heart. I was wrong. The canyonlands did have

a heart, a living heart, and that heart was Glen Canyon and the golden, flowing Colorado River.

In the summer of 1959 a friend and I made a float trip in little rubber rafts down through the length of Glen Canyon, starting at Hite and getting off the river near Gunsight Butte—The Crossing of the Fathers. In this voyage of some 150 miles and ten days our only motive power, and all that we needed, was the current of the Colorado River.

In the summer and fall of 1967 I worked as a seasonal park ranger at the new Glen Canyon National Recreation Area. During my five-month tour of duty I worked at the main marina and headquarters area called Wahweap, at Bullfrog Basin toward the upper end of the reservoir, and finally at Lee's Ferry downriver from Glen Canyon Dam. In a number of powerboat tours I was privileged to see almost all of our nation's newest, biggest and most impressive "recreational facility."

Having thus seen Glen Canyon both before and after what we may fairly call its damnation, I feel that I am in a position to evaluate the transformation of the region caused by construction of the dam. I have had the unique opportunity to observe firsthand some of the differences between the environment of a free river and a power plant reservoir.

One should admit at the outset to a certain bias. Indeed I am a "butterfly chaser, googly eyed bleeding heart and wild conservative." I take a dim view of dams; I find it hard to learn to love cement; I am poorly impressed by concrete aggregates and statistics in the cubic tons. But in this weakness I am not alone, for I belong to that ever-growing number of Americans, probably a good majority now, who have become aware that a fully industrialized, thoroughly urbanized, elegantly computerized social system is not suitable for human habitation. Great for machines, yes: but unfit for people.

Lake Powell, formed by Glen Canyon Dam, is not a lake. It is a reservoir, with a constantly fluctuating water level—more like a bathtub that is never drained than a true lake. As at Hoover (or Boulder) Dam, the sole practical function of this impounded water is to drive the turbines that generate electricity in the powerhouse at the base of the dam. Recreational benefits were of secondary importance in the minds of those who conceived and built this dam. As a result the volume of water in the reservoir is continually being increased or decreased according to the requirements of the Basin States Compact and the power-grid system of which Glen Canyon Dam is a component.

The rising and falling water level entails various consequences. One of the most obvious, well known to all who have seen Lake Mead, is the "bathtub ring" left on the canyon walls after each drawdown of water, or what rangers at Glen Canyon call the Bathtub Foundation. This phenomenon is perhaps of no more than aesthetic importance; yet it is sufficient to dispel any illusion one might have, in contemplating the scene, that you are looking upon a natural lake.

The utter barrenness of the reservoir shoreline recalls by contrast the aspect of things before the dam, when Glen Canyon formed the course of the untamed Colorado. Then we had a wild and flowing river lined by boulder-strewn shores, sandy beaches, thickets of tamarisk and willow, and glades of cottonwoods.   8

The thickets teemed with songbirds: vireos, warblers, mockingbirds and thrushes. On the open beaches were killdeer, sandpipers, herons, ibises, egrets. Living in grottoes in the canyon walls were swallows, swifts, hawks, wrens and owls. Beaver were common if not abundant: not an evening would pass, in drifting down the river, that we did not see them or at least hear the whack of their flat tails on the water. Above the river shores were the great recessed alcoves where water seeped from the sandstone, nourishing the semitropical hanging gardens of orchid, ivy and columbine, with their associated swarms of insects and birdlife.   9

Up most of the side canyon, before damnation, there were springs, sometimes flowing streams, waterfalls and plunge pools—the kind of marvels you can now find only in such small scale remnants of Glen Canyon as the Escalante area. In the rich flora of these laterals the larger mammals—mule deer, coyote, bobcat, ring-tailed cat, gray fox, kit fox, skunk, badger and others—found a home. When the river was dammed almost all of these things were lost. Crowded out—or drowned and buried under mud.   10

The difference between the present reservoir, with its silent sterile shores and debris choked side canyons, and the original Glen Canyon, is the difference between death and life. Glen Canyon was alive. Lake Powell is a graveyard.   11

For those who may think I exaggerate the contrast between the former river canyon and the present man-made impoundment, I suggest a trip on Lake Powell followed immediately by another boat trip on the river below the dam. Take a boat from Lee's Ferry up the river to within sight of the dam, then shut off the motor and allow yourself the rare delight of a quiet, effortless drifting down the stream. In that twelve-mile stretch of living green, singing birds, flowing water and untarnished canyon walls—sights and sounds a million years older and infinitely lovelier than the roar of   12 motorboats—you will rediscover a small and imperfect sampling of the kind of experience that was taken away from everybody when the oligarchs and politicians condemned our river for purposes of their own.

Lake Powell, though not a lake, may well be as its defenders assert the 13 most beautiful reservoir in the world. Certainly it has a photogenic backdrop of buttes and mesas projecting above the expansive surface of stagnant waters where the speedboats, houseboats and cabin cruisers play. But it is no longer a wilderness. It is no longer a place of natural life. It is no longer Glen Canyon.

The defenders of the dam argue that the recreational benefits available 14 on the surface of the reservoir outweigh the loss of Indian ruins, historical sites, wildlife and wilderness adventure. Relying on the familiar quantitative logic of business and bureaucracy, they assert that whereas only a few thousand citizens ever ventured down the river through Glen Canyon, now millions can—or will—enjoy the motorized boating and hatchery fishing available on the reservoir. They will also argue that the rising waters behind the dam have made such places as Rainbow Bridge accessible by powerboat. Formerly you could get there only by walking (six miles).

This argument appeals to the wheelchair ethos of the wealthy, upper- 15 middle-class American slob. If Rainbow Bridge is worth seeing at all, then by God it should be easily, readily, immediately available to everybody with the money to buy a big powerboat. Why should a trip to such a place be the privilege only of those who are willing to walk six miles? Or if Pikes Peak is worth getting to, then why not build a highway to the top of it so that anyone can get there? Anytime? Without effort? Or as my old man would say, "By Christ, one man's just as good as another—if not a damn sight better."

It is quite true that the flooding of Glen Canyon has opened up to the 16 motorboat explorer parts of side canyons that formerly could be reached only by people able to walk. But the sum total of terrain visible to the eye and touchable by hand and foot has been greatly diminished, not increased. Because of the dam the river is gone, the inner canyon is gone, the best parts of the numerous side canyons are gone—all hidden beneath hundreds of feet of polluted water, accumulating silt, and mounting tons of trash. This portion of Glen Canyon—and who can estimate how many cubic miles were lost?—*is no longer accessible to anybody.* (Except scuba divers.) And this, do not forget, was the most valuable part of Glen Canyon, richest in scenery, archaeology, history, flora and fauna.

Not only has the heart of Glen Canyon been buried, but many of the 17 side canyons above the fluctuating waterline are now rendered more difficult, not easier, to get into. This because the debris brought down into them by desert storms, no longer carried away by the river, must unavoidably build up in the area where flood meets reservoir. Narrow Canyon, for example, at the head of the impounded waters, is already beginning to silt up and to amass huge quantities of driftwood, some of it floating on the surface, some of it half afloat beneath the surface. Anyone who has tried to pilot a motorboat through a raft of half sunken logs and bloated dead cows will have his own thoughts on the accessibility of these waters.

Second, the question of costs. It is often stated that the dam and its 18 reservoir have opened up to the many what was formerly restricted to the few, implying in this case that what was once expensive has now been made cheap. Exactly the opposite is true.

Before the dam, a float trip down the river through Glen Canyon would 19 cost you a minimum of seven days' time, well within anyone's vacation allotment, and a capital outlay of about forty dollars—the prevailing price of a two-man rubber boat with oars, available at any army-navy surplus store. A life jacket might be useful but not required, for there were no dangerous rapids in the 150 miles of Glen Canyon. As the name implies, this stretch of the river was in fact so easy and gentle that the trip could be and was made by all sorts of amateurs: by Boy Scouts, Camp Fire Girls, stenographers, schoolteachers, students, little old ladies in inner tubes. Guides, professional boatmen, giant pontoons, outboard motors, radios, rescue equipment were not needed. The Glen Canyon float trip was an adventure anyone could enjoy, on his own, for a cost less than that of spending two days and nights in a Page motel. Even food was there, in the water: the channel catfish were easier to catch and a lot better eating than the striped bass and rainbow trout dumped by the ton into the reservoir these days. And one other thing: at the end of the float trip you still owned your boat, usable for many more such casual and carefree expeditions.

What is the situation now? Float trips are no longer possible. The only 20 way left for the exploration of the reservoir and what remains of Glen Canyon demands the use of a powerboat. Here you have three options: (1) buy your own boat and engine, the necessary auxiliary equipment, the fuel to keep it moving, the parts and repairs to keep it running, the permits and licenses required for legal operation, the trailer to transport it; (2) rent a boat; or (3) go on a commercial excursion boat, packed in with other sightseers, following a preplanned itinerary. This kind of play is only for the affluent.

The inescapable conclusion is that no matter how one attempts to cal- 21 culate the cost in dollars and cents, a float trip down Glen Canyon was much cheaper than a powerboat tour of the reservoir. Being less expensive, as well as safer and easier, the float trip was an adventure open to far more people than will ever be able to afford motorboat excursions in the area now.

All of the foregoing would be nothing but a futile exercise in nostalgia (so much water over the dam) if I had nothing constructive and concrete to offer. But I do. As alternate methods of power generation are developed, such as solar, and as the nation establishes a way of life adapted to actual resources and basic needs, so that the demand for electrical power begins to diminish, we can shut down the Glen Canyon power plant, open the diversion tunnels, and drain the reservoir.   22

This will no doubt expose a drear and hideous scene: immense mud flats and whole plateaus of sodden garbage strewn with dead trees, sunken boats, the skeletons of long-forgotten, decomposing water-skiers. But to those who find the prospect too appalling, I say give nature a little time. In five years, at most in ten, the sun and wind and storms will cleanse and sterilize the repellent mess. The inevitable floods will soon remove all that does not belong within the canyons. Fresh green willow, box elder and redbud will reappear; and the ancient drowned cottonwoods (noble monuments to themselves) will be replaced by young of their own kind. With the renewal of plant life will come the insects, the birds, the lizards and snakes, the mammals. Within a generation—thirty years—I predict the river and canyons will bear a decent resemblance to their former selves. Within the lifetime of our children Glen Canyon and the living river, heart of the canyonlands, will be restored to us. The wilderness will again belong to God, the people and the wild things that call it home.   23

In your journal, write the meanings of the following words:

- concrete *aggregates* (5)
- *aesthetic* importance (7)
- recessed *alcoves* (9)
- *oligarchs* and politicians (12)

- the wheelchair *ethos* **(15)**
- richest in . . . *archaeology* **(16)**
- preplanned *itinerary* **(20)**
- a *drear* and hideous scene **(23)**

QUESTIONS FOR WRITING AND DISCUSSION

1. Do you consider yourself an environmentalist—someone who is in favor of preserving wild rivers, designating wilderness areas, and forbidding mining, grazing, or the use of motorized vehicles in national parks? Or do you believe that federal lands, parks, and rivers should serve multiple uses? Explain, using a state or national park you have visited to give specific examples.

2. Which of Abbey's arguments did you find most persuasive? Which were least persuasive? Are there opposing arguments that Abbey does not answer? Explain, *referring to your own beliefs* outlined above.

3. An argument contains a *claim, reasons* that support the claim or refute the opposition, and *evidence.*

    - What sentence or sentences best illustrate Abbey's overall claim or thesis for this essay? Does he make a claim of fact or definition, value, cause, or solution—or some combination of these? Explain.
    - List the *reasons* Abbey gives to support his claim and refute the opposing arguments.
    - For *one* of his reasons, list the evidence, facts, examples, or testimony that Abbey gives.

4. Note passages in which Abbey's *appeal to character* is evident. Where is he most reasonable? Where is he most cantankerous or even misanthropic? Are these facets of his character consistent with the persona portrayed in paragraph 5? In your judgment, does his appeal to character help or hurt his argument? Explain.

5. Cite one sentence in which Abbey uses an *emotional appeal.* Does this sentence make his argument more effective?

6. Assume you are the controller of the Glen Canyon dam. Write a short response to Abbey explaining why his solution—to "open the diversion tunnels, and drain the reservoir"—is absurd. Choose either an adversarial or a Rogerian strategy, whichever would work best for Abbey.

7. On the Internet, visit several Glen Canyon websites, such as the site for draining the dam at *http://www.drainit.org/doa2001.htm*, a report on the "Decommissioning of Glen Canyon Dam" at *http://www.glencanyon.org*, or a tourism site such as *http://www.gorp.com*. What do each of these sites recommend about Glen Canyon dam? Who sponsors each site? What biases do each of these sites have? Do they support, refute, or revise Abbey's analysis and recommendations?

PROFESSIONAL WRITING

THREE PERSPECTIVES ON THE DEATH PENALTY

The three essays that follow, by Edward Koch, Robert Badinter, and John O'Sullivan, address the controversy surrounding the death penalty in the United States. In order to read these essays actively and critically, begin by writing down your ideas on the death penalty. List your own reasons why the death penalty should or should not be used. Should it be used only under certain circumstances? Are there circumstances under which it should not be used?

After you have written out your ideas, read all three essays. As you read—and reread—these essays, consider the following questions: Can there be three perspectives about an issue such as capital punishment? Are there other perspectives not described in these essays? Which of these writers makes the best argument to support his position? Which of these positions most closely agrees with yours? How exactly is your position different?

As you reread, also consider the different social and cultural contexts within which each essay was written. "Death and Justice," by Edward I. Koch, was written during one of his terms as mayor of New York City and appeared in The New Republic *in 1985 during a period of high crime rates. The second essay, "Death Be Not Proud," was written by Robert Badinter, a Senator and former Justice Minister of France. Badinter, was the prime mover behind France's decision to abolish the death penalty in 1981. Badinter's essay appeared in* Time International *in 2001 in response to the controversy surrounding the death penalty in Texas and Illinois at that time. The third essay, also titled "Death and Justice," appeared originally in the* Chicago Sun-Times *in 2001 and was reprinted in the* National Review Online. *The author, John O'Sullivan, is an editor-at-large for the* National Review *and writes a regular column on national and international political issues. The occasion of O'Sullivan's essay was the execution of Timothy McVeigh, the convicted bomber of the Murrah Federal Building in Oklahoma City. As you read, consider how each of these different contexts helps determine each writer's argument.*

DEATH AND JUSTICE

Edward I. Koch

Last December a man named Robert Lee Willie, who had been convicted of   *1*
raping and murdering an 18-year-old woman, was executed in the Louisiana state prison. In a statement issued several minutes before his death, Mr. Willie said: "Killing people is wrong. . . . It makes no difference whether it's citizens, countries, or governments. Killing is wrong." Two weeks later in South Carolina, an admitted killer named Joseph Carl Shaw was put to death for murdering two teenagers. In an appeal to the governor for clemency, Mr. Shaw wrote: "Killing is wrong when I did it. Killing is wrong when you do it. I hope you have the courage and moral strength to stop the killing."

It is a curiosity of modern life that we find ourselves being lectured on   *2*
morality by cold-blooded killers. Mr. Willie previously had been convicted of aggravated rape, aggravated kidnapping, and the murders of a Louisiana deputy and a man from Missouri. Mr. Shaw committed another murder a week before the two for which he was executed, and admitted mutilating the body of the 14-year-old girl he killed. I can't help wondering what prompted these murderers to speak out against killing as they entered the death-house door. Did their newfound reverence for life stem from the realization that they were about to lose their own?

Life is indeed precious, and I believe the death penalty helps to affirm   *3*
this fact. Had the death penalty been a real possibility in the minds of these murderers, they might well have stayed their hand. They might have shown moral awareness before their victims died, and not after. Consider the tragic death of Rosa Velez, who happened to be home when a man named Luis Vera burglarized her apartment in Brooklyn. "Yeah, I shot her," Vera admitted. "She knew me, and I knew I wouldn't go to the chair."

During my 22 years in public service, I have heard the pros and cons of   *4*
capital punishment expressed with special intensity. As a district leader, councilman, congressman, and mayor, I have represented constituencies generally thought of as liberal. Because I support the death penalty for heinous

crimes of murder, I have sometimes been the subject of emotional and outraged attacks by voters who find my position reprehensible or worse. I have listened to their ideas. I have weighed their objections carefully. I still support the death penalty. The reasons I maintained my position can be best understood by examining the arguments most frequently heard in opposition.

1. *The death penalty is "barbaric."* Sometimes opponents of capital punishment horrify with tales of lingering death on the gallows, of faulty electric chairs, or of agony in the gas chamber. Partly in response to such protests, several states such as North Carolina and Texas switched to execution by lethal injection. The condemned person is put to death painlessly, without ropes, voltage, bullets, or gas. Did this answer the objections of death penalty opponents? Of course not. On June 22, 1984, *The New York Times* published an editorial that sarcastically attacked the new "hygienic" method of death by injection, and stated that "execution can never be made humane through science." So it's not the method that really troubles opponents. It's the death itself they consider barbaric.

Admittedly capital punishment is not a pleasant topic. However, one does not have to like the death penalty in order to support it any more than one must like radical surgery, radiation, or chemotherapy in order to find necessary these attempts at curing cancer. Ultimately we may learn how to cure cancer with a simple pill. Unfortunately, that day has not yet arrived. Today we are faced with the choice of letting the cancer spread or trying to cure it with the methods available, methods that one day will almost certainly be considered barbaric and would certainly delay the discovery of an eventual cure. The analogy between cancer and murder is imperfect, because murder is not the "disease" we are trying to cure. The disease is injustice. We may not like the death penalty, but it must be available to punish crimes of cold-blooded murder, cases in which any other form of punishment would be inadequate and, therefore, unjust. If we create a society in which injustice is not tolerated, incidents of murder—the most flagrant form of injustice—will diminish.

2. *No other major democracy uses the death penalty.* No other major democracy—in fact, few other countries of any description—are plagued by a murder rate such as that in the United States. Fewer and fewer Americans can remember the days when unlocked doors were the norm and murder was a rare and terrible offense. In America the murder rate climbed 122 percent between 1963 and 1980. During that same period, the murder rate in New York City increased by almost 400 percent, and the statistics are even worse

in many other cities. A study at M.I.T. showed that based on 1970 homicide rates a person who lived in a large American city ran a greater risk of being murdered than an American soldier in World War II ran of being killed in combat. It is not surprising that the laws of each country differ according to differing conditions and traditions. If other countries had our murder problem, the cry for capital punishment would be just as loud as it is here. And I daresay that any other major democracy where 75 percent of the people supported the death penalty would soon enact it into law.

3. *An innocent person might be executed by mistake.* Consider the work   *8* of Adam Bedau, one of the most implacable foes of capital punishment in this country. According to Mr. Bedau, it is "false sentimentality to argue that the death penalty should be abolished because of the abstract possibility that an innocent person might be executed." He cites a study of the 7,000 executions in this country from 1893 to 1971, and concludes that the record fails to show that such cases occur. The main point, however, is this. If government functioned only when the possibility of error didn't exist, government wouldn't function at all. Human life deserves special protection, and one of the best ways to guarantee that protection is to assure that convicted murderers do not kill again. Only the death penalty can accomplish this end. In a recent case in New Jersey, a man named Richard Biegenwald was freed from prison after serving 18 years for murder; since his release he has been convicted of committing four murders. A prisoner named Lemuel Smith, who, while serving four life sentences for murder (plus two life sentences for kidnapping and robbery) in New York's Green Haven Prison, lured a woman corrections officer into the chaplain's office and strangled her. He then mutilated and dismembered her body. An additional life sentence for Smith is meaningless. Because New York has no death penalty statute, Smith has effectively been given a license to kill.

But the problem of multiple murder is not confined to the nation's   *9* penitentiaries. In 1981, 91 police officers were killed in the line of duty in this country. Seven percent of those arrested in the cases that have been solved had a previous arrest for murder. In New York City in 1976 and 1977, 85 persons arrested for homicide had a previous arrest for murder. Six of these individuals had two previous arrests for murder, and one had four previous murder arrests. During those two years the New York police were arresting for murder persons with a previous arrest for murder on the average of one every 8.5 days. This is not surprising when we learn that in 1975, for example, the median time served in Massachusetts for homicide was less than two-and-a-half years. In 1976 a study sponsored by the Twentieth Century Fund found that the average time served in the United States for first-degree murder is ten years. The median time served may be considerably lower.

4. *Capital punishment cheapens the value of human life.* On the contrary, it can be easily demonstrated that the death penalty strengthens the value of human life. If the penalty for rape were lowered, clearly it would signal a lessened regard for the victims' suffering, humiliation, and personal integrity. It would cheapen their horrible experience, and expose them to an increased danger of recurrence. When we lower the penalty for murder, it signals a lessened regard for the value of the victim's life. Some critics of capital punishment, such as columnist Jimmy Breslin, have suggested that a life sentence is actually a harsher penalty for murder than death. This is sophistic nonsense. A few killers may decide not to appeal a death sentence, but the overwhelming majority make every effort to stay alive. It is by exacting the highest penalty for the taking of human life that we affirm the highest value of human life.

5. *The death penalty is applied in a discriminatory manner.* This factor no longer seems to be the problem it once was. The appeals process for a condemned prisoner is lengthy and painstaking. Every effort is made to see that the verdict and sentence were fairly arrived at. However, assertions of discrimination are not an argument for ending the death penalty but for extending it. It is not justice to exclude everyone from the penalty of the law if a few are found to be so favored. Justice requires that the law be applied equally to all.

6. *Thou shalt not kill.* The Bible is our greatest source of moral inspiration. Opponents of the death penalty frequently cite the sixth of the Ten Commandments in an attempt to prove that capital punishment is divinely proscribed. In the original Hebrew, however, the Sixth Commandment reads, "Thou Shalt Not Commit Murder," and the Torah specifies capital punishment for a variety of offenses. The biblical viewpoint has been upheld by philosophers throughout history. The greatest thinkers of the 19th century—Kant, Locke, Hobbes, Rousseau, Montesquieu, and Mill—agreed that natural law properly authorizes the sovereign to take life in order to vindicate justice. Only Jeremy Bentham was ambivalent. Washington, Jefferson, and Franklin endorsed it. Abraham Lincoln authorized executions for deserters in wartime. Alexis de Tocqueville, who expressed profound respect for American institutions, believed that the death penalty was indispensable to the support of social order. The United States Constitution, widely admired as one of the seminal achievements in the history of hu-

10

11

12

manity, condemns cruel and inhuman punishment, but does not condemn capital punishment.

7. *The death penalty is state-sanctioned murder.* This is the defense with 13 which Messrs. Willie and Shaw hoped to soften the resolve of those who sentenced them to death. By saying in effect, "You're no better than I am," the murderer seeks to bring his accusers down to his own level. It is also a popular argument among opponents of capital punishment, but a transparently false one. Simply put, the state has rights that the private individual does not. In a democracy, those rights are given to the state by the electorate. The execution of a lawfully condemned killer is no more an act of murder than is legal imprisonment an act of kidnapping. If an individual forces a neighbor to pay him money under threat of punishment, it's called extortion. If the state does it, it's called taxation. Rights and responsibilities surrendered by the individual are what give the state its power to govern. This contract is the foundation of civilization itself.

Everyone wants his or her rights, and will defend them jealously. Not 14 everyone, however, wants responsibilities, especially the painful responsibilities that come with law enforcement. Twenty-one years ago a woman named Kitty Genovese was assaulted and murdered on a street in New York. Dozens of neighbors heard her cries for help but did nothing to assist her. They didn't even call the police. In such a climate the criminal understandably grows bolder. In the presence of moral cowardice, he lectures us on our supposed failings and tries to equate his crimes with our quest for justice.

The death of anyone—even a convicted killer—diminishes us all. But 15 we are diminished even more by a justice system that fails to function. It is an illusion to let ourselves believe that doing away with capital punishment removes the murderer's deed from our conscience. The rights of society are paramount. When we protect guilty lives, we give up innocent lives in exchange. When opponents of capital punishment say to the state: "I will not let you kill in my name," they are also saying to murderers: "You can kill in your *own* name as long as I have an excuse for not getting involved."

It is hard to imagine anything worse than being murdered while neigh- 16 bors do nothing. But something worse exists. When those same neighbors shrink back from justly punishing the murderer, the victim dies twice.

In your journal, write the meanings of the following words:

- I have represented *constituencies* **(4)**
- find my position *reprehensible* **(4)**
- the most *flagrant* form of injustice **(6)**
- the most *implacable* foes **(8)**
- this is *sophistic* nonsense **(10)**
- capital punishment is divinely *proscribed* **(12)**
- one of the *seminal* achievements **(12)**

PROFESSIONAL WRITING

DEATH BE NOT PROUD

Robert Badinter

I belong to a generation of Europeans for whom the United States embodies   *1*
democracy, progress and liberty. I went there as a student after the war. I have
never forgotten the warmth and friendship that the American people showed
me. In a word, I belong to that vanishing species: the Americanophile.

That is why I am writing this article. I don't believe that Americans   *2*
fully understand how their use of the death penalty has profoundly degraded
the country's image in the eyes of other democratic nations. Today, all the
Western democracies have abolished the death penalty. Almost all of Europe
has banished it. Can one seriously believe that, if it constituted an effective
instrument for fighting murderous crimes, the leaders of Europe's great states
would not have reinstated it long ago? Every study done in the abolitionist
countries has reached the same conclusion: the death penalty has never been
a deterrent to crime. In the U.S. itself, the murder rate is higher in Texas
than it is in the 12 states that have dropped the death penalty.

Today, 88% of all known executions in the world are carried out by   *3*
four countries: China, Iran, Saudi Arabia and the U.S. What, apart from the
death penalty, does the U.S. have in common with those countries? Useless
as an instrument to fight crime, capital punishment brings with it all the

evils of Western society: racism, social injustice, economic and cultural inequality. These traits are not unique to America, but they take on a particular intensity when viewed in light of the death penalty.

Capital punishment is infected by racism. African-Americans and Hispanics are the most at risk. Are they condemned to death more often than whites because their crimes are more atrocious or because they are black or Hispanic? This question alone should suffice in a democratic society to rule out the death penalty, as it has in South Africa.   *4*

The death penalty is not only racist but inegalitarian. Most prisoners on death row come from the poorest classes, those excluded from American society. They're criminals, we are told. Without a doubt. But has the society that puts them to death really given them the same chance as those more fortunate? Moreover, capital punishment strikes mainly those who don't have the money to hire competent, motivated and well-paid lawyers. Financial inequality before the law can lead to the worst possible consequences. Do Americans know that during a period of almost 20 years after the U.S. reinstated the death penalty, the overall rate of prejudicial error in the capital punishment system was 68%? Worse still, many innocent people have been condemned to death. Some have been saved in extremis, but how many others have been executed without anyone asking for a reconsideration of the trial? If a crime that goes unpunished is a challenge to society, the execution of an innocent person is the worst act that any community of free men can commit. It is the complete negation of justice. What kind of justice is it that, in order to avenge victims, becomes criminal itself by executing innocent people?   *5*

What about the barbaric practice, in the 21st century, of executing the feeble-minded and mentally defective, or the men and women whose crimes were committed when they were minors? What kind of society is it that treats adolescents as adults when it comes to sentencing them to death? Is this society ignorant of the fact that every adolescent is a human being in progress; that for every young murderer, part of the responsibility lies with the parents, the associates, the brief life he has lived so far—all of which means he cannot be considered guilty in the same way as an adult?   *6*

It is true that the suffering of the victims calls for both justice and punishment. But to make the execution of the criminal a bloody retribution for the victim's pain is a return to the darkest practices of the past. Other forms of punishment exist. The criminal's death does not bring the victim back. It merely adds one death to another, and adds society's injustices to the horror of the crime.   *7*

When France abolished the death penalty in 1981 and I gave the guillotine to a museum, there were 35 abolitionist nations in the world. Today, there are 108, *de facto* and *de jure,* among the 189 that belong to the U.N. Therefore, I ask my American friends: Where is your place in the world, you who aspire to assume its leadership, not just militarily and technologically, but also morally and culturally? Among the democrats who have banned the death penalty? Or alongside totalitarian China and fanatical Iran? 8

In your journal, write the meanings of the following words:

- the *Americanophile* (1)
- in the *abolitionist* countries (2)
- crimes are more *atrocious* (4)
- should *suffice* in a democratic society (4)
- not only racist but *inegalitarian* (5)
- the rate of *prejudicial* error (5)
- some have been saved *in extremis* (5)
- I gave the *guillotine* to a museum (8)
- *de facto* and *de jure* (8)

PROFESSIONAL WRITING

DEATH AND JUSTICE

John O'Sullivan

Of the many controversies swirling around the death penalty, whether or not Tim McVeigh's execution should be observed by the relatives of his victims is the most misleading. For it subtly discredits capital punishment by implying that it is a form of private revenge for the benefit of the victims' families. 1

Admittedly there is a link between justice and revenge. Bacon expressed   *2*
it well when he described revenge as "a kind of wild justice." When we
move; from a state of nature to a civilized society, however, we give up our
rights of self-protection and revenge in return for the state's promise of justice and retribution. And McVeigh's execution is the expression of that
public retribution rather than of private revenge.

The eighteenth century took this view even further, holding that pub-   *3*
lic retribution required a public execution. As Dr. Johnson pointed out, this
gave a certain dignity to the condemned man who was visibly paying for his
crimes. He would sometimes make a speech of repentance and admonition from the gallows: "Friends, be warned by my fate. Here is the dreadful consequence of a life of crime. I go now to seek mercy from the God who
will judge us all. Pray for my wretched soul. Etc."

We no longer hold public executions because we think ourselves more   *4*
civilized. In fact, we may merely be more squeamish. Restricting the seats
at an execution to a victim's family is arguably less justifiable than a public
gallows. For it treats a man's death not as an awesome punishment for a
terrible crime but as a means of emotional compensation for those he has
injured. Retributive justice is thus replaced by therapeutic revenge—a step
toward our sentimental modernity but away from a civilized rule of law.

Of course, some argue that the death penalty is uncivilized by its very   *5*
nature. But the death penalty, like all formal legal punishments, is a sign of
civilization. It is to civilization what lynching, vendettas, and vigilantism are
to barbarism and anarchy. Those who describe capital punishment as "barbaric" are generally defining "civilization" and "barbarism" quite arbitrarily
to mean whatever they like or dislike. Thus when they say, "The death
penalty is uncivilized," their words should be translated as "We don't like
the death penalty." That is not a statement about reality, nor a logical argument, but a pure expression of preference.

To be sure, some undoubtedly civilized European nations have aban-   *6*
doned the death penalty in favor of other punishments in the last few
decades. But the political elites in those countries usually did so over majority public opposition. What that demonstrates is not that Europe is more
civilized than the U.S. but that it is less democratic.

So we come finally to the argument that the death penalty is a cruel and   *7*
unnecessary punishment offensive to religious (and specifically Christian)
morality. In recent years something like this view has been adopted by no less
a figure than Pope John Paul II. This has raised difficult questions for Catholics
(and indeed other Christians) who have thus far supported capital punishment.

They will be helped through the theological thickets by a fine article 8
in the April issue of the religious magazine, *First Things,* by the newly created Cardinal Avery Dulles (the son of John Foster Dulles.) Cardinal Dulles
agrees with the Pope. But because the death penalty is a question that mixes
both moral and secular prudential judgments, he also makes room for con-
scientious disagreement by Catholics after prayerful consideration of the
Church's teaching.

The Cardinal's strongest points, as it seems to me, are that the death 9
penalty should not be imposed, first, if there is a serious risk of wrongful
execution and, second, if the legitimate purposes of punishment can be
equally well achieved by imprisonment. He feels that these considerations
override the traditional Christian endorsement of capital punishment. But
do they?

Take miscarriages of justice first. The number of known wrongful ex- 10
ecutions is tiny and the legal safeguards against them are so strict that very
few murderers ever reach the electric chair. The last federal execution, for
instance, took place 38 years ago. Above all, the arrival of DNA—which has
both exonerated some people on Death Row and increased public nerv-
ousness about capital punishment—ensures that the already low risk of
wrongful execution will now be reduced still further. Since there was a risk
of wrongful execution down the centuries when the Church supported capital punishment, our recent progress to a lesser risk strengthens the case for
it.

Nor can imprisonment effectively mimic the death penalty for the very 11
clear reason that it is less final. Some murderers are imprisoned, released,
and able to murder again. As Professor Paul G. Cassell pointed out in his
testimony to the House Judiciary Committee in 1993: "Of the roughly
52,000 state prison inmates serving time for murder in 1984, an estimated
810 had previously been convicted of murder and had killed 821 persons following those convictions. Executing each of these inmates following their
initial murder conviction would have saved 821 innocent lives."

Nor does life without parole entirely solve this problem: Five of the 12
murders were committed in prison. Again, we have no reason to think that
in the modern world imprisonment safeguards us as effectively as capital
punishment.

Where Cardinal Dulles does persuade me is in rejecting public execu- 13
tions on the grounds that, in our debased *Survivor* and MTV culture, they
would quickly be transformed from an awesome deterrent into bloodthirsty

Roman spectacles—unless, final irony, the death penalty is abolished even as our society spirals downwards into a new sort of barbarism which mingles casual cruelty with sentimentality and moral self-congratulation.

In your journal, write the meanings of the following words:

- public *retribution* **(2)**
- a speech of repentance and *admonition* **(3)**
- *retributive* justice **(4)**
- barbarism and *anarchy* **(5)**
- secular *prudential* judgments **(8)**
- *exonerated* some people on Death Row **(10)**

QUESTIONS FOR WRITING AND DISCUSSION

1. Each of these three authors is writing to a slightly different *audience*. Citing specific passages from each essay as illustration, describe the audience that each writer addresses.

2. What exactly is Edward Koch's thesis or overall claim? Find one or two sentences from his essay that clearly express his thesis. In paragraph 13, Koch says, "the state has rights that the private individual does not." Why is this statement important for Koch's thesis? Explain.

3. Where does Robert Badinter state his thesis most clearly? How is his thesis related to the fact that he is French and is responsible for abolishing the death penalty in France?

4. Is John O' Sullivan for or against the death penalty? What conditions would capital punishment have to meet in order for him to support it? Where does he state his conditional position most clearly?

5. Edward Koch's essay follows a classical argumentative organization. Look at the six-part classical structure in the "Shaping" section of this chapter. Does

Koch's essay follow the classical sequence outlined there (introduction, narration, partition, argument, refutation, and conclusion)? How does he revise or adapt this structure?

6. Compare the organization of Badinter's and O'Sullivan's essays. Which of the elements of a classical organization does each essay use? Where does each essay consider opposing positions and counter them with reasons and evidence?

7. Argumentative essays use appeals to reason, character, and emotion. Review all three essays, looking examples of each of these appeals by all three writers. Which writer is most logical? Which writer uses appeals to character most frequently? Are these appeals effective? Finally, find examples of appeals to emotion by all three writers. Which appeals are most effective and which are too emotional?

8. Evaluate all three essays based on their use of supporting evidence. Find examples, if you can, of statistics, specific references to crimes or criminals, and comparisons or analogies used by each writer. Which writer's evidence most effectively supports his argument?

9. In the preface to these essays, you were asked to consider how the *context* for the writing of each essay helped determine each writer's argument. Explain the influence that the writing context—the events occurring during the time of the writing of the essay, the writer's own occupation and experiences, and the place of publication—had on the argument of each writer.

10. On the Internet, use your browser or a database such as Electric Library to find more recent articles on capital punishment. Print out three or four of the most interesting articles and bring them to class. Be prepared to summarize the argument in each essay and to discuss how the new essays add to the conversation created in the three essays by Koch, Badinter, and O'Sullivan. What arguments are still being debated? What new perspectives do these articles bring to the discussion?

11. Consider the arguing essay that you are currently writing. Keeping your own particular context, purpose, and audience in mind, should you use Edward Koch's classical organization? How do you intend to respond to opposing or alternative viewpoints? Should you use all three kinds of appeals (to reason, to character, and to emotion)? What personal experiences, specific examples, statistics, quotations from authorities, and comparisons could you use?

12. Statistics can be effective support in an argumentative essay as long as the study is valid and the conclusions drawn from them are justifiable by the

study or poll methods. Read the following results taken from a poll published by the *Harris Poll*. Then answer these questions:

- Are these statistics most likely to support a writer's appeal to reason, to character, or to emotion? Refer to arguments in the essays to explain your choice.

- Which of the three essays by Koch, Badinter, and O'Sullivan do these statistics most clearly support? Explain.

- If any of these authors were to use the results of this poll, *where* in their essays should they cite these statistics and conclusions? Why?

- Read the "Methodology" paragraph and state in your own words what it means.

PROFESSIONAL WRITING

MORE THAN TWO-THIRDS OF AMERICANS CONTINUE TO SUPPORT THE DEATH PENALTY

Humphrey Taylor

Support for the death penalty remains very strong in the United States, even though almost everyone believes that innocent people are sometimes convicted of murder, and only a minority believes it is a deterrent.

The last few years have seen many reports of people being released from prison after DNA tests showed they were innocent of murders or rapes for which they had been wrongly convicted many years before. The state of Illinois has imposed a moratorium on capital punishment. But a large 69% to 22% majority of the public still favors capital punishment and this majority is actually somewhat higher than it was in 2001 and in 2000 (when it had fallen to 64% to 25%).

This majority support for the death penalty holds even though almost everyone (95%) believes that innocent people are sometimes convicted of murder. On average they believe that 11% of all those convicted are innocent. But the two-thirds of the public who support the death penalty seem to feel that that is an acceptable price to pay.

Certainly, there are some inconsistencies in public attitudes toward the *4*
death penalty, as there are on many issues. Only just over one-third of the
public (37%) say, when asked, that they would still support the death penalty
if they believed "that quite a substantial number of innocent people are
convicted of murder" and about half (47%) say they would oppose it. But
if 11% are wrongly convicted, is that not "substantial"?

Based on this and other polls, it seems very unlikely that a majority of *5*
Americans will actually oppose capital punishment any time soon, leaving
the United States as the only western democracy which executes murderers.

These are some results of the *Harris Poll*® of 993 adults, surveyed by *6*
telephone by Harris Interactive between December 10 and 16, 2003.

Other interesting results of this poll are: *7*

- Only 41% of all adults believe that the death penalty deters people
  from committing murder—the smallest number from among all of
  the *Harris Polls*® that asked this question in the last 27 years.
- A 36% plurality would still like to see an increase in the number of
  executions (versus 21% who favor a decrease, and 33% no change).
- African Americans believe that, on average, 23% of murder convictions are of innocent people, compared to 9% among whites and
  16% among Hispanics.

Methodology

The *Harris Poll*® was conducted by telephone within the United States be- *8*
tween December 10 and 16, 2003 among a nationwide cross-section of 993
adults (ages 18+). Figures for age, sex, race, education, number of adults

Table 10.1   Believe in Capital Punishment

"Do you believe in capital punishment, that is the death penalty, or are you opposed to it?"

	1965	1969	1970	1973	1976	1983	1997	1999	2000	2001	Dec 2003
	%	%	%	%	%	%	%	%	%	%	%
Believe in it	38	48	47	59	67	68	75	71	64	67	69
Opposed to it	47	38	42	31	25	27	22	21	25	26	22
Not sure/Refused	15	14	11	10	8	5	3	8	11	7	9

Base: All Adults

Table 10.2 Is Capital Punishment a Deterrent?

"Do you feel that executing people who commit murder deters others from committing murder, or do you think such executions don't have much effect?"

	1976	1983	1997	1999	2000	2001	Dec 2003
	%	%	%	%	%	%	%
Deters others	59	63	49	47	44	42	41
Not much effect	34	32	49	49	50	52	53
Not sure/Refused	7	5	2	4	7	7	6

Base: All Adults

and number of voice/telephone lines in the household were weighted where necessary to align them with their actual proportions in the population.

In theory, with a probability sample of this size, one can say with 95 percent certainty that the results have a statistical precision of ±3 percentage points of what they would be if the entire adult population had been polled with complete accuracy. Unfortunately, there are several other possible sources of error in all polls or surveys that are probably more serious than theoretical calculations of sampling error. They include refusals to be interviewed (non-response), question wording and question order, interviewer bias, weighting by demographic control data and screening (e.g., for likely voters). It is impossible to quantify the errors that may result from these factors.

These statements conform to the principles of disclosure of the National Council on Public Polls.

Arguing: The Writing Process

ASSIGNMENT FOR ARGUING

For this assignment, choose a subject that interests you or relates to your own experience. You may even choose a subject that you have already written about for this class. Then examine the subject for a debatable claim of fact or definition, value, cause and effect, or policy that you could make about it. If the claim is arguable, you have a focus for your arguing paper. Analyze your probable audience to guide your argumentative strategy. (Avoid ready-made pro–con subjects such as abortion, drinking age, drugs, and euthanasia *unless* you have clear beliefs based on your own experience.)

Arguments can appear in a wide range of genres, depending on your purpose and audience. Letters to the editor, essays for a college class, postings to an Internet forum, scripts for a debate, and political documents use the strategies of argument. As you select your topic, consider what audience and genre would most effectively meet the assignment, purpose, and audience.

> *You can write about anything, and if you write well enough, even the reader with no intrinsic interest in the subject will become involved.*
>
> —TRACY KIDDER, NOVELIST

CHOOSING A SUBJECT

If a journal entry suggested a possible subject, do the collecting and shaping strategies. Otherwise, consider the following ideas:

- Review your journal entries from previous chapters and the papers that you have already written for this class. Test these subjects for an arguable claim that you could make, opposing arguments you could consider, and an appropriate audience for an argumentative piece of writing.
- Brainstorm possible ideas for argumentative subjects from the other courses you are currently taking or have taken. What controversial issues in psychology, art, philosophy, journalism, biology, nutrition, engineering, physical education, or literature have you discussed in your classes? Ask current or past instructors for possible controversial topics relating to their courses.

- Newspapers and magazines are full of controversial subjects in sports, medicine, law, business, and family. Browse through current issues or on-line magazines looking for possible subjects. Check news items, editorials, and cartoons. Look for subjects related to your own interests, your job, your leisure activities, or your experiences.

- Interview your friends, family, or classmates. What controversial issues are affecting their lives most directly? What would they most like to change about their lives? What has irritated or angered them most in the recent past?

- If you are doing a community-service-learning project, consider one of the following possible topics: (1) Which of the agency's activities best meet the goals of the agency? Write an essay to the agency coordinator recommending a reallocation of resources to the most effective activities. (2) How might agency volunteers more usefully serve the agency in future projects? Write to your project coordinator recommending improvements that would better meet the dual goals of academic learning and agency service.

COLLECTING

NARROWING AND FOCUSING YOUR CLAIM   Narrow your subject to a specific topic, and sharpen your focus by applying the "Wh" questions. If your subject is "grades," your responses might be as follows.

Subject: Grades

- **Who:** College students
- **What:** Letter grades
- **When:** In freshman and sophomore years
- **Where:** Especially in nonmajor courses
- **Why:** What purpose do grades serve in nonmajor courses?

Determine what claim or claims you want to make. Make sure that your claim is *arguable*. (Remember that claims can overlap; an argument may combine several related claims.)

Claim of Fact or Definition

- Letter grades exist. (not arguable)
- Employers consider grades when hiring. (slightly more arguable, but not very controversial)
- Grades do not measure learning. (very arguable)

Claim About Cause or Effect

- Grades create anxiety for students. (not very arguable)
- Grades actually prevent discovery and learning. (arguable)

Claim About Value

- Grades are not fair. (not very arguable: "fairness" can usually be determined)
- Grades are bad because they discourage individual initiative. (arguable)
- Grades are good because they give students an incentive to learn. (arguable)

Claim About a Solution or Policy

- Grades should be eliminated altogether. (arguable—but difficult)
- Grades should be eliminated in humanities courses. (arguable)
- Grades should change to pass/fail in nonmajor courses. (arguable—and more practical)

Focusing and narrowing your *claim* helps determine what evidence you need to collect. Use your observing, remembering, reading, and investigative skills to gather the evidence. *Note:* An argumentative essay should not be a mathematical equation that uses only abstract and impersonal evidence. *Your experience* can be crucial to a successful argumentative essay. Start by doing the *remembering* exercises. Your audience wants to know not only why you are writing on this particular *topic,* but also why the subject is of interest to *you.*

REMEMBERING   Use *freewriting, looping, branching,* or *clustering* to recall experiences, ideas, events, and people who are relevant to your claim. If you are writing about grades, brainstorm about how *your* teachers used grades, how you reacted to specific grades in one specific class, how your friends or parents reacted, and what you felt or thought. These prewriting exercises will help you understand your claim and give you specific examples that you can use for evidence.

OBSERVING   If possible for your topic, collect data and evidence by observing, firsthand, the facts, values, effects, or possible solutions related to your claim. *Repeated* observation will give you good inductive evidence to support your argument.

INVESTIGATING   For most argumentative essays, some research or investigation is essential. Because it is difficult to imagine all the valid counterarguments, interview friends, classmates, family, coworkers, and authorities on your topic. From the library, gather books and articles that contain arguments in support of your claim. *Note:* As you do research in the library, print out articles or make photocopies of key passages from relevant sources to hand in with your essay. If you cite sources from your research, list them on a Works Cited page following your essay. (See Chapter 12 for the proper format.)

SHAPING

As you plan your organization, reconsider your rhetorical situation. Will the *genre* you have selected (letter, essay, Web site, brochure, Power Point presentation) help carry out your *purpose* for your intended audience? Is there a relevant *occasion* (meeting, anniversary, or response to news item) that your writing might focus on? What is the *cultural, social,* or *political context* for your writing? Finally, reconsider your *audience*. Try imagining one real person who might be among your readers. Is this person open-minded and likely to be convinced by your evidence? Does this person represent the opposing position? If you have several alternative positions, are there individual people who might represent, in your mind, each of these positions? After reconsidering your rhetorical situation, try the shaping strategies that follow.

> **" *No one can write decently who is distrustful of the reader's intelligence, or whose attitude is patronizing.* "**
> —E. B. WHITE,
> ESSAYIST

LIST OF "PRO" AND "CON" ARGUMENTS   Either on paper or in a computer file, write out your *claim,* and then list the arguments for your position (pro) and the arguments for the opposing positions (con). After you have made the list, match up arguments by drawing lines, as indicated. (On the computer file, move "Con" column arguments so they appear directly opposite the corresponding "Pro" column arguments.)

Claim: Grades should be changed to pass/fail in nonmajor courses.

Pro	Con
Grades inhibit learning by putting too much emphasis on competition	Grades actually promote learning by setting students to study as hard as possible.
Pass/fail grading encourages students to explore nonmajor fields.	Students should be encouraged to compete with majors. They may want to change majors and need to know if they can compete.
Grade competition with majors in the field can be discouraging.	
Some students do better without the pressure of grades; they need to find out if they can motivate themselves without grades, but they shouldn't have to risk grades in their major field to discover that.	If students don't have traditional grading, they won't take nonmajor courses seriously.

If some pro and con arguments "match," you will be able to argue against the con and for your claim at the same time. If some arguments do not "match," you will need to consider them separately.

DRAW CIRCLE OF ALTERNATIVE POSITIONS   If you are considering multiple alternative positions, put your claim in the middle of a circle and indicate the various positions or stakeholders on the outside of the circle. This diagram will help you identify the most important positions in the debate and will help you organize your writing. The following example is based on the claim that standardized testing in schools should put the students' needs first.

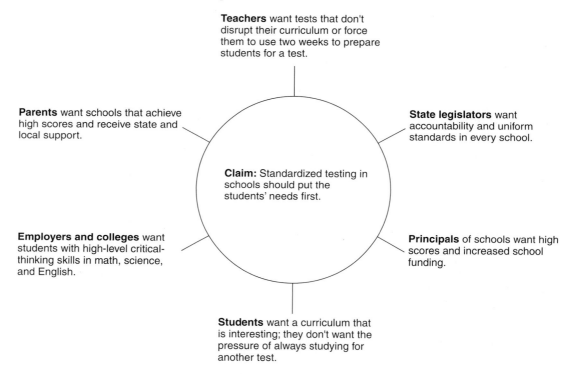

Teachers want tests that don't disrupt their curriculum or force them to use two weeks to prepare students for a test.

Parents want schools that achieve high scores and receive state and local support.

State legislators want accountability and uniform standards in every school.

Claim: Standardized testing in schools should put the students' needs first.

Employers and colleges want students with high-level critical-thinking skills in math, science, and English.

Principals of schools want high scores and increased school funding.

Students want a curriculum that is interesting; they don't want the pressure of always studying for another test.

Once you have a diagram for all the major alternative positions or stakeholders, decide the focus of your argument. For your purpose, audience, and context, you may want to focus just on the different goals of teachers, students, and parents. Or you may want to suggest how teachers, students, and parents should organize and force legislators to change the standardized tests or change how schools are funded based on test results.

OUTLINES FOR ARGUMENTS   For more than two thousand years, writers and speakers have been trying to determine the most effective means to persuade audiences. One of the oldest outlines for a successful argument comes from classical rhetoric. The following six-part outline is intended as a guideline rather than a rigid list. Test this outline; see if it will work for *your* argument.

Introduction:	Announces subject; *gets audience's interest and attention;* establishes a trustworthy character for the writer
Narration:	Gives *background*, context, statement of problem, or definition
Partition:	States thesis or *claim*, outlines or *maps* arguments
Argument:	Makes *arguments* and gives *evidence* for the claim or thesis
Refutation:	Shows why *opposing arguments* are not true or valid
Conclusion:	Summarizes arguments, suggests solution, *ties into the introduction or background*

Most arguments have these features, but not necessarily in this order. Some writers prefer to respond to or refute opposing arguments before giving the arguments in support of their claims. When con and pro arguments match, refuting an argument followed by the argument for your claim may work best. As you organize your own arguments, put your strongest argument last and your weakest argument either first or in the middle.

Because most short argumentative essays contain the introduction, narration, and partition all in a few introductory paragraphs, you may use the following abbreviated outlines for argument:

Outline 1   Introduction (attention getter, background, claim or thesis, map)
Your arguments
Refutation of opposing arguments
Conclusion

Outline 2   Introduction
Refutation of opposing arguments
Your arguments
Conclusion

Outline 3   Introduction
Refutation of first opposing argument that matches your first argument
Refutation of second opposing argument that matches your second argument, and so on
Additional arguments
Conclusion

For Rogerian arguments, you can follow one of the above outlines, but the emphasis, tone, and attitude are different:

Introduction: Attention getter, background
                       Claim (often downplayed to reduce threat)
                       Map (often omitted)
                       Appeal to character (crucial to Rogerian argument)

Opposing arguments: State opposing arguments fairly
                       Show where, how, or when those arguments may be
                       valid; establish common ground

Your arguments: State your position fairly
                       Show where, how, or when your arguments are valid

Resolution: Present compromise position
                       State your solution to the problem, and show its advantages to both sides

DEVELOPING ARGUMENTS   Think of your argument as a series of *because* statements, each supported by evidence, statistics, testimony, expert opinion, data, specific examples from your experience, or a combination of these.

THESIS OR CLAIM: Grades should be abolished in nonmajor courses

Reason 1   Because they may keep a student from attempting a difficult non-major course
            Statistics, testimony, data, and examples

Reason 2   Because competition with majors in the field can be discouraging
            Statistics, testimony, data, and examples

Reason 3   Because grades inhibit students' learning in nonmajor fields
            Statistics, testimony, data, and examples

You can develop each reason using a variety of strategies. The following strategies may help you generate additional reasons and examples:

Definition: Define the crucial terms or ideas. (What do you mean by
               learning?)

Comparison: Compare the background, situation, and context with another
               similar context. (What other schools have tried pass/fail grading
               for nonmajor courses? How has it worked?)

Process: How does or should a change occur? (How do nonmajors become
               discouraged? How should a school implement pass/fail in grading?)

Research Tips [_____] GO

When you draft your arguing essay, don't let your citations or direct quotations overpower your own argument. Two tactics will keep you in control of your argument:

First, always avoid "unidentified flying quotations" by *sandwiching* your quotations. *Introduce* quotations by referring to the author, the source, and/or the author's study. *Follow* quotations with a sentence explaining how the author's evidence supports your argument. For examples, see paragraphs 4 and 5 in the essay by student writer Crystal Sabatke at the end of this chapter.

Second, keep your direct quotations *short*. If possible, reduce a long passage to one sentence and incorporate the quoted material in the flow of your own language. For example, in her essay at the end of this chapter, Sabatke writes,

> According to Ruth Conniff, author of "Big Bad Welfare: Welfare Reform, Politics, and Children," the welfare reform discussion "indicates that what happens to children doesn't matter to Americans, so long as mothers are forced to work" (8).

These strategies may help you develop an argument coherently and effectively. If several strategies are possible, consider which would be most effective for your *audience*.

DRAFTING

You will never really know "enough" about your subject or have "enough" evidence. At some point, however, you must stop collecting and start your draft. The most frequent problem in drafting an argumentative essay is delaying the actual writing too long, until the deadline is too close.

For argumentative essays, start with a working order or sequence and sketch an outline on paper or in your head. Additional examples and appeals to reason, character, or emotion may occur to you as you develop your argument or refute opposing arguments. In addition, if you have done some research, have your notes, photocopies of key data, statistics, quotations, and citations of authorities close at hand. As you write, you will discover that some information or arguments simply don't fit into the flow of your essay. Don't force arguments into your draft if they no longer seem to belong.

REVISING

Argumentation is the most public of the purposes for writing. The rhetorical situation (purpose, audience, genre, occasion, and cultural context) plays a crucial role. As you revise, look at this larger context, not just at phrasing, words, or sentences. Test your argument by having friends or classmates read it. Explain your claim, your focus, and your intended audience, genre, and context. Ask them to look for counterarguments that you have omitted or for weaknesses, omissions, or fallacies in logic. But don't automatically change your draft. Take the advice that makes your overall purpose more effective for your audience.

Guidelines for Revision

- **When you finish your draft, reconsider the elements of the rhetorical situation** (writer, purpose, audience, genre, occasion, cultural context). Look at the big picture. What needs changing? What needs to be added? What parts are repetitious or not effective?

- **Ask a class member or friend to read your draft to determine the intended audience for your argument.** See which arguments your reader thinks would not be effective for your audience.

- **Use the Toulmin model to evaluate your essay.** Is your claim clearly stated? Does your claim have a qualifier? Do you note exceptions to your claim? Do you have warrant statements explaining how your data support your reasons and claim?

- **Which of your *because* arguments are most effective?** Least effective? Should you change the outline or structure that you initially chose?

- **Revise your draft to avoid fallacies or errors in reasoning.** Errors in logic create two problems: They can destroy your rational appeal and open your argument to a logical rebuttal, and they lessen your credibility—and thus reduce your appeal to your character. (Review the list of fallacies below.)

- **Support your reasons with evidence:** *data, facts, statistics, quotations, observations, testimony, statistics, or specific examples from your experience.* Check your collecting notes once again for additional evidence to add to your weakest argument. Is there a weak or unsupported argument that you should simply omit?

PEER RESPONSE

Writer: Before you exchange drafts with a peer reader, provide the following information about your essay:

1. a. Intended audience and genre
   b. Primary claim or thesis
   c. Opposing arguments that you refute
   d. Arguments supporting your claim
2. Write out one or two questions about your draft that you want your reader to answer.

Reader: Read the writer's entire draft. As you reread, answer the following questions:

1. **Arguments.** Without looking at the writer's responses above, describe the essay's (a) target audience, (b) primary claim, (c) opposing arguments that are refuted, (d) arguments supporting the claim. Which of these did you have trouble identifying? What additional pro or con arguments should the writer consider?

2. **Organization.** Identify the following parts of the writer's draft: introduction, narration, partition, argument, refutation, and conclusion. Does the writer need all of these for his or her particular subject and audience? Why or why not? Where could the writer clarify transitions between sections? Explain.

3. **Appeals.** Identify places where the writer appeals to reason, to character, and to emotion. Where could these appeals be stronger? Identify sentences where the writer is overly emotional or illogical (see the section "Revising Fallacies in Logic").

4. **Evidence.** Identify at least one paragraph in which the supporting evidence is strong. Then identify at least one paragraph in which the writer makes assertions without sufficient supporting evidence. What kind of evidence might the writer use—first-hand observation, personal examples, testimony from experts, interviews, statistics, or other? Explain.

5. **Revision plan.** List three key changes that the writer should make during the revision.

6. Answer the writer's questions.

(continued on next page)

(continued from previous page)

Writer: When your essay is returned, read the comments by your peer reader(s) and do the following:

1. Compare your descriptions of the audience, genre, claim, and pro and con arguments with your reader's descriptions. Where there are differences, clarify your essay.

2. Read all of your peer reader's responses. List revisions that you intend to make in each of the following areas: *audience, genre, arguments, organization, appeals,* and *supporting evidence.*

- **Signal the major arguments and counterarguments in your partition or map.** Between paragraphs, use clear transitions and paragraph hooks.
- **Could your essay be improved by visuals or special formatting?** Reconsider your genre and audience. If visuals might make your essay more effective, do a search on the computer. If you need help formatting your essay, check with a peer, a computer lab assistant, or your instructor.
- **If you cite sources in your essay, check the *accuracy* of your statistics, quotations, and source references.** (See Chapter 12 for the proper format of in-text documentation and the Works Cited page.)
- **Revise sentences to improve conciseness and clarity.**
- **Edit sentences for grammar, punctuation, and spelling.**

REVISING FALLACIES IN LOGIC Listed below are common fallacies in logic. Reread your draft or your peer's draft and revise as appropriate to eliminate these logical errors.

- **Hasty generalization:** Conclusion not logically justified by sufficient or unbiased evidence. If your friend Mary tells you that Professor Paramecium is a hard grader because he gave her a 36 percent on the first biology test, she is making a hasty generalization. It may be *true*—Prof P. may *be* a difficult grader—but Mary's logic is not valid. She cannot logically draw that conclusion from a sample of one; the rest of the class may have received grades of between 80 and 100.
- **Post hoc ergo propter hoc:** Literally, "after this, therefore because of this." Just because Event B *occurred after* Event A does not mean that A *necessarily caused* B. You washed your car in the morning, and it rained in the afternoon. Though we joke about how it always rains after we wash the

car, there is, of course, no causal relationship between the two events. "I forgot to leave the porch light on when I went out last night, and someone robbed my house": Without further evidence, we cannot assume that the lack of light contributed to the robbery. A more obvious cause might be the back door left unlocked.

- **Genetic fallacy:** Arguing that the origins of a person, object, or institution determine its character, nature, or worth. Like the post hoc fallacy, the genetic fallacy is an error in causal relationships.

> This automobile was made in Detroit. It'll probably fall apart after 10,000 miles.
> He speaks with a funny German accent. He's really stupid, you know.
> He started Celestial Seasonings Herb Teas just to make a quick buck; it's just another phony yuppie product.

The second half of each statement *may* or *may not* be true; the logical error is in assuming that the origin of something will necessarily determine its worth or quality. Stereotyping is frequently caused by a genetic fallacy.

- **Begging the question:** Loading the conclusion in the claim. Arguing that "pornography should be banned because it corrupts our youth" is a logical claim. However, saying that "filthy and corrupting pornography should be banned" is begging the question: The conclusion that the writer should *prove* (that pornography corrupts) is assumed in the claim. Other examples: "Those useless psychology classes should be dropped from the curriculum"; "Senator Swingle's sexist behavior should be censured by Congress"; "Everyone knows that our ineffective drug control program is a miserable failure." The writers must *prove* that the psychology classes are useless, that Senator Swingle is sexist, and that the drug program is a failure.
- **Circular argument:** A sentence or argument that restates rather than proves. Thus, it goes in a circle: "President Reagan was a great communicator because he had that knack of talking effectively to the people." The terms in the beginning of the sentence (*great communicator*) and the end of the sentence (*talking effectively*) are interchangeable. The sentence ends where it started.
- **Either/or:** An oversimplification that reduces alternatives to only two choices, thereby creating a false dilemma. Statements such as "Love it or leave it" attempt to reduce the alternatives to two. If you don't love your school, your town, or your country, you don't have to leave: A third choice is to change it and make it better. Proposed solutions frequently have an

either/or fallacy: "Either we ban boxing or hundreds of young men will be senselessly killed." A third alternative is to change boxing's rules or equipment. "If we don't provide farmers with low-interest loans, they will go bankrupt." Increasing prices for farm products might be a better alternative.

- **Faulty comparison or analogy:** Basing an argument on a comparison of two things, ideas, events, or situations that are similar but not identical. Although comparisons or analogies are often effective in argument, they can hide logical problems. "We can solve the meth problem the same way we reduced the DWI problem: Attack it with increased enforcement and mandatory jail sentences." Although the situations are similar, they are not identical. The DWI solution will not necessarily work for drugs. An analogy is an extended comparison that uses something simple or familiar to explain something complex or less familiar. "Solving a mathematics problem is like baking a cake: You have to take it one step at a time. First, you assemble your ingredients or your known data. . . ." Like baking, solving a problem does involve a process; unlike baking, however, mathematics is more exact. Changing the amount of flour in a recipe by 1 percent will not make the cake fall; changing a numeric value by 1 percent, however, may ruin the whole problem. The point, however, is not to avoid comparisons or analogies. Simply make sure that your conclusions are qualified; acknowledge the *differences* between the two things compared as well as the similarities.

- **Ad hominem (literally, "to the man"):** An attack on the character of the individual or the opponent rather than his or her actual opinions, arguments, or qualifications: "Susan Davidson, the prosecuting attorney, drinks heavily. There's no way she can present an effective case." This is an attack on Ms. Davidson's character rather than an analysis of her legal talents. Her record in court may be excellent.

- **Ad populum (literally, "to the people"):** An emotional appeal to positive concepts (God, mother, country, liberty, democracy, apple pie) or negative concepts (fascism, atheism) rather than a direct discussion of the real issue: "Those senators voting to increase the defense budget are really warmongers at heart." "If you are a true American, you should be for tariffs to protect the garment industry."

- **Red herring and straw man:** Diversionary tactics designed to avoid confronting the key issue. *Red herring* refers to the practice of dragging a smelly fish across the trail to divert tracking dogs away from the real quarry. A red herring occurs when writers avoid countering an opposing argument directly: "Of course equal pay for women is an important issue, but I wonder whether women really want to take the responsibility that comes with higher paying jobs. Do they really want the additional stress?" This writer diverts attention away from the argument about equal pay to another issue, stress—thus, a red herring. In the *straw man* diversion, the writer sets up an artificially easy argument to refute in place of the real issue. Former President Richard Nixon's famous "Checkers" speech is a good example. Accused of spending $18,000 in campaign gifts for personal use, Nixon described how he received Checkers, a little black-and-white spotted cocker spaniel dog. Because his daughter Tricia loved this dog, Nixon decided to keep it. Surely, there's nothing wrong with that, is there? The "Checkers" argument is a "straw man" diversion: Justifying his personal use of this gift was much easier than explaining how and why he spent the $18,000. Avoid red herring and straw man tactics by either refuting an argument directly or acknowledging that it has some merit. Don't just change the subject.

POSTSCRIPT ON THE WRITING PROCESS

In your journal, answer the following questions:

1. Describe how your beliefs about your subject changed from the time you decided on your claim to when you revised your essay. What caused the change in your views?

2. What opposing argument was most difficult to counter? Explain how you handled it.

3. Which was your strongest argument? Did you use logical appeals and evidence, or did you rely more on appeals to character or emotion? Explain.

4. How did your writing process for the argumentative essay change from the process for your previous essays? What steps or stages took longer? What stages did you have to go back and rework?

STUDENT WRITING

STUDENT WRITING

WELFARE IS STILL NECESSARY FOR WOMEN AND CHILDREN IN THE U.S.

Crystal Sabatke

Crystal Sabatke decided to write her arguing essay about changes in the welfare system that require women to work in order to receive certain welfare payments. She decided to focus particularly on readers who believe that welfare mothers will simply become lazy if they don't have to work for the money to support their families. She hopes that "by showing examples of positive welfare stories, I can show that mothers and their children are more important than saving a few cents per dollar." Reproduced below are Sabatke's notes for her audience analysis, her rough draft, the responses to her peer review workshop, and her final, revised draft.

Audience Analysis: Readers' Beliefs

My readers will assume that women on welfare who have children can go out and get jobs. That they should get jobs for the betterment of themselves and their children. That when they do get a job, their financial problems will be solved and that welfare will be a thing of the past. In order to shake these assumptions, I believe that emotional appeals should be used. Examples of factual women on welfare in negative situations that prevent them from getting jobs—children, low-income wage jobs, etc.

My readers also believe in the principle of a strong work ethic, the idea that if you work hard, you can achieve the "American Dream." I do feel that I should show how this principle is not applicable in certain situations—ones that my readers probably do not take into strong consideration.

Finally, I feel that my readers blindly value getting jobs more than taking care of children (even though these are the same people who hypocritically focus on family values). I think that family values should be focused on because this is something that is held in high regard by nearly every human being.

WELFARE IN THE UNITED STATES—
A NECESSITY WITHOUT PROGRAMMING

First Draft

What defines an American woman? Women in the United States play numerous roles; many are successful executives, mothers, wives, and scholars. Women have broken many barriers throughout U.S. history and have become, in general, a very successful group in society. But what about the women who haven't broken the barriers? What about the women who had children at a young age with a boyfriend or husband who left them alone soon after? What about the women who can't find a job because their education level hinders their prosperity? What about the women who can't seem to find their way above the poverty level and have to seek help from the government?

Throughout the United States, poverty is not abnormal—especially for women and children. With "44.6 percent of the children who lived in [female-headed households] poor in 1994, and almost half of all children who are poor living in female-headed households," (A) doesn't it seem ironic that the government is cutting welfare expenditures for women and children? Many government officials believe that "the welfare system and its recipients are the cause of the problem." (B) What the lawmakers aren't considering, however, is that poverty is essentially the catalyst in a circle of controversy, and that the only way out of the problems is to provide adequate educational opportunities for welfare recipients, along with ample child care programs and options and a sufficient minimum wage for all citizens. The answer is not ending welfare, but dealing with the problems of poverty in a realistic manner.

In contrast to opposing arguments, most women aren't poor and having children because they want more welfare money or because they are lazy, but because they don't have a sufficient education. As Nicholas Zill, a writer for *Public Health Reports,* states, "Girls and boys who become parents while they are still of school age are . . . predominantly those with low test scores and grades, who are disengaged from school or in active conflict with parents, teachers, or school authorities." (C) The government needs to provide for all Americans an education system that works not only for the successful student, but also for the students that are not doing well. Female students, especially, should be educated about birth control and negative outcomes of having children at younger ages. We should not be punishing and impeding children for the mistakes of their parents and the deficiencies of our education system. Welfare is indispensable for uneducated women and their children until a system of education and support can be initiated and proven successful.

For people opposing government assistance of the poor, another popular argument is that welfare needs to be ended in all forms, and women with children need to get jobs. According to Charles Murray, a strong oppressor of the welfare system in America and an advocate of family values, a "strict job program" needs to be established that will force women to "drop out of a welfare program altogether." (D) Essentially, to the opposition, "the welfare-reform discussion indicates that what happens to children doesn't matter to Americans, so long as mothers are forced to work." (E) Unfortunately, however, for women with children who either decide to go into or are forced into the job market, there isn't a child care system that works with mothers to make a "strict job program" successful. The truth is, there is a scarcity of child care options in this country, and the ones that are available are generally out of the price range of a welfare mother. Shouldn't children be put foremost in this debate? If our country is really focused on family values, shouldn't women have the option to stay home and give their children good care even if it means keeping them on welfare? Welfare is essential in providing a means for women to provide not only adequate care for their children, but positive values for their future.

Another category of women on welfare who are quite often overlooked are those mothers who have minimum-wage jobs and who still need government assistance. The current method of getting women into the workplace is the Job Training Partnership Act, or "the Government's biggest training program." (E) According to *The Wall Street Journal*, however, this program, which offers low-wage jobs such as fast food "is a sham" (E) and "actually led to lower wages for poor young women compared with a control group." (E) Once a woman is in the workplace, it is easy to assume that she will be removed from welfare and become an effective member of society. What is not taken into consideration, however, is that a minimum wage can hardly keep up with the needs of a single mother. "The average [welfare] recipient who gets a full-time job . . . makes $6.74 an hour—about $14,000 a year. Daycare for two children can easily cost $12,000." (E) It is obvious that after subtracting child care, this equation leaves a mother with virtually nothing left to provide herself and her children with necessities such as food, clothing, and shelter. The answer is clearly not to simply put women in low-wage-earning jobs. Until Washington can come up with a solution that involves education and child care assistance and has raised the minimum wage enough to support a mother with children, a welfare system still needs to be provided.

The answer is not ending welfare, but providing supplemental programs that can realistically assist a single mother. With the minimum wage being too low, child care costs being impractical, and education programs virtually nonexistent, it is not fair to assume that welfare can be abolished. Of course, there are problems with the current welfare system, but supplemental programming is the only way to effectively change these glitches.

Arguing Essay: Peer-Response Worksheet

To the Writer: Briefly describe the audience for this paper. (Be sure to include your audience's position on the issue you're writing about.) Also note what you want your readers to focus on as they read.

My audience is white, conservative males who are against any welfare. Please comment on my development—and I kind of gave up on my conclusion. How can I make it better?

To the Reader: Answer the following questions:

1. Underline the *claim/thesis*. Is it clear? Make suggestions for improvement.

    Bev: *Good thesis. It is clear and placed in a good spot, just after enough background and before the bulk of the paper. However, I would elaborate more on the "realistic manner" either in your thesis sentence or a separate sentence.*

    Amy: *The thesis is very clear—however, the sentence after it confused me.*

2. Is the claim adequately *focused*—narrow within manageable/defensible limits? Why or why not? Explain.

    Bev: *The claim is well focused and clear.*

    Amy: *Possibly even too focused. Reads more like an essay map than a thesis.*

3. Do you feel the writer needs to add any *qualifiers* or exceptions in order to avoid overgeneralizing? If yes, explain.

    Bev: *You sort of overgeneralize about women on welfare, but not too noticeably. Maybe some statistics concerning these women would help.*

    Amy: *Possibly qualify for 2 parent and singles—see paragraph #5.*

4. Does the paper deal with *opposing arguments*? How successful do you feel the paper is in conceding and/or refuting opposing arguments? Explain.

Bev: *Good job of laying out the opposing sides of the argument.*

Amy: *Opposition clearly stated each time and then refuted. No work needed on the ones you have stated. Does not take into consideration two-parent welfare families or singles. Will some of your claims work for them as well?*

5. Does the *evidence* support the reasons? Where is more evidence needed? What kind of evidence is needed?

Bev: *Your use of evidence is effective. However, I would suggest more evidence in the first body paragraph. You only have one quotation—maybe throw another one in there.*

Amy: *More statistics would be helpful, for example, test scores as related to teen pregnancy.*

6. What are *one* or *two* areas that you feel the writer should address *first* in revising this paper? What suggestions can you make for conducting those revisions?

Bev: *Good organization of the paper. You follow a clear layout and it is easy to follow. I would develop your quotations more in paragraph 2. You use good evidence. Just develop it more. In your conclusion, maybe if you tied it into the intro, it would help you out. Restate arguments that you made in the introduction.*

Amy: *The lead paragraph seems to give an essay map but doesn't. Possibly phrase some of the questions to relate to the paragraphs? Conclusion: Instead of summing up what you said, try an analysis of the problem and its solutions.*

7. Return the paper to the writer and discuss your comments.

Final Draft

Welfare Is Still Necessary for Women and Children in the U.S.

What defines an American woman? Women in the United States play numerous roles; many are successful executives, mothers, wives, and scholars. Women have broken many barriers throughout U.S. history and have become, in general, a very successful group in society. But what about the women who haven't broken the barriers? What about the women who had children at a young age with a boyfriend or husband who left them soon after? What about the women who can't find a job because their education   *1* level hinders their prosperity? What about the women who can't seem to find their way above the poverty level and have to seek help from the government?

In the United States, poverty is not abnormal—especially for women and children. With "44.6 percent of the children who lived in [female-headed households] in 1994, and almost half of all children who are poor living in female-headed households," doesn't it seem ironic that the government continues to cut welfare expenditures for women and children? (Wellstone 1). Many government officials believe that "the welfare system and its recipients are the cause of the problem" (Rank 1). What these lawmakers aren't considering, however, is that poverty is essentially the catalyst in a circle of controversy, and that the only way out of the problem is to provide adequate educational opportunities for welfare recipients, ample child care programs and options, and a sufficient minimum wage for all citizens. Until methods such as these are instituted, it is necessary for the government to maintain a supportive welfare system for the women and children of our country.

In refutation of opposing arguments, most women aren't poor and having children because they want more welfare money or because they are lazy, but because they don't have a sufficient education. As Nicholas Zill, a writer for *Public Health Reports,* states, "Girls and boys who become parents while they are still of school age are . . . predominantly those with low test scores and grades, who are disengaged from school or in active conflict with parents, teachers, or school authorities" (6). Recent studies by the National Center for Health Statistics show that "nearly one in every four children in the U.S. is born to a mother who has not finished high school" (Zill 2). The government needs to provide an educational system that focuses not only on the successful student, but also on the student who is performing poorly. Because "parent education is linked to children's economic well-being," positive programs need to be created that provide support and alternatives to mainstream education for students who are "high risk" or are not college-bound (Zill 3). Female students, specifically, should be educated about birth control and the negative consequences of having children at younger ages. Until our nation takes active measures to improve the educational system, welfare is necessary to support the children who are born because of the inadequacies of our schools. America should not be punishing and impeding children for the mistakes of their parents and the deficiencies of our school system. Welfare is indispensable for uneducated women and their children until a better system of education and support can be initiated and proven successful.

Another popular argument given by people who oppose welfare is that single women with children should be working, not accepting welfare.

According to Charles Murray, a strong critic of the welfare system, we need to institute a "strict job program" that will force women to "drop out of welfare altogether" (285). According to Ruth Conniff, author of "Big Bad Welfare: Welfare Reform Politics and Children," the welfare reform discussion "indicates that what happens to children doesn't matter to Americans, so long as mothers are forced to work" (8). Unfortunately, however, for single women with children who either decide to work or are forced into the job market, there isn't a child care system that could make a "strict job program" successful (Murray 285). With child care costing "about $116 a week for a toddler and $122 for an infant," not only is American day care economically insensitive, but day care options are limited as well (Conniff 8). According to Mark Robert Rank, author of "Winners and Losers in the Welfare Game," the "scarcity of affordable child care for low-income families" makes the current welfare system in this country a "losing game" (1). How can women be expected to get jobs when there aren't sufficient means to care for their children? Ruth Conniff wonders that if our country "is so concerned about family values, wouldn't make sense to let mothers stay home with their young children?" (8). Welfare is essential to provide means for women to supply not only adequate care for their children but also positive values for their children's future.

Another category of women on welfare who are quite often overlooked 5 are those mothers who have minimum-wage jobs and who still need government assistance. The current method of getting women into the work place is the Job Training Partnership Act, or "the Government's biggest training program" (Conniff 5). According to *The Wall Street Journal*, however, this program—which offers low-wage jobs such as fast-food work—has "actually led to lower wages for poor young women compared with a control group" (Conniff 5). Once a woman is in the workplace, many people assume that she will be removed from welfare and become an independent member of society. What is not considered, however, is that the minimum wage can scarcely keep up with the needs of a single mother. According to a survey done of welfare recipients in Dane County, Wisconsin, "the average [welfare] recipient who gets a full-time job ... makes $6.74 an hour—about $14,000 a year. Day care for two children can easily cost $12,000" (Conniff 7). It is obvious that after subtracting child care costs, this equation leaves a mother with virtually nothing left to provide herself and her children with necessities such as food, clothing, and shelter—making it necessary to stay on government assistance. Until the minimum wage has been raised to keep up with these strenuous living situations, Washington needs to continue providing welfare to help single mothers and their children survive.

One of the many roles that American women assume is often that of   6
a poverty-stricken single mother. With current education programs that
are not effective for "high-risk" women students, with child care costs that
are overwhelming, and with a minimum wage so low that it can't keep up
with the needs of single mothers, it is not fair to assume that welfare can
be abolished. As Michelle Tingling Clement of National Public Radio
states, "What [women] truly need is . . . education, skills development . . . and
not just any job but jobs that pay living wages with family health benefits
and child care" (2). Until programs that can realistically assist women and
children are created, welfare is still a definite necessity.

Works Cited

Clement, Michelle T. "Republicans Finalize Welfare Reform Package." *All Things
Considered.* National Public Radio. 15 Nov. 1998. Transcript.

Conniff, Ruth. "Big Bad Welfare: Welfare Reform Politics and Children." *The Progressive* 84 (1994): 1–10.

Murray, Charles. "Keeping Priorities Straight on Welfare Reform." *The Aims of Argument.* Ed. Timothy W. Crucius and Carolyn E. Channell. Mountain View,
CA: Mayfield, 1998. 285–88.

Rank, Mark Robert. "Winners and Losers in the Welfare Game." Editorial. *St.
Louis Post-Dispatch* 15 Sept. 1994: 1–2.

Wellstone, Paul. "If Poverty Is the Question." *The Nation Digital Edition* 4 Apr.
1997. 10 Oct. 1998 *http://www.thenation.com.*

Zill, Nicholas. "Parental Schooling and Children's Health." *Public Health Reports* 111
(1996): 1–10.

Questions for Writing and Discussion

1. Sabatke says that her audience consists of white, conservative males
who believe that everyone should have a job and no one should be on welfare.
Where in her essay does she address this audience? Could she revise her essay
to focus on this audience even more specifically? Explain.

2. Read Sabatke's first draft and then the responses by Bev and Amy on the
peer-response sheet. Which of Bev's and/or Amy's suggestions do you agree
with? What other suggestions might you give Sabatke? Which of the peer-
response suggestions does Sabatke take or ignore in her final draft? How
might Sabatke have improved her final version even more? Explain.

3. What opposing arguments does Sabatke consider? Choose one of her responses, and explain why you think the counterargument is or is not effective. Think of one additional counterargument that she might consider. Should she address that argument? Why or why not?

4. At what points in her essay should Sabatke give additional evidence? Should she use more statistics about welfare mothers? Should she give a more specific description of the current welfare system? Should she give evidence from case studies of welfare recipients? Explain your choices.

STUDENT WRITING

STANDARDIZED TESTS: SHOULDN'T WE BE HELPING OUR STUDENTS

Eric Boese

As standardized testing has increased in the nation's high schools in recent years, so have the attacks against these tests. Several universities have followed the University of California's lead and deemphasized the SAT test. High school tests, such as the Texas TAAS, California's Stanford 9, Minnesota's MJCA, or Colorado's CSAP, have come under fire because they seem to punish the poorer school districts mainly for having insufficient funds to compete with the wealthy suburban schools. Eric Boese, a student at Colorado State University, decided to write about the problems created by these standardized tests. His purpose, he explains, is to persuade his readers—primarily politicians who set testing policies—that "the use of standardized tests in the education system has to be changed."

Over the past few decades our nation's school systems have progressed with leaps and bounds. We have seen improvements in textbooks, technology, teacher resources, and so much more. The opportunities for children to excel going through primary education are enormous, greater now than they have ever been. Still we see so many children being held back. Funds are being used inefficiently, and our priorities have become a little mixed up. I'm talking about what it is that we actually teach in primary schools. Are we teaching students skills and giving them knowledge that will make them them better members of society or have we decided that it is more important to   1 teach kids how to do well on tests? The answer to this question you may not like, but it is an answer that we can do something about.

To begin working on a solution, we should first locate the source of the problem. As I have said, everything in the world of education is changing, and I have seen that there is one change in particular can go a long way towards explaining, and solving, our problem. This change is in the use of standardized tests. They have become a more important and more destructive component of our schools. Of course I'm not suggesting that we throw the tests out, for they can be a vital part of education. I hope to show how the current use of these tests is harming the educational process and show how we can use them in a more productive manner in the future.

Over the last ten years in Texas some interesting things have happened. The first was that, in 1990, an exam called the Texas Assessment of Academic Skills (TAAS) was administered for the first time in a number of schools (Weisman). The test was given in grades three through eight and was used as an exit exam early in school. A lot of stress was placed on this test because it was used to determine the longevity of the careers of teachers and administrators. Their jobs depended on the success of their students in taking the exam. In 1994 George W. Bush, the test's biggest supporter, mandated that it be administered statewide. Over six years, the pass rate of the test increased in all student populations (Weisman). The test appeared to be a huge success.

George W. Bush credited the better scores to the test challenging students to do better. I, however, credit it to how the test changed the way the schools function. An alarming article by Jonathan Weisman reviews just this case. He shows how improvements on the TAAS are not correlated to improvements on other standardized tests that were given to the same students. While the TAAS scores went up, the other scores did nothing. The biggest revelation in his article is when he explains why students raised their test scores on that exam and not on others. What he found was that teachers were teaching them how to take the exam. Student learning was compromised because too much stress was put on teachers to make sure their students scored well. Jonathan Weisman knows this to be true:

> In a study published by the Harvard Civil Rights Project in January, Professors Linda McNeil of Rice University and Angela Valenzuela of the University of Texas delivered a scathing assessment of the TAAS's impact on Texas classrooms, asserting that "behind the rhetoric of the test scores are a growing set of classroom practices in which test-prep activities are usurping a substantive curriculum."

Of course it didn't really take experts to figure this out. Anyone involved in the classrooms of these schools knew that was going on:

> Teachers protested that they were spending eight to ten hours a week in test-preparation drills and that their principals were pressuring them to spend even more. Only 27 percent said they believed the rising TAAS scores reflected increased learning and higher-quality teaching; half said the scores indicated nothing of the sort. (Weisman)

This is a situation that is simply unacceptable. Endorsing tests that have these kinds of side effects is pumping out graduating classes of test takers. It's causing students to become less capable of meeting challenges that will face them in college and in the future. Texas isn't the only place this is taking place, but it is a great example of the way our nation's schools will turn out if we allow the use of these tests to continue to spread.

In Texas there are still other factors that cause the test scores to be mis- 5 leading. There was legislation that allowed schools to exempt special-ed students from taking the test. The number of exemptions increased during the years that the test was administered (Weisman). From this we see that the students aren't even improving as much on the tests as the figures show.

The fact that students score better on this kind of exam reveals noth- 6 ing about their personal improvements. If used differently, however, the exams could be much more effective in meeting students' needs and less destructive of their education. We could eliminate undue stress on teachers and create better evaluations of students' abilities.

In other places than Texas, standardized tests are being used in coun- 7 terproductive ways. The biggest problem seems to be that the tests have too much riding on them. In her article "Test Case: Now the Principal's Cheating," Carolyn Kleiner gives some examples of how the stakes of standardized tests have been raised:

> Twenty-eight states now use standard exams to determine graduation and 19 to govern student promotion; a growing number also dole out performance-based bonuses for schools that show progress and threaten intervention, even closure, for those that don't.

Kleiner links the growing importance of the tests to an inevitable side effect, cheating. Of course there are more ways that tests have grown in importance, and yes, more downfalls. The results of standardized tests can have impacts on the jobs of teachers and principals, the money they will make, the reputation of a school or district, and the high school graduation rates. The scores can also affect school funding and various different community issues. People would rather send their children to school somewhere that has a reputation for scoring well on exams and that doesn't have funding problems. In extreme cases, test results can have effects on the property values of residents in a district. George Madaus notes that the test results "don't provide a full picture of a child's—or a school's—accomplishments" and says that "You can't use these tests by themselves to make any decisions" (Kantrowitz et al.). The tests have, however, been used to determine a number of the things above, and as a result, some drawbacks of the tests are that they affect student learning in the classroom, and they cause great stress to students and teachers.

In "Schools for Scandal," Thomas Toch and Betsy Wagner discuss how   8 standardized tests have ultimately led to a problem of educators cheating. The problem of cheating has been one that, until recently, involved students breaking the rules. The new problem we are seeing is that teachers and even principals have started to help their students cheat on some tests. Why would they do this, you ask? It's similar to the situation in Texas—high stakes tests put pressure on them. They are pressured by administrators, principals, and parents alike, all of whom want to see the students get good scores for their own benefit. For parents, good scores are expected, and they see them as being equivalent to their students' doing well in school. In other words, if they see that a school has scored poorly on any given test, they see it as a failure on the part of the school, a further incentive for schools to improve their scores.

It's not something may of us want to hear, but the need for high scores   9 has caused many school officials to encourage cheating as well as raise their school's score by any means possible. "In a national survey of educators in 1990, 1 in 11 teachers reported pressure from administrators to cheat on standardized tests" (Toch and Wagner). On top of the pressures of cheating, there is almost nothing stopping teachers from giving out answers. In most common standardized tests, security monitoring is minimal, answers are available to test givers (who are usually the teachers), and tests are used multiple times. This makes it easy for teachers not only to cheat, but to teach the material that they know will be covered on any given test. Researchers in Colorado found that tests scores dropped dramatically from a first test that teachers had the time to prepare their students for and a very similar test given only a few weeks later. University of Colorado testing expert Lorrie Shepard said, "Teachers are not teaching students skills and concepts. . . . They are teaching specific examples by rote memorization" (Toch and Wagner).

Due to cheating and various other issues, standardized tests reveal less   10 accurate scores each year. In other words, tests are getting worse at what they were designed to do: measure skill levels of students. The reason, Toch and Wagner mention, is that people want high scores. Many tests that challenge students are not being used by schools simply because they yield low scores. The basic skills covered by these tests are inflating scores and forcing teachers to focus on teaching remedial skills and not on the needs of the individual students. In "Education: Is That Your Final Answer?" Jodie Morse gives an example in which the problem is even worse:

> Educators say they have had to dumb down their lessons to teach the often picayune factoids covered by the exams. A study released last month by the University of Virginia found that while some schools had boosted their performance on Virginia's exam, teachers had to curtail field trips, elective courses and even student visits to the bathroom—all in an effort to cram more test prep into the school day. Says the study's author, education professor Daniel Duke: "These schools have become battlefield units."

Causing practices like these to occur in our nation's schools is unjustifiable. The inflation of scores doesn't stop there; tests are being reused to a point where most schools can manage to do very well on them. This creates a false impression of students' skills. The U.S. Department of Education agreed that "with respect to national averages, [school] districts and states are presenting inflated results and misleading the public." How can somebody defend a policy that diminishes the education of students for tests that don't accurately reflect student achievement or, in some cases, even challenge them to think on their own?

So far we have considered some of the many effects of our current testing system. It is equally important to review exactly what materials the tests cover and whether or not they are testing the right things. First of all, 80 percent of standardized tests used in America are produced by corporations (Toch and Wagner). Who says corporations know what should be on these tests in the first place? The relevancy and difficulty of tests are determined by people who have little or no concern for their effects on schools. They are not held accountable for the material covered on their exams and do not feel that security is their concern. Often-times, the corporations will make the materials on their tests easier because more schools will buy tests that make themselves look good. In other cases, the corporations simply don't know what to include in their tests for different grade levels. A side effect of corporations writing tests is that they usually recycle their tests and so they rarely "allow schools to return copies of their graded exams to students so they, and their teachers, might learn from their mistakes" (Toch and Wagner). Of the students I surveyed, none claimed that they had ever even learned their own scores on school-mandated standardized tests, and none claimed that they learned anything substantial from the exams that they had taken. On many exams, questions relating to students' advanced-thinking skills are almost nonexistent. Corporations are just not giving tests that are beneficial to students. This is the first change we need to make: either make the corporations answer to a selected group of educational officials or have somebody make tests that have the student in mind.

Along the same lines as above, we need to throw out the tests that are   *12* too difficult for students of any particular age group. Only a few people actually oppose this argument. New York State Education Commissioner Richard Mills said that "subjecting 9-year-olds to tests they can't pass is one of the strategies to change things for the better" (Ohanian). I wish somebody would explain this to me. Is this supposed to make students want to work harder because they failed miserably or is it going to discourage them? This may not be an opinion that is held by too many people, but it sure seems to be in some cases. In some states, like Massachusetts for example, students are required to take tests that can last up to 18 hours in order to graduate from high school. We can't expect this much of students who are only 18 years old; not many of them would be able to pass such a test if their classes weren't so focused on preparing them for it, and as we have seen, test preparation often adversely affects student learning.

A level of testing has to be found such that students will be challenged   *13* and yet they will not be overwhelmed. Standardized tests should include materials relevant to a student's grade level, some materials that would require the student to explore new ideas, and some questions designed to test a student's advanced-thinking skills. This test would cover materials that would be included in a normal school curriculum and therefore would take up less class time. A teacher could concentrate on students' needs again, and classes could cover more material, explore subjects more deeply and give students the education they deserve. There would be time to do more of what one student claims to love most about school, "getting into great conversations and developing ideas" (Selzer). A test that fits these criteria would give a more accurate evaluation of the student's skills and of the student's potential to succeed in higher-level and college courses. Such a test may not be easy to make, but it would definitely be worth the effort.

It's getting harder and harder to see the positive side of using today's   *14* standardized tests. Not only are the tests giving inaccurate evaluations of students' skills, but they are causing corruption in our schools and diminishing the opportunities for educational excellence of our students. I've discussed ideas for new tests that could be used, but that is not enough to make up for the disturbances involved with the importance of the tests. It is my opinion that we cannot allow these tests to undermine the current system. First of all, funding should not be determined by scores; it should be determined by need. Taxpayers in any given region would also be able to vote to increase funding for the schools that they support. I mentioned that, in Texas, for teachers and administrators the tests held an additional, personal importance. Determining who holds these positions needs a more personal evaluation than looking at test scores. We need to look at how their students are really improving and the effort they put into their students' education.

I'm sure that the public will still have the bias that their students should 15 be getting the best scores, but this is an issue that will have to be faced. They need to be shown that the test scores are a sign for teachers to read to determine the extra attention that some students may require, and this is what the test should be used for. There is no greater purpose for having these tests than for improving education. Many of the problems of the current system will prove to be very difficult to resolve, but any steps towards a new system are ones for the better.

It may all sound difficult now, but the state of our schools is in desperate 16 need of change. Pushing for more tests as so many people are doing is not the answer. I urge you to consider how bright children are being discouraged by an unproductive testing system and to be the person who puts the needs of the children first.

Works Cited

Kantrowitz, Barbara, Daniel McGinn, Ellise Pierce, and Erika Check. "When Teachers Are Cheaters." *Newsweek* 19 June 2000. 15 Apr. 2001 *http://www.elibrary.com*.

Kleiner, Carolyn. "Test Case: Now the Principal's Cheating." *U.S. News and World Report* 12 June 2000. 10 Apr. 2001 *http://www.elibrary.com*.

Morse, Jodie. "Education: Is That Your Final Answer?" *Time* 19 June 2000. 15 Apr. 2001 *http://www.elibrary.com*.

Ohanian, Susan. "Editorials: Standardized Schools." *The Nation* 18 Sep. 1999. 10 Apr. 2001 *http://www.elibrary.com*.

Selzer, Adam. "High-Stakes Testing: It's Backlash Time." *U.S. News & World Report* 3 Apr. 2000. 15 Apr. 2001 *http://www.usnews.com/usnews/issue/000403/education.htm*.

Toch, Thomas, and Betsy Wagner. "Schools for Scandal." *U.S. News & World Report* 27 Apr. 1992. 10 Apr. 2001 *http://www.elibrary.com*.

Weisman, Jonathan. "Only a Test." *The New Republic* 10 Apr. 2000. 15 Apr. 2001
http://www.thenewrepublic.com/041000/weisman041000.html.

In your journal, write the meanings of the following words:

- determine the *longevity* of the careers of teachers **(3)**
- test-prep activities are *usurping a substantive* curriculum **(4)**
- a further *incentive* **(8)**
- teach the often *picayune factoids* **(10)**
- preparation often *adversely* affects student learning **(12)**

QUESTIONS FOR WRITING AND DISCUSSION

1. In your journal, write three short paragraphs explaining your own experience with standardized tests. First, which tests have you taken, and when did you take them? Next, what was the purpose of the tests—to evaluate you or your school? Finally, describe the effect of these tests on your own education. Did they detract from the regular curriculum? Did they give you motivation and incentive to learn? Did they help you get into college?

2. Eric Boese uses a problem-solving format for his arguing essay. Which paragraphs describe the problems with standardized tests? List these problems. Which paragraphs indicate his solutions? What are his solutions? Is his essay clear or would you give him suggestions for improving his organization? Explain.

3. Boese writes that the intended audience for his essay is politicians who are in favor of increased use of standardized tests. Where does Boese address this audience? Where and how could he make his appeal to this audience even stronger? Write out actual sentences Boese could add to his essay.

4. On the Internet, read more recent articles on standardized testing. Has testing in high schools changed since Boese wrote his essay in 2001? Do more or fewer high schools give mandated tests? Has the quality of the tests improved? Do students and teachers like or dislike these tests? Explain.

Works of art—poetry, stories, and paintings—often choose earlier myths, stories, and legends for their subject. In *The Fall of Icarus*, Brueghel draws on the Greek myth of Daedalus and his son, Icarus, as told by the Roman poet Ovid. Several modern poets, including W. H. Auden and William Carlos Williams have written poems inspired by both the myth and Brueghel's painting (see highlight on page 559). To see how painting inspires poetry—and vice versa—see W. H. Auden's poem, "Musée des Beaux Arts" on page 560 as well as the journal exercises on page 562.

Pieter Brueghel
The Fall of Icarus (c. 1558)
Oil-tempera
Museum of Fine Arts, Brussels

11

Responding to Literature

In an Introduction to Literature class, you and a friend are assigned to work collaboratively on an essay about Eudora Welty's "A Worn Path." You are both interested in how Phoenix Jackson's journey contains images of the phoenix: a mythological bird said to live for five hundred years, after which it burns itself to death and then rises from its ashes to become youthful and beautiful again. You draft your essays separately and then read each other's drafts. At that point, you collaborate on a single essay, combining the best ideas and evidence from your separate drafts. Your collaborative essay shows how Phoenix Jackson is characterized by birdlike images, how she calmly faces images of fire and death on her journey, and how her grandson represents her rebirth.

In a film class, you watch Roman Polanski's *Tess,* an adaptation of Thomas Hardy's novel *Tess of the D'Urbervilles.* You decide to compare the film with the novel, focusing on four key episodes: the "strawberry scene," in which Tess meets Alec; the rape scene at night; the harvesting scene; and the final scene at Stonehenge. On the basis of your comparison, you argue that Polanski's interpretation (and the acting of Nastassia Kinski) retains Hardy's view of Tess as a victim of social and sexist repression.

R ESPONDING TO POEMS AND SHORT STORIES REQUIRES BOTH IMAGINATION AND CRITICAL-READING SKILL. AS READERS, WE ANTICIPATE, IMAGINE, FEEL, WORRY, ANALYZE, AND QUESTION. A STORY OR POEM IS LIKE AN EMPTY balloon that we inflate with the warm breath of our imagination and experience. Our participation makes us partners with the author in the artistic recreation.

First, readers must *imagine* and recreate that special world described by the writer. The first sentences of a short story, for example, throw open a door to a world that—attractive or repulsive—tempts our curiosity and imagination. Like Alice in *Alice in Wonderland,* we cannot resist following a white rabbit with pink eyes who mutters to himself, checks his watch, and then zips down a rabbit hole and into an imaginary world.

Here are three opening sentences of three very different short stories:

Young Goodman Brown came forth at sunset into the street at Salem village; but put his head back, after crossing the threshold, to exchange a parting kiss with his young wife.

—Nathaniel Hawthorne, "Young Goodman Brown"

As Gregor Samsa awoke one morning from uneasy dreams he found himself transformed in his bed into a gigantic insect.

—Franz Kafka, "The Metamorphosis"

The morning of June 27th was clear and sunny, with the fresh warmth of a full-summer day; the flowers were blossoming profusely and the grass was green.

—Shirley Jackson, "The Lottery"

Whether our imaginations construct the disturbing image of a "gigantic insect" or the seemingly peaceful picture of a perfect summer day, we actively recreate each story.

In a similar way, poems invite the reader to participate in actively creating characters, images, places, feelings, and reflections. Below are lines from several poems, each creating its own characters, places, images, and themes.

Because I could not stop for Death—
He kindly stopped for me—
The Carriage held but just Ourselves—
And Immortality.
—Emily Dickinson, "Because I could not stop for Death"

anyone lived in a pretty how town
(with up so floating many bells down)
spring summer autumn winter
he sang his didn't he danced his did.
   —e.e. cummings, "anyone lived in a pretty how town"

Tyger! Tyger! burning bright
In the forests of the night,
What immortal hand or eye
Could frame thy fearful symmetry?
   —William Blake, "The Tyger"

We real cool. We
Left school. We

Lurk late. We
Strike straight. We

Sing sin. We
Thing gin. We

Jazz June. We
Die soon.
   —Gwendolyn Brooks, "We Real Cool"

Two roads diverged in a yellow wood,
And sorry I could not travel both
And be one traveler, long I stood
And looked down one as far as I could
   —Robert Frost, "The Road Not Taken"

  Responding to literature also requires that readers *reread.* First, you should reread for yourself—that is, reread to write down your ideas, questions, feelings, and reactions. To heighten your role in re-creating a story or poem, you should note in the margins your questions and responses to main characters, places, metaphors and images, and themes that catch your attention: "Are the names of Hawthorne's characters significant? Is Young Goodman Brown really good? Is his wife, Faith, really faithful?" "Why does Emily Dickinson have her speaker personify Death as the driver of a carriage? Why does her speaker say that 'he *kindly* stopped for me'? What action is taking place?" Don't just underline or highlight passages. Actually *write* your questions and responses in the margins.

Second, you should reread with a writer's eye. In fiction, identify the major and minor characters. Look for conflicts between characters. Mark passages that contain foreshadowing. Pinpoint sentences that reveal the narrative point of view. Use the appropriate critical terms (character, plot, conflict, point of view, setting, style, and theme) to help you reread with a writer's eye and see how the parts of a story relate to the whole. Similarly, in poetry, look for character, key events, and setting, and *always* pay attention to images and metaphors, to voice and tone, to word choice, and to rhythm and rhyme. Each critical term is a tool—a magnifying glass that helps you understand and interpret the literary work more clearly.

In addition to rereading, responding to literature requires that readers *share* ideas, reactions, and interpretations. Sharing usually begins in small-group or class discussions, but it continues as you explain your interpretation in writing. A work of literature is not a mathematical equation with a single answer. Great literature is worth interpreting precisely because each reader responds differently. The purpose of literature is to encourage you to reflect on your life and the lives of others—to look for new ways of seeing and understanding your world—and ultimately to expand your world. Sharing is crucial to appreciating literature.

> Hawthorne doesn't come right out and say that people become disillusioned by experiencing evil. He shows how it actually happens in the life of young Goodman Brown.

> Shirley Jackson's "The Lottery" helps me see that the notion of human sacrifice and the idea of the human scapegoat still exist in our culture today.

> In "Because I could not stop for Death," Emily Dickinson uses personification and metaphors as vehicles for her own reflection and introspection.

Writing about your responses and sharing them with other readers helps you "reread" your own ideas in order to explain them fully and clearly to other readers.

RESPONDING TO A SHORT STORY

Read and respond to Kate Chopin's "The Story of an Hour." Use your imagination to help create the story as you read. Then *reread* the story, noting in the margin your questions and responses. When you finish rereading and annotating your reactions, write your interpretation of the last line of the story.

PROFESSIONAL WRITING

THE STORY OF AN HOUR

Kate Chopin

Kate O'Flaherty Chopin (1851–1904) was an American writer whose mother was French and Creole and whose father was Irish. In 1870, she moved from St. Louis to New Orleans with her husband, Oscar Chopin, and over the next ten years she gave birth to five sons. After her husband died in 1882, Chopin returned to St. Louis to begin a new life as a writer. Many of her best stories are about Louisiana people and places, and her most famous novel, The Awakening, *tells the story of Edna, a woman who leaves her marriage and her children to fulfill herself through an artistic career.*

1   Knowing that Mrs. Mallard was afflicted with a heart trouble, great care was taken to break to her as gently as possible the news of her husband's death.

2   It was her sister Josephine who told her, in broken sentences, veiled hints that revealed in half concealing. Her husband's friend Richards was there, too, near her. It was he who had been in the newspaper office when intelligence of the railroad disaster was received, with Brently Mallard's name leading the list of "killed." He had only taken the time to assure himself of its truth by a second telegram, and had hastened to forestall any less careful, less tender friend in bearing the sad message.

3   She did not hear the story as many women have heard the same, with a paralyzed inability to accept its significance. She wept at once, with sudden, wild abandonment, in her sister's arms. When the storm of grief had spent itself she went away to her room alone. She would have no one follow her.

4   There stood, facing the open window, a comfortable, roomy armchair. Into this she sank, pressed down by a physical exhaustion that haunted her body and seemed to reach into her soul.

5   She could see in the open square before her house the tops of trees that were all aquiver with the new spring life. The delicious breath of rain was in the air. In the street below a peddler was crying his wares. The notes of a distant song which someone was singing reached her faintly, and countless sparrows were twittering in the eaves.

There were patches of blue sky showing here and there through the clouds that had met and piled one above the other in the west facing her window. *6*

She sat with her head thrown back upon the cushion of the chair quite motionless, except when a sob came up into her throat and shook her, as a child who has cried itself to sleep continues to sob in its dreams. *7*

She was young, with a fair, calm face, whose lines bespoke repression and even a certain strength. But now there was a dull stare in her eyes, whose gaze was fixed away off yonder on one of those patches of blue sky. It was not a glance of reflection, but rather indicated a suspension of intelligent thought. *8*

There was something coming to her and she was waiting for it, fearfully. What was it? She did not know; it was too subtle and elusive to name. But she felt it, creeping out of the sky, reaching toward her through the sounds, the scents, the color that filled the air. *9*

Now her bosom rose and fell tumultuously. She was beginning to recognize this thing that was approaching to possess her, and she was striving to beat it back with her will—as powerless as her two white slender hands would have been. *10*

When she abandoned herself a little whispered word escaped her slightly parted lips. She said it over and over under her breath: "Free, free, free!" The vacant stare and the look of terror that had followed it went from her eyes. They stayed keen and bright. Her pulses beat fast, and the coursing blood warmed and relaxed every inch of her body. *11*

She did not stop to ask if it were not a monstrous joy that held her. A clear and exalted perception enabled her to dismiss the suggestion as trivial. *12*

She knew that she would weep again when she saw the kind, tender hands folded in death; the face that had never looked save with love upon her, fixed and gray and dead. But she saw beyond that bitter moment a long procession of years to come that would belong to her absolutely. And she opened and spread her arms out to them in welcome. *13*

There would be no one to live for during those coming years; she would live for herself. There would be no powerful will bending her in that blind persistence with which men and women believe they have a right to impose a private will upon a fellow creature. A kind intention or a cruel intention made the act seem no less a crime as she looked upon it in that brief moment of illumination. *14*

And yet she had loved him—sometimes. Often she had not. What did it matter! What could love, the unsolved mystery, count for in face of this *15* possession of self-assertion which she suddenly recognized as the strongest impulse of her being.

"Free! Body and soul free!" she kept whispering. *16*

Josephine was kneeling before the closed door with her lips to the key- *17* hole, imploring for admission. "Louise, open the door! I beg; open the door—you will make yourself ill. What are you doing, Louise? For heaven's sake open the door."

"Go away. I am not making myself ill." No; she was drinking in a very *18* elixir of life through that open window.

Her fancy was running riot along those days ahead of her. Spring days, *19* and summer days, and all sorts of days that would be her own. She breathed a quick prayer that life might be long. It was only yesterday she had thought with a shudder that life might be long.

She arose at length and opened the door to her sister's importunities. *20* There was a feverish triumph in her eyes, and she carried herself unwittingly like a goddess of Victory. She clasped her sister's waist, and together they descended the stairs. Richards stood waiting for them at the bottom.

Someone was opening the front door with a latchkey. It was Brently *21* Mallard who entered, a little travel-stained, composedly carrying his grip-sack and umbrella. He had been far from the scene of accident, and did not even know there had been one. He stood amazed at Josephine's piercing cry; at Richards's quick motion to screen him from the view of his wife.

But Richards was too late. *22*

When the doctors came they said she had died of heart disease—of joy *23* that kills.

RESPONDING TO A POEM

Read and respond to W. H. Auden's "Musée des Beaux Arts." Begin by examining the painting by Pieter Brueghel, *Landscape with the Fall of Icarus*, reproduced at the beginning of this chapter. Carefully read and reread the poem, comparing it with details in the painting. Then go online to find the description of Daedalus and Icarus described in the Roman poet Ovid's *Metamorphoses*. As you reread Auden's poem, pay particular attention to the detail in the description, to Auden's references to scenes not depicted in the painting, and to the language and word choice.

PROFESSIONAL WRITING

MUSÉE DES BEAUX ARTS

W. H. Auden

In the following poem, W. H. Auden reflects on the art and the theme of Pieter Brueghel's famous painting, Landscape with the Fall of Icarus *(c. 1558). Auden (1907–1973) was born in England, went to school at Oxford, and eventually moved to the United States. Auden describes and interprets Brueghel's vision of the Fall of Icarus, and Brueghel in turn visualizes and interprets the Roman poet Ovid's version of the story of Daedalus and his son, Icarus. In this Greek myth, according to Ovid, Daedalus fashions wings made out of feathers and wax in order to help them escape the island of Crete. Daedalus cautions his son not to fly too near the heat of the sun, but Icarus ignores his father's advice. When Icarus soars too high, the sun melts the wax in his wings, and he plunges into the ocean. In Brueghel's painting, only the white legs of Icarus are visible (in the lower right-hand corner of the painting) as he disappears into the water.*

About suffering they were never wrong,
The old Masters: how well they understood
Its human position: how it takes place
While someone else is eating or opening a window or just
    walking dully along;
How, when the aged are reverently, passionately waiting   5
For the miraculous birth, there always must be
Children who did not specially want it to happen, skating
On a pond at the edge of the wood:
They never forgot
That even the dreadful martyrdom must run its course   10
Anyhow in a corner, some untidy spot
Where the dogs go on with their doggy life and the torturer's
    horse
Scratches its innocent behind on a tree.
In Breughel's Icarus, for instance: how everything turns away
Quite leisurely from the disaster; the ploughman may   15
Have heard the splash, the forsaken cry,

But for him it was not an important failure; the sun shone
As it had to on the white legs disappearing into the green
Water, and the expensive delicate ship that must have seen
Something amazing, a boy falling out of the sky,   20
Had somewhere to get to and sailed calmly on.

Techniques for Responding to Literature

As you read and respond to a work of literature, keep the following techniques in mind.

- **Understanding the assignment and selecting a possible purpose and audience.** Unless stated otherwise in your assignment, your purpose is to *interpret* a work of literature. Your audience will be other members of your class, including the teacher.

- **Actively reading, annotating, and discussing the literary work.** Remember that literature often contains *highly condensed experiences.* In order to give imaginative life to literature, you need to reread patiently both the major events and the seemingly insignificant passages. In discussions, look for the differences between your responses and other readers' ideas.

- **Focusing your essay on a single, clearly defined interpretation.** In your essay, clearly state your main idea or thesis, focusing on a *single* idea or aspect of the piece of literature. Your thesis should *not be a statement of fact.* Whether you are explaining, evaluating, or arguing, your interpretation must be clearly stated.

- **Supporting your interpretation with evidence.** Because your readers will probably have different interpretations, you must show which specific characters, events, scenes, conflicts, images, metaphors, or themes prompted your response, and you must use these details to support your interpretation. *Do not merely **retell** the major events of the story or **describe** the main images in the poem*—your readers have already read your story or poem.

WARMING UP: JOURNAL EXERCISES

Read all of the following questions and then write for five minutes on two or three. These questions should help clarify your perceptions about literature or develop your specific responses to "The Story of an Hour" or to "Musée des Beaux Arts."

1. On your bookshelves or in the library, find a short story or poem that you read at least six months ago. Before you reread it, write down the name of the author and the title of the work. Note when you read it last and describe what you remember about it. Then reread the story or poem. When you finish, write for five minutes, describing what you noticed that you did not notice the last time you read it.

2. Write out the *question* that "The Story of an Hour" seems to ask. What is your answer to this question? What might have been Kate Chopin's answer?

3. The words *heart, joy, free, life,* and *death* appear several times in "The Story of an Hour." Underline these words (or synonyms) each time they appear. Explain how the meaning of each of these words seems to *change* during the story. Is each word used ironically?

4. Write out a dictionary definition of the word *feminism.* Then write out your own definition. Is Mrs. Mallard a feminist? Is Kate Chopin a feminist? What evidence in the story supports your answers?

5. Kate Chopin's biographer, Per Seyersted, says that Chopin saw that "truth is manifold" and thus preferred not to "take sides or point a moral." Explain how "The Story of an Hour" does or does not illustrate Seyersted's observations.

6. In Ovid's account of the myth of Daedalus and Icarus, the fisherman, shepherd, and plowman are "astonished" as they observe Icarus flying, and Ovid suggests that they might worship Icarus and Daedalus as gods. In what way does Brueghel revise Ovid's account? Explain how and why Brueghel changes this part of the myth.

7. Auden suggests that one theme of Brueghel's painting is that suffering is largely ignored by the general populace. Study Brueghel's painting again. What other themes or ideas are present in the painting that Auden does not mention? Explain another possible interpretation of the painting based on specific images or points of focus in the painting.

8. Auden says that the theme of Brueghel's painting is about suffering, but he also includes a description of "the miraculous birth" and children who "did

not specially want it to happen." Does this image distract from Auden's main point, or is the idea of the miraculous birth related to Auden's theme? Explain.

9. Literature often expresses common themes or tensions, such as the conflict between generations, the individual versus society, appearance versus reality, self-knowledge versus self-deception, and civilization versus nature. Which of these themes are most apparent in "The Story of an Hour" or in "Musée des Beaux Arts"? Explain your choices.

Purposes for Responding to Literature

In responding to literature, you should be guided by the purposes that you have already practiced in previous chapters. As you read a piece of literature and respond in the margin, begin by writing *for yourself.* Your purposes are to observe, feel, remember, understand, and relate the work of literature to your own life: What is happening? What memories does it trigger? How does it make you feel? Why is this passage confusing? Why do you like or dislike this character? Literature has special, personal value. You should write about literature initially in order to discover and understand its importance in your life.

When you write an interpretive essay, however, you are writing *for others.* You are sharing your experience in working with the author as imaginative partners in recreating the work. Your purposes will often be mixed, but an interpretive essay often contains elements of *explaining, evaluating, problem solving,* and *arguing.*

- **Explaining.** Interpretive essays about literature explain the *what, why,* and *how* of a piece of literature. What is the key subject? What is the most important line, event, or character? What are the major conflicts or the key images? What motivates a character? How does a character's world build or unravel? How does a story on poem meet or fail to meet our expectations? How did our interpretations develop? Each of these questions might lead to an interpretive essay that explains the *what, why,* and *how* of your response.

- **Evaluating.** Readers and writers often talk about "appreciating" a work of literature. *Appreciating* means establishing its value or worth. It may mean praising the work's literary virtues; it may mean finding faults or weaknesses. Usually, evaluating essays measure *both strengths and weaknesses,* according to specific criteria. What important standards for literature do you wish to apply? How does the work in question measure up? What kinds of readers might find this story worth reading? An evaluative essay cites evidence to show why a story is exciting, boring, dramatic, puzzling, vivid, relevant, or memorable.

- **Problem solving.** Writers of interpretive essays occasionally take a problem-solving approach, focusing on how the reader overcomes obstacles in understanding the story or poem, or on how the author solved problems in writing key scenes, choosing images and language, developing character, and creating and resolving conflicts. Particularly if you like to write fiction or poetry yourself, you may wish to take the writer's point of view: how did the writer solve (or fail to solve) problems of image, metaphor, character, setting, plot, or theme?

- **Arguing.** As readers share responses, they may discover that their interpretations diverge sharply from the ideas of other readers. Does "The Story of an Hour" have a feminist theme? Is it about women or about human nature in general? Is the main character admirable, or is she selfish? Is Auden's interpretation of Brueghel's painting faithful to Bureghel's conception, or does Auden impose his interpretation? Is Auden's the only way to interpret Bureghel's painting? In interpretive essays, writers sometimes argue for their beliefs. They present evidence that refutes an opposing or alternate interpretation and supports their own reading.

Most interpretive essays about literature are focused by these purposes, whether used singly or in combination. Writers should *select* the purpose(s) that are most appropriate for the work of literature and their own responses.

Responding to Short Fiction

Begin by noting in the margins your reactions at key points. *Summarize* in your own words what is happening in the story. Write down your *observations* or *reactions* to striking or surprising passages. Ask yourself *questions* about ambiguous or confusing passages.

After you respond initially and make your marginal annotations, use the following basic elements of fiction to help you *analyze how the parts of a short story re-*

late to the whole. Pay attention to how setting or plot affects the character, or how style and setting affect the theme. Because analysis artificially separates plot, character, and theme, look for ways to *synthesize* the parts: seeing how these parts relate to each other should suggest an idea, focus, or angle to use in your interpretation.

CHARACTER   A short story usually focuses on a *major character*—particularly on how that character faces conflicts, undergoes changes, or reveals himself or herself. *Minor characters* may be flat (one-dimensional), static (unchanging), or stereotyped. To get a start on analyzing character, diagram the *conflicts* between or among characters. Examine characters for motivation: What causes them to behave as they do? Is their behavior affected by *internal* or *external* forces? Do the major characters reveal themselves *directly* (through their thoughts, dialogue, and actions) or *indirectly* (through what other people say, think, or do)?

PLOT   *Plot* is the sequence of events in a story, but it is also the cause-and-effect relationship of one event to another. As you study a story's plot, pay attention to *exposition, foreshadowing, conflict, climax,* and *denouement.* To clarify elements of the plot, draw a time line for the story, listing in chronological order every event—including events that occur before the story opens. *Exposition* describes the initial circumstances and reveals what has happened before the story opens. *Foreshadowing* is an author's hint of what will occur before it happens. *Conflicts* within characters, between characters, and between characters and their environment may explain why one event leads to the next. The *climax* is the high point, the point of no return, or the most dramatic moment in a story. At the climax of a story, readers discover something important about the main character. *Denouement* literally means the "unraveling" of the complications and conflicts at the end of the story. In "The Story of an Hour," climax and denouement occur almost at the same time, in the last lines of the story.

NARRATIVE POINT OF VIEW   Fiction is usually narrated from either the first-person or the third-person point of view.

A *first-person narrator* is a character who tells the story from his or her point of view. A first-person narrator may be a minor or a major character. This character may be relatively *reliable* (trustworthy) or *unreliable* (naive or misleading). Although reliable first-person narrators may invite the reader to identify with their perspectives or predicaments, unreliable narrators may cause readers to be wary of their naive judgments or unbalanced states of mind.

A *third-person omniscient narrator* is not a character or participant in the story. Omniscient narrators are assumed to know everything about the characters and events. They move through space and time, giving readers necessary information at any point in the story. A *selective omniscient narrator* usually limits his or her focus to a single character's experiences and thoughts, as Kate Chopin focuses on Mrs. Mallard in "The Story of an Hour." One kind of selective omniscient point of view is *stream-of-consciousness narration,* in which the author presents the thoughts, memories, and associations of one character in the story. Omniscient narrators may be *intrusive,* jumping into the story to give their editorial judgments, or they may be *objective,* removing themselves from the action and the minds of the characters. An objective point of view creates the impression that events are being recorded by a camera or acted on a stage.

Reminder: As you reread a story, do not stop with analysis. Do not quit, for example, after you have identified and labeled the point of view. Determine how the point of view affects your reaction to the central character or to your understanding of the theme. How would a different narrative point of view change the story? If a different character told the story, how would that affect the theme?

SETTING   *Setting* is the physical place, scene, and time of the story. It also includes the social or historical context of the story. The setting in "The Story of an Hour" is the house and the room in which Mrs. Mallard waits, but it is also the social and historical time frame. *Setting is usually important for what it reveals about the characters, the plot, or the theme of the story.* Does the setting reflect a character's state of mind? Is the environment a source of tension or conflict in the story? Do changes in setting reflect changes in key characters? Do sensory details of sight, touch, smell, hearing, or taste affect or reflect the characters or events? Does the author's portrait of the setting contain images and symbols that help you interpret the story?

STYLE   *Style* is a general term that may refer to sentence structure and to figurative language and symbols, as well as to the author's tone or use of irony. *Sentence structure* may be long and complicated or relatively short and simple. Authors may use *figurative language* (Mrs. Mallard is described in "The Story of an Hour" as sobbing, "as a child who has cried itself to sleep continues to sob in its dreams"). A *symbol* is a person, place, thing, or event that suggests or signifies something beyond itself. In "The Story of an Hour," the open window and the new spring life suggest or represent Mrs. Mallard's new freedom. *Tone* is the author's attitude toward the characters, setting, or plot. Tone may be sympathetic, humorous, serious, detached, or critical. *Irony* suggests a double meaning. It occurs when the author or a character says or does one thing but means the opposite or something altogether different. The ending of "The Story of an Hour" is ironic: The doctors say Mrs. Mallard has died "of joy that kills." In fact, she has died of killed joy.

THEME The focus of an interpretive essay is often on the *theme* of a story. In arriving at a theme, ask how the characters, plot, point of view, setting, and style *contribute* to the main ideas or point of the story. The theme of a story depends, within limits, on your reactions as a reader. "The Story of an Hour" is *not* about relationships between sisters, nor is it about medical malpractice. It is an ironic story about love, personal freedom, and death, but what precisely is the *theme*? Does "The Story of an Hour" carry a feminist message, or is it more universally about the repressive power of love? Is Mrs. Mallard to be admired or criticized for her impulse to free herself? Do not trivialize the theme of a story by looking for some simple "moral." In describing the theme, deal with the complexity of life recreated in the story.

PROFESSIONAL WRITING

A Worn Path

Eudora Welty

Eudora Welty was born in Jackson, Mississippi, in 1909 and earned degress from Mississippi State College, the University of Wisconsin, and Columbia University. While she was writing short stories during the early 1930s, Welty held jobs with the Works Progress Administration, a Jackson radio station, and local newspapers. Like Flannery O'Connor and William Faulkner, Eudora Welty wrote stories and novels set in the American South. Her first major publication, A Curtain of Green and Other Stories, *appeared in 1941 and was followed by three more collections of short stories. Her novels include* Delta Wedding *(1946) and* The Optimist's Daughter *(1972), which won a Pulitzer Prize. Welty's collection of reviews and essays,* The Eye of the Story *(1978), and her brief autobiography,* One Writer's Beginnings *(1984), provide insight into her fiction and her life.*

It was December—a bright frozen day in the early morning. Far out in the country there was an old Negro woman with her head tied in a red rag, coming along a path through the pinewoods. Her name was Phoenix Jackson. She was very old and small and she walked slowly in the dark pine shadows, moving a little from side to side in her steps, with the balanced heaviness and lightness of a pendulum in a grandfather clock. She carried a thin, small cane made from an umbrella, and with this she kept tapping the frozen earth in front of her. This made a grave and persistent noise in the still air, that seemed meditative like the chirping of a solitary little bird.

She wore a dark striped dress reaching down to her shoe tops, and an 2 equally long apron of bleached sugar sacks, with a full pocket: all neat and tidy, but every time she took a step she might have fallen over her shoe-laces, which dragged from her unlaced shoes. She looked straight ahead. Her eyes were blue with age. Her skin had a pattern all its own of numberless branching wrinkles and as though a whole little tree stood in the middle of her forehead, but a golden color ran underneath, and the two knobs of her cheeks were illuminated by a yellow burning under the dark. Under the red rag her hair came down on her neck in the frailest of ringlets, still black, and with an odor like copper.

Now and then there was a quivering in the thicket. Old Phoenix said, 3 "Out of my way, all you foxes, owls, beetles, jack rabbits, coons, and wild animals! . . . Keep out from under these feet, little bob-whites. . . . Keep the big wild hogs out of my path. Don't let none of those come running my direction. I got a long way." Under her small black-freckled hand her cane, limber as a buggy whip, would switch at the brush as if to rouse up any hiding things.

On she went. The woods were deep and still. The sun made the pine 4 needles almost too bright to look at, up where the wind rocked. The cones dropped as light as feathers. Down in the hollow was the mourning dove— it was not too late for him.

The path ran up a hill. "Seem like there is chains about my feet, time 5 I get this far," she said, in the voice of argument old people keep to use with themselves. "Something always take a hold of me on this hill—pleads I should stay."

After she got to the top she turned and gave a full, severe look behind 6 her where she had come. "Up through pines," she said at length. "Now down through oaks."

Her eyes opened their widest, and she started down gently. But before 7 she got to the bottom of the hill a bush caught her dress.

Her fingers were busy and intent, but her skirts were full and long, so 8 that before she could pull them free in one place they were caught in another. It was not possible to allow the dress to tear. "I in the thorny bush," she said. "Thorns, you doing your appointed work. Never want to let folks pass—no sir. Old eyes thought you was a pretty little green bush."

Finally, trembling all over, she stood free, and after a moment dared to 9 stoop for her cane.

"Sun so high!" she cried, leaning back and looking, while the thick 10
tears went over her eyes. "The time getting all gone here."

At the foot of this hill was a place where a log was laid across the creek. 11

"Now comes the trial," said Phoenix. 12

Putting her right foot out, she mounted the log and shut her eyes. Lift- 13
ing her skirt, leveling her cane fiercely before her, like a festival figure in
some parade, she began to march across. Then she opened her eyes and she
was safe on the other side.

"I wasn't as old as I thought," she said. 14

But she sat down to rest. She spread her skirts on the bank around her 15
and folded her hands over her knees. Up above her was a tree in a pearly
cloud of mistletoe. She did not dare to close her eyes, and when a little boy
brought her a little plate with a slice of marblecake on it she spoke to him.
"That would be acceptable," she said. But when she went to take it there
was just her own hand in the air.

So she left that tree, and had to go through a barbed-wire fence. There 16
she had to creep and crawl, spreading her knees and stretching her fingers
like a baby trying to climb the steps. But she talked loudly to herself: she
could not let her dress be torn now, so late in the day, and she could not pay
for having her arm or her leg sawed off if she got caught fast where she was.

At last she was safe through the fence and risen up out in the clearing. 17
Big dead trees, like black men with one arm, were standing in the purple
stalks of the withered cotton field. There sat a buzzard.

"Who you watching?" 18

In the furrow she made her way along. 19

"Glad this not the season for bulls," she said, looking sideways, "and the 20
good Lord made his snakes to curl up and sleep in the winter. A pleasure
I don't see no two-headed snake coming around that tree, where it come
once. It took a while to get by him, back in the summer."

She passed through the old cotton and went into a field of dead corn. 21
It whispered and shook and was taller than her head. "Through the maze
now," she said, for there was no path.

Then there was something tall, black, and skinny there, moving be- 22
fore her.

At first she took it for a man. It could have been a man dancing in the 23
field. But she stood still and listened, and it did not make a sound. It was
as silent as a ghost.

"Ghost," she said sharply, "who be you the ghost of? For I have heard 24
of nary death close by."

But there was no answer—only the ragged dancing in the wind. *25*

She shut her eyes, reached out her hand, and touched a sleeve. She *26* found a coat and inside that an emptiness, cold as ice.

"You scarecrow," she said. Her face lighted. "I ought to be shut up for *27* good," she said with laughter. "My senses is gone, I too old. I the oldest people I ever know. Dance, old scarecrow," she said, "while I dancing with you." She kicked her foot over the furrow, and with mouth drawn down, shook her head once or twice in a little strutting way. Some husks blew down and whirled in streamers about her skirts.

Then she went on, parting her way from side to side with the cane, *28* through the whispering field. At last she came to the end, to a wagon track where the silver grass blew between the red ruts. The quail were walking around like pullets, seeming all dainty and unseen.

"Walk pretty," she said. "This the easy place. This the easy going." *29*

She followed the track, swaying through the quiet bare fields, through *30* the little strings of trees silver in their dead leaves, past cabins silver from weather, with the doors and windows boarded shut, all like old women under a spell sitting there. "I walking in their sleep," she said, nodding her head vigorously.

In a ravine she went where a spring was silently flowing through a hol- *31* low log. Old Phoenix bent and drank. "Sweet-gum makes the water sweet," she said, and drank more. "Nobody know who made this well, for it was here when I was born."

The track crossed a swampy part where the moss hung as white as lace *32* from every limb. "Sleep on, alligators, and blow your bubbles." Then the track went into the road.

Deep, deep the road went down between the high green-colored banks. *33* Overhead the live-oaks met, and it was as dark as a cave.

A black dog with a lolling tongue came up out of the weeds by the *34* ditch. She was meditating, and not ready, and when he came at her she only hit him a little with her cane. Over she went in the ditch, like a little puff of milkweed.

Down there, her senses drifted away. A dream visited her, and she *35* reached her hand up, but nothing reached down and gave her a pull. So she lay there and presently went to talking. "Old woman," she said to herself, "that black dog come up out of the weeds to stall you off, and now there he sitting on his fine tail, smiling at you."

A white man finally came along and found her—a hunter, a young *36* man, with his dog on a chain.

"Well, Granny!" he laughed, "what are you doing there?"   *37*

"Lying on my back like a June-bug waiting to be turned over, mister,"   *38* she said, reaching up her hand.

He lifted her up, gave her a swing in the air, and set her down. "Any-   *39* thing broken, Granny?"

"No sir, them old dead weeds is springy enough," said Phoenix, when   *40* she had got her breath. "I thank you for your trouble."

"Where do you live, Granny?" he asked, while the two dogs were growl-   *41* ing at each other.

"Away back yonder, sir, behind the ridge. You can't even see it from   *42* here."

"On your way home?"   *43*

"No, sir, I going to town."   *44*

"Why, that's too far! That's as far as I walk when I come out myself,   *45* and I get something for my trouble." He patted the stuffed bag he carried, and there hung down a little closed claw. It was one of the bob-whites, with its beak hooked bitterly to show it was dead. "Now you go on home, Granny!"

"I bound to go to town, mister," said Phoenix. "The time come around."   *46*

He gave another laugh, filling the whole landscape. "I know you old   *47* colored people! Wouldn't miss going to town to see Santa Claus!"

But something held Old Phoenix very still. The deep lines in her face   *48* went into a fierce and different radiation. Without warning, she had seen with her own eyes a flashing nickel fall out of the man's pocket onto the ground.

"How old are you, Granny?" he was saying.   *49*

"There is no telling, mister," she said, "no telling."   *50*

Then she gave a little cry and clapped her hands and said, "Git on away   *51* from here, dog! Look! Look at that dog!" She laughed as if in admiration. "He ain't scared of nobody. He a big black dog." She whispered, "Sic him!"

"Watch me get rid of that cur," said the man. "Sic him, Pete! Sic him!"   *52*

Phoenix heard the dogs fighting, and heard the man running and   *53* throwing sticks. She even heard a gunshot. But she was slowly bending forward by that time, further and further forward, the lids stretched down over her eyes, as if she were doing this in her sleep. Her chin was lowered almost to her knees. The yellow palm of her hand came out from the fold of her apron. Her fingers slid down and along the ground under the piece of money with the grace and care they would have in lifting an egg from under a sitting hen. Then she slowly straightened up, she stood erect, and the nickel was in her apron pocket. A bird flew by. Her lips moved. "God watching me the whole time, I come to stealing."

The man came back, and his own dog panted about them. "Well, I 54 scared him off that time," he said, and then he laughed and lifted his gun and pointed it at Phoenix.

She stood straight and faced him. 55

"Doesn't the gun scare you?" he said, still pointing it. 56

"No, sir, I seen plenty go off closer by, in my day, and for less than what 57 I done," she said, holding utterly still.

He smiled, and shouldered the gun. "Well, Granny," he said, "You must 58 be a hundred years old, and scared of nothing. I'd give you a dime if I had any money with me. But you take my advice and stay home, and nothing will happen to you."

"I bound to go on my way, mister," said Phoenix. She inclined her head 59 in the red rag. Then they went in different directions, but she could hear the gun shooting again and again over the hill.

She walked on. The shadows hung from the oak trees to the road like 60 curtains. Then she smelled wood-smoke, and smelled the river, and she saw a steeple and the cabins on their steep steps. Dozens of little black children whirled around her. There ahead was Natchez shining. Bells were ringing. She walked on.

In the paved city it was Christmas time. There were red and green 61 electric lights strung and crisscrossed everywhere, and all turned on in the daytime. Old Phoenix would have been lost if she had not distrusted her eyesight and depended on her feet to know where to take her.

She paused quietly on the sidewalk where people were passing by. A 62 lady came along in the crowd, carrying an armful of red-, green-, and silver-wrapped presents; she gave off perfume like the red roses in hot summer, and Phoenix stopped her.

"Please, missy, will you lace up my shoe?" She held up her foot. 63

"What do you want, Grandma?" 64

"See my shoe," said Phoenix. "Do all right for out in the country, but 65 wouldn't look right to go in a big building."

"Stand still then, Grandma," said the lady. She put her packages down 66 on the sidewalk beside her and laced and tied both shoes tightly.

"Can't lace 'em with a cane," said Phoenix. "Thank you, missy. I 67 doesn't mind asking a nice lady to tie up my shoe, when I gets out on the street."

Moving slowly and from side to side, she went into the big building and   *68*
into a tower of steps, where she walked up and around and around until her
feet knew to stop.

She entered a door, and there she saw nailed up on the wall the docu-   *69*
ment that had been stamped with the gold seal and framed in the gold
frame, which matched the dream that was hung up in her head.

"Here I be," she said. There was a fixed and ceremonial stiffness over   *70*
her body.

"A charity case, I suppose," said an attendant who sat at the desk be-   *71*
fore her.

But Phoenix only looked above her head. There was sweat on her face,   *72*
the wrinkles in her skin shone like a bright net.

"Speak up, Grandma," the woman said: "What's your name? We must   *73*
have your history, you know. Have you been here before? What seems to be
the trouble with you?"

Old Phoenix only gave a twitch to her face as if a fly were bothering   *74*
her.

"Are you deaf?" cried the attendant.   *75*

But then the nurse came in.   *76*

"Oh, that's just old Aunt Phoenix," she said. "She doesn't come for   *77*
herself—she has a little grandson. She makes these trips just as regular as
clockwork. She lives away back off the old Natchez Trace." She bent down.
"Well, Aunt Phoenix, why don't you just take a seat? We won't keep you
standing after your long trip." She pointed.

The old woman sat down, bolt upright in the chair.   *78*

"Now, how is the boy?" asked the nurse.   *79*

Old Phoenix did not speak.   *80*

"I said, how is the boy?"   *81*

But Phoenix only waited and stared straight ahead, her face very solemn   *82*
and withdrawn into rigidity.

"Is his throat any better?" asked the nurse. "Aunt Phoenix, don't you   *83*
hear me? Is your grandson's throat any better since the last time you came
for the medicine?"

With her hands on her knees, the old woman waited, silent, erect and   *84*
motionless, just as if she were in armor.

"You mustn't take up our time this way, Aunt Phoenix," the nurse   *85*
said. "Tell us quickly about your grandson, and get it over. He isn't dead,
is he?"

At last there came a flicker and then a flame of comprehension across *86* her face, and she spoke.

"My grandson. It was my memory had left me. There I sat and forgot *87* why I made my long trip."

"Forgot?" The nurse frowned. "After you came so far?" *88*

Then Phoenix was like an old woman begging a dignified forgiveness *89* for waking up frightened in the night. "I never did go to school, I was too old at the Surrender," she said in a soft voice. "I'm an old woman without an education. It was my memory fail me. My little grandson, he is just the same, and I forgot it in the coming."

"Throat never heals, does it?" said the nurse, speaking in a loud, sure *90* voice to Old Phoenix. By now she had a card with something written on it, a little list. "Yes. Swallowed lye. When was it—January—two-three years ago—"

Phoenix spoke unasked now. "No, missy, he not dead, he just the same. *91* Every little while his throat begin to close up again, and he not able to swallow. He not get his breath. He not able to help himself. So the time come around, and I go on another trip for the soothing medicine."

"All right. The doctor said as long as you came to get it, you could have *92* it," said the nurse. "But it's an obstinate case."

"My little grandson, he sit up there in the house all wrapped up, wait- *93* ing by himself," Phoenix went on. "We is the only two left in the world. He suffer and it don't seem to put him back at all. He got a sweet look. He going to last. He wear a little patch quilt and peep out holding his mouth open like a little bird. I remembers so plain now. I not going to forget him again, no, the whole enduring time. I could tell him from all the others in creation."

"All right." The nurse was trying to hush her now. She brought her a *94* bottle of medicine. "Charity," she said, making a check mark in a book.

Old Phoenix held the bottle close to her eyes and then carefully put it *95* into her pocket.

"I thank you," she said. *96*

"It's Christmas time, Grandma," said the attendant. "Could I give you *97* a few pennies out of my purse?"

"Five pennies is a nickel," said Phoenix stiffly. *98*

"Here's a nickel," said the attendant. *99*

Phoenix rose carefully and held out her hand. She received the nickel *100* and then fished the other nickel out of her pocket and laid it beside the new one. She stared at her palm closely, with her head on one side.

Then she gave a tap with her cane on the floor. *101*

"This is what come to me to do," she said. "I going to the store and buy *102* my child a little windmill they sells, made out of paper. He going to find it hard to believe there such a thing in the world. I'll march myself back where he waiting, holding it straight up in this hand."

She lifted her free hand, gave a little nod, turned round, and walked out *103* of the doctor's office. Then her slow step began on the stairs, going down.

QUESTIONS FOR WRITING AND DISCUSSION

1. Which of the following approximates your response(s) to the character of Phoenix Jackson: Surprise that she should be the subject of a story? Anger that no one helps her on her journey? Boredom that you just read a story in which nothing seems to happen? Puzzlement at her apparently senile behavior? Amazement at her determination and courage? Describe any other responses you may have.

2. According to legend, the Phoenix is a mythological bird that lives for five hundred years, burns itself to death, and then rises from its ashes in the freshness of youth to live through another life cycle. What *events, references,* and *images* in the story suggest that Welty's Phoenix Jackson is like the mythological bird?

3. One reader has suggested that during her journey, Phoenix encounters twelve obstacles (internal and external) that represent tests, or trials, of her faith and courage. How many of these tests can you find? Does she "pass" each test? What do these tests reveal about her character?

4. In an essay entitled "Is Phoenix Jackson's Grandson Really Dead?" Eudora Welty says, "The story is told through Phoenix's mind as she undertakes her errand. As the author is at one with the character as I tell it, I must assume that the boy is alive. As the reader, you are free to think as you like, of course: the story invites you to believe that no matter what happens, Phoenix for as long as she is able to walk and can hold to her purpose will make her journey." Explain how the boy's actual condition might affect your interpretation of the story.

5. Kate Chopin's "The Story of an Hour" and Eudora Welty's "A Worn Path" are both stories about love. By way of contrast, what do the character and behavior of Mrs. Mallard tell you about Phoenix? What do the character and behavior of Phoenix reveal about Mrs. Mallard?

PROFESSIONAL WRITING

THE LESSON

Toni Cade Bambara

Toni Cade Bambara is an activist for the African-American community on many fronts: political, cultural, and literary. She has worked for political and social causes in urban communities, taught African-American studies at half a dozen different colleges and universities, and is the author of several collections of short stories and novels, including Gorilla, My Love *(1972),* The Sea Birds Are Still Alive *(1977),* The Salt Eaters *(1980), and* If Blessing Comes *(1987). "The Lesson," which appears in* Gorilla, My Love, *dramatizes the gradual awakening of several children to the political and economic realities of contemporary urban life. As you read the story, pay attention to the narrator, Sylvia. What is the lesson, and what does Sylvia learn?*

Back in the days when everyone was old and stupid or young and foolish and me and Sugar were the only ones just right, this lady moved on our block with nappy hair and proper speech and no makeup. And quite naturally we laughed at her, laughed the way we did at the junk man who went about his business like he was some big-time president and his sorry-ass horse his secretary. And we kinda hated her too, hated the way we did the winos who cluttered up our parks and pissed on our handball walls and stank up our hallways and stairs so you couldn't halfway play hide-and-seek without a goddamn gas mask. Miss Moore was her name. The only woman on the block with no first name. And she was black as hell, cept for her feet, which were fish-white and spooky. And she was always planning these boring-ass things for us to do, us being my cousins, mostly, who lived on the block cause we all moved North the same time and to the same apartment then spread out gradual to breathe. And our parents would yank our heads into some kinda shape and crisp up our clothes so we'd be presentable for travel with Miss Moore, who always looked like she was going to church, though she never did. Which is just one of the things the grownups talked about when they talked behind her back like a dog. But when she came calling with some sachet she'd sewed up or some gingerbread she'd made or some book, why then they'd all be too embarrassed to turn her down and we'd get handed over all spruced up. She'd been to college and

1

said it was only right that she should take responsibility for the young ones' education, and she not even related by marriage or blood. So they'd go for it. Specially Aunt Gretchen. She was the main gofer in the family. You got some ole dumb shit foolishness you want somebody to go for, you send for Aunt Gretchen. She been screwed into the go-along for so long, it's a blood-deep natural thing with her. Which is how she got saddled with me and Sugar and Junior in the first place while our mothers were in a la-de-da apartment up the block having a good ole time.

So this one day Miss Moore rounds us all up at the mailbox and it's *2* puredee hot and she's knockin herself out about arithmetic. And school suppose to let up in summer I heard, but she don't never let up. And the starch in my pinafore scratching the shit outta me and I'm really hating this nappy-head bitch and her goddamn college degree. I'd much rather go to the pool or to the show where it's cool. So me and Sugar leaning on the mailbox being surly, which is a Miss Moore word. And Flyboy checking out what everybody brought for lunch. And Fat Butt already wasting his peanut-butter-and-jelly sandwich like the pig he is. And Junebug punchin on Q.T.'s arm for potato chips. And Rosie Giraffe shifting from one hip to the other waiting for somebody to step on her foot or ask her if she from Georgia so she can kick ass, preferably Mercedes's. And Miss Moore asking us do we know what money is, like we a bunch of retards. I mean real money, she say, like it's only poker chips or monopoly papers we lay on the grocer. So right away I'm tired of this and say so. And would much rather snatch Sugar and go to the Sunset and terrorize the West Indian kids and take their hair ribbons and their money too. And Miss Moore files that remark away for next week's lesson on brotherhood, I can tell. And finally I say we oughta get to the subway cause it's cooler and besides we might meet some cute boys. Sugar done swiped her mama's lipstick, so we ready.

So we heading down the street and she's boring us silly about what *3* things cost and what our parents make and how much goes for rent and how money ain't divided up right in this country. And then she gets to the part about we all poor and live in the slums, which I don't feature. And I'm ready to speak on that, but she steps out in the street and hails two cabs just like that. Then she hustles half the crew in with her and hands me a five-dollar bill and tells me to calculate 10 percent tip for the driver. And we're off. Me and Sugar and Junebug and Flyboy hangin out the window and hollering to everybody, putting lipstick on each other cause Flyboy a faggot anyway, and making farts with our sweaty armpits. But I'm mostly trying to figure how to spend this money. But they all fascinated with the meter ticking and Junebug starts laying bets as to how much it'll read when Flyboy can't hold his breath no more. Then Sugar lays bets as to how much it'll be when we get there. So I'm stuck. Don't nobody want to go for my plan, which is to jump out at the next light and run off to the first bar-b-que we can find. Then the driver tells us to get the hell out cause we there already. And the meter reads eighty-five cents. And I'm stalling to figure out the tip and Sugar say give him a dime. And I decide he don't need it bad as I do, so later for him. But then he tries to take off with Junebug foot still in the door so we talk about his mama something ferocious. Then we check out that we on Fifth Avenue and everybody dressed up in stockings. One lady in a fur coat, hot as it is. White folks crazy.

"This is the place," Miss Moore say, presenting it to us in the voice *4*
she uses at the museum. "Let's look in the windows before we go in."

"Can we steal?" Sugar asks very serious like she's getting the ground *5*
rules squared away before she plays. "I beg your pardon," say Miss Moore, and we fall out. So she leads us around the windows of the toy store and me and Sugar screamin, "This is mine, that's mine, I gotta have that, that was made for me, I was born for that," till Big Butt drowns us out.

"Hey, I'm goin to buy that there." *6*

"That there? You don't even know what it is, stupid." *7*

"I do so," he say punchin on Rosie Giraffe. "It's a microscope." *8*

"Whatcha gonna do with a microscope, fool?" *9*

"Look at things." *10*

"Like what, Ronald?" ask Miss Moore. And Big Butt ain't got the first *11*
notion. So here go Miss Moore gabbing about the thousands of bacteria in a drop of water and the somethinorother in a speck of blood and the million and one living things in the air around us is invisible to the naked eye. And what she say that for? Junebug go to town on that "naked" and we rolling. Then Miss Moore ask what it cost. So we all jam into the window smudgin it up and the price tag say $300. So then she ask how long'd take for Big Butt and Junebug to save up their allowances. "Too long," I say. "Yeh," adds Sugar, "outgrown it by that time." And Miss Moore say no, you never outgrow learning instruments. "Why, even medical students and interns and," blah, blah, blah. And we ready to choke Big Butt for bringing it up in the first damn place.

"This here costs four hundred eighty dollars," say Rosie Giraffe. So *12*
we pile up all over her to see what she pointin out. My eyes tell me it's a chunk of glass cracked with something heavy, and different-color inks dripped into the splits, then the whole thing put into a oven or something.

But for $480 it don't make sense.

"That's a paperweight made of semi-precious stones fused together 13
under tremendous pressure," she explains slowly, with her hands doing the
mining and all the factory work.

"So what's a paperweight?" asks Rosie Giraffe. 14

"To weigh paper with, dumbbell," say Flyboy, the wise man from the 15
East.

"Not exactly," say Miss Moore, which is what she say when you warm 16
or way off too. "It's to weigh paper down so it won't scatter and make your
desk untidy." So right away me and Sugar curtsy to each other and then to
Mercedes who is more the tidy type.

"We don't keep paper on top of the desk in my class," say Junebug, fig- 17
uring Miss Moore crazy or lyin one.

"At home, then," she say. "Don't you have a calendar and a pencil case 18
and a blotter and a letter-opener on your desk at home where you do your
homework?" And she know damn well what our homes look like cause she
nosys around in them every chance she gets.

"I don't even have a desk," say Junebug. "Do we?" 19

"No. And I don't get no homework neither," says Big Butt. 20

"And I don't even have a home," say Flyboy like he do at school to 21
keep the white folks off his back and sorry for him. Send this poor kid to
camp posters, is his specialty.

"I do," says Mercedes. "I have a box of stationery on my desk and a 22
picture of my cat. My godmother bought the stationery and the desk.
There's a big rose on each sheet and the envelopes smell like roses."

"Who wants to know about your smelly-ass stationery," say Rosie 23
Giraffe fore I can get my two cents in.

"It's important to have a work area all your own so that. . . ." 24

"Will you look at this sailboat, please," say Flyboy, cuttin her off and 25
pointin to the thing like it was his. So once again we tumble all over each
other to gaze at this magnificent thing in the toy store which is just big
enough to maybe sail two kittens across the pond if you strap them to the
posts tight. We all start reciting the price tag like we in assembly. "Hand-
crafted sailboat of fiberglass at one thousand one hundred ninety-five
dollars."

"Unbelievable," I hear myself say and am really stunned. I read it again 26
for myself just in case the group recitation put me in a trance. Same thing.

For some reason this pisses me off. We look at Miss Moore and she lookin at us, waiting for I dunno what.

"Who'd pay all that when you can buy a sailboat set for a quarter at 27 Pop's, a tube of glue for a dime, and a ball of string for eight cents? It must have a motor and a whole lot else besides," I say. "My sailboat cost me about fifty cents."

"But will it take water?" say Mercedes with her smart ass.   28

"Took mine to Alley Pond Park once," say Flyboy. "String broke. Lost 29 it. Pity."

"Sailed mine in Central Park and it keeled over and sank. Had to ask 30 my father for another dollar."

"And you got the strap," laugh Big Butt. "The jerk didn't even have a 31 string on it. My old man wailed on his behind."

Little Q.T. was staring hard at the sailboat and you could see he wanted 32 it bad. But he too little and somebody'd just take it from him. So what the hell. "This boat for kids, Miss Moore?"

"Parents silly to buy something like that just to get all broke up," say 33 Rosie Giraffe.

"That much money it should last forever," I figure.   34

"My father'd buy it for me if I wanted it."   35

"Your father, my ass," say Rosie Giraffe getting a chance to finally push 36 Mercedes.

"Must be rich people shop here," say Q.T.   37

"You are a very bright boy," say Flyboy. "What was your first clue?" 38 And he rap him on the head with the back of his knuckles, since Q.T. the only one he could get away with. Though Q.T. liable to come up behind you years later and get his licks in when you half expect it.

"What I want to know is," I says to Miss Moore though I never talk 39 to her, I wouldn't give the bitch that satisfaction, "is how much a real boat costs? I figure a thousand'd get you a yacht any day."

"Why don't you check that out," she says, "and report back to the 40 group?" Which really pains my ass. If you gonna mess up a perfectly good swim day least you could do is have some answers. "Let's go in," she say like she got something up her sleeve. Only she don't lead the way. So me and Sugar turn the corner to where the entrance is, but when we get there I kinda hang back. Not that I'm scared, what's there to be afraid of, just a toy store. But I feel funny, shame. But what I got to be shamed about? Got as much right to go in as anybody. But somehow I can't seem to get hold of the door, so I step away for Sugar to lead. But she hangs back too. And I look at her and she looks at me and this is ridiculous. I mean, damn, I have never ever been shy about doing nothing or going nowhere. But then Mercedes steps up and then Rosie Giraffe and Big Butt crowd in behind and shove, and next thing we all stuffed into the doorway with only Mercedes squeezing past us, smoothing out her jumper and walking right down the aisle. Then the rest of us tumble in like a glued-together jigsaw done all wrong. And people lookin at us. And it's like the time me and Sugar crashed into the Catholic church on a dare. But once we got in there and everything so hushed and holy and the candles and the bowin and the hand-kerchiefs on all the drooping heads, I just couldn't go through with the plan. Which was for me to run up to the altar and do a tap dance while Sugar played the nose flute and messed around in the holy water. And Sugar kept givin me the elbow. Then later teased me so bad I tied her up in the shower and turned it on and locked her in. And she'd be there till this day if Aunt Gretchen hadn't finally figured I was lyin about the boarder takin a shower.

Same thing in the store. We all walkin on tiptoe and hardly touch-in *41* the games and puzzles and things. And I watched Miss Moore who is steady watchin us like she waitin for a sign. Like Mama Drewery watches the sky and sniffs the air and takes note of just how much slant is in the bird formation. Then me and Sugar bump smack into each other, so busy gaz-ing at the toys, 'specially the sailboat. But we don't laugh and go into our fat-lady bump-stomach routine. We just stare at that price tag. Then Sugar run a finger over the whole boat. And I'm jealous and want to hit her. Maybe not her, but I sure want to punch somebody in the mouth.

"Watcha bring us here for, Miss Moore?" *42*

"You sound angry, Sylvia. Are you mad about something?" Givin me *43* one of them grins like she tellin a grown-up joke that never turns out to be funny. And she's lookin very closely at me like maybe she plannin to do my portrait from memory. I'm mad, but I won't give her that satisfaction. So I slouch around the store bein very bored and say, "Let's go."

Me and Sugar at the back of the train watchin the tracks whizzin by *44* large then small then gettin gobbled up in the dark. I'm thinkin about this tricky toy I saw in the store. A clown that somersaults on a bar then does chin-ups just cause you yank lightly at his leg. Cost $35. I could see me askin my mother for a $35 birthday clown. "You wanna who that costs what?" she'd say, cocking her head to the side to get a better view of the hole in my head. Thirty-five dollars could buy new bunk beds for Junior and Gretchen's boy. Thirty-five dollars and the whole household could go visit Granddaddy Nelson in the country. Thirty-five dollars would pay for the rent and the piano bill too. Who are these people that spend that much for performing clowns and $1,000 for toy sailboats? What kinda work they do and how they live and how come we ain't in on it? Where we are is who we are, Miss Moore always pointin out. But it don't necessarily have to be that way, she always adds then waits for somebody to say that poor people have to wake up and demand their share of the pie and don't none of us know what kind of pie she talkin about in the first damn place. But she ain't so smart cause I still got her four dollars from the taxi and she sure ain't gettin it. Messin up my day with this shit. Sugar nudges me in my pocket and winks.

Miss Moore lines us up in front of the mailbox where we started from, 45 seem like years ago, and I got a headache for thinkin so hard. And we lean all over each other so we can hold up under the draggy-ass lecture she always finishes us off with at the end before we thank her for borin us to tears. But she just looks at us like she readin tea leaves. Finally she say, "Well, what did you think of F. A. O. Schwarz?"

Rosie Giraffe mumbles, "White folks crazy."   46

"I'd like to go there again when I get my birthday money," says Mer- 47 cedes, and we shove her out the pack so she has to lean on the mailbox by herself.

"I'd like a shower. Tiring day," say Flyboy.   48

Then Sugar surprises me by sayin, "You know, Miss Moore, I don't 49 think all of us here put together eat in a year what that sailboat costs." And Miss Moore lights up like somebody goosed her. "And?" she say, urging Sugar on. Only I'm standin on her foot so she don't continue.

"Imagine for a minute what kind of society it is in which some people 50 can spend on a toy what it would cost to feed a family of six or seven. What do you think?"

"I think," say Sugar pushing me off her feet like she never done before, 51 cause I whip her ass in a minute, "that this is not much of a democracy if you ask me. Equal chance to pursue happiness means an equal crack at the dough, don't it?" Miss Moore is besides herself and I am disgusted with Sugar's treachery. So I stand on her foot one more time to see if she'll shove me. She shuts up, and Miss Moore looks at me, sorrowfully I'm thinkin. And somethin weird is goin on, I can feel it in my chest.

"Anybody else learn anything today?" lookin dead at me. I walk away 52 and Sugar has to run to catch up and don't even seem to notice when I shrug her arm off my shoulder.

"Well, we got four dollars anyway," she says.   53

"Uh hunh." *54*

"We could go to Hascombs and get half a chocolate layer and then go to *55*
the Sunset and still have plenty money for potato chips and ice cream sodas."

"Uh hunh." *56*

"Race you to Hascombs," she say. *57*

We start down the block and she gets ahead which is O.K. by me cause *58*
I'm going to the West End and then over to the Drive to think this day
through. She can run if she want to and even run faster. But ain't nobody
gonna beat me at nuthin.

QUESTIONS FOR WRITING AND DISCUSSION

1. Describe one incident when a parent, friend, or family member
   tried to get you to do something that you didn't want to do. How did you
   react? How was your behavior similar to or different from the reaction of
   Sylvia, the narrator in "The Lesson"?

2. Reread the opening sentence of the story. What does the first half of that
   sentence reveal about the character of the narrator? Does the rest of the story
   confirm that initial impression? Explain.

3. Locate at least one sentence or passage describing the reactions of each of the
   following children to the merchandise at F. A. O. Schwarz: Sylvia (the narrator), Sugar, Flyboy, Mercedes, Big Butt, Junebug, Rosie Giraffe, and Q.T.
   How do their reactions to the toys and their prices affect the narrator? Why
   does Bambara include all of these children in the story rather than tell it
   using just Miss Moore, Sylvia, and Sugar?

4. Miss Moore is the "teacher" for this "lesson," but what kind of teacher is she,
   and how do her students react to her? What strategies does she use to help
   the children learn? Are her methods effective? How do the children react to
   each other's learning? Does Miss Moore make some mistakes?

5. What evidence (cite specific sentences) suggests that Sylvia is learning more
   from this lesson than she wants to? What exactly is she learning? Describe
   what she might do in the future as a result of what she learns.

6. Explain how each of the following quotations from Sylvia's thoughts relates
   to the theme or main idea of "The Lesson":

White folks crazy.

I mean, damn, I have never ever been shy about doing nothing or going nowhere.

If you gonna mess up a perfectly good swim day least you could do is have some answers.

But ain't nobody gonna beat me at nuthin.

7. Write two paragraphs comparing and contrasting the "awakenings" of Mrs. Mallard in "The Story of an Hour" and Sylvia in "The Lesson." What—and how—does each character learn? How do they react to what they learn? What do we, as readers, learn?

Responding to Poetry

Poems often have characters, setting, and point of view, but they also have other features that are important to reading imaginatively and critically. Use the following literary terms to help focus your reading and response to poems.

Voice and Tone. The speaker in a poem is not necessarily the same as the author of the poem. When Robert Frost says in "The Road Not Taken," "Two roads diverged in a yellow wood, /And sorry I could not travel both," the "I" in the poem is not directly equivalent to Robert Frost. The "I" represents a speaker faced with this particular choice. *Tone,* the speaker's attitude toward the subject matter, is also important in the poem. A speaker's tone might be happy or sad, delighted or angry, serious or humorous, spontaneous or reflective, straightforward or ironic. In Frost's poem, the speaker's tone is serious and reflective when he says, in conclusion, "I took the one less traveled by, /And that has made all the difference." In Auden's poem, the speaker is a person explaining or interpreting a painting. Phrases such as "how well they understood its human position" or "In Bureghel's Icarus, for instance" reveal the speaker as knowledgeable and perhaps slightly academic. The speaker's tone is serious and reflective: he is praising the virtues of a painting by one of the Old Masters.

Word Choice. In poetry, diction and word choice are especially important. A poet might use academic language and formal phrasing or might use street language or slang. A poet might use short, emphatic words, or longer, more flowing language. Sometimes a poem juxtaposes formal and informal language.

Auden deliberately contrasts a more formal diction ("About suffering they were never wrong, /The Old Masters") with more informal and colloquial (spoken) language ("Anyhow in a corner, some untidy spot / Where the dogs go on with their doggy life and the torturer's horse / Scratches its innocent behind on a tree").

Figures of Speech: Similes, Metaphors, Symbols, Personification. Figures of speech enable poets to compress experience, to add emotional impact, or to make an experience vivid, dramatic, or memorable. *Simile* is a comparison using *like* or *as:* "My love is like a red, red rose." A *metaphor* creates a direct equivalency without using *like* or *as:* "My love is a red, red rose." William Blake uses metaphor when he writes, "Tyger! Tyger! burning bright / In the forests of the night." The tiger is not literally a burning fire, but the colors of his coat and his potentially violent spirit are directly compared to a fire. A word becomes a *symbol* when it represents something larger or more abstract than its literal meaning. The tiger in Blake's poem becomes a symbol because it represents something larger than itself: the potential for violence and perhaps natural evil in the world. Similarly, readers might argue that Auden uses Icarus to symbolize human suffering in the world. Finally, in *personification,* an abstraction or an inanimate object is given human qualities. Death, in Emily Dickinson's poem, is personified: like the driver of a carriage, it stops to pick up the speaker and carry her on toward eternity.

Sound, Rhyme, and Rhythm. Poets often use repetitions of sounds, of rhyming words, and of patterns of stressed (long) and unstressed (short) syllables. Emily Dickinson's poem, "Because I could not stop for death" uses an *iambic* pattern (one short syllable followed by one long syllable) to create a regular rhythm: "Because I could not stop for death— / He kindly stopped for me." Every second and fourth lines end with a rhyming word. William Blake rhymes the first and second lines and uses the *trochaic* pattern (one long syllable followed by one short syllable): Tyger! Tyger! burning bright / In the forests of the night." In contrast, W. H. Auden uses an open form, without a set rhythm of rhyme. Poets also use patterns or combinations of sounds to reflect the meaning of the poem. *Alliteration* is the repetition of consonant sounds, and *assonance* is the repetition of vowel sounds. "Tyger! Tyger! burning bright" uses the alliteration of the t's and g's in "Tyger! Tiger!" and the repeated b's and r's in "burning bright" to give emphasis and power to the lines. In e. e. cummings' poem, "anyone lived in a pretty how town," cummings repeats the "o" sound in several successive words to give a smooth easy flow to the language.

PROFESSIONAL WRITING: FIVE CONTEMPORARY POEMS

Aurora Levins Morales

Born in Puerto Rico in 1954 to a Jewish father and a Puerto Rican mother,
Aurora Levins Morales moved with her family to the United States in 1967.
She has published a collection of short stories and collaboratively written with
her mother, Rosario Morales, a book containing short stories, essays, and poetry:
Getting Home Alive *(1986). She currently lives near San Francisco.*

CHILD OF THE AMERICAS

I am a child of the Americas,
a light-skinned mestiza of the Caribbean,
a child of many diaspora,[1] born into this continent at a
   crossroads.

I am a U.S. Puerto Rican Jew   5
a product of the ghettos of New York I have never known.
An immigrant and the daughter and granddaughter of
   immigrants.
I speak English with passion: it's the tongue of my consciousness,
a flashing knife blade of crystal, my tool, my craft.

I am Caribeña,[2] island grown. Spanish is in my flesh,
ripples from my tongue, lodges in my hips: 10
the language of garlic and mangoes,
the singing in my poetry, the flying gestures of my hands.

I am of Latinoamerica, rooted in the history of my continent:
I speak from that body.

I am not african. Africa is in me, but I cannot return.   15
I am not taína.[3] Taíno is in me, but there is no way back.
I am not european. Europe lives in me, but I have no home
   there.

I am new. History made me. My first language was spanglish.[4]
I was born at the crossroads
and I am whole.   20

---

[1] **diaspora** "a scattering," referring to the dispersion of Jews from Israel.
[2] **Caribeña** Carribean woman
[3] **taína** a native Indian tribe in Puerto Rico
[4] **spanglish** a mixture of Spanish and English

Gary Soto

Gary Soto was born in Fresno, California, in 1952. Soto is the author of many books of fiction and poetry, including Black Hair *(1985),* Who Will Know Us? *(1990), and* Canto Familiar/Familiar Song *(1994). He currently lives in northern California.*

BLACK HAIR

At eight I was brilliant with my body.
In July, that ring of heat
We all jumped through, I sat in the bleachers
Of Romain Playground, in the lengthening
Shade that rose from our dirty feet.   5
The game before us was more than baseball.
It was a figure—Hector Moreno
Quick and hard with turned muscles,
His crouch the one I assumed before an altar
Of worn baseball cards, in my room.   10
I came here because I was Mexican, a stick
Of brown light in love with those
Who could do it—the triple and hard slide,
The gloves eating balls into double plays.
What could I do with 50 pounds, my shyness,   15
My black torch of hair, about to go out?
Father was dead, his face no longer
Hanging over the table or our sleep,
And mother was the terror of mouths
Twisting hurt by butter knives.   20

In the bleachers I was brilliant with my body,
Waving players in and stomping my feet,
Growing sweaty in the presence of white shirts.
I chewed sunflower seeds. I drank water
And bit my arm through the late innings.   25
When Hector lined balls into deep
Center, in my mind I rounded the bases
With him, my face flared, my hair lifting
Beautifully, because we were coming home
To the arms of brown people.

Joy Harjo

A prolific writer of poems and songs, Joy Harjo was born in Tulsa, Oklahoma, in 1951. Her books of poetry include She Had Some Horses *(1983),* The Woman Who Fell From the Sky *(1994), and* How We Became Human: New and Selected Poems *(2002). She has received the Josephine Miles poetry award and the American Indian Distinguished Achievement in the Arts award. She has lived in Colorado, California, and Hawaii.*

PERHAPS THE WORLD ENDS HERE

The world begins at a kitchen table. No matter what,
we must eat to live.

The gifts of earth are brought and prepared, set on the
table. So it has been since creation, and it will go on.

We chase chickens or dogs away from it. Babies teethe   5
at the corners. They scrape their knees under it.

It is here that children are given instructions on what
it means to be human. We make men at it,
we make women.

At this table we gossip, recall enemies and the ghosts   10
of lovers.

Our dreams drink coffee with us as they put their arms
around our children. They laugh with us at our poor
falling-down selves and as we put ourselves back
together once again at the table.   15

This table has been a house in the rain, an umbrella
in the sun.

Wars have begun and ended at this table. It is a place
to hide in the shadow of terror. A place to celebrate
the terrible victory.   20

We have given birth on this table, and have prepared
our parents for burial here.

At this table we sing with joy, with sorrow.
We pray of suffering and remorse.
We give thanks.   25

Perhaps the world will end at the kitchen table,
while we are laughing and crying,
eating of the last sweet bite.

Wislawa Szymborska

*Wislawa Szymborska was born in Poland in 1923. She is the author of many
books of poetry, including two that are translated into English:* Sounds, Feelings, Thoughts: Seventy Poems by Wislawa Szymborska *(1981) and* View
with a Grain of Sand: Selected Poems *(1995). She won the Nobel Prize in Literature in 1996. She currently lives in Cracow.*

END AND BEGINNING

TRANSLATED BY JOSEPH BRODSKY

After each war
somebody has to clear up
put things in order
by itself it won't happen.

Somebody's got to push
rubble to the highway shoulder
making way
for the carts filled up with corpses.

Someone might trudge
through muck and ashes,
sofa springs,
splintered glass
and blood-soaked rugs.

Somebody has to haul
beams for propping a wall,
another put glass in a window
and hang the door on hinges.

This is not photogenic
and takes years.
All the cameras have left already
for another war.

Bridges are needed
also new railroad stations.
Tatters turn into sleeves
for rolling up.

Somebody, broom in hand,
still recalls how it was,
Someone whose head was not
torn away listens nodding.
But nearby already
begin to bustle those
who'll need persuasion.

Somebody still at times
digs up from under the bushes
some rusty quibble
to add it to burning refuse.

Those who knew
what this was all about
must yield to those
who know little   40
or less than little
essentially nothing.

In the grass that has covered
effects in causes
somebody must recline,   45
a stalk of rye in the teeth,
ogling the clouds.

Yusef Komunyakka

*Born in 1947 in Bogalusa, Louisiana, Yusef Komunyakka served in Vietnam
before returning to earn degrees at the University of Colorado, Colorado State
University, and the University of California, Irvine. He has published many
books of poetry, including* Thieves of Paradise *(1998),* Pleasure Dome: New
& Collected Poems, 1975–1999 *(2001), and* Dien Cai Dau *(1988), in which
the poem "Facing It" appears. The photograph of the Vietnam Veterans Memorial was selected to appear with this poem. After you read the poem, consider how
effectively this photograph illustrates the themes and images in the poem.*

FACING IT

My black face fades,
hiding inside the black granite.
I said I wouldn't,
dammit: No tears.
I'm stone. I'm flesh.   5
My clouded reflection eyes me
like a bird of prey, the profile of night
slanted against morning. I turn
this way—the stone lets me go.
I turn that way—I'm inside   10
the Vietnam Veterans Memorial

again, depending on the light
to make a difference.
I go down the 58,022 names,
half-expecting to find   15
my own in letters like smoke.
I touch the name Andrew Johnson;
I see the booby trap's white flash.
Names shimmer on a woman's blouse
but when she walks away   20
the names stay on the wall.
Brushstrokes flash, a red bird's
wings cutting across my stare.
The sky. A plane in the sky.
A white vet's image floats   25
closer to me, then his pale eyes
look through mine. I'm a window.
He's lost his right arm
inside the stone. In the black mirror
a woman's trying to erase names: 30
No, she's brushing a boy's hair.

Paul Merideth, photographer

USA, Washington DC, man touching Vietnam Veterans Memorial.

QUESTIONS FOR WRITING AND DISCUSSION

1. In "Child of the Americas," Aurora Levins Morales compares the mixture of languages and cultures within her to geographical mixtures and crossroads. Find several places in the poem where Levins Morales makes this comparison. What kinds of figurative language does she use (simile, metaphor, or image)? Explain how these images help construct one of Levins Morales's themes in the poem.

2. In Greek mythology, Hector was a great Trojan warrior. Hector was killed by Achilles in the Trojan War, but his death was avenged by his brother, Paris. In "Black Hair," how does Gary Soto use the legend of Hector? Which lines suggest references to Hector, and how do these references relate to a theme in the poem?

3. Although Joy Harjo entitles her poem, "Perhaps the World Ends Here," the poem is about both beginnings and endings. What images or examples of figurative language illustrate the beginnings, and which refer to endings? In your own words, explain how Harjo does or does not resolve the conflicts between beginnings and endings.

4. Wislawa Szymborska's poem, "End and Beginning," echoes Harjo's theme of beginnings and endings in a poem about the aftermath of war. The end of war, Szymborska says, "is not photogenic / and takes years. / All the cameras have left already / for another war." What images in the poem suggest the hard, dirty, and thankless work required to rebuild a civilization? How do these images fit into Szymborska's overall theme in the poem?

5. In "Facing It," Yusef Komunyakka contrasts the realities outside the memorial wall with the reflections and images inside the wall. What does Komunyakka describe that is outside the wall? What does he see in the wall or in the reflections of the wall? What do you think Komunyakka means when he says of a white vet, "He's lost his right arm / inside the stone"? Explain how these images or reality and reflection help explain a major theme of the poem.

6. Do a comparison and contrast of two of the poems in this chapter. Your purpose is to compare lines, images, figures of speech, and themes in order to show how one poem relates to the other. How do the similarities and differences enhance your reading of one or both of the poems? Possibilities for

comparison include the poems by Aurora Levins Morales and Gary Soto, by Harjo and Szymborska, and by Szymborska and Komunyakka.

Responding to Literature: The Writing Process

ASSIGNMENT FOR RESPONDING TO LITERATURE

Choose one of the poems or short stories from this chapter (or a work of literature assigned in your class), reread and annotate the work, and share your responses with others in the class. Then write an interpretative essay. Assume that you are writing for other members of your class (including your instructor) who have read the work but who may not understand or agree with your interpretation.

COLLECTING

In addition to reading, rereading, annotating, and sharing your responses, try the following collecting strategies. Illustrations below are based on an interpretive essay about "The Story of an Hour."

- **Collaborative annotation.** In small groups, choose a work of literature or select a passage that you have already annotated. In the group, read each other's annotations. Then discuss each annotation. Which annotations does your group agree are the best? Have a group recorder record the best annotations.
- **Elements of poetry analysis.** Reread the paragraphs earlier in the chapter on voice and tone, word choice, figures of speech, and sound, rhyme, and rhythm. Focus on the elements that seem most important for the poem you have selected. After you have finished annotating, freewrite a paragraph explaining how these elements work together to create the theme or overall effect of the poem.
- **Elements of fiction analysis.** Reread the paragraphs defining character, plot, point of view, setting, and style. Choose three of these elements that

seem most important in the story that you are reading. Reread the story, annotating for these three elements. Then freewrite a paragraph explaining *how these three elements are interrelated or how they explain the theme.*

- **Time line.** In your journal, draw a time line for the story. List above the line everything that happens in the story. Below the line, indicate where the story opens, when the major conflicts occur, and where the climax and the denouement occur. For "The Story of an Hour," student writer Karen Ehrhardt drew the following time line:

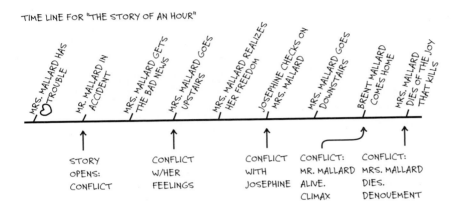

TIME LINE FOR "THE STORY OF AN HOUR"

- **Feature list.** Choose a character trait, repeated image, or idea that you wish to investigate in the poem or story. List, in order of appearance, every word, image, or reference that you find.
- **Scene vision or revision.** Write a scene for this story in which you change some part of it. You may *add* a scene to the beginning, middle, or end of the story. You may *change* a scene in the story. You may write a scene in the story from a different character's point of view. You may change the style of the story for your scene. How, for example, might Eudora Welty have described the opening scene of "The Story of an Hour"?
- **Draw a picture.** For your poem or short story, draw a picture based on images, characters, conflicts, or themes in the work of literature. Student writer Lori Van Sike drew the following picture for "The Story of an Hour" that shows how the rising and falling action of the plot parallels Mrs. Mallard's ascent and descent of the stairs.
- **Character conflict map.** Start with a full page of paper. Draw a main character in the center of the page. Locate the other major characters, internal forces, and external forces (including social, economic, and environmental

"The Story of an Hour"

Story Picture: The Rising/Falling Action

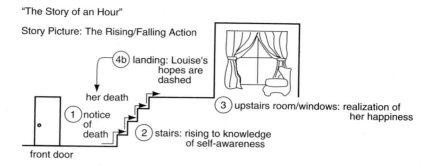

pressures) in a circle around the main character. Draw a line between each of these peripheral characters or forces and the main character. For his character conflict map for "The Story of an Hour," student writer Darren Marshall used images from his computer program to surround his picture of Mrs. Mallard.

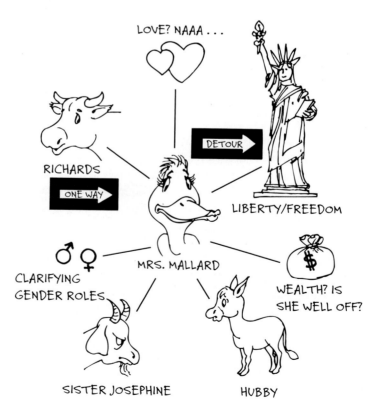

- **Background investigation.** Investigate the biographical, social, or historical context of the poem or story. Go online or to your library databases to find biographical information or other stories or poems by the same author. How does this background information increase your understanding or appreciation of the poem or story?
- **Reconsideration of purposes.** What idea, theme, or approach most interests you? Will you be explaining, evaluating, problem solving, or arguing? Are you combining purposes? Do these purposes suggest what kinds of information you might collect?

SHAPING

Test each of the following possible shapes against your ideas for your essay. Use or adapt the shape or shapes that are most appropriate for your own interpretation.

EXPLAINING RELATIONSHIPS Interpretative essays often analyze how the parts of a poem or story relate to the whole. As you explain these relationships, you should show how key images, lines, or scenes contribute to the overall theme or idea of the poem or story.

Introduction and thesis:	The details and images in the work reveal that the theme is X.
First scene, stanza, or group of lines:	How details and images establish the theme.
Second scene or group of lines:	How details and images relate to or build on previous images and contribute to the theme.
Third scene or group of lines:	How details and images continue building the theme.
Conclusion:	How the author highlights the key images or themes.

EVALUATING If your response suggests an evaluating purpose, you may wish to set up criteria for an effective poem or short story and then provide evidence showing how this poem or story does or does not measure up to your standards. Using criteria for a story, your essay might use the following outline:

Introduction and thesis:	Story X is highly dramatic.
Criterion 1:	A dramatic short story should focus on a character who changes his or her behavior or beliefs. Judgment and evidence for Criterion 1:

Criterion 2:	A dramatic story must have striking conflicts that lead to a crisis or a predicament. Judgment and evidence for Criterion 2:
Criterion 3:	A dramatic story should have a theme that makes a controversial point. Judgment and evidence for Criterion 3:
Conclusion:	Reinforces thesis.

ARGUING   During class discussion, you may disagree with another person's response. Your thesis may then take the form, "Although some readers believe this poem or story is about X, the poem or story can also be about Y.

Introduction and thesis:	Although some readers suggest the poem or story is about X, it is really about Y.
Body paragraphs:	State the opposing interpretation and give evidence for that interpretation. Then state your interpretation and give evidence (images, characters, events, points of conflict) supporting your interpretation.
Conclusion:	Clarifies and reinforces thesis.

INVESTIGATING CHANGES IN INTERPRETATION   Often, readers *change* interpretations during the course of responding to a piece of literature. Thus, your main point might be, "Although I initially believed X about the poem or story, I gradually realized the theme of the poem or story is Y." If that sentence expresses your main idea, you may wish to organize your essay following the chronology or the steps in the changes in your interpretation:

Introduction and thesis:	Although I initially thought X, I now believe Y.
Body paragraphs:	First step (your original interpretation of the story or poem and supporting evidence):
	Second step (additional or contradictory ideas and evidence that forced you to reconsider your interpretation):
	Third step (your final interpretation and supporting evidence):
Conclusion:	Shows how steps lead to thesis.

Note: One strategy you should not use is to simply retell the key parts of a poem or the plot of the story. Your audience has already read the poem or story. They want you to state your interpretation and then use details to show how and why your interpretation is credible. Although you will cite key characters, images, or events in the poem or story, you must explain how or why each of these details support your interpretation.

DRAFTING

To prepare to draft your essay, read through your annotations and gather your collecting and shaping notes. Some writers prefer to write one-sentence statements of their main ideas at the top of the page to keep them focused as they write. Other writers prefer to make rough outlines to follow, based on their adaptations of one of the preceding shaping strategies. When you begin drafting, you may wish to skip your introduction and start with the body of your essay. You can fill in the introduction after you have written a draft.

Once you start writing, keep your momentum going. If you draw a blank, reread what you have already written or look at your notes. If you cannot think of a particular word or are unsure about a spelling, draw a line _____ and keep on writing.

REVISING

Use the following guidelines as you read your classmates' drafts and revise your own essay. Be prepared to make changes in your ideas, organization, and evidence, as well as to fix problems in sentences and word choice.

Guidelines for Revisions

- **Clarify your main idea or interpretation.** Ask your readers to write, in one sentence, the main point of your interpretation. If their statements do not exactly match your main point, clarify your thesis. Your interpretation (not a statement of fact) should be clearly stated early in your essay.
- **Do not just summarize the poem or story.** Your readers have read the story or poem. Start with your interpretation; cite key images, metaphors, or lines that support your interpretation; and then explain why these images or key words are important.
- **Support each part of your interpretation with references to specific passages from the text.** Do not be satisfied with one piece of evidence. Find as many bits of evidence as possible. The case for your interpretation grows stronger with each additional piece of evidence.
- **Explain how each piece of evidence supports your interpretation.** Do not just cite several pieces of evidence and go on to your next point. Explain for your readers *how* the evidence supports your interpretation.

- **Define key terms in your essay.** If you are writing about the hero in a story, define what you mean by *hero* or *heroine*. If you are arguing that "The Story of an Hour" has a *feminist* theme, define *feminism.*
- **Signal the major parts of your interpretation.** Let your readers know when you shift to a new point. Use transitions and paragraph hooks at the beginning of body paragraphs.
- **Use the present tense as you describe the events in the story.** If you are describing the end of "The Story of an Hour," write, for example, "Mrs. Mallard descends the stairs and learns the 'good news' about her husband."
- **Quote accurately and cite page numbers for each reference.** Double-check your quotations to make sure they are accurate, word-for-word transcriptions. Following each direct quotation, cite page references as follows: In the first sentence, Kate Chopin says, "Mrs. Mallard was afflicted with a heart trouble" (479).

  In "Child of the Americas," the author states the central idea of the poem when she says, "I am of Latinoamerica, rooted in the history of my continent" (line 13).

  Note: The period goes outside the parentheses. See Chapter 12 for correct documentation style.
- **Revise your essay for sentence clarity and conciseness.** Read your essay aloud or have a classmate read it. Reduce unnecessary repetition. Use active verbs. Rework awkward or confusing sentences.
- **Edit your essay.** Check your essay for correct spelling, word choice, punctuation, and grammar.

POSTSCRIPT ON THE WRITING PROCESS

Before you turn in your essay, answer the following questions in your journal:

1. Explain what part of this essay (collecting ideas and evidence, focusing on your interpretation, shaping your essay, drafting, or revising) was most difficult for you. How did you work around the problems?

2. What do you like best about your essay? Refer to specific places in the essay (lead-in, thesis, pieces of evidence, ideas, conclusion). Which specific paragraphs do you like best? Why?

3. What did you learn about the story by writing your interpretation? What do you realize now that you did not understand when you first read the story?

4. If you had two more hours to work on this essay, what would you change? Why?

STUDENT WRITING

A WORN PATH

Julia MacMillan and Brett MacFadden

Julia MacMillan and Brett MacFadden collaboratively wrote their essay on the Phoenix imagery in Eudora Welty's "A Worn Path." They drafted their own essays separately and then collaborated on a revision that shared their interpretations and their best textual evidence. The following are their original separate notes and drafts, their plans for their collaborative revision, and their final revised interpretation. Read their separate versions first, and then see how they collaborated to produce their revised essay.

Rough Drafts

Julia MacMillan

The journey that Phoenix Jackson makes in Eudora Welty's "A Worn Path" is very similar to that made by the mythological phoenix on its way to rebirth. Much of the symbolism and figurative language throughout the story shows the succession of events that parallel a Phoenix-like ending to the old woman.

We can feel, almost from the beginning, that Phoenix's long life is coming to an end. She is described with "the two knots of her cheeks illuminated by a yellow burning under the dark" (289). In only a few more sentences, however, we hear the mourning dove, apparently mourning for Phoenix. The yellow burning under the dark is almost a desperate, final fiery burst in the face of oncoming death.

Her death is also foreshadowed in the mention of a buzzard, watching her from the tall, dead trees. She asks of him, "Who you watching?" as if she knows it is herself. Further in her journey, upon meeting the white hunter, her impending death as well as her expectation of it are shown. The little bob-white, "its beak hooked bitterly to show it was dead" (262), that the hunter is carrying on his bag quite forcefully shows us her death. The fact that she does not fear but expects this death is shown when the hunter points his gun at Phoenix, and she "stood straight and faced him" quite fearlessly (263). In not fearing this death and seeming to understand its nearness, Phoenix Jackson becomes more like the bird she is named for.

It is most clearly seen that the author intended her reader to see the Phoenix imagery when the grandson is introduced near the end of the story. On page 264, she "entered a door, and there she saw the document that had been stamped with the gold seal and framed in the gold frame, which matched the dream that was hung up in her head." The gold in this passage seems to represent flame—the flame of her funeral pyre and the dream in her head of perpetuation and reincarnation through her grandson's life. It is even more clearly stated when, once in the doctor's office, she goes into a strange trance, becoming unable to answer the agitated nurse's questions. When finally asked, "He isn't dead, is he?" "a flicker and then a flame of comprehension" come across her face" (265). These flames are symbolic of her death, yet they are caused by her remembering the importance of her grandson's life to her. This life is most precious to her, because it is through her grandson that Phoenix, like the mythological bird, will live again.

Brett MacFadden

In many ways Phoenix Jackson is like the mythical bird she is named after; her physical characteristics, her purpose in life, and her extreme age and nearness to death all support her likeness to the mythological phoenix.

The phoenix is a bird of myth that lives for five hundred years and then burns itself to death, rising from its ashes renewed and beautiful. Phoenix Jackson in the story "A Worn Path" by Eudora Welty is a very old black woman near the end of her life cycle who takes a long walk through the woods to town in order to get medicine for her ailing grandson. The core story is very simple, and it is because of this simplicity that the reader is forced to look beyond the core for a more complex tale. One of the first clues to the inner story is the name of the main character, Phoenix. With the knowledge of what a Phoenix is, we can find many clues supporting the idea of the old woman living her life as a Phoenix.

Throughout the short story, words and phrases that describe the old woman might also describe the mythological bird. Her skin is black with a "golden color underneath" (259) and the "two knobs of her cheeks were illuminated by a yellow burning under the dark" (259). Both the golden color and especially the yellow burning are colors of fire, symbolizing the bird's fiery death. A red rag that she wears on top of her head is also another color of flame. Her black, wrinkled skin can be thought of as looking quite like ashes, and assuming that her grandson is a blood relative, his skin should also be the color of charred ash. She is like a fire that is almost out. It is mostly black, but there is the small flicker of flame to show you it is not yet extinguished.

Assuming the reader chooses to believe that Phoenix does in fact have a grandson and he is in fact sick, then the main purpose of her trip is to get the boy his medicine. This idea goes along nicely with the phoenix theme because she is giving everything she has left for the benefit of her grandson. She is essentially burning herself up so that the new person can exist. We can assume from the physical appearance and actions of Phoenix that she is pretty nearly burnt out. Phoenix knows her grandson is the one with the potential now, and so she gives all the effort she has to get him his medicine. Her only wish is to see him rise from his sick bed.

There are many hints of Phoenix's extreme age. At one time she tells herself, "I is the oldest person I ever know" (261), indicating that she has lived longer than most. Another time the hunter that she comes across estimates that she is "a hundred years old" (263). Much of the imagery in the story symbolizes her oncoming death. The fact that it is winter can be seen as the winter of her life. Other death images include the big dead trees, the buzzard, the scarecrow she mistakes for a ghost, and the black dog that knocks her into the ditch.

Revised Draft

A SINGULAR PERPETUATION

Brett MacFadden and Julia MacMillan

Phoenix Jackson, in the story "A Worn Path," by Eudora Welty, is in many ways like the mythological bird she is named after. Her purpose in life, bird-like characteristics, and nearness to death all support a clear parallel between the character and her namesake. The story is very simple, and because of this simplicity the reader is forced to search for a more meaningful tale. One of the first clues to the inner story is the name of the main character, Phoenix. With the knowledge of what a phoenix is, it is possible to find many clues supporting the idea of the old woman living her life as a phoenix, burning herself out for the benefit of the new bird, her grandson.

The phoenix is a mythological bird who, after living for five hundred years, burns itself to ashes on a pyre and rises renewed to live another cycle. Phoenix Jackson journeys through the woods to town to get medicine for her ailing grandson. This idea parallels the phoenix theme, because she is making what appears to be her final journey, in order that her grandson may rise from his sickbed. The legend of the phoenix is one of singular perpetuation; only one exists in the world. This is shown when she tells the nurses that "We is the only two left in the world" (255). Phoenix is concerned because if both of them were to die, then it would result in the extinction of the species. As much as she worries about him surviving, she is confident that he, like the immortal bird, will survive. Speaking to the nurses again, she says, "He suffer and it don't seem to put him back at all. . . . He going to last" (265–66). As well as his immortality, his birdlike characteristics and dependence on Phoenix for his perseverance are shown when he peeps out of his quilt "holding his mouth open like a little bird" (266). He is her reincarnation, and she is devoted to his successful ascension.

Throughout the story many words and phrases that describe the old woman might also describe the mythological bird. Her skin is described as black with "a golden color underneath," and the "two knobs of her cheeks were illuminated by a yellow burning under the dark" (259). She wears on top of her head a red rag. Both the "golden color" and the "yellow burning," as well as the red of her rag, are colors of fire, symbolizing her approaching death. As she walks, the tapping of her umbrella sounds like "the chirping of a solitary little bird" (259). Her likeness to a bird is evidenced when, in passing a scarecrow in a field, she is frightened, as a bird would be. When startled by a dog, she falls into a ditch "like a little puff of milk-weed" (262). This gives the appearance that she is a light creature, mostly flame and feather. These birdlike characteristics of Phoenix seem to imply that the author intended her to represent the mythical bird.

The myth of the phoenix holds that when "its eyes begin to grow dim, it knows that the time of death has come" (Oswalt 239). When we are first introduced to the main character, as well as being old, she is described as having "eyes . . . blue with age" (259). Many images of death, some quite vivid, link Phoenix Jackson's impending death to that of the phoenix of myth. At one point in her journey she stoops and looks upward, exclaiming, "Sun so high! Time getting all gone here" (260). This clearly indicates her knowledge of her approaching death. Her death is also foreshadowed by the mention of several images that bombard us from the dawn of the story. Early on she reflects on the call of a mourning dove—mourning being something done in the wake of death. Later she comes upon a buzzard sitting in a dead tree. She asks of him, "Who you watching?" (261), as if she knows it is herself. Her death is foreshadowed further when walking through a cornfield she happens upon what she perceives to be a ghost. Upon closer inspection, the ghost turns out to be a scarecrow. However, she shows no fear approaching what she thinks is a ghost, which demonstrates that she is comfortable with dying. The black dog that knocks her into a ditch is another vivid image of death. Further in her journey, upon meeting a white hunter, her impending death as well as her expectation of it are shown. The little bob-white, "its beak hooked bitterly to show that it was dead" (262), that the hunter is carrying in his bag quite forcefully shows us her anticipated death. The fact that she does not fear but expects this death is shown when the hunter points his gun at Phoenix, and she "stood straight and faced him" quite fearlessly (263). In not fearing this death and seeming to understand its nearness, Phoenix Jackson becomes more like the bird she is named for.

A carefully wrought story, "A Worn Path" is more than a tale of an old   5
woman's formidable journey. It is the rebirth of an age-old myth wrapped in the cloak of conventionality. In examining some of the symbols, allusions, and the underlying legend, we find a well-hidden but evident parallel between the lives of the main character and her namesake, the phoenix.

Works Cited

Oswalt, Sabine G. *Concise Encyclopedia of Greek and Roman Mythology.* Chicago: Follett, 1969.

Postscript on the Collaborative Revision

We began this collaboration by reading each other's papers and rereading our own in order to find the strengths and weaknesses of each paper. Then together we combed through each paper, pulling out what we both agreed were our strongest points, and compiled these into a thesis. For our thesis, we used the second sentence in the first paragraph: "Her [Phoenix's] purpose in life, bird-like characteristics, and nearness to death all support a clear parallel between the character and her namesake."

Having decided on a thesis and a rough plan of action, we then went to the computer lab and began writing. At this point, the paper became more difficult because we had to narrow two papers into one and decide what we should omit. For example, Julia's paper discussed the emblem on the doctor's office wall as another symbol of Phoenix's fiery death. After discussing this scene, we decided that the symbolism was not strong enough and should be left out. We knew each other before deciding to write the collaborative essay, so we were both comfortable around each other and were able to say what we really thought about each other's writing. We knew also that our basic writing styles are opposing. Brett's is concise, and Julia's is more flowing. Our different writing styles had to be combined into one smooth style. We did this by having one person dictate and the other type, which caused an intertwining of our styles by the time the words hit the screen. We had fun working on this paper and learned quite a bit about collaboration in the process. For example, we found it challenging because we had to work on one sentence at a time, making sure each sentence was right before we went on to the next one. This process made the revision take far longer to complete than if it had been done by one person.

QUESTIONS FOR WRITING AND DISCUSSION

1. What are the best ideas or evidence in this essay? Explain the points at which you might disagree with the writers' interpretation.

2. Compare MacMillan's and MacFadden's drafts with the final version of their essay. Explain how their interpretation changed as they worked collaboratively on the final version. What did they add to their final version? What did they omit from the earlier drafts?

3. In the final version, MacMillan and MacFadden do not cite evidence from the final part of the story. Explain why the events in town support or do not support the Phoenix parallels.

4. Review the "Guidelines for Revisions." In the authors' essay, underline sentences that contain the *main idea*, that *define key terms*, that contain *evidence* or support, that *explain* how the evidence supports the thesis, that *signal* major parts of the interpretation, and that contain *accurate quotations*. Based on your annotations, what suggestions for further revision do you have for the authors?

STUDENT WRITING

DEATH: THE FINAL FREEDOM

Pat Russell

Following a class discussion of the feminist theme in Kate Chopin's "The Story of an Hour," Pat Russell wrote in his journal, "Is the story a feminist one? No. It is not just about feminism but about how people stifle their own needs and desires to accommodate those of their mate." In his essay, Russell argues that the traditional feminist reading limits the universal theme of the story. As you read his essay, see if you are persuaded by his argument.

The poor treatment of women and their struggle for an individual   *1*
identity make up a major underlying theme of Kate Chopin's stories. Although many regard Chopin's "The Story of an Hour" as a feminist story, today a more universal interpretation is appropriate. This story is not about the oppression of a woman, but about how people strive to maintain the normality and security of their relationships by suppressing their own individual wants and needs.

Evidence in favor of the feminist argument begins with the period the   *2*
story was written in, sometime around the turn of the century. Society prevented women from coming out of the household. Most women weren't allowed to run a business, and for that matter, they couldn't even vote. Their most important jobs were wife and mother. This background sets the tone for the main character's life. In the beginning we are told Mrs. Mallard has a "fair, calm face whose lines be-spoke repression" (414). There is also evidence that suggests her husband is ignorant of her ideas and forceful with his own. Chopin writes: "There would be no powerful will bending her in that blind persistence with which men and women believe they have a right to impose a private will upon a fellow creature" (415). In addition, Mrs. Mallard is described early as fearful and powerless, and later as a triumphant "goddess of Victory," indicating her rebirth. These citations suggest that this is a feminist story, but this label limits the meaning behind the story.

Many people who are unhappy with their marriages either fail to rec-   *3*
ognize their unhappiness or refuse to accept responsibility for it. I feel

sorry for those who don't recognize their unhappiness. However, it is pathetic to see someone such as Mrs. Mallard hold onto a relationship simply because she doesn't know how to let go. "And yet she had loved him—sometimes. Often she had not" (415). She continuously fell in and out of love with her husband until he "died," at which point she told herself that love didn't matter compared to the self-assertion "which she suddenly recognized as the strongest impulse of her being" (415). It is as if she has waited for all of her life for this moment; she prays for a long life, when only the day before she dreaded it. She weeps for him but at the same time compares her husband to a criminal, a man whom she has lived her life for, never once thinking of herself. But now "there would be no one to live for during those coming years; she would live for herself" (415). She is lucky in that she feels "free." Her emotional suppression is over, and she will no longer have anyone to blame for her unhappiness.

It is important not only to try to interpret the author's intended meaning of the story, but also to think about what message "The Story of an Hour" has for us today. As a feminist story, the lesson "The Story of an Hour" teaches is one-dimensional. Interpreting it as a story about the struggle of all people opens up the possibility of teaching others that selfishness and selflessness are both good, when used in moderation. In Mrs. Mallard's case, correcting this balance becomes a matter of life and death. In the face of her suppressor, her desperation for freedom forces her to choose death.

QUESTIONS FOR WRITING AND DISCUSSION

1. With what parts of Russell's interpretation do you agree? What additional evidence from the story might Russell cite in support of his interpretation? What ideas or sentences might you challenge? What evidence from the story might refute those statements?

2. Write out your definition of *feminism*. Where does or should Russell explain his definition? How should Russell clarify his definition?

3. Write out Russell's main idea or thesis. Explain why his thesis is an interpretation and not just a statement of fact.

4. What shaping strategy does Russell use to organize his essay?

5. Write out two other possible titles for Russell's essay. Explain why your alternate titles are (or are not) better than Russell's title.

Franz Marc, a German expressionist painter, is noted for his vivid and colorful paintings of horses and deer. His works contain recognizable figures but also expressionist and cubist elements that invite the viewer to tease out the meaning of his works. In addition, Marc's life and untimely death during World War I suggests parallels between his personal experiences and the subjects and styles of his paintings. A journal exercise on page 618 suggests using the art of Franz Marc to practice using library databases and evaluating the accuracy, reliability, and usefulness of sources found there.

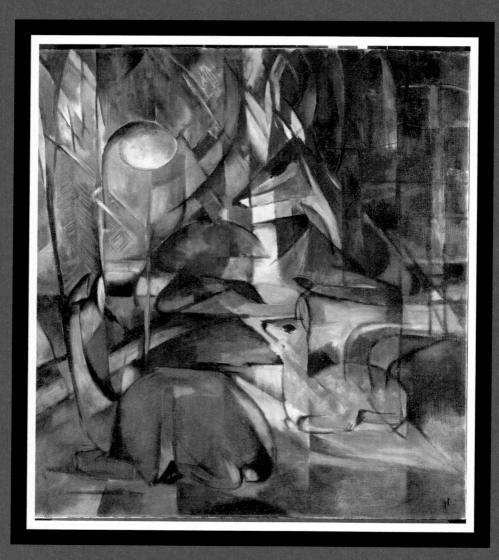

Franz Marc
Deer in the Forest II (1914)
Oil on Canvas, 110 × 100.5 cm
Staatliche Kunsthalle, Karlsruhe

12

Writing a Research Paper

While taking an art class, you become interested in the work of German artist Franz Marc and decide to examine how animals in his paintings help convey the central meaning of his work. You research key elements in the artist's life, his philosophy as a German expressionist, and his founding of Der Blaue Reiter (The Blue Rider). Focusing on *Deer in the Forest II*, you notice that Marc presents animals in harmony with their natural world that seems threatened by external forces shattering this peaceful scene. Writing for other students who are interested in twentieth-century art, you argue that Marc condemns people's inhumanity as he anticipates the devastating effects of World War I. The fact that he was killed in action near Verdun, France, in World War I helps highlight, you believe, the antiwar message of Franz Marc's work.

After spending two months in France living with a family and trying to understand their dinner conversation, you wonder why you—and other Americans—know so little about foreign languages. After reflecting on your inadequate background in French language and culture, you decide to investigate the current state of foreign-language studies in the United States. During your research, you discover that Americans know very little about foreign languages and cultures simply because foreign languages are rarely required of students either in high school or in college. You decide to write a research paper that documents the current state of foreign-language studies and demonstrates a need for a mandatory foreign-language requirement for secondary schools. You hope that it will persuade more students to study foreign languages and encourage some schools to revise their requirements.

> *Research is formalized curiosity. It is poking and prying with a purpose.*
> —ZORA NEALE HURSTON, NOVELIST AND FOLKLORE RESEARCHER

> *You know when you think about writing a book, you think it is overwhelming. But, actually, you break it down into tiny little tasks any moron could do.*
> —ANNIE DILLARD, NATURALIST, AUTHOR OF PILGRIM AT TINKER CREEK

4ᵉ Arrᵗ

PLACE DU PARVIS NOTRE-DAME

Although starting a research project sounds difficult and complicated, research is really a natural and enjoyable part of our everyday experience, both outside and inside college classrooms. We pride ourselves on being good detectives—whether it's window-shopping for a good bargain, finding the best used car, asking coworkers for tips on the best new restaurant in town, or reading up on a new diet. Even in college classes, curiosity leads us to explore new topics. Whenever we wonder about how global warming is affecting our weather, what makes the Internet work, how artists turn clay into beautiful pottery, or how the psychological fight-or-flight mechanism works, the seed for a research idea is planted in our minds.

At some point, the idea becomes a research question that we want to pursue by reading a variety of sources or doing field research. A *research question* sets forth the topic or controversy that we want to explore. What meanings or messages are behind the animal paintings of Franz Marc? What ethical problems arise when we test people for genetically based diseases? Should students in high school have a foreign language requirement? The research question then serves as a guide to start the research process. As we read and research further, we may need to revise our research question based on what we learn about the subject.

Like any other kind of writing, research-based writing takes place in a rhetorical situation. As a writer, you may start with your own research question, or you may have an occasion (an assignment in class or on the job) to write with a specific audience and genre already designated. As always, your purpose, the intended audience, the genre, and the social or cultural context are key factors in helping you focus and shape your research project.

Writing a source-based essay requires four specific skills that this chapter explains. First, you need to learn how to *access ideas and information* in the library, on the Internet, and from field research. Most school libraries have orientation sessions to help you learn which databases are most appropriate for your project. Second, you need to learn to *critically evaluate* your sources. While some Internet Web sites are reliable, many are not. Even reputable, published sources have a specific bias or point of view that affects the accuracy or reliability of the ideas and information. Third, you must *smoothly integrate* your sources by introducing the author and source, citing the relevant information, and indicating how or why the source is relevant to your point. Finally, you will learn how to *document your sources* in the text and in a Works Cited page.

This chapter outlines the key steps in the process of writing a source-based paper—preparing, locating, and evaluating sources; taking notes; collecting and shaping information; revising; and documenting your sources. As in other writing assignments presented in this text, the process is recursive. Often, you need to stop and retrace your steps, revise your research question, collect new information, or revise parts of your paper during the writing process. At the end of this chapter, student writer Kate McNerny's paper, "Foreign Language Study: An American Necessity," illustrates the important features of a source-based paper. Interspersed in the chapter, samples from her research log, her notes and drafts, and documentation illustrate various stages in one writer's process of writing a research paper.

Techniques for Writing a Research Paper

Like other kinds of writing, a research paper requires that you assess your purpose, audience, and possible genre, and then focus on a particular subject, develop your thesis, and support your position with convincing evidence: background information, facts, statistics, descriptions, and other results of interviews and research. The evidence that you present in a research paper, however, is more detailed than in a typical essay, and the sources are usually cited in the text and documented at the end of the paper.

In a sense, a research paper is like a scientific experiment. **Your readers should be able to trace your whole experiment—to see what ideas and evidence you worked with, where you found them, and how you used them in your paper.** If readers have any questions about the information you've presented or the conclusions you've reached, they can start with your sources and recreate or check the "experiment" for themselves. If they want to investigate your subject further, your sources will guide their reading. As you write your research paper, keep the following techniques in mind:

- **Using purpose, occasion, audience, genre, and context as your guides for writing.** Research is just a method of collecting and documenting ideas and evidence. The rhetorical situation still directs your writing.
- **Finding the best that has been written or said about your subject.** Instead of trying to reinvent the wheel, discover what other people or writers know and then build on what they have learned.
- **Critically evaluating your sources for accuracy, reliability, and bias.** Internet sources can be reliable, but they often represent people or

> *Criticism [is] a disinterested endeavor to learn and propagate the best that is known and thought in the world.*
> —MATTHEW ARNOLD, POET AND ESSAYIST

organizations with a pronounced bias or give inaccurate or misleading information.

- **Using sources to make *your* point.** As you gather information, you may revise your thesis in light of what you learn, but don't let the tail wag the dog: don't allow your sources to control you or your paper.
- **Documenting your sources, both in the text and at the end of the paper.** Avoid *plagiarism* by carefully and accurately acknowledging all ideas, information, paraphrases, or actual language that you find in your sources.

USING PURPOSE, AUDIENCE, AND GENRE AS GUIDES

Like any other kind of writing, research papers have a *purpose.* Reporting, explaining, evaluating, problem solving, and arguing are all purposes for research papers. Purposes may appear in combinations, as in a paper that summarizes current research and then proposes a solution to a problem. Research papers, however, are not just reports of other people's ideas or evidence. What you, the researcher, observe and remember and learn is important, too. Most subjects are not interesting until writers make them so. Your curiosity, your interest in the subject, your reason and intuition establish why the subject is worth researching in the first place—and why a reader would want to read the paper once it is finished.

Research papers have a defined *audience,* too. The subject you choose, the kind of research you do, the documentation format, the vocabulary and style you use—all should be appropriate for your selected audience. If you write a senior research paper in your major, you will write for a professor and for a community of people knowledgeable about your field. If you are a legal assistant or a junior attorney in a law firm, a superior may ask you to research a specific legal precedent. If you work for a manufacturer, a manager may assign you a research report on the sales and strategies of a competitor. Although your classmates and teacher will probably read the research paper that you write for this class, you will ask them to role-play your audience. They will try to read your paper from the point of view of a defined audience—an employer, a politician, a nutritionist, an artist, an astronomer, or a senior law partner. In fact, your instructor may ask you to send your paper to some person or persons who actually are part of your audience.

Finally, your research paper must follow a *genre* that fits your purpose and meets the expectations and needs of your audience. If you are researching advances in sports medicine for an audience of experts, you need to use the genre (article, pamphlet, thesis) used by experts in the field. If your paper is an academic article, you may have an abstract at the beginning, a section reviewing and evaluating current research, subsections for each of your main points, diagrams and charts for illustration, and an appendix with supplementary materials. If, however, you are writing primarily for jogging enthusiasts, your research-based paper may look more like an informal essay. Magazines and journals in the field illustrate a variety of appropriate forms for source-based papers. The student essay by Kate McNerny at the end of this chapter illustrates one typical genre.

FINDING THE BEST SOURCES

Accessing information from published sources, field sources, and Web sites is central to all research. To find good sources, you need to hone your detective skills. Unfortunately, Hollywood has promoted the myth that good detectives follow their suspects in high-speed car chases or through glamorous affairs. Of course, that's just fantasy. Detectives must do actual research—computer searches, paperwork, and legwork—to track down leads. Writers are, in a real sense, also detectives, constantly searching for key information from the best possible sources. For your own research project, be sure take your library's orientation session to learn how to access the most useful catalogs, indexes, and databases for your topic. Full-text databases such as *LexisNexis Academic, EBSCO Academic Search Premier, Contemporary Authors, Infotrak, New York Times,* and the *CQ Researcher* are just a few of the many indexes and databases that can help you with your research.

Research combines careful planning with good luck, mindless drudgery and moments of inspiration, many dead ends and a few rare discoveries. As coaches sometimes say, those who prepare and work hard make their own luck. The following excerpt from the introduction to Pauli Murray's *Proud Shoes: The Story of an American Family* recounts her research into her family genealogy, which included slaves, free blacks, some racially mixed family members, and other relatives who were white and socially prominent. Although her detective work took several years and involved both library and field research, her account reflects the problems and successes that all researchers experience.

My field research had the thrill of detection when the clues panned out. Rigorous discipline was needed for the drudgery of sifting through masses of documentary material in search of one relevant fact or one confirmation of a family legend. The trail of the Fitzgerald family led me into nearly a dozen localities in several states. It took me into musty basements of old courthouses to pore over dust-silted and sometimes indecipherable handwritten entries in old volumes. I found that each locality had its own captivating legends preserved in family papers; its traditions recorded in pamphlets and privately published little books; its stories printed in almanacs, newspapers, business directories. Almost every place had "the oldest living inhabitants" and their recollections. Most important, almost every locality had its own regional-history enthusiasts, who welcomed me into a fellowship of digging into the past. Some of them gave me expert guidance which improved the efficiency of my research and shortened my labors.

CRITICALLY EVALUATING YOUR SOURCES

With a computer and the Internet, it is easy to find books, articles, and Web sites that relate to your topic. It can be difficult, however, to find sources that are appropriate for your audience and purpose and are also accurate and reliable. If you are writing for an academic or professional audience, look for books and articles on the topic appropriate for your audience. Some databases, such as *Infotrak,* search popular newspapers and magazines. However, if you are writing for an academic or professional audience, you may want databases and indexes such as *LexisNexis* and subject indexes such as *Architectural Index, AGRICOLA, Art Abstracts, Biological Abstracts, ERIC, MEDLINE, PsycINFO,* or *Sociological Abstracts.*

Once you have found a source, learn to critically evaluate the source for accuracy, reliability, and bias. An article from a professional or academic journal such as *Science* or *The New England Journal of Medicine* will probably give accurate, up-to-date information. However, information from a popular magazine, a newspaper, or a Web site may not have accurate or reliable information or may have a personal or commercial bias. Read the sections later in this chapter on evaluating Internet and library sources. Examine your sources carefully. Who or what organization is the author or authors? Are they selling something? What is their point of view or bias? How recent, accurate, or reliable is their information? Failing to critically evaluate your sources may ruin all of your research efforts, so don't forget this important step!

USING SOURCES TO MAKE YOUR POINT

When your hard work does yield a source that has good information and ideas on your exact subject, don't be tempted to let that source take over your paper. If you start stringing together passages from only one or two key sources, you'll be summarizing rather than doing research. You'll be letting the sources tell you what to think, what information is important, or what conclusions to reach. Use your sources, then, to support *your* point. Write your own paper; don't let your sources write it for you.

DOCUMENTING YOUR SOURCES

Documenting your sources is an important part of writing a research paper. Documentation takes place in two stages: First, in the body or text of your paper, you give credit for any material that you have taken from your sources. Then, at the end of the paper, you include a list of Works Cited or Works Consulted that gives fuller information about these sources for your readers. If your readers doubt a fact or statistic, they can check your sources for themselves. If your readers want more information, your documentation enables them to track down the sources. ***Note:*** Decide on the documentation format (usually MLA or APA style) before you begin your research. You need to know what relevant bibliographical information you need to record in your notes.

Preparing Yourself for the Research Process

Writing a research paper involves the same process that you used in writing essays. The major difference is that each stage or dimension of the process takes longer. You may spend two weeks just collecting sources, reading articles and books, jotting down ideas, testing your ideas on classmates and friends, and narrowing and focusing your subject. And because you gather so much material, the shaping and organizing processes are also more demanding. Sometimes you may feel as if you're trying to put forty frogs in a dishpan: By the time you arrange ten, the first four have already jumped out. The revising also takes longer, partly because you have to include your documentation, but partly because the sections of the paper may not fit together as smoothly as you had hoped. There is really no way to rush research. If writing an ordinary paper is like fixing your lunch, then writing a research paper is like preparing Thanksgiving dinner. You can't microwave a research paper. Good things take time.

The first step in writing a research paper is to *readjust your inner clock*. Initially, you'll think that you're not making much progress. You'll think that you're in a slow-motion movie or that you're trying to jog through butter. However, once you readjust your inner clock, set more modest goals, and content yourself with a slower but more persistent pace, you've won half the battle. By reducing the pressure on yourself, you'll feel less frustrated when you reach a dead end and also readier to appreciate valuable information when you discover it.

To help you adjust mentally and physically to a new pace and an extended writing process, begin your preparation by making a research notebook, outlining a realistic timetable for the paper, and selecting a documentation format.

WARMING UP: JOURNAL EXERCISES

Do at least one of the following journal exercises to help get yourself into a research frame of mind or to discover a possible research subject:

1. Look again the painting by Franz Marc reproduced at the beginning of this chapter. Assume that paintings by Franz Marc are the subject of your research paper for your art class. First, do a search on Google for information about the author and some of his famous paintings. Print the first page of any sites that contain useful information about the author and his works. You should find Internet sites from the WebMuseum, from the Guggenheim Museum, and from the Franz Marc museum among others. Then, using EBSCO Academic Search Premier, enter "Franz Marc" in the search box and print out or e-mail yourself articles cited there from the *Art Journal*. Compare the length, detail, and usefulness of the articles you have found. Which of these sites or sources seem most or least reliable, and why? Which sources might be most or least useful for your paper, and why?

2. In the library, look in the computer catalog for books on a topic that you might select for your research paper. Go to the shelves where books on that topic are located. Choose one or two books and see if they refer to or cite other books in their *index* or *bibliography* at the end of the book. Take one book that has references to other works, go back to the library computer, and see if you can find any of those books or articles cited in the bibliography. Practicing this technique may suggest other *key words* for a search or other interesting and relevant sources that your computer search in the library did not initially cite. Be prepared to explain in class what other relevant books or articles you found using this research method.

3. In the library, find an issue of a magazine or newspaper published on or near the date and year of your birth. The issue may be on microfilm. Record the

date and title of the newspaper or magazine. Browse through the issue, looking at headlines, articles, advertisements, editorials, comics, weather, sports, local news, and so forth. As you look through the issue, record any items, facts, or historical incidents that interest you. Photocopy one page that you find especially interesting. Explain why that page captured your attention.

4. Sit down with a family member, friend, or classmate. On a sheet of paper, write down the subject of the most interesting course that you are currently taking. Hand the sheet of paper to that person and ask him or her to write down questions for an interview designed to find out *why* you like this course and *what* you like best about it. Then have that person interview you and record your responses. At the end of the interview, discuss your responses. What ideas could you research in order to explain to your interviewer what is interesting about this subject?

RESEARCH NOTEBOOK

Although some researchers still recommend using index cards for recording bibliographical entries and notes, for most shorter research projects (up to twenty pages), a notebook computer, a loose-leaf notebook, or a spiral notebook with pockets for additional papers and photocopies may be more functional. Divide your notebook into four sections: research log, bibliography, notes from sources (including photocopies), and drafts and ideas.

The *research log* section of your notebook serves as a scratch pad and log of your research progress. In it, you will record what you accomplish during each research session, potential references you need to check, reminders to yourself, questions to ask a librarian or your instructor, and notes about your problems, progress, and intended next steps. As you work, jot down what you did and what you still need to do. These notes about your problems, progress, questions, and next steps will help you maintain momentum on your research project. Each time you return to the library or to your research, you can check your notes to see what you need to do next.

4/26

4:30—6:00 p.m.

Still working on finding articles. EBSCO Academic Search Premier had several good articles. I tried using several search terms including "Foreign Language Study," "Foreign Language Requirements," and

"Foreign Language Education." Each gave me different results. When I tried searching in the ERIC database and put in "Foreign Language Study:" I got 7,000 articles! I need to narrow the search terms. LexisNexis had some good articles but not as many. I need to stop by the reference desk and ask about the best search terms.

April issue of <u>Education Digest</u> missing from the shelves. UGH—I hate that.

Question: Do I want to survey students to find out about typical attitudes toward taking foreign languages? What questions should I ask? Maybe I can try out some sample questions on some of my classmates.

Another question: Is this going to be an arguing paper? Is there a controversy? Are there multiple points of view about the problem or the best solution?

Remember that 5-6 p.m. is a good time to work in the library. Everyone clears out, so I don't have to fight over the Internet computers or the photocopiers.

In the *bibliography* section of your notebook, keep a list of every source that you consult, with complete information about each source. If your library's online catalog system shows the status of every source, be sure to print out every source you want to check. If you cannot print the source, you'll need to copy it in your notebook. Leave space between entries for additional information, such as call numbers. This list becomes *your working bibliography*. McNerny's bibliography included the following entries:

Hines, Marion E. "Foreign Language Curriculum Concerns in Times of Conflict." <u>Delta Kappa Gamma Bulletin</u> 70(2003): 15–22.

I retrieved this from the EBSCO Academic Search Premier, so i need to cite the database I found it in:

Hines, Marion E. "Foreign Language Curriculum Concerns in Times of Conflict." <u>Delta Kappa Gamma Bulletin</u> 70(Fall 2003): 15–22. <u>Academic Search Premier.</u> EBSCO. Colorago State U Lib. 23 May 2004 <http://o-web2.epnet.com.catalog.library. colostate.edu>.

Lambert, Richard D. "Some Issues in Language Policy for Higher Education." *The Annals of the American Academy of Political and Social Science* 532 (1994): 123:37.

H1.A4 Current issues in Current Periodicals Room: Older issues in stacks.

In the *source notes* section, leave plenty of pages to record direct quotations, paraphrases of key ideas, and facts from the sources in your bibliography list. Introduce each section with a reference to the author and a short version of the title. After each note, indicate the page number or numbers. One page of McNerny's notes contained the following entries:

Lambert, "Some Issues in Language Policy."

Lambert explains how the lack of coordination between secondary schools and higher education causes problems. As Lambert notes, "The result of this strong tradition of university autonomy is that in the United States, foreign language planning for higher education must take place one institution at a time and implementation of change must occur in house-to-house, hand-to-hand combat" (125).

Ranwez and Rogers, Status of Foreign Languages

91% of the 536 Colorado secondary schools responding to the questionnaire offered foreign languages, but 91% of schools responding didn't require any foreign language credits for graduation. pp. 99-100.

For your source notes section, make *photocopies* of any valuable source materials. Write author, title, and page numbers on each photocopied source.

In the *drafts and ideas* section of the notebook, jot down brainstorms, looping or clustering exercises, sketch outlines, trial drafts, and examples from your own experience. During a research project, ideas can come to you at any time. When they do, take time to write them down. This section of your notebook serves as a journal devoted solely to your research paper. One example from McNerny's drafts and ideas section records her personal experience with foreign languages:

4/29

I can remember my mom always telling me, "Take French classes, learn how to speak French so that you can go visit your cousins in France some day." At the time (junior high school) though, learning a foreign language was low on my priority list. I did take French classes for two years – but dropped out after my sophomore year and immediately lost any basic competency I might have acquired.

In college, I'd like to take a language again, but it never seems to fit with my schedule. But last year, as my mom had promised, I got the opportunity to visit my cousins in France. For some reason, the fact that I couldn't speak French didn't seem to me like it would be a big problem. That was until I stepped off the train at Gare du Nord in Paris and couldn't find the relative who was supposed to meet me. After frantically searching the entire station several times, I had to break down and ask for help. At the information desk a few completely butchered French phrases escaped my lips – only to be received by an unimpressed, unresponsive station attendant. He muttered something about dumb Americans and then pointed me off toward some unknown destination. Well I survived that ordeal – but at the same time swore to myself that I would never make another trip to France until I could speak the language.

RESEARCH TIMETABLE

Before you begin your research, write out a tentative schedule. Your instructor may assign due dates for specific parts of the paper (invention exercises, topic selection, working bibliography, rough draft), but you should make a schedule that fits your work habits and your weekly schedule.

The following schedule assumes that you have at least a month to work on your research paper. The amount of time required by each part depends on the amount of time you can work each day. On some days, you may have only thirty minutes. On other days, you may have several hours. The key is to do a little bit every day to keep your momentum going.

Prepare for research. Buy and organize a research notebook; set up a timetable; select a documentation format.	1–2 days
Choose a subject. Begin the narrowing and focusing process.	2–3 days
Collect sources. Find library sources; identify and find unpublished sources; do interviews or surveys; record personal experiences; browse sites on the Internet.	
Evaluate source materials; take *notes* on selected sources; *photocopy* sources.	12–14 days
Shape and outline ideas; *reread* notes and photocopies; *draft* sections of essay. Continue to *focus* thesis while rereading, planning, and drafting.	6–10 days
Revise draft. Get peer response, collect additional information, sharpen thesis, reshape or revise outline, cite sources in the text and in the bibliographical list, and edit and proofread the paper.	6–8 days

Tailor your schedule to your own temperament and work habits. If you like to work exactly to a schedule or even finish early, design your schedule so you can finish a day or two before the due date. If you are like most writers—you love to procrastinate or you are often up all night just before an assignment is due—then use your schedule to set early target dates, to get your momentum going. When you finish drafting your schedule, put a copy in the *research log* section of your notebook, so that you can check your progress as you work.

DOCUMENTATION FORMAT: MLA AND APA STYLES

A final step in preparing for the research paper is to select a documentation style. This chapter illustrates both the MLA and APA styles. If you are writing a paper for the humanities, follow the Modern Language Association (MLA) style set forth in the

MLA Handbook for Writers of Research Papers (6th ed., 2003). If you are writing a paper in the behavioral sciences, use the American Psychological Association (APA) style as described in the *Publication Manual of the American Psychological Association* (5th ed., 2001).

Leading academic and professional journals also illustrate the documentation styles customary in specialized fields. You may want to consult issues of those journals to determine the exact format for footnotes or in-text citation of sources. *Before you begin doing research, however, select a documentation style* that is appropriate for your subject, purpose, and audience. Then practice that style as you compile your working bibliography.

Research Paper: The Writing Process

ASSIGNMENT FOR THE RESEARCH PAPER

Choose a subject that strongly interests you and about which you would like to learn more. It may be a subject that you have already written about in this course. Research this subject in a library and, as appropriate, supplement your library research with questionnaires, interviews, Internet research, or other unpublished sources of information. Check with your instructor for suggested length, appropriate number or kinds of sources, and additional format requirements. Use a documentation style appropriate for your subject, purpose, and audience.

CHOOSING A SUBJECT

For this research paper, choose a subject in which you already have personal interest or experience. Start by rereading your journal entries for possible research subjects. Even a personal entry may suggest an idea. If you wrote about how you fainted in the gym during aerobics or weight training, you might research the potential dangers of exercising in high heat and humidity or sitting in a sauna after hard exercise. If you wrote a journal entry about a friend's drinking problem, you might like to read more about the causes and treatments of alcoholism.

In addition, reread the essays that you have written to see whether one of them refers to a possible research subject. If your observing essay, for example, was about a tattoo parlor that you visited, use that essay as the starting point for further investigation and research. Whom could you interview to find out more about tattooing? What is the history of tattooing? Why is it becoming more popular? What controversies surround its use? What resources does your library have? What sites can you find on the Internet? You might also use a topic from your remembering, reading, or investigating essays as starting places for additional reading and research. *Build on what you already know and what already interests you rather than launch into an entirely unknown subject.*

NARROWING AND FOCUSING YOUR SUBJECT   Once you have a tentative idea, remember that you'll need to narrow it, focus it, or otherwise limit the subject to make it appropriate for your audience and context. The topic of alcoholism is too general. Focus on a particular research question: "Do beer commercials on television contribute to alcoholism?" "Are there really positive effects of drinking moderate amounts of alcohol?" "What methods does Alcoholics Anonymous use to help people?" "Have DWI laws actually reduced the number of fatal automobile accidents?" Your research question may lead to a *thesis statement* that you will demonstrate in your research essay: "Although some studies show a definite link between consuming moderate amounts of red wine and reduced incidence of heart disease, the negative effects of alcohol consumption far outweigh the potential benefits."

Only after you've started your research, however, will you know whether your research question is still too broad (you can't begin to read everything about it in just two weeks) or too narrow (in two weeks, you can't find enough information about that question).

Two techniques may help narrow and focus your subject. You may wish to try these now, wait until you have done some initial reading, or do them several times during your collecting and shaping.

The first strategy is simply to think about your *purpose* and *audience*. The best way to focus your paper is to reflect on your purpose: What kinds of claims do you want to make about your topic? (If necessary, review the claims of fact, cause and effect, value, and policy outlined in Chapter 10, "Arguing.") As you collect articles, think about the kinds of claims you might want to make about your topic.

Claims of Fact: Are makers of hard liquor being discriminated against by not being allowed to advertise on TV? Is alcoholism a disease or just an addiction?

Claims of Cause and Effect: Does TV advertising increase alcohol consumption or just affect the brands that are consumed? Can students who are "recreational" drinkers become alcoholics? Do recovery programs like Alcoholics Anonymous really work?

Claims of Value: Does beer have any nutritional value? Are microbrews really made better or fresher than beers from larger breweries?

Claims of Policy: Do age-based drinking laws really work? Should liquor consumption be banned at campus sporting events? At dorms, fraternities, and sororities? At any campus function? Should makers of hard liquor be allowed to advertise on television?

Asking questions about your potential audience may also help you find a focus for your essay. If you are writing for a local audience, consider what they believe and what they might be interested in. Is the topic of alcohol regulation controversial? Who are your readers? What are they likely to believe on this issue? Profile your audience and brainstorm how you can connect your research question to those particular readers.

Question analysis is a second narrowing and focusing strategy. The who, what, when, where, and why questions that you use to focus your topic are the same questions that reference librarians use to help you focus your research in the library.

Who: What group of people is interested or affected?

What: How are key terms defined? What academic discipline is involved?

When: What is the period or time span?

Where: What continent, country, state, or town is involved?

Why: What are possible effects or implications?

Answering these questions—by yourself, in a group, or with a reference librarian—may suggest new angles, new avenues for research, or subtopics that could lead to a focus for your research paper. As you narrow your topic, you are narrowing and focusing the range of your research in the library. Student writer Kate McNerny, brainstorming with another class member, applied these questions to her subject about foreign-language study and came up with the following possibilities:

Foreign Language Study

Who?   Ans: I am interested in Americans. Specifically, I want to focus on why Americans should begin learning a foreign language early in school, in grade school, secondary school, and college. Learning a foreign language would affect how foreigners see us.

What?   Ans: Key terms defined – perhaps what
        "learning" means. Does it mean just basic
        speaking competency? Probably. If I could
        have asked a few simple questions in the Gare du
        Nord, I wouldn't have felt so stupid. Academic
        discipline – learning the foreign language is
        important, but <u>culture</u> is part of it, too. History
        should teach us about foreign cultures. So
        should psychology – do the Japanese think
        differently from the Spanish? Why did the
        French seem rude and Italians friendly?
        Do I want to research the psychology of
        languages? I don't think so.

When?   Ans: I really want to know why foreign
        language studies are currently not emphasized.
        But what about trends – is it getting better or
        worse? Are more people learning foreign
        languages than a few years ago? I don't know.

Where? Ans: In the United States. In my home town.
        Why is it that in the French schools, children
        as a matter of course learn several languages
        while we aren't required to learn any?

        Supposedly, we are the "melting pot" for
        many different languages and cultures, but
        we don't know each other's languages.

Why?   Ans. I can make a long list of the effects
        – We can't communicate when we're tourists.
        – We can't read anything printed in their
          language.
        – We don't understand their culture.
        – We don't even understand the cultures of
          the millions of Americans from other
          cultures.
        – We isolate ourselves in business, too.

        To avoid these effects, I want to argue
        for stronger foreign language requirements
        in secondary schools and colleges.

As a result of her question analysis, McNerny decided to discuss both language and culture, to focus on the current conditions, and to recommend that secondary schools require foreign languages. *In any research, however, what you look for and what you find are always different. You will need to modify your focus as you read and learn.*

COLLECTING

With ideas for a tentative subject, a possible purpose, and an audience, you can focus on collecting information. Collecting data for your research paper will require identifying and locating published and unpublished sources, evaluating your sources and choosing those that are the most appropriate for your needs, and then taking notes on your selected sources. *Remember, however, that finding sources—like writing itself—is an ongoing and recursive process.* You often identify new sources after you have taken notes on others. Although you may begin your search in the online catalog, in the reference section, or on the Internet, as you narrow and focus your topic or draft sections of your paper, you may come back and recheck the online catalog, basic references, periodical indexes, or bibliographies.

Use *informal contacts* with friends or acquaintances as an integral part of your collecting process. Friends, family members, business associates, or teachers may be able to suggest key questions or give you some sources: relevant books and magazine articles, television programs that are available in transcript, or local experts on your subject.

UNPUBLISHED SOURCES Although the library may be your main source of information, other sources can be important, too. You may *interview* authorities on your subject or design a *questionnaire* to measure people's responses. (Interviews and questionnaires are discussed in Chapter 6.) *Phone calls* and *letters* to experts, government agencies, or businesses may yield background information, statistics, or quotations. *Notes from classes, public lectures,* or *television programs* are useful sources. Use a tape recorder to ensure that you transcribe your information accurately. A *scientific experiment* may even be appropriate. *Unpublished public documents,* such as deeds, wills, surveyors' maps, and environmental impact statements, may contain gold mines of information. Finally, don't ignore the most obvious sources: your room, the attic in your home, or your relatives may have repositories of valuable unpublished data—private letters, diaries, old bills, or check stubs.

For her research paper, Kate McNerny decided to conduct an informal survey of attitudes toward foreign languages. She recorded the responses in the *drafts and ideas* section of her research notebook. When she drafted her paper, she used some of these responses in the introduction to her paper:

> Q: Should foreign languages be required in Junior and Senior High?
>
> A: (Mindy, 21, student) Yes, I think its a good idea – It would have been more valuable to me than some of the other required classes I took – like P.E.
>
> A: (Jodi, 22, student) No, I had a hard enough time with English. Besides, I don't think I'd ever need to use it.
>
> A: (Roger, 23, carpenter) Yes, I was in Europe last year and missed out on a lot because I couldn't speak any other language. Europeans don't speak English as much as we hear they do, but most of the people I met there spoke at least two languages.
>
> A: (Jim, 49, contractor) No, I've never gone to Europe and never needed to speak another language for any other reason. I had enough trouble getting through other classes.
>
> A: (Carolyn, 59, teacher) Yes, when I was teaching there were few language classes available. But as a reading teacher I can see many ways in which language studies would have enhanced our program.

PRIMARY AND SECONDARY SOURCES Some sources—accounts of scientific experiments, transcripts of speeches or lectures, questionnaires, interviews, private documents—are known as *primary sources.* They are original, firsthand information, "straight from the horse's mouth." Secondhand reports, analyses, and descriptions based on primary sources are known as *secondary sources*. Secondary sources may contain the same information, but they are once-removed. For example, a lecture or experiment by an expert in food irradiation is a primary source; the newspaper report of that lecture or experiment is a secondary source.

The distinction between primary and secondary sources is important for two related reasons. First, secondary sources may contain errors. The newspaper account, for example, may misquote the expert or misrepresent the experiment. If possible, therefore, find the primary source—a copy of the actual lecture or a published article about the experiment. Second, finding the primary sources may make your research document more persuasive through an appeal to character (see Chapter 10, "Arguing"). If you can cite the original source—or even show how some secondary accounts distorted the original experiment—you will gain your readers' trust and faith. Not only does uncovering the primary data make your research more accurate, but your additional effort makes all your data and arguments appear more credible.

LIBRARY SOURCES   Before you begin collecting information, acquaint yourself with the library itself. If you have not already done so, inquire at the information desk about library tours, or walk through the library with a friend or classmate. Locate the *reference section;* the *online catalog* for books and articles; the *indexes* for newspapers, journals, and magazines; the *microfilm room;* the *stacks;* and the *government documents* section. Don't assume that because you've used one library, you can immediately start your research in a new library. Remember: *Librarians* themselves are valuable sources of information. Use their expertise early in your research.

BACKGROUND INFORMATION AND GENERAL REFERENCE   Before you consult the online catalog, you may need a *general overview* of your subject. Start with an encyclopedia, dictionary, almanac, or biography for background information. Many people associate encyclopedias with their grade-school "research"—when they copied passages out of *The World Book* or *Collier's Encyclopedia*. But encyclopedias are an excellent source of basic information and terminology that may help you focus, narrow, and define your subject. *Use them as background reading, however, not as major sources.*

In addition to the general encyclopedias, there are hundreds of references—one or two might just save you hours of research in the library and lead you directly to key facts or important information on your topic. (You may wish to begin your collecting in the reference room or check there only after you have collected information from other books and articles. Often these references are more valuable *after* you have done some reading on your subject.) Beyond the standard college dictionary or thesaurus, the *Oxford English Dictionary,* known as the *OED,* or *Webster's Third New International Dictionary of the English Language* may help you find key ideas or definitions.

There are also many specialized dictionaries for scientific terms, slang words, symbols, and a host of other specialized vocabularies. If you need facts, figures, or statistics, consult the *World Almanac,* the *Book of Facts,* or the *Statistical Abstracts of the United States.* If your subject is a person, look at *Who's Who in America,* or check one of the references that indexes collections of biographies. *Biography and Genealogy Master Index* and *Biographical Dictionaries* reference more than three million biographical sketches.

The *librarian* is still the most valuable resource for your research. At some point during your research in the library, probably after you have a focused topic and have collected some sources, talk to a reference librarian. For many writers, asking for help can be really intimidating. To make the process of asking for help as painless— and productive—as possible, try saying something like the following: "Hi, I'm Kate McNerny. I'm doing a research project for my college writing course. My topic is foreign-language study in the United States. I'm trying to find information about the current state of foreign-language study in the United States and collect some arguments for increasing requirements in secondary schools and colleges. Here's what I've found so far [explain what you've done]. What additional reference books, Web sites, indexes, dictionaries, or bibliographies might help me in my research?" The resulting conversation may be the most productive five minutes of your entire library research. After you've talked to the librarian once, it will be easier to return and ask a question when you hit a snag.

THE ONLINE CATALOG   The good news for researchers in the twenty-first century is that computerized databases have revolutionized the whole process of library research. In most university libraries, a computer terminal can, in a few seconds, give you information that used to require hours of searching card catalogs or printed indexes. You can easily locate books, articles, and government documents relevant to your topic. You can find the library call numbers and locations of sources. You can determine if a source is available or checked out and get an abstract or a short description of a source. For some systems, you can print out the bibliographical information so that you don't have to take notes. Often, you can print out whole articles right there.

The only bad news is that nearly every online catalog system is different. Some colleges have OPACs (online public access catalogs) that allow you to access the library's holdings. Your college may use OCLC Online Computer Library System), which is the largest of the public access catalogs, or you may use systems such as

> ❝*Knowledge is of two kinds. We know a subject ourselves, or we know where we can find information upon it.*❞
> —SAMUEL JOHNSON, FROM JAMES BOSWELL'S LIFE OF JOHNSON

NOTIS, RLIN, MELVYL, CARL, or SAGE. But whatever system your library uses, you need to spend time learning the tricks of that particular database. Don't try to learn the system by yourself. Take a library orientation tour. Collect the library's handouts about its computerized databases. Ask the librarians for help. And don't wait until your research paper is assigned to walk into the library. If you have to learn a new computer system *and* write your paper at the same time, you will be inviting massive frustration.

When McNerny started her search in her library's online databases, she chose EBSCO Academic Search Premier, a database that has many full-text citations. After looking at the abstract and the article, she decided to email herself an article by Marion Hines and the accompanying abstract so she could print them later. She printed out the article and the citation so she would have all the information necessary for completing her bibliographical entry. A slightly edited version of the citation appears below.

Author:	Hines, Marion E.
Source:	Delta Kappa Gamma Bulletin; Fall 2003, Vol 70 Issue 1, p. 15, 7p.
Subject Terms:	LINGUISTS; UNIVERSITIES & colleges; SCHOOLS; EDUCATION; LANGUAGE & languages; NATIONAL security; GLOBALIZATION
Reviews & Products:	*Tongue-Tied American, The* (Book)
People:	SIMON, Paul
Abstract:	Argues that globalization and national security dictate the inclusion of foreign language study in the core curricula of American schools, colleges and universities. Statement from Paul Simon, former senator and author of the book, "The Tongue-Tied American: Confronting the Foreign Language Crisis"; Purpose of the National Virtual Translation Center; Fact which aggravates the shortages of U. S. linguists.
Persistent link to this record:	*http://0-search.epnet.com.catalog.library.colostate.edu:80/ direct.asp?an=11264017&db=aph*
Database:	Academic Search Premier

Five pieces of information from this citation are especially helpful and worth noting. First, the **source line** gives the key bibliographic information needed for the citation: place and date of publication with volume and page numbers. Second, the

subject terms (sometimes including **descriptors**) give other key words that might be helpful in searching databases. In addition to the key words *foreign language study,* this line suggests that the words *universities, schools, education,* or *globalization* might also be helpful search terms. Third, the **abstract** summarizes the main ideas or focus of the article. Fourth, the **persistent link** gives the URL at which McNerny could find this article if she didn't have her printed copy and needed to check a fact or quotation. Fifth, the **database** indicates that she found this article on Academic Search Premier. This information is necessary to include in the bibliographic entry on the Works Cited or References page. *Always print out this citation page so you have accurate information for your own citations.*

SEARCH STRATEGY   As you practice with you library's online system, you'll discover that the *search strategy* you use and the *key words* you enter become very critical. Should you use a *word* or a *subject* search? You need to *practice with your library's system* to see *how it works.* Next, you need to pay careful attention to the key words you enter. If you are writing an essay about teenagers' psychological problems, entering the word *teen* may get you nowhere, while entering the word *adolescent* or even *teenage* may hit the jackpot. To help with your key-word search, try the following. First, make a list in your research notebook of all the possible terms that may relate to your subject. When you do a search, note the other possible terms or headings given on the computer terminal.

If you are having trouble gathering information on your topic, be sure to consult a librarian and discuss your search strategy and the list of key words you are using for your search.

INTERNET SOURCES   Where should you start your search for relevant sources—in the library databases or on the Internet? The answer to that question depends on your topic, your purpose, and your audience. But the recent explosion of Web sites indicates that, for many writers and topics, the Internet may well be the place to start. The immense variety of sources makes the Internet a great place to do your browsing—especially if you're not quite sure exactly what your topic will be or what angle you wish to investigate. Other writers—especially those who are already sure of their focus—may wish to begin with an online search in their library and to save their Internet research for later, when they want to find sources they cannot locate in the library. Whatever choice you make, you will probably want to browse the Internet at some point during your research.

Especially if you are not an expert at Internet research, you should think about the strengths and weaknesses of Internet research. The strengths of Internet research are many:

The Library of Congress

SEARCH

Get It Online . . . Words, Pictures & Sound

more than a library

American Memory
US History & Culture

THOMAS
Legislative Information

Global Gateway
World Culture & Resources

Exhibitions
Online Galleries

America's Library
Log On, Play Around
Learn Something

Wise Guide
It's Fun to Know History

More Online Collections...

Find It ...
- Search Our Catalogs
- Advanced Search
- Research Centers
- Index A-Z
- Site Map
- Ask a Librarian

- Today in History
  October 29

Especially For ...
- Researchers
- Law Researchers
- Librarians & Archivists
- Teachers
- Kids & Families
- Publishers
- Persons with Disabilities
- Blind Persons
- Newcomers

Information & Services
- US Copyright Office
- National Digital Preservation Program

- About the Library
- Visit / Tour
- Philanthropy
- Jobs / Fellowships
- Shop

News & Events
Veterans History and 'Voices of War'
New Book Tells Veterans' Stories

Katherine Dunham Collection
New Site on Dancer, Choreographer

Featured Webcast
Authors at the 2004 Book Festival

MORE Complete News & Events

- The Internet has a mind-boggling number of sources and Web pages.
- The Internet can have an amazing retrieval speed for sources from around the world.
- The Internet gives you the ability to chat with other people who share similar interests.
- The Internet gives you personal access—from your library or your home—to key information from libraries, businesses, organizations, and governments.

Unfortunately, doing research on the Internet does have drawbacks that are often related to its strengths. Internet enthusiasts often praise the Web for creating a democratic space where every person and site is equal. On the downside, however, librarians often shudder at doing research on the Internet simply because everything is so decentralized and disorganized. There are other problems as well:

- The sheer number of possible sources on the Internet may make finding the exact source you need very difficult.
- Browsing on the Web may be fun, but you may spend hours going from one site to the next without making any real progress.
- The increasing commercialization of Web sites may interfere with locating relevant information.

- Waiting for a source to download from a busy site can be tedious and frustrating.
- Sources on the Internet may not be accurate or reliable—and thus not appropriate for your paper.

With realistic estimations about the Internet's virtues and faults, however, you should be able to find relevant and even exciting sources that will help you learn about your topic and communicate your findings to your audience.

Note: As you continue to read in this section of the chapter, you may want to open a connection to the Internet so you can check out several of the sites. Also, remember to start making bookmarks for any sites you want to revisit later.

Internet Browsers and Search Engines

Once you have an idea for a possible topic, you can begin searching sites on the Internet for relevant information. If you need to review the basics of Internet research and terminology, refer to the Internet glossary on page 636. If you are sitting at a computer with a browser, such as Netscape or Internet Explorer, you can begin working on your topic right now by accessing one of the popular search engines described below. Of course, there are actually hundreds of such searching tools available on the Web, but the ones described here can get you started.

The following search engines are listed in order of their usefulness, as judged by Search Engine Watch, a site devoted to up-to-date ratings and comparisons of search engines. Some search engines that researchers used to depend on, such as Alta Vista, Lycos, and Excite, are in decline or have merged with other search engines. The best search engines on the Web today are Google and Yahoo!. Many people, of course, use the popular AOL search (powered by Google) or MSN search (powered by Inktomi and LookSmart). The best advice is to try more than one search engine for your particular subject and use what works best.

Google *http://www.google.com* Google has quickly become the highest rated engine because of its huge index and the high relevancy of its responses.

Yahoo *http://www.yahoo.com* Yahoo!, one of the oldest search engines on the Web, still provides excellent searches. Among other services, you can check Web sites that have been evaluated by a human editor.

Ask Jeeves *http://www.askjeeves.com* Initially, Ask Jeeves was entirely a "natural language" search that allowed users to ask questions. It gets results now from a search engine that it owns, Teoma.

AllTheWeb *http://www.alltheweb.com* This search engine is gaining popularity because, although powered by Yahoo!, it is sometimes easier to use and also gives results for video and MP3 searches.

HotBot *http://www.hotbot.com* Hotbot's virtue is its ability to combine results from Yahoo!, Google, and Teoma.

Alta Vista *http://www.altavista.com* Started in 1995, Alta Vista is one of the oldest search engines and, though declining in popularity, still produces good results through Yahoo!'s search engine.

Highbeam Research *http://www.highbeam.com/library/index* Formerly known as Electric Library, Highbeam Research is not really a search engine, but it offers an article-retrieval service and accesses over 32 million documents from nearly three thousand sources.

Of course, Web sites and search engines are constantly changing. But the good news is that you can find comparative reviews and data about the various research tools and search engines on the Internet. Access **Search Engine Watch** at *http://searchenginewatch.com* for reviews and comparisons of popular and specialized search engines.

BASIC INTERNET GLOSSARY

The URL (uniform resource locator) is the address that identifies each Internet site. In the address that follows, for example, **http** stands for "Hypertext Transfer Protocol," **www** stands for World Wide Web, **Yahoo** is the manager of the Web site, and **.com** indicates a commercial site:

URL: *http://www.yahoo.com*

In addition to commercial (**.com**), you can access a variety of locations, including educational (**.edu**), governmental (**.gov**), noncommercial (**.org**), military (**.mil**), and networking (**.net**). Other URLs can access gopher sites (**gopher://**), ftp (**ftp://**), newsgroups (**news://**), and so forth.

Note: URLs have no spaces between any letters, periods, or slashes. URLs must be typed with complete accuracy—one missed slash or period or letter and your computer will not be able to find the correct address.

As you get started doing research on the Internet, acquaint yourself with the following key terms and definitions. If you know the basic language for navigating the **Internet,** you won't remain a newbie very long.

blog A blog (short for Web log) is a journal available on the Web. Blogs are usually updated daily by the owner of the log. Updating a blog is called "blogging."

bookmark Your computer's browser (see below) exables you to record each URL that you want to remember, so the next time you want to visit that site, you merely have to click on the right line in your bookmark rather than type out a complete URL string. Remember to bookmark sites that look promising as you do your research!

browser Your computer needs a browser such as Netscape or Internet Explorer to help you access Telnet, gopher, or Web sites on the Internet. (A browser is not the same as a search engine such as Yahoo! or Google.)

cyberspace The online world created in electronic space or on the Internet.

FTP The File Transfer Protocol is the set of commands that enables you to transfer files between two sites on the Internet.

home page The home page is usually the first page of any Web site, and it identifies the author of the page, the location or sponsor of the site, and the basic information about the site.

html Hypertext Markup Language is the computer code used to write pages on the Web.

hyperlink Often just called *links,* these are highlighted words, icons, or bits of graphic that you can click on to move to a related site. A hypertext is simply a collection of documents or graphics connected by these links.

listserv A listserv is a mail list that enables users to conduct an ongoing e-mail conversation about a particular topic.

MOO A multiuser domain, object-oriented, provides a space in which people can meet at a given time to discuss a particular topic.

MUD A multiuser domain (or dungeon) enables simultaneous communication, often by role-playing a certain character or persona.

newsgroup Any group of people who post messages on Usenet. Usenet is a network that gives access to an electronic discussion group.

search engine A program that enables Internet users to find relevant sites on the Internet. Popular search engines or search tools include Yahoo! and Google.

This short list is just the tip of the iceberg of Internet terminology. If you want to know about **ASCII, baud rates, bytes, cookies, flame wars, MIMEs, POPs, spam, Veronica, WYSIWYC,** or literally hundreds of other terms, visit one of the dozens of Internet glossaries available online, such as the Internet Literacy Consultants'

Glossary of Internet Terms at *http://www.matisse.net/files/glossary.html*. Check out this site and make a bookmark so you can return whenever you have a question.

Tips for Doing Research on the Internet

If you are still learning to use the Internet, here are some tips that may save you quite a bit of time during your research.

- If it takes more than a couple of minutes to get files from your site, click on the "Stop" button and try another source.
- Use the "bookmark" or "favorites list" to record your best sites. You may even want to organize your favorites or bookmarks into a folder designated specifically for the topic of this paper.
- Make sure your browser is set so that the location (URL), title, date, and page are recorded on the copies you print. If they do not appear, ask your laboratory monitor or teacher for assistance.
- The time of day you access the Internet may be crucial. Obviously, 3 A.M. is a good time for minimal Net traffic, but you do need your sleep. Log on at different times of the day to find out when is best for your location.
- Make sure you have enough information from your source (author, title, title of work, full URL address, and date of visit) so that you can write an in-text citation and a references citation in either MLA or APA format. (See the sections on MLA and APA citation of on-line sources later in this chapter.)

Useful Research Addresses

In some cases, instead of browsing through a search engine such as Google or Yahoo! you may wish to go directly to a reliable and relevant site. Here are a few you may wish to visit as you research your topic. Each of these sites offers links to other relevant sites.

- **Eric** *http://www.cal.org/ericll* Your library will probably have an ERIC (Educational Resources Information Center) database that you can conveniently search, but if you are not at a library, you can access the ERIC site at this URL. You may even order readymade searches on popular topics such as "English Only/English Plus," "Teaching ESL Abroad," or "Peace Corps Language Teaching Materials."
- **The Library of Congress** *http://lcweb.loc.gov* The Library of Congress site can give you direct access to an immense range of government and library resources.

- **News Index** *http://www.newsindex* News Index is one of many news and newspaper indexes. News Index searches the current issue and archives of over three hundred newspapers and news sources. Also use Google and Yahoo! to find specific newspapers with searchable indexes.
- ***The New York Times*** *http://www.nytimes.com* You will need to register with *The New York Times*, but then you can access the current paper or do a key-word search of the archives for relevant articles, editorials, and feature stories.
- **Online Writing Centers** Check out the online writing centers at the following addresses for help with writing as well as with finding relevant research strategies and sites: Colorado State University Online Writing Center at *http://writing.colostate.edu* or the Purdue University Online Writing Lab at *http://www.owl.trc.purdue.edu*.
- **Popular Magazines** Many magazines, such as *Mother Jones* and *Utne* have home pages that allow you to access articles and participate in online listservs or "salon" conversations on current issues. Use your search engine to find their URLs.
- **Uncover** *http://www.ingenta.com* Uncover has changed to Ingenta, but it still accesses over 11 million articles and 26,000 publications. If you access Uncover from a library, the service is free of charge.
- **U.S. Government Printing Office** *http://www.access.gpo/gov/su_docs/ index.html* The Government Printing Office (GPO) is the largest publisher in the world, and the GPO Access site allows you to find government publications on almost every topic imaginable.

EVALUATING INTERNET SOURCES

Evaluating sources on the Internet requires much more care and attention than judging print sources. Printed sources in the library have often been screened and filtered for accuracy and reliability, whereas often Web sources may represent simply one person's opinion, reaction, or point of view. Even more problematic is our inability to judge the context of the information. When we read an article in *The New York Times*, for example, we can expect a certain level of accuracy and reliability; conversely, when we read an article in a supermarket tabloid, we know we should expect very little accuracy. We know not to quote a tabloid article about diet supplements when we are writing an academic paper about health and nutrition. Even in the television media, we know when we're watching *CNN News* and when we're seeing an infomercial. On the Internet, however, we may have very few context cues to help us judge what we're reading.

Internet sources must be evaluated with a critical eye. Unless you critically appraise your sources, you don't know whether the site you are using was written by a sixth-grader doing research for a class assignment, a grandmother doing her first Web page, a wild-eyed radical, or a neighborhood dog. When we find a source, we need to ask some key questions: Who is the author? Is the author an expert, a salesperson, or a person with a reason to be biased? What organization is publishing this information? Where did the author find his or her sources? Can we verify the information in other reliable sources? How current is this information? As you read and download texts from the Internet, pay particular attention to the six criteria below. (These criteria are adapted from guidelines designed by Elizabeth E. Kirk, the Library Instruction Coordinator for the Milton S. Eisenhower Library at Johns Hopkins University and are available at *http://milton.mse.jhu.edu:8001/research/ education/net.html*.)

"On the Internet, nobody knows you're a dog."

- **Authorship.** Who is the author? Is the author well known? Are the author's credentials or biographical information available on the Internet or elsewhere? Does the author have a reason to be biased? The less you know about the author, the more cautious you need to be about using the source.

If you decide to use a document by a questionable authority, indicate exactly what you know or don't know about the author's credentials.

- **Publishing organization.** Does the site indicate the organization responsible for the text? Is there information in the header or footer indicating the organization, Webmaster, or designer of the home page? Is this organization recognized in its field? Is the organization selling something? *If you know the source is not authoritative or has a commercial basis, indicate the organization's identity if you quote from the site.*

- **Point of view or bias.** Every document or text has a point of view or bias—but some biases may mean that the site's information is not reliable or accurate. Does the author or the organization have a commercial, political, philosophical, religious, environmental, or even "scientific" agenda? *When you use a source with highly selective or biased information or perspectives, indicate the author's probable bias or agenda when you cite the text.*

- **Knowledge of the literature.** Reliable sources refer to other texts available or published in that discipline or field. Look for documents that have in-text citation or reference to other sources, a fair and reasonable appraisal of alternative points of view, and a bibliography. *Any source that has no references to other key works may simply be one writer's opinion and/or may contain erroneous information.*

- **Accuracy and reliability.** Can the information in the text be verified for accuracy? Are the methods of gathering information indicated? Has this study been replicated elsewhere? *If you have reason to believe the source is not reliable or accurate, find other sources.*

- **Currency.** Depending on your purpose and audience, currency may or may not be important. If you are writing about the reception of Shakespeare's plays, information from texts written in the seventeenth century may be more relevant than current ones. If you are writing about stem cell research or about censorship on the Internet, however, you need the most current available information. Can you determine the date the text was written? Can you find the date the information was posted on the site? Are cited statistics based on recent data? *You may use information from an older study, but acknowledge that it is dated and supplement it with more recent studies.*

As you gather sources from the Internet, be skeptical! Question the authority of the texts you find. If you think the source is not reliable, trust your judgment and don't use it. If the text seems accurate and reliable, but you cannot verify all of these criteria, indicate the problems in the source when you introduce your citation:

Certainly Mind Extension University is in the business of selling online education, but they may be right when they claim that distance learning is the wave of the future.

Karen Levine is a Spanish teacher at Thousand Oaks High School and has sponsored school-to-school exchange programs, but her testimonial for the International Education Forum's program—an exchange program for which she has worked—should be balanced against recommendations of other foreign-language exchange programs.

If you have a question about the reliability, relevance, or accuracy of any source, check with your instructor or a librarian. *If you decide to use any questionable or biased sources, you need to qualify their findings and data when you introduce the source.* Otherwise, your reader may believe that your argument is based on biased, inaccurate, or unreliable data.

EVALUATING LIBRARY SOURCES   Even with published library sources, you should appraise your sources with a critical eye, just as you do for Internet and Web sources. Just because something is published or printed does not mean that it is relevant, current, accurate, or reliable. Some sources will not relate specifically to your topic; others will be too superficial or too technical. Some will be out of date; others will be biased or simply inaccurate. Evaluate your printed sources based on the following criteria:

- **Sources should be relevant.** The sources you select should be relevant to your subject, your purpose, and your intended audience. If your narrowed topic is still too general, all your sources will look relevant. In that case, narrow your subject even more. Sources must also be relevant to your purpose. If you are writing an argumentative research paper, for example, you need sources representing both sides of the issue. If you are proposing a solution to a problem, look for sources describing the problem or the solution. Finally, sources should be appropriate for your intended audience. The articles that Kate McNerny found in *Foreign Language Annals* were more appropriate for her academic audience than was a brief and superficial article she found in *Parents* magazine.
- **Sources should be current.** As a rule of thumb, look for the most current sources—especially those on scientific or technical subjects. Research and data on AIDS are more accurate and complete now than they were in 1990. Sometimes, however, older books and articles are important. If you are doing historical research about the Great Depression in the United States, you may want to read key documents from the 1930s. In every

academic discipline, some sources remain authoritative for decades. When you find that many writers refer to a single source, it may be valuable regardless of its date of publication.

- **Sources should be reliable.** Check for possible biases in articles and books. Don't expect the National Rifle Association to give an unbiased report on gun-control legislation. Don't assume that representatives of right-to-life or prochoice groups will objectively represent the full range of facts about abortion. Because at least some bias is inevitable in any source, locate and use a variety of sources representing several points of view. If you are in doubt about an author's point of view or credibility, consult experts in the field or check book reviews. *Book Review Digest,* for example, contains references to reviews that may indicate the author's reputation or reliability.

AVOIDING PLAGIARISM

As you collect your sources, make notes, and draft your essay, be sure to give credit to your sources. Plagiarism occurs when we use the language, ideas, or visual materials from another person or text without acknowledging the source. Use the following guidelines to avoid plagiarism.

- Do not use language, ideas, or graphics from any essay, text, or visual image that you find *online,* in the *library,* or from *commercial sources* without acknowledging the source.
- Do not use language, ideas, or visuals from *any other student's essay* without acknowledging the source.

Students who plagiarize typically fail the course and face disciplinary action by the university.

Sometimes, however, students create problems by rushing or by not knowing how to quote or paraphrase accurately and fairly. You can avoid this *inadvertent* plagiarism by quoting accurately from your sources, by paraphrasing using your own words, and by citing your sources accurately.

Let's assume that you are working with the following passage, taken from the opening paragraph of an article by Marion E. Hines, "Foreign Language Curriculum Concerns in Times of Conflict," which appeared in the *Delta Kappa Gamma Bulletin* in 2003:

The United States' chronically weak language resources and lack of linguistic preparedness are invariably exposed when events such as the war in

Iraq and the September 11 terror strikes threaten the balance of power, peace or detente in global affairs. In order to regain or maintain a competitive edge, the government offers grants to encourage the restructuring of curriculum, to "retool" educators, and to infuse new technologies. The efforts have been heroic, but they have not succeeded in correcting the overall problem.

Plagiarism: Every college needs to require a foreign language, in part because we need to communicate better in times of crisis. *Events such as the war in Iraq and the terror strikes of September 11* have exposed our *lack of linguistic preparedness.* Better knowledge of foreign languages would help us communicate with people from different cultures or religions.

Explanation: This writer uses several phrases lifted directly from the source (see italics) without using quotation marks or acknowledging the source.

Proper Citation: Every high college needs to require a foreign language in part because we need to communicate better in times of crisis. Marion E. Hines, an assistant professor in modern languages and linguistics at Howard University, argues that "the United States' chronically weak language resources and lack of linguistic preparedness" result in our inability to communicate with people from different cultures or religions (15).

Explanation: In this passage, the writer cites the author before introducing the quotation, uses quotation marks for words and phrases that appear in the article, and uses the proper citation format at the end of the sentence. This article by Marion E. Hines would also be cited in the Works Cited or References page at the end of the essay.

As you take notes and write your drafts, practice using proper citation practices. If at any point you have a question about how to cite your sources accurately, recheck the sections in this chapter or ask your instructor.

TAKING NOTES   Taking careful notes from both published and unpublished sources is, of course, fundamental to accurate documentation. When a source appears relevant and useful, do the following:

1. **Record complete bibliographical information in the bibliography section of your research notebook (or in your computer notebook).** For many online library systems, you will be able to print out the bibliographical information

you need right from your computer terminal. For *books*, you need authors, editors, titles, volumes, publishers, places of publication, and years of publication.

For *articles*, you need authors; article titles; magazine or journal titles; volume numbers or dates, months, and years of publication; and beginning and ending page numbers. As Kate McNerny did in her log, leave a space between each entry to record call numbers or locations of documents:

(Book): Freed, Barbara F., ed. <u>Second Language Acquisition in a Study Abroad Context.</u> Philadelphia: John Benjamins, 1995.
   HF5549.A2P38   Current Periodical Room

(Article): Brady, Robert I. "English-Only Rules Draw Controversy."
   <u>HR Focus</u> June 1996: 20.
   P118.2.S433   1995   First Floor East

If the source is unpublished—such as a telephone conversation, a letter, or a public document in the country courthouse—record all the information about it that your readers will need to identify and consult the source themselves. (See the "Documenting Sources" section in this chapter.)

2.   **Record notes in the source notes section of your research notebook.**
   Identify each entry with the author's name and the title. If your notes fill two or more pages, put the author and title at the top of each page. Write on only one side of each page. Briefly *summarize* the main points made in the source, note specific information useful to you, paraphrase key ideas, transcribe interesting quotations, and jot down your own brief comments, questions, and memories. Place page numbers immediately following each paraphrase or quotation. Use direct quotation rather than paraphrase when the actual words in the source are more concise, authoritative, or persuasive than your paraphrase might be. *Be sure that direct quotations are accurate, word-for-word transcriptions from the original.*

3.   **Photocopy important sources for later rereading and reference.** Make sure all photocopies clearly show authors, titles, and page numbers. (For some research projects, your instructor may request photocopies of every source you paraphrase or quote.) *Tip:* If you photocopy several pages, *copy title pages or the magazines' covers,* and staple the copies together. Then, you will have all the necessary bibliographical information, and you can underline key passages or make notes on the photocopies themselves.

4. **As you read sources and take notes, record your own reactions and ideas in the drafts-and-ideas section of your research or computer notebook.** Be an active reader of your sources. When you agree or disagree with what you are reading, stop for a minute and jot down your ideas. When you think of a comparison, a process, a way to analyze or evaluate something, possible causes and effects, or examples from your own experience, *write out your ideas as completely as you can, right then, while they're fresh in your mind.* Don't get so absorbed in taking notes that you forget to record your own ideas. You don't have to collect twenty sources and *then* do a draft; instead, draft ideas *as* you collect information.

> *"Writing is the hardest work in the world not involving heavy lifting."*
> —PETE HAMILL,
> JOURNALIST

SHAPING

Once you've collected information for your research paper, you may feel overwhelmed by the task of shaping it into a coherent form. You can assert control over your data, however, and shape them into coherent form by reconsidering your purpose and thesis. *Reread your own notes and especially your draft sections from your research notebook.* Then, in the draft section of your notebook, answer the following questions:

> *"Writing a book is not as tough as it is to haul 35 people around the country and sweat like a horse five nights a week."*
> —BETTE MIDLER,
> SINGER, ACTOR,
> AUTHOR

Subject:	What is your general subject?
Narrowed topic or question:	What aspect of your subject is most interesting to you now? What question will you answer or explain?
Purpose:	Is your purpose primarily to inform, explain, evaluate, describe a problem and propose a solution, or argue a claim?
Working thesis:	What thesis, claim, or proposal do you want to impress upon your readers?
Audience:	Analyze your audience. How can you interest them in your subject? What aspects of your collected data are most appropriate for your audience?
Genre:	What genre will work best for your assignment or your purpose and audience? Find a sample of your genre and analyze its features. Will graphics and images be appropriate for this genre and audience?

As you shape, draft, and revise your research paper, you may continue to refocus your topic and question, refine your thesis, or revise your sense of audience.

SHAPING STRATEGIES

Your goal now is to design some order, sequence, plan, or outline for your research paper. Forcing yourself to write an outline, however, simply may not work. You should have an idea from your previous papers about how your writing process works best, but if you're stuck, feeling frustrated, or overwhelmed, try several of the following strategies:

- *Review strategies for shaping* that are appropriate for your particular purpose. If you are arguing for a certain claim, reread the shaping strategies discussed in Chapter 10. If you are evaluating something or analyzing a problem and proposing a solution, review the strategies discussed in Chapter 8 or 9.
- *Explain to a friend or classmate your purpose, audience, and working thesis.* Then try to explain how you might proceed.
- *Try freewriting, looping, or clustering* to develop a plan.
- *Reread your notes and drafts* from your research notebook.
- *Take a break.* Let your ideas simmer for a while. Go for a walk. Work on assignments for another course. Go jogging or swimming. Let your mind run on automatic pilot for a while—the information and ideas in your mind may begin organizing themselves into an initial "sketch outline" without your conscious effort.
- *Try branching or treeing your main ideas.* On paper or at the chalkboard, begin with your topic and draw the trunk and main branches of your topics. Try to explain your sketch or chalkboard drawing to someone.

Think of these activities as a circle: Begin at any point, work in either direction, and repeat them as necessary. When something starts to work, stay with it for a while. If you start to block or become frustrated, go on to the next activity.

WORKING OUTLINE   If the shaping activities helped you discover a basic design or plan, translate it into a working outline. If not, you may need to begin drafting in order to discover an outline. Kate McNerny decided to follow a pattern for writing an argument. Although she modified it considerably to change her purpose to problem solving, the sketch outline helped her organize her ideas and source material so she could begin drafting.

Introduction: Comments—quotations from informal survey—why people feel they don't need to know a foreign language.
Mention study on misconceptions of school-aged children about Russian children.

I. Narration:	Foreign-language studies' position in other countries as opposed to U.S.
	Mention "Official English" here?
	Include example of European requirements?
	Statistics on how many Americans are actually competent in another language.
	Mention bills to require a state language?
	U.S. position in world as far as power, trade.
II. Partition:	American students should be required to study a foreign language throughout the six years of junior and senior high school. To increase number of students studying foreign language, we need changes in administrators and teachers, changes in students, and changes in state and national policies.
III. Arguments:	An increase in number of students studying foreign languages would:
	Help to improve diplomatic relations with other countries—peace cannot be achieved without this.
	Change Americans' attitudes toward foreigners and change foreigners' attitudes toward Americans.
	Facilitate international trade and other business.
	Increase jobs for students abroad and at home.
	Without requirement, no incentive for many students.
IV. Refutation:	Not necessary because other countries can speak English. (This is more an argument against learning a language, not against a requirement.)
	Not essential for quality education.
	As requirement, would detract from other important subjects.
	Not enough federal, state, or local money to change number of foreign-language courses offered.
Conclusion:	Call for action on part of federal government.
	Contrary to popular belief, we are not an isolated country.
	A required study of languages will bring us one step closer to global understanding and peace.

ORGANIZING YOUR NOTES With a rough outline as a guide, reread your draft ideas, notes, and photocopies, and label them according to headings and subheadings in your working outline (for instance, I: Intro; II: Background and History; III: Required Changes; IV: Advantages of Changes; and V: Conclusion). Before you remove pages from the source notes section of your notebook or unstaple photocopied articles or sections of books, *make sure each entry or photocopy contains the author, title, and page numbers.* Now you are ready to arrange your notes and copies for use during drafting. Organize your notes into groups according to each section of your working outline. Reread each group, deciding which information should come first, in the middle, or last.

DRAFTING

At this point, some of the most difficult work is behind you. Congratulate yourself—there aren't many people who know as much as you do right now about your subject. You are an authority: You have information, statistics, statements, ideas from other writers and researchers, and your own experiences and observations at your fingertips. As you write, remember your purpose and audience. What is your purpose—to inform, explain, evaluate, offer a solution, or argue? Who exactly is your audience? What arguments and evidence will convince them? Your sources will become the evidence and support for *your ideas.* Remember that your voice and point of view should unify the information for your reader.

Many writers prefer to start a draft with the first main idea, leaving the introduction until later. As you write, you may discover a quotation, example, or narrative that doesn't fit anywhere else but that would be a perfect lead-in. Or you may already know how you want to start, using an idea that will help organize and direct your thoughts. As you draft, be guided by your working outline and your notes. Avoid copying passages verbatim from your own notebook ideas; instead, reread your notes and express those ideas in language that fits the idea you're working on.

If you get stuck, go back and reread what you have drafted so far or reread the source notes and ideas that you have assembled from your notebook and photocopies. Try to maintain your momentum by writing as quickly as possible. Don't be upset if the natural flow of your writing suggests a slightly different order or deviates from your working outline. Consider the new possibility. You may have discovered a better way to shape your material. If you are missing some fact or quotation, just leave a long line and keep writing. Later you can find the source and add the material you need.

USING GRAPHICS

As you draft your essay, you may need to decide whether to include data and statistics in your sentences or add graphics, charts, or other visuals to emphasize your point. Writing on foreign-language requirements, for example, imagine that you have photocopied pages from an article by the Department of Modern and Classical Languages at the University of Connecticut, "A National Study on Secondary to Postsecondary Foreign Language Articulation." You have photocopied the following two paragraphs and accompanying figures.

Reason for Studying a Foreign Language

When administrators and teachers were asked to state the main reason students study a foreign language, the overwhelming majority (83% and 84% respectively) felt it was to fulfill a requirement. Only 5% of administrators and 8% of teachers believed students learn a foreign language for enjoyment or interest [Figure 1]. Students were also asked the main reason they studied foreign languages. For more than half (56%) of the students, the stated reason was to fulfill a requirement. About one out of four (24%) students studied a language because they find it interesting or they like it.

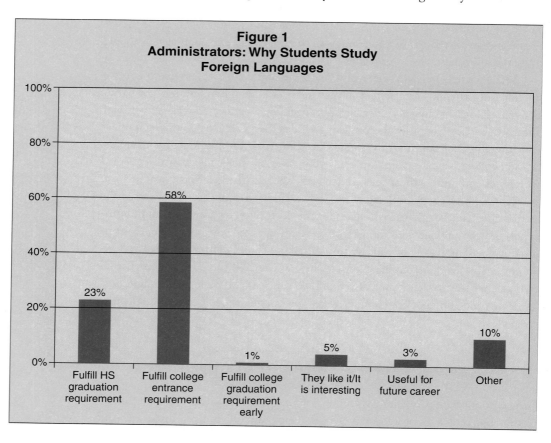

Figure 1
Administrators: Why Students Study Foreign Languages

However, when given the opportunity to list all the reasons they studied a foreign language, students selected the following: 52% to fulfill a high school graduation requirement, 44% to fulfill a college entrance requirement, 43% due to interest or enjoyment, 15% for traveling, 13% for a future career, 8% to learn the language of ethnic heritage, and 7% to fulfill a college graduation requirement early. An additional 6% gave other reasons for learning a foreign language [Figure 2].

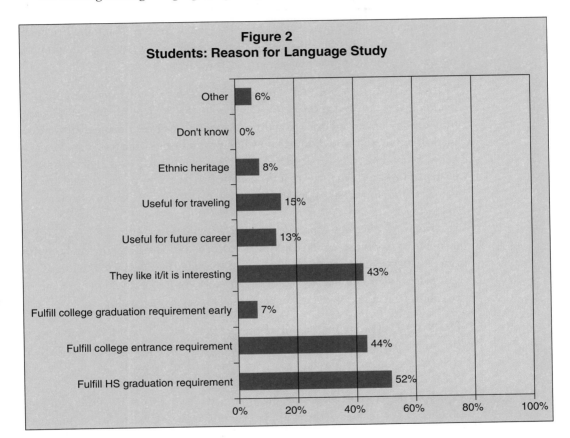

Figure 2
Students: Reason for Language Study

As you draft, decide when you want to make your point by using data in your sentences and when you want to add a graph for illustration. In this example, you might want to cite the statistic in the first sentence of the first paragraph ("According to this study, approximately 83% of administrators indicated that students took a foreign language primarily because of high school or college requirements"). The accompanying bar graph would help make the point, but might not be necessary.

However, in the second paragraph, including all the percentages would make your argument too tedious and dry. Using the bar graph with a short introduction would make the point much more concisely.

USING SOURCES Proper use of sources requires both creativity and scrupulous honesty. On the one hand, you want to use other people's information and ideas when and where they serve *your* purpose and *your* ideas. A research paper is not simply a long string of quotations connected by a few transitions. On the other hand, the sources you cite or quote must be used *fairly* and *honestly*. You must give credit for other writers' ideas and information. You must quote accurately, cite your sources in your text, and document those sources accurately.

WHAT SOURCES TO CITE You must cite a source for any fact or bit of information that is not *general knowledge*. Obviously, what is "general knowledge" varies from one writer and audience to another. **As a rule, however, document any information or fact that you did not know before you began your research.** You may know, for example, that America spends more money on defense than it does on education. However, if you state that the defense budget for the previous year is greater than the total amount spent on education for the past forty years, then cite the source for that fact.

Knowing when you must cite a source for an idea, however, can be tricky. You do not need to indicate a source for *your* ideas, of course. But if you find a source that agrees with your idea, or if you suspect that your idea may be related to ideas from particular source, cite that source. A citation gives your idea additional credibility: you show your reader that another authority shares your perception.

HOW TO CITE SOURCES In the text of your research paper, you will need to cite your sources according to either the Modern Language Association (MLA) style or the American Psychological Association (APA) style. Remember: Choose either the MLA style or the APA style and stick with it. Don't mix styles.

According to the MLA style, the in-text citation contains the author and page number of your source (Torres 50). No comma appears between author and page number. (If the author is unknown, identify the title and page number of your source. Underline book titles; place quotation marks around article titles.)

According to the APA style, the in-text citation contains author and date (Torres, 1996). Use a comma between author and date. If you refer to a page number, it should appear after the author and date (Torres, 1996, p. 50). Use a *p.* (or *pp.* for more than one page) before the page number(s).

The in-text citation (either MLA or APA) refers readers to the end of your paper, where you give complete information about each source in a "Works Cited"

(MLA) or "References" (APA) list. For illustration purposes, the following examples use MLA style. See the "Documenting Sources" section (pp. 599–615) for examples of both APA and MLA styles.

IDENTIFY CITED REFERENCES (MLA STYLE)   Once you have decided that a fact, a paraphrase, or a direct quotation contributes to your thesis and will make a strong impression on your reader, use the following guidelines for in-text citation.

- **Identify in the text the persons or source for the fact, paraphrased idea, or quotation:**

As two foreign-language teachers noted, "Like it or not, we are members of a world community consisting of hundreds of nations, and our fates are closely intertwined" (Long and Long 366).

Note: The parentheses and the period *follow* the final quotation marks.

- **If you cite the author in your sentence, the parentheses will contain only the page reference:**

According to Paul Simon, former member of the President's Commission on Foreign Language, the United States should erect a sign at each port of entry that reads, "WELCOME TO THE UNITED STATES—WE CANNOT SPEAK YOUR LANGUAGE" (1).

- **Use block format (separated from the text by a blank line, indented ten spaces, and double-spaced) for quotations of five lines or more:**

Educator Gerald Unks points out two instances in which a lack of language proficiency caused companies to initiate fatal marketing programs.

> When Pepsi-Cola went after the Chinese market, "Come Alive with Pepsi" was translated into Chinese in Taiwan as "Pepsi Brings Your Ancestors Back from the Dead." No Sale! General Motors sought to sell its Nova in South America, oblivious to the fact that "No va" in Spanish means "It doesn't go." (24)

Note: In block quotations, the final period comes *before* the parentheses.

- **Vary your introductions to quotations:**

Educator Gerald Unks claims that "only 15 percent of American high school students study a foreign language. Only 8 percent of our colleges require credit in a foreign language for admission (down from 34 percent in 1966)" (24).

The problem is that high school students are not taking foreign languages, and most colleges no longer require a foreign language for admission: "Only 15 percent of American high school students study a foreign language. Only 8 percent of our colleges require credit in a foreign language for admission (down from 34 percent in 1966)" (Unks 24).

- **Edit quotations when necessary to condense or clarify.** Use three ellipsis points or spaced periods (. . .) if you omit words from the middle of a quoted sentence:

As two foreign language teachers noted, "We are members of a world community . . . and our fates are closely intertwined" (Long and Long 366).

If you omit words from the end of a quoted sentence or omit sentences from a long quoted passage, place a period after the last word quoted before the omission; follow it with three ellipsis points—for a total of four periods. (Be sure that you have a complete sentence both before and after the four periods.)

Paul Simon advises us that our nation's lack of language proficiency may have been a partial cause of our disastrous policies in Vietnam:

Vietnam and the Middle East have taught us that our security position is not solely a matter of dealing with the Warsaw Pact countries or the giants among the nations. Before our heavy intervention in Vietnam, fewer than five American-born experts on Vietnam, Cambodia, or Laos . . . could speak with ease one of the languages of that area. . . . What if—a big if—we had had . . . a mere twenty Americans who spoke Vietnamese fluently, who understood their culture, aspirations, and political history? Maybe, just maybe, we would have avoided that conflict. (9)

Note: The first line is indented five spaces because in the source the quotation begins a new paragraph.

In some cases you may want to change the wording of a quotation or add explanatory words of your own to clarify your quotation. If you do so, clearly indicate your changes or additions by placing them within square brackets:

As Simon suggests, if only a few Americans knew Vietnamese, then "maybe, just maybe, we would have avoided [the Vietnam War]" (9).

REVISING

You have been revising your research essay since the first day of the project. You thought about several subjects, for example, but you chose only one. You started with a focus but revised it as you thought, read, and wrote more. You initially tested your ideas in the draft section of your research notebook, but you revised those ideas as you drafted. At this point, you are just continuing your revising; now, however, you have a complete draft to revise.

Start the revision of your complete draft by taking a break. Fix your schedule so that you can do something else for a couple of days. When you return and reread your draft, be prepared to be flexible. If there is something missing in your data, prepare yourself to track down the information. If a favorite source or quotation no longer seems relevant, have the courage to delete it. If an example on page 4 would work better as a lead-in for the whole paper, reorder your material accordingly. If the evidence for one side of an argument appears stronger than you initially thought, change your position and your thesis. *Being willing to make such changes is not a sign of poor research and writing. Often, in fact, it demonstrates that you have become more knowledgeable and sophisticated about your subject.*

After you have finished your rough draft, ask friends or classmates to give you their responses. Accept their criticism gracefully, but ask them to explain *why* they think certain changes would help. Would they help to make your purposes clearer? Would they be more appropriate for your audience? Don't be intimidated and feel that you must make every change that readers suggest. You must make the final decisions.

> *"What makes me happy is rewriting. . . . It's like cleaning house, getting rid of all the junk, getting things in the right order, tightening things up."*
> —ELLEN GOODMAN, JOURNALIST

DOCUMENTING SOURCES

Both the MLA and APA documentation styles require citation of sources in the text of your paper, followed by a Works Cited (MLA style) or References list (APA style) at the end of your paper. Use footnotes only for content or supplementary notes that explain a point covered in the text or offer additional information. *Note:* MLA in-text documentation and Works Cited documentation are explained here. See pages 666–673 for APA in-text documentation and References format.

IN-TEXT DOCUMENTATION: MLA STYLE   In the MLA style, give the author's name and the page numbers in parentheses following your use of a fact, paraphrase, or direct quotation from a source. These in-text citations then refer your readers to the complete documentation of the source in a Works Cited or Works Consulted list at the end of the paper.

As you cite your sources in the text, use the following guidelines:

If you cite the author in the text, indicate only the page number in parentheses:

> According to Vicki Galloway, Project Director for the American Council on the Teaching of Foreign Languages, a student's horizons will not be broadened by "grammar lectures and manipulative classroom exercises" (33).

If the author is unknown, use a short version of the title in the parentheses:

> Most students in the United States would be surprised to learn that the Communist Party in Russia actually sponsors rock concerts (A Day in the Life 68).

If the source is unpublished, cite the name or title used in your bibliography:

> In an informal interview, one university administrator noted that funding of foreign-language study has steadily decreased over the past ten years (Meyers).

If the source is from the Internet or the Web, use the author, or if there is no author, use the title:

> Many websites now provide detailed information about how to plan a study-abroad semester or year (Foreign Language).

If your bibliography contains more than one work by an author, cite the author, a short title, and page numbers. The following examples show various ways of citing a reference to Paul Simon, *The Tongue-Tied American:*

> In The Tongue-Tied American, Simon explains that students can earn a doctorate degree in the United States without ever studying a foreign language (2).

> As Simon notes, "It is even possible to earn a doctorate here without studying any foreign language" (Tongue-Tied 2).

> In the United States, one can earn a doctorate degree without studying a single foreign language (Simon, Tongue-Tied 2).

Note: Use a comma between author and title but not between title and page number.

If a source has two authors, cite both authors' names in the text or in the parentheses:

> A recent study sampling 536 secondary schools revealed that 91 percent did not require foreign-language credits for graduation (Ranwez & Rodgers 98).

If a source has three or more authors, give the name of the author listed first in your bibliography followed by the abbreviation *et al.,* meaning "and others":

> Teachers should integrate the study of history, culture, politics, literature, and religion of a particular region with the study of language (Berryman et al. 96).

If a source has several volumes, precede the page number with the volume number and a colon, as indicated:

> Language and grammar can be taught with real-life contexts or scenarios (Valdman 3:82).

If you are citing a quotation or information from a source that itself cites another source, use the abbreviation *qtd. in* for "quoted in" to indicate that you have used an indirect source for your information or quotation. (If possible, however, check the original source.)

> As Sue Berryman and her colleagues explain, "The course is developed as a world tour during which time the students take a vicarious trip . . . to become saturated in every aspect of a particular area of the globe" (qtd. in Simon 96).

If you cite two or more authors as sources for a fact, idea, or plan, separate the citations with a semicolon, as follows:

> Most recently, two prominent foreign language educators have published plans to coordinate foreign-language studies (Lambert 9–19; Lange 70–96).

CONTENT OR SUPPLEMENTARY NOTES   You may use footnote numbers in the text of your paper to refer to a Notes section at the end of the paper. If you have an important idea, a comment on your text, or additional information or sources *that would interrupt the flow of your ideas in the text,* you may use that idea or comment in your supplementary Notes section. During her research, for example, McNerny read about the movement to make English the "official language" of the United States. She didn't want to digress in her paper, so she described the controversy in a supplementary note at the end of the paper. Here is a first draft of that note:

> [1]Several states currently have bills before their legislatures to make English the "official language." Proponents of these bills argue that immigrants need incentives to learn English. Many opponents from ethnic and civil rights groups believe these bills are racist (McBee 64). If Americans were all educated in foreign languages, these bills would be unnecessary. Americans' ignorance and fear of foreign languages are probably a reason that these bills are so popular.

WORKS CITED LIST: MLA STYLE   After you have revised your essay and are certain that you will not change any in-text documentation, you are ready to write your list of sources. Depending on what you include, it will be one of the following:

- A Works Cited list (only those works actually cited in your essay)
- A Works Consulted list (works cited and works you read)
- A Selected Bibliography (works cited and the most important other works)
- An Annotated List of Works Cited (works cited, followed by a short description and evaluation of each source)

A Works Cited list alphabetically orders, by author's last name, all published and unpublished sources cited in your research paper. If the author is unknown, alphabetize by the first word (excluding *A, An,* or *The*) of the title. As a general rule, underline or italicize titles of books, periodicals, and newspapers, but use quotation marks to enclose titles of newspaper and magazine articles. Use the following abbreviations for missing information (other than an unknown author): n.p. (no place of publication given), n.p. (no publisher given), n.d. (no date of publication given), or n. pag. (no pagination in source). The first line of each citation begins at the left margin, and succeeding lines are indented five spaces. Double-space the entire Works Cited list.

Following are examples of MLA-style entries in a Works Cited list, organized by kind of source: books, articles, and unpublished sources. Use these as models for your own Works Cited list. For additional information and examples, see *MLA Handbook for Writers of Research Papers* (6th ed., 2003).

Note: In your essay or manuscript, citations of titles of articles, poems, and short stories should be surrounded by quotation marks ("The Story of an Hour"). Titles of books, plays, novels, magazines, journals, or collections should be underlined (Caramelo, National Geographic). Underlining indicates to a publisher that a title should be placed in italics. When your essay or manuscript is published, underlining is then replaced by italics (*Caramelo, National Geographic*). If you wish to use italics in your Works Cited list to indicate underlining, check with your instructor.

BOOKS: MLA STYLE

Order the information as follows, omitting information that does not apply:

Author's last name, first name. "Title of Article or Part of Book." Title of Book. Ed. or Trans. Name. Edition. Number of volumes. Place of publication: Name of publisher, Date of publication.

A Book by One Author

Cisneros, Sandra. Caramelo. New York: Random, 2002.

Additional Books by Same Author

Morrison, Toni. Song of Solomon. New York: Knopf, 1977.

———— Jazz. New York: Knopf, 1992.

A Book with Two or Three Authors

Conklin, Nancy F., and Margaret A. Lourie. <u>A Host of Tongues: Language</u>
<u>Communities in the United States.</u> New York: Free Press, 1983.

Padilla, Amando M., Halford H. Fairchild, and Concepcion M. Valadez. <u>Foreign</u>
<u>Language Education.</u> Newbury Park, CA: Sage, 1990.

A Book with More Than Three Authors

Abrams, M. H. et al. <u>The Norton Anthology of English Literature.</u> 7th ed. New
York: Norton, 2000.

An Unknown or Anonymous Author

<u>New York Public Library Student's Desk Reference.</u> New York: Prentice, 1993.

A Book with an Author and an Editor

Austen, Jane. <u>Pride and Prejudice.</u> Ed. Mark Schorer. Boston: Houghton, 1956.

[The names of well-known publishers are often shortened to the first key word.
Thus, "Houghton Mifflin Co." becomes "Houghton," and "Harcourt Brace Jovanovich, Inc." becomes simply "Harcourt."]

An Edited Book

Myers, Linda, ed. <u>Approaches to Computer Writing Classrooms.</u> Albany: State U of
New York P, 1993.

A Translation

Allende, Isabel. <u>Paula.</u> Trans. Margaret Sayers Peden. New York: HarperCollins,
1996.

An Article or Chapter in an Edited Book

Sophocles. <u>Electra.</u> Trans. David Grene. <u>Greek Tragedies</u>. Ed. David Grene and
Richmond Lattimore. Vol 2. Chicago: U of Chicago P, 1960. 2 vols. 45–109.

A Work in More Than One Volume

Morrison, Samuel Eliot, and Henry Steele Commager. <u>The Growth of the American</u>
<u>Republic.</u> 2 vols. New York: Oxford UP, 1941.

A Work in an Anthology

Chopin, Kate. "The Awakening." <u>The Harper Single Volume American Literature.</u>
Ed. Donald McQuade et al. 3rd ed. New York: Longman, 1999.

An Encyclopedia or Dictionary Entry

"Don Giovanni." <u>The Encyclopedia Americana.</u> 2004 ed.

A Government Document: Known Author

Juhnke, Gerald A. <u>Addressing School Violence: Practical Strategies &</u>
<u>Interventions.</u> ERIC Counseling and Student Services Clearinghouse.
Greensboro, NC: GPO, 2001.

[*GPO* stands for "Government Printing Office."]

A Government Document: Unknown Author

United States. Maternal and Child Health Bureau. <u>Babies Sleep Safest on Their</u>
<u>Backs: Reduce the Risk of Sudden Infant Death Syndrome (SIDS).</u> Bethesda,
MD: GPO, 2001.

An Unpublished Dissertation

Burnham, William A. "Peregrine Falcon Egg Variation, Incubation, and Population
Recovery Strategy." Diss. Colorado State U, 1984.

A Pamphlet

<u>Guide to Raptors.</u> Denver: Center for Raptor Research, 2003.

PERIODICALS: MLA STYLE

For all articles published in periodicals, give the author's name, the title of the article, and the name of the publication. For newspapers and magazines, add complete dates and inclusive page numbers. Use the first page number and a plus sign if an article is not printed on consecutive pages. For most professional journals, add volume numbers, issue numbers if appropriate, years of publication, and inclusive page numbers.

An Article in a Weekly or Biweekly Magazine

Hersh, Seymour M. "Chain of Command." <u>The New Yorker</u> 17 May 2004: 38–43.

An Article in a Monthly or Bimonthly Magazine

Appenzeller, Tim. "The End of Cheap Oil." <u>National Geographic</u> June 2004:
80–109.

Morrison, Ann M., Randall P. White, and Ellen Van Velsor. "Executive Women:
Substance Plus Style." <u>Psychology Today</u> Aug. 1987: 18+.

An Unsigned Article in a Magazine

"E-Commerce Takes Off." <u>Economist</u> 15–21 May 2004: 9.

An Article in a Professional Journal

Many professional journals have continuous page numbers throughout the year. The first issue of the year begins with page 1, but every issue after that begins with the number following the last page number of the previous issue. For such journals, give volume followed by the year.

> Swope, Christopher. "Panel OKs Bill to Make English Official Government
> Language." <u>Congressional Quarterly Weekly Report</u> 54 (1996): 2128–29.

[For page numbers over 100, use only two digits for the final page citation: 2128–29.] If each issue of a professional journal begins with page 1, cite the volume number followed by a period, then the issue number and year. In the following example, the article is in Volume 9, Issue 1, published in January 1987.

> Brodkey, Linda. "Writing Ethnographic Narratives." <u>Written Communication</u> 9.1
> (1987): 25–50.

An Article in a Newspaper

Omit the introductory article (*New York Times* instead of *The New York Times*). If the masthead indicates an edition (late ed.), include it in your entry. Newspaper articles do not usually appear on consecutive pages, so indicate the page number on which the article begins and then put a "[plus]" sign to indicate that the article continues on later pages. Indicate section numbers (A, B, C) when appropriate.

> Harmon, Amy. "In New Tests for Fetal Defects, Agonizing Choices for Parents."
> <u>New York Times</u> 20 June 2004, late natl. ed.: A1+.

An Unsigned Article in a Newspaper

> "A Jet Crash That Defies Resolution" <u>Los Angeles Times</u> 5 Sept. 2001: A1.

An Editorial

> Fish, Stanley. "When Principles Get in the Way." Editorial. <u>New York Times</u> 26
> Dec. 1996, late ed.: A27.

A Published Interview

> Lamm, Richard D. "Governments Face Tough Times." With Robert Baun.
> <u>Coloradoan</u> [Ft. Collins, CO] 30 Nov. 1995: B9.

An Unsigned Editorial in a Newspaper

> "A Primary Choice: Mark Green." <u>New York Times</u> 2 Sept. 2001, sec. 5:8.

A Review

> Iovine, Julie V. "Hi, Honey, I'm at the Airport." Rev. of *The Terminal,* dir. Steven
> Spielberg. <u>New York Times</u> 9 May 2004, late ed.:A36.

> Rosen, Charles, and Henri Zerner. "Scenes from the American Dream." Rev. of
> <u>Norman Rockwell: Pictures for the American People</u> by Maureen Hart
> Hennessey and Anne Knutson. <u>New York Review of Books</u> 8 Oct. 2000:
> 16–20.

ELECTRONIC AND INTERNET SOURCES: MLA STYLE

The World Wide Web and the Internet are still changing, so even the latest MLA guidelines, available in the sixth edition of the *MLA Handbook for Writers of Research Papers* (2003), will continue to change. The current abbreviated basic features of an electronic or Internet citation, given below, appear in complete form on the MLA home page at *http://www.mla.org*. Use the specific citations following this list as models for your own citations. For additional examples, consult the MLA home page or the most recent edition of the *MLA Handbook for Writers of Research Papers*.

1.   Name of author (if known)
2.   Title of article, short story, poem, or short work within a book, periodical, or database
3.   Title of book (underlined)
4.   Name of the editor or translator (if relevant), preceded by appropriate abbreviation, such as *Ed.* or *Trans.*
5.   Publication information for any print version of the source
6.   Title of periodical, database, scholarly project, or site (underlined), or for a site with no title, a description such as *home page*
7.   Name of the editor of the project or database (if available)
8.   The volume number, issue number, or other version number of the source
9.   Date of electronic publication, update, or posting
10.   Name of the subscription service and—if the library is a subscriber—the name and city (and state abbreviation, if necessary) of the library
11.   For a posting to a discussion list or forum, the name of the list or forum
12.   The number of pages, paragraphs, or sections, if they are numbered
13.   The name of any organization sponsoring the Web site
14.   Date when researcher accessed the source or site
15.   Electronic address or URL of the source in angle brackets. ***Note:*** If a URL must be divided between two lines, break it only after a slash. Do not use a hyphen.

A Book

Austin, Jane. <u>Pride and Prejudice.</u> Ed. Henry Churchyard. 1996. 7 Sept. 2001
    <http:www.pemberley.com/janeinfo/pridprej.html>.

A Poem

Carrol, Lewis. "Jabberwocky." 1872. 6 Mar. 1998
    <http://www.jabberwocky.com/carroll/jabber/jabberwocky.html>.

A Scholarly Project

The History Channel.com. 2004. History Channel. 21 June 2004
    <http://www.historychannel.com/>.

A Document Within an Online Scholarly Project

"Monet, Claude." Britannica Online. September 2001. Encyclopaedia Britannica.
    7 Sept. 2001 <http://members.eb.com>.

An Article in a Scholarly Journal

Mossman, Mark. "Acts of Becoming: Autobiography, Frankenstein, and the
    Postmodern Body." Postmodern Culture 11.3 (2001). 10 Sept. 2001
    <http://jefferson.village.virginia.edu/pmc/current.issue/11.3mossman.html>.

An Article in a Magazine

Smith, Dakota. "Black Women Ignore Many of Media's Beauty Ideals. Utne.com
    17 June 2004. 23 June 2004
    <http://www.utne.com/webwatch/2004_153/news/11244-1.html>.

An Anonymous Article in a Magazine

"The First Private Rocket Ship Soars into Space." USNews.com 22 June 2004.
    26 June 2004
    <http://www.usnews.com/usnews/tech/nextnews/nexthome.htm>.

A Work from an Online Database

[To cite online material from a database to which a library subscribes, complete the
citation by giving the name of the database (underlined), the name of the service (if
available), the name of the library, and the date of access, followed by the URL of
the service's home page, in angle brackets.]

Hines, Marion E. "Foreign Language Curriculum Concerns in Times of Conflict."
    Delta Kappa Gamma Bulletin 70 (Fall 2003): 15–22. Academic Search
    Premier. EBSCO. Colorado State U Lib. 23 May 2004
    <http://0-web2.epnet.com>.

Jost, Kenneth. "Could the Terrorist Attacks Have Been Prevented?" CQ
    Researcher 4 June 2004. CQ Researcher. Colorado State U Lib. 26 June 2004
    <http://0-library.cqpress.com>.

An Article in a Newspaper

Safire, William. "The Great Cash Cow." NYTimes.com 23 June 2004. 25 June 2004
    <http://www.nytimes.com/2004/06/23/opinion/23SAFI.html>.

An Editorial

Regan, Tom. "The New Political Correctness and the GOP." Editorial. <u>Christian Science Monitor</u> 2 Feb. 1999. 3 Feb. 1999.
  <http://www.csmonitor.com/atcmonitor/commop/regan/>.

A Letter to the Editor

Fuld, Leonard. Letter. <u>New York Times on the Web</u> 4 Sept. 2001. 6 Sept. 2001.
  <http://www.nytimes.com/2001/09/05/opinion/LOCELL.html>.

Posting to a Discussion List

Mitchell, Kerri. "Composition Philosophies and Rhetoric." Online posting. 24 Sept. 2003. Syllabase Discussion Group. 17 Jan. 2004.
  <http//writing.colostate.edu/Syllabase/classroom/communication/discussion/display_message.asp?Message ID=23726>.

A Professional Site

<u>The Official Website of the Nobel Foundation.</u> The Nobel Foundation. Aug. 2004. 10 Sept. 2004 <http://www.nobel.se/>.

A Personal Web Page

Palmquist, Michael. Home page. Jan. 2003. 10 Sept. 2003.
  <http://lamar.ColoState.EDU/~mp/>.

Synchronous Communications (MOOs, MUDs)

Grigar, Dene. Online defense of dissertation "Penelopeia: The Making of Penelope in Homer's Story and Beyond." 25 July 1995. LinguaMOO. 25 July 1995.
  <telnet://lingua.utdallas.edu:8888>.

A Publication on CD-ROM, Diskette, or Magnetic Tape

"World War II." <u>Encarta.</u> CD-ROM. Seattle: Microsoft, 1999.

Godwin, M. E. "An Obituary to Affirmative Action and a Call for Self-Reliance." <u>ERIC.</u> CD-ROM. SilverPlatter. Oct. 1992.

An E-Mail Communication.

Gogela, Anne. "RE: Teaching British Literature Survey." E-mail to the author. 30 May 2004.

OTHER SOURCES: MLA STYLE

For unpulished sources, give relevant information that may help your reader identify or locate the source.

Computer Software

Microsoft Word. Computer Software. Microsoft, 2004.

A Film

The Terminal. Dir. Steven Spielberg. Perf. Tom Hanks and Catherine Zeta-Jones. Dreamworks, 2004.

A Recording

Carey, Mariah. "Hero." Music Box. Sony Songs, Inc, Columbia Records, 1993.

A Television or Radio Program

"Not Quite Dead." Narr. Mike Wallace. Sixty Minutes. CBS. WCBS, New York. 13 Apr. 1997.

A Letter

McCarthy, Cormac. Letter to the author. 22 Feb 2003.

A Lecture or Speech

Evans, Pierre. Lecture on Colorado Raptors. U of Colorado, Boulder. 17 Sept. 2003.

If title is unknown, list type of oral presentation such as *Reading, Speech,* or *Lecture.*

A Personal Interview

Miller, J. Philip. Personal interview. 19 Mar. 2004.

A Personal Survey

Morgan Library Interlibrary Loan Questionnaire. Personal survey. 15 March 2000.

A Cartoon

Roberts, Victoria. Cartoon. New Yorker 13 Jan. 1997: 47.

An Advertisement

Give the name of the product or company followed by the label, *Advertisement,* not underlined or in italics. Follow with the usual publication information.

Escape Hybrid by Ford. Advertisement. National Geographic May 2004: 2.

A Painting, Sculpture, or Photograph

Indicate the artist's name first, followed by the title, the museum or collection, the owner if indicated, and the city.

Marc, Franz <u>Deer in the Forest II.</u> Staatliche Kunsthalle, Karlsruhe.

Vermeer van Delft, Jan. <u>The Astronomer.</u> Louvre, Paris.

IN-TEXT DOCUMENTATION: APA STYLE   In the APA style, give the author's name and date in parentheses following your use of a summary or paraphrase. If you quote material directly, give author's name, date, and page number. (Use *p.* for one page and *pp.* for more than one page.) These citations will direct your reader to your "References list," where you give complete bibliographical information. As you cite your sources, use the following guidelines:

If you do not cite the author in the text, give author, date, and page in parentheses at the end of the citation. If you are specifically citing a quotation or a part of a source, indicate the page with *p.* or the chapter with *chap:*

> A recent study of elementary school students studying a foreign language showed that participants from bilingual households "invariably scored higher than participants from English-speaking only households" (Cortes, 2002, p. 320).

If you cite the author in the text, indicate the date in parentheses immediately following the author's name, and cite the page number in parentheses following the quotation:

> According to Vicki Galloway (1984), a student's horizons will not be broadened by "grammar lectures and manipulative classroom exercises" (p. 33).

If you cite a long direct quotation (40 or more words), indent the passage five spaces from the left margin. Omit the enclosing direct quotation marks. Place the period at the end of the passage, not after the parentheses that include the page reference:

> In an article explaining the strategic value of foreign language study, Hines (2003) argues that our response has been inadequate:
>
> > The United States' chronically weak language resources and lack of linguistic preparedness are invariably exposed when events such as the war in Iraq and the September 11 terror strikes threaten the balance of power, peace or détente in global affairs. (15)

If you are paraphrasing or summarizing material (no direct quotations), you may omit the page number:

> According to Coxe (1984), many top American businesspeople agree that students who combine some business or economics training with fluency in Japanese have unlimited job possibilities.

Note: Although the APA style manual says that writers may omit page citation for summaries and paraphrases, check with your instructor before you omit page references. If you have previously cited the author and date of a study, you may omit the date:

> In addition, Coxe points out that many top American businesspeople agree that students who combine some business or economics training with fluency in Japanese have unlimited job possibilities.

If the work has between two and five authors, cite all authors in your text or in parentheses in the first reference. *Note:* In your text, write "Frith and Mueller"; in a parenthetical citation, use an ampersand "(Frith & Mueller)":

> Frith and Mueller (2003) cite another recent example of foreign-language ignorance in marketing. When the California Milk Processor Board wanted an ad agency to translate the "Got Milk?" campaign into Spanish, the unfortunate translation came out as "Are you lactating?" (p. 33).

> Two researchers cited another recent example of foreign language ignorance in marketing. When the California Milk Processor Board wanted an ad agency to translate the "Got Milk?" campaign into Spanish, the unfortunate translation came out as "Are you lactating?" (Frith & Mueller, 2003, p. 33).

For subsequent citations, cite both names each time if a work has two authors. If a work has three to five authors, give the last name of the first author followed by *et al.* Include the year for the first citation within a paragraph:

> Shedivy et al. (2004) found similar results. . . .

If a work has six or more authors, use only the last name of the first author and the abbreviation *et al.* followed by the date for the first and subsequent in-text and parenthetical citations:

> Teachers should integrate the study of history, culture, politics, literature, and religion of a particular region with the study of language (Berryman et al., 1988).

If a work has no author, give the first few words of the title and the year:

> Most students in the United States would be surprised to learn that the Russian government sponsored rock concerts (A Day in the Life, 1988).

If the source is from the Internet or the Web, use the author, or if there is no author, use the title:

> Many Web sites now provide detailed information about how to plan a study-abroad semester or year (Foreign Language, 2004).

If the author is a corporation, cite the full name of the company in the first reference:

> Foreign-language study must be accompanied by in-depth understanding and experience of culture (University of Maryland, 1990).

If the source is a personal communication (letter, memo, interview, phone conversation), cite in text but do not include in your "References" list (personal communications are not recoverable data):

> As Professor Devlin (personal interview, September 21, 2003) explained, "Foreign-language study encourages students to see their own language and culture from a fresh perspective."

If you are citing a government document, give the originating agency, its abbreviation (if any), the year of publication, and (if you include a direct quotation) the page number:

> Newcomers to a foreign culture should "pay attention to their health as well as their grammar. What the natives regularly eat may be dangerous to a foreigner's constitution" (Department of Health and Human Services [DHHS], 1989, p. 64).

If your citation refers to several sources, list the authors and dates in alphabetical order:

> Several studies (Frith & Mueller, 2003; Hines, 2002; Simon, 1980) have documented severe deficiencies in Americans' foreign-language preparation.

REFERENCES LIST: APA STYLE   If you are using the APA style, you should make a separate list, titled References (no underlining or quotation marks), that appears after your text but before any appendixes. Include only sources actually used in preparing your essay. List the sources cited in your text *alphabetically,* by author's last name. Use only *initials* for authors' first and middle names. If the author is unknown, alphabetize by the first word in the title (but not *A, An,* or *The*). In titles, capitalize only the first word, proper names, and the first word following a colon. As in MLA reference style, begin first line of each reference flush left and indent subsequent lines five spaces. Double-space the entire References list. ***Note:*** APA now recommends using italics—not underlining—for titles of books, journals, and other documents.

Following are samples of APA-style reference list entries. For additional information and examples, consult the *Publication Manual of the American Psychological Association* (5th ed., 2001).

BOOKS: APA STYLE

A Book by One Author

Cisneros, S. (2002). *Caramelo.* New York: Random.

A Book by Several Authors

Corbett, P. J., Myers, N., & Tate, G. (2000). *The writing teacher's sourcebook (4th ed.)* New York: McGraw-Hill.

Additional Books by Same Author

Morrison, T. (1977). *Song of Solomon.* New York: Knopf.

Morrison, T. (1992). *Jazz.* New York: Knopf.

A Book with Two or More Authors

Conklin, N. F., & Lourie, M. A. (1983). *A host of tongues: Language communities in the United States.* New York: Free Press.

An Unknown or Anonymous Author

New York Public Library student's desk reference (1993). New York: Prentice Hall.

Note: In titles of books and journals, capitalize the first word, the first word after a colon, and any proper names. (New York Public Library is a proper name.)

A Book with an Author and an Editor

Austen, J. (1956). *Pride and prejudice* (M. Schorer, Ed.). Boston: Houghton Mifflin.

Note: The APA style usually uses the full name of publishing companies.

A Work in an Anthology

Chopin, K. (1989). The story of an hour. In E. V. Roberts & H. E. Jacobs (Eds.), *Literature: An introduction to reading and writing* (pp. 304–306). Englewood Cliffs, NJ: Prentice Hall.

Note: Titles of poems, short stories, essays, or articles in a book are not underlined or italicized or put in quotation marks. Only the title of the anthology is underlined or italicized.

A Translation

Lefranc, J. R. (1976). *A treatise on probability* (R. W. Mateau & D. Trilling, Trans.). New York: Macmillan. (Original work published 1952).

An Article or Chapter in an Edited Book

Sophocles. (1960). *Electra* (D. Grene, Trans.). In D. Grene & R. Lattimore (Eds.), *Greek tragedies* (Vol. 2, pp. 45–109). Chicago: University of Chicago Press.

A Government Document: Known Author

Machenthun, K. M. (1973). *Toward a cleaner aquatic environment.* Environmental
Protection Agency. Office of Air and Water Programs. Washington, DC: U.S.
Government Printing Office.

A Government Document: Unknown Author

Maternal and Child Health Bureau. (2001). *Babies sleep safest on their backs:
Reduce the risk of sudden infant death syndrome (SIDS).* Bethesda, MD: U.S.
Government Printing Office.

PERIODICALS: APA STYLE

The following examples illustrate how to list articles in magazines and periodicals
according to APA style. ***Note:*** Do *not* underline or italicize or put quotation marks
around titles of articles. Do italicize titles of magazines or periodicals. Cite the volume number for magazines and omit the *p.* or *pp.* before any page numbers. If an article is not printed on continuous pages, give all page numbers, separated by commas.

An Article in a Weekly or Biweekly Magazine

Hersh, S. M. (2004, May 17). Chain of command. *The New Yorker,* 38–43.

An Article in a Monthly or Bimonthly Magazine

Dunbar, D. (1997, February). White noise. *Travel and Leisure,* 27, 106–110, 150–158.

An Unsigned Article in a Magazine

E-commerce takes off. (2004, 15–21 May). *Economist,* 371, 9.

An Article in a Journal with Continuous Pagination

Italicize the volume number and do not include *pp.* Also, APA style requires repeating all number digits: Write 2552–2555.

Sady, S. P. (1986). Prolonged exercise augments plasma triglyceride clearance.
Journal of the American Medical Association, 256, 2552–2555.

An Article in a Journal That Paginates Each Issue Separately

Italicize the volume number followed by the issue number in parentheses.

Brodkey, L. (1987). Writing ethnographic narratives. *Written Communication, 9* (1),
25–50.

An Article in a Newspaper

Use *p.* or *pp.* before newspaper section and page numbers.

Harmon, A. (2004, June 20). In new tests for fetal defects, agonizing choices for
parents. *New York Times,* p. A1.

An Unsigned Article in a Newspaper

A jet crash that defies resolution. (2001, September 5). *Los Angeles Times*, p. A1.

An Editorial

Fish, S. (1996, December 26). When principles get in the way. [Editorial.] *New York Times*, p. A27.

An Unsigned Editorial

European summit of uncertainty. (1994, January 7). [Editorial.] *Los Angeles Times*, p. B6.

ELECTRONIC AND INTERNET SOURCES: APA STYLE

The World Wide Web and the Internet are still changing, so even the latest APA guidelines, available in the fifth edition of the *Publication Manual of the American Psychological Association* (2001), will continue to change. The basic features of an electronic or Internet citation, given in abbreviated form below, are available for downloading from the APA home page at *http://www.apa.org/journals/webref.html*. Use the specific citations following this list as models for your own citations.

1. Name of author (if given)
2. Title of article (with APA capitalization rules)
3. Title of periodical or electronic text (italicized)
4. Volume number and/or pages (if any)
5. If information is retrieved from an electronic database (e.g., ABI/FORM, PsychINFO, Electric Library, Academic Universe), give the name of the database. (No library address or URL needed.)
6. Use the words "Retrieved" (include date here) "from" (give the URL here). (Use the words "Available from" to indicate that the URL leads to information on how to obtain the cited material rather than the complete address of the material itself.)
7. Do not use angle brackets around URL.
8. If citation ends with the URL, do not end URL with a period.

Note: APA style does not cite personal communications such as e-mail in a reference list. Cite such references in the text only.

An Article in a Journal

Mossman, M. (2001, May). Acts of becoming: Autobiography, Frankenstein, and the postmodern body. *Postmodern Culture 11*, 68–89. Retrieved September

10, 2001, from http://jefferson.village.edu/pmc/current.issue/
11.3mossman.html

An Article in an Internet-Only Journal

Fredrickson, B. L. (2000, March 7). Cultivating positive emotions to optimize health
and well-being. *Prevention & Treatment, 3*, Article 0001a. Retrieved
November 20, 2000, from
http://journals.apa.org/prevention/volume3/pre0030001a.html

An Article in a Newspaper

Greenhouse, L. (2004, June 25) Justices, in 5–4 vote, raise doubts on sentencing
rules. *New York Times.* Retrieved June 27, 2004, from
http://www.nytimes.com.

Message Posted to an Online Forum

Etter, B. (2001, August 24). Composition philosophies and rhetoric. Message
posted to http://writing.colostate.edu/SyllaBase/classroom/
communication/discussion/display_message.asp?MessageID=16232

A Work from an Online Database

Hines, M. E. (2003, Fall). Foreign language curriculum concerns in times of conflict.
Delta Kappa Gamma Bulletin, 70, 15–22. Retrieved May 23, 2004, from
Academic Search Premier database.

OTHER SOURCES: APA STYLE

In the APA system, unpublished letters and interviews are personal communica-
tions and do not represent recoverable data. Therefore, they should not appear in a
References list. Do, however, cite personal letters or interviews in your text. (See
"In-Text Documentation: APA Style.")

A Review

Rosen, C., & Zerner, H. (2000, October 8). Scenes from the American dream.
[Review of the book *Norman Rockwell: Pictures for the American people].*
New York Review of Books, 16–20.

A Published Interview

Lamm, R. (1995, November 30). Governments face tough times. [Interview with
Baun, R.] *Coloradoan,* p. B9.

Computer Software

Microsoft word. Vers. 5.0 [Computer software]. (1992). Microsoft.

A Film

Spielberg, S. (Director). (2004). *The terminal* [Film]. Dreamworks.

A Recording

Carey, M. (1993). Hero. On *Music box* [CD]. New York: Columbia Records.

A Television or Radio Program

Bogdonich, R. (Producer). (1997, April 13). *Sixty Minutes.* New York: WCBS.

EDITING AND PROOFREADING   Edit your paper for conciseness, clarity, and accuracy of grammar, spelling, and punctuation. See your handbook for assistance in revising errors and improving usage. Check your direct quotations to make sure they are *accurate, word-for-word transcriptions* of the originals. Make sure that your in-text citation of sources is accurate. Proofread both the text *and* the Works Cited or References section. Finally, have someone else proofread your research paper for typos, spelling errors, missing words, or confusing sentences.

POSTSCRIPT ON THE WRITING PROCESS

As your final entry in your research notebook, answer the following questions:

1. Reread your research log section. Compare your initial schedule with your actual progress. What parts of the research paper took longer than you anticipated? What took less time?

2. Describe your intended *audience* for this essay. Where in the essay do you indicate or address this audience?

3. What *genre* did you select for your writing? Describe the main features of this genre. Where might this genre be published? Does it typically contain visuals or graphics? Refer to several passages that you felt you were successful at imitating the key features of this genre.

4. Describe your overall *purpose* or purposes for your essay. Were you narrating, informing, explaining, evaluating, problem-solving, or arguing? Did you have different purposes at different parts of your essay? Cite several passages from your essay to illustrate your purpose(s).

5. What was the most difficult problem you encountered while writing the research paper? How did you try to solve that problem?

6. What do you like best about the final version of your paper? Why? What do you like least? What would you change if you had two more days to work on your paper?

STUDENT WRITING

FOREIGN LANGUAGE STUDY: AN AMERICAN NECESSITY

Kate McNerny

Kate McNerny's purpose was to persuade students, administrators, and ordinary citizens that learning the language and culture of a foreign country is important, both to people as individuals and to America as a nation. In this paper, she uses interviews, library research, research on the Internet, and her own experience to alert her readers to the seriousness of the problem and to recommend a solution. She argues that American schools should require students to study at least one foreign language during junior and senior high school. McNerny follows the MLA style for in-text documentation, supplementary notes, and Works Cited list. The marginal annotations highlight key features of her research paper.

1"   ½"
McNerny 1

Kate McNerny

Professor Thomas

English 101

/double space

/double space

Foreign-Language Study: /double space

An American Necessity

"Why should I learn a foreign language—everyone speaks English!" "I would never use another language—I never plan to leave the United States." "I had a hard enough time learning English!" These are only a few of the excuses people have given for opposing foreign-language studies, and unfortunately they represent the ideas of more than a few American citizens. In possibly the most multicultural nation in the world, it is ironic that so many people— who themselves have come from foreign cultures and foreign languages—should want to remain isolated from international languages and cultures. A recent indication of the backlash against foreign languages came when the House of Representatives passed legislation recommending that English should be the official language of the U.S. Government.[1] In addition, twenty-three states already have Official English laws on the books (Swope 2128; Torres 51). Because these attitudes are so widespread, we need a national policy supporting foreign-language study in elementary and secondary schools. If we are to continue to develop as a people and a nation, we must be able to communicate with and understand the cultures of people from countries around the globe.

Historically, Americans' attitudes toward foreign languages have swayed from positive to negative, depending on current

1"   1"

1"

For her lead-in, McNerny uses quotations she collected in her informal survey.

*McNerny gives first version of her **thesis** for her problem-solving essay: "We need a national policy supporting foreign-language study." McNerny presents historical background on the problem.*

McNerny 2

events around the world. Theodore Huebener's study <u>Why Johnny Should Learn Foreign Languages</u> shows how attitudes reflect the times. In 1940, in an isolationist period before World War II, a committee of the American Youth Commission issued a report labeling foreign-language studies as "useless and time-consuming" (Huebener 13). An even more appalling statement came from a group of Harvard scholars. They suggested that "foreign language study is useful primarily in strengthening the student's English. . . . For the average student, there is no real need at all to learn a foreign language" (Huebener 14). With such attitudes, it is no wonder that students and administrators ignored foreign language programs during the 1940s and 1950s.[2] Through the years, each international crisis has brought a renewed interest in foreign languages. Just as the advent of Sputnik in the late 1950s was followed by a surge of interest in learning foreign languages, the terrorist attacks of September 11, 2001 have created more interest in languages less commonly taught in the United States (Hines 20).

Despite some occasional surges of interest, however, foreign-language study still holds the weakest position of any major subject in American secondary schools. A recent study of foreign-language programs reports that "only 15 percent of American high school students study a foreign language. Only 8 percent of [American] colleges require credit in a foreign language for admission (down from 34 percent in 1966)" (Unks 24). Because available programs at the junior and senior high school level are generally limited in variety

Ellipsis points indicate material omitted from the source.

The superscript number refers the reader to the "Notes" page for McNerny's comment on the history of the problem.

Square brackets in quoted material indicate a word added by McNerny to clarify the sentence.

McNerny 3

and scope, only a small percentage of those students who take a foreign language ever become fluent in it. A 1984

"Let me put this in terms you'll understand. First, you'll have to tell me what language you're speaking."

www.CartoonStock.com

study that sampled 536 secondary schools revealed that most offered a foreign language, but 91 percent did not require foreign-language credits for graduation (Ranwez and Rodgers 98). In contrast, most European countries require all students to learn at least one and often two foreign languages. Norway, Spain, France, Sweden, Italy, England, Germany, and Finland all require at least one foreign language. According to Rune Bergentoft, currently a Mellon Fellow at the National Foreign Language Center, "Several [European] countries require knowledge of two foreign languages for entry to the upper

McNerny included the cartoon at this point to illustrate Americans' stubborn ignorance of foreign languages.

In-text citation for a source with two authors.

secondary school; in the Netherlands, the requirement is three foreign languages" (18).

The United States cannot continue to lag behind other countries in language capability. As two foreign-language researchers noted, "We are members of a world community consisting of hundreds of nations, and our fates are closely intertwined" (Long and Long 366). It is time to change attitudes and to recognize that in order to successfully interact with its "world community," the United States must drastically change its foreign-language practices and policies. American students should be encouraged to start their language studies in elementary school and required to study at least one foreign language during their six years of junior and senior high school.

How do we encourage more students to study a foreign language in our elementary and secondary schools? The solution requires changes on the part of administrators and teachers, changes in the attitudes and experiences of students themselves, and changes in our state and national foreign language policies.

School administrators across the country often oppose the idea of requiring foreign languages because they cannot see the contribution these studies make to the overall goals of the schools' curriculum. In a recent survey, New Jersey secondary school administrators "rated social studies objectives as contributing most to the attainment of high priority goals, and foreign language as contributing least" (Koppel 437). These administrators fail to realize that language studies can add a valuable dimension to a social studies program. Educators can use a combined program to

McNerny restates her thesis, using more specific language: "American students should be . . . required to study at least one foreign language during . . . junior and senior high school."

*McNerny's **essay map:** The solution requires changes by administrators, by students, and by national policymakers.*

*Notice **punctuation** for in-text citation: Source appears in parentheses after the quotation marks but **before** the period.*

McNerny 5

emphasize a global perspective in language and cultural studies. "The world looks and sounds different when one is 'standing in the shoes' of another, speaking another language, or recognizing another's point of view based on an alternative set of values" (Bragaw 37). This global awareness is crucial in our increasingly interdependent world.

Likewise, teachers need to continue to make changes in their foreign-language courses to attract more students. More and more primary and secondary language courses already focus on cultural issues more than grammar, but now they need to use all the computer, on-line, and Internet resources currently available to attract and motivate their students. Linguist Mark Warschauer, in a preface to papers collected at a conference on Global Networking in Foreign Language Learning, asserts that "foreign language learners can communicate rapidly and inexpensively with other learners or speakers of the target language around the world. With the World Wide Web, learners can access a broad array of authentic foreign language materials . . . or they can develop and publish their own materials to share with others across the classroom or across the globe" (ix). Teachers need to make use of the Internet communication possibilities to help motivate and interest their students.

Of course, students themselves need motivation in order to enroll in foreign-language classes. Many students simply fail to see why they will ever need to use a foreign language. I used to belong to that group. I remember my mom always telling me, "Take French classes. Learn how to speak French so you can visit your cousins in

*McNerny uses **personal experience** in her research paper. Her experience provides a great example of why students can benefit from studying a foreign language.*

McNerny 6

France someday." At the time, during junior high, I did take French
classes for a while, but then dropped them when my schedule
became "too busy." Then, as my mom had promised, I got the
opportunity to visit my cousins in France. For some reason, the fact
that I couldn't speak French didn't really hit me—until I stepped off
the train at Gare du Nord in Paris and couldn't find the relative who
was supposed to meet me. After frantically searching the entire
station several times, I had to break down and ask for help. At the
information desk, a few completely butchered French phrases
escaped my lips—only to be received by an unimpressed,
unresponsive station attendant. He muttered something about
dumb Americans. Then, with a wave of his hand, he gestured
toward some unknown destination. I did survive that painful ordeal,
but I vowed I wouldn't embarrass myself—and other Americans—
again.

Another way to change students' attitudes is to encourage
them to participate in exchange programs or study-abroad
programs.[3] Again, the Internet and the World Wide Web offer
students and their teachers immediate access to a variety of
exchange and study-abroad programs. The World Wide Web has
hundreds of sites related to foreign-language study that can
help both teachers and students. The International House
World Organization, at http://www. international-house.org,
is "a worldwide network of language schools sharing a common
commitment to the highest standards of teaching and training"
(International). Students wishing to find out about exchange
and study-abroad programs should browse the Web, perhaps

McNerny 7

beginning at a site such as Foreign Language Study Abroad
Service at http://www.netpoint.net/~flsas. The Foreign Language
Study Abroad Service was started in 1971 and is, according to
its home page, "the oldest study abroad service in the U.S."
(Foreign).

Study-abroad programs and exchange programs help students
learn the language, but just as important, they enable students to
learn about different cultures. In his resource book, Teaching Culture,
H. Ned Seelye, Director of Bilingual-Bicultural Education for the State
of Illinois, cites just one of many cultural lessons that American
students—and tourists—need to learn:

> At a New Year's Eve celebration in an exclusive
> Guatemalan hotel, one American was overheard telling
> another, "You see all these people? They're all my wife's
> relatives. And every damn one of them has kissed me
> tonight. If another Guatemalan man hugs and kisses me
> I'll punch him right in the face!" The irritated American
> was disturbed by two things: the extended kinship
> patterns of the group and the abrazo de ano neuvo as
> executed by the men (he did not complain of the female
> abrazos). Both customs—close family ties that extend to
> distant relatives and the abrazo given as a greeting or
> sign of affection devoid of sexual overtures—elicited
> hostility in the American who was bored by unintelligible
> language and depressed by nostalgia and alcohol. (85)

In order to prevent such linguistic and cultural misunderstandings,
more and more Americans should take advantage of study-abroad

*McNerny introduces the
author, the title of the
book, and the author's
credentials to lend au-
thority to the quoted
passage.*

*At the end of the quota-
tion, McNerny cites only
the page number, since
she has already intro-
duced the author. The
page number follows the
period in indented block
quotations.*

*McNerny does not end
her paragraph with a
quotation; instead, she
shows how this evidence
supports her point.*

McNerny 8

and exchange programs that will acquaint them with a variety of
cultures and languages.

Finally, in order to coordinate our schools' foreign-language
studies, America needs changes in our state and national foreign-
language policies to ensure that every child will receive some basic
instruction in foreign languages and culture. Changes in our foreign-
language requirements would not only promote cultural
understanding but also would strengthen U. S. international relations
in business and diplomacy. International trade is continually
increasing in the United States and has created a demand for
businesspeople competent in foreign languages. Many top American
businesspeople agree that students who combine some business or
economics training with fluency in Japanese have unlimited job
possibilities (Coxe 194). Company executives simply cannot expect to
make efficient, sound decisions in their international markets without
understanding and speaking the language of the country they are
dealing with (Huebener 45). Educator Gerald Unks points out two
instances in which a lack of language proficiency caused companies
to initiate fatal marketing programs:

> When Pepsi-Cola went after the Chinese market, "Come
> Alive With Pepsi" was translated into Chinese in Taiwan
> as "Pepsi Brings Your Ancestors Back from the Dead." No
> Sale! General Motors sought to sell its Nova in South
> America oblivious to the fact that "No va" in Spanish
> means "It doesn't go." (24)

Another recent example of foreign-language ignorance in
marketing occurred when the California Milk Processor Board

McNerny 9

wanted an ad agency to translate the "Got Milk?" campaign into Spanish. The unfortunate translation initially cam out as "Are you lactating?" (Frith & Mueller 33). These examples illustrate that business people need thorough competence in, not just a rudimentary knowledge of, foreign languages.

Finally, proficiency in foreign languages and cultures is important not only for business and trade overseas, but also for jobs in America. Required foreign-language study would help our future citizens understand and appreciate our multicultural heritage—and help them become employable. Verada Bluford, writing in Occupational Outlook Quarterly, argues that as our country "becomes more involved in foreign trade, tourism, and international cooperative ventures, the number of jobs open to fluent speakers of a foreign language increases" (25). Bluford explains that there are "language-centered jobs" such as teaching, translating, and interpreting, but there are also "language-related jobs," such as jobs in marketing and finance, engineering, airlines, banking, and government, where language skills are necessary. These "language-related jobs" will go to students who have language skills in addition to some other skill (Bluford 26). A foreign-language requirement, whether mandated by each state or by Congress, would make all Americans better citizens of the world and their own country.

The need for required language study in the United States is urgent. Some states already require schools to introduce children to some foreign language during their grade school years (Kuo 2). For example, North Carolina, Arkansas, Louisiana, Arizona, and Oklahoma already have laws, and Oregon has a proposed law that

Before quoting from Bluford, McNerny names the author and the journal from which the article is taken.

McNerny begins her conclusion, citing precedents and calling for state and federal administrators to support a foreign-language requirement.

McNerny 10

will require all tenth-graders to know a language other than English (Kuo 2). Since some individual schools and states realize the benefits of foreign-language requirements, Congress should guide all the states and formulate a national foreign-language policy that would make all our schools more like the European model.

Although the ideas and the plans for a national policy exist, often the funds do not. Some funds can be diverted from within school districts, but the federal government must take some initiative. The current administration spends endless time and money subsidizing business interests and propping up weak foreign economies. Since foreign-language knowledge contributes strongly to success in both these areas, however, it would be practical for the administration also to support expansion of language studies. Instead, it continues to reduce funding for special programs, including language studies centers and international teaching facilities (Unks 25). Realistically, a foreign-language requirement in junior and senior high school cannot be initiated without the support of both local school districts and the federal government. Americans must acknowledge the fact that they are not isolated from the rest of the world. Successful interaction in the "world community" depends on our ability, as a nation, to effectively communicate with and understand people from other countries. Understanding, communication, and world peace cannot be achieved without cultural awareness and foreign-language proficiency.

1"
Notes

½"
McNerny 11

[1]Americans not only hesitate to take a foreign language but also seem bent on keeping foreign languages officially "out of sight." The debate over "official English" has spilled over into the workplace, in the form of "English-only" rules in business. Robert Brady, writing in HR Focus, reviews the two sides of the English-only debate: "Advocates of English-only rules argue that a single language promotes good organizational communications, ensures workplace safety, improves service to the English-speaking customer base, and avoids discrimination" (20). On the other side, Brady says, opponents believe that requiring employees to speak English goes against the melting-pot heritage of our country—and may violate Title VII of the Civil Rights Act (20). Many opponents from ethnic and civil rights groups believe these bills and rules are racist (McBee 64). Americans' ignorance of foreign languages (and the fear that ignorance breeds) is an important cause of the popularity of both the "official English" laws and the "English-only" rules.

1"

1"

[2]One of the most disturbing facts is that although Huebener's study was done in 1961, very little has changed in over forty years. Except for slight changes in statistics, dates, and names of wars, Americans have remained strikingly insular in their attitudes toward foreign languages and foreigners.

[3]Recent figures on study-abroad programs illustrate the huge gap between the number of foreign students who study in the United States and U.S. students who study abroad. In an article on language learning and study abroad, Barbara Freed gives the following figures: "Close to half a million international students

1"

Content notes are placed on a separate page and double-spaced. Use raised footnote numbers and indent the first line five spaces.

In her notes, McNerny includes her ideas about "English-only" and "official English," which would have been digressive in the text of her paper.

In this footnote, McNerny puts statistics that didn't seem to fit in the flow of her paragraph but are relevant to study-abroad programs.

1"

McNerny 12

came to the United States to study in 1993–94 [while] approximately 71,000 American undergraduates participated in study abroad programs" (3). That means that nearly ten times more foreign students study English in the United States than American students study foreign languages abroad.

1"

1"

1"

1"

½"
McNerny 13

Works Cited

Bergentoft, Rune. "Foreign Language Instruction: A Comparative Perspective." The Annals of the American Academy of Political and Social Science 532 (1994): 8–34.

Bluford, Verada. "Working with Foreign Languages." Occupational Outlook Quarterly 38.4 (1994): 25–28.

Brady, Robert I. "English-Only Rules Draw Controversy." HR Focus June 1996: 20.

Bragaw, Donald H., and Helene Zimmer-Loew. "Social Studies and Foreign Language: A Partnership." Education Digest Dec. 1985: 36–39.

Coxe, Donald. "The Back Page." Canadian Business Feb. 1984: 194.

Foreign Language Study Abroad Service. 21 Feb. 2003 http://www.netpoint.net/flas..

Freed, Barbara F. "Language Learning and Study Abroad." Second Language Acquisition in a Study Abroad Context. Ed. Barbara F. Freed. Philadelphia: John Benjamins, 1995, 3–33.

Frith, Katherine T., and Barbara Mueller. Advertising and Societies: Global Issues. New York: P. Lang, 2003.

Hines, Marion E. "Foreign Language Curriculum Concerns in Times of Conflict." Delta Kappa Gamma Bulletin 70 (Fall 2003): 15–22. Academic Search Premier. EBSCO. Colorado State U Lib. 3 Dec. 2003 <http://0-web2.epnet.com>.

Huebener, Theodore. Why Johnny Should Learn Foreign Languages. New York: Chilton, 1961.

International House: The Worldwide Language Teaching Organization. Jan. 2003. 2 Mar. 2003 http://www.international-house.org.

1"

1"   1"

The Works Cited list begins a new page. List the entries alphabetically by the author's last name. If no author is given, list by the first word in the title. Double-space all lines.

Indent five spaces after first line of each entry.

Book

Internet Web Page

1"
½"
McNerny 14
Works Cited

Article from a journal with contiguous pagination.

Koppel, Irene E. "The Perceived Contribution of Foreign Language to High Priority Education Goals." Foreign Language Annals 15 (1982): 435–37.

Kuo, Fidelius. "Foreign Language Proposal in Washington State Worthy." Northwest Asian Weekly 9 Dec. 1994: 4.

For inclusive page numbers over 100, use only the last two digits in the second number (366–68).

Long, Delbert H., and Roberta A. Long. "Toward the Promotion of Foreign Language Study and Global Understanding." Education 105 (1985): 366–68.

McBee Susanna. "A War over Words." U.S. News and World Report 6 Oct. 1986: 64.

Ranwez, Alain D., and Judy Rodgers. "The Status of Foreign Languages and International Studies: An Assessment in Colorado." Foreign Language Annals 17 (1984): 97–102.

1"

Seelye, H. Ned. Teaching Culture: Strategies for Foreign Language Educators. Skokie, IL: National Textbook, 1974.

1"

Swope, Christopher. "Panel OKs Bill to Make English Official Government Language." Congressional Quarterly Weekly Report 54 (1996): 2128–29.

Torres, Joseph. "The Language Crusade." Hispanic 9.6 (1996): 50–54.

Article from a monthly magazine

Unks, Gerald. "The Perils of Our Single-Language Policy." Education Digest Mar. 1985: 24–27.

Warschauer, Mark. Preface. Telecollaboration in Foreign Language Learning. By Warschauer. Ed. Mark Warschauer. Honolulu: Second Language Teaching & Curriculum Center, 1996.

1"

Appendix: Writing Under Pressure

The main chapters of this text describe purposes for writing and strategies for collecting, shaping, drafting, and revising an essay. These chapters assume that you have several days or even weeks to write your paper. They work on the premise that you have time to read model essays, time to think about ideas for your topic, and time to prewrite, write several drafts, and receive feedback from other members of your class. Much college writing, however, occurs on midterm or final examinations, when you may have only fifteen to twenty minutes to complete the whole process of writing. When you must produce a "final" draft in a few short minutes, your writing process may need drastic modification.

A typical examination has some objective questions (true/false, multiple-choice, definition, short-answer) followed by an essay question or two. For example, with just twenty-five minutes left in your Western Civilization midterm, you might finish the last multiple-choice question, turn the page, and read the following essay question:

> Erich Maria Remarque's *All Quiet on the Western Front* has been hailed by critics the world over as the "twentieth century's definitive novel on war." What does Remarque's novel tell us about the historical, ideological, national, social, and human significance of twentieth-century warfare? Draw on specific illustrations from the novel, but base your observations on your wider perspective on Western civilization. Good luck!

Overwhelmed by panic, you find the blood drains from your face and your fingers feel icy. You now have twenty-two minutes to write on the "historical, ideological, national, social, and human significance of twentieth-century warfare." Do you have to explain everything about modern warfare? Must you use specific examples from the novel? Good luck, indeed! Everything you remembered about the novel has now vanished. Bravely, you pick up your pen and start recounting the main events of the novel, hoping to show the instructor at least that you read it.

You can survive such an essay examination, but you need to prepare yourself emotionally and intellectually. Following is some advice from senior English majors who have taken dozens of essay examinations in their four years of college. These seniors answer the question, "What advice would you give to students who are preparing to take an essay examination?"

> Even though I'm an English major, I'm perfectly petrified of writing impromptu essays. My advice is to calm yourself. Read the question. Study key words and concepts. Before beginning an essay question, write a brief,

informal outline. This will organize your ideas and help you remember them as well. Take a deep breath and write. I would also recommend *rereading* the question while you are writing, to keep you on track.

The first step is to know the material. Then, before you begin, read the instructions. Know what the teacher expects. Then try to organize your thoughts into a small list—preferably a list that will become your main paragraphs. Don't babble to fill space. Teachers hate reading nonsense. Reread what you've written often. This will ensure that you won't repeat yourself. Proofread at the end.

Organization is important but difficult in a pressure situation. Well-organized essays do have a tendency to impress the professor, sometimes more than information-packed essays. Organize your notes and thoughts about those notes as you study (not necessarily in a chronological order, but rather in a comprehensible order). Good luck.

Read the question carefully.

Get your thoughts in order.

Write what the question asks, not what you wish it asked.

Don't ramble.

Give textual facts or specific examples.

Summarize with a clear, understandable closing.

Proofread.

Keep calm. Your life doesn't depend on one test.

My advice would be first to learn how to consciously relax and practice writing frequently. *Practice!!!* It's important to practice writing as much as possible in any place possible, because the more writing you do, the better and easier it becomes. Also, your belief that it *can* be done is critical!

Know the information that you will be tested on well enough so that you can ask yourself tough and well-formed questions in preparation. You should be able to predict what essay questions your professor will ask, at least generally. I always go to the test file or ask friends for sample essay questions that I can practice on. Then I practice writing on different areas of the material.

The common threads in these excerpts of advice are to know your audience, analyze key terms in the question, make a sketch outline, know the material, practice writing before the test, and proofread when you finish writing. Knowing how to read the question and practicing your writing before the test will help you relax and do your best.

KNOW YOUR AUDIENCE

Teachers expect you to answer a question exactly as it is asked, not just to give the information that you know. Because teachers must read dozens of essays, they are impressed by clear organization and specific detail. As one senior says, teachers hate babble because they cannot follow the thread of your argument. Although they demand specific examples and facts from the text, they want you to explain how these examples *relate* to the overall question. In a pile of two hundred history exams graded by one professor, margins featured comments like "Reread the question. This doesn't answer the question." "What is your main point? State your main point clearly." "Give more specific illustrations and examples." Keep this teacher in mind as you write your next essay response.

ANALYZE KEY TERMS

Understanding the key terms in the question is crucial to writing an essay under pressure. Teachers expect you to respond to *their* specific question, not just to write down information. They want you to use your writing to *think* about the topic—to analyze and synthesize the information. In short, they want you to make sense of the information. Following are key terms that indicate teachers' expectations and suggest how to organize your answer.

Discuss: A general instruction that means "write about." If the question says *discuss,* look for other key words to focus your response.

Describe: Give sensory details or particulars about a topic. Often, however, this general instruction simply means "discuss."

Analyze: Divide a topic into its parts, and show how the parts are related to each other and to the topic as a whole.

Synthesize: Show how the parts relate to the whole or how the parts make sense together.

Explain: Show relationships between specific examples and general principles. Explain what (define), explain why (causes/effects), and/or explain how (analyze process).

Define: Explain what something is. As appropriate, give a formal definition, describe it, analyze its parts or function, describe what it is not, and/or compare and contrast it with similar events or ideas.

Compare: Explain similarities and (often) differences. Draw conclusions from the observed similarities and differences.

Contrast: Explain key differences. Draw conclusions from the observed differences.

Illustrate: Provide specific examples of an idea or process.

Trace: Give the sequence or chronological order of key events or ideas.

Evaluate: Determine the value or worth of an idea, thing, process, person, or event. Set up criteria and provide evidence to support your judgments.

Solve: Explain your solution; show how it fixes the problem, why it is better than other alternatives, and why it is feasible.

Argue: Present both sides of a controversial issue, showing why the opposing position should not be believed or accepted and why your position should be accepted. Give evidence to support your position.

Interpret: Offer your understanding of the meaning and significance of an idea, event, person, process, or work of art. Support your understanding with specific examples or details.

MAKE A SKETCH OUTLINE

The key terms in a question should not only focus your thinking but also suggest how to organize your response. Use the key terms to make a sketch outline of your response. You may not regularly use an outline when you have more time to write an essay, but the time pressure requires that you revise your normal writing process.

Assume that you have twenty-five minutes to read and respond to the following question from a history examination. Read the instructions carefully, note the key terms, and make a brief outline to guide your writing. Answer *one* of the following. Draw on the reading for your answer. (25 pts)

1. Define globalization, then explain both the advantages and disadvantages of globalization for both modern and third-world countries. Based on your explanation, argue for or against globalization as a means of improving the standard of living in both modern and third-world countries.

2. Explain the arguments that the United Nations does and does not play a positive role in international relations (discuss and illustrate both sides of the argument). Then take a stand—citing the evidence for your position.

Let's assume that because you know more about the United Nations, you choose the second question. First, you should identify and underline key words in the question. The subject for your essay is the *United Nations* and its role in *international relations.* You need to *explain* the reasons why the UN does or does not have a positive effect on international relations. You will need to *discuss* and *illustrate* (give specific examples of) both sides of the controversy. Finally, you need to *take a stand* (argue) for your belief, citing *evidence* (specific examples from recent history) of how the UN has or has not helped to resolve international tensions.

Based on your rereading and annotation of the key words of the question, make a quick outline or list, perhaps as follows:

I. Reasons (with examples) why some believe the UN is effective

A. Reason 1 + example

B. Reason 2 + example

II. Reasons (with examples) why some believe the UN is not effective

A. Reason 1 + example

B. Reason 2 + example

III. Reasons why you believe the UN is effective

Refer to reasons and examples cited in I, above, but explain why these reasons and examples outweigh the reasons cited in II, above.

With this sketch outline as your guide, jot down reasons and examples that you intend to use, and then start writing. Your outline will make sure that you cover all the main points of the question, and it will keep your essay organized as you concentrate on remembering specific reasons and examples.

JOURNAL EXERCISE

For practice, analyze at least one question from two of the following subject areas. First, underline key terms. Then, in your journal explain what these terms ask you to do. Finally, sketch an outline to help organize your response. If you are not familiar with the topics, check a dictionary or encyclopedia. (Do not write the essay.)

Biology

- Describe the process by which artificial insulin was first produced.
- What is reverse transcriptase and how was it used in genetic engineering?
- Humans—at least most of us—walk on two legs as opposed to four. How might you account for this using a Darwinian, Lamarckian, and Theistic model?

History

- Discuss the significant political developments in the English colonies in the first half of the eighteenth century.
- Account for the end of the Salem witchcraft delusion, and discuss the consequences of the outbreak for Salem Village.

Human Development

- Discuss evidence for nature versus nurture effects in human development.
- Contrast Piaget's, Vygotsky's, and Whorf's ideas on connections between language and thought.

Humanities

- How and why did early Christian culture dominate the Roman Empire? In terms of art and architecture, discuss specific ways in which the early Christians transformed or abolished the Greco-Roman legacy.

Literature

- Aristotle wrote that a tragedy must contain certain elements, such as a protagonist of high estate, recognition, and reversal, and should also evoke pity and fear in the audience. Which of the following best fits Aristotle's definition: *Hamlet, Death of a Salesman,* or *The Old Man and the Sea?* Explain your choice.

Philosophy

- On the basis of what we have studied in this class, define "philosophy." Taking your major subject of study (for example, biology, history, literature), discuss three philosophical problems that arise in this field.

- Write an essay explaining the following statement. Be clear in your explanation and use specific examples. "Egoism allows for prudent altruism."

Political Science
- Evaluate the achievements of the current administration's policy in Africa.
- Analyze the role of force in the contemporary international system.

Psychology
- Contrast Freud's and Erikson's stage theories of personality.
- What is meant by triangulation of measurement (multiple methodology)?

KNOW THE MATERIAL

It goes without saying that you must know the material in order to explain the concepts and give specific examples or facts from the text. But what is the best way to review the material so that you can recall examples under pressure? The following three study tactics will improve your recall.

First, read your text actively. Do not just mark key passages in yellow highlighter. Write marginal notes to yourself. Write key concepts in the margin. Ask questions. Make connections between an idea in one paragraph and something you read earlier. Make connections between what you read in the text and what you heard in class.

Second, do not depend only on your reading and class discussion. Join or form a study group that meets regularly to review course material. Each person in the group should prepare some question for review. Explaining key ideas to a friend is an excellent way to learn the material yourself.

Finally, use your writing to help you remember. Do not just read the book and your notes and head off for the test. Instead, review your notes, *close* your notebook, and write down as much as you can remember. Review the assigned chapters in the text, close the book, and write out what you remember. If you can write answers to questions with the book closed, you know you're ready for an essay examination.

JOURNAL EXERCISE

Get out the class notes and textbook for a course that you are currently taking. Annotate your notes with summary comments and questions. In the margins, write out the key ideas that the lecture covered. Then write out questions that you still have about the material. Open your textbook for that class. Annotate the margins of the chapter that you are currently reading. Write summary comments about important material. Write questions in the margins about material that you do not understand. Note places in the text that the instructor also covered in class.

PRACTICE WRITING

As several of the senior English majors suggested, practicing short essays *before* an examination will make you feel comfortable with the material and reduce your panic. A coach once noted that while every athlete wants to win, only the true winners are willing to *prepare* to win. The same is true of writing an examination. Successful writers have already completed 80 percent of the writing process *before* they walk into an examination. They have written notes in the margins of their notebooks and textbooks. They have discussed the subject with other students. They have closed the book and written out key definitions. They have prepared questions and practiced answering them. Once they read a question, they are prepared to write out their "final" drafts.

JOURNAL EXERCISE

For an upcoming examination in one of your other courses, write out three possible essay questions that your instructor might ask. For each question, underline the key words, and make a sketch outline of your response. Set your watch or timer for fifteen minutes, and actually write out your response to *one* of your questions.

PROOFREAD AND EDIT

In your normal writing process, you can put aside your draft for several days and proofread and edit it later. When you are writing under pressure, however, you need to save three or four minutes at the end to review what you have written. Often, you may be out of time before you have finished writing what you wanted to say about the question. At this point, one effective strategy is to draw a line at the end of what you have written, write "Out of Time," and then write one or two quick sentences explaining what you planned to say: "If I had more time, I would explain how the UN's image has become more positive following the crises in Israel and Iraq." Then use your remaining two or three minutes to reread what you have written, making sure that your ideas are clear and that you have written in complete sentences and used correct spelling and punctuation. If you don't know how to spell a word, at least write "sp?" next to a word to show that you think it is spelled incorrectly.

SAMPLE ESSAY QUESTIONS AND RESPONSES

The following are sample essay questions, students' responses, and instructors' comments and grades.

HISTORY 100: WESTERN CIVILIZATION
Examination II over Chapter 12, class lectures, and Victor Hugo's *The Hunchback of Notre Dame*

Essay I (25 Points)

What was the fifteenth-century view of "science" as described in *The Hunchback*? How did this view tend to inhibit Claud Frollo in his experiments in his closet in the cathedral?

ANSWER 1

The fifteenth-century view of "science" was characterized by superstition and heresy. In *The Hunchback of Notre Dame*, for example, we see superstition operating when the king's physician states that a gunshot wound can be cured by the application of a roasted mouse. Claud Frollo, a high-ranking church official, has a thirst for knowledge, but unfortunately it pushes beyond the limits of knowledge permitted by the church. When he works in his closet on the art of alchemy and searches for the "Philosopher's Stone" (gold), he is guilty of heresy. Frollo has read and mastered the arts and sciences of the university and of the church, and he wants to know more. He knows that if he presses into the "Black Arts," the Devil will take his soul. And indeed, the "Devil" of passion does. Frollo feels inhibited because many of the experiments he has performed have made him guilty of heresy and witchcraft in the eyes of the church. And this seems to be the case in almost anything "new" or out of the ordinary. La Esmeralda, for instance, is declared "guilty" of witchcraft for the training of her goat. Her goat appears to have been possessed by the Devil himself, when, in fact, all the girl is guilty of is training the goat to do a few simple tricks. All in all, the fifteenth-century view of "science" was one not of favor, but of oppression and fear. Thankfully, the Renaissance came along!

An excellent response. Your focus on superstition and heresy along with the specific examples of the roasted mouse, the "Philosopher's Stone," and La Esmeralda's goat illustrate the fifteenth-century view of science and its inhibiting effect. Grade: A

ANSWER 2

The fifteenth-century view of science was that according to the Bible, God was the creator of all, and as to scientific theory, the subject was moot. No one was a believer in the scientific method—however, we do find some science going on in Claud Frollo's closet, alchemy. At that time he was trying to create gold by mixing different elements together. Though alchemy seems to be the only science of that time period, people who practiced it kept it to themselves. We even find King Louis IX coming to Frollo, disguised, to dabble in a little of the science himself. At this time people were rejecting the theory of the Earth revolving around the sun because, as a religious ordeal, God created the Earth and man, and they are the center of all things, so there were no questions to be answered by science, because the answer was God.

Give more examples from the novel and show how the fifteenth-century view actually inhibited Frollo. Otherwise, generally good response. (Why was creating the Earth such a religious "ordeal"?) Grade: B

ANSWER 3

According to The Hunchback of Notre Dame, the view of "science" in the fifteenth century was basically alchemy, that is, being able to turn base metals into gold. Everything else that we would regard as scientific today was regarded as sorcery or magic in the fifteenth century. What inhibited Claud Frollo in his experiments of turning base metals into gold was that, according to the laws of alchemy, one needed "The Philosopher's Stone" to complete the experiment, and Claud Frollo was unable to find this particular stone.

Needs more specific illustrations from the novel. Frollo is inhibited by his lack of scientific method and the censure of the church. Underline title of novel: The Hunchback of Notre Dame. Grade: C

ANSWER 4

During the period that the *Hunchback* took place, the attitude toward science was one of fear. Because the setting was in the medieval world, the people were afraid to admit to doing some things that were not being done by a majority of people. The overall view during that period was to keep one's own self out of trouble. The fright may be the result of the public executions which were perhaps Claud Frollo's deterrent in admitting to performing acts of science which others are uneducated in. Claud Frollo was outnumbered in the area of wanting to be "educated" and he kept to himself because he feared the people. He was in a position that didn't give him the power to try and overcome people's attitude of fear toward science. If he tried, he risked his life.

State your ideas more clearly. Your response doesn't answer the question. Very limited in your examples of science. Grade: D

BIOLOGY 220: ECOLOGY
FINAL EXAMINATION

Essay II (20 Points)

Water running down a mountainside erodes its channel and carries with it considerable material. What is the basic source of the energy used by the water to do this work? How is the energy used by water to do this work related to the energy used by life in the stream ecosystem?

ANSWER 1

The process begins with the hydrologic cycle. The sun radiates down and forces evaporation. This H_2O gas condenses and forms rain or snow, which precipitates back to earth. If the precipitation falls on a mountain, it will eventually run down the hillside and erode its channel. (Some water will evaporate without running down the hill.) The energy used by water to do its work relates directly to the energy used by life in the stream system. The sun is an energy input. It is the source of energy for stream life just as it is the source of energy for the water. Through photosynthesis, the energy absorbed by the stream is used by higher and higher trophic levels. So the sun is the energy source for both running water and the life in the stream. It all starts with solar energy.

Good response. Clear focus on the hydrolic cycle, photosynthesis, and solar energy and the source of energy for both the stream and its ecosystems. Grade: A

ANSWER 2

Ultimately, the sun is the basic source of energy that allows water to do the work it does. Solar power runs the hydrologic cycle, which is where water gets its energy. Heat evaporates water and allows molecules to rise in the atmosphere, where it condenses in clouds. Above the ground, but still under the effects of gravity, water has potential energy at this point. When enough condensation occurs, water drops back to the ground, changing potential energy to kinetic energy, which is how water works on mountainsides to move materials. As water moves materials, it brings into streams a great deal of organic matter, which is utilized by a number of heterotrophic organisms. That is the original source of energy for the ecosystems and also how energy used by water is related to the energy that is used by life in streams.

Very clear explanation of the hydrolic cycle, but response doesn't explain how source of energy for the stream ecosystem is related, through photosynthesis, to solar energy. Grade: B

ANSWER 3

The actual energy to move the water down the mountains is gravitational pull from the center of the earth. The stream's "growth" from the beginning of the mountaintop to the base starts out with being a heterotrophic system. This is because usually there is not enough light to bring about photosynthesis for the plants and in turn help other organisms' survival, so the streams use outside resources for energy. Once the stream gets bigger (by meeting up with another stream), it is autotrophic. It can produce its own energy sources. When the water reaches the base and becomes very large, it falls back to a heterotrophic system because the water has become too deep for light to penetrate and help with photosynthesis.

Reread the question. The basic source of energy is solar power. You almost discover the answer when you discuss photosynthesis, but after that, you get off track again. Grade: C−

Credits

Index